The
Encyclopedia
of
Garden
Flowers

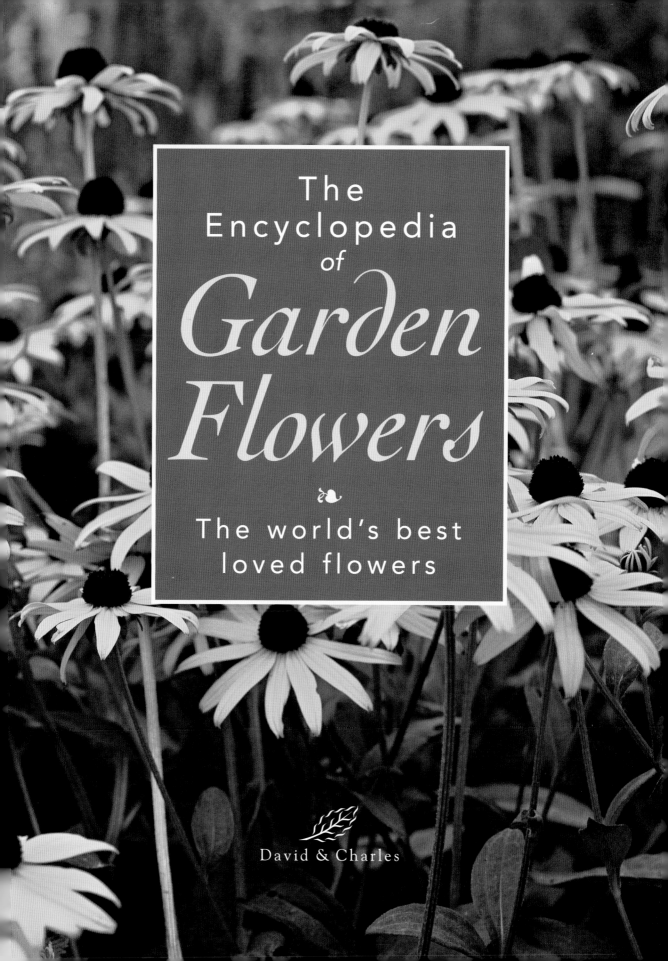

The Encyclopedia of Garden Flowers

The world's best loved flowers

David & Charles

Publisher	Gordon Cheers
Associate publisher	Margaret Olds
Project manager	Dannielle Doggett
Art director	Stan Lamond
Chief consultant	Kate Bryant
Consultant	Tony Rodd
Writers	Kate Bryant
	Geoff Bryant
Illustrations	Spike Wademan
Hardiness zone map	Bart Geerts
	John Frith
Senior editor	Margaret Malone
Editors	Loretta Barnard
	Denise Imwold
	Janet Parker
Picture research	Gordon Cheers
Photo library	Alan Edwards
Cover design	Stan Lamond
	Heather McNamara
Design concept	Cathy Campbell
Designers	Claire Edwards
	Louise Fitzgerald
	Pippa Hurst
	Kerry Klinner
Typesetting	Heather McNamara
	Dee Rogers
Index	Heather McNamara
Production	Bernard Roberts
Foreign rights	Sarah Minns
Publishing assistant	Erin King

Photography credits appear on page 704

A DAVID & CHARLES BOOK

First published in the UK in 2004

Copyright © Global Book Publishing Pty Ltd 2003, 2004

Photos and illustrations from the Global Photo Library

All rights reserved. No part of this publication may be reproduced, stored in a retrieval system, or transmitted, in any form or by any means, electronic or mechanical, by photocopying, recording or otherwise, without prior permission in writing from the publisher.

A catalogue record for this book is available from the British Library.

ISBN 0 7153 1840 3

Printed in Hong Kong by Sing Cheong Printing Company Ltd.

for David & Charles

Brunel House   Newton Abbot   Devon

Visit our website at www.davidandcharles.co.uk

David & Charles books are available from all good bookshops; alternatively you can contact our Orderline on (0)1626 334555 or write to us at FREEPOST EX2110, David & Charles Direct, Newton Abbot, TQ12 4ZZ (no stamp required UK mainland).

The moral rights of all contributors have been asserted.

Color separation Pica Digital Pte Ltd, Singapore

1 2   3 4 5 07 06 05 04 03

Photographers
Global Book Publishing would be pleased to hear from photographers interested in supplying photographs.

Captions for the preliminary pages

Page 1: Eschscholzia californica

Pages 2–3: Rudbeckia hirta

Page 4: Iris sibirica *'Tropic Night'*

Page 5: Lupinus *'Candy Floss'*

Pages 6–7: Hibiscus rosa-sinensis *'Mary Wallace'*

Pages 8–9: Lilium, *Asiatic Hybrid, 'Connecticut King' (yellow flowers)* and Delphinium *species (blue flowers)*

Pages 46–47: Dahlia, *Decorative, 'Ernte Dank'*

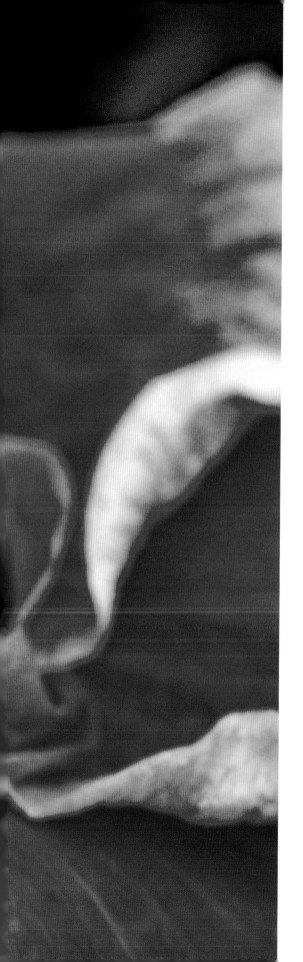

CONTENTS

THE COLORFUL
GARDEN

GROWING FLOWERS

Flowers play an essential part in our lives. Not only do they appeal to our sense of beauty and provide tremendous pleasure through their colors and fragrance, but also they are often laden with symbolic meaning. A well-chosen bouquet offers comfort to the bereaved, expresses admiration for a loved one, and conveys respect for a colleague. A world without flowers would feel empty indeed.

Growing flowers in the garden is a richly rewarding and satisfying activity. It is soothing to the soul in a frenzied society; it provides us with an opportunity to nurture living things; and, almost inevitably, it connects us to the earth in a way that few other activities do.

This book is full of inspiring ideas for hundreds of flowering plants. Some will be familiar to the British reader and others will be less well known, and Latin names are given throughout as well as common names (some of which are particular to the USA). Due to the UK's variable climate, some of the recommended plants will only do well in very sheltered gardens in the mildest regions of the country. However with a little research, planning and experimentation, many should thrive in a frost free conservatory or greenhouse.

There are suggestions in this book for cultivars that may also be less well known to the British reader. Again this opens up a rich vein of new planting opportunities to have fun with. They are generally available from specialist suppliers who will give advice on how and where to grow them—they are also available via the internet.

Planning a garden offers the opportunity for much creative stimulation. It is exciting to evaluate the many features of each plant, choose the most suitable, and finalize what will go where. Equally exciting is thinking about the mood or feeling of the garden. When selecting the plants, the blooms are only one consideration; the size, shape, texture, and fragrance of the plants, as well as the spatial layout of the garden and the landscaping, can be just as important. It is through a careful combination of the above that the mood of the proposed garden is established—be it of drama, tranquility, tasteful charm, or barely controlled chaos.

Considering Color

Blossom color is what guides most gardeners in their plant purchases and understandably so. But it is worth planning in advance how certain colors work before deciding what will go where. For instance, saturated and bright colors such as clear orange, deep yellow, and red stand up well to bright midday summer light but tend to disappear at dusk. White, pink, and blue often appear dull, washed out, and without nuance in the glaring, high-summer sun but pop into view as the light fades into dusk. Consider such factors when positioning plants.

Creating a color scheme is another area that can be considered. Schemes may involve contrasting or harmonious colors; can explore variations in tints and tones of favorite colors; rely on brights or pastels; or revolve around single colors. Of course, some gardeners eschew the idea of a color scheme entirely, preferring a splashy paintbox effect.

It is also worth noting that, while the flowers a plant produces are the most typical source of color in the garden, many herbaceous perennials, shrubs, and even trees offer colorful fruit, bark, leaves, and stems to add to the mix.

Consider the peeling bark and golden yellow leaves of ninebark (*Physocarpus opulifolius* 'Dart's

ABOVE LEFT *Achieve year-round interest in the garden with plants such as camellias. This graceful* camellia sasanqua *'Otome-Sazanka' is frost hardy to -5° C, 23° F. It does best in a hot, sunny site on neutral to acid soil.*

Gold'); the delicate, feath-ery twiggy branches of *Acer palmatum* 'Senkaki', the orange-scarlet berries of *Berberis* 'Barbarossa' and the dazzling silver-white leaves of *Elaeagnus umbellata*.

Creating Year-Round Interest

Careful planning can result in continuous interest throughout the year. Annuals, perennials, climbers, shrubs, and trees provide endless options for fra-grance and color during the warmer months, including autumn. Planning for excitement from early winter through early spring is more challeng-ing, but an ever-increasing number of options exist.

Plants that bloom in the autumn and winter are especially valuable and often possess fragrance like witch hazel *(Hamamelis × intermedia)* whose flowers are frost resistant and wintersweet *(Chimonanthus praecox)* which benefits from the shelter of a south or west facing wall in cold areas. Some sasanqua camellias *(Camellia sasanqua* cultivars*)* bloom in autumn with many fragrant flowers. They need protection in temperatures lower than –5°C, 23°F and do best on a hot, sunny site. *Clematis cirrhosa* is useful for its lacy, evergreen leaves and produces cream flowers in late winter and early spring in frost free weather. Other features of winter interest include the long lasting red berries on the bare branches of the winterberry *(Ilex verticillata)*; the crimson or yellow dogwoods *(Cornus stolonifera* and *C. alba* cultivars which if grown in full sun give the best winter colour)*; and of course broadleaf ever-greens and conifers,which provide valuable struc-ture and a green backdrop to the winter garden.

(*Cupressus sempervirens*) and the Rocky Mountain juniper (*Juniperus scopulorum* 'Skyrocket'), while superb horizontal effects are provided by the flat flowerheads of *Achillea* 'Coronation Gold' and the horizontal branches of shrubs like *Viburnum plicatum* var. *tomentosum* 'Mariesii'.

Plants with a weeping habit provide a graceful air to a garden. Examples include fuchsias and wisteria whose flowers create a drooping effect; *Itea ilicifolia* and *garrya elliptica* with their lovely catkins; the common laburnum tree *(Laburnum anagyroides)*; and the flowering cherry tree *(Prunus* species*)*.

At the other end of the spectrum are spiky plants, which range from the tiny, dense, miniature thrift *(Armeria caespitosa)* and fluffy-looking tufted hair grass *(Deschampsia cespitosa)* to yucca *(Yucca* species*)* and New Zealand flax *(Phormium* species*)*. As well, round or ball-shaped plants can also be highly effective and include *Euphorbia characias* and *Santolina neapolitana* 'Edward Bowles'.

Texture

Sometimes overlooked are the subtle differences that a plant's texture brings to a garden. Choose from the rough or prickly leaves of *Gunnera* ; spiny leaves or flowers such as those of sea holly *(Eryngium* species*)*; or shiny or smooth leaves of *Bergenia* species. Fuzzy and woolly leafed plants such as lambs's tongue *(Stachys byzantina)* and mullein *(Verbascum bombyciferum)* also offer texture, as do the crimped and crinkled leaves of honeybush *(Melianthus major)*, *Acaena* 'Blue

Using Height and Layers

The clever arranging of tall, medium, and small plants can lend a three-dimensional quality to the garden and can make a space seem larger than it actually is. It can lend a sense of enclosure to some spaces and openness to others. As the largest plant in the garden, trees also provide a feeling of protection and offer shade. Also tall perennials like graceful ornamental grasses (*Miscanthus sinensis* var.*) or bamboo (*Phyllostachys nigra*), as well as any number of shrubs, can effectively screen one area from another and provide a backdrop for smaller plants. Climbers can also create a sense of height and dimension, whether growing up a wall or up into a tree or large shrub.

Plant Shapes

Variously shaped plants can provide contrast and visual interest when juxtaposed. Plants that have a narrow vertical shape include the Italian cypress

Haze', or the cinquefoil, *Potentilla peduncularis*.

Flower Forms

Visit any garden nursery and you will soon appreciate the many different ways in which flowers have evolved. There are spires, globes, and elegant plumes of flowers. Solitary flowers contrast with dense clusters of blooms, and umbels with upturned rays of starry flowers, such as *Angelica sylvestris* 'Vicar's Mead', compete for attention with ray-flowers like those of the daisy family, including coneflower (*Echinacea purpurea*). Shape can range from cup-shaped to tubular to pompon, with much in between; petal arrangement varies from single to fully double; and habit moves through 180 degrees, from erect to pendent.

Fragrance

The sudden sweet scent of a flower can be a real pleasure. Position scented plants where their fragrance may be best appreciated, such as entry-ways and sitting areas. Some of the most famously fragrant plants include angel's trumpet (*Brugmansia* species), citrus (*Citrus* species), gardenia (*Gardenia jasminoides*)—all three of which are frost tender. Hardier plants include lily-of-the-valley

(*Convallaria majalis*), sweet pea (*Lathyrus odoratus*), daphne (*Daphne odora*), some of the lilies (*Lilium* species), magnolia (*Magnolia* species), mock orange (*Philadelphus* species), and the very fragrant common lilac (*Syringa vulgaris*).

A number of plants possess strongly aromatic foliage: lavender (*Lavandula* species) and rock rose (*Cistus* species) have volatile oils in the leaves that scent the air in hot weather. Scented geraniums (*Pelargonium* species) are lovely for edging and window boxes. Many sages (*Salvia*) also have scented leaves, including the carmine red-flowering pineapple sage (*S. elegans*) and peach sage (*S. dorisiana*), with hot pink flowers and a deliciously peachy-pineapple scented leaf. Most of these aromatic plants need protecting from winter frost.

ABOVE *The daisylike pink ray florets form a pretty ring around the dark orange center of* Echinacea purpurea *'Magnus'. Plant en masse for a really spectacular effect.*

BELOW *Grow lavenders such as* Lavandula stoechas *along a border, where its long-stalked spikes of richly aromatic flowers can be brushed against and their scent released.*

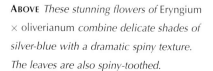

ABOVE *These stunning flowers of* Eryngium × oliverianum *combine delicate shades of silver-blue with a dramatic spiny texture. The leaves are also spiny-toothed.*

CHOOSING THE RIGHT PLANT

LEFT *When grouping plants together, their feeding and watering requirements, as well as height and growth rate, need to be compatible, otherwise they may need to be separated later on.*
BELOW *When seeking inspiration for your garden, plants such as this* Cercis canadensis *can provide ideas for color, shape, and texture that are in harmony with the environment.*

more cosmopolitan place and, largely, the focus has shifted toward its aesthetic qualities where gardeners are seeking plants for their textures, shapes, colors, and other properties. This is very much part of the fun of gardening, but it also requires a focused idea and a good eye.

Over time, knowledge and experience are gained by experimenting with different plants and plant combinations. However, you can save yourself much heartache by making good initial choices. Researching plants on the internet and in books are two excellent starting points. Speaking with a professional horticulturist at a local nursery will provide further direction. When assessing individual plants, it is important to determine their requirements and tendencies in the garden.

When considering plants that

Creativity, knowledge, and hard work are all needed to produce a vibrant and rewarding garden. Inspiration will help in visualizing a desired look, and dedication and hard work go a long way towards developing and implementing the plan. But knowledge is of equal importance, as this can help you choose plants that will be best suited to the needs of your garden.

look good together, it is vital that their rate of growth and eventual size are on the same scale. Make sure they have similar needs, such as light, water and soil requirements.

Artistry and Experimentation

Inspiration comes to people unexpectedly. It can be initiated by a simple, familiar, unremarkable detail seen for the first time in a very different light, or by the sight of something new and spectacular, never seen before. For gardeners, the enormous numbers of plants on offer can be almost overwhelming. In the past, the garden was mostly designed to maximize productivity, usually in a very practical lay-out. Today, the garden has evolved into a far

Climatic Factors

Climatic conditions play an important part in how plants grow and how we garden. It can be very satisfying to meet the challenges the weather throws up, and often involves exploiting its effects to the gardener's advantage. The easy route to success is to choose plants that suit the prevailing conditions. However, although some plants will only grow well in their native habitats, it is possible to adapt the conditions to allow many others to thrive.

The British Isles has a maritime climate, which is influenced by the warm air currents and rain from the surrounding oceans. Westerly regions can benefit from the warm air and sea currents coming from the Gulf Stream. This means that winters here are on the whole milder and frosts are generally not as prolonged.

Frost is a great hazard in gardening in the UK and thought to be more important than average minimum temperatures. The risk of spring frost in an area determines the date after which you can safely sow or plant out tender plants. The onset of the autumn frost signals the end of the growing season. We use the terms hardy, frost hardy and half hardy to determine what temperatures a plant can withstand. Hardy plants can tolerate temperatures down to –5°F (–15°C), frost hardy plants are safe above 23°F (–5°C) and half hardy plants need protection below temperature of 32°F (0°C).

In this book (especially in the A–Z section) there is reference to US Hardiness Zones 1 to 12. Broadly speaking, UK temperatures equate to US Hardiness zone 8 (annual min. temp. 10°F to 20°F, –12°C to –7°C) and zone 9 (20°F to 30°F, –7°C to –1°C).

RIGHT *Plants suited to a climate can add color to the garden when least expected. The long-lasting fruits of the fully hardy Malus 'Red Sentinel' bring vibrancy to a winter garden.*
BELOW *Large bodies of water can moderate a region's temperature, allowing the area to support less hardy plants. Choose plants that grow naturally along coastal paths and river banks.*

Exceptions to this would be if you garden in very sheltered conditions or in the mild west and south west which is roughly equivalent to Zone 10 (30°F to 40°F, –1°C to +4°C) or in very cold, exposed areas which would be equivalent to Zone 7 (0°F to 10°F, –16° to –12°C). It is always advisable to check with your nursery or supplier about temperatures and conditions required by particular plants before you buy.

When referring to the A–Z in this book you may find plants recommended which would only survive UK conditions in the most sheltered and mild areas (eg. orchids, cacti, bromeliads, tender flowers and shrubs). Such plants are generally frost tender and will do best in a greenhouse or conservatory.

LEFT Use your garden's microclimates creatively: Crinodendron hookerianum is a forest dweller from Chile that can be established in a sheltered damp spot.

these conditions. On a more localized scale, there can be variations within the confines of a single garden. For example, the south side of the house under an overhang offers an entirely different growing opportunity to a low, shady spot where water naturally collects or drains. A southern aspect will be the warmest, most protected site and will usually sustain tender plants longer than more exposed sites. A shady spot where water collects is usually the last place to dry out, making it suitable for plants that require moist, cool, shady sites.

Topography, Site and Microclimates
Every region has a number of influences that affect the suitability for planting. Bodies of water, prevailing winds, hills, mountains, valleys, slopes, forests, fields, buildings, urban areas, and many other features interact, creating microclimates that offer varying growing opportunities for different plants. Very windy and exposed sites or very wet areas are always challenging for a gardener, however it is still possible to find interesting plants that do well in

ABOVE Container grown plants can be placed in areas of the garden where the conditions are most suitable and moved to a sheltered position when there is a risk of frost or heavy winds.

LEFT AND RIGHT The garden was formerly a much more dedicated place, with culinary, cultural, and agricultural roots. Today, the emphasis is on personal taste and beauty, as people try to bring nature into their lives.

CARING FOR YOUR GARDEN

The amount of care a garden requires over time is directly related to its design. Naturally, the choice of plants is important, but it is the planning and preparation that goes into the garden space that is the most important factor in creating a beautiful and satisfying garden that requires minimum maintenance.

Soil Preparation

Of all the planning factors to consider, the most over-looked, yet crucial, is soil preparation. Before you can decide what you are going to plant in your garden it is essential to evaluate your soil. Establish your soil type (according to its clay, silt and sand content), its pH (acidity or alkalinity) and available nutrients, so you can work out which soil amendments to add. Home soil-testing kits are available at garden centers.

Most perennials and shrubs appreciate a well-drained, nutrient-rich, yet moisture-retentive soil. Depending on the composition and structure of the native soil, amendments in the form of composted organic matter (leaf mold, Canadian sphagnum peat moss, mushroom compost, and compost comprised of kitchen waste, bark, or manure) can be added to a depth of approximately 2 ft (0.6 m) to improve the soil structure. If the soil is comprised of heavy clay or if it drains poorly, the addition of organic matter will increase the soil's drainage and aeration. If it is sandy, gravelly, or nutrient-poor, it will improve the soil's ability to retain water. In certain cases, adequate quantities of sand, grit, or similar materials can improve drainage. This is important for plants with an aversion to poorly draining soil such as many alpine and Mediterranean plants.

Watering

The amount of watering needed in a garden depends on many factors, not least the amount of rainfall in an area, but also whether the plants are appropriate to the climate and site, and whether the soil has been well prepared. Careful planning can greatly minimize the frequency of watering tasks in a garden. Plants that require extra water can be grouped together, preferably in an area that is close to a hose or watering system. Plants that can tolerate less water can be planted in areas that are less accessible to water. Moisture-loving plants can be used in low-lying or poorly drained areas. Simple tips such as watering in the morning and early evening to reduce evaporation will help you collaborate with nature rather than fight it, thus saving much time and energy.

ABOVE *Rosa, Large-flowered (Hybrid Tea), 'Tendresse'. Roses will grow in most well-drained, medium loamy soils in which compost or organic manure has been incorporated.*

LEFT *The color of Hydrangea macrophylla flowers varies considerably, depending on the pH level of the soil. Acid soils produce blue flowers and alkaline soils produce reds and pinks.*

Remember that it takes quite a few years for a plant's root system to become sufficiently established to tolerate long dry periods. Not even "drought-tolerant" plants can survive drought until their roots are firmly established. The use of mulch during this period is particularly helpful.

ABOVE *As hot weather approaches, regular watering is important, particularly when rainfall is sporadic.*
LEFT *The old-fashioned watering can is a practical and satisfying method of watering the plants in a small garden.*

Fertilizing

Supplementary nutrients are sometimes useful but gardeners often over fertilize—an expensive habit that contributes to water pollution and causes some plants to make weak disease-prone growth. There is no use feeding a plant more than its roots are able to take up. Generally, a slow-release fertilizer that breaks down gradually is best, particularly if applied early in the growing season. Quick-release fertilizer should generally be reserved for plants such as vegetables, seedlings, annuals, and potted plants that need a boost for rapid growth. It is also worth considering whether extra growth is desirable on a plant. For instance, except where the soil is notably nutrient-poor, there is rarely reason to fertilize dwarf fruit trees with nitrogen, as they are at their most pleasing when modestly sized.

Sometimes nitrogen deficiency causes reduced growth and a lack of potassium can lead to leaf discoloration, however unless local soils are deficient in a particular nutrient or micronutrient, a balanced slow-release fertilizer is best to stimulate growth. Most established woody plants need only a layer of organic mulch, preferably the plants' own fallen leaves.

LEFT From left to right: Cedar chips, pine needles, and coconut husks make good mulching materials. The best time to apply mulch is in winter—make sure to remove weeds beforehand.

Mulching

Material that is spread on the surface of the soil to suppress weeds, conserve moisture, and protect the soil from washing away is known as mulch. Left to themselves, plants provide their own mulch when they drop leaves, which break down over time and cover the surface. Materials such as bark or wood chips, pine needles, grass clippings, chopped leaves, nutshells, and coconut husks also gradually break down, thus improving the condition of the soil. Organic mulch that breaks down fairly rapidly also encourages earthworms and microbes; these, in turn, improve the aeration and health of the soil. As the mulch decomposes, it should be replaced. Mulches made from materials such as gravel, rocks, and pebbles are sometimes used because they are more durable or for aesthetic reasons. They should be used with care, however, as they are more permanent and hard to rearrange.

Weeding

The chore of weeding is much minimized by the application of mulch. However, new or neglected gardens sometimes have severe perennial weed problems and it can take a few years of attention to control, much less eradicate, some persistent invaders. Depending on the weed in question, options include consistent hand-pulling and digging, thickly applied mulch, landscape fabric, solarizing (a technique making use of the heat of the summer sun to "fry" weed seeds on the surface of the soil), and—as a last resort—herbicide. (If choosing to use herbicide, always seek out the least toxic option first, and make sure you follow the directions on the label with particular care.)

A lot of garden weeds are annuals that grow rapidly, often in early spring, before setting seed and dying. Their seeds generally sprout the following season. By pulling them out before they set seed, you can minimize their numbers greatly every year. Mulching is the most highly effective way of suppressing annual weeds.

Pruning

Careful pruning can transform an unexciting shrub or tree into a shapely work of art. Pruning is generally done to improve a plant's health, to improve flowering, and for aesthetic reasons. Thus, diseased and dead wood is first removed, followed by pruning for improved flowering and shape.

When caring for woody plants including shrubs and trees, minor pruning can be done in spring—

ABOVE Pruning may be necessary if the tree or shrub outgrows its allotted space. Make the first cut on the underside of the branch, close to the branch collar.

after flowering is complete for spring-bloomers, and before growth begins for those that bloom later in the season. The aim is to encourage the plant to produce more "flowering wood" that is most likely to flower prolifically the following season. As different species are best pruned at different times, a comprehensive pruning book should be consulted. More serious pruning of woody plants and trees is best done during winter dormancy or in earliest spring for evergreens. For major pruning work, consult a manual, as trees in particular need to be pruned correctly if they are to heal properly.

RIGHT *A herbaceous perennial climber, the everlasting sweet pea (Lathyrus grandiflorus) needs to be deadheaded promptly, and the long shoots trimmed back in winter.*
BELOW *The ancient art of topiary involves shaping plants by meticulous pruning. Evergreen trees and shrubs are favored topiary subjects because of their dense foliage.*

Shrubs and trees are often at their best when their individual growth habit is accentuated. Thus, an open style of pruning that allows the plant's natural shape, as well as bark and leaves, to be seen, is desirable. Shearing is best reserved for hedges and topiary, as this type of pruning stimulates tight growth and crowded foliage, which can cause some plants to develop disease and insect problems.

Prune herbaceous perennials in early spring. Simply cut all the previous year's dead growth off at the base. In most climates, spring is also the time to divide overgrown clumps of perennials.

ANNUALS AND PERENNIALS

At the heart of the flower garden are annuals, biennials, and perennials. They offer an almost unrivalled choice of brilliantly colored blooms, are tolerant of a wide range of gardening situations and conditions and can provide an ongoing display of colorful flowers or foliage in the garden.

Annuals are plants that germinate, grow, flower, set seed, and die within a period of one year or less. Most annuals are grown from seed, and it can be enormously satisfying to watch the young plant emerge, grow, then burst into glorious bloom, often in the space of just a few months. Annuals are commonly classed as hardy. These often self seed and overwinter outdoors and start to grow in spring, or may be planted before the last frost. Half hardy plants include many tender perennials treated as annuals. Then there are frost tender plants that complete their lives between the first and last frost. Common annuals include petunias [Petunia], wax begonias [Begonia, Semperflorenscultorum Group]), and zinnias (Zinnia).

It is important to choose annuals according to your climate. Colorful annuals such as pansies (Viola × wittrockiana) and sweet peas (Lathyrus odoratus) typically require cool temperatures to develop strong root systems.

Annuals such as marigolds (Tagetes species), cosmos (Cosmos bipinnatus), and sunflowers (Helianthus annuus) require warmth to grow and flower well They must be started indoors or purchased as germinated seedlings and planted outdoors after the soil is sufficiently warm in spring and the danger of frost has completely passed.

A wide selection of annual seedlings is available at most garden centers in spring. When purchasing young seedlings, look for plants that are well-rooted but not overgrown. Some unusual annuals may be available only through specialist seed catalogs.

Biennials take two growing seasons to complete their life cycle, growing during the first season and flowering during the second before setting seed and dying. Biennials include hollyhocks (Alcea rosea), common foxgloves (Digitalis purpurea), and ornamental cabbages (Brassica species). To grow biennials from seed, plant in late spring or summer, as directed by the seed packet, either directly in the ground or in trays or small pots for later transplanting. They will flower the following growing season.

Perennials, which live for more than two years, are the mainstay of many flower gardens. The diversity of colors and shapes of perennial plants's foliage and blossoms is almost endless. In

ABOVE Today, many old-fashioned cottage garden flowers such as poppies (Papaver species) are grown as much for their traditional associations as for their bright and cheerful flowers.

LEFT Annuals like these petunias will grow strongly with regular water, fertilizer, and removal of spent flowers. This keeps the plant's energy focused on producing new flowers.

ABOVE *Combine annuals and perennials to achieve maximum effect in a cottage garden. Select colorful and fragrant plants to create a visual and olfactory delight.*

RIGHT *Annuals such as marigolds (*Tagetes *species) are undemanding plants that will add a splash of color to the garden. Removing spent blooms will prolong the flowering season.*

terms of growth habit, perennials come in a variety of forms. Herbaceous perennials such as peonies *(Paeonia species),* and some of the ornamental grasses die down to the ground in winter and resprout from the roots in spring. The tops of some perennials—such as cardinal flowers *(Lobelia cardinalis)*—die back and are replaced by a rosette of leaves that overwinter, putting on fresh growth in spring. Evergreen perennials persist throughout the year in essentially the same form and include plants such as pinks *(Dianthus species).*

Throughout history, there have been various ideas promoted concerning the mixing of perennials and annuals in gardens. During the Victorian period, for instance, annuals were bedded out by themselves in elaborate patterns—a high-maintenance, high-impact type of gardening that is rarely seen today outside of corporate or park plantings. Today, most gardeners prefer to grow annuals, perennials and shrubs in mixed borders,pots and baskets. Plant bold masses of color in bedding schemes, use dwarf varieties to provide color in tricky spots or gaps, and create interest with the shape, form, and foliage of perennials while more slow-growing plants like shrubs and trees establish themselves. The choice really is endless.

SHRUBS

Until recently, shrubs have been given short shrift in the popular mindset, viewed as a kind of plain green garden furniture, useful for foundation plantings around a house or garage. But an increasing number of beautiful shrubs is available, with multiple seasons of interest and more assets than just solid evergreen foliage or a fleeting show of flowers.

Generally defined as long-lived woody plants, distinct from trees by being under 10–15 ft (3–4.5 m) in height and clothed with leaves right down to the ground instead of having a bare trunk crowned with leaves, shrubs can range from subshrubs (small shrubs that are woody only at the base, such as *Salvia* species) to large woody plants that can be pruned either as trees or shrubs, such as elderberry (*Sambucus*).

An example of a shrub that has much to offer, yet is relatively rare even in the mild gardens to which it is suited, is the hybrid mahonia, *Mahonia × media* 'Arthur Menzies'. With spiky-looking foliage and sprays of yellow flowers in late winter, this 8–12 ft (2.4–3.5 m) high evergreen shrub makes an elegant and bold addition to the garden.

Dwarf serviceberry (*Amelanchier ovalis* 'Pumila') is also rarely grown, in spite of its useful size—about 3–4 ft (0.9–1.2 m) high—and its cold-hardiness down to –30°F (–34°C). It has attractive bluish green leaves that turn yellow and orange in autumn, and pretty clusters of white flowers in mid-spring.

Classics such as huge-flowered blue mophead hydrangeas (*Hydrangea macrophylla*) and camellias (*Camellia japonica*) will always be beloved garden plants. But many other, equally as interesting,

ABOVE *Use taller shrubs, such as* Mahonia × media *'Charity' shown here, to form a substantial colorful framework around which complementary plants can be added.*

RIGHT *Even when not in flower, shrubs—particularly those with colored, textured, or variegated foliage—can create maximum impact.*

species and varieties can be found within the stable ranks of these popular genera and can add considerable distinction to plantings. For instance, there is the beautiful and unusual *Hydrangea aspera,* Villosa Group. Attaining a height of around 12 ft (3.5 m) or more, this award-winning group of plants has fuzzy dark green leaves and large lacecap flowers with purple to purple-blue, fertile inner flowers and large, pinkish purple or lilac-white, sterile outer flowers.

There is also a vast array of species camellias that are rarely grown but offer a serene beauty. Many of

the species have smaller flowers than those of the *C. japonica* hybrids and have thus been overlooked for garden cultivation.

Today, camellias with attractive leaves or smaller, but exquisitely shaped and sometimes fragrant blossoms are increasingly grown and appreciated. These include *Camellia tsaii,* a species with numerous, small, white flowers and shiny, willowy, wavy-edged leaves, and the tea camellia (*Camellia sinensis*), with round ivory buds; small, white or pink, lightly fragrant flowers with fluffy yellow stamens; and glossy dark green leaves. The dried leaves of the tea camellia are the source of black tea, and the plant is a fun conversation piece as well as being attractive both in bud and in flower.

ABOVE *Give a classic look to any garden using hydrangeas for landscaping, to define areas in the garden, for mass plantings, or as a single specimen.*

RIGHT *Camellias, such as Camellia japonica 'Candy Apple', are popular garden shrubs, admired both for their gorgeous flowers and their lustrous leaves.*

Depending on the climate, autumn to spring is the best time to plant shrubs. Planting in autumn allows roots to establish while the ground is still warm, but can be done in winter during mild weather when the ground is not frozen. Spring planting could cause top growth to develop before roots establish and will require extra watering if there is an early dry spell. Disturbing the roots of pot-bound plants is best avoided in summer.

Shrubs are a vital addition to any garden, providing colorful flowers, foliage, fruit, and bark, as well as fragrance and interesting foliar texture. Prudent selection will ensure color and interest in the garden throughout the year. Large shrubs can be used in mixed borders to provide structure and backdrop. They can also provide visual screens, shade, and delineate space within the garden. When well-pruned, many shrubs are attractive enough to stand on their own as specimens.

TREES

Providing shelter, structure, and beauty, well-chosen trees lend dignity and grace to the landscape and play a vital role in the life of the planet, moderating temperatures and producing oxygen. Generally defined as tall woody plants with one dominant trunk, or a few trunks, and a crown of foliage, trees are distinguished from shrubs by being taller than 10–15 ft (3–4.5 m), and are often much taller. However, some trees grow as shrubs, due to pruning or cold temperatures, while some shrubs can attain treelike proportions.

In urban situations, trees quiet the noise, mitigate air pollution, and provide a sense of calm and in summer, trees can have a cooling effect by shading buildings from the sun. Windbreaks and hedges can reduce heating bills, as well as screening unsightly views.

As well as serving a variety of utilitarian purposes, trees form the living backbone of the garden,

LEFT *Most magnolias become statuesque and elegant with age and make fine specimen shrubs and trees, particularly for lawns and open areas.*

offering beauty through their blossoms, fruit, foliage, bark, and structure. Healthy trees, particularly large ones, also produce an ineffable feeling of security in humans. Particularly when trees are in scale to their settings, a sense of harmony is created: for wide open areas and near large structures, large trees look appropriate, while small trees are in scale with small structures and confined areas, making them feel more spacious.

Trees include some of Earth's largest and oldest living entities—the oldest recorded living tree, a bristlecone pine *(Pinus aristata)* growing in California's Sierra Nevada, is some 4,800 years old—and, though it is unlikely that such ages will be achieved in the back garden, it is nevertheless important to choose and position a tree carefully. Some trees grow quickly but are short-lived; others are investments in the future, growing more slowly perhaps but often living longer.

Some practical issues to consider when choosing and positioning trees include the tree's cold or heat tolerance; rate of growth; height and width; foliage (evergreen or deciduous); possible litter from flowers, leaves, or fruit; root system; and potential pest and disease problems.

Flowering trees such as flowering cherry *(Prunus species)* and crabapple *(Malus species)* are landscape classics, providing some of the most gloriously beautiful and fragrant spring flowering displays imaginable in cool- to cold-winter climates. Cherries also offer fine yellow and orange autumn foliage and distinctive shiny bark, while the bright orange, red, or yellow fruits of crabapples sometimes

LEFT *Often heralding winter's end and the beginning of spring, magnificent blossoms cover the bare branches of the flowering cherry, such as* Prunus sargentii *shown here.*

ABOVE *Shade, depth, height, texture, color, and contrast can all be provided by careful selection of trees, thereby creating a peaceful garden sanctuary for relaxation and enjoyment.*
RIGHT Crepe myrtle (Lagerstroemia indica) *is a half hardy landscaping subject, producing long panicles of colorful summer flowers, followed by fiery autumn foliage*

decorate the tree until after the leaves have dropped.

In milder areas and sheltered gardens, crepe myrtle *(Lagerstroemia* species) offer four seasons of beauty: summer flowers in flashy pinks, reds, and purples, as well as white; exceptional red, orange, or yellow autumn color; beautiful, smooth, brown- and cream-mottled bark to admire when the leaves are gone in winter; and, very often, coppery red new growth in spring.

Another choice for sheltered gardens are wattles *(Acacia)* and *Eucalyptus*. These fast-growing broadleaf evergreen trees range in form from shrubs to large trees. They have fluffy flowers mostly in cream to yellow shades, and pretty green, silvery, pinkish, or bluish, evergreen foliage. Some *Acacia* species have fragrant flowers and most *Eucalyptus*

species have strongly scented foliage. Both wattles and eucalypts are excellent choices for mild, dry areas, as once they are established they have minimal water requirements.

The genus *Magnolia*, among the most ancient seed-bearing plants still in existence, includes a diverse group of shrubs and trees ranging from the cold-hardy early-blooming star magnolia *(Magnolia stellata)* to the unusual, somewhat tender, evergreen *Magnolia delavayi*, noted for its fragrant blooms that often open at night.

Trees are a vital part of the landscape, providing a framework for other plants and lending grace and beauty to the garden. Choosing the right tree is not difficult, as long as the many practical factors are taken into account along with aesthetic preferences.

FLOWERING GROUND COVERS

Ground covers are low-growing plants, grown en masse to eliminate lawn maintenance, help retain steep banks, suppress weeds, and create swathes of color. Many perennials, grasses, climbers, shrubs, and bulbs are suitable to use as ground covers. Densely planting an area can create the effect of a ground cover, whether the same plant is used throughout or a tapestry of species is chosen. Ground covers can be totally prostrate or can reach up to 4 ft (1.2 m) in height—any taller, and they are simply massed perennial or shrub beds.

LEFT Bergenia cordifolia 'Red Start' is a good ground cover and rockery plant, valued as much for its heart-shaped leaves as for its flowers.
BELOW LEFT Ideal for rock gardens, Iberis sempervirens is a low spreading subshrub, with dense rounded heads of white flowers and attractive dark green leaves.
BELOW Clivia miniata 'Kirstenbosch Yellow' has creamy yellow flowers. In mild regions, clivias can be used in borders but need protection against. frost.

Properly chosen ground covers are often a practical alternative to lawn grass, as they don't require much maintenance and, once established, are self-mulching and rarely need trimming. On steep banks, narrow strips between paths and buildings, and in areas underneath trees where grass struggles, many ground covers will thrive. Best of all, there are many beautiful flowering ground covers that will serve the purpose.

When landscaping with ground-cover plants, care should be taken that the plants chosen are suitable for the site and the amount of care available. Factors to consider include the plant's cold and heat tolerance; moisture, light, drainage, and soil-quality requirements; ultimate dimensions; rate of growth; plus leaf and flower size and color. It is also worth considering whether an evergreen or deciduous ground cover is desired.

If weed suppression is the aim, then the ground cover you choose should grow quickly and create a thick mat of growth that effectively chokes out weeds. Some plants are better at this than others, but in any case, weeds should be completely removed prior to planting.

Many people overlook native ground covers, but these are well adapted to the local climate and, once established, can thrive with minimal effort on the part of the gardener. Flowering plants are also sometimes overlooked as ground covers, but except in the most difficult situations, there is no reason to stick with plain green foliage plants unless a uniform green color is sought.

Wide-spreading flowering shrubs abound, and make good ground covers by providing rapid horizontal coverage. The wide-spreading prostrate wattle *Acacia pravissima* 'Golden Carpet', with profuse, bright yellow, honey-scented flowers, and the creeping *Ceanothus griseus* 'Yankee Point', with fluffy heads of medium-blue flowers, are suitable for sheltered gardens in milder climates. These evergreen shrubs have a low spreading habit, appreciate sun, and are tolerant of drought and heat.

ABOVE Erica cinerea *f.* alba *'C. D. Eason' is a widely spreading low shrub with erect sprays of rose purple flowers. Most cultivars in this species will provide a sea of color in summer.

RIGHT Veronica austriaca *subsp.* teucrium *'Shirley Blue' grows to 10 in (25 cm) high, and is suitable for a rock garden or as a ground cover. It flowers from late spring to mid-summer.*

In colder areas, numerous low-flowering shrubs can be used, including bluebeard (*Caryopteris* × *clandonensis*), covered in blue flowers in summer and reaching 2 × 2 ft (0.6 × 0.6 m), and the wide-spreading Nikko slender deutzia (*Deutzia gracilis* 'Nikko'), with arching stems to 2 ft (0.6 m) clothed in small pure white flowers. Low-growing heaths and heathers (*Erica* and *Calluna* species) provide swathes of purple, pink, or white blooms and their dense evergreen foliage successfully suppresses most weeds.

Many flowering perennials, planted en masse, make excellent ground covers. These include *Bergenia* species, lily-of-the-valley (*Convallaria majalis*), candytuft (*Iberis* species), and speedwell (*Veronica* species). Perennials with fibrous roots and

a thick growth habit are also especially valuable for use as ground covers.

In mild areas the fibrous-rooted *Agapanthus* species can make fine ground covers with their strappy elegant leaves and bright showy flowers and includes several hardier species that can be grown in cooler climates. The evergreen species make especially nice ground covers. They do best in full sun and the crowns need to be protected with mulch in the winter

Flowering climbers such as jasmine (*Jasminum* species), honeysuckle (*Lonicera* species), and climbing hydrangea (*Hydrangea anomala* subsp. *petiolaris*) can be used to cover banks and bare areas of ground, providing thick foliage and flower cover.

selections are sometimes prone to disease but new cultivars have been developed to resist disease and, as a result, these exquisite trees are now regaining popularity in the garden.

Known as juneberry, shadblow, or serviceberry, depending on what part of the world you're in, *Amelanchier* trees have fuzzy silver buds that open to reveal exceedingly pretty white flowers early in the season and, usually, dark fruits that are appreciated by birds. An added bonus with virtually all species of *Amelanchier* is the bright orange autumn foliage.

FRUIT TREES

Many fruit trees are grown as much for their ornamental attributes as for their fruit. However, increasingly, numerous fruit-bearing trees are selected precisely for their ornamental features, which include showy, sometimes double flowers, large and colorful fruits that persist well into winter, and fiery autumn foliage.

Closely related to their fruiting cousins, the apple and the cherry, the flowering crabapple *(Malus species)* and flowering cherry *(Prunus species)* are classic ornamental trees. Both types of tree produce a lavish display of white, pink, or red blossoms in spring. Crabapples follow the display of flowers with fruit that is usually showy and that makes good jam and jelly. As an added bonus, the flowers of both are usually sweetly fragrant. Older

In general, frost-tender citrus trees *(Citrus* species) are primarily selected for the edible characteristics of their fruit. But, as it happens, the flowers are lovely and intensely fragrant, and the trees themselves are attractive, with glossy evergreen leaves and rounded forms. There is variation among citrus in frost- and disease-tolerance, as well as heat requirements. Most require temperatures of 41°F–50°F, 5°C–10°C and in cooler areas are grown in pots in conservatories where they may simply be grown for the fragrant flowers and not be expected to produce ripe fruit. Citrus trees make fine specimen plants to enjoy in the right conditions.

HERBS

Cultivated since ancient times, herbs have traditionally been valued for medicinal and culinary purposes, their fragrance, and also for general household use. Although they are rarely grown in gardens for medicinal purposes today, a dozen or so culinary herbs are essential plants for many gardeners (and cooks). These include basil (*Ocimum basilicum*), parsley (*Petroselinum crispum*), spearmint (*Mentha spicata*), thyme (*Thymus vulgaris*), oregano (*Origanum vulgare*), sweet marjoram (*Origanum marjorana*), and chives (*Allium schoenoprasum*).

Many culinary herbs are easy and gratifying to grow, if somewhat frost-tender. Appreciating plenty of sun and warmth, most make fine pot subjects and can often be overwintered in a bright windowsill. Many herbs are easy to start from seed, as well, and those that don't overwinter can be replaced in spring. Culinary herbs are best planted close to the kitchen door, where they may be easily harvested for cooking.

Just as satisfying is to grow herbs purely for their ornamental qualities and fragrance. Rosemary (*Rosmarinus officinalis*), sage (*Salvia officinalis*), and

LEFT *In warm climates,* Lavandula dentata *is in flower most of the year. It has rich purple flower spikes and narrow gray-green leaves that are bluntly toothed.*

lavender (*Lavandula* species) are widely grown in flower gardens, and numerous ornamental cultivars exist of each. They include prostrate rosemary (*Rosmarinus* 'Irene'), which is marvelous hanging down rock walls; *Salvia officinalis* 'Purpurascens', with dark, smoky, purple foliage; and the many species and selections of lavender, from the silver-leafed, woolly, Lisa Marie lavender (*Lavandula lanata* 'Lisa Marie') to the fat-spiked, purple, Otto Quast Spanish lavender (*L. stoechas* 'Otto Quast').

The popular Mediterranean herbs such as sage, rosemary, thyme, and lavender are often incorporated into perennial borders, contributing fragrance and pretty flowers that are attractive to bees. They may need protection during cold weather however. Herbs with fragrant foliage are wonderful when placed beside paths, where they are frequently brushed against in passing, thus releasing their delightful scent. Often used in pots, the scented geraniums such as *Pelargonium crispum*, have particularly delicious and pungent leaf oils.

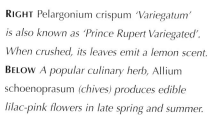

RIGHT Pelargonium crispum *'Variegatum' is also known as 'Prince Rupert Variegated'. When crushed, its leaves emit a lemon scent.*
BELOW *A popular culinary herb,* Allium schoenoprasum *(chives) produces edible lilac-pink flowers in late spring and summer.*

BULBS, CORMS, AND TUBERS

Plants that possess an underground storage system are known as bulbs, and there are a wide array of beautiful flowering plants that fall into this category. The bulb is a common adaptation that simply means the plant may be dug up, dried, and sold, usually without foliage, while at rest (dormant). The rest period coincides with a period of adverse weather, usually drought, in the bulbs's native habitat. Most "Dutch" bulbs like daffodils (*Narcissus*) and tulips (*Tulipa*) are planted in the autumn and bloom in spring—although there are also bulbs that are planted in spring and bloom in summer or autumn. Typically included under the rubric of bulbs are true bulbs, rhizomes, corms, and tubers, as well as tuberous-rooted plants. The differences between these types of storage systems are mostly technical but it can be useful to understand the basic differences.

A true bulb consists of an underground stem base containing an embryonic plant surrounded by scales and wrapped in a protective papery tunic. Examples include crinum (*Crinum*), lily (*Lilium*), grape hyacinth (*Muscari*), daffodil, and tulip.

Corms, which are shaped like bulbs but composed of solid tissue instead of scales, are essentially swollen underground stem bases wrapped in a tunic of the dried bases of the previous season's leaves. Corms include crocus (*Crocus*), autumn crocus (*Colchicum*), crocosmia (*Crocosmia*), gladiolus (*Gladiolus*), corn lily (*Ixia*), and harlequin flower (*Sparaxis*). Corms, like true bulbs, often have a brief and finite flowering period, quickly followed by dormancy.

Rhizomes are also underground stems modified for storage—examples include lily-of-the-valley (*Convallaria majalis*), crimson flag (*Schizostylis coccinea*), bearded iris (*Iris* hybrids), and calla lily (*Zantedeschia* species). In both rhizome and corm, the older part often dies seasonally and is replaced

RIGHT *Narcissus 'Quail' is a delightful daffodil that enlivens the garden in mid-spring with its bright yellow flowers.*
BELOW *Suitable for a mixed border or woodland garden, Muscari armeniacum 'Blue Spike' bears dense bunches of blue flowers in early spring.*

ELOW *'Ascari' is an exotic* Lilium *Oriental Hybrid, with fragrant pink flowers marked in red and yellow.*

by new growth. Some rhizomes have evergreen foliage that never completely disappears during dormancy.

Tubers are swollen underground stems with a fleshy non-scaly structure, possessing multiple growth points. Some examples include *Cyclamen* and *Begonia*. Some tubers and tuberous-rooted perennials bloom almost indefinitely once they have developed sufficient foliage for the season, unlike true bulbs, corms, and many rhizomes, whose blooms are fleeting and followed by dormancy.

With flowers that are sometimes large and fleshy, sometimes smaller and delicate, bulbous plants possess some of the most voluptuous exquisitely formed blossoms outside of the orchid family. Many bulbs make good cut flowers and, planted in large swathes, bulbs provide a floral display that few plants can rival. True bulbs and corms that flower then become dormant play a special role in the perennial garden: they can be layered, rising to flower and then disappearing as the perennials's leaves emerge.

Mass plantings of bulbs underneath trees in woodland areas can create a huge impact. Blossoming in the dappled light underneath deciduous trees, woodland bulbs such as wood anemone *(Anemone nemorosa)*, Greek windflower *(A. blanda)*, and snowdrop *(Galanthus* species) are among the earliest to bloom in the garden, signifying spring.

In grassy wilder areas of the garden, plants such as *Narcissus pseudonarcissus* and *N. poeticus* look natural and, in some climates, will slowly colonize. Camass *(Camassia* species) and some crocus, particularly the lavender-blue *Crocus tomasinianum*, can be planted in lawns or meadows that are cut short in autumn. Peeking through the cut grass in late winter to early spring, they have usually finished blooming and their foliage has died right down by the time of the next mowing.

Given rich, well-drained soil, tulips, crocus species, and many small species of narcissus thrive in all aspects except deep shade. These bulbs look good in gravel gardens planted with *Yucca*, lavenders, creeping rosemary, *Euphorbia* species, shrubby *Penstemon*, rock rose *(Cistus* species), and other drought-adapted plants.

CACTI AND SUCCULENTS

Featuring plants from many botanical families and from virtually every part of the world, succulents are defined most simply as plants that store water for an extended period during some part of the year. Possessing thick fleshy leaves, stems, or roots designed to maximize water storage, succulents have adapted to situations where fresh water is not steadily available such as in semi-desert habitats, along seashores where the available water is saline, and in the canopy of tropical rainforests, where the only available water must be captured in the form of rain or mist.

Succulent plants can be found in tropical, sub-tropical and temperate climates throughout the world and are particularly abundant in Africa and the Americas, but true cacti are only naturally found in the Americas.

Succulents have been used throughout human history for a host of purposes including medicine, food, drink, fiber, and shelter. *Aloe vera*, the earliest recorded succulent, was used for treating wounds at least as far back as late Sumerian times, and the native peoples of the Americas have traditionally relied on succulents, including cacti, for many medicinal, ceremonial, and other purposes.

Succulents play a special role in the garden, not only because they are tolerant of drought and fit well with modern low-water landscapes but also because they suggest, with their forms, colors, and textures, a dramatic, otherworldly, heat-drenched environment, even when planted in temperate climates. Some of the plants's water-conserving mechanisms also give them their distinctive appearance: common among succulents are such features as glossy, waxy, powdery, hairy, or scaly surfaces. The colors of most succulents's stems and leaves are muted but, when the flowers are bright, the subtle foliage only intensifies the colors.

Succulents look good planted in swathes, as solitary specimens, and in pots, where they often thrive. Low-growing succulents can be massed in beds and grown in pots outdoors and indoors as house plants. In mild areas large, spiky succulents, such as many *Euphorbia* and the succulentlike *Yucca*, look bold and modern in the garden and are

LEFT Delosperma *species, like* D. brunnthaleri, *are useful low-growing plants, suitable for underplanting. Min temp 41°F, 5°C. Frost tender*
FAR LEFT *With minimal water requirements, plants like* Lampranthus aurantiacus *can bring color to dry areas. Min temp 41°F, 5°C. Frost tender*

substantial enough to stand alone as specimens, although they are most attractive underplanted with low-growing smaller-leafed flowering succulents like ice plants *(Delosperma* and *Lampranthus* species both min temp 41°F, 5°C). Taking a cue from a succulent's native habitat can reveal ideal planting companions but many exotic plants from similar environments work well on a sheltered site, including drought-tolerant species of rock rose *(Cistus),* manzanita *(Arctostaphylos),* Texas or autumn sage *(Salvia greggii), Gazania,* blanket flower *(Gaillardia),* blue oat grass *(Helictotrichon sempervirens),* and California poppy *(Eschscholzia californica).*

While many succulents are cold-sensitive, there are a number that tolerate temperatures of 20°F (–7°C) and lower. They include not only succulent perennial plants commonly grown in temperate gardens such as stonecrop *(Sedum)* and houseleek *(Sempervivum)* but also a number of more unusual species of cactus that are rarely seen outside their native habitat in spite of their relative ease of cultivation.

Frost-hardy cacti may seem like a contradiction, as cacti so thoroughly symbolize the hot desert, but some grow at high elevations and in environments that are frosty in winter. These include the claret cup cactus, *Echinocereus triglochidiatus,* with scarlet to crimson flowers and the pink- to purple-flowered lacy cactus, *E. reichenbachii* from Oklahoma. However they do not thrive in cold and wet climates and would be better grown indoors in the UK.

Succulents and cacti are a diverse group of plants, ranging in size, shape, blossom type and color, and cultural preferences. Well-drained soil is necessary for almost all species and lean soil is often ideal. However, given their few requirements, these are remarkably easy-care plants.

LEFT *The unusual shapes of cacti, like* Echinocereus coccineus, *form natural sculptures and do better indoors.*
BELOW *Some plants, like hardy* Sedum spathulifolium *'Purpureum', offer plump, fleshy, colorful foliage.*

CLIMBING PLANTS

Climbers are among the most versatile of plant groups from a design perspective, able to scale walls, drape across fences, scramble up trees, provide cover for banks, and wind their way up arbors, trellises, pergolas, and pillars.

Climbers lend height and dimension to the garden, lifting the eye upward and filling in spaces that would otherwise remain empty. With the help of a suitable trellis, a blank wall or the corner of a building can be clothed with a beautiful flowering vine. Smaller climbers, such as hybrid clematis, can be trained into large shrubs whose bloom period is brief, thus providing an additional season of flowers.

There is a great diversity of flower types among climbing plants, from the bright orange tubular-shaped flowers of the common trumpet creeper (*Campsis radicans*) and scarlet trumpet honeysuckle (*Lonicera* × *brownii* 'Dropmore Scarlet') to the intoxicatingly fragrant lipped flowers of the giant Burmese honeysuckle (*L. hildebrandiana*) and early Dutch honeysuckle (*L. periclymenum* 'Belgica'). The candy-colored papery bracts of *Bougainvillea* (min

temp 45°F-50°F, 7°C-10°C) provide intense color in conservatories.

Annual climbers such as morning glory (*Ipomoea tricolor*) and black-eyed Susan vine (*Thunbergia alata*) can provide quick and colorful coverage for small garden structures, with long-lasting, reliable, summer flowers. (Both half hardy min 32°F, 0°C).

Evergreen climbers such as ivy (*Hedera*) are best for cloaking structures or views that you wish to obscure, while deciduous climbers will only create a screen during the summer months, losing their leaves in the autumn. Many deciduous climbers with woody frameworks also provide winter interest, offering sinuously twining trunks (*Wisteria*), or beautiful, peeling, cinnamon-colored bark (*Hydrangea anomala* subsp. *petiolaris*). Most wisteria and climbing hydrangea leaves turn a fine clear yellow in autumn before they drop.

There are many methods of attachment among climbers, and supports should be selected to suit the climbing methods of the chosen plant. Climbing methods include the twisting leaf stalks

LEFT *Annual climbers, such as Black Eyed Susan* (Thunbergia alata), *have attractive flowers and can be trained to grow up small structures.*
BELOW Bougainvillea *species, scrambling climbers, are loved for their vibrant colors and do best grown in a conservatory.*

ABOVE *Climbing by tendrils,* Passiflora *species produce gorgeous flowers. Many bear edible fruit, the most well known being the passionfruit.*

used by clematis to attain height; tendrils used by climbers such as the annual sweet pea (*Lathyrus odoratus*); and side and twisting terminal shoots produced by passion climbers (*Passiflora* species) and grape climbers (*Vitus* species). These types of climbers can have trouble with large smooth posts and do best with finer supports that they can easily grasp or encircle.

Self-clinging climbers such as climbing hydrangea (*Hydrangea anomala* subsp. *petiolaris*) and common trumpet creeper (*Campsis radicans*) use aerial rootlets or adhesive discs to grasp on to flat surfaces.

Trailing or scandent climbing shrubs such as winter jasmine (*Jasminum nudiflorum*) simply send out long supple shoots that should be tied to a support. Bougainvillea (*Bougainvillea* hybrids) and many roses employ long sharp thorns or prickles to scramble through trees and up structures. Scrambling climbers can also cascade along banks and walls.

As well as types of attachment, the growth rate and ultimate size of climbers vary. More delicate climbers are suitable for small structures such as wirework arches or training through shrubs, while climbers with more rampant growth are best reserved for sturdy structures. However, with diligent pruning, large climbers such as wisteria can be grown on small trellises. Most climbers need little more maintenance than

ABOVE *Climbing roses—Large-flowered or Cluster-flowered— are a classic choice for gardens needing an elegant touch.*
TOP *Most* Clematis *species are deciduous, and can be grown to scramble up through trees and shrubs and up trelliswork.*

regular pruning and removal of old growth.

Climbing plants are a kind of fabric that weaves a garden together, filling in empty spaces, connecting structures to the garden, disguising fences and walls, screening unwanted views, softening hard lines and edges, and—very often—providing the luxury of blossoms to boot throughout the seasons. There is a suitable climber for nearly every garden situation— the challenge lies in narrowing down the many attractive choices.

ORCHIDS

Often regarded with a kind of reverence, orchids are undeniably special among flowering plants and have been much sought after in the West since the discovery by Europeans of the economically important vanilla *(Vanilla planifolia)* in 1510. Attributed with a variety of properties including aphrodisiacal ones, orchids and particularly orchid blossoms represent adventure, exoticism, eroticism, and opulence. Perhaps due to many orchids's deceptive reproductive habits, they have a reputation for fertility, mystery, even evil. Historically, they have been among the most highly prized, and therefore costly, plants in cultivation, with large sums paid for rare specimens.

Nevertheless, most of them are easy to grow in cultivation, provided their basic needs are met. These include five basic requirements: light, moisture, air circulation, humidity, and nutrients. Fortunately, due to the diverse habitats in which orchids originate, there are suitable orchids for a wide array of interior and some garden situations.

Comprising probably the largest family in the plant kingdom, the members of Orchidaceae include about 900 genera, 20,000 species, and over 100,000 hybrids and cultivars, with more wild discoveries and many more hybrids every year.

The subsequent range of size, shape, color, and fragrance among orchid flowers is legendary. Individual flowers range in size from microscopic to approximately 8 in (20 cm) in diameter, in shape from flat to nearly tubular, and are arranged in racemes, spikes, or clusters of one to several dozen blossoms. Color range is breathtaking: jewel-tone pinks, reds, and purples to yellows, browns, greens, nearly black, and even a true blue. Some orchid blossoms are pure single colors while others are multicolored, often intricately marked and patterned. Some cultivated orchids have no fragrance or just a light sweet odor but others are intensely fragrant, some particularly so at night. A few, in order to attract specific pollinators, smell of carrion.

Leaves range from tiny to more than 3 ft (0.9 m) across and can be wide and pleated, plump and fleshy, thin and grassy, or hard and leathery. Some orchid leaves last for years; others drop off yearly and are replaced. Some orchids have exquisitely patterned foliage with mottling, checks, or stripes, occasionally overlaid with a glistening sheen, other times bristling with soft hairs.

Orchid plants also vary tremendously in form and include primarily underground species that lack chlorophyll (saprophytes); soil-dwelling (terrestrial) perennial herbs; rock-dwelling species (lithophytes); and others (epiphytes) that cling to the bark of trees and shrubs, gathering moisture and nutrients from rain, fog, and dew. These tree-dwelling types make up more than half of all known orchid species.

Hardy orchids, so called because they originate from the temperate areas of the world, are primarily terrestrial and include *Bletilla*, lady's slipper orchids, some other Cypripedium species, and Indian crocus *(Pleione)*.

Many orchids originate in the tropics and subtropics, and outside of those regions, such as in the UK, they are grown indoors as house plants or in greenhouses—though they can be

LeLeft The fascinating reproductive structures of orchids include elaborate and colorful blossoms. Pleione El Pico 'Pheasant' has a red-spotted daintily frilled lip.

placed outdoors during summer in warmer areas. Some, such as the jewel orchid *(Ludisia discolor)*, are quite adaptable to household conditions, appreciating shade, warmth, and even tolerating rather dry air.

There is an almost limitless number of stunning orchids to choose from. The key to their successful cultivation is to begin by selecting varieties that are suitable to the conditions at hand. Those who choose the right orchids for their home, garden or greenhouse will be rewarded with long-lived, healthy plants that produce some of the most extravagantly beautiful flowers known to humankind.

ABOVE RIGHT *Less hardy orchids, such as Dendrobium speciosum, do best in an intermediate greenhouse with a minimum winter night temperature of 55°F-60°F, 13°C-15°C.*
RIGHT *Orchids are produced in every shade and color combination —seen here is Cymbidium Pontiac 'Trinity'.*

BROMELIADS

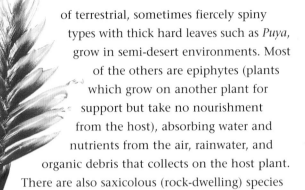

Including some 2,700 species and many more hybrids, bromeliads are an increasingly popular group of perennial herbs known for their stiff rosettes of foliage and brightly colored unusually shaped flowers.

Bromeliads are virtually all New World plants, growing from sea level up to 14,000 ft (4,270 m) and from cool mountain ranges and tropical rainforests to hot semi-deserts. Most come from South America, primarily Brazil, but they are also found from Chile and Argentina, through Central America and the Caribbean, as far north as coastal Virginia in the USA. Most are found in tropical rainforests but some, particularly a group of terrestrial, sometimes fiercely spiny types with thick hard leaves such as *Puya*, grow in semi-desert environments. Most of the others are epiphytes (plants which grow on another plant for support but take no nourishment from the host), absorbing water and nutrients from the air, rainwater, and organic debris that collects on the host plant. There are also saxicolous (rock-dwelling) species that grow on stony outcrops and sheer cliff faces.

Many bromeliads have stiff rosettes of leaves that overlap at the base, creating a funnellike structure that collects water. As well as storing moisture for the plant's own use, the collected water is used by rainforest tree frogs that rely on such "tank" bromeliads during part of their life cycle. To take advantage of scarce rainfall and fog, bromeliad leaves have specialized scales designed to absorb moisture when it is present and provide a shield against moisture loss when water is scarce and when the sun is hot.

The best-known member of Bromeliflorae is the pineapple (*Ananas comosus*), discovered as a cultivated crop among the Carib Indians during Columbus's second voyage to the New World in 1493. Within 50 years of this discovery, the pineapple had been widely disseminated and was cultivated in a number of tropical regions for commerce. By the end of the eighteenth century, the collection and propagation of ornamental bromeliads had begun in earnest, as collectors discovered their unusual and colorful flowers and foliage.

ABOVE *Rather aptly known as painted feather, the elegant plumelike flowers of* Vriesea *'Mariae' are a highly decorative plant.*

LEFT *Providing a glorious indoor display, the basal rosette of leaves of* Aechmea *species, such as* A. pineliana, *serves as a water reservoir.*

BELOW Aechmea *species such as* A. gamosepala *often have brightly colored flowers contrasting with equally highly colored bracts.*

Except for the pineapple fruit, bromeliads are grown today as ornamentals. There is an incredible diversity of flower and leaf shape and color, as well as plant size, which can vary from less than 1 in (25 mm) to 20 ft (6 m) in height. Common genera include *Aechmea*, vase plant (*Billbergia*), *Neoregelia*, air plant (*Tillandsia*), and *Vriesea*, with some 56 currently described

ABOVE *Although the native habitat of most* Guzmania *species is tropical rainforest, they make superb indoor plants.*
RIGHT *If they are to do well,* Billbergia *species need a position offering shade, warmth, and humidity (min temp 41°F, 5°C).*

genera. Extensively hybridized, most recent bromeliad selections have colorful flowers and foliage forms. Leaves are striped, barred, mottled, or uniformly colored in shades of green, bluish green, yellow-green, silver, gray, red, purple, and almost black. Flowers appear in many hues of pink, purple, red, blue, silver, white, and green. Flower spikes can be cupped, bracted, branched, upright, or pendent.

The requirements of care for most bromeliads are minimal, as long as suitable species are chosen for a given situation. They make curiously fascinating and beautiful specimens in the home, warm conservatory or greenhouse. Some take full sun, some prefer partial shade, and there are species appropriate for both humid and dry conditions. Many appreciate being regularly misted

and others like to go dry between waterings.

Bromeliads are generally inexpensive, easy to grow, demand little special care when correctly situated, and offer brilliant, colorful, long-lasting flowers and dramatic ornamental foliage. Varying tremendously in size, texture, and color, they can fulfill numerous functions in return for very little effort.

Illustrated Guide to

FLOWER TYPES

F lowers are the plant's reproductive center, producing seed in a protected chamber, the ovary, which develops into the fruit. To ensure this, flowers have evolved into a wide range of colors, sizes, and shapes. With cultivation, this diversity has only increased.

STRUCTURE

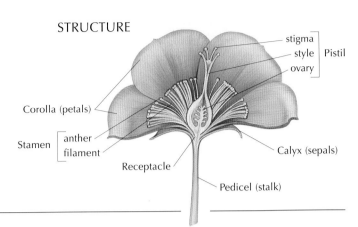

SHAPES

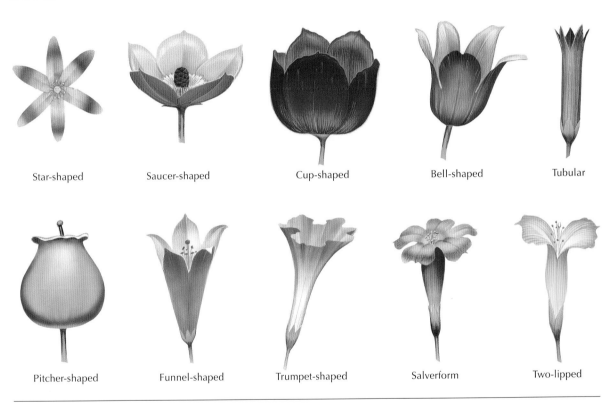

Star-shaped   Saucer-shaped   Cup-shaped   Bell-shaped   Tubular

Pitcher-shaped   Funnel-shaped   Trumpet-shaped   Salverform   Two-lipped

ORIENTATION

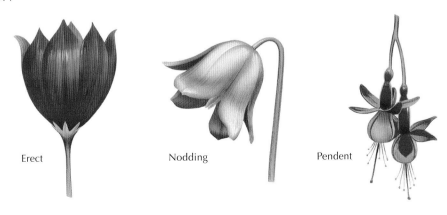

Erect   Nodding   Pendent

INFLORESCENCES

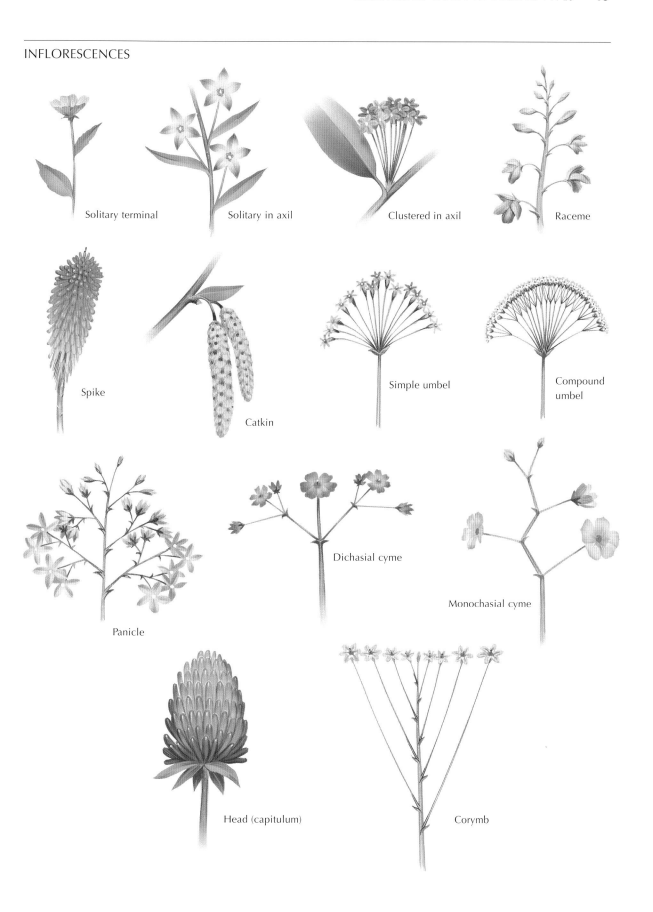

Solitary terminal

Solitary in axil

Clustered in axil

Raceme

Spike

Catkin

Simple umbel

Compound umbel

Panicle

Dichasial cyme

Monochasial cyme

Head (capitulum)

Corymb

Illustrated Guide to
LEAF TYPES

Leaves have adapted to a multitude of environments in order to successfully capture the sun's vital energy, and to allow the passage of water out of the plant through their cells. The result is a wonderful variety in the shape, size, and arrangement of leaves.

STRUCTURE

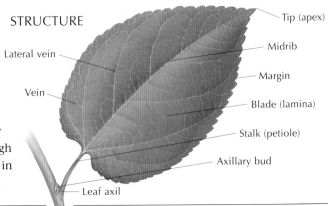

- Lateral vein
- Vein
- Tip (apex)
- Midrib
- Margin
- Blade (lamina)
- Stalk (petiole)
- Axillary bud
- Leaf axil

SHAPES

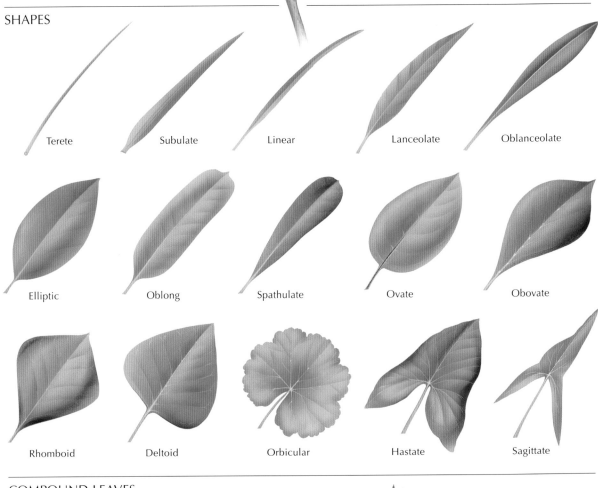

| Terete | Subulate | Linear | Lanceolate | Oblanceolate |

| Elliptic | Oblong | Spathulate | Ovate | Obovate |

| Rhomboid | Deltoid | Orbicular | Hastate | Sagittate |

COMPOUND LEAVES

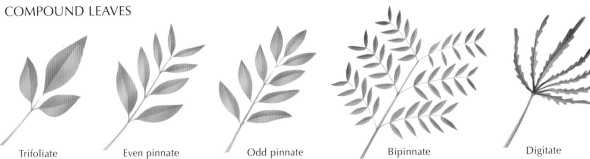

| Trifoliate | Even pinnate | Odd pinnate | Bipinnate | Digitate |

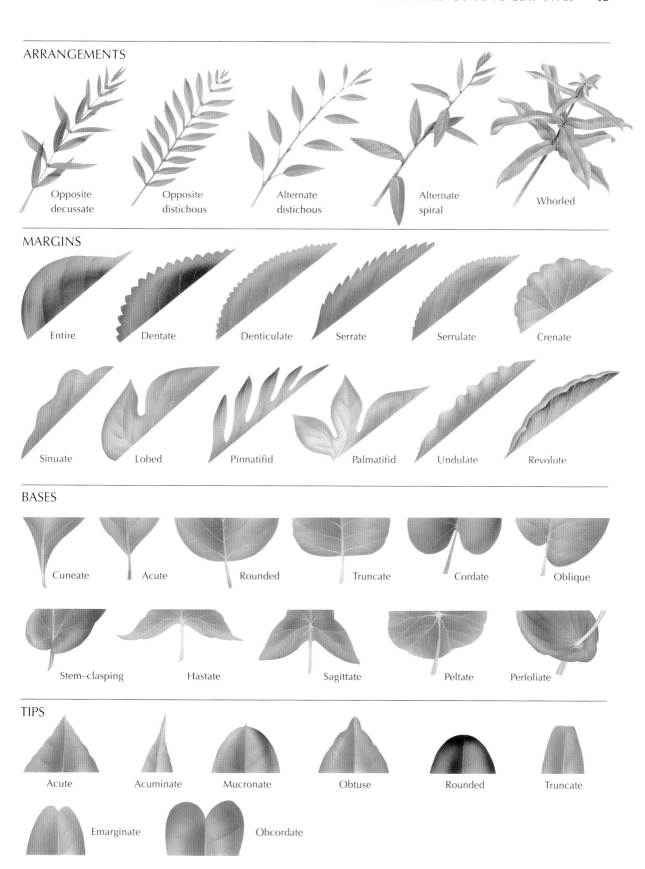

ARRANGEMENTS

Opposite decussate

Opposite distichous

Alternate distichous

Alternate spiral

Whorled

MARGINS

Entire

Dentate

Denticulate

Serrate

Serrulate

Crenate

Sinuate

Lobed

Pinnatifid

Palmatifid

Undulate

Revolute

BASES

Cuneate

Acute

Rounded

Truncate

Cordate

Oblique

Stem–clasping

Hastate

Sagittate

Peltate

Perfoliate

TIPS

Acute

Acuminate

Mucronate

Obtuse

Rounded

Truncate

Emarginate

Obcordate

A–Z OF FLOWERS

ABUTILON

This genus belonging to the mallow family is represented in most warm parts of the world, but the majority of its 150 species are from South or Central America; the remainder are mainly from Australia and Africa. Most are shrubs with slender tough-barked twigs but a few are annuals, perennials, or even small trees. Leaves vary from heart-shaped to jaggedly lobed, their margins toothed in most species; twigs and leaves may be clothed with bristly hairs. The common name Chinese lantern alludes to the pretty, pendent, bell-shaped flowers seen in many species; these can appear in shades ranging from white and pale pink to yellow, orange, and deep bronzy red.

CULTIVATION

These plants are easily grown in the garden or indoors in pots in a well-lit position. They like well-drained soil of moderate fertility, in light shade or bright sun. In cool climates keep plants indoors until the worst frosts are past, and then plant out for a great summer display. Propagate from tip cuttings in late summer.

ABOVE Abutilon × hybridum *'Ashford Red' is a popular cultivar, notable for its brilliant red flowers and large leaves.*

Favorites	Flower Color	Blooming Season	Flower Fragrance
Abutilon × hybridum 'Ashford Red'	red	spring to autumn	no
Abutilon × hybridum 'Canary Bird'	bright yellow	spring to autumn	no
Abutilon × hybridum 'Souvenir de Bonn'	orange	spring to autumn	no
Abutilon megapotamicum	red and yellow	spring to autumn	no
Abutilon pictum	orange	summer to autumn	no
Abutilon × suntense	purple, mauve	spring to autumn	no

ABOVE *With its yellow lantern flowers, Abutilon ×
hybridum 'Canary Bird' makes an ideal garden plant.*
LEFT *Abutilon × suntense is
distinctive for its cheerful
violet flowers and light
green leaves. It needs plenty
of space however, as it is
a tall and vigorous grower.*
BELOW *There are two forms
of the popular garden plant
Abutilon megapotamicum;
one is an erect shrub, the
other almost prostrate. Both
forms have bell-shaped red-
and-yellow flowers.*

Top Tip

Prune off leading
shoots in late
winter if a compact
form is desired, but
note that some
cultivars display
their blooms best
on long arching
branches.

Plant Height	Plant Width	Hardiness Zone	Frost Tolerance
10 ft (3 m)	10 ft (3 m)	8–11	yes
10 ft (3 m)	10 ft (3 m)	8–11	yes
10 ft (3 m)	7–10 ft (2–3 m)	8–11	yes
18 in (45 cm)	5 ft (1.5 m)	8–10	yes
12 ft (3.5 m)	7–15 ft (2–4.5 m)	9–12	yes
15 ft (4.5 m)	8 ft (2.4 m)	8–9	yes

ACACIA

The genus *Acacia* consists of at least 1,200 species of which over 900 are Australian; its other major centers are Africa and warmer parts of the Americas. In Australia, they are invariably known as wattles. Most are shrubs or small to medium-sized trees, displaying a wide range of leaf shapes and sizes, some quite bizarre. Flowers are small and densely crowded into spikes; throughout winter or spring they form an abundant display of blossom, often a brilliant golden yellow. In African and some tropical American species, sharp spines range along the branches. These may be extremely large and fierce-looking and, in a few species, the spines are much thicker than the branchlets that bear them.

CULTIVATION

Most acacias are fast growers and are useful plants for restoring vegetation to denuded areas, as well as being suitable for ornamental or landscape use—though their quick growth habit is offset by a short life. They require well-drained soil and full sun. If disease sets in, replacing the plants may be the best solution. Propagation is mostly from seed.

ABOVE Acacia paradoxa *may be highly ornamental but it also makes a formidable barrier hedge: beneath its masses of large golden yellow flower balls hide needle-like spines.*
BELOW *Though quite a tall spreading shrub in the wild,* Acacia pravissima *is usually smaller in cultivation. It has drooping branches and small, triangular, olive green, leaf-like stalks. Golden yellow flowers appear in spring.*

Favorites

	Flower Color	Blooming Season	Flower Fragrance	Plant Height	Plant Width	Hardiness Zone	Frost Tolerance
Acacia baileyana	golden yellow	winter to early spring	yes	6–20 ft (1.8–6 m)	10–20 ft (3–6 m)	8–9	yes
Acacia dealbata	pale to bright yellow	late winter to spring	yes	80 ft (24 m)	20–35 ft (6–10 m)	8–10	yes
Acacia farnesiana	golden yellow	winter to spring	yes	15 ft (4.5 m)	15–25 ft (4.5–8 m)	10–12	yes
Acacia longifolia	bright yellow	winter to spring	yes	6–25 ft (1.8–8 m)	6–10 ft (1.8–3 m)	9–12	yes
Acacia paradoxa	yellow	late winter to spring	yes	10–12 ft (3–3.5 m)	10–12 ft (3–3.5 m)	8–11	yes
Acacia pravissima	golden yellow	spring	yes	10–25 ft (3–8 m)	10–20 ft (3–6 m)	8–11	yes

LEFT Acacia farnesiana *is a native of tropical America. It is widely cultivated for its decorative value and for the essential oil obtained from its flowers, which is used in perfume.*

BELOW Acacia baileyana *is one of the most popular of all the wattles. A small yet elegant tree, it has feathery silver-gray leaves that contrast with the yellow flowers borne in profusion from winter to spring.*

ACHILLEA

ABOVE *Spreading perennials such as Achillea umbellata are suitable for informal garden arrangements. If planting in a mixed border, choose plants that will not overwhelm the delicate silver-gray leaves and small white flowers of this species.*

This genus of 100-odd species of clumping or mat-forming perennial plants is a member of the large Asteraceae (daisy) family. Achillea species grow throughout Europe and northern and western Asia in a range of habitats including alpine. Some species can be invasive. The foliage is usually finely divided with a fern-like appearance and is often aromatic. The daisy-like flowerheads are flattened or rounded, comprising numerous small flowers in white, pale cream, lemon, and pink. A number of cultivars are available in brighter shades, and these make excellent border plants. The genus is named after Achilles, the hero of Greek mythology, who is said to have known of the plant's wound-healing qualities.

CULTIVATION

Most species are easily grown in well-drained soil in full sun. They can tolerate quite poor conditions and are fairly frost hardy. Alpine and dwarf species require perfect drainage and protection from winter rain if downy-leaved. Propagation is by division or seed.

Top Tip

Achillea are hardy plants that will multiply rapidly. After the flowers have died down in winter, prune the clumps back to stimulate strong regrowth in spring.

BELOW *Achillea millefolium cultivars provide abundant ground cover with their attractive dark to sea green leaves. Take care, however, as they can be invasive.*

Favorites

	Flower Color	Blooming Season	Flower Fragrance	Plant Height	Plant Width	Hardiness Zone	Frost Tolerance
Achillea ageratifolia	white	summer	yes	12 in (30 cm)	6–8 in (15–20 cm)	3	yes
Achillea 'Coronation Gold'	golden yellow	spring to summer	yes	3 ft (0.9 m)	18 in (45 cm)	4–10	yes
Achillea millefolium	white to pink	summer	yes	24 in (60 cm)	24 in (60 cm)	3–10	yes
Achillea 'Terracotta'	deep orange to yellow	late spring to autumn	yes	18 in (45 cm)	24 in (60 cm)	3–10	yes
Achillea tomentosa	bright yellow	summer to early autumn	yes	12 in (30 cm)	18 in (45 cm)	4–10	yes
Achillea umbellata	white	summer	yes	8 in (20 cm)	12 in (30 cm)	4–10	yes

RIGHT Achillea millefolium boasts a number of pretty cultivars. This one, 'Paprika', bears vibrant red flower-heads with golden yellow disc florets. Colors tend to fade with age.

BELOW RIGHT Achillea 'Terracotta' has fern-like foliage and produces an abundance of orange to faded yellow flowers.

Top Tip

The genus name *Aconitum* comes from the Greek and can be translated as "unconquerable poison." This plant is very toxic; use caution when handling it, especially around children.

BELOW *This beautiful plant, Aconitum 'Stainless Steel', is ideal for the front of a border where its pale blue flowers and silver green foliage can be admired.*

ACONITUM

Belonging to the buttercup family, this genus contains about 100 species of mostly tuberous biennials and perennials occurring primarily in the northern temperate zones. Completely dormant over winter, they quickly develop a clump of deeply lobed leaves from which emerge erect flower stems bearing clusters of pendulous, hooded, or helmet-shaped flowers, usually white, creamy yellow, or mauve-blue to purple in color. The flowering season may last from summer to autumn. The plants's sap contains several highly toxic alkaloids, principally aconitine, which has a long history of deliberate use as a poison, especially in animal traps, hence the common names of the genus: wolfsbane and badgers's bane. Aconitine is used medicinally in controlled doses to slow the heart rate.

CULTIVATION

Species in this genus are mostly very hardy and easily grown in full or half sun. The soil should be moist, humus-rich, and well-drained. Take care when cutting flowerheads, as the foliage may irritate the skin. Propagate these plants by division when dormant or raise from seed.

ABOVE RIGHT Aconitum altissimum *is native to the European Alps. A handsome robust plant, the tall stems are crowned by clusters of yellow flowers.*

RIGHT Aconitum napellus *var.* giganteum *is a vigorous grower and a good choice for garden cultivation. It bears purple-blue flowers on tall erect stems.*

BELOW Aconitum carmichaelii *is a highly rewarding garden plant, notable for its long-lasting, large, deep blue flowers.*

Favorites	Flower Color	Blooming Season	Flower Fragrance	Plant Height	Plant Width	Hardiness Zone	Frost Tolerance
Aconitum altissimum	lemon yellow	summer	no	4 ft (1.2 m)	18 in (45 cm)	4–8	yes
Aconitum carmichaelii	purple, mauve, blue	autumn	no	3–6 ft (0.9–1.8 m)	12–15 in (30–38 cm)	3–9	yes
Aconitum lycoctonum	purple, occasionally yellow	summer	no	3–5 ft ft (0.9–1.5 m)	12 in (30 cm)	5–8	yes
Aconitum napellus	deep purple-blue	summer	no	4 ft (1.2 m)	12 in (30 cm)	3–9	yes
Aconitum 'Spark's Variety'	deep purple-blue	summer	no	5 ft (1.5 m)	18 in (45 cm)	6–9	yes
Aconitum 'Stainless Steel'	pale lilac-blue	late summer to autumn	no	3 ft (0.9 m)	30 in (75 cm)	4–9	yes

LEFT *At the center of Aechmea fasciata there is a cluster of reddish pink bracts containing light blue flowers that age to rose red. This plant has silvery leaves.*
BELOW *The distinctive feature of Aechmea weilbachii is its red stem that bears purple-blue flowers, followed by oval fruit.*

Top Tip

These plants need plenty of water during the growing season—keep the central cup filled with water, and fertilize monthly with a mixture that is low in nitrogen.

AECHMEA

Within this large genus of approximately 240 species and 500 cultivars there is a wonderful variety of form, size, and color. The species are mostly epiphytic in their natural environment—that is, they grow on another plant for support—and are found mainly in the humid regions of Central America down to the cooler areas of southern Brazil and Argentina. The rosette-forming foliage ranges in color from shiny green to silver, and the edges of the leaves have teeth that vary from very fine to almost vicious. Their dramatic spear-like flowerheads can vary from short to elongated, and many have bright red bracts beneath the flower branches that attract hummingbirds as pollinators.

CULTIVATION

An extremely popular genus, plants are mostly grown in cultivation in pots with some form of shade. In mild areas they are best grown indoors; outdoors they need a moist humus-rich soil. Propagation is mainly by offsets, but some species can be raised from seed.

ABOVE Aechmea miniata *is a striking Brazilian native, notable for its spiny channelled leaves. As seen above, the popular form* A. miniata *var.* discolor *has red and blue flowers, while its leaves have maroon or rose undersides.* **LEFT** *Also from Brazil,* Aechmea ornata *var.* hoehneana *has strappy green leaves. The erect red bracts are extremely eye-catching, and the flowerhead is a short bristly cylinder bearing many small flowers with blue petals.*

Favorites

	Flower Color	Blooming Season	Flower Fragrance	Plant Height	Plant Width	Hardiness Zone	Frost Tolerance
Aechmea fasciata	light blue; red-pink bracts	summer	no	18 in (45 cm)	20 in (50 cm)	10–12	no
Aechmea fulgens	violet	summer	no	18 in (45 cm)	15 in (38 cm)	11–12	no
Aechmea miniata var. *discolor*	red and blue	summer	no	12–15 in (30–38 cm)	24 in (60 cm)	10–12	no
Aechmea ornata var. *hoehneana*	blue; red bracts	summer	no	24 in (60 cm)	3 ft (0.9 m)	10–12	no
Aechmea recurvata	pale pink, purple; red bracts	summer	no	8 in (20 cm)	20 in (50 cm)	9–12	no
Aechmea weilbachii	blue-purple; red bracts	summer	no	27 in (70 cm)	12 in (30 cm)	10–12	no

LEFT *There are several* Agapanthus *hybrids and selections available, most of them evergreen. This is an attractive* Agapanthus praecox *cultivar.*

Top Tip

Protect *Agapanthus* species from slugs and snails, which can damage young plants. They also need regular watering in spring and summer, as well as loamy soil.

AGAPANTHUS

Commonly known as the lily-of-the-Nile, this is a southern African genus of just 10 species of fleshy-rooted perennials. They have long, strappy, fleshy leaves that form dense clumps of evergreen or deciduous foliage. Tall stems bear blue flowers that are bell-shaped or tubular. In frost-free climates, flowers of evergreens appear over a long season, elsewhere only in summer. This genus makes an ideal border plant due to its narrow upright shape, and dwarf forms are superb in rockeries or containers. In Greek, *Agapanthus* means the flower of love, although the reason for this name is unclear.

CULTIVATION

Agapanthus species are easily grown in full sun or part-shade in any well-drained soil. They are hardy plants and will withstand drought and poor soil, although these situations will affect flower production. Propagate by division in winter or from seed.

LEFT *Also known as the African lily, Agapanthus 'Lilliput' is a charming dwarf cultivar. The plant bears many deep blue flowers, and the narrow leaves are sparse. 'Lilliput' is useful in containers, mass displays, or borders.*

LEFT Agapanthus inapertus *is a many-flowered deciduous species. It has pendent clusters of deep bluish tubular flowers that are unusual in that they do not face the sun. The leaves are bluish green.*

RIGHT *The most popular species in this genus,* Agapanthus praecox *is loved for its starburst flowers that bloom in summer. The evergreen foliage is attractive in its own right and is a year-round asset in the garden.*

Favorites	Flower Color	Blooming Season	Flower Fragrance	Plant Height	Plant Width	Hardiness Zone	Frost Tolerance
Agapanthus africanus	blue-purple	summer to early autumn	no	18 in (45 cm)	18 in (45 cm)	8–10	yes
Agapanthus campanulatus	pale to deep blue	mid- to late summer	no	36 in (90 cm)	18 in (45 cm)	7–11	yes
Agapanthus inapertus	deep blue-purple	late summer to autumn	no	5 ft (1.5 m)	24 in (60 cm)	8–11	yes
Agapanthus 'Lilliput'	deep blue	mid- to late summer	no	18 in (45 cm)	15 in (38 cm)	8–10	yes
Agapanthus praecox	mauve-blue	summer	no	3 ft (0.9 m)	24 in (60 cm)	9–11	no
Agapanthus 'Rancho White'	white	summer	no	18 in (45 cm)	24 in (60 cm)	9–11	no

AGASTACHE

A member of the mint family (Lamiaceae), this genus of 20 species of aromatic upright or spreading perennials is found in North America, Japan, and nearby parts of China. The leaves are usually lance- to heart-shaped with finely lobed or toothed edges. The small flowers are borne in terminal spikes, which vary in length, depending on the species. The flowers appear in summer, and may be white, pink, mauve-blue, or purple, though cultivars occur in a wider color range. Several species have a mint-like flavor and are used in herbal teas or as mint substitutes. Most species have mildly sedating and pain relieving effects and have been used medicinally wherever they occur.

BELOW *From North America, Agastache foeniculum bears decorative clusters of light purple flowers with violet bracts. This species tolerates cold and wet more than others in the genus.*

CULTIVATION

Although intolerant of repeated hard frosts, these plants grow quickly and can be treated as annuals in cold areas. All species can be easily grown in any sunny position with good, moist, well-drained soil. Propagate from basal cuttings of non-flowering stems or seed. Deadhead old flowers so that re-blooming will take place later in the season.

Top Tip

Agastache plants are a welcome addition to mixed borders and herb gardens. They can also be successfully grown as container plants indoors.

LEFT *There are a number of* Agastache *hybrid cultivars available in a wide range of colors. 'Blue Fortune' is a bushy variety with pale blue to lilac flower spikes.* BELOW *The toothed triangular leaves of* Agastache foeniculum *(also known as anise hyssop) have the aroma and flavor of anise, and are used in herbal teas.*

Favorites

	Flower Color	Blooming Season	Flower Fragrance	Plant Height	Plant Width	Hardiness Zone	Frost Tolerance
Agastache aurantica **'Apricot Sunrise'**	deep orange, ageing to apricot	summer to autumn	no	30 in (75 cm)	24 in (60 cm)	7–10	yes
Agastache **'Blue Fortune'**	blue	summer to autumn	no	36 in (90 cm)	18–30 in (45–75 cm)	4–10	yes
Agastache **cana**	red-pink	late summer to autumn	no	24–36 in (60–90 cm)	18 in (45 cm)	5–10	yes
Agastache **foeniculum**	light purple	mid-summer to early autumn	no	3–5 ft (0.9–1.5 m)	3–4 ft (0.9–1.2 m)	3–10	yes
Agastache **rupestris**	orange and purple-pink	summer to autumn	no	18–30 in (45–75 cm)	18 in (45 cm)	7–10	yes
Agastache **'Tutti Frutti'**	purple-red	summer	no	3–4 ft (0.9–1.2 m)	12–24 in (30–60 cm)	8–10	yes

ALLIUM

This genus of around 700 species of bulbous perennials and biennials includes many familiar plants such as the onion, leek, chive, garlic, and ornamental onion. *Allium* is the type genus for its family, the Alliaceae, and occurs in dry areas of the Northern Hemisphere. The foliage may be fine and grassy, strappy, or hollow and tubular. The flowers are generally borne in rounded heads atop long stems, and are often brightly colored. Many species are famed for their taste and pungency, and form vital ingredients in the world's cuisines. Some, especially garlic, have a long history in herbal medicine and folklore, and the ornamental species are not without an air of mystery, too. In European traditions *Allium moly* was thought to be a protection against demons, and Homer attributed to it magical properties that allowed Ulysses to enter Circe's lair.

CULTIVATION

Most alliums thrive in fairly light soil in a sunny well-drained position. Ample water is important during foliage development and flowering but thereafter the plants can be allowed to dry off. Propagate by gathering offsets and bulbils or from seed.

Favorites	Flower Color	Blooming Season	Flower Fragrance
Allium cristophii	pinkish-purple	late spring to summer	no
Allium karataviense	pale purple-pink to white	summer	no
Allium moly	golden yellow	summer	no
Allium paradoxum	white	spring	no
Allium porrum	gray-green to red	summer	no
Allium sphaerocephalon	pink to red-purple	summer	no

RIGHT Allium karataviense *'Ivory Queen' bears up to 50 tiny star-shaped flowers in each flowerhead. The leaves occur in shades of gray-green or purple-gray, and are often tinged at the edges with red.*

Plant Height	Plant Width	Hardiness Zone	Frost Tolerance
24 in (60 cm)	24 in (60 cm)	7–9	yes
4–10 in (10–25 cm)	18 in (45 cm)	3–9	yes
15 in (38 cm)	12 in (30 cm)	4–9	yes
12 in (30 cm)	8 in (20 cm)	5–9	yes
36 in (90 cm)	18 in (45 cm)	5–10	yes
36 in (90 cm)	18 in (45 cm)	4–10	yes

ABOVE LEFT *This bulbous perennial,* Allium cristophii, *is striking for its large pink to purple flowerheads that turn black as the seeds ripen. Cut and use in dried flower arrangements.*

ABOVE *These leeks,* Allium sphaerocephalon, *make delightful garden plants when planted en masse. Their round to bell-shaped heads bear tightly packed reddish purple flowers.*

Top Tip

Don't worry that by planting garlic or onion species in the garden their distinctive scent will soon take over. The pungent aroma is usually only noticeable when the leaves are crushed or bruised.

RIGHT *Justifiably known as golden garlic,* Allium moly *produces dense umbels of golden yellow flowers. This cultivar, 'Jeannine', is ideal for border planting, as it has quite stiff tall stems and large flowerheads.*

LEFT Native to Chile, the sunny Alstroemeria aurea is one of the easiest species to grow. The clear orange to yellow flowers are flecked with red, and appear over summer. Grow in containers or mixed borders to show off their flowers to advantage.

ALSTROEMERIA

Commonly called Peruvian lily or lily of the Incas, this genus of around 50 species of fleshy rooted perennials is found in South America, often at altitude. Celebrated for their long-lasting beautifully marked flowers, they are equally notorious for their vigorous roots and self-sowing nature. At least 1 species, *Alstroemeria psittacina,* is considered a weed in some areas. The leaves are mid-green, usually lance-shaped, and slightly twisted. Tall wiry stems terminate in a many-flowered head of 6-petalled lily-like blooms that occur in many shades. The famous botanist Linnaeus named the genus after one of his pupils, Claus von Alstroemer (1736–1794), who sent him the seeds in 1753 from Spain.

BELOW The Peruvian lily produces many long-lasting beautifully colored flowers; factors which have made them popular with commercial gardeners. Alstroemeria 'Apollo' has large white flowers with tiger-like gold and brown markings.

CULTIVATION

Some species can be a little frost tender, which can be managed by insulating the roots with mulch. However, most are easily grown in any sunny position with moderately fertile well-drained soil that can be kept moist during the flowering season. Propagate by division when dormant or from seed.

Favorites

Favorites	Flower Color	Blooming Season	Flower Fragrance	Plant Height	Plant Width	Hardiness Zone	Frost Tolerance
Alstroemeria 'Apollo'	white	summer	no	30 in (75 cm)	24 in (60 cm)	8–9	yes
Alstroemeria aurea	orange with maroon streaks	summer	no	3 ft (0.9 m)	18 in (45 cm)	7–9	yes
Alstroemeria, Dr Salter's Hybrids	yellow, orange, red, pink	summer	no	24 in (60 cm)	24 in (60 cm)	7–9	yes
Alstroemeria, Dutch Hybrids	various	summer	no	24 in (60 cm)	24 in (60 cm)	8–10	yes
Alstroemeria, Ligtu Hybrids	various	summer	no	24 in (60 cm)	24 in (60 cm)	7–9	yes
Alstroemeria pelegrina	white and pink or purple	summer to autumn	no	12–24 in (30–60 cm)	24 in (60 cm)	8–10	yes

LEFT AND BELOW *There are countless excellent hybrids to choose from, and most are prolific flowerers. The award-winning Dutch Hybrid,* Alstroemeria 'Fuego', *left, with its bright red and gold flowers, is one fine example. Similarly, Ligtu Hybrids such as that shown below come in a range of flower colors, from cream and pink to red.*

Top Tip

Alstroemeria plants need plenty of sunlight and shelter to thrive. Protect from strong wind. They do well planted in a clump in a border and with herbaceous perennials.

AMARANTHUS

There are about 60 species of weedy annuals and short-lived perennials in this exotic-looking genus, which is a member of the Amaranthaceae family. They have a worldwide distribution, often being found in wasteland areas. Species range in form from prostrate to tall, with unusual, long, often drooping tassels of many small blood red or green flowers. Foliage can be just as striking, ranging in color from red to gold to green. Individual flowers are either male or female, and each sex may be borne on separate plants. Some species are cultivated as leaf or grain crops in tropical areas, while those with dramatic flowers or colorful foliage are ideal for summer bedding displays, in containers and in hanging baskets.

CULTIVATION

Amaranthus are easily grown in well-drained fertile soil in full sun. Protect tall varieties from strong wind. In cooler climates sow seed under glass in early spring and plant out after the danger of frosts has passed. In warmer areas seed can be sown outdoors later in the season.

ABOVE LEFT Amaranthus hypochondriacus 'Pygmy Torch' is a dwarf bushy annual grown for its upright spikes of deep red flowers.
LEFT Unlike most species in the Amaranthus group, A. tricolor cultivars are valued for their eye-catching leaves, rather than their flowers. Colors vary from green and gold to crimson, often in the same plant, as is the case with 'Joseph's Coat'.

Top Tip

Plenty of sun and a sheltered site will ensure healthy and vigorous plants. Prune when young to promote growth, and water regularly during dry periods to prolong the flowering season.

ABOVE *This erect annual,* Amaranthus cruentus, *has dark green to purple leaves that provide a lush back-drop for its long arching branches of red flowers.*
RIGHT *The pendent tassel-like flowering spikes of* Amaranthus caudatus *'Green Tails', featuring tiny pale green flowers, are indeed like the trailing tail of some strange creature.*

Favorites

	Flower Color	Blooming Season	Flower Fragrance	Plant Height	Plant Width	Hardiness Zone	Frost Tolerance
Amaranthus caudatus	purple-crimson	summer to early autumn	no	3–5 ft (0.9–1.5 m)	18–30 in (45–75 cm)	8–11	no
Amaranthus caudatus 'Green Tails'	light green	summer to early autumn	no	3–5 ft (0.9–1.5 m)	18–30 in (45–75 cm)	8–11	no
Amaranthus cruentus	dark red	summer to early autumn	no	to 6 ft (to 1.8 m)	18 in (45 cm)	8–11	no
Amaranthus hypochondriacus	crimson	summer to early autumn	no	3–4 ft (0.9–1.2 m)	12–18 in (30–45 cm)	8–11	no
Amaranthus tricolor	green, red	summer	no	3 ft (0.9 m)	18 in (45 cm)	8–11	no
Amaranthus tricolor 'Joseph's Coat'	green, red	summer	no	3 ft (0.9 m)	18 in (45 cm)	8–11	no

ABOVE Amelanchier × grandiflora 'Rubescens' bears flowers flushed with pink, opening from darker pink buds.

AMELANCHIER

This genus consists of 30 or so species of deciduous shrubs and small trees valued for their attractive white spring blossom; all but 2 species are native to North America and Mexico. They have smallish oval or elliptical leaves on slender stalks, often downy beneath and with finely toothed margins. The star-shaped flowers, each with 5 narrow petals, are borne in small sprays that create clouds of pretty white blooms. This attractive, if brief, feature makes them suitable as ornamental plants; the silvery down on the leaves and the autumn foliage color of some species is equally as appealing. Fruits are edible when ripe and are an important food for wildlife, especially birds: hence the common name serviceberry.

CULTIVATION

Amelanchier species are mostly woodland plants that prefer moist sheltered sites and are most effective when planted against a backdrop of darker foliage. They are prone to the same pests and diseases as apples and pears, including the dreaded fireblight. Propagation is normally from seed; cultivars are grafted.

LEFT *The fruits of* Amelanchier *species are small and spherical or pear-shaped, such as on this* A. denticulata *tree. They mostly ripen to blue-black and are edible, although often not palatable until overripe.*

Top Tip

These handsome plants are most at home in woodland situations, though certain species tolerate boggy ground and do well at the edge of a pond or stream.

ABOVE Amelanchier × grandiflora *is a hybrid of* A. arborea *and* A. laevis. *A spreading, almost shrubby tree, its leaves change from bronze to green to orange-red as the seasons progress. White flowers appear in mid-spring.*

RIGHT Amelanchier spicata *is another plant highly valued for its foliage: its leaves are covered in soft down when new and turn shades of gold, orange, and red in autumn.*

Favorites	Flower Color	Blooming Season	Flower Fragrance	Plant Height	Plant Width	Hardiness Zone	Frost Tolerance
Amelanchier alnifolia	white	late spring to early summer	no	12 ft (3.5 m)	12 ft (3.5 m)	3–9	yes
Amelanchier arborea	white	spring	no	20 ft (6 m)	30 ft (9 m)	4–9	yes
Amelanchier denticulata	white	spring	no	10 ft (3 m)	6 ft (1.8 m)	8–10	no
Amelanchier × grandiflora	white	spring	no	20 ft (6 m)	30 ft (9 m)	4–9	yes
Amelanchier laevis	white	spring	no	25 ft (8 m)	25 ft (8 m)	4–9	yes
Amelanchier spicata	white-pink	spring	no	8 ft (2.4 m)	10 ft (3 m)	4–9	yes

Favorites	Flower Color	Blooming Season	Flower Fragrance
Anemone blanda	white, blue, pink	spring	no
Anemone hupehensis	white to mauve	late summer to autumn	no
Anemone × hybrida	white-pink	late summer to autumn	no
Anemone multifida	white-cream	summer	no
Anemone nemorosa	white-cream	early spring	no
Anemone sylvestris	white	spring and early summer	yes

ABOVE Anemone × hybrida *contains over 30 cultivars. These are popular choices for their robust nature and often large blooms. Colors range from delicate white to deep pink.*

ANEMONE

Widespread in the temperate regions of both hemispheres, this buttercup family (Ranunculaceae) genus encompasses around 120 species of perennials. A large and versatile group, their colorful, wide-open, bowl-shaped flowers are generally borne on wiry stems that hold them well above the clumps of finely divided foliage. Most species flower in spring shortly after the foliage appears but some continue into early summer and a few bloom in autumn. Most likely the genus name is derived from the Greek *anemos*, meaning wind, hence its common name windflower, but some consider it to come from *Naamen*, a variation on the name Adonis. According to legend, it was his blood that gave *Anemone coronaria* its red flowers.

CULTIVATION
Some species, appropriately known as wood anemones, prefer woodland conditions with dappled shade but most are happy in a sunny perennial or flower border with moist well-drained soil. Propagation is either by division in winter when dormant or, in the case of the strains grown as annuals, by seed.

Top Tip

Anemones can be divided into 2 main groups: tuberous and rhizomatous types that flower mainly in spring; and those with fibrous roots that flower in autumn.

Plant Height	Plant Width	Hardiness Zone	Frost Tolerance
8 in (20 cm)	6 in (15 cm)	6–9	yes
24–36 in (60–90 cm)	15 in (38 cm)	6–10	yes
4–5 ft (1.2–1.5 m)	7 ft (2 m)	6–10	yes
12 in (30 cm)	6 in (15 cm)	2–8	yes
3–6 in (8–15 cm)	12 in (30 cm)	5–9	yes
12 in (30 cm)	12 in (30 cm)	4–9	yes

ABOVE *Long cultivated in Japan,* Anemone hupehensis *var.* japonica *is taller than the species and produces pinkish purple flowers.*

LEFT *Given time,* Anemone blanda *will naturalize in a variety of sites, covering an area in color. Here, 'White Splendour' makes a vibrant display; other hybrids occur in shades of blue and pink.*

BELOW Anemone nemorosa *'Robinsoniana' produces flowers in the palest shades of lavender. Vigorous, it will quickly cover an area.*

ANIGOZANTHOS

Top Tip

These plants are highly valued for use as cut flowers, though most will grow well outdoors in frost-free regions. Plant in a border and water well to prolong flowering over summer.

ABOVE RIGHT *The common name for* Anigozanthos *is kangaroo paw, a reference to the flowers. As seen on A.* Bush Gems Series, *'Bush Nugget', the blooms are covered on the outside in woolly hairs, and open at the end into claw-like lobes.*

This genus contains 11 species of ever-green clump-forming perennials, all of which are confined naturally to southwestern Australia. The foliage is usually dark green and varies from grassy to iris-like, with sword-shaped leaves. Tubular-shaped furry blooms—thought to resemble a kangaroo's paw—are borne on slender branching stems, usually during the warmer months. Flowers occur in green and deeper shades of gold, pink, red, and russet brown, depending on the species. They make excellent cut flowers as they last well when cut, and many new varieties have been developed with the florist trade in mind. A very different use for flowers of *Anigozanthos* plants is the addition of floral extracts to shampoos and conditioners.

CULTIVATION

Plant in a sunny position with good drainage. Most plants perform better if watered well during the growing season but will tolerate drought. Blackened foliage is a sign of ink disease, which can be very damaging, as can slugs and snails. Propagation is most often by division. Species may be raised from seed.

LEFT Anigozanthos flavidus *is one of the hardiest of the kangaroo paws, and can adapt to a variety of climates and soils. In Australia, this species is attractive to native birds.*

Favorites

	Flower Color	Blooming Season	Flower Fragrance	Plant Height	Plant Width	Hardiness Zone	Frost Tolerance
Anigozanthos **Bush Gems** Series, 'Bush Haze'	bright yellow	spring	no	18 in (45 cm)	18 in (45 cm)	9–11	no
Anigozanthos **Bush Gems** Series, 'Bush Nugget'	pale orange and green	spring	no	18 in (45 cm)	18 in (45 cm)	9–11	no
Anigozanthos **Bush Gems** Series, 'Bush Ruby'	deep orange to red	spring	no	18 in (45 cm)	18 in (45 cm)	9–11	no
Anigozanthos flavidus	yellow, green, red	spring	no	3–5 ft (0.9–1.5 m)	3 ft (0.9 m)	9–11	no
Anigozanthos manglesii	yellow-green	mid-spring to early summer	no	1–4 ft (0.3–1.2 m)	15–24 in (38–60 cm)	9–11	no
Anigozanthos 'Pink Joey'	dusky pink	late spring to mid-summer	no	20 in (50 cm)	3 ft (0.9 m)	9–11	no

ABOVE *The bright yellow flowers of the hardy plant* Anigozanthos *Bush Gems Series, 'Bush Haze' appear on the end of tall red stems.*
LEFT *'Bush Ruby' is another plant in the popular Bush Gems Series. As with other cultivars in this series, it has greater resistance to ink disease than most species. A compact plant, its orange-red blooms appear throughout spring.*

ANTHURIUM

Well-loved as house plants everywhere, this genus is from the American tropics and encompasses around 900 species of evergreen perennials. The large leaves, which are elliptical, lance-shaped, or arrowhead-shaped, are usually held upright on stiff stems that emerge from a stout rootstock. The distinctive flowerheads are made up of a flattened, shield-shaped, petal-like bract known as a spathe. This surrounds a protruding cylindrical spike embedded with many tiny flowers, called the spadix. Both the spathe and spadix tend to be the same color, usually bright red, though other colors occur among the hybrids. *Anthurium* plants last well as cut flowers and are an important industry in Hawaii, where at the peak of production in the 1980s around 30 million flower stems were shipped to the world's markets.

CULTIVATION

Anthurium species in the wild are mostly epiphytic, but do adapt well to greenhouse, container, and garden cultivation, thriving in bright humid conditions with moist humus-rich soil. Although completely intolerant of frost, they cope surprisingly well with cool conditions. Humidity and prolonged warmth, however, are required for flowering.

ABOVE *An erect epiphyte,* Anthurium andraeanum *has dark green leaves, a heart-shaped red-colored spathe, and a white spadix with a yellow tip.*

RIGHT Anthurium scandens *is epiphytic in the wild, and has green to purple colored flowers. Its many-seeded berries are white, turning purple as they ripen.*

Top Tip

For successful indoor use, these tropical plants need bright light, warm moist conditions, and protection from drafts. Spray leaves with water several times daily.

RIGHT *Remarkable for its curling spadix and brilliant red spathe,* Anthurium scherzerianum *is also noteworthy for its relative tolerance to cold.*

BELOW *Anthurium veitchii is an upright epiphyte with dark green glossy leaves. Its delicate spreading spathe is pale green to ivory, with a cream-colored spadix.*

Favorites	Flower Color	Blooming Season	Flower Fragrance	Plant Height	Plant Width	Hardiness Zone	Frost Tolerance
Anthurium andraeanum	bright red	all year	no	24 in (60 cm)	8–12 in (20–30 cm)	11–12	no
Anthurium crystallinum	green	all year	no	24 in (60 cm)	24 in (60 cm)	11–12	no
Anthurium scandens	green to purple	all year	no	3 ft (0.9 m)	12 in (30 cm)	11–12	no
Anthurium scherzerianum	bright red	all year	no	15–30 in (38–75 cm)	12 in (30 cm)	10–12	no
Anthurium umbrosum	green and purplish	all year	no	3 ft (0.9 m)	3 ft (0.9 m)	10–12	no
Anthurium veitchii	pale green to creamy white	most of the year	no	4 ft (1.2 m)	4 ft (1.2 m)	11–12	no

ANTIRRHINUM

Naturally occurring in the temperate Northern Hemisphere, this genus of around 40 species of annuals, perennials, and subshrubs belongs in the figwort family (Scrophulariaceae). The best-known types are the garden annuals, loved by children for the way the mouth of the flower opens and closes with squeezing, hence they are commonly called snapdragon—although the genus name means nose-like. Most species are compact plants that form a low shrubby mound of simple rounded to lance-shaped leaves, sometimes with a gray-green tint. Flowering stems develop from late spring and carry heads of the familiar 2-lipped tubular blooms from early summer into autumn. Snapdragon seed is rich in oil, which in former times was extracted and used like olive oil.

Favorites	Flower Color	Blooming Season	Flower Fragrance
Antirrhinum grosii	white, purple spots	summer	no
Antirrhinum hispanicum	mauve-pink	all year	no
Antirrhinum majus	white, yellow, pink, red, purple	summer to mid-autumn	no
Antirrhinum majus, **Sonnet Series**	white, yellow, pink, red, purple	summer to mid-autumn	no
Antirrhinum molle	light pink, white	summer	no
Antirrhinum sempervirens	white, cream	summer	no

CULTIVATION

Snapdragons grow best in a fertile, moist, humus-rich soil in full sun. The Mediterranean species are reasonably drought tolerant but still need moisture to flower well. Deadhead to extend the flowering season. Tall plants may need staking. Rust diseases can cause problems in humid conditions. Propagation is usually by seed, though perennials will grow from cuttings of non-flowering stems.

Top Tip

Although they are short-lived perennials, *Antirrhinum majus* cultivars are best treated as annuals. Older plants are at greater risk of disease, and flower quality fades after the first year.

RIGHT Antirrhinum *'Sonnet White'* makes a spectacular display over summer and into autumn. Its bushy habit, clear white blooms, and ability to tolerate wet weather makes it ideal for informal garden layouts.

Plant Height	Plant Width	Hardiness Zone	Frost Tolerance
8 in (20 cm)	12 in (30 cm)	7–10	yes
10 in (25 cm)	12 in (30 cm)	7–10	yes
10–30 in (25–75 cm)	12–18 in (30–45 cm)	6–10	yes
24 in (60 cm)	18 in (45 cm)	6–10	yes
6–8 in (15–20 cm)	8–12 in (20–30 cm)	8–10	yes
6–8 in (15–20 cm)	8–12 in (20–30 cm)	8–10	yes

LEFT Antirrhinum *'Sonnet Pink'* produces 2-lipped pink-purple flowers; other cultivars in this series have bronze, crimson, red, white, or yellow blooms.

AQUILEGIA

This genus belongs to the buttercup family (Ranunculaceae), and contains around 70 species found over much of the temperate and subarctic Northern Hemisphere. These clump-forming perennials have fine-stemmed, often blue-green foliage that emerges from a woody rootstock. The flowering stems usually reach above the foliage and carry attractive, spurred, bell-shaped, often pendulous flowers in shades of blue and purple, as well as red, yellow, and white. The flowering period can vary among the species; some bloom through much of late spring and summer, others are short-flowering. In contrast to its common name, granny's bonnet, *Aquilegia* is derived from the Latin *aquila* (eagle) and *lego* (to gather), suggesting that the spurs situated at the base of the flower resemble the closing talons of an eagle.

CULTIVATION

This is an adaptable genus, with species and varieties suitable for a range of situations including woodlands, rockeries, and perennial borders. Generally, a cool-winter climate and a position in partial shade with cool, moist, humus-rich, well-drained soil is best. Certain species can be very attractive to aphids. Propagation is usually by seed, though some species can be divided when dormant.

LEFT Aquilegia vulgaris, *with its gently nodding flowers, is the eponymous granny's bonnet. Hybrids occur in shades of red, white or green, as well as bicolors like 'Rougham Star'.* **RIGHT** *The Songbird Series is well-loved for its large up-right blooms in a wide range of colors.*

LEFT Aquilegia caerulea *is the Colorado state flower, and occurs naturally from New Mexico to Montana. It bears bicolored white and lilac-blue flowers with slender spurs on erect stems.*
BELOW *The hybrid cultivar* Aquilegia *'Crimson Star' has mid-green leaves and upright stems, each one bearing 2 to 3 pendent flowers with ruby red sepals and creamy white petals.*

Top Tip

These plants are fairly easy to grow, and are suited to sunny herbaceous borders. As they hybridize freely, plant different types some distance apart.

Favorites

	Flower Color	Blooming Season	Flower Fragrance	Plant Height	Plant Width	Hardiness Zone	Frost Tolerance
Aquilegia caerulea	blue and white	late spring to early summer	no	24 in (60 cm)	12 in (30 cm)	3–9	yes
Aquilegia canadensis	red and yellow	late spring to early summer	no	24–36 in (60–90 cm)	12 in (30 cm)	3–9	yes
Aquilegia 'Crimson Star'	crimson and ivory	late spring to mid-summer	no	24 in (60 cm)	12 in (30 cm)	3–10	yes
Aquilegia flabellata	blue-purple	summer	no	18 in (45 cm)	10–15 in (25–38 cm)	5–10	yes
Aquilegia, Songbird Series	blue, purple, pink, white	spring to early summer	no	24–36 in (60–90 cm)	18 in (45 cm)	3–10	yes
Aquilegia vulgaris	blue, pink, red, purple, white	late spring to early summer	no	3 ft (0.9 m)	18 in (45 cm)	3–10	yes

Left Arctotis, Harlequin Hybrid 'Red Devil' bears bright red flowers from mid-summer to autumn, which contrast with the attractive silvery green leaves.

Arctotis

Known as the African daisy, this genus is naturally occurring from the southern tip of Africa northwards to Angola. It consists of around 50 species of low-spreading annuals and perennials that often produce masses of large and brightly colored flowerheads. The leaves are simple, usually lance-shaped, and frequently have felted undersides. For much of the year in mild climates the daisy-like flowers top the foliage, appearing in a wide range of colors. Modern strains now cover most of the color spectrum except blue. The name *Arctotis* comes from the Greek and means bear's ear, which is what the individual petals on the flower are though to resemble.

Cultivation
African daisies thrive in light well-drained soil, and full sun. They are drought tolerant but flower much more heavily if watered well during the growing season. Propagation is by seed, though the perennial species grow readily from cuttings of the non-flowering stems.

Favorites	Flower Color	Blooming Season	Flower Fragrance
Arctotis acaulis	yellow-orange to red	mid-summer to autumn	no
Arctotis fastuosa	orange	mid-summer to autumn	no
Arctotis, Harlequin Hybrids	yellow, orange, pink, red, white	summer to autumn	no
Arctotis, Harlequin Hybrid 'Flame'	orange-red	summer to autumn	no
Arctotis, Harlequin Hybrid 'Red Devil'	bright red	summer to autumn	no
Arctotis venusta	yellow, orange, pink, white	mid-summer to autumn	no

Top Tip

If you deadhead the flowers after the first flush of summer blooms, flowering will continue for a longer period. *Arctotis* plants need lots of sun, but do not tolerate very hot or humid conditions.

BELOW Arctotis acaulis *is a spreading perennial that flowers late in the season. The blooms range in color from yellow to red, and have a blackish purple center.*

ABOVE Arctotis, *Harlequin Hybrid 'Flame' is one of the most popular plants in this group, as it has striking orange-red flowers. These hybrids generally produce their best flowers in the first year.*

LEFT Arctotis venusta *is commonly known as the blue-eyed African daisy because of its deep bluish gray eye, which is surrounded by a bright yellow ring.*

Plant Height	Plant Width	Hardiness Zone	Frost Tolerance
12 in (30 cm)	24 in (60 cm)	9–11	no
12–24 in (30–60 cm)	12 in (30 cm)	9–11	no
18–20 in (45–50 cm)	12 in (30 cm)	9–11	no
18–20 in (45–50 cm)	12 in (30 cm)	9–11	no
18–20 in (45–50 cm)	12 in (30 cm)	9–11	no
24 in (60 cm)	15 in (38 cm)	9–11	no

Argyranthemum

Often treated as perennials, the 24 or so members of this genus from the Canary Islands and Madeira are evergreen shrubs, part of the huge daisy family. Most species are low spreading, though some are erect, and have rather crowded leaves clustered at the tips of brittle stems; the leaves vary from coarsely toothed to deeply dissected, and have a slightly aromatic or bitter smell when bruised. Flowers rise above the foliage, borne on long stems. Of the numerous cultivars, the majority have double or semi-double flowerheads in shades varying from white through pink to rose-purple. In the original 'single' forms, each head consists of a ring of ray florets around an eye of tiny yellow disc florets. Flowers appear over a long season.

Cultivation

Argyranthemum plants are marginally frost hardy and in cold climates need to be brought under shelter over winter. For permanent outdoor use they prefer a temperate climate. Soil should be very well drained and not too rich, and a sunny position is essential. Propagate from tip cuttings in autumn for a spring and summer display.

RIGHT *Argyranthemum 'Butterfly', with its cheerful yellow and white blooms, makes a welcome sight in spring. The long-stemmed flowers are excellent for bedding or borders, and appear over a long season. They are also favorites as cut flowers.*

ABOVE *Argyranthemum gracile is appreciated for the simplicity of its white flowerheads and golden central disc floret.*
LEFT *Recent interest in the genus has produced various new cultivars designed for garden use. Argyranthemum 'Donnington Hero' is one such example.*

BELOW *As its name suggests, Argyranthemum 'Petite Pink' is a neat subshrub. Pale pink flowers with yellow disc florets appear on slender stems above gray-green leaves. This is a good container plant.*

Top Tip

Young plants can be shaped by gently pinching out growing tips; pruning lanky old plants should be done with caution as they often die if cut back hard.

Favorites	Flower Color	Blooming Season	Flower Fragrance	Plant Height	Plant Width	Hardiness Zone	Frost Tolerance
Argyranthemum 'Butterfly'	yellow and white	spring to autumn	no	18 in (45 cm)	24 in (60 cm)	8–11	yes
Argyranthemum 'Donnington Hero'	white	spring to summer	no	24 in (60 cm)	24 in (60 cm)	8–11	yes
Argyranthemum frutescens	white	late spring to early summer	no	27 in (70 cm)	27 in (70 cm)	8–11	yes
Argyranthemum gracile	white	late spring to early summer	no	36 in (90 cm)	24 in (60 cm)	9–11	yes
Argyranthemum maderense	pale yellow	late spring to early summer	no	36 in (90 cm)	20 in (50 cm)	9–11	yes
Argyranthemum 'Petite Pink'	pale pink	late spring to early summer	no	12 in (30 cm)	12 in (30 cm)	8–11	yes

ARISAEMA

This genus of about 150 tuberous perennials is a member of the Araceae (arum) family. Species are found in Africa, North America, and Asia, usually growing in moist woodland. Their ornamental leaves and stems and bizarre flowers make them interesting garden subjects. Leaves may be compound or divided and the stems are often mottled in pink to purplish shades. The large hooded flower spathes may be yellow, green, brown, red, or pink, striped or mottled. They surround the spadix, a central column of small true flowers, which varies from short and clublike to long and drooping. Dense clusters of orange-red berries form on the spadix following the flowers.

CULTIVATION

Grow frost-tolerant species in a sheltered, semi-shaded, or woodland position in a moist, cool, peaty soil. Cover with protective mulch over winter and guard from slugs. Tropical species grown in the greenhouse require a deep pot in an equal mix of leaf mould, grit, and slightly acid loam. Propagate from seed or division of the tubers.

ABOVE The new tubular spathe emerges from the basal leaf-like bracts of this Arisaema concinnum plant.

TOP RIGHT The hooded spathe of Arisaema amurense grows up to 5 in (12 cm) long, striped with dark purple or green.

Favorites	Flower Color	Blooming Season	Flower Fragrance	Plant Height	Plant Width	Hardiness Zone	Frost Tolerance
Arisaema amurense	purple and white	spring	no	18 in (45 cm)	6 in (15 cm)	5–9	yes
Arisaema concinnum	green and white	early summer	no	20 in (50 cm)	12 in (30 cm)	8–10	yes
Arisaema kishidae	green and white	early summer	no	18 in (45 cm)	12 in (30 cm)	5–9	yes
Arisaema limbatum	deep purple and white	early summer	no	15 in (38 cm)	10 in (25 cm)	6–9	yes
Arisaema ringens	purple and green	early summer	no	12 in (30 cm)	4 in (10 cm)	6–9	yes
Arisaema sikokianum	deep purple	spring to early summer	no	12–20 in (30–50 cm)	6 in (15 cm)	7–9	yes

BELOW *This Japanese species,* Arisaema kishidae, *is a stocky plant whose flowers are nonetheless striking: the brown-green spathe, mottled white, surrounds a slender spadix.*

RIGHT *Most* Arisaema *plants bear a single flower spike in spring or early summer, held aloft on flowering spikes that may vary considerably in height.* Arisaema limbatum *has a deep purple spathe, striped with white, and a pale green spadix.*

Top Tip

These plants are generally fairly hardy and can be planted outdoors in light or dappled shade. Provide ample water during the growing season. Protect from slugs.

Favorites	Flower Color	Blooming Season	Flower Fragrance
Aristolochia californica	cream	summer	no
Aristolochia clematitis	yellow to brown	late spring to mid-summer	no
Aristolochia fimbriata	purple-brown	autumn	no
Aristolochia littoralis	maroon and white	summer	no
Aristolochia macrophylla	yellow-green, purple-brown	late spring to early summer	no
Aristolochia tomentosa	yellow, green, purple	summer	no

ARISTOLOCHIA

This genus contains about 300 species and is a member of the Aristolochiaceae (birth-wort) family. Plants range from strong climbers to perennials, both deciduous and evergreen, and are found throughout tropical and temperate regions. Stems are usually thick and fissured, and leaves are often heart-shaped and vary from smooth-edged to lobed. The weird, contorted, tubular flowers are mottled in shades of pink, purple, brown, and ivory; they range in size from very small to gigantic and many have an offensive odor. Insects, lured to the flowers by the strong odor, act as a medium for pollination as they become dusted with pollen while in the flower's bladder-like interior. The common name, birthwort, comes from the herbal use of some species as an aid during childbirth.

CULTIVATION

Many of the vigorous climbers are not very hardy, and they are better suited to the green-house in cooler regions. Where suitable, grow outdoors in sun or part-shade in a rich well-drained soil. Climbers require support and can be pruned in late winter. Propagate from soft-wood cuttings, division, or seed.

ABOVE *A netting of white veins and markings color the maroon flowers of* Aristolochia littoralis. *This twining species quickly reaches 20 ft (6 m) high.*
TOP LEFT Aristolochia clematitis *has heart-shaped mid-green leaves and bears clusters of curiously shaped yellow or yellowish brown flowers during summer.*

Plant Height	Plant Width	Hardiness Zone	Frost Tolerance
15 ft (4.5 m)	4 ft (1.2 m)	7–10	yes
36 in (90 cm)	24 in (60 cm)	5–9	yes
7 ft (2 m)	36 in (90 cm)	10–12	no
20 ft (6 m)	8 ft (2.4 m)	10–12	no
20–30 ft (6–9 m)	10 ft (3 m)	4–9	yes
35 ft (10 m)	10 ft (3 m)	8–10	yes

RIGHT *The maroon flowers of* Aristolochia fimbriata *have a heavily netted surface of yellow veins and markings, and the edges are fringed by long hairs. The large, heart-shaped, dark green leaves are etched with lighter veining.*

BELOW *A vigorous twining species,* Aristolochia californica *is commonly known as the California Dutchman's pipe due to its unusual flowers, which are cream in color with purplish veins and purple-brown lobed lips.*

Top Tip

As many of these plants have malodorous flowers, and some also have leaves that give off an unpleasant odor when crushed or bruised, select a planting position away from high traffic and entertaining areas.

ARMERIA

This genus comprises around 80 species of herbaceous and shrubby perennials found in Eurasia, North Africa, and the American Pacific coast. They form dense cushion-like clumps of simple linear leaves above which in spring and summer rounded heads of tiny flowers are borne on slender stems. Flowers may be white, pink, or nearly red. The genus was named *Armeria,* the Roman word for *Dianthus* (or carnation), because of a supposed resemblance between the 2 genera, though in fact they are not from the same family. The common name of *Armeria* is thrift—that is, to thrive—which refers to the plant's ability to grow well even under harsh conditions.

CULTIVATION
Known as coastal plants, the species actually occur in a wide range of environments and are easily cultivated, being especially at home in rockeries. Most are quite hardy and prefer moist well-drained soil and a position in full or half sun. Propagate by seed, cuttings, or the careful division of well-established clumps.

ABOVE LEFT *Though compact in size,* Armeria maritima *'Bloodstone' is certainly eye-catching. Throughout spring and summer it produces many deep pink to red flowers.*
ABOVE Armeria alliacea *is a robust perennial that bears white, occasionally red-purple, flowers on tall stems that may grow up to 20 in (50 cm) in height.*

Favorites

	Flower Color	Blooming Season	Flower Fragrance	Plant Height	Plant Width	Hardiness Zone	Frost Tolerance
Armeria alliacea	white to red-purple	summer	no	20 in (50 cm)	20 in (50 cm)	5–9	yes
Armeria 'Bee's Ruby'	deep pink	early summer	no	12 in (30 cm)	10 in (25 cm)	5–9	yes
Armeria girardii	lavender-pink	late spring to summer	no	10 in (25 cm)	12 in (30 cm)	6–9	yes
Armeria juniperifolia	light to deep pink	late spring	no	3 in (8 cm)	6 in (15 cm)	5–9	yes
Armeria maritima	white to deep red	spring to summer	no	4 in (10 cm)	8 in (20 cm)	4–9	yes
Armeria 'Westacre Beauty'	pink	spring to summer	no	6 in (15 cm)	12 in (30 cm)	4–9	yes

RIGHT *A mass of pink flowerheads is borne above the gray-green foliage of* Armeria juniperifolia. *Place this hummock-forming plant at the front of a border.*
BELOW Armeria maritima *is ideally suited to this rock garden. In this example, a mass of narrow sea green leaves appears as a cushion to a profusion of red flowers.*

Top Tip

A favorite of the cottage garden, *Armeria* flowers can also be used fresh or dried in floral arrangements. Try tall-stemmed brightly colored cultivars such as 'Bee's Ruby'.

ARTEMISIA

This genus of about 300 species of evergreen herbs and shrubs is spread throughout northern temperate regions with some also found in southern Africa and South America. It is a member of the large daisy family, but most species bear small white or yellow flowers. The beauty of these plants lies in their attractive foliage, which is well dissected and of palest gray to silver. The overall appearance is often soft and silky, and various species can be used to good effect in a border or clipped and used as a low hedge. The plants are often aromatic. Tarragon, the popular culinary herb, is a member of this genus.

CULTIVATION

These shrubs are perfect for hot dry climates as most can withstand considerable drought. They should be grown in full sun in light well-drained soil. Prune back quite hard in spring to prevent legginess and lightly clip at flowering time if the flowers are not wanted. Propagation is usually from softwood or half-hardened cuttings in summer.

Top Tip

The foliage of some *Artemisia* species is not only decorative but also quite aromatic; plant those species in the garden for a natural way to ward off leaf-eating insects.

FAR RIGHT *Commonly known as white mugwort,* Artemisia lactiflora *is native to China. It is tall growing and has dark green foliage. The cultivar 'Guizhou' has purple stems and creamy white flowerheads.*

ABOVE Artemisia vulgaris *was thought by ancient herbalists to have magical properties. This bushy cultivar, 'Oriental Limelight', has yellow and green leaves.*
LEFT Artemisia *'Powis Castle' has a delightfully sprawling habit. It occurs naturally in southwestern regions of the USA.*

BELOW *The yellow-brown flowers of* Artemisia alba *'Canescens' are insignificant; the attraction of this plant lies mainly in its distinctive, fluffy, silver leaves.*

Favorites	Flower Color	Blooming Season	Flower Fragrance	Plant Height	Plant Width	Hardiness Zone	Frost Tolerance
Artemisia alba	yellowish	late spring to early summer	no	36 in (90 cm)	36 in (90 cm)	8–10	yes
Artemisia dracunculus	creamy white to yellow	late summer	no	36 in (90 cm)	12 in (30 cm)	6–9	yes
Artemisia lactiflora	white	summer	no	4–5 ft (1.2–1.5 m)	18 in (45 cm)	5–9	yes
Artemisia ludoviciana	brownish gray	summer	no	4 ft (1.2 m)	24 in (60 cm)	4–10	yes
Artemisia 'Powis Castle'	silvery	late summer	no	24–36 in (60–90 cm)	3–6 ft (0.9–1.8 m)	6–10	yes
Artemisia vulgaris	red-brown	summer to autumn	no	4–8 ft (1.2–2.4 m)	36 in (90 cm)	4–10	yes

ASCLEPIAS

This American and African genus consists of over 100 species and includes annuals, perennials, subshrubs, and shrubs among its number. The shrubs are generally upright many-branched plants with simple, narrow, elliptical to lance-shaped leaves. They produce heads of small 5-petalled flowers that are followed by inflated seed pods, sometimes oddly shaped and variable in length. Upon ripening, the seed pods open to reveal rows of tightly packed small seeds, each with a small parachute of silky down, hence the common name of silkweed. All parts of the plants exude a milky sap if cut, which may irritate the skin. This sap is the origin of the genus's other common name, milkweed.

CULTIVATION

Asclepias plants are easily grown in any light well-drained soil with full sun. They will, however, bear more luxuriant foliage and a greater profusion of flowers if well-fed and watered. The shrubby species are generally rather frost tender but grow so readily and quickly from seed that they can be treated as annuals or short-lived perennials.

ABOVE *Common in South America, the cultivar Asclepias curassavica 'Silky Gold' produces yellow-gold flowers and has attractive lance-shaped leaves.*
RIGHT *Asclepias incarnata is a herbaceous perennial from eastern U.S.A. It bears delightful clusters of pinkish purple flowers.*

LEFT *Native to southwestern U.S.A., Asclepias linaria is a sun-loving shrubby perennial with needle-like leaves and clusters of white flowers.*

Top Tip

Asclepias plants, particularly the shrubby species, can be trimmed to shape if necessary but do not cut back to bare wood as the plants can be slow to recover if pruned to excess.

ABOVE *Bold strappy leaves and bright orange-red flowers are features of* Asclepias curassavica, *a plant that is considered invasive in warmer climates.*

RIGHT *Butterflies flock to the hot-colored flowers of* Asclepias tuberosa, *which is why this plant is commonly known as butterfly weed. It needs lots of sun and well-drained soil.*

Favorites	Flower Color	Blooming Season	Flower Fragrance	Plant Height	Plant Width	Hardiness Zone	Frost Tolerance
Asclepias curassavica	orange-red	summer to autumn	no	36 in (90 cm)	24–36 in (60–90 cm)	9–12	no
Asclepias incarnata	pinkish purple	mid-summer to early autumn	no	4 ft (1.2 m)	24 in (60 cm)	3–8	yes
Asclepias linaria	white	spring and summer	no	36 in (90 cm)	36 in (90 cm)	9–11	no
Asclepias speciosa	pinkish purple	summer	no	36 in (90 cm)	24 in (60 cm)	2–9	yes
Asclepias subulata	yellowish white	spring to autumn	no	3–5 ft (0.9–1.5 m)	36 in (90 cm)	9–11	no
Asclepias tuberosa	orange-red, orange, yellow	summer	no	24–36 in (60–90 cm)	12 in (30 cm)	3–9	yes

Favorites	Flower Color	Blooming Season	Flower Fragrance
Aster alpinus	violet-blue	summer	no
Aster amellus	pink to purple-blue	late summer to autumn	yes
Aster × frikartii	violet-blue	late summer to early autumn	no
Aster novae-angliae	violet-purple	late summer to early autumn	no
Aster novi-belgii	light to dark purple	late summer to mid-autumn	no
Aster radula	mauve to violet	summer	no

ABOVE *Known as a rough-leafed aster, Aster radula occurs naturally in wet woodlands or swamps. In summer it bears pale violet flowers with a yellow disc on tall stems.*

RIGHT *Aster × frikartii 'Mönch' is a delightful plant for the garden. Upright and free-flowering, it produces a profusion of long-lasting lavender-blue flowers.*

Top Tip

Provide protection from strong winds. Taller perennials may benefit from staking if planted in an exposed area. When the flowers have faded, trim the long stems down to ground level and tidy the clumps.

ASTER

Found over much of the temperate Northern Hemisphere and into South America, this group of 250 species of mainly herbaceous perennials is the type genus for the daisy family, the Asteraceae. They are upright plants that often sprawl under the weight of their foliage and flowers, and have simple linear to lance-shaped leaves that are sometimes hairy and/or serrated along the edges. Most species bloom in late summer and autumn, producing large heads of small to medium-sized daisies in a wide range of colors, including white, pink, and blue. Asters feature in several Greek and Roman god myths; the ancient Greeks also believed that asters would repel snakes and serve as an antidote to their venom.

CULTIVATION

Mostly very frost resistant, asters have a preference for well-drained fertile soil that remains moist during the growing season. A sunny, airy, open position ensures maximum flower production and minimum mildew, which can cause problems in humid conditions. Cut back hard after flowering, and propagate by winter division or spring softwood cuttings.

Plant Height	Plant Width	Hardiness Zone	Frost Tolerance
6–12 in (15–30 cm)	18 in (45 cm)	3–9	yes
18–24 in (45–60 cm)	18 in (45 cm)	4–9	yes
30 in (75 cm)	15 in (38 cm)	5–9	yes
5 ft (1.5 m)	24 in (60 cm)	4–9	yes
4 ft (1.2 m)	36 in (90 cm)	3–9	yes
4 ft (1.2 m)	36 in (90 cm)	5–9	yes

ABOVE *The clump-forming* Aster alpinus *flourishes in situations such as this sunny corner of a rock garden. It has hairy, violet to blue ray florets with pretty golden disc florets.*

BELOW Aster novae-angliae, *New England aster, is most often found in the form of its cultivars. 'Andenken an Alma Potschke' is an award-winning compact plant that has vibrant crimson-pink flowerheads above a dense mass of mid-green leaves.*

ASTILBE

Found mainly in temperate East Asia, this perennial genus of the saxifrage family (Saxifragaceae) includes just 12 species but has been extensively selected and hybridized to produce many garden plants. The shiny toothed leaves sprout directly from the plant's fleshy stem and soon form a generous foliage clump. Striking long-stemmed plumes of tiny flowers appear during spring and summer in colors ranging from white to shades of pink, mauve, and red. Surprisingly, given their showy nature, the genus name *Astilbe* actually means without brilliance, coming from the Greek *a* (without) and *stilbe* (brilliance). That is because, although the flowerheads are bright, each flower on its own is tiny and rather dull.

CULTIVATION

Astilbe plants are not drought tolerant nor do they thrive in the hot summer sun; instead they prefer light, moist, humus-rich woodland soil and dappled sunlight. They often thrive around pond margins as they tolerate being waterlogged, especially in winter. To propagate, divide clumps in winter when dormant, then replant immediately.

BELOW LEFT Astilbe japonica *'Deutschland' is grown for its springtime profusion of tiny white flowers borne on plume-like panicles. Foliage is dark to bright green.*
BELOW Astilbe × arendsii *refers to a group of hybrids derived from 4 East Asian species. They are valued for their pretty feathery spikes. 'Gloria', below, has deep pink flowers; lilac, white, crimson, and coral pink forms are also available.*

Top Tip

Astilbe flowers can be cut and used in fresh flower arrangements, but they do not last long. For more satisfying results, bring some indoors as pot plants when the flowers are at their best.

ABOVE *Another hybrid from the* Astilbe × arendsii *group, 'Fanal' grows up to 24 in (60 cm). Like many hybrids in this group, it is a striking plant. It has dark leaves and long-lasting, star-shaped, crimson-red flowers.*

RIGHT Astilbe chinensis *'Visions' is an attractive clump-forming plant with toothed, hairy, dark green leaves and dense fluffy spikes of pink-red flowers.*

Favorites

	Flower Color	Blooming Season	Flower Fragrance	Plant Height	Plant Width	Hardiness Zone	Frost Tolerance
Astilbe × arendsii	white to purple-pink	summer	no	24–48 in (60–120 cm)	24 in (60 cm)	6–10	yes
Astilbe chinensis	white flushed with pink or red	summer	no	24 in (60 cm)	24 in (60 cm)	6–10	yes
Astilbe japonica	white	summer	no	36 in (90 cm)	24–36 in (60–90 cm)	5–10	yes
Astilbe koreana	ivory	summer	no	24 in (60 cm)	24 in (60 cm)	6–10	yes
Astilbe simplicifolia	white	summer	no	12 in (30 cm)	18 in (45 cm)	7–10	yes
Astilbe thunbergii	white, turning pink with age	early summer	no	24 in (60 cm)	24–36 in (60–90 cm)	7–10	yes

LEFT *Astrantia carniolica is a native of the southern Alps. It has white flowers with pinkish tints.*

ASTRANTIA

This genus of about 10 species of perennials is mainly European, though it also occurs westwards to Asia, favoring alpine meadows or woodlands. Its most distinguishing feature is its sprays of flowers, which appear above the clump-forming hand-shaped foliage. The small pastel-toned flowers are borne on neat dome-shaped flowerheads and are surrounded by a ring of papery bracts, which are often more showy than the true flowers inside. This genus is variously referred to as masterwort or pin-cushion flower. The name *Astrantia* probably comes from the Latin *aster,* meaning star, re-ferring to the star-shaped flowerheads. These plants are best grown in informal garden situations. They also make excellent dried flowers.

CULTIVATION

Apart from an intolerance of prolonged dry conditions, *Astrantia* plants grow freely in any cool-temperate garden with moderately fertile free-draining soil. The foliage may be more lush in the shade, which is of particular con-sideration with the variegated cultivars, but they usually flower best with at least half-sun. Propagate by division when dormant or from seed, which needs stratification.

Top Tip

Astrantia plants can be grown in cottage gardens, woodland gardens, or herbaceous bor-ders. They make great cut flowers because of their straight wiry stems.

BELOW *Astrantia major bears clusters of delicate white or pink flowerheads that resemble daisies. This species originates from cen-tral and eastern Europe.*

BELOW Astrantia major *has a number of cultivars available in a wide variety of colors.* A. major *subsp.* involucrata *'Moira Reid' (pictured) flowers earlier in the season than the species, and has large green-tipped flowers.*

ABOVE *A favorite in cottage gardens,* Astrantia major *'Ruby Wedding' bears ruby red flowers on distinctive maroon stems throughout the summer months.*

Favorites	Flower Color	Blooming Season	Flower Fragrance	Plant Height	Plant Width	Hardiness Zone	Frost Tolerance
Astrantia carniolica	white tinged pink	summer	no	18–24 in (45–60 cm)	24 in (60 cm)	4–9	yes
Astrantia carniolica **'Rubra'**	deep pink with silvery tints	summer	no	18–24 in (45–60 cm)	24 in (60 cm)	4–9	yes
Astrantia major	pink, white, purple, green	summer	no	12–36 in (30–90 cm)	18 in (45 cm)	6–9	yes
Astrantia major **'Ruby Wedding'**	deep red	summer	no	12–36 in (30–90 cm)	18 in (45 cm)	6–9	yes
Astrantia major **subsp.** *involucrata* **'Moira Reid'**	white	summer	no	12–36 in (30–90 cm)	18 in (45 cm)	6–9	yes
Astrantia maxima	pale pink	summer	no	36 in (90 cm)	12 in (30 cm)	5–9	yes

BANKSIA

This genus is easy to recognize, with its bold flowering spikes, attractive foliage, and interesting fruiting cones. All but one of the approximately 75 species are endemic to Australia. Species range from woody low-growing shrubs to low-branching trees, though they all feature the large cylindrical or globular-shaped flower spikes made up of hundreds of densely packed small flowers in colors of pale orange and burnished gold to rosy pink and deep scarlet. As the flowers die they develop into large, woody, fruiting cones. The thick leathery leaves are usually long and narrow with toothed edges. The genus name comes from Sir Joseph Banks, the renowned English botanist who first documented the plants on his travels to Australia with Captain Cook.

CULTIVATION

Most species prefer an open sunny position and well-drained sandy soil. Some banksias are moderately frost tolerant and once established will withstand dry conditions. Taking cut flowers will encourage flower production and thicken up the foliage. Propagate from seed in early spring or autumn.

BELOW *The hairpin banksia,* Banksia spinulosa, *is found on hillsides along the east coast of Australia, and is popular with gardeners. It has yellow flower spikes with orange to red styles.*

LEFT *Proving extremely tolerant of coastal conditions,* Banksia integrifolia *is an ideal plant for seaside gardens. The colorful display of nectar-rich flowers, produced over a long flowering season, will also attract birdlife to the garden.*

Top Tip

Banksias will benefit from a light pruning, rewarding keen gardeners with more flowers and denser foliage. To maintain the shape and appearance of the bush, lightly prune the tips regularly.

ABOVE *Once flowering has ceased,* Banksia serrata *continues to make a striking impression, bearing its trademark woody cones among the attractive saw-toothed leaves.*
RIGHT *The cylindrical yellow flower spikes of* Banksia speciosa *create a perfect foil to the foliage. The gray-green leaves have silvery undersides, and are sharply toothed, with the serrations extending to the midrib of the leaf.*

Favorites

	Flower Color	Blooming Season	Flower Fragrance	Plant Height	Plant Width	Hardiness Zone	Frost Tolerance
Banksia ericifolia	yellow to orange-brown	autumn to late winter	no	10–20 ft (3–6 m)	6–12 ft (1.8–3.5 m)	9–10	no
Banksia integrifolia	pale yellow	summer to winter	no	15–80 ft (4.5–24 m)	10–25 ft (3–8 m)	8–11	yes
Banksia marginata	pale yellow	late summer to winter	no	6–30 ft (1.8–9 m)	6–10 ft (1.8–3 m)	8–10	yes
Banksia serrata	cream to yellow-green	summer to winter	no	10–70 ft (3–21 m)	6–25 ft (1.8–8 m)	9–11	no
Banksia speciosa	light yellow	summer to autumn	no	10–15 ft (3–4.5 m)	10–25 ft (3–8 m)	9–10	no
Banksia spinulosa	golden yellow	autumn to winter	no	3 ft (0.9 m)	4 ft (1.2 m)	9–11	no

Favorites	Flower Color	Blooming Season	Flower Fragrance
Begonia boliviensis	orange-red	summer	no
Begonia bowerae	white	winter to early spring	no
***Begonia,* Cane-stemmed**	white, pink orange, red	early spring to autumn	no
***Begonia,* Rex-cultorum Group**	white, pink	early spring	no
***Begonia,* Semperflorens- cultorum Group**	white, pink, red	summer or all year	no
***Begonia,* Tuberhybrida Group**	orange, red, pink, yellow, white	summer	no

ABOVE *Begonia 'Pin-up Flame' bears gorgeous yellow and orange-red flowers and is an ideal selection for container planting. The Tuberhybrida Group—of which it is a member—is famed for its large, showy, saucer-shaped flowers, which come in single or double form, in a wide range of colors.*

Top Tip

The many varieties of begonia offer a range of choices for the keen gardener. Some are suitable for basket planting, others as bedding annuals, while some cultivars are suited to terrarium planting.

BEGONIA

This genus belongs to the Begoniaceae family and contains around 900 species of perennials, shrubs, and climbers that are found throughout the tropics and subtropics. The most diverse species occur in the Americas. These clump-forming plants have olive green to bright green foliage that may vary greatly in color, texture, and shape but is often lobed and covered in fine hairs. There is usually a single female flower surrounded by 2 or more male flowers, appearing in shades of white, yellow, orange, red, and pink. Begonias were named after Michel Bégon, a fifteenth-century Governor of Santo Domingo and later of French Canada, known today as Quebec.

CULTIVATION

Outside of tropical climates, begonias are best grown as indoor container plants. They grow well in a bright but not a sunny position with cool, moist, humus-rich soil and need to be watered and fed well. Begonias are susceptible to fungal diseases so they need to have good air flow around them.

ABOVE *The glossy, heart-shaped leaves of Begonia 'Merry Christmas'—a member of the Rex-cultorum Group—have a rosy pink central heart, edged in dark green, and are sometimes flecked with silver highlights. During autumn and winter, this attractive foliage is complemented by rosy pink flowers.*

Plant Height	Plant Width	Hardiness Zone	Frost Tolerance
36 in (90 cm)	36 in (90 cm)	10–11	no
10 in (25 cm)	12 in (30 cm)	10–12	no
5 ft (1.5 m)	4 ft (1.2 m)	10–11	no
8–12 in (20–30 cm)	18–24 in (45–60 cm)	10–12	no
12 in (30 cm)	12 in (30 cm)	9–11	no
18 in (45 cm)	24 in (60 cm)	9–11	no

ABOVE *The variegated light and dark green leaves of Begonia bowerae 'Tiger' provide a contrast to the small, pure white flowers borne in early summer. It is particularly suited to indoor situations, where it will flower reliably.*
BELOW *An easy-care plant, the intense red blooms of Begonia, Semperflorens-cultorum Group, 'Prelude Scarlet' are produced from summer through to winter's first frosts.*

LEFT *Contrasting shades of pink, and somewhat crimped petal edges, combine to create the attractive, double, summer-flowering blooms of Begonia 'Roy Hartley', a member of the Tuberhybrida Group.*

BELOW *A lovely example of the Picotee group of cultivars in the Tuberhybrida Group, Begonia 'Mardi Gras' bears snow white double blooms, becoming creamier at the center, with crimson-edged petals.*

BELOW *Lovely full blooms in the softest apricot color, slightly darker at the petal's edge, are the signature of Begonia, Tuberhybrida Group, 'Apricot Delight'.*

ABOVE *Begonia 'Pinafore' bears small, soft pink flowers on slender stems. Glossy leaves, dark green above and deep red beneath, add interest to this low-growing plant.*

LEFT *The glossy dark green leaves of* Begonia, *Semperflorens-cultorum Group, 'Prelude Bicolor' provide a perfect foil for the coral pink-edged white flowers, which are held above the leaves on long stems.*

ABOVE *A reliable performer,* Begonia, *Semperflorens-cultorum Group, 'Senator Scarlet' creates a dramatic impact when used as a bedding plant, with its vivid red flowers appearing among leaves of the darkest green.*

BERGENIA

Curiously known as pigsqueak, this genus of the saxifrage family (Saxifragaceae) is made up of 8 species of perennials that are found in Asia, extending from Afghanistan to Mongolia. Sprouting from tough woody stems, the large leathery leaves are broad and light green in color. The 5-petalled flowers grow in clusters on long stems and open in spring. Most species produce flowers in shades of pink but some garden forms occur in white, mauve, and red. *Bergenia* is named after an eighteenth-century German botanist, Karl August von Bergen. The common name pigsqueak comes from the sound the wet leaves make when rubbed between the fingers.

CULTIVATION

Bergenia species thrive in sun or shade with humus-rich soil. Planting in partial shade with cool moist conditions will develop lush foliage, whereas full sun will produce flowers at the expense of the leaves. This adaptable genus is extremely suitable as a ground cover or as a rockery plant.

ABOVE *Originating from China,* Bergenia emeiensis *is a relative newcomer to Western gardens. It has proven particularly useful in hybridization work.*
LEFT *The attractive pink-hued blooms of* Bergenia crassifolia *are carried on long stalks to emerge through the lush foliage.*

Top Tip

Bergenia species will withstand less than ideal soil conditions and some neglect. However, they will benefit from the removal of old flowers and dead leaves.

ABOVE Bergenia ciliata *is popular for both its handsome foliage and attractive flowers. The large, rounded, glossy leaves are around 12 in (30 cm) wide, and are interspersed with pretty clusters of blooms during the flowering season.*
RIGHT *The autumn foliage of* Bergenia cordifolia *'Perfecta' is spectacular, as the glossy heart-shaped leaves take on fiery hues of scarlet and gold. The purple-pink flowers, held on long stems, appear in late winter.*

Favorites

	Flower Color	Blooming Season	Flower Fragrance	Plant Height	Plant Width	Hardiness Zone	Frost Tolerance
Bergenia 'Abendglut'	magenta-red	spring	no	8–12 in (20–30 cm)	18–24 in (45–60 cm)	3–8	yes
Bergenia ciliata	pink, white	early spring	yes	12 in (30 cm)	18 in (45 cm)	5–9	yes
Bergenia cordifolia	purple-pink	late winter to early spring	no	24 in (60 cm)	30 in (75 cm)	3–9	yes
Bergenia crassifolia	rose pink to magenta	early spring	no	18 in (45 cm)	18 in (45 cm)	3–9	yes
Bergenia emeiensis	white flushed pink	early spring	no	8 in (20 cm)	18 in (45 cm)	8–9	yes
Bergenia × *schmidtii*	rose pink	late winter to early spring	no	12 in (30 cm)	24 in (60 cm)	5–10	yes

Billbergia

This genus belongs to the large bromeliad family (Bromeliaceae) and consists of around 65 species of evergreen perennials and about 500 cultivars. Most species are epiphytic or rock dwelling and come from Mexico and the warmer regions of Central and South America. The leaves form a tubular rosette and range in color from dull olive green to gray-green with a variety of attractive markings. Showy stalked flower clusters emerge from the leaf rosettes. The flowers are globular to cylindrical and have side spikes of blue-green to navy blue petals. Bright pink or red banner-like bracts appear underneath the flowerhead. *Billbergia* plants are commonly referred to as vase plants because the central hollow of the plant acts as an important storage area for water between rainfalls.

Cultivation

Most plants in this genus are easy to grow and are suitable for both indoor and outdoor planting. If planting outside, keep the plant in a sheltered humid spot in a porous fast-draining soil mix or a mound of stones. Use the shoots that grow from the base of the plant for propagation.

ABOVE *As the name indicates,* Billbergia venezuelana *is a native of Venezuela. When in flower it grows to about 36 in (90 cm) tall, and has numerous brightly colored bracts.*

Favorites	Flower Color	Blooming Season	Flower Fragrance	Plant Height	Plant Width	Hardiness Zone	Frost Tolerance
Billbergia distachia	green-blue	summer	no	20 in (50 cm)	20 in (50 cm)	9–12	no
Billbergia nutans	green-blue	spring	no	20 in (50 cm)	Indefinite	9–12	no
Billbergia pyramidalis	magenta	late summer to mid-winter	no	20 in (50 cm)	10 in (25 cm)	9–12	no
Billbergia sanderiana	lavender-pink and pale green	autumn	no	20–24 in (50–60 cm)	24 in (60 cm)	9–12	no
Billbergia venezuelana	pink-red and yellow-green	autumn-winter	no	36 in (90 cm)	24 in (60 cm)	9–12	no
Billbergia zebrina	pink-red and yellow-green	autumn-winter	no	36 in (90 cm)	24 in (60 cm)	9–12	no

LEFT Billbergia zebrina *is a very hardy plant from South America. Its green leaves are banded in silver or white, and may develop bronze tints in strong light.*

Top Tip

If grown as indoor plants, *Billbergia* species need to be potted in a mixture composed of leaf mold, bark, and sand. They do best if placed in a warm sunny position.

RIGHT *The striking features of* Billbergia pyramidalis *are the panicles of magenta-pink flowers tipped in pale blue that appear in summer.* **FAR RIGHT** *Known as the friendship plant,* Billbergia nutans *is valued for its long narrow leaves, and flowers of light green and dark blue, with pink bracts.*

BOUGAINVILLEA

Known for their brilliant floral displays and ground-covering power, bougainvilleas are strong-growing climbers and trailers from the tropics and subtropics of South America. Their wonderful colors come not from their true flowers, which are small cream tubes, but from the leafy bracts that surround them. The leaves are simple, elliptical, and taper to a fine point. Rather than climb by tendrils or twining, bougainvilleas use their sharp thorns to gain a hold and then develop a framework of strong stems. This genus was named in honor of the sixteenth-century explorer and scientist, Louis Antoine de Bougainville, who made the first French voyage around the world.

CULTIVATION

All species do well in warm to hot climates in full sun and some species will tolerate light frosts. Although drought tolerant, they need plenty of moisture during the flowering season. Overfeeding will produce masses of foliage but very little in the way of colorful bracts. Most cultivars can be propagated from cuttings.

ABOVE *The vibrant bracts of* Bougainvillea *'Sundance' in fiery hues appear amid the mid-green leaves. This cultivar can give a distinct tropical feel to the garden.*

RIGHT *Inconspicuous, white, tubular flowers are held within vivid scarlet bracts, scattered throughout the foliage of* Bougainvillea *'Scarlett O'Hara'.*

Favorites	Flower Color	Blooming Season	Flower Fragrance
Bougainvillea **'Barbara Karst'**	red bracts	spring to autumn	no
Bougainvillea × *buttiana*	orange-pink to red bracts	spring to autumn	no
Bougainvillea glabra	purple bracts	spring to autumn	no
Bougainvillea **'Miss Manila'**	pinkish orange bracts	spring to autumn	no
Bougainvillea **'Scarlett O'Hara'**	scarlet to crimson bracts	spring to autumn	no
Bougainvillea **'Sundance'**	orange-pink bracts	spring to autumn	no

Top Tip

Be sure to wear protective gloves when pruning or handling bougainvilleas, as their thorns are dangerously sharp.

BELOW LEFT Bougainvillea *'Miss Manila'* is a vigorous climber that produces tiny insignificant flowers within lovely orange bracts that gradually fade to pink.
BELOW The papery bracts of Bougainvillea × buttiana *'Raspberry Ice'* are a spectacular cerise color, while the mid-green leaves are edged in creamy yellow.

Plant Height	Plant Width	Hardiness Zone	Frost Tolerance
10–20 ft (3–6 m)	8–12 ft (2.4–3.5 m)	10–12	no
25–40 ft (8–12 m)	10–20 ft (3–6 m)	10–12	no
15–30 ft (4.5–9 m)	10–20 ft (3–6 m)	10–12	no
25–40 ft (8–12 m)	10–20 ft (3–6 m)	10–12	no
25–40 ft (8–12 m)	10–20 ft (3–6 m)	10–12	no
10–20 ft (3–6 m)	8–12 ft (2.4–3.5 m)	10–12	no

BRUGMANSIA

Belonging to the South American potato family (Solanaceae), this genus contains just 5 species of large evergreen shrubs or small trees. Extensive hybridization, however, has produced a wide range of garden forms. The large downy leaves shield impressively long, hanging, trumpet-like flowers with flared lobes that curve delicately back towards the base of the flower. Colors range from white, cream, and yellow to pink and red. *Brugmansia* species generally flower in spring and autumn and can look quite spectacular when flowering en masse. Most plants bear fragrant flowers, with their scent being more noticeable in the evening. The common name of angel's trumpet comes from the shape of the flower but belies the dangerous effect of the narcotic substances found in all parts of the plant.

CULTIVATION

Frost tender and best suited to mild climates, these plants prefer full or half sun and deep, moist, humus-rich, well-drained soil. During the summer growing season they need to be watered and fed well. Regular trimming will help keep the plant in a dense rounded shape. Propagate from half-hardened cuttings.

Top Tip

Prune brugmansias in early spring, removing old, dead, or surplus stems, to encourage an abundant display of flowers throughout the blooming season.

RIGHT *The boldly-colored, trumpet-shaped flowers of the red angel's trumpet,* Brugmansia sanguinea, *make a spectacular impact in the garden.*

BELOW LEFT *In soft colors of cream, yellow, or apricot, the elegant, trumpet-shaped flowers of* Brugmansia aurea *exude a sweet fragrance in the evening.*

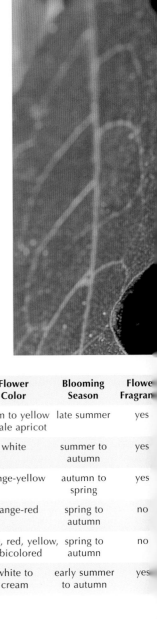

Favorites	Flower Color	Blooming Season	Flower Fragrance
Brugmansia aurea	cream to yellow or pale apricot	late summer	yes
Brugmansia × candida	white	summer to autumn	yes
***Brugmansia* 'Charles Grimaldi'**	orange-yellow	autumn to spring	yes
***Brugmansia* 'Inca Queen'**	orange-red	spring to autumn	no
Brugmansia sanguinea	orange, red, yellow, or bicolored	spring to autumn	no
Brugmansia suaveolens	white to cream	early summer to autumn	yes

ABOVE *The attractive, bell-shaped, fragrant flowers of* Brugmansia suaveolens *are usually white, though there are also pink and yellow forms. With regular pruning, this species can make an attractive garden shrub.*
BELOW Brugmansia × candida *is a fast-growing species with slender trumpets of cream to white, delicately veined in green. The scented flowers appear in profusion from summer to autumn and occasionally bloom at other times.*

Plant Height	Plant Width	Hardiness Zone	Frost Tolerance
12–20 ft (3.5–6 m)	10–15 ft (3–4.5 m)	10–12	no
10–20 ft (3–6 m)	6–10 ft (1.8–3 m)	10–12	no
6–12 ft (1.8–3.5 m)	5–8 ft (1.5–2.4 m)	10–12	no
12–15 ft (3.5–4.5 m)	10–12 ft (3–3.5 m)	9–11	no
12–15 ft (3.5–4.5 m)	12 ft (3.5 m)	9–11	no
12–20 ft (3.5–6 m)	8–12 ft (2.4–3.5 m)	10–12	no

BUDDLEJA

This genus consists of about 100 species of deciduous, semi-deciduous, and evergreen shrubs and small trees from America, Asia, and South Africa, and includes many tropical and subtropical species. The attractive leaves are large, pointed, often crepe-textured, and usually grow in opposite pairs on the stem. Most species are grown for their flowers, however, and there are many decorative cultivars to choose from. Small, usually fragrant, flowers form loose branching clusters, and occur in shades of pink, mauve, reddish purple, orange, and yellow. The genus can be spelt *Buddleja* or *Buddleia* and is named after the seventeenth-century English botanist Adam Buddle.

CULTIVATION

These plants are hardy, quick growing, salt tolerant, and will thrive in any soil type. They prefer full sun and good drainage. Pruning in early spring will keep the plant tidy. Propagate from half-hardened cuttings in summer.

ABOVE *The name of the South African species* Buddleja salviifolia *derives from the plant's similarity in appearance to members of the sage* (Salvia) *genus.*
BELOW *A native of Argentina and Chile,* Buddleja globosa *features tight bobble-like clusters of orange-yellow flowers.*

Top Tip

The nectar-rich flowers of *Buddleja davidii* varieties often attract feeding butterflies to the garden in summer.

ABOVE Buddleja × weyeriana *is a cross between* B. davidii *and* B. globosa. *The petals of its orange-yellow flowers can sometimes be flushed soft purple.*

Favorites

	Flower Color	Blooming Season	Flower Fragrance	Plant Height	Plant Width	Hardiness Zone	Frost Tolerance
Buddleja alternifolia	mauve-pink	late spring to early summer	yes	15 ft (4.5 m)	12 ft (3.5 m)	5–9	yes
Buddleja davidii	purple, pink, white, red	summer	yes	10–20 ft (3–6 m)	10–20 ft (3–6 m)	4–10	yes
Buddleja fallowiana	pale lavender	summer and early autumn	yes	10 ft (3 m)	10 ft (3 m)	8–9	yes
Buddleja globosa	orange-yellow	late spring and early summer	yes	10–20 ft (3–6 m)	10–20 ft (3–6 m)	7–9	yes
Buddleja salviifolia	mauve	late autumn and winter	yes	10–25 ft (3–8 m)	10–15 ft (3–4.5 m)	8–10	yes
Buddleja × weyeriana	orange-yellow	summer to autumn	yes	15 ft (4.5 m)	10 ft (3 m)	6–9	yes

LEFT Buddleja davidii *'Nanho Blue' has bluish purple flowers clustered on 6-in (15-cm) long panicles. The tiny flowers are highly aromatic, and the flower spikes may be cut and placed in a vase to add both color and fragrance to the home.*

CALCEOLARIA

This genus of around 300 species includes annuals, perennials, and even some small shrubs, and is found from Mexico to the southern tip of South America. The leaves tend to be light green and are covered with fine hairs and small glands that make them sticky to the touch. They are known as slipper flower or ladies's purse, due to the distinctive pouchlike shape of the flowers, which is common to almost all species. The flowers are 2-lipped, with a small hooded upper lip and a large lower lip that is inflated to form a kind of pouch. Yellow, orange, and red shades dominate. *Calceolaria* plants are usually grown as pot plants or in hanging baskets, as the blossoms are rather fragile.

CULTIVATION

While *Calceolaria* plants vary in their frost hardiness and sun tolerance, they all prefer cool moist soil conditions. Work in plenty of high-humus compost before planting. The shrubby species tend to become rather untidy after a few years, and although pruning can rejuvenate them, replacement with new plants may be more successful. The seed germinates well, but tip cuttings strike so quickly that this is a more successful method of propagation.

ABOVE 'Sunset Red' is one of the many cultivars of the Calceolaria, *Herbeohybrida* Group. It has deep red flowers and is suitable for massed bedding.

LEFT A hybrid of uncertain parentage, Calceolaria 'John Innes' has cheerful yellow and red flowers that bloom throughout summer.

Top Tip

A liquid fertilizer applied every few weeks to indoor plants will improve the size and color of the flowers. Make sure not to give them too much water.

Favorites

	Flower Color	Blooming Season	Flower Fragrance	Plant Height	Plant Width	Hardiness Zone	Frost Tolerance
Calceolaria biflora	yellow	summer	no	4–12 in (10–30 cm)	12 in (30 cm)	7–9	yes
Calceolaria, Herbeohybrida Group	various	spring to summer	no	8–18 in (20–45 cm)	6–12 in (15–30 cm)	9–11	no
Calceolaria, Herbeohybrida Group, 'Sunset Red'	red and yellow	spring to summer	no	8 in (20 cm)	10 in (25 cm)	9–11	no
Calceolaria integrifolia	bright yellow	summer	no	2–5 ft (0.6–1.5 m)	2–5 ft (0.6–1.5 m)	8–10	yes
Calceolaria 'John Innes'	yellow with deep red markings	summer	no	6 in (15 cm)	12 in (30 cm)	7–9	yes
Calceolaria uniflora var. *darwinii*	yellow, white, and red	summer	no	4 in (10 cm)	12 in (30 cm)	6–9	yes

LEFT *'Goldbouquet' is one of many named cultivars of* Calceolaria integrifolia. *These woody-based plants are suitable in pots, borders, and hanging baskets, and require lots of sun.*

BELOW *From Patagonia,* Calceolaria uniflora *var.* darwinii *has whimsical tri-colored flowers with a large lower lip. If grown indoors, it requires a well-ventilated spot away from strong sun.*

LEFT *With its aromatic pale green foliage and profuse yellow flowers,* Calendula officinalis *is a useful plant for poor soil or terrain where drifts of color are needed.*
RIGHT *An award-winning dwarf cultivar,* Calendula officinalis *'Fiesta Gitana' adds a splash of sunny colors to the garden.*

CALENDULA

Found throughout the Mediterranean and on the nearby Atlantic Islands, this daisy family (Asteraceae) genus comprises around 20 species of somewhat aromatic annuals and perennials that are commonly known as marigolds. These small bushy plants have simple lance- to spatula-shaped leaves that are sometimes downy and toothed at their tips. Bright yellow to golden orange flowers, often double in the garden forms, appear over many months and may carry on through winter in mild areas. The name *Calendula* comes from the Latin *calendae* (first day of the month), and refers to the long flowering season, as calendulas bloom almost all year round. Several species, especially *Calendula officinalis*, have a long history of herbal and culinary use.

CULTIVATION

Calendulas are easily grown in full or half sun in any reasonably fertile well-drained soil. Deadhead routinely to prolong flowering and keep a watch for fungal diseases. Propagation is mainly from seed, though the perennials may be divided. They often naturalize and may become slightly invasive.

Favorites	Flower Color	Blooming Season	Flowe Fragran
Calendula officinalis	yellow, gold, orange, apricot	spring to autumn	no
Calendula officinalis 'Bon Bon'	yellow, orange, apricot	spring to autumn	no
Calendula officinalis 'Fiesta Gitana'	cream, yellow, gold, orange	spring to autumn	no
Calendula officinalis 'Greenheart Orange'	orange, green center	spring to autumn	no
Calendula officinalis 'Indian Prince'	orange, backed red-brown	spring to autumn	no
Calendula officinalis, Pacific Beauty Series	orange, yellow	spring to autumn	no

Top Tip

Calendulas have healing and anti-septic properties, and are popular in herbal remedies. The petals can also be used for herbal teas or added to salads to provide color and piquancy.

BELOW *With a large bright green "heart" surrounded by fluffy orange petals, it is easy to see how* Calendula officinalis *'Greenheart Orange' acquired its name.*

LEFT *Easy-care sun-loving* Calendula officinalis, *Pacific Beauty Series cultivars come in a wide range of colors, including bicolored forms.*

Plant Height	Plant Width	Hardiness Zone	Frost Tolerance
24 in (60 cm)	24 in (60 cm)	6–10	yes
8–10 in (20–25 cm)	12 in (30 cm)	6–10	yes
12 in (30 cm)	15 in (38 cm)	6–10	yes
24 in (60 cm)	18 in (45 cm)	6–10	yes
18 in (45 cm)	18 in (45 cm)	6–10	yes
18–24 in (45–60 cm)	18 in (45 cm)	6–10	yes

CALLISTEMON

Commonly known as bottlebrush, this Australian genus of about 30 species of highly ornamental evergreen shrubs and small trees includes a large range of hybrids and cultivars. They have leathery linear or lance-shaped leaves arranged spirally around the stem, and new growth is often richly colored, usually pink or bronze. Callistemons are famed for their showy flowers, which when massed together in terminal spikes form cylindrical bottlebrush-like shapes. The flowers usually open in spring and summer, and sometimes again in autumn, and are followed by long-lasting, round, woody seed capsules crowded into a cylindrical group along the stem. The main flower colors are generally in shades of pink, red, cream, or green, although many cultivars have extended this range even further. The flowers are highly attractive to small nectar-feeding birds. Callistemons offer a colorful display over long periods and will fit into most landscape situations. Many of the larger species are suitable for use as street plantings in mild climates.

ABOVE RIGHT *The bright red flowers of* Callistemon polandii *are a welcome sight in a mild-climate winter garden.*

Top Tip

The colorful, sun-loving, and adaptable bottlebrush looks particularly attractive in a shrub border or along the wall of a house. Monthly fertilizing is advised.

Favorites	Flower Color	Blooming Season	Flower Fragrance	Plant Height	Plant Width	Hardiness Zone	Frost Tolerance
Callistemon citrinus	bright red to crimson	late spring to autumn	no	10 ft (3 m)	8 ft (2.4 m)	8–11	no
Callistemon citrinus 'Splendens'	carmine red	late spring to autumn	no	8 ft (2.4 m)	8 ft (2.4 m)	8–11	no
Callistemon 'Mauve Mist'	mauve-pink	summer	no	6–12 ft (1.8–3.5 m)	6–12 ft (1.8–3.5 m)	8–11	no
Callistemon polandii	red	winter and early spring	no	15 ft (4.5 m)	8 ft (2.4 m)	9–12	no
Callistemon rigidus	deep red	summer	no	4–12 in (10–30 cm)	8 in (20 cm)	9–10	no
Callistemon viridiflorus	greenish yellow	late spring and summer	no	8 ft (2.4 m)	8 ft (2.4 m)	8–10	no

CULTIVATION

Most bottlebrushes prefer moist, well-drained, slightly acid soil in a sunny position and are only marginally frost tolerant. All species respond well to pruning in the final days of flowering, which prevents the seed capsules from forming and stimulates bushier growth and a greater number of flowers next season. The lower branches of the larger species can be removed, leaving the top to branch out. Most species are propagated from the fine seed, though selected forms and cultivars are grown from half-hardened tip cuttings.

ABOVE RIGHT Callistemon *'Mauve Mist' is a dense rounded shrub that bears mauve-pink flowers in summer.*
RIGHT *'Burgundy' is a cultivar of* Callistemon citrinus. *It has dense foliage and a profusion of wine red flowers in spikes up to 4 in (10 cm) long.*
LEFT *Native to Tasmania,* Callistemon viridiflorus *is somewhat frost tolerant. Its flowers are greenish yellow and appear in late spring and summer.*
BELOW Callistemon citrinus *provides a mass of red flower spikes in spring and occasionally in autumn. Several forms and cultivars are available.*

CALOCHORTUS

This group of around 60 species of bulbs is found in the Americas, especially the western regions of the U.S.A. Variously known as mariposa tulip, sego lily, or fairy lantern, most species form a clump of narrow grassy leaves, and in spring and summer wiry stems carry flowers with 3 petals and 3 petallike sepals. The flowers, which cover a wide color range and are often beautifully marked, may be upright or nodding, and when upward facing they can be rather tuliplike. The genus name *Calochortus* comes from the Greek *kallos* (beautiful) and *chortos* (grass). In the past, Native Americans ate the bulbs of certain species. *Calochortus nuttallii* is the state flower of Utah.

CULTIVATION

Although mainly very hardy, mariposa tulips require a climate that is warm and dry in summer. Plant in full sun in gritty free-draining soil—a rockery or raised bed is ideal. Water well from late winter on but allow them to dry off after flowering. Propagate by division in autumn or raise from seed.

BELOW RIGHT Calochortus tolmiei *can survive in poor soil in its native habitat on the west coast of the U.S.A. Its white to lilac flowers are bearded on the inside with violet hairs.*

BELOW Calochortus monophyllus *is one of the pretty, upward-facing, tuliplike species. The flowers are a clear yellow.*

ABOVE *The spring flowers of* Calochortus luteus *are extremely interesting. They are bell-shaped and yellow, with reddish brown spots and markings. There are also fine hairs inside.*

ABOVE Calochortus albus *is also known as the fairy lantern or white globe lily. It has pretty globe-shaped flowers and is native to southern California.*

RIGHT *The flowers of Calochortus splendens are white to pale lilac. The plant needs good soil and part-shade.*

Favorites

	Flower Color	Blooming Season	Flower Fragrance	Plant Height	Plant Width	Hardiness Zone	Frost Tolerance
Calochortus albus	white	spring to early summer	no	8–20 in (20–50 cm)	4 in (10 cm)	5–9	yes
Calochortus luteus	yellow	spring	no	8–20 in (20–50 cm)	3 in (8 cm)	5–10	yes
Calochortus monophyllus	yellow	spring	no	6–10 in (15–25 cm)	4 in (10 cm)	5–9	yes
Calochortus nuttallii	white to yellow	late spring to summer	no	6–15 in (15–38 cm)	4 in (10 cm)	5–9	yes
Calochortus splendens	pale pinkish lilac	late spring to early summer	no	12–24 in (30–60 cm)	4 in (10 cm)	5–10	yes
Calochortus tolmiei	white, cream, or pale mauve	spring to early summer	no	6–15 in (15–38 cm)	4 in (10 cm)	5–10	yes

RIGHT *Camassia cusickii is native to northeastern Oregon, and produces starry pale blue flowers on tall slender spikes.*

CAMASSIA

This genus of 5 species of bulbs belongs to the hyacinth family (Hyacinthaceae) and occurs mainly in western North America. The Latin name *Camassia* comes from the Native American name, which is usually transliterated as *Quamash*. The meaning of the name is unclear, but what is known is that the edible bulbs were an important element in the diet of the native peoples. As garden plants they are tough and very adaptable, and 1 species, *Camassia leichtlinii,* has been extensively developed into garden forms. *Camassia* species have long narrow leaves, and in late spring and early summer they produce heads of 6-petalled flowers atop strong stems, rather reminiscent of some of the *Agapanthus* species.

CULTIVATION

The plants are mostly frost hardy and easily grown in fertile well-drained soil that does not dry out. Plant in full or half sun. Species may be raised from seed, but these take up to 5 years to bloom. Most garden plants are cultivars and may be propagated by division during winter.

LEFT *Now largely grown for its delicate pale blue flowers,* Camassia quamash *was once a significant part of the Native American diet.*

RIGHT *Camassia leichtlinii is particularly attractive for its gentle colors. Its slender flower stems are pale green, complemented by a covering of soft white flowers.*

Top Tip

These bulbous perennials are ideal for borders in temperate climates. The dead flowers tend to persist on the plant, so they need to be trimmed off periodically.

Favorites

	Flower Color	Blooming Season	Flower Fragrance	Plant Height	Plant Width	Hardiness Zone	Frost Tolerance
Camassia cusickii	blue	late spring to early summer	no	24–36 in (60–90 cm)	6 in (15 cm)	5–9	yes
Camassia leichtlinii	creamy white	late spring	no	2–4 ft (0.6–1.2 m)	6 in (15 cm)	4–9	yes
Camassia leichtlinii 'Semiplena'	creamy white	late spring	no	2–4 ft (0.6–1.2 m)	6 in (15 cm)	4–9	yes
Camassia leichtlinii subsp. *suksdorfii*	blue to violet	late spring	no	24–36 in (60–90 cm)	6 in (15 cm)	4–9	yes
Camassia quamash	blue	spring and early summer	no	8–30 in (20–75 cm)	6 in (15 cm)	4–9	yes
Camassia scilloides	blue, violet, white	late summer	no	8–30 in (20–75 cm)	4 in (10 cm)	4–9	yes

RIGHT Camassia leichtlinii *subsp.* leichtlinii *is also known as* C. leichtlinii *'Alba'. It bears racemes of creamy white flowers in late spring.*

CAMELLIA

Well-loved throughout the world for their undoubted beauty, this genus contains nearly 300 evergreen shrubs or small trees, as well as innumerable cultivars. They are native to the mountainous regions of eastern Asia, which may yet produce new species. Camellias have glossy, mid- to dark green, toothed leaves and bear short-stalked flowers that bloom during the colder months, many in mid-winter when the plants are semi-dormant. Of the many cultivars, most adopt a formal, upright, shrubby stance, though smaller, bushy, less formal cultivars are becoming increasingly popular. There are camellias for all situations, be it a formal garden or a woodland setting. *Camellia japonica* is the state flower of Alabama.

ABOVE *Glossy dark foliage provides a wonderful backdrop for the large, pure white, semi-double flowers of* Camellia japonica *'Silver Waves'.*

LEFT *Upright in habit,* Camellia *'Night Rider' bears small semi-double blooms in darkest black-red.*

BELOW Camellia japonica *'Drama Girl' bears large semi-double flowers shaded deep salmon pink to rose pink.*

CULTIVATION

Plant camellias in late autumn and winter, withholding nutrition and additional water during this time. Shaded or semi-shaded positions, acid to neutral soils, dry winters, and wet summers suit the majority. A freely draining site and purpose-designed potting mixes are essential for all species. Propagate by grafting, or from cuttings in late summer to winter.

LEFT Camellia sasanqua *'Jennifer Susan'* has lovely semi-double blooms. The pale pink petals are somewhat curled, giving a soft delicate appearance to this stunning cultivar.

Favorites

	Flower Color	Blooming Season	Flower Fragrance	Plant Height	Plant Width	Hardiness Zone	Frost Tolerance
Camellia hiemalis	white or pale pink	winter and early spring	no	10 ft (3 m)	8 ft (2.4 m)	7–10	yes
Camellia hiemalis **'Chansonette'**	pink-lavender	winter and early spring	no	10 ft (3 m)	8 ft (2.4 m)	8–10	yes
Camellia japonica	red	late autumn to early spring	no	15 ft (4.5 m)	8 ft (2.4 m)	7–10	yes
Camellia japonica **'Nuccio's Gem'**	white	late autumn to early spring	no	15 ft (4.5 m)	8 ft (2.4 m)	7–10	yes
Camellia lutchuensis	white	winter	yes	8 ft (2.4 m)	6–12 ft (1.8–3.5 m)	8–10	no
Camellia **'Night Rider'**	blackish red	mid-winter to late spring	yes	6–12 ft (1.8–3.5 m)	4–8 ft (1.2–2.4 m)	7–10	yes
Camellia nitidissima	pale gold	winter	yes	10 ft (3 m)	10 ft (3 m)	10–11	no
Camellia pitardii	pink, white	winter to early spring	no	10–20 ft (3–6 m)	8–12 ft (2.4–3.5 m)	8–10	yes
Camellia reticulata	pinkish red	mid-winter to early spring	no	12–20 ft (3.5–6 m)	10 ft (3 m)	8–10	yes
Camellia reticulata **'Captain Rawes'**	carmine	mid- to late spring	no	12–20 ft (3.5–6 m)	10 ft (3 m)	8–10	yes
Camellia saluensis	white, pink, red	late winter to early spring	no	10–15 ft (3–4.5 m)	8–15 ft (2.4–4.5 m)	7–10	yes
Camellia sasanqua	pink to carmine	early autumn to early winter	yes	15 ft (4.5 m)	10 ft (3 m)	8–11	yes
Camellia sasanqua **'Shishigashira'**	pinkish red	autumn to winter	no	6–10 ft (1.8–3 m)	10 ft (3 m)	8–10	yes
Camellia sinensis	white	winter	no	8–20 ft (2.4–6 m)	8 ft (2.4 m)	9–12	no
Camellia tsaii	white	winter	yes	10–20 ft (3–6 m)	15 ft (4.5 m)	10–11	no
Camellia × *williamsii*	white to pink	late winter to spring	no	10–15 ft (3–4.5 m)	8 ft (2.4 m)	7–10	yes
Camellia × *williamsii* **'Bow Bells'**	rose pink	winter to spring	no	10 ft (3 m)	8 ft (2.4 m)	7–10	yes
Camellia × *williamsii* **'Donation'**	pink	late winter to early spring	no	10–15 ft (3–4.5 m)	8 ft (2.4 m)	7–10	yes

FLOWER FORM, SIZE, AND COLOR

Due to extensive hybridization, camellia flowers are wonderfully diverse. To make them easier to identify, gardeners have recognized a number of flower forms, sizes, and petal markings. Flower forms are divided into single, semi-double, formal double, and informal double—the latter categories also include peony-form and anemone-form types—and petal colors range between shades of white, pink, rose red, puce, scarlet, dark red, and purple-red. On some varieties, the stamens can be pronounced or almost invisible, with their colors ranging between yellow, white, and a rarely seen but spectacular bright red. As well, some bear attractively bronzed limpid new growth, while a few are sweetly scented. It is worth remembering that some cultivars bear flowers that discolor in rough weather, particularly the whites and paler shades, while a few others retain disfiguring spent blooms. For the amateur gardener, however, camellias remain a great choice for their abundance of blooms and bold foliage.

RIGHT *The rich deep pink petals of* Camellia sasanqua *'Paradise Belinda' are highlighted by the central mass of gold stamens, some of which bear tiny pink and white petaloids.*

BELOW *Superb, glossy, dark green leaves and gorgeous, shell pink, double blooms are the trademark characteristics of* Camellia sasanqua *'Jean May'.*

LEFT Camellia sasanqua *'Shishigashira' bears deep rosy pink-red semi-double flowers among lush glossy foliage. This cultivar is a particularly good ground cover or espalier plant.*

ABOVE RIGHT *The often very large semi-double flowers of Camellia reticulata 'Pink Sparkle' feature ruffled pink petals around the dull gold stamens.*

RIGHT *Camellia × williamsii 'Buttons 'n' Bows' has beautiful formal double flowers in shades of pink. The inner petals are palest pink; the color gradually deepens to a rich pink at the outermost petals.*

BELOW *Autumn-flowering* Camellia sasanqua *'Yuletide' is a lovely cultivar with single red flowers and golden yellow stamens.*

ABOVE Camellia pitardii *is a slow-growing species that can reach a height of 20 ft (6 m) and is equally useful as a bonsai specimen. Seen above is the cultivar 'Sprite', a small, pink, double form.*

Top Tip

As the sun and wind can damage camellia petals, causing unsightly brown marks, these plants do best if sited in a spot with some protection from the elements.

ABOVE *Spring-flowering* Camellia × williamsii *'Francis Hanger' is an extremely hardy cultivar with single snow white flowers and glossy crinkled leaves.*
RIGHT Camellia nitidissima, *known as golden camellia, has soft yellow petals surrounding a mass of gold stamens.*

LEFT *The simple elegance of* Camellia lutchuensis *is seen in its single white flowers and wonderful fragrance.*
BELOW Camellia japonica *'William Honey' bears attractive, medium-sized, carmine-streaked white flowers.*

ABOVE Camellia japonica *'Virginia Franco Rosea'* is a particularly striking example of the formal double camellia. Layers of overlapping pink petals are perfectly complemented by the lustrous deep green leaves.

ABOVE *With its crisp, white, formal double flowers and glossy dark green leaves,* Camellia japonica *'Nuccio's Gem is a hardy award-winning cultivar.*
LEFT Camellia hiemalis *'Chansonette', a formal double type, has lovely pink petals, sometimes with lilac overtones.*

ABOVE *Award-winning* Camellia × williamsii *'Donation'*
bears a profusion of pink semi-double flowers during spring.
This evergreen shrub is a particulary hardy cultivar.

ABOVE *A delicate edging*
of rich rose pink adorns
the milky white semi-
double blooms of Camellia
sasanqua *'Wahroongah'.*
LEFT *Carmine-flowered*
Camellia reticulata *'Captain*
Rawes' is named in honor
of the man who, in 1820,
brought the first C. reticulata
to England from China.

Top Tip

Campanula species thrive on plenty of sunshine. Although they are hardy and can handle the cold, they require excellent drainage for best results.

CAMPANULA

Widespread in the northern temperate zones, *Campanula* is made up of around 300 species of annuals, biennials, and perennials, and is the type genus for the bellflower family (Campanulaceae). Growth habit and size varies, but the species can be divided into 3 broad groups: trailing types suitable for rockeries; low mounding forms whose flowers are among the foliage; and those with a basal foliage clump and tall upright flower stems. The leaves are mostly lance- to heart-shaped and nearly always have toothed or lobed edges. The flowers, usually bell-shaped, have 5 petals or lobes that are often reflexed at the tips. Named from the Latin *campana* (bell), species have been cultivated since medieval times and were once used medicinally.

CULTIVATION

Mostly very hardy, *Campanula* species grow in sun or partial shade and do best in humus-rich well-drained soil. Rockery types need grittier soil; tall varieties may need staking. Propagate by division, from cuttings, or from seed as appropriate for the growth form. Cut back after flowering to encourage further growth.

ABOVE Campanula lactiflora *(milky bellflower) produces flowers from late spring to late summer that are white to light blue, lavender-blue, violet, or dark lilac-blue. This cultivar, 'Loddon Anna', is popular for its pale lilac-pink flowers.*
BELOW Campanula garganica *'Dickson's Gold' is so named because the foliage can be yellow-gold before the flowers appear in summer, depending on the amount of sun it gets. This attractive plant is suitable for edges and rock gardens.*

Favorites	Flower Color	Blooming Season	Flower Fragrance	Plant Height	Plant Width	Hardiness Zone	Frost Tolerance
Campanula carpatica	blue, purple, white	late spring to summer	no	12 in (30 cm)	12–24 in (30–60 cm)	3–9	yes
Campanula cochleariifolia	blue, mauve	summer	no	3 in (8 cm)	12 in (30 cm)	6–9	yes
Campanula garganica	blue, mauve	summer	no	2 in (5 cm)	12 in (30 cm)	5–9	yes
Campanula lactiflora	white to purple-blue	summer	no	4–5 ft (1.2–1.5 m)	24 in (60 cm)	5–9	yes
Campanula punctata	creamy white to pale pink	early summer	no	12 in (30 cm)	15 in (38 cm)	4–8	yes
Campanula takesimana	pink-flushed white	summer	no	20 in (50 cm)	36 in (90 cm)	5–9	yes

RIGHT *A feature of Campanula carpatica is the bell-shaped upturned flowers. As seen here, the flowers of 'Alba' are large and white.*
BELOW *The pendent flowers of Campanula takesimana have maroon spots inside. This spreading plant is a native of Korea, and makes a suitable ground cover.*

CAMPSIS

This genus is a member of the bignonia family (Bignoniaceae), and consists of 2 species of deciduous vines, one found in China and Japan, the other native to the U.S.A. Commonly known as trumpet creeper or vine, *Campsis* species are vigorous growers that can cling to most surfaces by using pads of aerial roots, and they can be trained onto walls in the same way as ivy. The large leaves are feather-like, with elliptical leaflets that have toothed edges. In summer and autumn, clusters of large, trumpet-shaped, 5-lobed flowers appear, usually in orange-red shades, less often yellow or crimson. Flowers are nectar-rich and very attractive to hummingbirds and honeyeaters. The name *Campsis* comes from the Greek *kampa* (bent), refer-ring to the curved stamens.

CULTIVATION

Although these vines are hardy, late frosts can cause severe damage, so prune established plants in spring after frosts. Plant in full sun with moist, humus-rich, well-drained soil. Suckers often emerge some distance from the main plant and have the potential to be invasive. Propagate by cuttings or layering, from rooted suckers or seed.

ABOVE *Campsis radicans* f. *flava (syn. 'Yellow Trumpet') has delicate yellow flowers, and the leaves are paler than those of the species.*

RIGHT *Known as the Chinese trumpet creeper,* Campsis grandiflora *grows very quickly, and produces brilliant red to orange flowers that are larger than those of* C. radicans.

Favorites	Flower Color	Blooming Season	Flower Fragrance
Campsis grandiflora	scarlet to orange	late summer to autumn	no
Campsis grandiflora **'Morning Charm'**	peach	late summer to autumn	no
Campsis radicans	orange to red	late summer to autumn	no
Campsis radicans **f. flava**	yellow	late summer to autumn	no
Campsis × *tagliabuana*	orange to red	summer	no
Campsis × *tagliabuana* **'Madame Galen'**	orange-red	summer	no

Plant Height	Plant Width	Hardiness Zone	Frost Tolerance
10–30 ft (3–9 m)	10 ft (3 m)	7–11	yes
10–30 ft (3–9 m)	10 ft (3 m)	7–11	yes
15–30 ft (4.5–9 m)	10 ft (3 m)	4–10	yes
15–30 ft (4.5–9 m)	10 ft (3 m)	4–10	yes
8–20 ft (2.4–6 m)	10 ft (3 m)	6–11	yes
8–20 ft (2.4–6 m)	10 ft (3 m)	6–11	yes

Top Tip

Campsis species grow well against a warm sunny wall. They can be trained to grow on a pillar, fence, or tree, and may need extra support.

BOTTOM *Developed in Italy during the 1850s,* Campsis × tagliabuana *can be shrub-like rather than climbing in its growth habit.*

BELOW *Considered a weed in its native southeastern U.S.A.,* Campsis radicans *is popular elsewhere for its prolific display of colorful orange to red flowers.*

CANNA

Found throughout the tropics and subtropics of the Americas, and widely naturalized elsewhere, there are just 9 species in this genus. Cannas are vigorous perennial plants with strong, upright, reed-like stalks that sprout from rhizomes and bear long lance-shaped leaves. Heads of lily-like flowers—generally in shades of yellow, tangerine, and red, either as solid colors or in patterns—appear throughout the growing season. They make excellent pot plants and are effective in mass plantings. The common name Indian shot comes from the story that the hard, round, black seeds were sometimes substituted for buckshot; the seeds are certainly hard enough, but they are so light that their range would have been very limited.

CULTIVATION

Although often tropical in origin, most species can withstand light frosts when dormant if their roots are well insulated with mulch. Plant in full sun in moist, humus-rich, well-drained soil, and feed well. Propagation of selected forms is by division in early spring. Seeds will often self-sow but rarely result in superior plants.

ABOVE *The bright voluptuous canna is an asset to any tropical garden.* Canna iridiflora *has gorgeous pink flowers and interesting bluish green leaves.*

LEFT *The flowers of* Canna *'Erebus' are salmon pink, and similar in shape to the gladiolus. Cannas are easy to grow, especially in areas with warm climates.*

Favorites	Flower Color	Blooming Season	Flower Fragrance
Canna 'Erebus'	dark red	summer to autumn	no
Canna 'Intrigue'	orange-red	summer to autumn	no
Canna iridiflora	pink to orange	summer to autumn	no
Canna 'Phasion'	orange	summer to autumn	no
Canna 'Pretoria'	orange	summer to autumn	no
Canna 'Wyoming'	orange	summer to autumn	no

LEFT Canna 'Phasion' is a hot-colored flamboyant cultivar. As well as its orange flowers, the plant has large leaves dramatically striped in red, green, and yellow.
BELOW The flowers of many cannas, such as 'Pretoria', have intense colors, but cultivars are also available in more subtle shades of cream, salmon, and pink.

Top Tip

Cannas are not restricted to the tropics—they will happily grow in cold climates in a container or green-house. Divide the clumps for easy propagation.

Plant Height	Plant Width	Hardiness Zone	Frost Tolerance
6 ft (1.8 m)	20 in (50 cm)	8–12	no
7 ft (2 m)	20 in (50 cm)	8–12	no
10 ft (3 m)	20 in (50 cm)	9–12	no
6 ft (1.8 m)	20 in (50 cm)	8–12	no
6 ft (1.8 m)	20 in (50 cm)	8–12	no
8 ft (2.4 m)	20 in (50 cm)	8–12	no

CATHARANTHUS

Although related to the common periwinkle (*Vinca*), the 8 annuals and perennials of this genus are far less hardy and will not tolerate frost. All species are native to Madagascar, and they are bushy plants with simple elliptical leaves on semi-succulent stems. Flat 5-petalled flowers, mainly in pink and mauve shades, appear at the stem tip and leaf axils. Though considered a weed in the tropics and subtropics, the widely cultivated species *Catharanthus roseus* is a perennial often grown as a greenhouse plant or as a summer bedder in temperate gardens. Although highly toxic in its natural form, this species is the source of the drugs known as vinca alkaloids that are used to treat Hodgkin's disease and lymphocytic leukemia.

RIGHT *Catharanthus roseus 'Cooler Blush' is one of the Cooler Series cultivars. It has delicate pale pink flowers with a conspicuous dark pink eye. The petals are broad and overlapping.*

CULTIVATION

These plants are very easily grown in part-shade, and can withstand strong sunlight. They are drought tolerant, but flower more heavily with summer moisture. Water moderately in the growing season. Gently pinch back to encourage bushiness. In cool climates with winter frost, bring indoors or discard and replace in spring. Propagate from seed or half-hardened summer cuttings.

LEFT *The cultivars in the Pacifica Series of Catharanthus roseus come in a wide range of beautiful colors. 'Pacifica Punch' has magenta-pink flowers that are darker in the center.*

Top Tip

Tip prune *Catharanthus* species to maintain their fullness, but don't get too enthusiastic—over-pruning can discourage flowering. A bit of liquid fertilizer once a month is also recommended.

ABOVE Catharanthus roseus *is also referred to as "old maid" or the "Madagascar periwinkle." As seen here, the cultivar 'Albus' has dainty white flowers with a yellow eye. A sunny to partly sunny spot is ideal for this plant.*

LEFT *'Stardust Orchid' is one of the most striking cultivars of* Catharanthus roseus. *With its bright magenta flowers featuring a white center and yellow eye, this plant is ideally used as a colorful border for a garden path.*

Favorites

	Flower Color	Blooming Season	Flower Fragrance	Plant Height	Plant Width	Hardiness Zone	Frost Tolerance
Catharanthus roseus	white, pink, red	spring to autumn	no	24 in (60 cm)	24 in (60 cm)	9–12	no
Catharanthus roseus 'Albus'	white	spring to autumn	no	24 in (60 cm)	24 in (60 cm)	9–12	no
Catharanthus roseus 'Blue Pearl'	lilac-blue	spring to autumn	no	12–18 in (30–45 cm)	18 in (45 cm)	9–12	no
Catharanthus roseus 'Cooler Series'	white to pink	spring to autumn	no	15–18 in (38–45 cm)	18 in (45 cm)	9–12	no
Catharanthus roseus, Pacifica Series	lilac, pink, white, red	spring to autumn	no	12–15 in (30–38 cm)	18 in (45 cm)	9–12	no
Catharanthus roseus, Victory Series	red, white, rose, carmine	spring to autumn	no	12–15 in (30–38 cm)	18 in (45 cm)	9–12	no

CATTLEYA

ABOVE Cattleya loddigesii *originates from Brazil. 'Blue Sky' is a well-loved cultivar with lilac-blue tints and a yellow center. Other color varieties of the species are available.*

This genus, from tropical America, is one of the most popular groups of orchids in cultivation. These rock and tree dwellers have showy, colorful, long-lasting, and sometimes fragrant flowers produced on stout plants with club-shaped to cylindrical bulb-like stems, known as pseudobulbs. They are topped with 1 (unifoliate) or 2 (bifoliate), dull green, leathery leaves. Most species require warmth in winter, though many of the Brazilian, bifoliate, autumn-flowering types will stand cooler winter temperatures for short periods of time while dormant if kept dry. Healthy plants will develop an extensive system of thick white roots, which are long-lived and freely branch. Thousands of hybrids have been developed within the genus, with many of the larger flowering types grown commercially for cut flower production and often used in corsages.

CULTIVATION

Cattleyas must have unimpeded drainage and prefer a coarse bark-based medium. The plants can be grown in porous pots or hanging baskets with suitable coarse fibrous compost. After several years, it may be necessary to repot them when dormant.

Favorites	Flower Color	Blooming Season	Flower Fragrance	Plant Height	Plant Width	Hardiness Zone	Frost Tolerance
Cattleya aurantiaca	orange-yellow to red	summer	no	12 in (30 cm)	12 in (30 cm)	10–12	no
Cattleya bicolor	greenish brown and red	summer to autumn	no	18–24 in (45–60 cm)	18 in (45 cm)	10–12	no
Cattleya, **Bifoliate Hybrids**	white, pink, red, yellow-orange	spring or autumn	no	18 in (45 cm)	18 in (45 cm)	10–12	no
Cattleya loddigesii	white, tinted pink to lilac	autumn to winter	yes	24 in (60 cm)	18 in (45 cm)	10–12	no
Cattleya skinneri	rose pink to bright purple	winter to spring	yes	12 in (30 cm)	12 in (30 cm)	10–12	no
Cattleya, **Unifoliate Hybrids**	pink, white	spring or autumn	yes	18 in (45 cm)	18 in (45 cm)	11–12	no

Top Tip

Cattleyas make wonderful house plants, but need reasonably high humidity and protection from intense sunlight— indirect or dappled light is preferred.

ABOVE *Bow Bells 'July' is one of the Unifoliate Hybrids and a purebred* Cattleya. *You will often find these gorgeous ruffled specimens for sale in flower shops.*
RIGHT *The characteristics of* Cattleya bicolor *are its fleshy petals and white staminal column. 'Golden Gate' is a striking combination of chartreuse and purple-red.*
BELOW Cattleya *Chocolate Drop* × × Laeliocattleya *is a soft apricot and pink Bifoliate Hybrid, but it also contains some of the rich maroon of its parent Chocolate Drop.*

CEANOTHUS

Native to North America, and commonly known as the Californian lilac, this genus of around 50 species of evergreen and deciduous shrubs and small trees belongs to the buckthorn (Rhamnaceae) family. Plants are characterized by deep green foliage and vivid blue flowers. Size and shape of the leaves vary, but they are usually small, with noticeable veining, and shallow-toothed edges. The individual flowers are tiny but are borne in rounded heads or conical branching clusters. As well as shades of blue they may be white, cream, or occasionally pink. In common with *Monarda*, the leaves of some species were used as a tea substitute during the American Revolution.

CULTIVATION

Hardiness varies, with the common western U.S.A. natives being more tender than the few eastern species in cultivation. Plant in full sun with moist well-drained soil. They are drought tolerant but need regular watering when in flower. Propagate from cuttings, by layering, or raise from seed.

Top Tip

Ceanothus plants are undemanding and are tolerant of coastal conditions. Low-growing varieties are suited to rock-garden planting or for use as a ground cover.

TOP *During the flowering season, the lustrous mid-green leaves of* Ceanothus thyrsiflorus *are highlighted with flowers in shades of blue, earning it the common name of blueblossom.* **LEFT** *From mid- to late spring* Ceanothus incanus *bears lightly fragranced, fluffy, white blossoms. This thorny evergreen shrub has dull gray-green leaves with paler undersides.*

Favorites

	Flower Color	Blooming Season	Flower Fragrance	Plant Height	Plant Width	Hardiness Zone	Frost Tolerance
Ceanothus americanus	white	summer	no	24–36 in (60–90 cm)	3–5 ft (0.9–1.5 m)	4–9	yes
Ceanothus 'Dark Star'	purple-blue	late spring	yes	6 ft (1.8 m)	10 ft (3 m)	7–9	yes
Ceanothus × delileanus 'Gloire de Versailles'	pale blue	mid-summer to autumn	yes	12 ft (3.5 m)	5 ft (1.5 m)	7–9	yes
Ceanothus griseus	violet-blue	spring	no	10 ft (3 m)	10 ft (3 m)	8–10	yes
Ceanothus incanus	creamy white	spring	yes	10 ft (3 m)	12 ft (3.5 m)	8–10	yes
Ceanothus thyrsiflorus	pale to dark blue	spring to early summer	no	6–20 ft (1.8–6 m)	20 ft (6 m)	7–9	yes

LEFT *The oval leaves of* Ceanothus griseus *var.* horizontalis *'Hurricane Point' are extremely glossy, and are interspersed with clusters of pale blue blooms during spring.*

BELOW *From summer to autumn, the dark green leaves of* Ceanothus × delileanus *'Gloire de Versailles' are accompanied by delicately scented pale blue flowers.*

CELOSIA

Found in the tropics of Asia, Africa, and the Americas, this genus of around 50 species of annuals and perennials is a member of the amaranth family (Amaranthaceae). The annual *Celosia argentea* is the only widely cultivated species, and it has been developed into many variably flowered and colored seedling strains. They are upright plants, some growing up to 6 ft (1.8 m) tall, though most are far smaller. Most have simple lance-shaped leaves and tiny vivid yellow, orange, or red flowers massed in upright plumes or combs. Commonly known as cockscomb or woolflower, the genus name *Celosia* comes from the Greek word *keleos* (burning), which is an apt description of the flamelike color and shape of the flowerhead.

CULTIVATION

Although as annuals they can be grown far outside their natural tropical range, *Celosia* plants do need ample warmth to perform well. Plant in fertile well-drained soil in full sun and water well. Raise from seed.

BELOW Celosia spicata *begins blooming from the base of the flower spike. Opening to reveal purplish pink flowers, they gradually fade to silvery pink.*

Favorites	Flower Color	Blooming Season	Flower Fragrance	Plant Height	Plant Width	Hardiness Zone	Frost Tolerance
Celosia argentea, Plumosa Group	yellow to red, purple	summer to autumn	no	24 in (60 cm)	18 in (45 cm)	10–12	no
Celosia argentea, Plumosa Gp, 'Castle Mix'	gold, pink, red, cream	summer to autumn	no	18 in (45 cm)	12 in (30 cm)	10–12	no
Celosia argentea, Plumosa Gp, 'Forest Fire'	bright scarlet	summer to autumn	no	30 in (75 cm)	18 in (45 cm)	10–12	no
Celosia spicata	purplish pink	summer to autumn	no	24–36 in (60–90 cm)	12 in (30 cm)	10–12	no
Celosia 'Startrek Lilac'	deep rose	summer to autumn	no	4 ft (1.2 m)	24 in (60 cm)	10–12	no
Celosia 'Venezuela'	yellow, red, cerise	summer to autumn	no	24 in (60 cm)	18 in (45 cm)	10–12	no

LEFT *Members of the* Celosia argentea, *Plumosa Group—so named for their plumelike blooms—come in a range of fiery colors, including vibrant reds, hot oranges, and golden yellows.*

RIGHT *The feathery flowers of* Celosia argentea, *Plumosa Group, 'Castle Mix' are popular for their colorful mix of hot shades.*

BELOW Celosia argentea, *Plumosa Group, 'Forest Fire' has magnificent plumes of bright red flowers, and rich purple-brown leaves.*

Top Tip

Cut *Celosia* blooms and hang in a dry and well-ventilated location. The dried flowers are ideal for indoor arrangements, with their excellent color retention properties.

CENTAUREA

Widespread in the temperate zones, this daisy family (Asteraceae) genus, commonly known as cornflower or knapweed, encompasses around 450 species of annuals, perennials, and subshrubs. They are a variable lot, though most are readily identifiable by their thistle-like flowerheads, which emerge from an egg-shaped whorl of bracts. The flowerheads often have distinctly different inner and outer florets, with those on the outer having narrow petals. Flower colors include white, yellow, pink, mauve, and blue. Plant size varies greatly, but common features are feather-like foliage, often silver-gray, and an upright habit. *Centaurea* was named after Chiron the Centaur, the Greek mythological figure famed for his healing powers, because some species have been used to treat wounds.

CULTIVATION

Plant in light well-drained soil in full sun. Good ventilation will lessen any mildew problems. Annuals such as the common cornflower (*Centaurea cyanus*) are raised from seed; perennials may be propagated by division or from softwood cuttings of non-flowering stems.

LEFT Centaurea dealbata 'Steenbergii' has an erect habit, reaching a height of 36 in (90 cm), and produces lovely large flowerheads in bright cerise.

RIGHT An early-flowering species, Centaurea montana has a wispy outer floret of violet-blue and an inner floret of rosy pink-red.

ABOVE *Thistle-like in appearance, Centaurea macrocephala, the globe cornflower, has overlapping brown bracts around the base of the golden yellow flowerheads.*

Favorites	Flower Color	Blooming Season	Flower Fragrance	Plant Height	Plant Width	Hardiness Zone	Frost Tolerance
Centaurea cyanus	purplish blue	spring to summer	no	24–36 in (60–90 cm)	6 in (15 cm)	5–10	yes
Centaurea dealbata	pink	late spring to summer	no	36 in (90 cm)	24 in (60 cm)	4–9	yes
Centaurea macrocephala	yellow	summer	no	36 in (90 cm)	24 in (60 cm)	4–9	yes
Centaurea montana	violet-blue	early summer	no	30 in (75 cm)	24 in (60 cm)	3–9	yes
Centaurea rothrockii	pale purple, cream center	mid-summer to early autumn	no	4–5 ft (1.2–1.5 m)	24 in (60 cm)	6–10	yes
Centaurea simplicicaulis	rose pink	late spring to early summer	no	10 in (25 cm)	24 in (60 cm)	3–9	yes

Top Tip

Cornflowers will
bloom reliably over
a long season.
Deadheading will
often encourage
a further show
of flowers and
increased flower
production.

LEFT *The dainty white outer
floret surrounding the rose-
tinged inner floret gives
Centaurea montana 'Alba'
a delicate lacy appearance.*

CERCIS

This small genus of 6 or 7 deciduous trees and shrubs is found in the temperate zone from North America to Southeast Asia and is grown for the showy spring flowers. The leaves are alternate and mostly broadly egg-shaped. The flowers are pea-shaped, with 5 petals in a squat calyx, usually borne on bare stems before or with the early leaves. The fruit is a flat legume with a shallow wing along the edge. In North America, this genus is commonly known as the redbud, but in some parts of the world it is known as the Judas tree. Tradition holds that it was a *Cercis* tree from which Judas hanged himself after betraying Christ.

Top Tip

As *Cercis* species do not transplant well, consideration should be given to their suitability and long-term needs when choosing a site to plant.

CULTIVATION

Cercis species prefer a moderately fertile soil that drains well, and exposure to sun for most of the day. All species are frost hardy. Some early shaping is needed to select a main leader, but little regular pruning is needed after that. They do not respond well to transplanting. Propagation is usually from freshly harvested seeds, which need pre-soaking in hot water to soften the hard coat. Half-hardened cuttings may be taken in summer or early autumn.

ABOVE *Red, pink, or purple flowers cover the bare stems of* Cercis canadensis *before the attractive heart-shaped leaves appear.*

RIGHT *The flowers of* Cercis siliquastrum *are followed by bean-like pods which contain up to 12 seeds. The decorative pods persist on the stems until winter.*

Favorites	Flower Color	Blooming Season	Flower Fragrance	Plant Height	Plant Width	Hardiness Zone	Frost Tolerance
Cercis canadensis	lilac-pink to crimson	spring to early summer	no	15–30 ft (4.5–9 m)	20 ft (6 m)	5–9	yes
Cercis canadensis 'Forest Pansy'	lilac-pink to crimson	spring to early summer	no	15–30 ft (4.5–9 m)	20 ft (6 m)	5–9	yes
Cercis chinensis	lavender to red-purple	spring to early summer	no	12–15 ft (3.5–4.5 m)	15 ft (4.5 m)	6–9	yes
Cercis griffithii	mauve to purple	spring to early summer	no	15–20 ft (4.5–6 m)	15 ft (4.5 m)	7–9	yes
Cercis occidentalis	pink to magenta	spring	no	15 ft (4.5 m)	12 ft (3.5 m)	7–9	yes
Cercis siliquastrum	pinkish magenta	spring	no	20–30 ft (6–9 m)	15–20 ft (4.5–6 m)	7–9	yes

BELOW *The slender maroon seed pods of* Cercis griffithii *are similar in shape to those of* C. siliquastrum, *but are smaller and contain fewer seeds.*

CHAENOMELES

This genus belonging to the Rosaceae family, and commonly known as flowering quince, has 3 species of spiny, deciduous shrubs that are native to the high-altitude woodlands of Japan and China. Some species grow into small trees up to 20 ft (6 m) tall. Their early pink, red, or white flowers appear before the leaves on last year's wood and are highly valued. The leaves are alternate, serrated, oval, and deep green. The flowers, usually with 5 petals, unless double, are cup-shaped and appear from late winter to late spring, singly or in small clusters. The roughly apple-shaped, rounded, green fruit turns yellow when ripe and is used in jellies and preserves.

CULTIVATION

Chaenomeles species will grow in most soils, except for very alkaline types. In too rich a soil they will produce more foliage and less flowers. Generally, a well-drained moderately fertile soil, in sun or part-shade, will give best results. In colder climates, they will carry more flowers if grown against a south wall. They can also be used for hedging and as ornamental shrubs. Half-hardened cuttings can be taken in summer or autumn. Seed can be sown in autumn in containers with protection from winter frosts or in a seedbed in the open ground.

ABOVE *From early spring, lovely saucer-shaped blossoms, in shades of pink to light red, cover the dark stems of* Chaenomeles × californica.

LEFT *Select* Chaenomeles × superba *'Rowallane' for situations requiring a low-growing plant. This cultivar will add vibrant color to the garden, producing clusters of bright red flowers.*

Favorites

	Flower Color	Blooming Season	Flower Fragrance	Plant Height	Plant Width	Hardiness Zone	Frost Tolerance
Chaenomeles × *californica*	pink to red	spring	no	6 ft (1.8 m)	8 ft (2.4 m)	5–10	yes
Chaenomeles cathayensis	pink-flushed white	early to mid-spring	no	8–15 ft (2.4–4.5 m)	10 ft (3 m)	5–10	yes
Chaenomeles japonica	orange-red	late winter to early spring	no	36 in (90 cm)	6 ft (1.8 m)	6–9	yes
Chaenomeles speciosa	pink to red	winter to summer	no	6–10 ft (1.8–3 m)	10–15 ft (3–4.5 m)	6–9	yes
Chaenomeles × *superba*	white, pink to orange-scarlet	spring	no	3–6 ft (0.9–1.8 m)	8 ft (2.4 m)	6–10	yes
Chaenomeles × *superba* 'Rowallane'	bright red	spring	no	36 in (90 cm)	6 ft (1.8 m)	6–10	yes

LEFT *A quirky cultivar,* Chaenomeles speciosa *'Toyo Nishiki' produces clusters of pink, red, and white flowers on the same branch and sometimes in the same cluster.*

BELOW *Appearing in clusters along the bare stems of the previous year's growth, the flowers of* Chaenomeles × superba *are produced in a range of colors including red, pink, and orange.*

Top Tip

Easy-to-grow, this adaptable genus is ideal for cutting. From early spring cut stems can be brought indoors to add long-lasting vibrant color to the home.

CHRYSANTHEMUM

Numerous species in this once-large genus have been moved to other genera, leaving just 5 European and North African annual species plus a number of hybrids known as florists's chrysanthemums, which are sorted into groups based on flower form. Perennials originally from China, where they have been cultivated for over 2,500 years, chrysanthemums were used medicinally and for flavoring as well as for ornamental purposes. The Japanese adopted chrysanthemums and frequently use them in their art as a symbol of longevity and happiness. The annual species are small plants that closely resemble their daisy family (Asteraceae) relatives and are mainly used for summer bedding or in borders.

ABOVE Chrysanthemum, *Single, 'Megatime' bears pink daisylike flowers with a greenish yellow central disc. This plant prefers slightly acidic well-drained soil.*

CULTIVATION

The annuals thrive in a sunny position with light well-drained soil. Florists's chrysanthemums prefer a heavier richer soil and will tolerate some shade. They also need pinching back when young and disbudding to ensure the best show of flowers. Annuals are raised from seed; the florists's forms are propagated by division when dormant or from half-hardened summer cuttings.

RIGHT Chrysanthemum, *Spoon-shaped, 'Energy Time' has semi-double rich red blooms with golden yellow centers.*

ABOVE *Chrysanthemum, Incurved, 'Creamest' and 'Gold Creamest' are popular exhibition flowers.*
LEFT *The daisylike blooms of Chrysanthemum, Single, 'Tiger' look wonderful in mass plantings. The flowers are orange-yellow with a flat central disc.*

Favorites	Flower Color	Blooming Season	Flower Fragrance	Plant Height	Plant Width	Hardiness Zone	Frost Tolerance
Chrysanthemum, Anemone-centered	white, pink, red, yellow, orange	late summer to autumn	no	2–4 ft (0.6–1.2 m)	18–30 in (45–75 cm)	5–10	yes
Chrysanthemum, Incurved	white, pink, red yellow, orange	late summer to autumn	no	2–4 ft (0.6–1.2 m)	18–30 in (45–75 cm)	5–10	yes
Chrysanthemum, Pompon	white, pink, red yellow, orange	late summer to autumn	no	2–4 ft (0.6–1.2 m)	18–30 in (45–75 cm)	5–10	yes
Chrysanthemum, Quill-shaped	white, pink, red yellow, orange	late summer to autumn	no	2–4 ft (0.6–1.2 m)	18–30 in (45–75 cm)	5–10	yes
Chrysanthemum, Reflexed	white, pink, red, yellow, orange	late summer to autumn	no	2–4 ft (0.6–1.2 m)	18–30 in (45–75 cm)	5–10	yes
Chrysanthemum, Single	white, pink, red yellow, orange	late summer to autumn	no	1–4 ft (0.3–1.2 m)	18–30 in (45–75 cm)	5–10	yes
Chrysanthemum, Spider-form	white, pink, red yellow, orange	late summer to autumn	no	2–4 ft (0.6–1.2 m)	18–30 in (45–75 cm)	5–10	yes
Chrysanthemum, Spoon-shaped	white, pink, red yellow, orange	late summer to autumn	no	2–4 ft (0.6–1.2 m)	18–30 in (45–75 cm)	5–10	yes
Chrysanthemum, Spray	white, pink, red yellow, orange	late summer to autumn	no	2–4 ft (0.6–1.2 m)	18–30 in (45–75 cm)	5–10	yes
Chrysanthemum weyrichii	white to pink	summer to autumn	no	6–12 in (15–30 cm)	12–24 in (30–60 cm)	5–9	yes
Chrysanthemum yezoense	white	autumn to early winter	no	12–18 in (30–45 cm)	18–30 in (45–75 cm)	6–9	yes
Chrysanthemum zawadskii	white, pink	late summer to mid-autumn	no	12–24 in (30–60 cm)	12–24 in (30–60 cm)	5–9	yes

Top Tip

Chrysanthemums make great pot specimens. Use a good organic potting mixture and do not over-water. Fertilize in summer.

RIGHT Chrysanthemum, *Single, 'Splendid Reagan' is another chrysanthemum ideal for mass plantings. The cerise flowers are set off by the greenish yellow center.* **BELOW** Chrysanthemum, *Spray, 'Fiji' has pale pink flowers. It is an excellent cut flower and a popular exhibition choice, with several blooms on each stem.*

RIGHT Chrysanthemum, *Anemone-centered, 'Score'* has flowers that appear in sprays. The flowers are pink with raised pincushion centers that are deeper pink.

BELOW RIGHT *The bright pink blooms of* Chrysanthemum, *Anemone-centered, 'Weldon' have a large, yellow, cushionlike central disc.*

BELOW *Deep pink blooms fading to pale pink at the petal tips are the hallmark of* Chrysanthemum, *Single, 'Harlekjin', an extremely attractive cultivar.*

LEFT Chrysanthemum, *Spider-form, 'Mixed Spider' bears double blooms with long narrow florets that are often coiled at the ends. It comes in an array of colors.*

ABOVE Chrysanthemum, *Pompon, 'Furore' has small, spherical, green flowerheads that are white at the edges. Because the plant is bushy, it is very suitable for use in a border.*

LEFT *Rich dark green leaves are the perfect foil for the pale pink flowerheads of* Chrysanthemum weyrichii. *It is a small mat-forming* Chrysanthemum *species.*
RIGHT Chrysanthemum, *Spoon-shaped, 'Dublin' will benefit from mulching in winter, especially in cooler areas. It has gorgeous red flowers with yellow centers.*
BELOW Chrysanthemum, *Spoon-shaped, 'Yellow Biarritz' is another excellent exhibition flower. The tips are yellow and the inside of the bloom is orange-brown.*

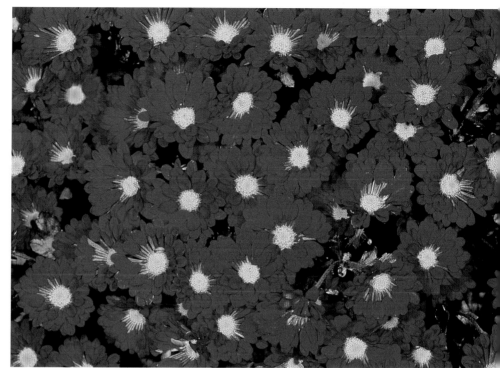

BELOW Chrysanthemum, *Anemone-centered, 'Sunny Le Mans' has flowers that are yellow with orange centers. Several blooms are produced per stem, so they make great cut flowers.*

Favorites	Flower Color	Blooming Season	Flower Fragrance
Cistus × *aguilarii*	white	summer	no
Cistus creticus	pink-purple, deep crimson	summer	no
Cistus ladanifer	white with crimson blotch	summer	no
Cistus × *pulverulentus*	rose pink to purple pink	summer	no
Cistus × *purpureus*	pink to magenta; dark red blotch	summer	no
Cistus salviifolius	white; yellow at base	summer	no

CISTUS

This genus is made up of around 20 species of resinous evergreen shrubs from the Mediterranean region and nearby Atlantic islands. Commonly known as rock roses, they have simple, gray-green to bright green, elliptical leaves, sometimes shallowly toothed. The foliage and young stems are often sticky to the touch and covered with fine downy hairs. Reminiscent of single roses, the flowers have 5 crepe-like petals and a central boss of golden stamens. They come in white or pink shades, sometimes with contrasting central blotches. The aromatic resin, known as gum labdanum, has a history dating back to Ancient Greek and Roman times and is still used as a fragrant binding agent by perfumers.

CULTIVATION

Although they are frost-tolerant, these temperate-climate plants are not suitable for harsh winter conditions. Situate in full sun with light, gritty, free-draining soil. While they are drought and heat resistant, rock roses flower better if well watered and fed. Propagate from cuttings or seed.

ABOVE *The 2-in (5-cm) wide flowers of* Cistus × pulverulentus *have bright pink to purple-pink papery petals around a center of golden yellow stamens.*

ABOVE LEFT *With lovely flowers in pink to magenta,* Cistus × purpureus *is a resilient species, well suited to coastal conditions.*

Top Tip

Tip prune young plants to encourage thicker growth. Established plants will remain tidy if they are given a light trim and old stems are removed.

Plant Height	Plant Width	Hardiness Zone	Frost Tolerance
4 ft (1.2 m)	4 ft (1.2 m)	8–10	yes
3 ft (0.9 m)	3 ft (0.9 m)	7–9	yes
5 ft (1.5 m)	5 ft (1.5 m)	8–10	yes
24 in (60 cm)	36 in (90 cm)	8–10	yes
4 ft (1.2 m)	4 ft (1.2 m)	7–10	yes
30 in (75 cm)	36 in (90 cm)	7–9	yes

BELOW Cistus ladanifer *has crisp white-petalled flowers, often marked with a dark red basal spot, and fragrant dark green leaves.*

RIGHT Cistus × aguilarii *bears large, snow white, showy flowers, with the papery petals surrounding bright gold stamens.*

Citus

Grown in most of the warmer countries of the world, this genus comprises around 20 species of evergreen shrubs and small trees that are greatly valued for their edible fruits and aromatic volatile oils. Highly ornamental, the citrus family crops longer than any other fruit tree, and the dark glossy foliage holds its attractive appearance throughout the year. The fragrant, white, star-shaped flowers appear singly or in clusters at different times of the year, depending on the variety. The tough skin of the fruit, dotted with many tiny cavities that are filled with oil, encloses a white "pith" of varying thickness. Within this, the characteristic juice-filled segments are contained.

ABOVE Citrus limon 'Meyer' bears thin-skinned fruit that is less acid than other lemons and provides excellent juice. It is relatively disease resistant and makes a good tub plant.
BELOW The Sweet Orange Group of Citrus × aurantium includes the common eating oranges. 'Valencia' is the best variety for juicing; the fruit appears in spring and summer.

Cultivation

In frost-free conditions most *Citrus* plants thrive in fertile well-drained soil in a sunny position protected from the wind. During the growing season they need plenty of water and regular applications of nitrogenous fertilizer to promote growth and fruit size. In general, *Citrus* plants need little pruning, except to remove shoots below the graft union and, when mature, to remove damaged or dead branches and reduce overcrowding within the tree. Propagation is by budding or grafting the desired *Citrus* species onto a suitable rootstock.

Top Tip

Citrus species make excellent decorative and fruiting trees for large pots. They should receive plenty of sunlight and be protected from frosts and wind.

ABOVE *Citrus sinensis is the state flower of Florida. This cultivar, 'Washington Navel', is known as the sweet orange.*
RIGHT *As the name implies, the desert lime (Citrus glauca) is drought tolerant. White spring flowers are followed by yellow-green fruits that contain a tasty, juicy, acid pulp.*

Favorites

	Flower Color	Blooming Season	Flower Fragrance	Plant Height	Plant Width	Hardiness Zone	Frost Tolerance
Citrus × aurantium	white	spring to summer	yes	20–35 ft (6–10 m)	20 ft (6 m)	9–11	no
Citrus glauca	white	spring	yes	6–10 ft (1.8–3 m)	8 ft (2.4 m)	9–12	no
Citrus ichangensis	white	spring	yes	5–15 ft (1.5–4.5 m)	6 ft (1.8 m)	9–10	no
Citrus limon	white	most of year	yes	20 ft (6 m)	5–20 ft (1.5–6 m)	9–11	no
Citrus reticulata	white	spring	yes	10–15 ft (3–4.5 m)	5–10 ft (1.5–3 m)	9–11	no
Citrus sinensis	white	spring to summer	yes	20–40 ft (6–12 m)	10–15 ft (3–4.5 m)	9–11	no

CLARKIA

A fuchsia family (Onagraceae) genus of 33 species of annuals, commonly known as godetia, *Clarkia* species are found mainly in western North America. They develop quickly from spring to be in flower by the summer solstice. The leaves are small, linear to lance-shaped, and sometimes toothed, but the foliage is of little consequence as it soon disappears under an abundance of large, brightly colored, dark-blotched, 4-petalled flowers, usually in pink, red, and mauve shades. Borne on leafy slender stems, they make splendid cut flowers. The genus was named by the Scottish botanist David Douglas after the North American explorer Captain William Clark (1770–1838).

CULTIVATION

An easily cultivated temperate-climate genus, it requires only a bright sunny position with moderately fertile well-drained soil. Deadhead frequently to encourage continued flowering. Propagate from seed, which can be sown in autumn in areas with mild winters.

ABOVE RIGHT Clarkia pulchella *is a hardy annual that is excellent in a border or in a cottage garden. Because it is pretty and sturdy, children find it fun and satisfying to grow.*

RIGHT *The common names of* Clarkia amoena *are farewell to spring and satin flower. The plant's flowering season is the first 3 weeks in summer.*

Top Tip

When growing clarkias, make sure that the soil is slightly acid. If the soil is too fertile, clarkias do not flower well. They also dislike heat and humidity.

RIGHT Clarkia unguiculata *naturally occurs in California. It produces small flowers, 1 in (25 mm) in diameter, in a range of colors.* **BELOW** *Clarkia amoena. Many cultivars have been developed from this species. Grace and Satin Series cultivar flowers have contrasting centers, and Satin Series plants are smaller and shrubbier than the species.*

Favorites	Flower Color	Blooming Season	Flower Fragrance	Plant Height	Plant Width	Hardiness Zone	Frost Tolerance
Clarkia amoena	pink	summer	no	30 in (75 cm)	12 in (30 cm)	7–11	yes
Clarkia amoena, **Grace Series**	lavender-pink, pink to red	summer	no	24–30 in (60–75 cm)	12 in (30 cm)	7–11	yes
Clarkia amoena, **Satin Series**	various	summer	no	8 in (20 cm)	8 in (20 cm)	7–11	yes
Clarkia concinna	red	spring to early summer	no	15 in (38 cm)	18 in (45 cm)	8–11	yes
Clarkia pulchella	pink to lavender	spring to summer	no	8–20 in (20–50 cm)	12 in (30 cm)	9–11	no
Clarkia unguiculata	pink, salmon, red, purple	summer	no	12–36 in (30–90 cm)	8 in (20 cm)	7–11	yes

CLEMATIS

Known by many as Virgin's bower or traveller's joy, the 200 species in this genus belong to the buttercup family (Ranunculaceae) and encompass a wide range of plants. Mainly climbing or scrambling, though sometimes shrubby or perennial, deciduous or evergreen; flowering at any time and in any color; occurring in both northern and southern temperate zones and at higher altitudes in the tropics—there seems to be a clematis for any season and place. Their leaves may be simple or pinnate, and their flowers are nearly always showy, with 4 to 8 petallike sepals. Numerous fluffy seed heads follow. The name Virgin's bower comes from a German legend that Mary and Jesus sheltered under clematis during their flight into Egypt.

ABOVE Clematis 'The President' is a beautiful member of the Patens Group. It is a free-flowering large-bloomed hybrid; its purple flowers have the added interest of silver undersides.

CULTIVATION

The general rule is that the foliage should be in the sun while the roots are kept cool and moist. Incorporate plenty of humus-rich compost before planting, and water well. Clematis wilt disease is a problem in many areas. Propagate from cuttings or by layering. Species may be raised from seed but sex will be undetermined before flowering.

ABOVE Clematis, *Patens Group, 'Fireworks'* has stunning, large, pink and mauve striped flowers. It requires part-shade to full sun, fairly moist soil, and plenty of fertilizer during the growing season.

Top Tip

Clematis vines can become tangled; they need yearly pruning to achieve maximum flowering. Pruning techniques vary, depending on the plant group.

LEFT *The Jackmanii hybrids are vigorous, fast growing, and very floriferous.* Clematis 'Sunset' (pictured) has deep rose pink flowers.

ABOVE *This elegant hybrid in the Texensis Group is known as* Clematis *'Princess Diana'. These plants prefer warm dry areas, and are fast growing.*

Favorites	Flower Color	Blooming Season	Flower Fragrance	Plant Height	Plant Width	Hardiness Zone	Frost Tolerance
Clematis armandii	white	spring	yes	10–15 ft (3–4.5 m)	6–10 ft (1.8–3 m)	5–9	yes
Clematis cirrhosa	cream	late winter to early spring	no	8–10 ft (2.4–3 m)	5 ft (1.5 m)	7–9	yes
Clematis, Diversifolia Group	blue-violet, rose pink	summer to early autumn	no	3–6 ft (0.9–1.8 m)	3 ft (0.9 m)	5–9	yes
Clematis, Florida Group	white to purple	late spring to summer	no	8 ft (2.4 m)	3 ft (0.9 m)	7–9	yes
Clematis, Forsteri Group	white to greenish yellow	mid-spring to early summer	yes	8–12 ft (2.4–3.5 m)	10 ft (3 m)	8–10	yes
Clematis integrifolia	purple-blue	summer	no	24 in (60 cm)	24 in (60 cm)	3–9	yes
Clematis, Jackmanii Group	pink, red, blue to purple	summer to autumn	no	7–20 ft (2–6 m)	5–10 ft (1.5–3 m)	5–9	yes
Clematis, Lanuginosa Group	white to red to violet	summer to autumn	no	8–12 ft (2.4–3.5 m)	5–8 ft (1.5–2.4 m)	5–9	yes
Clematis macropetala	violet-blue	spring to early summer	no	6–10 ft (1.8–3 m)	5 ft (1.5 m)	3–9	yes
Clematis, Patens Group	white, blue, red, purple	late spring to summer	no	6–12 ft (1.8–3.5 m)	5–8 ft (1.5–2.4 m)	5–9	yes
Clematis, Texensis Group	pink, red	summer to mid-autumn	no	6–12 ft (1.8–3.5 m)	3–6 ft (0.9–1.8 m)	5–9	yes
Clematis, Viticella Group	white to red to purple	summer to early autumn	no	8–12 ft (2.4–3.5 m)	5–8 ft (1.5–2.4 m)	6–9	yes

RIGHT Clematis, *Diversi-folia Group, 'Arabella'* produces mauve-purple flowers from mid-summer to early autumn. It flowers freely, has a scrambling habit, and will climb with support.

BELOW LEFT Clematis, *Texensis Group, 'Etoile Rose'* is a small-flowered climber, blooming in autumn. It produces clusters of nodding, open, bell-shaped flowers with paler tips.

ABOVE Clematis, *Viticella Group, 'Madame Julia Correvon'* has open bell-shaped flowers in a stunning shade of wine red that appear from summer until late autumn.

ABOVE Clematis *'Comtesse de Bouchaud'* is a strong easy-to-grow climber, and is one of the original large-flowered hybrids of the Jackmanii Group.

RIGHT The Viticella Group includes deciduous vines from southern Europe and western Asia. *'Ville de Lyon'* (pictured) has carmine-red flowers with dark margins.

RIGHT Clematis, *Lanuginosa Group, 'Ruby Glow'* is a delightful Canadian variety with distinctive rosy purple blooms. It flowers from late spring to autumn and grows up to 8 ft (2.4 m). Little or no pruning is needed.

ABOVE *The violet-blue flowers of* Clematis macropetala *are followed by silvery pink seed heads. The foliage is pale to mid-green, and there are a number of cultivars available.*

ABOVE Clematis, *Forsteri Group, 'Early Sensation'* produces white flowers in winter and spring. It is a good climbing plant and needs a sunny protected position for best results.

LEFT *A* Clematis *Patens Group cultivar, 'Daniel Deronda' is also the title of an 1876 novel by George Eliot. The plant has semi-double bluish purple flowers that can reach up to 8 in (20 cm) in diameter.*

ABOVE Clematis *'Duchess of Edinburgh'* is a cultivar of the Florida Group. This plant is less robust than other clematis, but is very frost hardy, bearing double white flowers.
RIGHT Clematis armandii *needs a sunny spot, and liberal pruning after the flowering season. 'Snowdrift' (pictured) is an attractive white-flowered cultivar.*

LEFT *There are many cultivars of* Clivia miniata. *'Vico Yellow' is one of several cream and yellow forms available—it has creamy white flowers with a yellow throat.*

BELOW *The flowers of* Clivia caulescens *are narrow, funnel shaped, and pendent, and come in a range of warm colors. The plant's leaves can be up to 6 ft (1.8 m) in length.*

CLIVIA

Named not for Robert Clive of India (general and colonial administrator) but instead for his granddaughter, Lady Charlotte Clive, Duchess of Northumberland, this amaryllis family (Amaryllidaceae) genus is made up of just 4 species of perennials from southern Africa. They are commonly known as Kaffir lilies. Clump-forming with stocky rhizomes, they have long, bright green, strappy leaves and at various times, depending on the species, produce strong flower stems topped with heads of large funnel-shaped flowers in yellow, orange, and red shades.

CULTIVATION

Tolerating only light frost but otherwise easily grown, *Clivia* plants are superb as greenhouse container specimens. Outdoors they are best grown in dappled shade. Water well during the warmer months and allow to dry off for winter. They are usually propagated by division.

Favorites

	Flower Color	Blooming Season	Flower Fragrance	Plant Height	Plant Width	Hardiness Zone	Frost Tolerance
Clivia caulescens	orange, red, pinkish red	spring to summer	no	24 in (60 cm)	18 in (45 cm)	10–11	no
Clivia × cyrtanthiflora	salmon pink	summer to autumn	no	18–24 in (45–60 cm)	18 in (45 cm)	9–11	no
Clivia miniata	orange to scarlet; yellow throat	spring	no	18 in (45 cm)	18 in (45 cm)	9–11	no
Clivia miniata 'Flame'	red-orange	spring	no	18 in (45 cm)	18 in (45 cm)	9–11	no
Clivia miniata 'Kirstenbosch Yellow'	creamy white; golden mid-stripe	spring	no	18 in (45 cm)	18 in (45 cm)	9–11	no
Clivia miniata 'Striata'	red-orange	spring	no	18 in (45 cm)	18 in (45 cm)	9–11	no

Top Tip

Dark red berry-like fruits often follow the colorful flowers of *Clivia* species. These showy fruits can make an unusual yet highly attractive addition to fresh flower arrangements.

ABOVE Clivia miniata *is commonly known as the bush lily or fire lily. The cultivar 'Striata' has salmon red flowers with a yellow throat, as well as striped cream and green leaves.* **RIGHT** *Originally from South Africa,* Clivia miniata *is extremely popular in its native country.* C. miniata *var.* citrina *has pretty, yellow, funnel-shaped flowers.*

ABOVE *An easily grown cultivar, Colchium speciosum 'Album' displays its goblet-shaped, weather-resistant, white flowers in autumn.*

COLCHICUM

This genus of around 45 species of corms is found from eastern Europe to northern Africa and eastwards to China. Although not related to the true crocuses, the common name of autumn crocus is an apt description of the habit and appearance of many of the species. The plants are dormant and leafless in summer. Their flowers have 6 petals, usually in 2 whorls, and start to appear from early autumn before the foliage develops. Double-flowered forms are available. This genus is famous as the source of the cancer treatment drug colchicine, a mutagen that affects cell division; it is sometimes used by plant breeders to produce new cultivars.

CULTIVATION

Hardy and adaptable plants that are great favorites with enthusiasts of rockery gardens, *Colchicum* species thrive in zones that have 4 distinct seasons. Some species require a hot dry summer to flower well, but most plants are happy in any fertile well-drained soil in either full or half sun. They also do well in containers.

ABOVE Colchium specio-sum 'The Giant' is a robust perennial producing violet-pink flowers with white bases. The flowers are larger than those of other species.

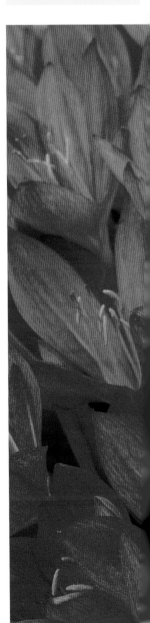

Favorites

	Flower Color	Blooming Season	Flower Fragrance	Plant Height	Plant Width	Hardiness Zone	Frost Tolerance
Colchicum agrippinum	lilac-pink	early autumn	no	3–4 in (8–10 cm)	2 in (5 cm)	5–9	yes
Colchicum autumnale	lilac-pink	late summer to mid-autumn	no	4–6 in (10–15 cm)	3 in (8 cm)	5–9	yes
Colchicum cilicicum	pinkish purple	autumn	no	4 in (10 cm)	3 in (8 cm)	4–9	yes
Colchicum parnassicum	lilac-pink	autumn	no	4–6 in (10–15 cm)	3 in (8 cm)	5–9	yes
Colchicum speciosum	lilac-pink; white throat	autumn	no	7 in (18 cm)	4–6 in (10–15 cm)	6–9	yes
Colchicum speciosum 'Album'	white	autumn	no	7 in (18 cm)	4–6 in (10–15 cm)	6–9	yes

LEFT Colchium cilicicum *needs deep soil and full sun to produce its purplish pink funnel-shaped flowers. Lance-shaped leaves grow to 15 in (38 cm) long.*
BELOW *When the lilac-pink flowers of* Colchicum parnassicum *appear, it is said to be an early sign of autumn. They grow in clusters and are quite large.*

COLUMNEA

Named by Linnaeus in honor of Italian botanist Fabius Columna (1567–1640), this mainly epiphytic genus from the African violet family (Gesneriaceae) consists of around 160 shrubby species native to the New World tropics. They have slightly arching pendulous stems that form a crown of foliage. The leaves are small, oval to lance-shaped, in opposite pairs, and usually downy, as are the stems and outer whorls of the tubular flowers. Orange and red are the common flower colors, but white, yellow, pink, and maroon also occur.

CULTIVATION

Intolerant of frost, *Columnea* plants do best as house or greenhouse plants outside of the sub-tropics. They are nearly always grown in hanging baskets so that their trailing flower stems may be best appreciated. They prefer steady temperatures, not necessarily hot, but not widely varying; they need dappled light and shelter from cold drafts. Allow to dry in winter. Propagate from half-hardened tip cuttings.

ABOVE *With a prolonged flowering season, the attractively colored blooms of* Columnea *'Early Bird' are always a welcome addition to the garden.*
LEFT *Native to Costa Rica,* Columnea microphylla *bears red flowers. The leaves surface is dotted with red hairs.*

Top Tip

Most *Columnea* species prefer high humidity. For best results grow them in an open compost mix containing sphagnum moss, peat, or charcoal, and mist regularly.

RIGHT *The dark green leaves of* Columnea gloriosa *have a covering of soft hairs. This appealing plant produces hooded scarlet flowers, with striking yellow markings.*

LEFT *The reddish orange flowers of* Columnea scandens *are followed by small globular fruit. This plant has given rise to a number of hybrids, often planted in hanging baskets.*

Favorites	Flower Color	Blooming Season	Flower Fragrance	Plant Height	Plant Width	Hardiness Zone	Frost Tolerance
Columnea arguta	red	autumn to winter	no	6 ft (1.8 m)	18 in (45 cm)	11–12	no
Columnea 'Early Bird'	orange with yellow throat	most of the year	no	10 in (25 cm)	15 in (38 cm)	10–12	no
Columnea gloriosa	scarlet with yellow throat	autumn to spring	no	6 ft (1.8 m)	18 in (45 cm)	11–12	no
Columnea microphylla	red with yellow markings	autumn to spring	no	6 ft (1.8 m)	24 in (60 cm)	11–12	no
Columnea scandens	red with yellow markings	spring to summer	no	12 in (30 cm)	24 in (60 cm)	11–12	no
Columnea schiedeana	lemon yellow, mottled dull red	spring to autumn	no	18 in (45 cm)	36 in (90 cm)	11–12	no

CONSOLIDA

A Eurasian buttercup family (Ranunculaceae) genus of around 40 species, consolidas are the annual cousins of the delphiniums, with which they were once grouped. Commonly known as larkspurs, most grow to 18–36 in (45–90 cm) tall with fine feathery foliage; about half their height is taken up with upright sometimes branching heads of 5-petalled flowers. Pretty in the garden, they also make excellent cut flowers. Their name comes from the Latin *consolida*, meaning to make whole, referring to the medicinal use of the plant to heal wounds. The juice of the leaves has also been used in herbal preparations, but parts of the plant, especially the seeds, are poisonous.

CULTIVATION

Plant in fertile well-drained soil in full sun. The plants thrive under most conditions and will often self-sow, though the flowers of wild seedlings rarely amount to much. They may need staking. Raise from seed.

Top Tip

The taller *Consolida* cultivars produce flowers that are suitable for drying, as well as cutting. They may need to be staked when they become top-heavy.

RIGHT Consolida, *Giant Imperial Series*, 'Blue Spire' *has several vertical stalks that are 4 ft (1.2 m) high. Its double flowers are a lovely shade of rich violet-blue.*
BELOW Consolida, *Giant Imperial Series*, 'White King' *looks superb in a cottage garden or border. Thin the plants to create space, and flower size will increase.*

ABOVE Consolida, *Giant Imperial Series, 'Pink Perfection' produces soft pink double flowers on straight tall stems. They are superb as cut flowers.*

Favorites	Flower Color	Blooming Season	Flower Fragrance	Plant Height	Plant Width	Hardiness Zone	Frost Tolerance
Consolida ajacis	pink, white, purple	summer	no	4 ft (1.2 m)	10–12 in (25–30 cm)	7–10	yes
Consolida 'Frosted Skies'	pale blue, darker edges	spring to summer	no	18–24 in (45–60 cm)	12 in (30 cm)	7–10	yes
Consolida, Giant Imperial Series	white, pink, red, mauve, blue	spring to summer	no	2–4 ft (0.6–1.2 m)	12 in (30 cm)	7–10	yes
Consolida, Giant Imperial Series, 'Miss California'	salmon pink	spring to summer	no	24–36 in (60–90 cm)	12 in (30 cm)	7–10	yes
Consolida, Giant Imperial Series, 'Rosalie'	deep pink	spring to summer	no	24–36 in (60–90 cm)	12 in (30 cm)	7–10	yes
Consolida regalis 'Blue Cloud'	deep blue	summer to early autumn	no	15–30 in (38–75 cm)	15–30 in (38–75 cm)	7–10	yes

CONVALLARIA

Better known as lily-of-the-valley, this plant has been cultivated since at least 1000 B.C., which is not surprising considering its unique and intense fragrance and the ease with which it grows. The sole species in the genus is a low-spreading perennial found over much of the northern temperate zone. Its vigorous rhizomes can colonize a large area, and in spring it produces bright green lance-shaped leaves and short-stemmed flower-heads with their well-known white bell-shaped blooms. A pale pink-flowered form is available. These are followed by red berries. When seventeenth-century herbalists prescribed lily-of-the-valley to strengthen the heartbeat they were correct, because it contains glycoside compounds that have been used in modern-day heart medications.

ABOVE *'Hardwick Hall', a cultivar of* Convallaria majalis, *is characterized by very wide green leaves edged with pale green.*

Top Tip

Lily-of-the-valley can be grown indoors in a container, then planted outside after flowering. A top-dressing of leaf mold is recommended in autumn.

CULTIVATION

Plant in dappled shade with deep, moist, well-drained soil. A cool winter is required for proper dormancy. The rhizomes, known as pips, are somewhat invasive in loose soil. Propagate by division.

RIGHT Convallaria majalis *'Prolificans' bears inflorescences of fragrant white flowers. The flowers do not have the distinctive bell shape of the species—some people have described them as malformed.*

LEFT *The pink-flowered varieties of* Convallaria majalis *are referred to as* C. majalis *var.* rosea. *Like the species, they are valued for their beautiful sweet perfume.*

BELOW *Although lily-of-the-valley (*Convallaria majalis*) is now one of the most popular flowers in the world, it was once considered bad luck to cultivate this plant.*

Favorites	Flower Color	Blooming Season	Flower Fragrance	Plant Height	Plant Width	Hardiness Zone	Frost Tolerance
Convallaria majalis	white	late spring to early summer	yes	8–12 in (20–30 cm)	12 in (30 cm)	3–9	yes
Convallaria majalis 'Aureomarginata'	white	late spring to early summer	yes	8–12 in (20–30 cm)	12 in (30 cm)	3–9	yes
Convallaria majalis 'Hardwick Hall'	white	late spring to early summer	yes	8–12 in (20–30 cm)	12 in (30 cm)	3–9	yes
Convallaria majalis 'Prolificans'	white	late spring to early summer	yes	8–12 in (20–30 cm)	12 in (30 cm)	3–9	yes
Convallaria majalis var. *rosea*	pink	late spring to early summer	yes	8–12 in (20–30 cm)	12 in (30 cm)	3–9	yes
Convallaria majalis 'Variegata'	white	late spring to early summer	yes	8–12 in (20–30 cm)	12 in (30 cm)	3–9	yes

CONVOLVULUS

This genus comprises around 200 species
of twining climbers, soft-stemmed shrubs,
and herbaceous perennials from many temperate regions. The leaves are mostly narrow
and textured, and shrubby species should be
trimmed regularly to encourage density of
growth. The flared funnel-shaped flowers
appear in succession over a long period from
summer to autumn. Blooms appear in a wide
range of colors, from white and pink to crimson. The genus name comes from the Latin
convolvo (to intertwine), which describes the
twisting nature of the plants.

CULTIVATION

Most are hardy plants adaptable to a range of
soils and situations, and all prefer full sun. They
are easily propagated from cuttings.

ABOVE Convolvulus tricolor
*is a bushy spreading plant,
ideal for a hanging basket or
as a ground cover. Flowers
are strikingly patterned with
bands of purple-blue and
white surrounding a vivid
yellow center.*
LEFT *A fast-growing evergreen perennial,* Convol-
vulus sabatius *bears pretty
pale mauve flowers. It does
best in sunny rocky situ-
ations with some protec-
tion from the elements.*

Top Tip

Most *Convolvulus* plants are easy to grow in full sun with dry to moist well-drained soil. Take care to manage plants properly as some can become invasive, such as *C. althaeoides.*

BELOW *The rosy pink flowers of* Convolvulus althaeoides *are highly beguiling, but this species can be difficult to manage. Grow in a pot to contain its root system.*

LEFT *Known as silverbush,* Convolvulus cneorum *has silky silvery foliage and white flowers. A compact plant, it is excellent in mass plantings or rocky crevices.*

Favorites	Flower Color	Blooming Season	Flower Fragrance	Plant Height	Plant Width	Hardiness Zone	Frost Tolerance
Convolvulus althaeoides	pink to purple	mid- to late summer	no	6 in (15 cm)	24 in (60 cm)	8–10	yes
Convolvulus boissieri	pink-flushed white	early summer	no	3 in (8 cm)	15 in (38 cm)	7–10	yes
Convolvulus cneorum	white; yellow at base	spring to summer	no	24 in (60 cm)	36 in (90 cm)	8–10	yes
Convolvulus lineatus	pink	summer	no	6 in (15 cm)	24 in (60 cm)	7–10	yes
Convolvulus sabatius	pale to deep lilac-blue	summer to early autumn	no	6–8 in (15–20 cm)	36 in (90 cm)	8–11	yes
Convolvulus tricolor	dark purple-blue, white, and yellow	summer	no	8–12 in (20–30 cm)	12–24 in (30–60 cm)	8–11	yes

COREOPSIS

Found in the Americas, especially in south-western U.S.A. and Mexico, the 80-odd annuals and perennials in this daisy family (Asteraceae) genus are heavy-flowering compact plants that are indispensable for summer color. Most are tall shrubby plants, with narrow leaves that can be lobed. The flowers of the species are nearly always golden yellow, though garden forms occur in many shades. The tips of the ray florets are often toothed as if cut with pinking shears. The flowers of some species yield a golden orange dye. Both the common name of tickseed and the meaning of the Greek word *koreopsis* (bug-like), from which the genus name is derived, refer to the appearance of small black seeds.

CULTIVATION

Plant in a sunny position with light well-drained soil. *Coreopsis* species flower better with summer moisture but are quite drought tolerant. All may be raised from seed, and the perennials will also grow from divisions or small basal cuttings of non-flowering stems.

Top Tip

Coreopsis flowers are both pretty and extremely versatile. They are equally at home in a meadow garden, a herbaceous border, or in a cut flower arrangement.

ABOVE Coreopsis verticillata 'Moonbeam' is a compact perennial from southwestern U.S.A. It features lemon yellow flowers that measure up to 1 in (25 mm) in diameter. **BELOW** Coreopsis rosea is the only plant in this genus with pink flowers. This cultivar, 'American Dream', is a dense bush that is slightly shorter than the species.

ABOVE Coreopsis tinctoria *has bright, red-centered, yellow flowers, and provides a colorful summer display in the fields and prairies of southwestern regions of the U.S.A.*
RIGHT Coreopsis *'Sunray' is an annual cultivar, and while it is best suited to a meadow garden, it is also useful as a cut flower. Its double flowerheads are deep yellow and are carried singly on long stems.*

Favorites	Flower Color	Blooming Season	Flower Fragrance	Plant Height	Plant Width	Hardiness Zone	Frost Tolerance
Coreopsis grandiflora	golden yellow	late spring to summer	no	12–24 in (30–60 cm)	12–24 in (30–60 cm)	6–10	yes
Coreopsis lanceolata	golden yellow	late spring to summer	no	24 in (60 cm)	18 in (45 cm)	3–11	yes
Coreopsis rosea	pink or red with yellow center	summer to early autumn	no	24 in (60 cm)	12 in (30 cm)	4–8	yes
Coreopsis 'Sunray'	deep yellow	spring to summer	no	20–30 in (50–75 cm)	12–24 in (30–60 cm)	6–10	yes
Coreopsis tinctoria	yellow with maroon center	summer to autumn	no	3–4 ft (0.9–1.2 m)	12–18 in (30–45 cm)	4–10	yes
Coreopsis verticillata	yellow	summer to early autumn	no	24–36 in (60–90 cm)	18 in (45 cm)	6–10	yes

CORNUS

There are about 40 species of deciduous and evergreen trees and shrubs in this genus, which is commonly known as dogwood. A few are ornamental and grown in the garden for their autumn leaf color, their colored winter stems, and their branches covered in blankets of "flowers," which may be composed of large petals or wide decorative bracts surrounding small insignificant flowers. The simple oval leaves are usually opposite each other, and the fleshy fruits have stones.

CULTIVATION

Requirements include sun or semi-shade, good drainage, and a fertile neutral to acid soil. Plants chosen for their winter stem color are best grown in full sun and cut back in early spring. In the right conditions *Cornus* species are easily grown but, if pushed to their limits, they may fail to flower or may fall victim to mildew, leaf spot, and crown canker. Propagate the multi-stemmed species by layering of sucker growths, from hardwood cuttings taken in summer or autumn, or from seed, which should be cleaned of flesh and cold-stratified for at least 3 months. The large-bracted species can be raised from seed (also stratified), half-hardened cuttings in summer, or by grafting in the case of prized cultivars.

LEFT Cornus mas *'Macrocarpa' is a sun-loving shrubby tree. Its yellow flowers are followed by glossy red fruits that are used in making jams and jellies.*

RIGHT *In summer,* Cornus kousa *has a mass of green and white flowers, and in autumn the oval wavy-edged leaves turn crimson-bronze. The fruits are pink or red-tinted.*

ABOVE *The flowering dogwood* Cornus florida *is the state flower of both Virginia and North Carolina. It is a highly ornamental spreading tree native to eastern U.S.A.*
LEFT *Commonly known as the creeping dogwood,* Cornus canadensis *is a mat-forming herbaceous perennial. The leaves turn fiery red in autumn.*

Favorites	Flower Color	Blooming Season	Flower Fragrance	Plant Height	Plant Width	Hardiness Zone	Frost Tolerance
Cornus alba	white to creamy white	late spring to early summer	no	6–10 ft (1.8–3 m)	10 ft (3 m)	4–9	yes
Cornus alternifolia	white to lemon yellow	early summer	no	25 ft (8 m)	20 ft (6 m)	3–9	yes
Cornus canadensis	cream with white bracts	summer	no	8 in (20 cm)	36 in (90 cm)	2–8	yes
Cornus capitata	white with lemon yellow bracts	summer	no	30 ft (9 m)	40 ft (12 m)	8–10	yes
Cornus controversa	white	early summer	no	50 ft (15 m)	50 ft (15 m)	5–9	yes
Cornus florida	green with white to pink bracts	late spring to early summer	no	20 ft (6 m)	25 ft (8 m)	5–9	yes
Cornus kousa	green with cream bracts	early summer	no	20 ft (6 m)	15 ft (4.5 m)	5–9	yes
Cornus mas	golden yellow	mid-winter to early spring	no	15–25 ft (4.5–8 m)	15 ft (4.5 m)	5–8	yes
Cornus officinalis	yellow	late winter	no	15 ft (4.5 m)	15 ft (4.5 m)	6–8	yes
Cornus × rutgersiensis	white, cream, pink	spring	no	20 ft (6 m)	25–30 ft (8–9 m)	5–9	yes
Cornus sanguinea	white	late spring to summer	no	12 ft (3.5 m)	8 ft (2.4 m)	6–8	yes
Cornus stolonifera	white	summer	no	7 ft (2 m)	12 ft (3.5 m)	2–10	yes

RIGHT *The hybrid Cornus ×
rutgersiensis was developed
at Rutgers University
in New Jersey.
Its autumn
foliage is often
a bright red.
The cultivar
'Aurora', seen here, has
rounded, white, velvety
bracts ageing to a rich
yellow-cream.*

Top Tip

Dogwoods are
picturesque trees
that look beautiful
in every season;
they are superb in
woodland gardens,
or featured by the
edge of a reflective
pool or pond.

ABOVE Cornus officinalis *is
grown for its yellow flowers
that appear on bare stems
in late winter, its red edible
fruits, and its richly colored
autumn foliage.*
RIGHT *Commonly known
as the American dogwood,*
Cornus stolonifera *has
orange-red autumn leaves.
This cultivar, 'Flaviramea',
displays white star-shaped
flowers from early summer
followed by spherical bluish
white fruit in autumn.*

LEFT Cornus alternifolia *'Argentea' is a deciduous bushy shrub with white variegations on the leaves, tiered branches, and a delicate veil-like appearance.*
BELOW *The horizontal spreading branches of* Cornus controversa *are carried in well-separated tiers on which the white upturned flowers lie. The fruits are blue-black.*

LEFT *The Sonata Series cultivars of* Cosmos bipinnatus *are considerably smaller than the species. Their lovely pink, white, and crimson flowers have a tufted yellow center.*
BELOW Cosmos sulphureus *is a fast-growing annual. Its foliage is coarser than that of other* Cosmos *species, and its habit is more spreading. This cultivar, 'Cosmic Yellow', has cheerful golden yellow flowers that appear in summer.*

COSMOS

This daisy family (Asteraceae) genus, commonly known as Mexican aster, is found in the Americas from the tropics to the warm temperate zones. There are about 26 species, including annuals and perennials, of which 3 are commonly grown. The common annual *Cosmos bipinnatus* has fine feathery foliage and showy, large, open flowers with 8 ray florets. It is available in many colors and varieties from dwarf to 6 ft (1.8 m) tall. The common perennial species have broader leaves and smaller flowers but are valued for their colors and scent. Native Americans treated the young tops of *C. sulphureus* as a vegetable.

CULTIVATION

Annuals should be planted out only when all danger of frost has passed. The perennials will tolerate occasional moderate frosts. Plant in a protected sunny spot with moist well-drained soil. Do not overfeed or the plants may become top-heavy—they may need staking anyway. Propagate the annuals from seed and the perennials from basal cuttings.

Favorites	Flower Color	Blooming Season	Flow Fragra
Cosmos atrosanguineus	dark maroon	mid-summer to autumn	ye
Cosmos bipinnatus	pink, red, purple, white	summer to autumn	n
Cosmos bipinnatus 'Sea Shells'	crimson, pink, white	summer to autumn	n
Cosmos bipinnatus, Sensation Series	pink, white	summer to autumn	n
Cosmos bipinnatus, Sonata Series	crimson, pink, white	summer to autumn	n
Cosmos sulphureus	yellow to red	summer	n

LEFT *Despite their elegant appearance,* Cosmos *plants are moderately priced and easy to grow. C. bipinnatus 'Sonata Carmine'—from the Sonata Series—has stunning rich red flowers.*

BELOW Cosmos bipinnatus *plants have fine wiry stems, and even the slightest breeze seems to make them dance. Another advantage of this species is that it can be grown directly from seed, which germinates quickly— a great project for children.*

Top Tip

Cosmos species are great cut flowers. Cut them immediately after they open and place in warm water first, moving the flowers to a deep vase of cool water after a few minutes.

Plant Height	Plant Width	Hardiness Zone	Frost Tolerance
24 in (60 cm)	18 in (45 cm)	8–10	yes
5–6 ft .5–1.8 m)	18 in (45 cm)	8–11	no
36 in (90 cm)	18 in (45 cm)	8–11	no
36 in (90 cm)	18 in (45 cm)	8–11	no
8–24 in 5–60 cm)	12 in (30 cm)	8–11	no
4 ft (1.2 m)	18 in (45 cm)	8–11	no

LEFT Crataegus viridis *is native to southeastern U.S.A. This beautiful cultivar, 'Winter King', has bright red spherical fruits in winter, attractive silver-gray bark, and hardly any thorns.*
BELOW LEFT Crataegus per-similis 'Prunifolia Splendens' *adds a wealth of color to the garden throughout the year. It has white flowers in late spring and early summer, scarlet autumn leaves, and red winter fruits.*

CRATAEGUS

This genus of the Rosaceae family contains around 200 species. Most are spiny large shrubs or small trees. The leaves are alternate, simple or lobed, some toothed, and deep green in color. The small white to pink flowers have 5 sepals and/or petals depending on the species, and are carried in flat-topped clusters or are solitary. They are followed by nutlets, the fleshy covering of which is edible. The color of the fruits can be black, yellow, or bluish green, but the majority are bright red. *Crataegus laevigata* and *C. monogyna* have been used as hedging plants for centuries. These trees are commonly known as hawthorns.

CULTIVATION

Grow in sun or partial shade in any soil. Cultivars may be budded in summer or grafted in winter. Sow seeds as soon as ripe in a position protected from winter frosts. Germination may take up to 18 months. Some hawthorns are prone to fireblight.

Favorites

	Flower Color	Blooming Season	Flower Fragrance	Plant Height	Plant Width	Hardiness Zone	Frost Tolerance
Crataegus laevigata	white to pink	late spring	no	25 ft (8 m)	25 ft (8 m)	5–9	yes
Crataegus × lavallei	white	late spring to early summer	no	25 ft (8 m)	15–20 ft (4.5–6 m)	6–10	yes
Crataegus monogyna	white	late spring	yes	30 ft (9 m)	25 ft (8 m)	4–9	yes
Crataegus persimilis 'Prunifolia Splendens'	white	late spring to early summer	no	20 ft (6 m)	20 ft (6 m)	5–9	yes
Crataegus punctata	white	early summer	no	25–35 ft (8–10 m)	30 ft (9 m)	4–9	yes
Crataegus viridis	white	spring	no	40 ft (12 m)	12 ft (3.5 m)	4–9	yes

LEFT Crataegus × lavallei *is a French hybrid. It has toothed oval leaves that are similar to rose leaves. White spring flowers are followed by red fruits in winter.*
BELOW *Originating from eastern U.S.A.,* Crataegus punctata *is a highly ornamental species. It produces masses of white blossoms and large pear-shaped fruits.*

Top Tip

Prune *Crataegus* branches to get rid of excessive twiggy growth, and trim hawthorn hedges in autumn or after flowering. Many species have long sharp thorns, so take special care when pruning.

CRINUM

Found throughout the tropics and subtropics, this is a genus of around 130 species of bulbs belonging to the amaryllis family (Amaryllidaceae). Leaves are usually long and strappy, may be evergreen or deciduous, and range from no more than about 2 in (5 cm) long in the smallest species to well over 3 ft (0.9 m) in the largest. Strong flower stems develop in the center of the foliage clump and carry heads of large, often fragrant, 6-lobed, trumpet-shaped flowers in shades of white or pink. Round seed pods follow. The genus name comes from the Greek *krinon* (a lily), and though poisonous, extracts of the bulbs have been used medicinally, mainly in poultices for wounds.

CULTIVATION

Few species will tolerate any but the lightest frosts, and all prefer a warm climate. Although often found in damp ground, they grow just as well in moist well-drained soil. Plant in full or half sun with the bulb neck above the surface. Propagation is mainly from seed.

BELOW Crinum × powellii *'Album' is the white form of this popular hybrid. It is usually easily cultivated, but may need staking.*
BELOW LEFT Crinum × powellii *has light to mid-green strap-like foliage and bears umbels of fragrant deep pink blooms from late summer to autumn.*

Top Tip

Crinum species are best planted in spring and should be kept well-watered during the growing season. Keep moist after flowering.

ABOVE Crinum moorei *is quite a cold-hardy species and will grow well in light to deep shade. The soft pink flowers are borne on stems that are up to 36 in (90 cm) high.*
RIGHT Crinum americanum, *the southern swamp lily, bears up to 6 pure white flowers, growing up to 5 in (12 cm) long.*

Favorites	Flower Color	Blooming Season	Flower Fragrance	Plant Height	Plant Width	Hardiness Zone	Frost Tolerance
Crinum americanum	white	spring to autumn	yes	20 in (50 cm)	18 in (45 cm)	9–11	no
Crinum bulbispermum	white to pink; red mid-stripe	late spring	yes	24 in (60 cm)	18 in (45 cm)	6–10	yes
Crinum 'Ellen Bosanquet'	deep reddish pink	summer	no	18–24 in (45–60 m)	18 in (45 cm)	8–11	yes
Crinum erubescens	white	summer to autumn	yes	36 in (90 cm)	4 ft (1.2 m)	9–12	no
Crinum moorei	white to pink	late summer to early autumn	yes	36 in (90 cm)	24 in (60 cm)	8–11	yes
Crinum × powellii	pink	late summer to autumn	yes	3–5 ft (0.9–1.5 m)	24 in (60 cm)	7–10	yes

CROCOSMIA

BELOW *The vibrant orange-red blooms of* Crocosmia masoniorum *make striking cut flowers. Their appeal and appearance is enhanced by the mid-green, pleated, sword-shaped leaves.*

The 7 species of corms in this South African iris family (Iridaceae) genus are widely cultivated as ornamentals, though some of them are considered weeds in various parts of the world. They have long sword-shaped leaves, sometimes conspicuously veined or pleated, that may be near-evergreen in mild climates. Flowering occurs mainly during summer and autumn, when arching sprays of usually 6-petalled flowers in bright orange and red shades appear. Cultivars cover a wider color range from yellow to rusty brown, and they last well when cut. The genus name, derived from the Greek *krokos* (saffron) and *osme* (smell), was given because the classifying botanist noticed a saffron-like scent when water was spilt on a dried specimen. They are commonly known as montbretia.

CULTIVATION

Surprisingly hardy, they are easily grown in full or half sun in moist well-drained soil. In areas where the soil freezes, the corms may be stored dry over winter and replanted in spring. Propagate from offsets, which are often numerous.

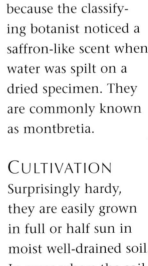

Top Tip

Plant corms 3–4 in (8–10 cm) deep in early spring, and water well during the warmer months. *Crocosmia* plants multiply freely once established.

LEFT Crocosmia 'Rowallane Yellow' bears graceful golden yellow flowers that face upward to
the sky. The slender wiry stems and pleated
leaves are a rich mid-green.

BELOW The elegant, trumpet-shaped, orange-red
flowers of Crocosmia pottsii are borne in sprays
from late summer until early autumn. They make
excellent cut flowers.

Favorites

	Flower Color	Blooming Season	Flower Fragrance	Plant Height	Plant Width	Hardiness Zone	Frost Tolerance
Crocosmia × *crocosmiiflora*	yellow to orange-red	summer	no	24–36 in (60–90 cm)	24 in (60 cm)	7–11	yes
Crocosmia 'Emily McKenzie'	yellow to orange; red markings	late summer	no	24 in (60 cm)	24 in (60 cm)	7–11	yes
Crocosmia 'Lucifer'	red	summer	no	3–4 ft (0.9–1.2 m)	3 in (8 cm)	7–11	yes
Crocosmia *masoniorum*	orange to flame red	late summer	no	4 ft (1.2 m)	18 in (45 cm)	7–11	yes
Crocosmia *pottsii*	red-tinged orange	late summer	no	36 in (90 cm)	18 in (45 cm)	7–11	yes
Crocosmia 'Rowallane Yellow'	golden yellow	late summer	no	36 in (90 m)	18 in (45 cm)	7–11	yes

CROCUS

For many, the first peeping blooms of this well-known genus of late winter- and early spring-flowering corms herald the beginning of spring. The genus is made up of around 80 species spread from central Europe to northern Africa and central Asia. Most have short grassy leaves that emerge with or after the flower buds. The flowers are 6-petalled short-stemmed goblets with up to 4 blooms per head and occur in a wide range of colors, especially yellow and purple shades. A member of the iris family (Iridaceae), the genus name comes from the Greek word *krokos* (saffron), which is produced from the dried stigmas of the plant. Saffron has always been among the most expensive spices, and this is one of the few cases where a plant is cultivated for its stamens.

CULTIVATION

Of variable hardiness, but mostly very tough, crocuses thrive in cool, moist, humus-rich soil. Propagate by dividing established clumps or raise from seed.

ABOVE *The pretty flowers of* Crocus sieberi *'Tricolor' appear from spring to early summer, each one in shades of purple, white, and yellow.*

TOP Crocus tommasinianus *is a favorite of many: it is easy to grow, copes with all soil types, and is among the first to flower each season.*

Favorites	Flower Color	Blooming Season	Flower Fragrance	Plant Height	Plant Width	Hardiness Zone	Frost Tolerance
Crocus chrysanthus	creamy yellow to gold	late winter to early spring	no	2 in (5 cm)	2 in (5 cm)	4–9	yes
Crocus serotinus	pale to deep purple	autumn	yes	2–3 in (5–8 cm)	2 in (5 cm)	5–9	yes
Crocus sieberi	lilac-blue with yellow throat	late winter to spring	no	3 in (8 cm)	1 in (25 mm)	7–9	yes
Crocus speciosus	violet-blue; deep blue veining	autumn	yes	6 in (15 cm)	2 in (5 cm)	3–8	yes
Crocus tommasinianus	lavender-blue; silver highlights	late winter to spring	no	4 in (10 cm)	1 in (25 mm)	5–9	yes
Crocus vernus	white, pink, mauve, purple	spring to early summer	no	6 in (15 cm)	2 in (5 cm)	4–9	yes

Top Tip

Crocuses perform especially well in the leafy soil found under deciduous trees. For best results, plant them where they will receive sun at flowering time.

LEFT *The autumn-flowering* Crocus serotinus *subsp.* salz-mannii *is a lovely plant for open grassy or rocky areas. Its lilac blooms are sometimes veined a darker purple shade.*

ABOVE Crocus speciosus *has unusually large, open, purple to blue flowers that are borne on leafless stems. A rewarding garden plant, it grows easily under trees and bushes.*

CYCLAMEN

Very distinctive in both leaf and flower, the 19 species in this primrose family (Primulaceae) genus are tuberous perennials found in Europe, around the Mediterranean shores, and in western Asia. Also known as Persian violets or sowbread, cyclamens occur in a range of sizes but are otherwise similar. From their flattened tubers emerge gray-green to blue-green heart-shaped leaves, often attractively patterned silver-gray. Downward-facing flowers in white, pink, purple, or red shades are borne one per stem and have large reflexed petals. Cyclamen is an ingredient in numerous interesting herbal recipes, one of which is a "love cake" that supposedly causes anyone eating it to fall irretrievably in love.

CULTIVATION

The tubers need perfect drainage. Add grit and fibrous compost, and plant the tuber with its top at or just above soil level. Most prefer dappled shade. Propagate from seed as established clumps flower better if left undivided.

ABOVE *The mid- to dark green leaves of* Cyclamen hederifolium *are tinged purple underneath. Pink blooms appear in autumn.*
BELOW *The so-called florist's cyclamen,* C. persicum *is a popular indoor and conservatory plant that can have a long flowering season.*

Top Tip

If growing from seed, soak for a good 12 hours and then rinse well. Sow seed in the cooler months for best results, and leave the tubers undisturbed.

LEFT *There are a number of cultivars of* Cyclamen persicum, *all easily grown, but best suited to indoor cultivation. They like high humidity—this can be achieved by standing the pot on a tray of pebbles.*

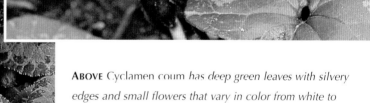

ABOVE *Cyclamen coum has deep green leaves with silvery edges and small flowers that vary in color from white to shades of pink, usually with a crimson base.*

Favorites	Flower Color	Blooming Season	Flower Fragrance	Plant Height	Plant Width	Hardiness Zone	Frost Tolerance
Cyclamen cilicium	soft pink, darker at petal base	autumn to early spring	yes	2 in (5 cm)	4 in (10 cm)	7–9	yes
Cyclamen coum	light to dark purple-pink	winter to early spring	no	2–4 in (5–10 cm)	4–6 in (10–15 cm)	6–9	yes
Cyclamen hederifolium	pink, darker at petal base	autumn	yes	4–6 in (10–15 cm)	6 in (15 cm)	5–9	yes
Cyclamen persicum	white, pink, red, purple	winter	yes	8–12 in (20–30 cm)	12 in (30 cm)	9–10	no
Cyclamen purpurascens	pale to dark purple-red	summer	yes	4 in (10 cm)	4 in (10 cm)	5–9	yes
Cyclamen repandum	white, pink, red	spring	yes	4–6 in (10–15 cm)	6–8 in (15–20 cm)	6–9	yes

CYMBIDIUM

This genus includes some 50 or so species, distributed throughout Asia and down to Australia. Most of the mountain species are terrestrial, with upright to arching flower spikes bearing blooms in many colors. In the lowlands, most cymbidiums take to the trees as epiphytes, growing in high light. Many of these species have long pendent clusters of flowers and thick leathery leaves. Tens of thousands of hybrids have been artificially created over the past century, and they are often loosely categorized by their flower size. Today, these hybrids form the basis of an important pot plant and cut flower industry in temperate climates. Traditionally, the main flowering season has been winter to spring, however selective breeding is expanding this.

CULTIVATION

Today, most hybrid cymbidiums are grown in commercial orchid composts, which are generally free draining but retain some moisture. The epiphytic species prefer a mix incorporating a high percentage of coarse bark. In the main, they like to be kept moist year-round, with extra watering and fertilizing from spring to autumn, while they are actively growing. Most of the cool-growing species and complex hybrids need a night-time drop in temperature of at least 50°F (10°C) during summer evenings, to help initiate flowering for the following season. This can be manipulated by giving the plants a regular light misting of water at sunset during the warmer months.

Top Tip

In summer, cymbidiums need good ventilation, filtered sunlight, and regular watering and misting. In winter, the plants need full sun, and not as much water.

LEFT Cymbidium erythrostylum *is native to Vietnam, and is a highly desirable species because its flowers are very large in comparison to the leaves.*

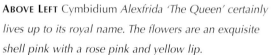

ABOVE LEFT Cymbidium *Alexfrida 'The Queen'* certainly lives up to its royal name. The flowers are an exquisite shell pink with a rose pink and yellow lip.

ABOVE Cymbidium lowianum *'Tiger'* × C. ormoulu *is a striking hybrid, taking its flower color from its parent* C. lowianum, *a sturdy species from the mountains of Asia.*

LEFT Cymbidium tracyanum *makes an excellent addition to a cut flower arrangement because of its greenish yellow flowers with dramatic reddish brown spots and stripes. The species bears arching racemes of up to 20 flowers.*

Favorites

	Flower Color	Blooming Season	Flower Fragrance	Plant Height	Plant Width	Hardiness Zone	Frost Tolerance
Cymbidium Alexfrida 'The Queen'	shell pink; rose and yellow lip	spring	no	36 in (90 cm)	24 in (60 cm)	10–11	no
Cymbidium erythrostylum	white; yellow lip and red veining	spring to summer	no	12 in (30 cm)	18 in (45 cm)	9–11	no
Cymbidium goeringii	cream with red markings	winter to spring	yes	8–12 in (20–30 m)	12 in (30 cm)	9–11	no
Cymbidium lowianum	green; cream lip with red markings	spring	no	36 in (90 cm)	36 in (90 cm)	10–11	no
Cymbidium sinense	yellow and maroon; cream lip	autumn to spring	yes	24 in (60 cm)	18 in (45 cm)	9–11	no
Cymbidium tracyanum	yellow-green with red markings	spring	no	36 in (90 cm)	36 in (90 cm)	9–11	no

CYTISUS

This genus of about 50 species belongs to the pea family and consists mainly of ever-green shrubs, although species can vary in form from prostrate shrubs to small trees. Most are native to Europe, with a few found in western Asia and northern Africa. All have typical pea-flowers, which appear from late spring and into early summer. The broom-like twiggy growths—hence the well-known common name of the genus, broom—are sometimes almost leafless. The fruit is a flattened legume containing small hard-coated seeds. Brooms are useful ornamen-tally for their hardiness and showy flowers.

Top Tip

Brooms tolerate most conditions, and make a suit-able seaside plant. They prefer slightly acidic soil. If the soil has a high alkaline content, add iron sulfate.

CULTIVATION

Brooms need a free-draining soil, preferably slightly acidic but fairly low in fertility. An exposed sunny position gives the best display of flowers. Spent flowers and shoots should be removed after flowering, together with some of the older shoots, in order to open up the center of the plant and encourage new growth from the base. The typical arching habit of the plant should be maintained. Most species can be propagated from short-tip cuttings of the ripened current year's growth, taken in late autumn or early winter.

BELOW Cytisus scoparius *is a widely grown medium-sized shrub. It is generally valued for its yellow flowers, but along the west coast of the U.S.A. and in Hawaii it is thought to be invasive.*

ABOVE Cytisus × kewensis *has tiny hairy leaves and a semi-prostrate habit with trailing stems. It produces masses of creamy white flowers in spring.*

Favorites	Flower Color	Blooming Season	Flow Fragra
Cytisus battandieri	yellow	summer	ye
Cytisus × kewensis	cream to lemon yellow	spring	ye
Cytisus × praecox	creamy white to pale yellow	spring	n
Cytisus purgans	golden yellow	spring to early summer	ye
Cytisus scoparius	golden yellow	late spring to early summer	n
Cytisus supranubius	rose-tinged white	late spring	y

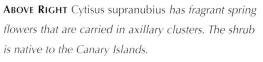

ABOVE RIGHT Cytisus supranubius *has fragrant spring flowers that are carried in axillary clusters. The shrub is native to the Canary Islands.*

RIGHT *The flowers of* Cytisus × praecox *'Warminster' are usually held in long sprays on the outer stems, and are heavily perfumed. The leaves have a silky texture.*

Plant Height	Plant Width	Hardiness Zone	Frost Tolerance
12 ft (3.5 m)	15 ft (4.5 m)	7–9	yes
12 in (30 cm)	5 ft (1.5 m)	6–9	yes
4 ft (1.2 m)	5 ft (1.5 m)	6–9	yes
36 in (90 cm)	36 in (90 cm)	6–9	yes
7 ft (2 m)	5 ft (1.5 m)	5–9	yes
10 ft (3 m)	8 ft (2.4 m)	9–10	no

DAHLIA

Beloved by gardeners everywhere, this daisy family genus consists of around 30 species of tuberous rooted perennials and sub-shrubs. They have attractive foliage, with deep to bright green lobed leaves, hollow stems, and bold flowerheads that, due to much cultivation, may vary greatly. Dahlias can be broadly divided into tall border plants and low-growing bedding dahlias, though a more detailed classification sorts them into 10 groups based on the size and type of flowerhead; this ranges from tiny pompon to large giant-flowered cactus types. Colors include shades of white and cream to bright yellow and deep red. Mostly native to Mexico, these flamboyant plants were originally cultivated by the Aztecs for their large edible roots.

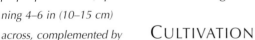

ABOVE *One of the Decor-ative cultivars,* Dahlia *'Ted's Choice' bears beautiful full purple-pink blooms, span-ning 4–6 in (10–15 cm) across, complemented by rich green foliage.*

CULTIVATION

Plant dahlias in a sunny open position with fertile, free-draining, humus-rich soil. In cold climates, where frozen or waterlogged soil is likely to occur, the tubers should be lifted and stored near-dry in a frost-free place. Most species can be propagated by dividing the tubers or by taking cut-tings off young shoots.

LEFT *Recently introduced,* Dahlia *'Lilac Taratahi' is a Cactus dahlia. Bursting open on elegant tall stems, the ray florets of lilac-pink quill-like petals give the lovely full blooms a delicate appearance.*

ABOVE *Bringing hot tropical colors to the garden,* Dahlia *'Tout-à-Toi' is a Decorative dahlia with fiery orange-red petals turning golden yel-low toward the base.*

Top Tip

When planting dahlias, select a site that is sheltered from strong winds. Even in a protected spot, dahlias will often need staking to prevent them falling over.

ABOVE *The snow white flowers of* Dahlia *'My Love' are a stunning addition to any garden. This Semi-cactus dahlia is popular for floral arrangements, particularly bridal bouquets.*

Favorites	Flower Color	Blooming Season	Flower Fragrance	Plant Height	Plant Width	Hardiness Zone	Frost Tolerance
Dahlia, Anemone-flowered	white to pink, red, yellow, orange	summer to autumn	no	2–6 ft (0.6–1.8 m)	12–24 in (30–60 cm)	8–11	yes
Dahlia, Ball	white to pink, red, yellow, orange	summer to autumn	no	1–6 ft (0.3–1.8 m)	12–24 in (30–60 cm)	8–11	yes
Dahlia, Cactus	white to pink, red, yellow, orange	summer to autumn	no	4–6 ft (1.2–1.8 m)	18–30 in (45–75 cm)	8–11	yes
Dahlia coccinea	yellow, orange to dark red	summer to autumn	no	10 ft (3 m)	4 ft (1.2 m)	8–11	yes
Dahlia, Collarette	white to pink, red, yellow, orange	summer to autumn	no	4 ft (1.2 m)	18 in (45 cm)	9–11	yes
Dahlia, Decorative	white to pink, red, yellow, orange	summer to autumn	no	3–6 ft (0.9–1.8 m)	18–30 in (45–75 cm)	8–11	yes
Dahlia imperialis	lavender, pink, white	late autumn to winter	no	12–20 ft (3.5–6 m)	5–10 ft (1.5–3 m)	9–11	yes
Dahlia merckii	white to pink or purple	summer to autumn	no	2–5 ft (0.6–1.5 m)	36 in (90 cm)	8–11	yes
Dahlia, Pompon	white to pink, red, yellow, orange	summer to autumn	no	12–36 in (30–90 cm)	12–24 in (30–60 cm)	8–11	yes
Dahlia, Semi-cactus	white to pink, red, yellow, orange	summer to autumn	no	4–6 ft (1.2–1.8 m)	18–30 in (45–75 cm)	8–11	yes
Dahlia, Single	white to pink, red, yellow, orange	summer to autumn	no	1–5 ft (0.3–1.5 m)	12–24 in (30–60 cm)	8–11	yes
Dahlia, Waterlily	white to pink, red, yellow, orange	summer to autumn	no	3–5 ft (0.9–1.5 m)	18–30 in (45–75 cm)	8–11	yes

LEFT *Flowering from early summer to early autumn, Dahlia 'Gay Princess' is a Waterlily dahlia with rich green foliage and 4–6 in (10–15 cm) wide flowers in shades of pink or white.*

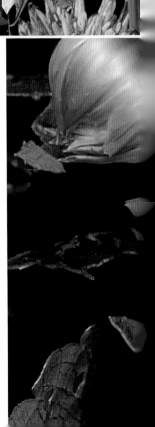

ABOVE *While* Dahlia *'Explosion' is classed as a Semi-cactus type of dahlia, it is often called a "dinner-plate dahlia," as its huge red-striped yellow flower-heads are as large as the name suggests.*

LEFT Dahlia *'Aurwen's Violet' is a Pompon dahlia. With mid-green leaves and a hemispherical head of purple-red petals held on tall thin stems, this elegant plant reaches a height of up to 36 in (90 cm).*

LEFT Dahlia *'Golden Charmer'* is a Semi-cactus dahlia with broad florets of yellow-bronze petals. The large flowerheads are 4–6 in (10–15 cm) across.

BELOW Fast-growing Dahlia *'Alfred Grille'* can reach a height of 4–6 ft (1.2–1.8 m). This lovely Cactus dahlia has wispy blooms in shades of yellow and pink.

LEFT *With large leaves and single large flowers in pink, lavender, or white, Dahlia imperialis is a native of Central America. This species can reach a height of up to 20 ft (6 m).*

RIGHT *A member of the Decorative dahlias, Dahlia 'Suffolk Punch' has attractive dark foliage, and bears lovely, bright purple-pink, double blooms.*

BELOW *A Semi-cactus dahlia with bright vermilion petals, Dahlia 'Red Pygmy' is an ideal border plant. Growing to a height of only 22 in (55 cm), it will not overshadow its neighbors.*

BELOW *Dahlia 'Kelvin Floodlight' is an award-winning Decorative dahlia. The stunning, sunny yellow, double blooms are dinner-plate sized.*

ABOVE *Slender tall stems carry the light orange, bronze-tinged, double blooms of Dahlia 'Hamilton Lillian', a Decorative dahlia that can grow to 5 ft (1.5 m) high.*
TOP *Dahlia 'White Cactus' is a stunning example of the Cactus dahlias. The white petals are incurved along part of their length to give a quill-like appearance.*
LEFT *Gorgeous double blooms in the richest of bright reds are the trademark of Dahlia 'My Valentine'. This beautiful plant is a member of the Decorative dahlia group.*

Favorites	Flower Color	Blooming Season	Flower Fragrance
Daphne × *burkwoodii*	light pink	mid-to late spring	yes
Daphne caucasica	white	late spring to early summer	yes
Daphne cneorum	pale to deep pink	spring	yes
Daphne genkwa	lilac	spring	yes
Daphne × *napolitana*	rose pink	spring	yes
Daphne odora	purple-pink to white	mid-winter to spring	yes

ABOVE *The flowers of* Daphne odora *are popular for their wonderful perfume; they also make a reasonably long-lasting display when cut and placed in a vase.*

DAPHNE

This genus includes 50 or so evergreen and deciduous shrubs indigenous to Europe, North Africa, and temperate and subtropical Asia. They vary in habit and may be erect, rounded, or spreading. The leaves are mostly simple, smooth-edged, oval-shaped, and often a dull green or slightly glossy color. Small scented flowers, usually in delicate shades of white, cream, yellow, or pink, grow singly or in rounded clusters. The fruit that follows the flowers can also be very colorful, ranging from white and pink to red and purple. Famed for their fragrance, daphnes are at home in rock gardens, as well as in mixed borders alongside plants such as camellias and rhododendrons.

CULTIVATION

Daphnes generally prefer moist, cool, humus-rich, and well-drained soil. Once established, the plant needs to be mulched well and the roots should not be disturbed. Small-leafed species prefer light conditions, while those with larger leaves need some shade. Propagate from seed, cuttings, or by layering.

Top Tip

Grow one of the smaller species of *Daphne* in a window box or container placed near a doorway; on a warm day the delightful fragrance of the flowers will be carried indoors.

Plant Height	Plant Width	Hardiness Zone	Frost Tolerance
5 ft (1.5 m)	5 ft (1.5 m)	5–9	yes
7 ft (2 m)	5 ft (1.5 m)	6–8	yes
8 in (20 cm)	7 ft (2 m)	4–9	yes
5 ft (1.5 m)	5 ft (1.5 m)	5–9	yes
30 in (75 cm)	30 in (75 cm)	8–10	yes
5 ft (1.5 m)	5 ft (1.5 m)	8–10	yes

ABOVE *Its long flowering season and masses of scented blooms ensure that* Daphne × napolitana *is a popular choice with gardeners.*

LEFT Daphne × burkwoodii, *a hybrid between* D. cneorum *and* D. caucasica, *and has a number of forms, all with beautifully variegated foliage.*

BELOW *The low-growing habit of* Daphne cneorum *makes it ideal for rockeries or alpine troughs.*

DELOSPERMA

This genus is one of several genera known as ice plants. It contains about 150 species of annuals, perennials, and subshrubs found throughout southern and eastern Africa. Species are generally drought tolerant and are excellent for desert gardens. They have dense yellow-green foliage that is made up of small, fleshy, and usually cylindrical leaves growing in opposite pairs on the stem. During spring and summer, the daisy-like flowers are borne in vivid shades of white, yellow, orange-red, and bright magenta, with the result that the spreading species form boldly-colored carpets of blooms. Several species have been used in herbal and traditional medicines, and recent studies show that they contain fairly high concentrations of a mildly hallucinogenic drug (dimethyltryptamine).

CULTIVATION

Delosperma species prefer full sun in a sheltered spot with light, gritty, well-drained soil. They are ideally suited for coastal areas and rockeries. A few species will tolerate light frosts. Propagate from seed or cuttings.

BELOW *The flowers of* Delosperma nubigenum *are only small but compensate for this with their brightness; flowers are mostly vibrant yellow or orange-red.*

LEFT *A prostrate succulent perennial,* Delosperma cooperi *has cylindrical light green leaves that provide excellent ground coverage Its bright magenta flowers have contrasting white anthers and can grow up to 2 in (5 cm) in diameter.*

Top Tip

These hardy southern African species will perform best if water is withheld during autumn, allowing the plants to harden off for winter. During the growing period, water regularly, applying fertilizer every 3 weeks.

ABOVE Delosperma sutherlandii *occurs naturally in the grasslands and rocky areas of Transvaal and Natal in South Africa. Its purple-pink blooms are among the largest flowers of the ice plants, growing up to 2¹/₂ in (6 cm) wide.*
RIGHT *The trailing succulent* Delosperma lehmannii *is an ideal choice for any sunny dry rock crevice or corner. It bears triangular-shaped gray-green leaves and pale yellow flowers that usually open in the afternoon.*

Favorites	Flower Color	Blooming Season	Flower Fragrance	Plant Height	Plant Width	Hardiness Zone	Frost Tolerance
Delosperma congestum	bright yellow	summer to early autumn	no	2 in (5 cm)	10 in (25 cm)	8–10	yes
Delosperma cooperi	magenta	mid- to late summer	no	2–3 in (5–8 cm)	18–24 in (45–60 cm)	9–11	no
Delosperma lehmannii	lemon yellow	summer	no	6 in (15 cm)	24 in (60 cm)	9–11	no
Delosperma nubigenum	bright yellow to orange-red	late spring to summer	no	1 in (25 mm)	36 in (90 cm)	7–11	yes
Delosperma sphalmanthoides	pink-purple	spring to summer	no	2 in (5 cm)	12 in (30 cm)	9–11	no
Delosperma sutherlandii	magenta	summer	no	2 in (5 cm)	6 in (15 cm)	8–11	yes

Favorites	Flower Color	Blooming Season	Flower Fragrance
Delphinium, Belladonna Group	blue, white	early to late summer	no
Delphinium, Elatum Group	blue, white	summer to autumn	no
Delphinium grandiflorum	blue, white, violet	summer	no
Delphinium 'Michael Ayres'	dark violet	summer	no
Delphinium nudicaule	red and yellow	late spring to mid-summer	no
Delphinium, Pacific Hybrids	blue, white, purple	early to mid-summer	no

ABOVE *Commonly known as butterfly delphinium, D. grandiflorum is a tufted short-lived perennial, often grown as an annual. Large flowers in shades of white, bright blue, or violet, such as the cultivar 'Tom Pouce' above, bloom throughout the summer months.*

DELPHINIUM

This genus contains around 250 species of annuals and perennials native to mainly temperate zones in the Northern Hemisphere, and belongs to the widely cultivated buttercup family (Ranunculaceae). The light to bright green leaves are usually hand-shaped and slightly hairy. Delphiniums are generally thought to have tall erect flower stems but many species have short branching ones. All species, however, grow striking flowers along much of the length of the stem. Characteristic flower colors include blue and deep purple, though some species have white, red, or pale green flowers. Delphinium comes from the Greek *delphin* (dolphin) and describes the shape of the nectar-containing spurs found at the base of the flower.

CULTIVATION

Plant in full sun with moist, fertile, well-drained soil. Any withered foliage must be cut back to maintain the vigorous growth of the plant. Annuals and species can be propagated from seed, whereas hybrids and cultivars can be propagated by division or from cuttings.

Top Tip

There cannot be many plants more suited to a border or feature bed than delphiniums and, in particular, *D. elatum* is a perfect choice. Stake, if necessary, for extra support.

Plant Height	Plant Width	Hardiness Zone	Frost Tolerance
4 ft (1.2 m)	24 in (60 cm)	3–9	yes
3–6 ft (0.9–1.8 m)	24 in (60 cm)	3–9	yes
18 in (45 cm)	12 in (30 cm)	3–9	yes
5 ft (1.5 m)	18 in (45 cm)	3–9	yes
24 in (60 cm)	8 in (20 cm)	5–7	yes
5 ft (1.5 m)	30 in (75 cm)	7–9	yes

ABOVE AND LEFT
Delphinium elatum *and its hybrids make up the Elatum Group which contains many popular garden forms. Plants produce tall spikes tightly packed with flowers, which are ideal for cutting. 'Sungleam', above, bears cream-colored flowers and 'Albert Shepherd', left, has soft purple-blue blooms lightly flushed with pink.*

CENTER LEFT *A favorite with gardeners, Delphinium 'Michael Ayres' is an award-winning plant. Tall spikes grow up to 6 ft (1.8 m) and produce a profusion of flowers along its length in deep violet shades with distinct black eyes.*

LEFT *This stunning flower belongs to* Dendrobium wardianum, *a deciduous epiphyte. Flowers are white, with magenta-tipped ends, and have a yellow and maroon-spotted center.*
RIGHT Dendrobium bigib-bum *var.* compactum *produces rather beautiful pink-colored flowers. Its dark green leaves are some-times edged with purple.*

DENDROBIUM

Extremely popular with orchid growers, this large genus contains about 1,200 species native to quite a large area that ranges from India, Sri Lanka, and Southeast Asia through to New Guinea, Australia, and the Pacific Islands. With so many species, the genus boasts an amazing diversity of plant habit, flower form, and color. Examples range from soft-stemmed epiphytic species that grow on other plants for support, to varieties that grow on the naked surfaces of rocks. The leaves may be long and elongated or oblong-shaped. Flowers come in a dazzling mix of color, shape, and size, and are borne singly or in clusters along the stem. Plants are dormant during the dry season, bursting into flower after rainfall to produce the next season's growth.

CULTIVATION

The cultivation of particular species varies dramatically, though generally a very well-drained mixture of bark and charcoal, often with a bit of added sphagnum moss, is ideal. Propagation is by division or cuttings, depending on the species.

Favorites	Flower Color	Blooming Season	Flow Fragra
Dendrobium bigibbum	white, mauve to magenta, pink	autumn to winter	no
Dendrobium binoculare	yellow	early summer	ye
Dendrobium kingianum	pink, red, mauve, purple, white	late winter to spring	ye
Dendrobium Thanaid Stripes	cerise with darker veining	most of the year	ne
Dendrobium wardianum	white with red, purple, yellow	spring to autumn	ye
Dendrobium White Fairy	white flushed palest pink	autumn to winter	ye

Top Tip

These plants are best grown in containers, and once established they dislike disturbance. Use stakes to give the flower stems extra support.

BELOW *A compact plant, Dendrobium Thanaid Stripes produces its lovely pink-striped blooms all year round, but especially from mid-summer to late winter.*

LEFT *The clump-forming Dendrobium kingianum is found in eastern Australia, where it is known as pink rock orchid. Its perfumed flowers appear in shades ranging from pale pink to mauve, red, and white.*

Plant Height	Plant Width	Hardiness Zone	Frost Tolerance
3 ft (0.9 m)	12 in (30 cm)	11–12	no
24 in (60 cm)	12 in (30 cm)	10–12	no
6–12 in 15–30 cm)	6 in (15 cm)	9–11	no
4 ft (1.2 m)	24 in (60 cm)	11–12	no
3 ft (0.9 m)	12 in (30 cm)	10–12	no
24–36 in 50–90 cm)	24 in (60 cm)	11–12	no

DEUTZIA

This genus consists of around 60 species of deciduous and evergreen shrubs from temperate Asia and Central America. The pale green leaves range from oval-pointed to lance-shaped, often with serrated edges, and grow in opposite pairs on the stem. Most of the commonly grown species are spring-flowering with the small 5-petalled flowers growing in a profusion of clustered sprays that reach above the foliage. The flowers are usually white or pink and may be scented. These plants are ideal for a mixed shrub border; the peeling bark of certain species also adds to their interest.

CULTIVATION

Most *Deutzia* species are frost hardy, preferring fertile soil, a sheltered position, and sun during the day. Pruning after flowering will maintain a framework of strong branches. Propagate from seed or half-hardened summer cuttings.

ABOVE *A deciduous species from the Himalayas,* Deutzia compacta *has fine branches and pointed dark green leaves. Flowers are white, open quite late, and are carried in small heads.*
RIGHT Deutzia × magnifica *is a hybrid shrub of uncertain parentage. It has strong upright growth with finely toothed leaves that are gray and felt-like beneath. Dense clusters of white flowers appear in early summer.*

Favorites

	Flower Color	Blooming Season	Flower Fragrance	Plant Height	Plant Width	Hardiness Zone	Frost Tolerance
Deutzia compacta	white	early to mid-summer	no	6 ft (1.8 m)	8 ft (2.4 m)	6–9	yes
Deutzia crenata	white	spring	no	8 ft (2.4 m)	5 ft (1.5 m)	6–9	yes
Deutzia gracilis	white	early to mid-summer	yes	3 ft (0.9 m)	3 ft (0.9 m)	4–10	yes
Deutzia × hybrida	pink	early summer	no	5–7 ft (1.5–2 m)	5 ft (1.5 m)	5–9	yes
Deutzia × magnifica	white	early summer	no	7 ft (2 m)	6 ft (1.8 m)	5–9	yes
Deutzia setchuenensis	white	summer	no	7 ft (2 m)	6 ft (1.8 m)	6–9	yes

Top Tip

This graceful and ornamental genus is widely cultivated and is a mainstay of temperate gardens due to its frost-hardy nature. All are suitable for a shrub border or as specimen plants.

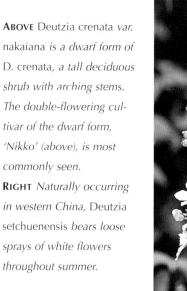

ABOVE Deutzia crenata *var.* nakaiana *is a dwarf form of* D. crenata, *a tall deciduous shrub with arching stems. The double-flowering cultivar of the dwarf form, 'Nikko' (above), is most commonly seen.*
RIGHT *Naturally occurring in western China,* Deutzia setchuenensis *bears loose sprays of white flowers throughout summer.*

DIANTHUS

O ften just simply referred to as pinks, this large genus belongs to the carnation family (Caryophyllaceae). It consists of around 300 species of perennials and a few annuals occurring throughout Europe, Asia, and southern Africa. Their foliage is fairly unremarkable—consisting of mostly small, blue-gray, tufted mounds—but this is more than compensated for by the flowers, which are borne singly or in clusters on wiry flower stems. Hugely popular as cut flowers and garden plants, there are thousands of cultivars whose flowers vary greatly in size, color, and pattern. This centuries-old flower gets its common name of pink from the petal edges, which appear to be cut with pinking shears. The state flower of Ohio is *Dianthus caryophyllus*.

LEFT *Exuding a clove-scented fragrance, Dianthus 'Monica Wyatt' is a Pink type. With fluffy double blooms featuring soft pink petals that have a rose red base, its delicate coloring and texture belie its hardiness.*

CULTIVATION

This genus varies in hardiness and size; most of the species are ideal for rockeries or small perennial borders, others are suitable for alpine troughs. They are best planted in full sun with gritty well-drained soil. Propagate perennials by layering or from cuttings in summer and annuals from seed in autumn.

LEFT Dianthus gratianopolitanus 'Baker's Variety' has grassy foliage and pink single flowers with a wonderful spicy fragrance.
BELOW A member of the Perpetual-flowering Carnations, Dianthus 'Crimson Tempo' produces gorgeous rich red double flowers throughout the year.

RIGHT Dianthus *'Carmine Letitia Wyatt'* produces rich pink, fragrant, semi-double flowers that are deeper pink toward the center. This Pink type can reach a height of up to 10 in (25 cm).

Top Tip

Dianthus plants suit a range of applications from border plantings to ground covers for shady spots. Many can be used for cut flowers, adding color and fragrance indoors.

Favorites	Flower Color	Blooming Season	Flower Fragrance	Plant Height	Plant Width	Hardiness Zone	Frost Tolerance
Dianthus alpinus	deep pink to crimson	summer	no	6 in (15 cm)	4 in (10 cm)	4–9	yes
Dianthus, **Annual Pinks**	white to pink or red, bicolored	late spring to early autumn	no	8–12 in (20–30 cm)	8–12 in (20–30 cm)	7–10	yes
Dianthus barbatus	pink to red, purple, white	late spring to early summer	yes	18–24 in (45–60 cm)	12 in (30 cm)	4–10	yes
Dianthus, **Border Carnations**	white, pink, lemon, purple, bicolored	spring to early summer	yes	18–24 in (45–60 cm)	12 in (30 cm)	6–9	yes
Dianthus carthusianorum	deep pink to purple, white	summer	no	8 in (20 cm)	8 in (20 cm)	3–9	yes
Dianthus caryophyllus	pink, purple, white, bicolored	summer	yes	12–30 in (30–75 cm)	12–15 in (30–38 cm)	8–10	yes
Dianthus deltoides	white, light pink to red	summer	no	6–8 in (15–20 cm)	12 in (30 cm)	3–10	yes
Dianthus gratianopolitanus	dark pink	summer	yes	6–8 in (15–20 cm)	15 in (38 cm)	5–9	yes
Dianthus, **Malmaison Carnations**	white, pink, red	most of year	yes	18–30 in (45–75 cm)	12–18 in (30–45 cm)	9–11	yes
Dianthus pavonius	pale pink to crimson	summer	no	4 in (10 cm)	6–10 in (15–25 cm)	4–9	yes
Dianthus, **Perpetual-flowering Carnations**	white, pink, red, yellow, bicolored	all year	yes	3 ft (0.9 m)	12 in (30 cm)	8–11	yes
Dianthus, **Pinks**	white, pink to crimson	late spring to early autumn	yes	6–18 in (15–45 cm)	18 in (45 cm)	5–10	yes

LEFT Dianthus *'Lemsii'*, with its fragrant pink flowers, is a dwarf Pink. With a spreading habit, this plant forms large carpets of foliage and flowers in summer.

RIGHT *The deep pink buds of* Dianthus *'Valda Wyatt' open to reveal double pink flowers that are somewhat darker at the center. These stunning Pink-type flowers are clove scented.*
BELOW Dianthus *'Delphi' is a Perpetual-flowering Carnation producing full, double, snow white blooms.*

RIGHT *The sweetly fragrant flowers of* Dianthus barbatus *'Auricula-eyed Mixed' come in a wide range of colors and have a well-defined eye.*

BELOW RIGHT *For areas in need of an infusion of color,* Dianthus deltoides *will produce rapid results. Flowers in shades of pink, red, and white, often red-eyed, are borne throughout summer.*

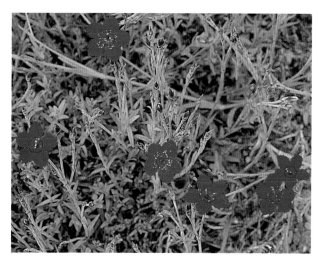

ABOVE *A Perpetual-flowering Carnation,* Dianthus *'Mambo' is very hardy. Providing year-round color, it bears double apricot flowers with subtle tinges of salmon pink.*

DIASCIA

A bout 50 species of annuals and perennials from southern Africa make up this member of the figwort family (Scrophulariaceae). Species are mostly low and spreading, forming a mound of stems with small, serrated-edged, elliptical leaves, though some plants are erect or semi-erect. In summer these mounds are covered with small stalks bearing tiny 5-lobed flowers that are usually pink but also come in colors ranging from red-pink through to pale apricot and even maroon. The name *Diascia* comes from the Greek *di* (two) and *askos* (a sac), which refers to the pair of nectar-containing spurs found at the back of the flower. The plant's common name, twinspur, is also derived from this distinctive structure.

CULTIVATION

This genus is tolerant of light to moderate frosts. They need a sunny position with moist, fertile, well-drained soil. Water well during dry periods. Most species can be propagated from seed as soon as ripe or in early spring.

ABOVE *From summer to autumn, pretty flowers decorate the foliage of* Diascia *'Langthorn's Lavender'.*
BELOW Diascia vigilis *bears an abundance of clear pink flowers with rich maroon centers, flecked with gold.*

Top Tip

These plants are superb in hanging baskets and containers, though they need good drainage. They also make a great impact when planted in the garden in generous drifts of 3 to 5 plants.

ABOVE Diascia 'Twinkle' is rewarding for its lush green foliage and long-blooming pale magenta flowers.

LEFT Diascia 'Little Dancer' is an excellent container plant and is particularly prolific. Its wonderful bright pink flowers almost smother the dense compact foliage beneath.

Favorites	Flower Color	Blooming Season	Flower Fragrance	Plant Height	Plant Width	Hardiness Zone	Frost Tolerance
Diascia fetcaniensis	rose pink	summer to early autumn	no	12 in (30 cm)	20 in (50 cm)	8–10	yes
Diascia integerrima	purple-pink	summer	no	18 in (45 cm)	3–4 ft (0.9–1.2 m)	8–10	yes
Diascia 'Langthorn's Lavender'	lavender	summer to autumn	no	12 in (30 cm)	12 in (30 cm)	8–10	yes
Diascia 'Little Dancer'	bright pink	summer to autumn	no	8 in (20 cm)	8 in (20 cm)	8–10	yes
Diascia 'Twinkle'	dusky pink	summer to autumn	no	18 in (45 cm)	18 in (45 cm)	8–10	yes
Diascia vigilis	pink	summer to early winter	no	20 in (50 cm)	24 in (60 cm)	8–10	yes

DICENTRA

This genus of 19 species of annuals and perennials is a member of the poppy family (Papaveraceae). Naturally occurring across temperate Asian and North American habitats, it is commonly referred to as bleeding heart—a reference to the shape and color of its pendulous flowers. Apart from red and purple, flowers occur in shades of white, pink, and yellow, hanging gracefully from upright or slightly arching stems. This clump-forming genus has gray-green to blue-green fern-like foliage. Many species have unusually shaped flowers that lend themselves to a wide variety of common names such as lady's locket and Dutchman's breeches. The slightly ominous name, stagger weed, refers to the effect the foliage has on animals that graze on the plant.

CULTIVATION

Dicentra species thrive in a climate with clearly defined seasons and are happiest in cool, moist, humus-rich soil and dappled sunlight. Propagate from seed in autumn or by division in late winter.

ABOVE *The finely arching stems of Dicentra formosa 'Aurora' bear creamy yellow flowers above attractive blue-green foliage.*
LEFT *Dicentra 'Bacchanal' makes a glorious bushy addition to a perennial border. Pendulous burgundy flowers hang above ferny bright green foliage.*

Top Tip

Dicentra plants usually flower throughout spring and early summer. Ample watering will encourage a longer-lasting display of the attractive lacy foliage.

ABOVE Dicentra spectabilis *'Alba' produces pure white flowers and softly shaded green leaves.*

BELOW *Clearly demonstrating why this genus is called bleeding heart, the flowers of* Dicentra spectabilis *hang gracefully in a row. The outer petals are a rich pink, and the inner petals are white.*

Favorites	Flower Color	Blooming Season	Flower Fragrance	Plant Height	Plant Width	Hardiness Zone	Frost Tolerance
Dicentra 'Bacchanal'	burgundy	mid- to late spring	no	18 in (45 cm)	24 in (60 cm)	3–9	yes
Dicentra eximia	light to dark pink, white	summer to early autumn	no	18–24 in (45–60 cm)	18 in (45 cm)	4–8	yes
Dicentra formosa	pink to red	spring and summer	no	18 in (45 cm)	36 in (90 cm)	3–9	yes
Dicentra 'Langtrees'	white tinged with pink	mid-spring to mid-summer	no	12 in (30 cm)	18 in (45 cm)	3–9	yes
Dicentra scandens	yellow, white	summer	no	12 ft (3.5 m)	24 in (60 cm)	4–9	yes
Dicentra spectabilis	rose pink and white	late spring to summer	no	24–36 in (60–90 cm)	18–24 in (45–60 cm)	2–9	yes

ABOVE *The cylindrical nodding flowers of* Digitalis obscura *vary from yellow to reddish brown to faded orange, and are often spotted red inside.*

DIGITALIS

This genus consists of around 20 species of biennials and perennials from North Africa, Europe, and Central Asia, and is a member of the figwort family (Scrophulariaceae). They are mainly clump-forming plants with whorls of simple, smooth-edged, mid-green leaves that decrease in size as they grow up the erect flower spike. These branching stems bear pure white, pink, and sometimes yellow flowers throughout spring and summer, which are instantly recognizable by their hanging, 2-lipped, tubular bell shape. The common name foxglove refers to the curious shape of the flowers, which are thought to look a little like finger gloves. The medicinal properties of this genus have been appreciated since ancient times, and it is still used in the treatment of heart ailments.

CULTIVATION

Digitalis species are easily grown in moist humus-rich soil. Most thrive in woodland conditions but are also suitable for open borders. Cut flowering stems down to the ground when flowering has finished to encourage the growth of new flower spikes. Propagate from seed in autumn or by division.

ABOVE RIGHT *The softly shaded yellow flowers of* Digitalis ciliata *attract bees, birds, and butterflies to the garden. It is also suitable for indoor cultivation.*

LEFT Digitalis grandiflora *is a short-lived perennial that bears pale lemon yellow flowers, etched inside with fine brown lines. Leaves are rich green and veined.*

Top Tip

Digitalis species are widely appreciated for their tall spikes of vibrantly colored flowers; remove dead flowers to encourage a secondary flush of blooms.

BELOW *Throughout early summer the tall flowering spikes of Digitalis parviflora are covered in a mass of red-brown flowers, veined with violet, each with a purple-brown lip.*

Favorites	Flower Color	Blooming Season	Flower Fragrance	Plant Height	Plant Width	Hardiness Zone	Frost Tolerance
Digitalis ciliata	cream to pale yellow	late spring to early summer	no	18 in (45 cm)	18 in (45 cm)	6–10	yes
Digitalis ferruginea	golden brown; red-brown veins	summer	no	4 ft (1.2 m)	18 in (45 cm)	7–10	yes
Digitalis grandiflora	lemon yellow	early to mid-summer	no	3 ft (0.9 m)	18 in (45 cm)	4–9	yes
Digitalis obscura	yellow to brown	late spring to mid-summer	no	12–24 in (30–60 cm)	18 in (45 cm)	4–8	yes
Digitalis parviflora	red-brown	early summer	no	24 in (60 cm)	12 in (30 cm)	4–9	yes
Digitalis purpurea	purple, pink, white, yellow	summer	no	3–6 ft (0.9–1.8 m)	24 in (60 cm)	5–10	yes

ECHINACEA

Naturally occurring in the eastern U.S.A. and closely allied to *Rudbeckia*, this genus of 9 species belongs to the daisy family (Asteraceae). Commonly known as coneflowers, these strongly upright shrubby perennials develop quickly in spring to be in full flower by summer. Their simple leaves are a typical pointed lance shape, but their flowers are distinctive, having a dome-like central cone and large drooping ray florets that are usually purple-pink. Among the earliest American genera to enter European cultivation, arriving in 1640, *Echinacea* is extensively used in herbal medicines, probably more so than any other genus. It is thought to boost the immune system and is a popular cold preventative.

CULTIVATION

Very hardy and adaptable plants, they do best in full sun in well-drained soil that remains moist during the growing season. *Echinacea* plants can grow quite tall and may need staking in exposed positions. Propagate from seed, from root cuttings, or by division.

Top Tip

Echinaceas do not take well to disruption. If you must divide to increase your stock, do so very carefully, retaining the shoots. Fertile soil and mulching are also recommended.

ABOVE Echinacea purpurea *'Magnus' is an especially pretty cultivar, with large pinkish purple flowers that have bold orange-red centers. The blooms are well-suited for use in a vase on their own or in a mixed flower arrangement.*

RIGHT Echinacea angusti-folia *has narrow pale pink or purple ray florets surrounding a high brown cone. Its leaves are hairy and linear. The plant is considered to be an aphrodisiac.*

ABOVE Echinacea purpurea *is the most popular of all the* Echinacea *species, and is commonly known as the purple coneflower. It has lance-shaped leaves, and its pink-purple blooms make good cut flowers.*

RIGHT *'White Swan' is one of several* Echinacea purpurea *cultivars. It looks lovely in a border, a meadow, or as a cut flower, as its fragrant, white, daisy-like blooms have a contrasting green to coppery orange center.*

Favorites	Flower Color	Blooming Season	Flower Fragrance	Plant Height	Plant Width	Hardiness Zone	Frost Tolerance
Echinacea angustifolia	purple or pink	summer	no	5 ft (1.5 m)	18 in (45 cm)	4–9	yes
Echinacea pallida	purple	summer	no	4 ft (1.2 m)	24 in (60 cm)	5–9	yes
Echinacea purpurea	pinkish purple	summer	no	2–4 ft (0.6–1.2 m)	24 in (60 cm)	3–10	yes
Echinacea purpurea 'Magnus'	deep pink-purple	summer	no	24–36 in (60–90 m)	24 in (60 cm)	3–10	yes
Echinacea purpurea 'White Lustre'	white	summer	no	18–30 in (45–75 cm)	24 in (60 cm)	3–10	yes
Echinacea purpurea 'White Swan'	white	summer	yes	18–24 in (45–60 cm)	18 in (45 cm)	3–10	yes

Top Tip

Extremely hardy and robust, *Echinocereus* species are well suited to the testing conditions of a desert garden, and are equally at home in a greenhouse collection.

ECHINOCEREUS

This group of around 60 species of cacti is found from the southern areas of the U.S.A. to central Mexico. They vary considerably in size and growth habit, many with pronounced ribs, spiny stems, and green stamens, and most producing lateral branches and flowers that emerge through the epidermis. Spines vary from almost absent to very fierce; some are highly colored and comb-shaped. Many have large, funnel-shaped, diurnal flowers in bold shades of purple, red, orange, and yellow. The edible fleshy fruits that follow are spherical to egg-shaped, green or red, splitting open vertically to reveal black or brown seeds. The genus name comes from the Latin *echinos* (hedgehog) and *cereus* (candle), referring to the spiny fruit.

CULTIVATION

Grow these plants in a rich well-drained soil in full sun to half shade. Withhold watering during winter, although occasional misting may be required. Some species require low temperatures or frost to flower. Propagate from seed germinated under glass until seedlings start to grow, and then replant in small pots. Cuttings of some species may be rooted in sand.

RIGHT *During the flowering season of* Echinocereus coccineus, *bright orange-red flowers are produced that open during daylight hours.*
BELOW *Small spines in shades of red, white, and brown add textural color to the ribbed stems of* Echinocereus rigidissimus.

Favorites	Flower Color	Blooming Season	Flow Fragra
Echinocereus coccineus	scarlet, yellow at center	spring to summer	no
Echinocereus engelmannii	lavender to purple-red	summer	no
Echinocereus reichenbachii	pink to purple	spring to summer	n
Echinocereus rigidissimus	pink-red to magenta	summer	n
Echinocereus triglochidiatus	scarlet	spring to summer	n
Echinocereus viridiflorus	green	spring	y

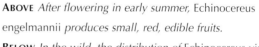

ABOVE *After flowering in early summer,* Echinocereus engelmannii *produces small, red, edible fruits.*

BELOW *In the wild, the distribution of* Echinocereus viridi-florus *subsp.* davisii *is confined to a small area of Texas; in cultivation, it makes a great pot plant for a desert garden.*

Plant Height	Plant Width	Hardiness Zone	Frost Tolerance
3 in (8 cm)	4 in (10 cm)	6–11	yes
10–18 in (25–45 cm)	10–24 in (25–60 cm)	8–11	yes
8 in (20 cm)	4 in (10 cm)	8–11	yes
2–12 in (5–30 cm)	2–5 in (5–12 cm)	8–11	yes
6–12 in (5–30 cm)	18–36 in (45–90 cm)	8–11	yes
1–4 in (.5–10 cm)	1–3 in (2.5–8 cm)	4–10	yes

ECHINOPS

Commonly known as globe thistle, this mainly Eurasian genus of 120-odd annuals and perennials belongs to the daisy family (Asteraceae). The popular *Echinops ritro* has been in cultivation for over 400 years and was a favorite with the Victorians both as a garden plant and for its dried flowers. *Echinops* species grow strongly from early spring, producing a basal clump of silver-gray to almost steel blue leaves that may be simple or featherlike, and are usually spine-tipped at the lobes. The round flowerheads are usually metallic purple-blue; they are without ray florets, but are enclosed in similarly colored bracts. *Echinops* is from the Greek meaning "like a hedgehog," which is an apt description for the spiky flowerheads.

CULTIVATION

Hardiness varies, but most species are frost tolerant. They will also withstand summer heat but prefer not to dry out. Moist, humus-rich, well-drained soil is best. Deadhead the flowers frequently to prolong flowering. Cut plants back to ground level in autumn or early winter. Propagate by division when dormant, or raise from seed.

Top Tip

Echinops plants will thrive on neglect, and can be used in herbaceous borders or meadow gardens. They are also suitable for cutting and in dried flower arrangements.

ABOVE RIGHT Echinops ritro *'Blue Glow' is a sturdy cultivar with light blue flowers. If you plan to dry out the flowers, cut them before the pollen appears.*
RIGHT Echinops sphaerocephalus *is a tall plant with large silvery gray flowerheads. Its gray-green leaves are long and jagged, with hairy undersides.*

ABOVE RIGHT *The globose flowerheads of Echinops ritro start off as metallic blue, then age to purple-blue. The plant's leaves are stiff and spiny.*

RIGHT *Echinops bannaticus 'Taplow Blue' has bright blue-purple flowers, whereas the flowers of the species are pale blue-gray. The stems are gray and woolly.*

Favorites	Flower Color	Blooming Season	Flower Fragrance	Plant Height	Plant Width	Hardiness Zone	Frost Tolerance
Echinops bannaticus	blue-gray to blue	mid- to late summer	no	4 ft (1.2 m)	24 in (60 cm)	3–9	yes
Echinops bannaticus 'Taplow Blue'	blue-purple	mid- to late summer	no	4 ft (1.2 m)	24 in (60 cm)	3–9	yes
Echinops ritro	blue to purplish blue	summer	no	36 in (90 cm)	36 in (90 cm)	3–9	yes
Echinops ritro 'Blue Glow'	light blue	summer	no	36 in (90 cm)	18 in (45 cm)	3–9	yes
Echinops sphaerocephalus	gray	mid- to late summer	no	6 ft (1.8 m)	3 ft (0.9 m)	3–9	yes
Echinops sphaerocephalus 'Arctic Glow'	white	mid- to late summer	no	30 in (75 cm)	18 in (45 cm)	3–9	yes

ECHIUM

Spread throughout the Mediterranean and nearby Atlantic islands, this borage family (Boraginaceae) genus of 40 species of biennials, perennials, and shrubs includes several spectacular flowering plants. All have hairy leaves, usually a simple elongated lance-shape, and often in basal rosettes. Some plants are small and bushy, some form clumps of rosettes with tall flower stems, and others are woody shrubs with conical flower spikes. The flowers are small, 5-petalled, usually purple-blue, and heavily massed to produce an intense burst of color. Several *Echium* species have been used medicinally, and viper's bugloss *(Echium vulgare)* was once considered a cure for snakebite, though it is now better known for the honey made from its nectar.

ABOVE *Native to the Canary Islands,* Echium pininana *flowers during its second year, producing tiny blue-toned flowers on tall spikes up to 12 ft (3.5 m) high.*

CULTIVATION

Of variable hardiness, most species require a bright sunny position with light, gritty, well-drained soil that remains moist during the flowering season. Propagation is by division, from basal cuttings, or from seed, depending on the growth form. Some species self-sow readily in milder climates, so pruning of the old flower spikes is recommended.

Favorites	Flower Color	Blooming Season	Flower Fragrance	Plant Height	Plant Width	Hardiness Zone	Frost Tolerance
Echium amoenum	purple-red	spring to summer	no	6 in (15 cm)	6 in (15 cm)	7–9	yes
Echium candicans	purplish blue	spring to summer	no	4–7 ft (1.2–2 m)	6–10 ft (1.8–3 m)	9–10	no
Echium pininana	blue to lavender blue	mid- to late summer	no	8–12 ft (2.4–3.5 m)	3 ft (0.9 m)	9–10	yes
Echium plantagineum	red to blue-purple	late spring to summer	no	24 in (60 cm)	12 in (30 cm)	9–10	yes
Echium vulgare	blue, white, pink, purple	summer	no	24–36 in (60–90 cm)	12 in (30 cm)	7–10	yes
Echium wildpretii	red to purple	spring to summer	no	6 ft (1.8 m)	12 in (30 cm)	9–10	no

ABOVE Echium vulgare *'Blue Bedder'* is an excellent choice for the seaside garden or border planting.
LEFT *Native to Madeira,* Echium candicans *bears tall spikes covered with masses of tiny blue-purple flowers.*

Top Tip

Ideally suited to use in the garden border setting, *Echium* species flower reliably, tolerate a range of soil types, and require minimal pruning to keep in good order.

LEFT *Initially forming a rosette of narrow leaves,* Echium wildpretii *flowers during its second year. Tall spikes bear masses of rose to coral red flowers, earning this species its common name—tower of jewels.*

EPIMEDIUM

Variously known as barrenwort or bishop's hat, this genus of 25 species of rhizome-rooted herbaceous perennials is found from southern Europe to Japan. The leaves, which are roughly heart-shaped with shallowly lobed or toothed edges, are sometimes evergreen in mild climates but are usually deciduous and may color well in autumn. Sprays of small, dainty, 4-petalled flowers appear in spring as the new leaves expand. The flowers may be white, yellow, pink, or red, depending on the species, and may continue into early summer. *Epimedium* extracts, sometimes known as "Yang tonics," are used extensively in traditional Chinese medicines and are also found in commercially available herbal pick-me-ups.

CULTIVATION

Very hardy and suitable as ground covers for woodland situations, in rockeries, or perennial borders, these tough little plants are easily grown in partial shade in fertile, moist, humus-rich, well-drained soil. Propagate by division in late winter just as the new growth appears, or raise from seed.

TOP *Easy-to-grow Epimedium × versicolor is perfect for adding color to shady spots in the garden.*
ABOVE *The dainty flowers of Epimedium acuminatum are held on stems above the heart-shaped leaflets.*

Top Tip

Though relatively slow-growing, *Epimedium* species do well in shady spots, and are ideal for planting under trees. They are equally happy in containers, and are a versatile addition to the small garden.

RIGHT *Similar to the species but producing larger flowers, slow-growing* Epimedium pinnatum *subsp.* colchicum *spreads to create a mat of color. Bright yellow blooms appear among the dark green leaves during the spring flowering season.*

Favorites	Flower Color	Blooming Season	Flower Fragrance	Plant Height	Plant Width	Hardiness Zone	Frost Tolerance
Epimedium acuminatum	purple and pale pink	mid-spring to early summer	no	12 in (30 cm)	18 in (45 cm)	7–9	yes
Epimedium grandiflorum	white, pink, violet, yellow	spring	no	8–12 in (20–30 cm)	12 in (30 cm)	4–9	yes
Epimedium × perralchicum	bright yellow	spring	no	15 in (38 cm)	24 in (60 cm)	6–9	yes
Epimedium pinnatum	yellow; purple-brown spurs	late spring to early summer	no	8–12 in (20–30 cm)	8–12 in (20–30 cm)	6–9	yes
Epimedium platypetalum	yellow	spring	no	6 in (15 cm)	8 in (20 cm)	6–9	yes
Epimedium × versicolor	yellow and pink with red spurs	spring	no	12 in (30 cm)	12 in (30 cm)	5–9	yes

LEFT *Delicate yellow flowers are held above the heart-shaped leaves of* Epimedium platypetalum *in spring. During autumn, the leaves take on purplish tones, ensuring that the plant adds color and interest to the garden throughout the year.*

Top Tip

Prudent selection of ericas can ensure year-round color in the garden. There are varieties available that flower in each season of the year.

ERICA

This genus in the family Ericaceae includes around 750 species of evergreen shrubs ranging in form from small subshrubs to trees that are widely distributed from Madagascar, Africa, and the Atlantic Islands to the Middle East and Europe. Its habitat includes wet and dry heathland and moorland—hence the common name of heath. Most of the plants are frost tender except for the European species, which are generally tolerant of frost. The small needle-like leaves are linear with rolled edges, whorled, and rarely opposite. Flowers are bell-shaped or tubular, and the predominant colors are shades of pink and white, but all colors occur, except blue. Some species yield a yellow dye. The majority are cultivated for ornamental use in gardens.

CULTIVATION

Ericas prefer full sun or partial shade. The winter-growing heaths are lime tolerant and will grow in alkaline soil, while the summer-flowering ones like acid soil; both types can be grown in neutral soil. Propagate by taking half-hardened cuttings in mid- to late summer, or by layering in spring.

ABOVE Erica vagans *'Mrs. D. F. Maxwell' is a popular shrub, noted for its dense coverage of flowers.*
BELOW *With a broad bushy habit,* Erica × darleyensis *is a tough reliable shrub that is tolerant of climatic variations.*

Favorites

Favorites	Flower Color	Blooming Season	Flow Fragr
Erica canaliculata	pale pink	winter to early spring	n
Erica carnea	purple-pink	winter to spring	n
Erica cinerea	white, purple, pink	summer to early autumn	n
Erica × darleyensis	white to pink	late winter to early spring	n
Erica lusitanica	white	winter to spring	y
Erica vagans	white to mauve-pink	mid-summer to mid-autumn	r

ABOVE *The vibrantly hued flowers of* Erica cinerea *f. alba 'Hardwick's Rose' provide a burst of color in the garden.*

RIGHT *From late winter to early spring,* Erica carnea *'Pink Spangles' bears masses of deep pink flowers.*

Plant Height	Plant Width	Hardiness Zone	Frost Tolerance
6 ft (1.8 m)	4 ft (1.2 m)	8–10	no
12 in (30 cm)	22 in (55 cm)	5–9	yes
24 in (60 cm)	30 in (75 cm)	5–9	yes
24 in (60 cm)	24 in (60 cm)	6–9	yes
10 ft (3 m)	3 ft (0.9 m)	8–10	yes
30 in (75 cm)	30 in (75 cm)	5–9	yes

ERYNGIUM

This genus derives its name from a Greek word meaning thistle, and indeed many of its 230-odd species of annuals, biennials, and perennials are thistle-like, though they belong in the carrot family (Umbelliferae), not among the composites. While they are widely distributed, most of the cultivated species—which are commonly known as sea holly—come from Eurasia and North and South America. The leaves are often lance-shaped or featherlike, and edged with spine-tipped teeth. Strong flower stems, usually branching at the top, carry hemispherical heads of minute flowers backed by spiny bracts that give the head much of its color, often a metallic silver-blue. The roots have long been used medicinally and appear to have anti-inflammatory properties.

RIGHT *The blue-mauve flowerheads of* Eryngium *'Jos Eijking' are surrounded by narrow silvery green bracts tinged at the base with purple tones.*

CULTIVATION

Hardiness varies with the species. Plant in a sunny position in light very well-drained soil, otherwise roots will rot during the winter months. Water well when growing, but otherwise allow to dry off. Propagate species from seed and selected forms from root cuttings or by division in spring.

RIGHT *Commonly known as Miss Willmott's ghost,* Eryngium giganteum *has green or blue cone-shaped flowerheads surrounded by large, silvery, snowflake-shaped bracts.*

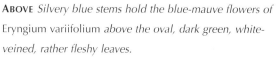

ABOVE *Silvery blue stems hold the blue-mauve flowers of Eryngium variifolium above the oval, dark green, white-veined, rather fleshy leaves.*

RIGHT *As its name indicates, the flowerheads of* Eryngium amethystinum *are indeed a lovely amethyst color. Delicate silvery green bracts form a collar around the flowerheads.*

Favorites

	Flower Color	Blooming Season	Flower Fragrance	Plant Height	Plant Width	Hardiness Zone	Frost Tolerance
Eryngium alpinum	gray-blue to white	mid-summer to early autumn	no	30 in (75 cm)	18 in (45 cm)	3–9	yes
Eryngium amethystinum	gray-blue to amethyst	mid- to late summer	no	30 in (75 cm)	30 in (75 cm)	7–10	yes
Eryngium giganteum	pale green to blue	summer	no	3–4 ft (0.9–1.2 m)	30 in (75 cm)	6–9	yes
Eryngium 'Jos Eijking'	mauve-blue	summer	no	24 in (60 cm)	18 in (45 cm)	5–9	yes
Eryngium planum	blue	summer	no	36 in (90 cm)	18 in (45 cm)	5–9	yes
Eryngium variifolium	blue-gray to mauve	summer	no	18 in (45 cm)	10 in (25 cm)	7–10	yes

Favorites	Flower Color	Blooming Season	Flower Fragrance
Erysimum bonannianum	lemon yellow	late spring to early winter	yes
Erysimum 'Bowles' Mauve'	bright mauve	late winter to summer	no
Erysimum 'Gold Shot'	golden yellow	late spring	yes
Erysimum kotschyanum	yellow to orange-yellow	summer	yes
Erysimum 'Sunlight'	bright yellow	early summer	no
Erysimum 'Wenlock Beauty'	mauve and yellow	early to late spring	no

ERYSIMUM

Formerly listed under *Cheiranthus*, this genus consists of 80 or so annuals, perennials, and subshrubs. *Erysimum* species are found mainly in Europe, western Asia, and western North America, and are popularly known as wallflowers. They have simple narrow leaves, are mainly evergreen, and range from rockery dwarfs to medium-sized shrubs. Flower stems, tall in the larger species, appear mainly over spring and summer, and also in winter in mild climates. The heads carry dense clusters of small 4-petalled blooms that are often richly fragrant. The petals are usually yellow but may also be orange, red, or mauve. The old genus name, *Cheiranthus*, meaning "hand-flower," refers to the custom dating to the Middle Ages when the sweetly scented flowers were often carried in the hand at festivals and events.

CULTIVATION

Wallflowers like cool summers and mild winters. Plant in a sunny open position in moist well-drained soil. If perennials become woody they should be cut back hard. Annuals are raised from seed; perennials are propagated from cuttings of non-flowering stems.

ABOVE LEFT *Low-growing* Erysimum kotschyanum *is native to Turkey. Throughout the flowering season, bright golden yellow flowers appear among the densely clustered dull green leaves.*

ABOVE *In favorable climates* Erysimum 'Bowles' Mauve' *can flower throughout the year. Appearing among the gray-green leaves, the dark purple-black buds open to reveal bright mauve flower*

Plant Height	Plant Width	Hardiness Zone	Frost Tolerance
6–12 in (15–30 cm)	12 in (30 cm)	8–10	yes
30 in (75 cm)	4 ft (1.2 m)	6–11	yes
18 in (45 cm)	12 in (30 cm)	5–8	no
4 in (10 cm)	10 in (25 cm)	6–9	yes
3–4 in (8–10 cm)	18 in (45 cm)	6–9	yes
18 in (45 cm)	18 in (45 cm)	5–8	yes

RIGHT Erysimum *'Gold Shot' has clusters of fragrant golden yellow flowers and mid-green leaves. This charming sun-loving plant is an ideal choice for rockery, border, or container planting.*

Top Tip

Choose evergreen long-flowering wallflowers for container planting. The container can be moved around the garden wherever color and/or fragrance is needed.

RIGHT *Endemic to Sicily and its surrounding islands, Erysimum bonannianum prefers rocky terrain. This species bears clusters of lemon yellow flowers that carry a mild fragrance.*

Favorites	Flower Color	Blooming Season	Flower Fragrance
Eschscholzia caespitosa	bright yellow	summer	yes
Eschscholzia caespitosa 'Sundew'	light yellow	summer	yes
Eschscholzia californica	yellow to orange-red	spring to autumn	no
Eschscholzia californica 'Purple Gleam'	violet-purple	spring to autumn	no
Eschscholzia lobbii	yellow	spring	no
Eschscholzia mexicana	yellow with orange center	late winter to spring	no

ABOVE *The lovely clear yellow flowers of* Eschscholzia lobbii *are followed by fruit with rough seeds. These charming flowers close up in overcast weather.*

RIGHT *A brilliant scarlet when they first bloom, the open single flowers of* Eschscholzia californica *'Single Red' gradually turn a vibrant orange-red.*

Top Tip

Undemanding annuals, these plants are ideal for filling large areas of ground with color. They require little care and reward with colorful blooms.

ESCHSCHOLZIA

Native to western North America and now widely naturalized, this poppy family (Papaveraceae) genus is made up of around 8 annuals and short-lived perennials. Commonly known as California poppies, they have fine feathery foliage, which is often a rather grayish green, and in summer produce masses of bright, golden yellow, 4- to 8-petalled blooms that only open on sunny days. Modern seed strains flower in a wide color range. Long seed capsules follow. The genus was named in 1820 after Johann Friedrich Eschscholz (1793–1831), leader of the Russian expedition on which it was first collected in 1816. The seeds were among the many taken to England by the Scottish botanist David Douglas.

CULTIVATION

Very easily grown in any sunny position in light, gritty, well-drained soil, *Eschscholzia* species often self-sow and naturalize, especially in gravel riverbeds. Most are very frost hardy and tolerate poor soil. Deadhead regularly to prolong flowering. Raise from seed in spring, which is best sown directly where the plants are to grow as they do not transplant well.

Plant Height	Plant Width	Hardiness Zone	Frost Tolerance
6 in (15 cm)	6 in (15 cm)	7–10	yes
6 in (15 cm)	6 in (15 cm)	7–10	yes
8–12 in (20–30 cm)	12 in (30 cm)	6–11	yes
8–12 in (20–30 cm)	12 in (30 cm)	6–11	yes
4–8 in (10–20 cm)	8 in (20 cm)	7–10	yes
8 in (20 cm)	8 in (20 cm)	7–11	yes

BELOW Eschscholzia californica, *the state flower of California, produces lovely cup-shaped flowers in bright shades of orange and yellow over a long flowering season.*

EUCALYPTUS

Most of the approximately 700 species in this genus of evergreen trees are native to Australia. They belong to the myrtle family, noted for its aromatic leaves. Eucalypts range in size from immense, single-trunk, forest trees to the small multi-stemmed shrubs called mallees. Various distinctive bark types have given rise to many common names such as gums, boxes, stringybarks, and ironbarks. The eucalypt flower bud has an enlarged floral receptacle and a cap, which covers numerous stamens and is shed when the flower opens. The many fluffy stamens may be white, cream, yellow, pink, or red. Eucalypts are adaptable to a wide range of climatic conditions and are cultivated in many parts of the world.

CULTIVATION

Most species are fast growing and long lived, and once established require little artificial watering or fertilizer. They are best suited to warm-temperate or semi-arid regions. Frost hardiness varies, as do requirements for moist or dry conditions. Propagate from seed, which germinates readily.

Top Tip

Pruning is not essential, though many *Eucalyptus* species can be cut back and shaped if desired.

LEFT Eucalyptus woodwardii thrives in hot dry climate areas with a low summer rainfall. It is a tall upright tree with smooth gray bark.

ABOVE Eucalyptus cinerea has ornamental juvenile foliage that is silvery gray. **LEFT** The tallowwood (Eucalyptus microcorys) is an excellent hardwood tree. **ABOVE LEFT** Eucalyptus leucoxylon has pink- and red-flowered forms that are sold under the name 'Rosea'.

Favorites

	Flower Color	Blooming Season	Flower Fragrance	Plant Height	Plant Width	Hardiness Zone	Frost Tolerance
Eucalyptus cinerea	creamy white	summer	no	30–50 ft (9–15 m)	20–30 ft (6–9 m)	8–10	yes
Eucalyptus gunnii	creamy white	summer	no	30–80 ft (9–24 m)	20–30 ft (6–9 m)	7–9	yes
Eucalyptus leucoxylon	white, cream, pink, red	autumn to spring	no	30–60 ft (9–18 m)	20–30 ft (6–9 m)	9–11	no
Eucalyptus microcorys	creamy white	summer	no	60–100 ft (18–30 m)	20–40 ft (6–12 m)	10–12	no
Eucalyptus pauciflora	white to cream	spring to summer	no	30–60 ft (9–18 m)	15–30 ft (4.5–9 m)	7–9	yes
Eucalyptus woodwardii	lemon yellow	winter to spring	no	20–50 ft (6–15 m)	15–30 ft (4.5–9 m)	9–11	no

EUCOMIS

This mainly South African genus, which is made up of 15 species of bulbs, is classified in the hyacinth family (Hyacinthaceae). The species have glossy, light green, strappy leaves and form large clumps of basal foliage rosettes. In summer they produce long stems bearing simple, star-shaped, mostly green to white flowers with an interesting tuft of foliage at the top, rather like that atop a pineapple—hence they are commonly known as pineapple lilies. (As well, the genus name comes from the Greek *eukomos,* which means lovely haired.) The flower stems are often arching and may fall over under their own weight. They make attractive cut decorations and last for weeks in water. The bulbs are edible and were used as a food source by tribespeople in Africa.

CULTIVATION

Of variable hardiness, the most commonly cultivated species in this genus are reasonably tough. In frosty areas they can be safely stored for winter indoors as dormant bulbs in moist soil. Plant out in full sun in moist, humus-rich, well-drained soil. Propagation is usually by division, but *Eucomis* species can be raised from seed and may self-sow.

ABOVE *The summer display of purple-edged greenish flowers of* Eucomis bicolor *is followed by bright green fruits. A crown of light green bracts tops the flower stem.*

Top Tip

Use *Eucomis* species indoors as a potted plant to create an interesting focal point. If repotted each year, they will thrive and flower for years.

ABOVE *Beneath the tuft of mid-green bracts, this* Eucomis comosa *hybrid bears creamy white flowers on tall purple-spotted stems*

LEFT *Emerging from rosette of strappy leaves, the stems of* Eucomis zambesiaca *are covered with masses of white flowers and topped by bright green bracts.*

ABOVE *Greenish white flowers add tonal and textural contrast to the fresh bright green of the strappy leaves, thick stems, and rosette of stem-top bracts of* Eucomis autumnalis.

Favorites	Flower Color	Blooming Season	Flower Fragrance	Plant Height	Plant Width	Hardiness Zone	Frost Tolerance
Eucomis autumnalis	greenish white to green	summer to autumn	no	18–30 in (45–75 cm)	24 in (60 cm)	7–10	yes
Eucomis bicolor	green, edged with purple	summer	no	15–24 in (38–60 cm)	18 in (45 cm)	8–10	yes
Eucomis comosa	greenish white; purple markings	late summer to autumn	no	30–36 in (75–90 cm)	30 in (75 cm)	8–11	yes
Eucomis **'Sparkling Burgundy'**	pale green to pale purple	mid- to late summer	no	18–24 in (45–60 cm)	18 in (45 cm)	7–10	yes
Eucomis pallidiflora	greenish white	summer	no	18–30 in (45–75 cm)	30 in (75 cm)	8–10	yes
Eucomis zambesiaca	white	late summer	no	12–18 in (30–45 cm)	15 in (38 cm)	8–10	yes

EUPHORBIA

This large genus of around 2,000 species of annuals, perennials, shrubs, and trees, both evergreen and deciduous, is distributed throughout the world. It covers a diverse range of forms and natural habitats, from the spiny and succulent cactuslike species of hot dry areas to leafy perennials from cooler temperate climates. The true flowers, borne singly or in clusters, are very small and insignificant, but are often accompanied by long-lasting, colorful, petallike bracts. All species contain a poisonous milky sap that can cause severe skin irritation and, sometimes, temporary blindness on contact with the eyes. The purgative qualities of the sap are acknowledged in the common name spurge, from the Latin word *expurgare*, meaning to purge.

CULTIVATION

The diversity of form makes it difficult to generalize cultivation requirements. Consider the plant's natural habitat, and provide similar growing conditions. Because of the toxicity of the sap, care should always be taken when handling these plants. Some species are propagated from seed or by division, while others grow from stem-tip cuttings.

Favorites	Flower Color	Blooming Season	Flower Fragrance	Plant Height	Plant Width	Hardiness Zone	Frost Tolerance
Euphorbia amygdaloides	greenish yellow	mid-spring to early summer	no	30–36 in (75–90 cm)	12 in (30 cm)	7–9	yes
Euphorbia characias	greenish yellow	spring	no	4 ft (1.2 m)	4 ft (1.2 m)	8–10	yes
Euphorbia cyparissias	yellow-green	late spring to early summer	no	8–15 in (20–38 cm)	8–12 in (20–30 cm)	4–9	yes
Euphorbia griffithii	orange to red	summer	no	36 in (90 cm)	36 in (90 cm)	5–10	yes
Euphorbia keithii	yellow to green	spring to summer	no	6–20 ft (1.8–6 m)	5–8 ft (1.5–2.4 m)	9–11	no
Euphorbia marginata	green and white	late summer to autumn	no	12–36 in (30–90 cm)	24 in (60 cm)	7–11	yes
Euphorbia × *martinii*	yellow-green; dark red center	spring to mid-summer	no	36 in (90 cm)	36 in (90 cm)	7–10	yes
Euphorbia milii	scarlet, crimson, yellow	most of the year	no	12–24 in (30–60 cm)	36 in (90 cm)	10–11	no
Euphorbia myrsinites	yellow-green	spring to summer	no	4–8 in (10–20 cm)	12 in (30 cm)	5–9	yes
Euphorbia myrsinites subsp. *pontica*	yellow-green tinged with red	spring	no	4–8 in (10–20 cm)	12 in (30 cm)	5–9	yes
Euphorbia nicaeensis	yellow to greenish yellow	late spring to mid-summer	no	30 in (75 cm)	18 in (45 cm)	5–8	yes
Euphorbia pulcherrima	bright red bracts, yellowish flowers	winter to early spring	no	10 ft (3 m)	10 ft (3 m)	10–11	no

LEFT Euphorbia myrsinites *subsp.* pontica *is a good rock-garden plant requiring light well-drained soil.*
RIGHT *Oval-shaped, blue-green, succulent leaves are one of the best features of* Euphorbia myrsinites, *along with its whorls of bracts.*

Top Tip

One of the most popular *Euphorbia* species is the poinsettia from Mexico (*E. pulcherrima*), which needs fertile soil and plenty of sunshine to grow successfully.

BOVE Euphorbia × martinii, *which bears distinctive chareuse flowerheads, is best planted in a sheltered spot.*
GHT *Bright orange bracts and small yellow flowers give e cultivar* Euphorbia griffithii *'Fireglow' its name.*

ABOVE Euphorbia characias *will readily self-seed if it is planted in a well-drained site where it receives plenty of sunshine. It is native to the Mediterranean region.*

BELOW *Commonly known as ghostweed,* Euphorbia marginata *has eye-catching white and green bracts. This fast-growing plant prefers well-drained soil.*

ABOVE Euphorbia characias *'Portuguese Velvet', with its long, bluish green, feather-shaped leaves, is very suitable for a rock garden or a mixed border.*

RIGHT *Valued for its bright red bracts that resemble a large flower, the poinsettia (*Euphorbia pulcherrima*) has long been popular as a Christmas decoration in many parts of the world.*

ABOVE *A semi-succulent shrub,* Euphorbia milii *is an ideal plant for courtyards or in rock gardens. The orange-yellow flowers are surrounded by red bracts.*

RIGHT Euphorbia keithii *is a tall cactuslike plant with gray-blue spines and tiny yellow flowers that appear in spring and continue well into the summer months.*

Favorites	Flower Color	Blooming Season	Flo Frag
Eustoma grandiflorum	white, blue, pink, purple	mid-spring to summer	r
Eustoma grandiflorum **'Echo Blue'**	violet-blue	mid-spring to summer	r
Eustoma grandiflorum **'Echo White'**	white	mid-spring to summer	r
Eustoma grandiflorum **'Echo Yellow'**	pale yellow	mid-spring to summer	r
Eustoma grandiflorum **'Forever Blue'**	violet-blue	mid-spring to summer	r
Eustoma grandiflorum **'Lilac Rose'**	lilac-pink	mid-spring to summer	r

ABOVE Eustoma grandiflorum *'Echo Blue' is one of the Echo Series cultivars. Its double flowers are somewhat roselike in appearance and are an appealing shade of violet-blue.*

EUSTOMA

Formerly classified as *Lisianthus*, these long-stemmed gentian relatives (family Gentianaceae) are widely cultivated as cut flowers. Also commonly known as prairie gentians or Texas bluebells, there are 3 annual or short-lived perennial species in this genus, which are found from southern U.S.A. to northern South America. They form clumps of succulent oval to narrowly elliptical leaves, and from spring to summer produce showy funnel- to bell-shaped flowers. Species sometimes carry their flowers singly, but the cultivated plants have long stems that produce a profusion of eye-catching blooms in a wide range of color. *Lisianthus* means "bitter flower;" this refers to the taste of the flowers, which were traditionally used in herbal medicine by Native Americans.

CULTIVATION

Eustoma plants are usually cultivated as annual Slow growing, they need lengthy warm conditions to flower well. Plant in full or half su in fertile, moist, well-drained soil. The flower stems are best staked. Propagation can be fro cuttings, but it is better to raise plants from seed. Sow in early autumn for spring flowers.

Plant Height	Plant Width	Hardiness Zone	Frost Tolerance
18–30 in (45–75 cm)	12 in (30 cm)	9–11	no
18–24 in (45–60 cm)	12 in (30 cm)	9–11	no
18–24 in (45–60 cm)	12 in (30 cm)	9–11	no
18–24 in (45–60 cm)	12 in (30 cm)	9–11	no
8 in (20 cm)	12 in (30 cm)	9–11	no
12–18 in (30–45 cm)	12 in (30 cm)	9–11	no

ABOVE *'Lilac Rose' is an especially pretty cultivar of* Eustoma grandiflorum, *with delicate lilac-pink flowers.*
LEFT Eustoma grandiflorum *'Forever Blue' has violet-blue flowers, and is much smaller than the species.*

Top Tip

Although *Eustoma* species are classified as perennials, they do not perform very well beyond their first season. It is advised to replace the plants after flowering with fresh stock.

LEFT *A white-flowered variety,* Eustoma grandiflorum *'Forever White' makes an excellent container plant. The cut flowers will last for up to 3 weeks.*

FELICIA

Commonly known as the kingfisher daisy due to its brilliant blue flowers, this genus includes around 80 species of annuals, perennials, and subshrubs naturally occurring from southern Africa to the Arabian Peninsula. Mainly low-growing plants, they have simple oblong leaves that are often covered with fine bristly hairs. The daisylike flowers are made up of a central yellow disc floret surrounded by a brightly colored flowerhead, which is often sky blue, although it may be pink or white. *Felicia* species bloom throughout much of spring and summer, and are suitable for rock gardens, containers, and beds. The genus was named for Herr Felix, a nineteenth-century mayor of Regensburg, a town on the Danube.

CULTIVATION

These plants are reasonably hardy but will only withstand light frost. The perennials and subshrubs are best suited to a mild climate with warm summers and dry winters. Plant in full sun with light, gritty, well-drained soil. Propagate from cuttings taken in late summer or autumn, or from seed in spring.

Top Tip

These plants need a little attention to keep them tidy. Regular deadheading and pruning of straggly stems will control spread and extend the flowering season.

Favorites	Flower Color	Blooming Season	Flower Fragrance	Plant Height	Plant Width	Hardiness Zone	Frost Tolerance
Felicia amelloides	sky blue	spring to early summer	no	12–18 in (30–45 cm)	30 in (75 cm)	9–11	no
Felicia amelloides 'Variegata'	sky blue	spring to early summer	no	12–18 in (30–45 cm)	30 in (75 cm)	9–11	no
Felicia bergeriana	blue	late winter to early spring	no	8 in (20 cm)	8 in (20 cm)	9–11	no
Felicia filifolia	mauve to white	spring	no	36 in (90 cm)	36 in (90 cm)	9–11	no
Felicia fruticosa	mauve, white, purple	spring	no	2–4 ft (0.6–1.2 m)	3 ft (0.9 m)	9–11	no
Felicia 'Spring Melchen'	blue, pink, white	spring	no	12 in (30 cm)	18 in (45 cm)	9–11	no

LEFT *Among the mid-green needle-like leaves, tiny mauve or white flowers cover the stems of Felicia filifolia.*
BELOW *A small evergreen shrub, Felicia fruticosa bears an abundance of flowers, in shades of pink, purple, and white, throughout the spring months.*

FORSYTHIA

T his genus of about 7 species of deciduous
shrubs belongs to the Oleaceae family and
occurs mainly in open woodland in eastern
Asia, with the exception of 1 species, which
derives from southeastern Europe. The simple,
narrow, blunt-toothed leaves grow in opposite
pairs on the softwooded stems, which branch
upwards from the ground. The starry bright
yellow flowers are a cheerful sight in early
spring, appearing as they do sometimes before
the season's new leaves. Some species have
slightly hanging branches that can be trained
over a support to form an attractive wall plant.
The bright blossoms are believed to herald the
beginning of spring in China and Japan, and
as such are highly valued.

CULTIVATION

These frost-hardy plants are easy to grow. They
need an open sunny position, a well-drained
fertile soil, as well as adequate water in summer
and freezing temperatures in winter to encourage flowering. Propagate from soft-tip cuttings
in summer or hardwood cuttings in winter.

ABOVE RIGHT Forsythia
suspensa *is well suited to
training on a wall, which is
an ideal way to feature its
abundant golden flowers
each spring. In autumn, the
long leaves turn yellow.*
RIGHT Forsythia 'Northern
Sun' *is a strong-growing
tall shrub that produces a
magnificent display of yellow flowers in spring. The
flower buds are almost as
hardy as the stem wood.*

Top Tip

Flowers are borne on the over-wintered year-old shoots; remove older shoots when flowering has finished to make room for new shoots that arise from the base.

ABOVE Forsythia ovata 'Tetragold' has large golden yellow flowers and a denser habit than its parent, a compact bushy species from Korea.

RIGHT A moderate to fast grower, Forsythia 'Arnold Dwarf' roots easily in moist soil, and makes a lovely ground cover. It has bright green leaves and small pale yellow flowers.

Favorites	Flower Color	Blooming Season	Flower Fragrance	Plant Height	Plant Width	Hardiness Zone	Frost Tolerance
Forsythia 'Arnold Dwarf'	yellow-green	early spring	no	18–36 in (45–90 cm)	6 ft (1.8 m)	4–9	yes
Forsythia × *intermedia*	yellow	spring	no	10 ft (3 m)	10 ft (3 m)	5–9	yes
Forsythia 'Northern Gold'	golden yellow	spring	no	5–8 ft (1.5–2.4 m)	5–7 ft (1.5–2 m)	4–9	yes
Forsythia 'Northern Sun'	clear yellow	spring	no	10 ft (3 m)	8 ft (2.4 m)	4–9	yes
Forsythia ovata	yellow	early spring	no	5 ft (1.5 m)	10 ft (3 m)	5–9	yes
Forsythia suspensa	golden yellow	early spring	no	10 ft (3 m)	8 ft (2.4 m)	4–9	yes

FREMONTODENDRON

There are 3 species of evergreen shrubs in this genus from southwestern North America and Mexico. The lobed leaves vary in shape from almost rounded to a pointed oval, while color varies from dull to dark green. The eye-catching flowers are large, bowl-shaped, and have 5 petallike sepals, usually a bright golden color, though one extremely rare species has copper-colored flowers. Flowers are borne in flushes from spring onwards, sometimes appearing for many months. The genus gets its unusual common name, flannel bush, from the dense covering of fine bronze bristles on the stems, undersides of the leaves, flower buds, and seed capsules. These may irritate the skin if brushed.

CULTIVATION

These shrubs require a sunny sheltered site and in cool climates they need the protection of a wall. Poor dry soils suit them best as rich soils produce an excess of foliage rather than flowers. Once established, they should not be moved. Avoid over-watering. Propagate from seed and softwood or half-hardened cuttings.

BELOW Fremontodendron *decumbens is a rare and endangered species from the Sierra Nevada range. It forms a low spreading shrub whose copper flowers last for 9 months of the year.*

LEFT *Another endangered species,* Fremontodendron mexicanum *is found in San Diego and Baja California. Its sunny yellow flowers are almost starlike in appearance. They can grow up to 3 in (8 cm) wide.*

Top Tip

A little care is needed with these plants. Rich soils can reduce the plant's life span, as can too much moisture and root disturbance. Key factors are sunshine, shelter, and protection from frost.

ABOVE Fremontodendron californicum *is at home both in the wild and in cultivation, and has produced numerous cultivars such as the woody ornamental 'Margo' (seen above). All are fast growers and flower young.*

RIGHT Fremontodendron *'California Glory' is a hybrid between* F. californicum *and* F. mexicanum. *It has proved superior to either parent, being hardier, more vigorous, and capable of producing a heavier crop of characteristically cheerful, large, yellow flowers.*

Favorites	Flower Color	Blooming Season	Flower Fragrance	Plant Height	Plant Width	Hardiness Zone	Frost Tolerance
Fremontodendron 'California Glory'	yellow	late spring to mid-autumn	no	20 ft (6 m)	12 ft (3.5 m)	8–10	yes
Fremontodendron californicum	yellow	spring to summer	no	20 ft (6 m)	12 ft (3.5 m)	8–10	yes
Fremontodendron decumbens	coppery yellow	spring to autumn	no	24 in (60 cm)	10 ft (3 m)	8–10	yes
Fremontodendron 'Ken Taylor'	orange-yellow	spring to autumn	no	4–6 ft (1.2–1.8 m)	10 ft (3 m)	8–10	yes
Fremontodendron mexicanum	golden yellow	spring to mid-autumn	no	20 ft (6 m)	12 ft (3.5 m)	9–11	yes
Fremontodendron 'Pacific Sunset'	bright yellow	spring to summer	no	20 ft (6 m)	12–15 ft (3.5–4.5 m)	8–10	yes

LEFT *Native to northwestern U.S.A. and northeastern Asia,* Fritillaria camschatcensis *has pendent bell-shaped flowers in shades of dark purple, maroon-brown, and sometimes green-purple.*

Top Tip

Not every *Fritillaria* species is easy to grow; good species to start with are *F. imperialis, F. meleagris,* and *F. michailovskyi.* Use in herbaceous borders or pots.

FRITILLARIA

A member of the lily family, this genus of about 100 species includes some rare species that are coveted by many plant collectors. Most are native to the Balkans and the Mediterranean, though species also occur in much of the temperate areas of the Northern Hemisphere. The leaves are narrow and simple with tubular or bell-shaped pendulous flowers borne on erect stems. Petals may be alternately colored, striped, or speckled, often in rather unusual colors, such as chocolate, lime green, sulfur yellow, dusky rose, and even gray. Both the genus and common name (fritillary) derive from the Latin word *fritillus,* meaning checkered dice box, an image suggested by the alternately colored flower petals.

CULTIVATION

These generally frost-hardy plants prefer a climate with distinct seasons. Most species grow well in rockeries or woodland conditions in part-shade with moist, humus-rich, very well-drained soil. Propagation is by seed.

BELOW *Commonly known as the snake's head fritillary, Fritillaria meleagris is highly appreciated for its maroon, green, or purple flowers, which are strikingly etched or checkered with purple.*

BOVE *This unusual-looking species,* Fritillaria imperialis, *ears up to 8 red to yellow flowers in a tight pendent clus-r, which is crowned with a tuft of upright leaf-like bracts.* *FT The small and graceful* Fritillaria michailovskyi *has nce-shaped clear green leaves and bell-shaped flowers. hese are a rich purple-brown color, with yellow tips.*

Favorites

	Flower Color	Blooming Season	Flower Fragrance	Plant Height	Plant Width	Hardiness Zone	Frost Tolerance
Fritillaria camschatcensis	purple-black, maroon, green	summer	no	10–18 in (25–45 cm)	3–4 in (8–10 cm)	4–9	yes
Fritillaria imperialis	yellow, orange, red	late spring to early summer	no	5 ft (1.5 m)	10–12 in (25–30 cm)	4–9	yes
Fritillaria meleagris	white, green, pink to purple	spring	no	12 in (30 cm)	6 in (15 cm)	4–9	yes
Fritillaria michailovskyi	purple-brown edged in yellow	summer	no	8 in (20 cm)	3 in (8 cm)	7–9	yes
Fritillaria pallidiflora	pale yellow	late spring to early summer	no	15 in (38 m)	6 in (15 cm)	3–9	yes
Fritillaria persica	dark purple	spring	no	3 ft (0.9 m)	12 in (30 cm)	5–9	yes

FUCHSIA

There are about 100 species of evergreen or deciduous spreading or climbing shrubs and small to medium-sized trees in this genus, almost all of which come from South and Central America, with a few from New Zealand. They have long mid- to deep green leaves growing in whorls on stems but it is their arresting flowerheads that have attracted the interest of gardeners and have given rise to many thousands of hybrids and cultivars. The hanging flowers are mostly tubular, growing singly or in clusters along the stem and come in shades of red, white, pink, and purple, as well as bicolored. Fuchsias are ideal in hedges, hanging baskets, or trained on espaliers.

CULTIVATION

Moderately frost hardy to frost tender, these plants require moist but well-drained fertile soil in sun or partial shade, and some shelter from wind. Propagate the species from seeds and cuttings. Cultivars are propagated from softwood cuttings in spring or half-hardened cuttings in late summer.

ABOVE *The hybrid* Fuchsia *'Mrs Popple' is a popular choice for its frost tolerance and brightly colored single flowers. A vigorous grower, plant this shrub in a border.*

Favorites	Flower Color	Blooming Season	Flower Fragrance	Plant Height	Plant Width	Hardiness Zone	Frost Tolerance
Fuchsia arborescens	rose purple	mid-autumn to spring	no	8–20 ft (2.4–6 m)	6 ft (1.8 m)	9–11	no
Fuchsia boliviana	pale pink to scarlet	all year long	no	12 ft (3.5 m)	3–4 ft (0.9–1.2 m)	10–11	no
Fuchsia denticulata	orange-red, red	summer to autumn	no	4–8 ft (1.2–2.4 m)	4 ft (1.2 m)	9–11	no
Fuchsia 'Eva Boerg'	white, pink, and purple-pink	late spring to summer	no	24 in (60 cm)	3 ft (0.9 m)	9–11	no
Fuchsia magellanica	red, purple	late spring to early winter	no	10 ft (3 m)	6–10 ft (1.8–3 m)	7–10	yes
Fuchsia 'Mrs Popple'	bright red and purple	late spring to autumn	no	3 ft (0.9 m)	3 ft (0.9 m)	8–11	yes
Fuchsia 'Orange Flare'	light orange to orange-red	late spring to autumn	no	4 ft (1.2 m)	3 ft (0.9 m)	9–11	no
Fuchsia paniculata	lavender-pink	mid autumn to spring	no	12–15 ft (3.5–4.5 m)	8 ft (2.4 m)	9–11	yes
Fuchsia procumbens	orange, green, and purple	summer	no	2 in (5 cm)	3–4 ft (0.9–1.2 cm)	9–10	yes
Fuchsia 'Swingtime'	red and white	late spring to autumn	no	24 in (60 cm)	18–30 in (45–75 cm)	9–11	no
Fuchsia thymifolia	white to pink	late spring to autumn	no	3–10 ft (0.9–3 m)	3–10 ft (0.9–3 m)	8–11	yes
Fuchsia triphylla	orange to coral red	summer to early autumn	no	30 in (75 cm)	2–4 ft (0.6–1.2 m)	9–11	no

RIGHT *A large erect shrub native to Central America,* Fuchsia arborescens *bears striking panicles of pinkish purple tubular flowers. The round fruit is purple and wrinkled when ripe.*

BELOW Fuchsia magellanica *var.* molinae *is a pale pink-flowered cultivated variant of* F. magellanica. *It can make an attractive hedge.*

ABOVE Fuchsia procumbens *is a prostrate, spreading, evergreen subshrub. Small heart-shaped leaves offset the upward-facing flowers, which have greenish to pale orange tubes and purple-tipped green sepals; there are no petals. This is a good plant for a rock garden.*

Top Tip

Most fuchsias are frost tender and benefit from being potted up and sheltered over winter. Hardy types can stay in the ground but need generous mulching to protect their root systems.

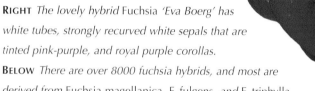

RIGHT *The lovely hybrid* Fuchsia *'Eva Boerg' has white tubes, strongly recurved white sepals that are tinted pink-purple, and royal purple corollas.*
BELOW *There are over 8000 fuchsia hybrids, and most are derived from* Fuchsia magellanica, F. fulgens, *and* F. triphylla. *'Billy Green', a* F. triphylla *hybrid, is a vigorous upright plant with olive green leaves and pink flowers.*

GAILLARDIA

Discovered in the Rocky Mountains around 1825, this genus of around 30 species of annual, biennial, and perennial daisies (family Asteraceae) occurs mainly in the southern U.S.A. and Mexico. The common name of blanket flower comes from a Native American legend of a blanket maker who the spirits rewarded with an ever-blooming blanket of flowers on his grave. Appropriately, these small mounding plants are covered in summer and autumn with vivid flowerheads. The ray florets are typically red at the center with a yellow outer half. Cultivated garden forms occur in warm tones and have long flowering periods.

ABOVE *One of the taller cultivars available, reaching up to 24 in (60 cm) high, Gaillardia 'Burgunder' produces flowerheads of burgundy red petals around a red to yellow disc floret.*
RIGHT *Gaillardia × grandiflora 'Indian Yellow' bears a profusion of sunny yellow blooms during summer. Regular removal of any spent flowers will prolong the flowering season well into autumn.*

CULTIVATION

Hardiness varies, though they are so easily cultivated that replacing any winter casualties is no problem. Plant in full sun in well-drained soil that remains moist during the growing season. Propagate from seed or basal cuttings.

Favorites	Flower Color	Blooming Season	Flower Fragrance	Plant Height	Plant Width	Hardiness Zone	Frost Tolerance
Gaillardia **'Burgunder'**	dark red	summer to autumn	no	20–24 in (50–60 cm)	18 in (45 cm)	5–10	yes
Gaillardia **'Dazzler'**	orange-yellow; dark red center	summer to autumn	no	24–36 in (60–90 cm)	18–24 in (45–60 cm)	5–10	yes
Gaillardia × **grandiflora**	orange, yellow, red, and maroon	early summer to early autumn	no	36 in (90 cm)	18 in (45 cm)	5–10	yes
Gaillardia **'Kobold'**	dark red, tipped with yellow	late spring to early autumn	no	12 in (30 cm)	30 in (75 cm)	5–10	yes
Gaillardia **pulchella**	red, yellow; red and yellow	summer to autumn	no	18–24 in (45–60 cm)	18 in (45 cm)	8–10	yes
Gaillardia pulchella, **Plume Series**	red, yellow	summer to autumn	no	10–18 in (25–45 cm)	24–36 in (60–90 cm)	8–10	yes

BOVE *Sunflowerlike in
 pearance,* Gaillardia
*obold' brings dazzling
 lor to the garden, with its
  d disc florets and yellow-
 ped red petals.*

GHT *Pictured here in the
 ld,* Gaillardia pulchella
*s plump cone-shaped
 sc florets in rich maroon,
 rounded by deep red
 tals with yellow tips.*

GALANTHUS

Probably the most welcome harbinger of spring, this normally late winter-flowering Eurasian genus of 15 bulbs in the amaryllis family (Amaryllidaceae) also includes a few species that bloom in autumn. The narrow grassy leaves usually break through shortly after mid-winter, followed by short flower stems that each carry 1 pendulous, white, mildly scented, 6-petalled flower. The inner 3 petals are short and green-tipped. Double-flowered forms are also available. Familiarly known as snowdrop, the genus name *Galanthus* comes from the Greek *gala* (milk) and *anthos* (a flower), referring to the color of the flower. According to Christian legend, the snowdrop first bloomed to coincide with the Feast of Purification held on February 2, known as Candlemas Day.

ABOVE Galanthus plicatus, the Crimean snowdrop, hails from Turkey and Eastern Europe. The inner petals of the snow white flowers are marked with green.

CULTIVATION

Galanthus plants perform best in cool-temperate climates and thrive in woodland or rockery conditions. They prefer dappled shade; moist humus-rich soil; and, while very hardy, do need watering during dry times. They may be propagated from seed but usually multiply quickly enough so that division after the foliage dies back is more practical.

Top Tip

Do not allow divided snowdrop bulbs to dry out. Plant promptly, at a depth of 3 in (8 cm), and a similar distance apart.

RIGHT *As the graceful, nodding, white flowers of Galanthus 'S. Arnott' burst open, they fill the winter garden with a delicious honey fragrance.*

Favorites

	Flower Color	Blooming Season	Flower Fragrance	Plant Height	Plant Width	Hardiness Zone	Frost Tolerance
Galanthus elwesii	white with green markings	late winter to spring	yes	10 in (25 cm)	6 in (15 cm)	6–9	yes
Galanthus ikarae	white with green markings	winter	no	6 in (15 cm)	4 in (10 cm)	6–9	yes
Galanthus nivalis	white with green markings	late winter	yes	6 in (15 cm)	8 in (20 cm)	4–9	yes
Galanthus nivalis 'Flore Pleno'	white	late winter	no	6 in (15 cm)	8 in (20 cm)	4–9	yes
Galanthus plicatus	white with green markings	late winter to early spring	no	8 in (20 cm)	6 in (15 cm)	6–9	yes
Galanthus 'S. Arnott'	white	late winter to spring	yes	8 in (20 cm)	6 in (15 cm)	4–9	yes

BELOW *Slender 6–8 in (15–20 cm) high stems carry the dainty, nodding, white flowers of* Galanthus nivalis, *the common snowdrop.*

RIGHT *Blue-green foliage offsets the large, white, scented flowers of* Galanthus elwesii. *Each of the inner petals has delicate green markings.*

Gardenia

This genus in the madder family (Rubiaceae) consists of around 250 species, the majority found in the tropics of Africa and Asia. Mostly evergreen shrubs or small trees, they have opposite or whorled, simple, shiny, deep green leaves. The fragrant, large, tubular to funnel-shaped flowers can be white or yellow and are produced singly or in semi-double and double forms along or at the ends of branches. The fruit is a leathery or fleshy berry with many seeds. Gardenias are attractive landscape subjects and make wonderful container plants. The beautiful flowers have made this genus popular in cultivation throughout the world and a favorite with florists; they are popular flowers for corsages and buttonholes. The flowers of some species are used to perfume tea.

Cultivation

Most species perform best in a well-drained, humus-rich, acidic soil. When in growth, mulch with good quality compost and fertilizer, with adequate summer watering. In cool climates grow in a heated greenhouse, as gardenias are frost tender. Propagate from seed or leafy tip or half-hardened cuttings in late spring and summer.

RIGHT *A native of South Africa, Gardenia thunbergia is commonly known as the starry gardenia. It has shiny, leathery, green leaves and single, fragrant, white to cream flowers.*

ABOVE *Appearing after the flowers, the brownish gray to green, egg-shaped fruits of* Gardenia thunbergia *can persist on the branches for several years.*

LEFT *A glorious fragrance coupled with beautiful, semi-double, ivory blooms are the signature characteristics of* Gardenia augusta *'Magnifica'.*

Top Tip

Contrary to their elegant appearance, gardenias are quite resilient evergreen shrubs. They can tolerate sun or part-shade, but do not do well in desert climates.

Favorites	Flower Color	Blooming Season	Flower Fragrance	Plant Height	Plant Width	Hardiness Zone	Frost Tolerance
Gardenia augusta	white, creamy white	summer to autumn	yes	4–7 ft (1.2–2 m)	3–6 ft (0.9–1.8 m)	10–11	no
Gardenia augusta 'Kleim's Hardy'	white	summer to autumn	yes	24–36 in (60–90 cm)	24–36 in (60–90 cm)	9–11	no
Gardenia augusta 'Mystery'	white	mid-summer to early autumn	yes	4 ft (1.2 m)	4 ft (1.2 m)	10–11	no
Gardenia augusta 'Radicans'	white	summer to autumn	yes	6–12 in (15–30 cm)	24–36 in (60–90 cm)	10–11	no
Gardenia augusta 'Veitchii'	white	summer to autumn	yes	3–4 ft (0.9–1.2 m)	6 ft (1.8 m)	10–11	no
Gardenia thunbergia	white, cream	mid-spring to summer	yes	8–15 ft (2.4–4.5 m)	8 ft (2.4 m)	9–11	no

Favorites	Flower Color	Blooming Season	Flower Fragrance
Gazania 'Blackberry Ripple'	burgundy and white	late spring to summer	no
Gazania, Chansonette Series	orange, pink, red, yellow	summer	no
Gazania 'Christopher Lloyd'	bright pink and green	late spring to summer	no
Gazania linearis	orange-yellow	summer to autumn	no
Gazania rigens	orange-yellow	spring to summer	no
Gazania rigens 'Variegata'	orange-yellow	spring to summer	no

GAZANIA

Commonly known as treasure flowers, the 16 species of annuals and perennials in this daisy family (Asteraceae) genus are found mainly in South Africa, with a few species extending the range to the tropics. They are low-growing, near-evergreen, clump-forming plants with simple, narrow, lance-shaped, sometimes downy leaves with pale undersides. Their flowers, which appear throughout the warmer months, are the main attraction as they are large, brightly colored, often interestingly marked, and showy. While the species usually have yellow or orange flowers, garden forms are available in a huge color range. The genus was named for Theodore of Gaza (1398–1478), who translated the botanical texts of Theophrastus from Greek into Latin.

CULTIVATION
Apart from being somewhat frost tender and resenting wet winters, they are easily grown in any sunny position in gritty free-draining soil. Propagate by division or from basal cuttings in autumn, or raise from seed in late winter.

ABOVE *Gazanias open in full sun and close up during overcast weather and at dusk. Sun-loving* Gazania rigens *opens to reveal bright yellow daisylike flowers.*
ABOVE LEFT *With bright pink petals marked emerald green at the base,* Gazania 'Christopher Lloyd' *is an ideal choice when a colorful ground cover is required.*

Plant Height	Plant Width	Hardiness Zone	Frost Tolerance
6 in (15 cm)	24 in (60 cm)	9–11	no
8 in (20 cm)	10 in (25 cm)	8–10	no
6 in (15 cm)	18 in (45 cm)	9–11	no
8–12 in (20–30 cm)	12–18 in (30–45 cm)	9–11	no
6 in (15 cm)	24–36 in (60–90 cm)	9–11	no
6 in (15 cm)	24–36 in (60–90 cm)	9–11	no

RIGHT *Attractive green and cream variegated leaves distinguish* Gazania rigens *'Variegata' from the species. The large, open, yellow-orange flowers are distinctly marked black with a white eye toward the petal base.*

BELOW *Creamy white petals streaked with dark purple-pink and highlighted in yellow toward the base are the trademarks of* Gazania *'Blackberry Ripple'. These features are accented by the silvery gray leaves.*

Top Tip

Gazanias can add color to the seaside garden, as they are extremely tolerant of coastal conditions. Most species are able to withstand poor dry soils, but appreciate additional humus under these conditions.

GENTIANA

This genus of 400 or so species of annuals, biennials, and perennials is widely distributed and is the type genus for its family, the Gentianaceae. Although they range from tiny tufted alpines to species with tall erect flower stems, most form a compact clump of simple pointed leaves, sometimes in rosettes. The flowers, which may be borne singly among the foliage or clustered on upright or over-arching stems, are trumpet- or bell-shaped, and mostly brilliant blue. If not blue, many gentian flowers are white, cream, yellow, or purple. Some gentians have medicinal uses, and the name honors Gentius, King of Illyria, who in 180 B.C. was cited by Pliny as having discovered these properties.

CULTIVATION

Gentiana species generally prefer a climate with distinct seasons. They grow best in sun or part-shade in moist, well-drained, humus-rich soil. The small species thrive in rockeries or flower borders. Propagate by division in early spring or raise from fresh seed in autumn.

ABOVE *Sky blue funnel- or bell-shaped flowers adorn* Gentiana ternifolia *during autumn. Long stems hold the flowers above the deep green foliage.*

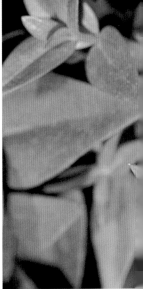

LEFT *Spectacular trumpet-shaped flowers in the deep est of sapphire blues are the trademark features of the versatile cultivar* Gentiana acaulis 'Rannoch'. *This plant is perfect for adding color to a rock garden.*

LEFT *The white-throated, purple-blue, 2 in (5 cm) wide flowers of* Gentiana septemfida *are held aloft on arching stems above the mid-green leaves.*
BELOW Gentiana clusii *is ideally suited to border planting or for use as a contrast in the rock garden, where the rich blue flowers provide interesting highlights to the area.*

Top Tip

Mostly alpine species, *Gentiana* plants do not do well under the searing heat of the sun in warmer climates, and should be sited where they are given some shade.

Favorites	Flower Color	Blooming Season	Flower Fragrance	Plant Height	Plant Width	Hardiness Zone	Frost Tolerance
Gentiana acaulis	deep blue, green spotted interior	spring to early summer	no	4 in (10 cm)	12 in (30 cm)	3–9	yes
Gentiana asclepiadea	violet-blue	late summer to early autumn	no	24 in (60 cm)	18 in (45 cm)	6–9	yes
Gentiana clusii	deep blue, green spotted interior	summer	no	4 in (10 cm)	12 in (30 cm)	7–9	yes
Gentiana makinoi	pale blue to violet-blue	summer	no	20 in (50 cm)	6 in (15 cm)	6–9	yes
Gentiana septemfida	dark blue to blue-purple	late summer	no	6–12 in (15–30 cm)	12 in (30 cm)	3–9	yes
Gentiana ternifolia	sky blue	autumn	no	3 in (8 cm)	12 in (30 cm)	5–7	yes

GERANIUM

The plants often called "geraniums" in fact belong in the genus *Pelargonium*. While both genera are members of the geranium family (Geraniaceae), the true geraniums are a very different group of over 300 species of perennials and subshrubs that are at times evergreen, and are widespread in the temperate zones. Their often finely hairy leaves are usually hand-shaped, with toothed lobes. They bloom in spring and summer and have simple, flat, 5-petalled flowers in pink or purple-blue shades, less often white or darker purple-black. The plant's common name, cranesbill, is attributed to the shape of its long narrow fruits, which somewhat resemble a crane's long beak. The genus name *Geranium* is derived from the Greek word *geranos* (crane).

CULTIVATION

Most species are hardy and will grow in a wide range of conditions, preferring sun or semi-shade and moist humus-rich soil. The roots can be invasive. Geraniums are appealing as ground covers, in rockeries, and as part of flower borders. Propagate by division or from cuttings or seed; these plants may self-sow.

ABOVE *With bright cerise petals and dark, almost black, velvety centers contrasting with the yellow-green leaves, Geranium 'Ann Folkard' is a striking cultivar.*
LEFT *Named for a noted English plantsman, Geranium sanguineum 'Alan Bloom' is an attractive bushy cultivar with bright pink flowers and mid- to dark green foliage.*

ABOVE *Gray-green leaves complement the strongly red-veined pink flowers of* Geranium cinereum *'Ballerina'.*
LEFT *From spring to summer, white-centered violet-pink flowers are featured among the mid-green lobed leaves of* Geranium sylvaticum *'Mayflower'.*

Favorites

	Flower Color	Blooming Season	Flower Fragrance	Plant Height	Plant Width	Hardiness Zone	Frost Tolerance
Geranium **'Ann Folkard'**	magenta with black center	mid-summer to mid-autumn	no	24 in (60 cm)	36 in (90 cm)	6–9	yes
Geranium **cinereum**	white, pale pink	late spring to early summer	no	6 in (15 cm)	12 in (30 cm)	5–9	yes
Geranium **maderense**	magenta-pink	late winter to late summer	no	5 ft (1.5 m)	4–5 ft (1.2–1.5 m)	9–10	no
Geranium **'Patricia'**	magenta	late spring to early summer	no	12–18 in (30–45 cm)	24 in (60 cm)	5–9	yes
Geranium **phaeum**	purple-black, maroon, mauve	late spring to early summer	no	30 in (75 cm)	18 in (45 cm)	5–10	yes
Geranium **pratense**	white, violet, blue	summer	no	24–36 in (60–90 cm)	24 in (60 cm)	5–9	yes
Geranium **renardii**	white with purple veins	early summer	no	12 in (30 cm)	12 in (30 cm)	6–9	yes
Geranium **sanguineum**	magenta to crimson	summer	no	8 in (20 cm)	12 in (30 cm)	5–9	yes
Geranium **sessiliflorum**	white	summer	no	6 in (15 cm)	12 in (30 cm)	7–9	yes
Geranium **'Sue Crûg'**	mauve-pink with darker veins	late spring to early summer	no	8 in (20 cm)	12 in (30 cm)	4–9	yes
Geranium **sylvaticum**	white, pink, purple	late spring to summer	no	30 in (75 cm)	24 in (60 cm)	4–9	yes
Geranium **tuberosum**	purple-pink	spring to early summer	no	8–10 in (20–25 cm)	12 in (30 cm)	7–10	yes

RIGHT *The pink flowers of Geranium 'Sue Crûg' have petals that become darker toward the center, and are delicately streaked with burgundy veining. The flowers are produced on stems above the mid-green foliage. This pretty cultivar grows to 15 in (38 cm) high.*

ABOVE *Geranium 'Patricia', a cross between* G. endressii *and* G. psilostemon, *bears maroon-eyed magenta flowers. Dark green foliage provides a perfect backdrop for the blooms.*
RIGHT *Rich purple flowers, larger than those of the species, are borne on nodding stems amid the yellow-green leaves of* Geranium phaeum *'Lily Lovell'.*
BELOW *The snow white petals of* Geranium pratense *'Splish-splash' are streaked and mottled with lilac-blue. This unusually colored cultivar grows to 24 in (60 cm) high.*

RIGHT *Native to the Mediterranean region, Geranium tuberosum has open purple-pink flowers. The pretty heart-shaped petals are highlighted with darker pink veining.*

ABOVE Geranium pratense *produces flowers in shades of white, blue, and violet, often accented with veining. The hairy, lobed, dark green leaves take on attractive bronze hues during the autumn months.*

Top Tip

Easily divided, geraniums can be used to fill any bare patches in the garden. They can quickly fill an area, and may need to be thinned out and pruned to maintain a tidy appearance.

GLADIOLUS

When people think of *Gladiolus*, the plants that most often come to mind are those tall-spiked large-flowered hybrids derived primarily from South African species. However, this iris family (Iridaceae) genus includes 180-odd species of corms distributed from Europe to western Asia and South Africa, many of which are quite different from the showy hybrids. Those species with less colorful flowers are sometimes scented. The name *Gladiolus* comes from the Latin *gladius* (a sword), and refers to the long sword-shaped foliage of most species; this feature has also given rise to the common name, sword lilies. Roasted *Gladiolus* corms were a food source for southern African tribes and are reputed to taste like chestnuts.

CULTIVATION
Plant the corms in full sun in well-drained soil, at 4 times their own depth. In cold areas corms will survive outdoors if planted below freezing depth; otherwise lift them and store dry for winter. Propagation is by growing on the tiny cormlets.

ABOVE Gladiolus communis subsp. byzantinus *is a hardy vigorous—even invasive— perennial with flowering spikes of deep pink blooms.*
ABOVE LEFT *In autumn the narrow leaves of* Gladiolus tristis *first emerge, heralding the appearance in spring of pale yellow blooms. Their scent is released at night.*

Top Tip

If growing gladioli for cut flowers, choose cultivars— with their large showy blooms— rather than species. Cut when the lower flowers open.

BELOW *Exotic, understated, and with a heady scent, Gladiolus callianthus bears a succession of pure white blooms with a bolt of dark maroon at the throat.*

Favorites

	Flower Color	Blooming Season	Flower Fragrance	Plant Height	Plant Width	Hardiness Zone	Frost Tolerance
Gladiolus callianthus	white with red markings	late summer to early autumn	yes	36 in (90 cm)	2 in (5 cm)	9–11	no
Gladiolus communis	pink with red or white	spring to summer	no	36 in (90 cm)	10 in (25 cm)	6–10	yes
Gladiolus 'Green Woodpecker'	greenish with red markings	summer	no	5 ft (1.5 m)	12 in (30 cm)	8–11	no
Gladiolus 'Red Beauty'	red	summer	no	5 ft (1.5 m)	12 in (30 cm)	8–11	no
Gladiolus tristis	creamy yellow	spring	yes	2–5 ft (0.6–1.5 m)	8 in (20 cm)	7–10	no
Gladiolus viridiflorus	yellow-green and dull pink	late autumn to winter	no	6–12 in (15–30 cm)	6 in (15 cm)	8–10	yes

LEFT Gypsophila repens 'Rosa Schönheit' forms a carpet of tiny, star-shaped, pink flowers amid narrow blue-green leaves.
BELOW LEFT Perfect for a range of situations including rockeries and hanging baskets, Gypsophila muralis 'Gypsy' bears masses of tiny, double, pink flowers.

GYPSOPHILA

Related to the carnations and commonly known as baby's breath, the 100-odd annuals and perennials in this genus occur naturally throughout Eurasia. They range from spreading mat-forming plants studded with pink or white blooms to upright shrubby species with billowing heads of tiny flowers. Their simple linear to lance-shaped leaves are sometimes rather fleshy and often blue-green. The flowering season is only short lived, but it can be prolonged by resowing every 3 weeks to give continuous blooms. *Gypsophila paniculata* and its cultivars are popular cut flowers that are often used by florists to add to bunches of brighter bolder blooms as backing foliage. They can also be used successfully in dried flower arrangements.

CULTIVATION

Gypsophila means chalk-loving, but most species are happy in any neutral to slightly alkaline soil that is fertile, moist, and well-drained. Mat-forming species are excellent rockery plants. Plant in full sun. Larger types will often rebloom if cut back after their first flush. Propagate from basal cuttings or seed.

Top Tip

Not fussy about soil type, summer-flowering baby's breath will quickly fill bare areas of the garden where a burst of color and speedy coverage are needed.

ABOVE The starry flowers and dainty foliage of Gypsophila muralis 'Garden Bride' form an airy cloud of pale pink when used in rockeries, borders, and window boxes.

RIGHT *Perfect as a cascading spillover plant,*
Gypsophila repens has clusters of tiny pink
or white flowers and blue-green leaves.

Favorites	Flower Color	Blooming Season	Flower Fragrance	Plant Height	Plant Width	Hardiness Zone	Frost Tolerance
Gypsophila cerastoides	white with pink veins	late spring to summer	no	3 in (8 cm)	6 in (15 cm)	5–10	yes
Gypsophila elegans	white, pink	summer	no	24 in (60 cm)	12 in (30 cm)	6–10	yes
Gypsophila muralis	pale pink to white	mid-summer to early autumn	no	6–12 in (15–30 cm)	12–18 in (30–45 cm)	7–10	yes
Gypsophila paniculata	white, pink	spring to summer	no	2–4 ft (0.6–1.2 m)	4 ft (1.2 m)	4–10	yes
Gypsophila paniculata 'Bristol Fairy'	white	summer	no	2–4 ft (0.6–1.2 m)	4 ft (1.2 m)	4–10	yes
Gypsophila repens	white, pink, lilac	summer	no	8 in (20 cm)	12–20 in (30–50 cm)	4–9	yes

HEBE

This genus consists of about 100 species of evergreen shrubs primarily native to New Zealand, although a handful come from South America and Australia. Species grow in a wide range of habitats, from coastal areas to alpine regions, and may be shrubby, treelike, compact, or sprawling. There are 2 distinct foliage groups: those with oval to lance-shaped leaves, and those with smaller compressed leaves that give the plants the appearance of conifers; these are known as whipcord hebes. While some species are grown for their attractive light to dark green foliage, most are grown for their abundant spikes of small tubular-shaped flowers in shades of white, pink, deep purple, and crimson.

CULTIVATION

Most hebes prefer a sunny position and will tolerate a wide range of soil conditions. Several of the species perform well in coastal situations. They vary in terms of frost hardiness, with the bigger-leafed species being more frost sensitive than the smaller-leafed species. Prune after flowering to maintain a tidy compact shape. Propagation of the species is from seed or half-hardened cuttings in late summer.

ABOVE Hebe *'Great Orme'* is an attractive rounded shrub that makes a useful hedging plant. It is valued for its elegant long spikes of pink flowers that gradually fade to white, which last well when cut.

BELOW Hebe *'Blue Clouds'* has lilac-blue flowers that bloom for a long period beginning in summer. The glossy green leaves are a winter attraction.

Top Tip

Hebes benefit from
an application of
liquid fertilizer
each month dur-
ing the growing
season. During
winter they should
only be watered
periodically.

ABOVE Hebe ochracea *has a modest habit, making it suitable for a range of garden locations. It has yellow-green foliage and small white flowers. It does not take well to pruning.*
RIGHT *Small blue-gray leaves are the distinctive feature of Hebe pinguifolia 'Pagei'. In spring and into autumn, the branches are topped with masses of small white flowers.*

Favorites

	Flower Color	Blooming Season	Flower Fragrance	Plant Height	Plant Width	Hardiness Zone	Frost Tolerance
Hebe 'Blue Clouds'	lilac-blue	summer to autumn	no	24–36 in (60–90 cm)	24–36 in (60–90 cm)	7–9	yes
Hebe 'Caledonia'	violet	spring to autumn	no	20 in (50 cm)	18 in (45 cm)	7–9	yes
Hebe 'Great Orme'	bright pink	summer to autumn	no	4 ft (1.2 m)	4 ft (1.2 m)	8–10	yes
Hebe 'Nicola's Blush'	pale pink	summer to autumn	no	24–30 in (60–75 cm)	24–30 in (60–75 cm)	7–9	yes
Hebe ochracea	white	mid- to late summer	no	18 in (45 cm)	3 ft (0.9 m)	6–9	yes
Hebe pinguifolia	white	spring to autumn	no	8–12 in (20–30 cm)	18–30 in (45–75 cm)	6–9	yes

HEDYCHIUM

This genus, commonly known as ginger lily or garland lily, is a member of the ginger family and includes some 40 species of perennials native to tropical Asia, the Himalayan region, and Madagascar. Strong canelike stems with large deep green leaves, similar to the canna lily, emerge from heavy fleshy rhizomes. Ginger lilies are grown for their colorful and

highly fragrant flowerheads, which are made up of a number of slender mostly tubular-shaped flowers that have protruding anthers. The flowers appear in summer and are mainly yellow or pink in color, although in some species they can be bright red. The fragrant roots of several *Hedychium* species are used in Indian Ayurvedic medicine.

ABOVE *Dense spikes of bright red flowers and long, pointy, mid-green leaves make* Hedychium greenei *one of the more spectacular ginger lilies. It does best in moist soil.*
LEFT Hedychium gardnerianum, *or Kahili ginger, bears bright orange seed pods containing shiny red seeds in late autumn.*

CULTIVATION

These plants are mostly tolerant of light frosts and are capable of reshooting from the rootstock. They are best planted in sun or shade with moist, humus-rich, well-drained soil. Cut back the stems of spent flowers and any old unproductive canes to encourage new growth. Water liberally during the growing season and add liquid fertilizer once a month. Propagate by division or from seed.

Favorites	Flower Color	Blooming Season	Flower Fragrance	Plant Height	Plant Width	Hardiness Zone	Frost Tolerance
Hedychium coccineum	orange, pink, red, white	late summer to autumn	yes	3–7 ft (0.9–2 m)	4–8 ft (1.2–2.4 m)	8–11	yes
Hedychium coronarium	white with yellow markings	summer to autumn	yes	6–8 ft (1.8–2.4 m)	6–10 ft (1.8–3 m)	9–12	no
Hedychium densiflorum	orange, yellow	summer to early autumn	yes	3–8 ft (0.9–2.4 m)	6 ft (1.8 m)	8–11	yes
Hedychium gardnerianum	yellow and red	late summer to autumn	yes	4–6 ft (1.2–1.8 m)	4–6 ft (1.2–1.8 m)	8–11	yes
Hedychium greenei	orange-scarlet	late summer to autumn	no	3–5 ft (0.9–1.5 m)	3–5 ft (0.9–1.5 m)	9–12	no
Hedychium spicatum	white and orange	summer to early autumn	no	3–5 ft (0.9–1.5 m)	5 ft (1.5 m)	8–11	yes

Top Tip

When the foliage of *Hedychium* species dies down, the fleshy stems can be lifted and overwintered, to be replaced in spring.

ABOVE *Ginger lilies such as* Hedychium spicatum *benefit from an application of a balanced liquid fertilizer when spring growth begins.*
RIGHT *Hedychium coccineum* produces beautiful blooms varying in color from coral to orange and red, with pink stamens.

HELENIUM

This mainly North American genus belongs to the daisy family and contains about 40 species of annuals, biennials, and perennials. Most species form an upright foliage clump and have simple, lance-shaped, light green leaves, usually covered with fine hairs. From mid-summer until well into autumn they produce large daisylike flowerheads, consisting of a central cone or disc floret surrounded by large and often slightly drooping ray florets. The central disc is usually yellow as may be the surrounding ray florets, although more often these are in contrasting shades of orange or red. *Helenium* species are commonly known as sneezeweed because Native Americans traditionally used the powdered flowers from certain species to make snuff.

CULTIVATION

Hardiness varies but most species are very frost tolerant. Plant them in a sunny open position in moist well-drained soil. Deadhead regularly to prolong the flowering period. Propagate by division, from cuttings taken from shoots at the base of the plant, or from seed.

Favorites	Flower Color	Blooming Season	Flower Fragrance
Helenium autumnale	yellow	late summer to mid-autumn	no
Helenium bigelovii	yellow and reddish brown	summer	no
Helenium 'Blopip'	yellow and green-brown	summer to early autumn	no
Helenium hoopesii	yellow-orange and brown	summer	no
Helenium 'Waldtraut'	yellow-orange and brown	late summer to early autumn	no
Helenium 'Wyndley'	yellow and brown	mid-summer to early autumn	no

Top Tip

Helenium species are easy to grow and do not require much attention. The taller varieties may need staking and can be planted along fences.

ABOVE *The yellow-brown central disc of* Helenium *'Wyndley' is surrounded by petals of rich butter yellow. It flowers for a long period.* **LEFT** Helenium *'Blopip' has large heads of sunflower-like blooms in a rich shade of yellow, and with a lovely greenish brown center. It is suitable for border planting.*

Plant Height	Plant Width	Hardiness Zone	Frost Tolerance
5 ft (1.5 m)	18 in (45 cm)	3–9	yes
3 ft (0.9 m)	12 in (30 cm)	7–9	yes
18 in (45 cm)	12 in (30 cm)	4–9	yes
3 ft (0.9 m)	18 in (45 cm)	3–9	yes
3 ft (0.9 m)	24 in (60 cm)	4–9	yes
30 in (75 cm)	24 in (60 cm)	4–9	yes

BELOW Helenium autumnale *is a perennial with daisylike bright yellow flowers that have a lighter central disc. It benefits from a layer of mulch around the base of the plant.*

BELOW *The cheerful blooms of* Helenium *'Waldtraut' are coppery red to brown and, like all* Helenium *species, make excellent long-lasting cut flowers for indoor decoration.*

HELIANTHUS

BELOW Helianthus annuus 'Ring of Fire' will indeed bring fiery colors to the garden, with its large flowerheads of bright red and golden yellow.

It is not hard to see why this genus has the common name sunflower: it not only accurately describes the shape of the blooms but also refers to the way the flowerhead turns to follow the sun during the day. This genus contains about 70 annuals and perennials, mostly from the Americas, and is probably best known for the common or giant sunflower, *Helianthus annuus*, which is widely grown as a garden plant as well as commercially for its seeds and the oil extracted from them. This spectacular species is also the state flower of Kansas. Plants are usually tall, with hairy and often sticky leaves, and tall bristly stems. The flowerheads grow above the foliage and are large, daisylike, and nearly always yellow.

CULTIVATION

Plant sunflowers in a sunny open position that has fertile, moist, and well-drained soil. Propagate the annuals from seed and the perennials either by division or from cuttings taken from the base of the plant.

RIGHT Helianthus annuus 'Ruby Eclipse' bears large flowerheads of rich ruby red petals tipped with pale yellow. This cultivar is a pollenless sunflower.

Top Tip

Allergy sufferers will appreciate the pollenless sunflower cultivars that are now available, while birds will enjoy the nutritious seed heads that develop in the central disc.

ABOVE *A compact grower reaching 36 in (90 cm) high, Helianthus annuus 'Teddy Bear' has attractive, fluffy, double flowerheads of bright golden yellow.*

RIGHT *Native to central U.S.A., the dark-centered, sunny yellow, 2 in (5 cm) wide flowers of* Helianthus salicifolius *are daisylike in appearance.*

Favorites

	Flower Color	Blooming Season	Flower Fragrance	Plant Height	Plant Width	Hardiness Zone	Frost Tolerance
Helianthus annuus	yellow	summer to early autumn	no	8–15 ft (2.4–4.5 m)	24 in (60 cm)	4–11	yes
Helianthus annuus 'Ring of Fire'	yellow and brick red	summer to early autumn	no	3–5 ft (0.9–1.5 m)	18 in (45 cm)	4–11	yes
Helianthus annuus 'Ruby Eclipse'	ruby red	summer to early autumn	no	6 ft (1.8 m)	18 in (45 cm)	4–11	yes
Helianthus maximiliani	golden yellow	summer and autumn	no	5–10 ft (1.5–3 m)	30 in (75 cm)	6–11	yes
Helianthus × multiflorus	golden yellow	late summer to mid-autumn	no	3–6 ft (0.9–1.8 m)	3 ft (0.9 m)	5–9	yes
Helianthus salicifolius	golden yellow	late summer to autumn	no	6–8 ft (1.8–2.4 m)	3 ft (0.9 m)	4–9	yes

HELLEBORUS

RIGHT *Helleborus niger, or Christmas rose, can be difficult to cultivate and often requires protection from winter weather. The stunning white flowers are well worth the effort.*

BELOW *Although it is a pretty plant with pale green flowers, the long dark green leaves of Helleborus foetidus emit an unpleasant smell when crushed. Once established, the plant will self-seed quite quickly.*

This genus comprising 15 species belongs to the buttercup family (Ranunculaceae) and is found in temperate zones from Europe to western China. They are mostly low-growing plants with hand-shaped, often toothed, short-stemmed, deep green leaves that emerge from a fleshy root-stock. The simple, 5-petalled, bowl-shaped flowers appear from mid-winter through to spring and occur in unusual shades of green, dusky pink, and maroon, as well as white. At the center of the flower are prominent, green, nectar-containing sacs and a number of yellow stamens. Commonly known as the lenten rose or winter rose, the perennials of this species were favorites of Gertrude Jekyll (1843–1935), a passionate English expert gardener and designer.

CULTIVATION

Helleborus species prefer cooler climates and woodland conditions with deep, fertile, humus-rich, well-drained soil and dappled shade. Some of the smaller types of plants are suitable for rockeries. Many species benefit from having old foliage removed when the plants are dormant. Propagate by division or from seed.

Favorites	Flower Color	Blooming Season	Flo Fragr
Helleborus argutifolius	pale green	late winter to early spring	n
Helleborus foetidus	green with red margins	mid-winter to mid-spring	n
***Helleborus* 'Halliwell Purple'**	pinkish purple	mid-winter to early spring	r
Helleborus lividus	greenish with pink-purple tint	mid-winter to early spring	
Helleborus niger	white, pink; greenish center	early winter to early spring	
Helleborus orientalis	white, cream, green, purple	mid-winter to mid-spring	

Top Tip

All *Helleborus* species are toxic and the sap can cause skin irritation, so exercise caution when handling. Keep out of reach of children.

RIGHT Helleborus 'Halliwell Purple' bears slightly drooping, saucer-shaped, dusky rose-colored flowers and has mid-green leaves.

LEFT Helleborus lividus *has deep green or bluish green glossy leaves and attractive light green flowers. Its compact habit makes it suitable as a border plant.*
BELOW Helleborus orientalis, *or lenten rose, is valued for its large saucer-shaped blooms that come in a range of colors.*

Plant Height	Plant Width	Hardiness Zone	Frost Tolerance
4 ft (1.2 m)	24 in (60 cm)	6–9	yes
30 in (75 cm)	18 in (45 cm)	6–10	yes
18 in (45 cm)	18–24 in (45–60 cm)	6–10	yes
18 in (45 cm)	12 in (30 cm)	7–9	yes
12 in (30 cm)	12–18 in (30–45 cm)	3–9	yes
2–24 in (0–60 cm)	18–24 in (45–60 cm)	6–10	yes

HEMEROCALLIS

Once grouped with the true lilies, this small genus of 15 species of fleshy-root perennials from temperate East Asia is now the type genus for its own family, the Hemerocallidaceae. The plants form clumps of grassy or iris-like leaves with funnel- to bell-shaped flowers held aloft on sturdy stems. Flowers come in a variety of forms and in shades of warm yellow, apricot, red and mauve. Individual flowers last only a day—hence the common name of daylily—although the plants do produce a succession of blooms lasting from late spring until autumn. All parts, especially the buds and flowers, are edible and may be added to salads or used as a colorful garnish. Stamens can be used as a saffron color substitute.

CULTIVATION

Hemerocallis plants are hardy and are easily grown in a sunny or partly shaded position with fertile, moist, well-drained soil. The flowers turn to face the sun, which is an important consideration when positioning the plants in the garden. Propagation is usually by division.

ABOVE Hemerocallis fulva, *a clump-forming perennial, prefers a sunny position and is popular for its tall, orange, trumpet-shaped flowers.*
BELOW *Lavender-blue flowers with a bright yellow center make* Hemerocallis *'Prairie Blue Eyes' a valuable addition to the garden, particularly among shrubs and on the edges of paths.*

Top Tip

Every few years it is a good idea to lift and divide clumps of daylilies as this will help to maintain vigor. Evergreen daylilies should be divided in spring.

Favorites

Favorites	Flower Color	Blooming Season	Flower Fragrance	Plant Height	Plant Width	Hardiness Zone	Frost Tolerance
Hemerocallis 'Buzz Bomb'	orange-red and yellow	summer to early autumn	no	24 in (60 cm)	18–24 in (45–60 cm)	5–11	yes
Hemerocallis fulva	orange-brown	summer to early autumn	no	3 ft (0.9 m)	24 in (60 cm)	4–11	yes
Hemerocallis 'Green Flutter'	yellow with green tints	summer to early autumn	no	20 in (50 cm)	3 ft (0.9 m)	5–11	yes
Hemerocallis lilioasphodelus	lemon yellow	early summer	yes	3 ft (0.9 m)	3 ft (0.9 m)	4–9	yes
Hemerocallis 'Prairie Blue Eyes'	mauve-blue	summer to early autumn	no	27 in (70 cm)	30 in (75 cm)	5–11	yes
Hemerocallis 'Stella de Oro'	bright yellow	summer	no	12 in (30 cm)	18 in (45 cm)	5–11	yes

ABOVE Hemerocallis *'Buzz Bomb' displays its showy orange-red blooms* *in summer. It looks particularly effective in mass plantings.*

RIGHT *The lemon yellow blooms of* Hemerocallis lilioasphodelus *have pleasant fragrance and are pleasing to the eye.*

HIBISCUS

This genus of over 200 annual or perennial herbs, shrubs, or trees is found throughout warm-temperate, subtropical, and tropical regions of the world. The species are mostly grown for their large, open, bell-shaped flowers, which grow as single flowers or in clusters. They are made up of 5 overlapping petals with a central column of fused stamens surrounded by a darker coloring in the center of the flower. Colors include white, yellow, and orange as well as dramatic pinks, purples, and reds. The beautiful flowers are followed by a fruit capsule. The light to dark green simple leaves grow alternately on the stem and take the shape of an outspread hand. *Hibiscus brackenridgei* is the state flower of Hawaii.

LEFT The cultivar Hibiscus rosa-sinensis 'Eileen McMullen' is grown for its stunning blooms of orange-red, attractively edged with yellow and featuring golden stamens.

CULTIVATION

Most species of hibiscus are susceptible to drought and are frost tender, needing a position in full sun with a rich and moist soil. The annuals are best grown from seed, while perennial varieties of hibiscus are propagated from seed or by division.

Top Tip

Hibiscus species are usually easy to grow, but they do need a warm position, and regular watering and feeding during the growing season. To keep the plant shape, trim after flowering.

LEFT Hibiscus rosa-sinensis 'Persephone' bears its single red-centered, pink flowers throughout summer. The glossy dark green leaves have toothed edges.

ABOVE *Another favorite cultivar is Hibiscus rosa-sinensis 'Jason Blue', with its bright yellow blooms and pale pink center. It needs lots of sunshine.*

RIGHT *Hibiscus syriacus 'Boule de Feu' responds well to pruning in the first 2 years of growth, and rewards this treatment with dusky pink flowers.*

Favorites

	Flower Color	Blooming Season	Flower Fragrance	Plant Height	Plant Width	Hardiness Zone	Frost Tolerance
Hibiscus brackenridgei	yellow	spring and early summer	no	10 ft (3 m)	5 ft (1.5 m)	10–12	no
Hibiscus moscheutos	white, pink, red	summer to early autumn	no	3–8 ft (0.9–2.4 m)	3 ft (0.9 m)	5–9	yes
Hibiscus mutabilis	whitish pink to deep pink	summer to autumn	no	6–15 ft (1.8–4.5 m)	5–12 ft (1.5–3.5 m)	8–12	yes
Hibiscus rosa-sinensis	red to dark red	mid-summer to early winter	no	5–15 ft (1.5–4.5 m)	4–8 ft (1.2–2.4 m)	9–12	no
Hibiscus schizopetalus	pink, red	summer to autumn	no	10–12 ft (3–3.5 m)	3–5 ft (0.9–1.5 m)	10–12	no
Hibiscus syriacus	white, pink, purple; red base	summer to autumn	no	10 ft (3 m)	6 ft (1.8 m)	5–10	yes

RIGHT *The aptly named* Hibiscus syriacus *'Red Heart' bears its white flowers over a long period in the warmer months. The leaves are coarsely toothed.*

BELOW Hibiscus mutabilis, *or cotton rose, is a large spreading shrub with attractive 5-petalled flowers that open white and age to pink or red.*

BOTTOM *Long arching branches and pendulous reddish pink flowers with an extra long stamen make* Hibiscus schizopetalus *one of the more unusual species.*

RIGHT Hibiscus rosa-sinensis *'Rosalind' bears semi-double flowers with ruffled petals in the most dazzling shades of orange and yellow. The vibrant coloring of this cultivar adds a tropical atmosphere to the garden.*

LEFT *The rich ruby red blooms of* Hibiscus moscheutos *'Lord Baltimore' make a striking contrast with the large mid-green leaves. Grow this plant in a sheltered spot.*
BELOW *The pale pink, almost white, double flowers of* Hibiscus mutabilis *'Plena' account for the popularity of this freely branching large shrub.*

HIPPEASTRUM

Also known as amaryllis and knight's star lily, this genus of around 80 species belongs to the bulb family and is indigenous to the Americas. They produce long, straplike, rather fleshy leaves and magnificent, large, funnel-shaped flowers borne on strong flower stems. The flowers are made up of 6 petals occurring in 2 whorls of 3 petals with widely varying patterns. Flowers bloom in late winter, and are white, pink, or red; different species show an even wider color range. There are many common cultivars. The name *Hippeastrum* comes from the Greek *hippos* (horse) and *astrum* (of the flower), and refers to the resemblance between the shape of the flowerhead and a horse's head.

CULTIVATION

Grow outdoors in frost-free areas or as greenhouse plants in cooler climates. Plant with the tip of the bulb exposed, in moist humus-rich soil. Plenty of water and feeding during the growing period will encourage large flowers. Allow the bulb to dry off after the foliage dies down and flowering finishes. These plants can only be grown from bulbs.

Top Tip

All *Hippeastrum* make suitable potted house plants and flower well indoors. They grow best in a good-quality loam-based potting mix.

BELOW LEFT Hippeastrum *'Pamela' is valued because it is a profuse bloomer, bearing glorious scarlet flowers that measure up to 10 in (25 cm) in length.*

BELOW Hippeastrum *'Picotee'* has beautiful white flowers, each petal edged with a fine red line. It needs warmth and light to produce its best blooms.

ABOVE Hippeastrum *'Christmas Star'*, with its red, white, and green flowers, makes a festive yuletide decoration.
LEFT The large, single, deep red flowers of Hippeastrum *'Royal Velvet'* lend a tropical warmth to the home when they appear on a potted indoor plant in winter.

Favorites

	Flower Color	Blooming Season	Flower Fragrance	Plant Height	Plant Width	Hardiness Zone	Frost Tolerance
Hippeastrum **'Christmas Star'**	red and white; greenish throat	late winter to mid-summer	no	18–24 in (45–60 cm)	12 in (30 cm)	9–12	no
Hippeastrum × *johnsonii*	red with white streaks	late winter to spring	no	18–24 in (45–60 cm)	12 in (30 cm)	7–11	no
Hippeastrum **'Pamela'**	scarlet	late winter to mid-summer	no	18–24 in (45–60 cm)	12 in (30 cm)	9–12	no
Hippeastrum **papilio**	greenish white; red markings	spring to early summer	no	18–30 in (45–75 cm)	12 in (30 cm)	9–12	no
Hippeastrum **'Picotee'**	white, edged with red	late winter to mid-summer	no	12–18 in (30–45 cm)	12 in (30 cm)	9–12	no
Hippeastrum **'Royal Velvet'**	deep red	late winter to mid-summer	no	18–24 in (45–60 cm)	12 in (30 cm)	9–12	no

HYACINTHUS

RIGHT Hyacinthus orientalis 'Blue Jacket' bears long spikes covered with purple-blue blooms and long, erect, bright green leaves. The bulbs flower best in their first year.

The type genus for its family, the Hyacinth-aceae, *Hyacinthus* contains just 3 species of spring-flowering bulbs found throughout western and central Asia. The glossy green leaves are narrow and straplike, rolling slightly inward toward the center of the plant. The flowers, a widely flared tubular bell-shape, are crowded in clusters on sturdy flower spikes. The garden cultivars come in a range of colors, from white to creamy yellow and shades of pink, red, and purple. Although famed for its scent, only 1 species, the common *Hyacinthus orientalis*, is especially fragrant. According to Greek mythology, this flower grew from the bleeding wound of Hyacinth, a boy loved by the god Apollo.

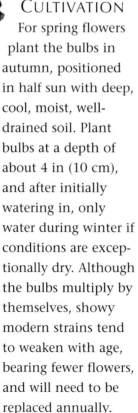

CULTIVATION

For spring flowers plant the bulbs in autumn, positioned in half sun with deep, cool, moist, well-drained soil. Plant bulbs at a depth of about 4 in (10 cm), and after initially watering in, only water during winter if conditions are exceptionally dry. Although the bulbs multiply by themselves, showy modern strains tend to weaken with age, bearing fewer flowers, and will need to be replaced annually.

ABOVE Hyacinthus orientalis 'Queen of the Pinks' lives up to its name by bearing a host of pink flowers in spring. Spent flower stems should be removed.
RIGHT The sweet scent of Hyacinthus orientalis 'Jan Bos' makes this a garden favorite. The waxy deep pink blooms look wonderful in mass plantings.

Right Hyacinthus orientalis *'Amethyst'* makes an excellent container plant. Make sure the soil is well drained and keep moist during the growing season.

Favorites	Flower Color	Blooming Season	Flower Fragrance	Plant Height	Plant Width	Hardiness Zone	Frost Tolerance
Hyacinthus orientalis	white, pink, blue to purple	early to mid-spring	yes	8–12 in (20–30 cm)	3 in (8 cm)	5–9	yes
Hyacinthus orientalis **'Blue Jacket'**	blue with purple stripes	mid-spring	yes	8–12 in (20–30 cm)	3 in (8 cm)	5–9	yes
Hyacinthus orientalis **'Carnegie'**	white	mid-spring	yes	8–12 in (20–30 cm)	3 in (8 cm)	5–9	yes
Hyacinthus orientalis **'City of Haarlem'**	creamy yellow	mid-spring	yes	8–12 in (20–30 cm)	3 in (8 cm)	5–9	yes
Hyacinthus orientalis **'Jan Bos'**	deep pink	mid-spring	yes	8–12 in (20–30 cm)	3 in (8 cm)	5–9	yes
Hyacinthus orientalis **'Pink Pearl'**	dark pink, lighter edges	mid-spring	yes	8–12 in (20–30 cm)	3 in (8 cm)	5–9	yes

Top Tip

Flowering potted hyacinths make a lovely gift. Because they are available in colors ranging from blue and pink to purple and white, there's a hyacinth to suit everyone.

RIGHT *Like all hyacinths, Hyacinthus orientalis 'Pink Pearl' makes a good cut flower. Changing the water daily will result in longer lasting blooms.*

BELOW *With deliciously perfumed, white-centered, deep purple-blue flowers, Hyacinthus orientalis 'Blue Magic' is a popular choice for the garden.*

ABOVE *Hyacinthus orientalis 'Carnegie' displays pure white flowers densely crowded onto a bright green stem.*

RIGHT *Wear gloves when planting hyacinth bulbs, such as* Hyacinthus orientalis *'Queen of the Night', as they can irritate sensitive skin.*

LEFT *From the middle of spring,* Hyacinthus orientalis *'City of Haarlem' produces tall flower spikes smothered with fragrant creamy yellow blooms. Plant this popular cultivar alongside contrasting single-colored daffodils (*Narcissus *species) and tulips (*Tulipa *species) for a stunning floral display.*

LEFT Hydrangea macrophylla *'Ami Pasquier' is a slow-growing mophead hydrangea that bears crimson-pink flowers that are streaked purple in the center.*

HYDRANGEA

There are about 100 species of deciduous and evergreen shrubs, trees, and climbers in this genus. They are native to eastern Asia and North and South America, where they grow in moist woodland areas. Though famed for their profusion of cheerful blooms, the foliage, with large oval leaves, often with serrated edges, makes a pleasant backdrop. Flowerheads are made up of very small fertile flowers surrounded by larger, eye-catching, 4-petalled, sterile florets. They may be conical, flat-topped (lacecap), or rounded (mophead), and usually emerge in spring and summer. Colors range from white through to red, purple, and blue and, in *Hydrangea macrophylla,* these can vary depending on the soil—acid soils produce blue flowers and alkaline soils produce reds and pinks.

CULTIVATION

This is an adaptable genus suitable for a range of situations. Position in sun or dappled shade with good composted soil, and feed lightly. Propagate from seed or tip cuttings in spring, or hardwood cuttings in winter.

ABOVE Hydrangea arborescens *subsp.* radiata *produces an interesting creamy white flowerhead, where the majority of the flowers in the cluster are sterile.*

Favorites

	Flower Color	Blooming Season	Flower Fragrance	Plant Height	Plant Width	Hardiness Zone	Frost Tolerance
Hydrangea arborescens	creamy white	late spring and summer	no	8 ft (2.4 m)	8 ft (2.4 m)	6–9	yes
Hydrangea involucrata	white and mauve	late summer	no	18–36 in (45–90 cm)	3–6 ft (0.9–1.8 m)	7–10	yes
Hydrangea macrophylla	pink and blue	summer	no	3–6 ft (0.9–1.8 m)	8 ft (2.4 m)	6–10	yes
Hydrangea paniculata	creamy white to pinkish white	late summer to early autumn	no	10–20 ft (3–6 m)	8 ft (2.4 m)	5–10	yes
Hydrangea quercifolia	white fading to pink	mid-summer to mid-autumn	no	4–8 ft (1.2–2.4 m)	8 ft (2.4 m)	5–10	yes
Hydrangea serrata	white, pink, blue	summer to autumn	no	4 ft (1.2 m)	4 ft (1.2 m)	6–10	yes

RIGHT Hydrangea macrophylla 'Parzifal' is one of the many mophead hydrangeas in cultivation. Easily grown, it does best in an alkaline soil. **BELOW** Blue hydrangeas, such as Hydrangea macrophylla 'Blue Sky', need an acid soil to produce their richly colored flowerheads. Application of an acidic fertilizer can also help.

ABOVE *A classic lacecap variety, Hydrangea macro-phylla 'Buchfink' has a central circle of tiny fertile flowers surrounded by crimson sterile florets.*

RIGHT *The pale pink, almost white, flowers of Hydrangea involucrata 'Hortensis' appear in late summer, ringed by dark green leaves.*

Top Tip

Hydrangeas are equally at home in borders, in group plantings, or in containers, but they do need some protection from cold winds.

BELOW *Maintain the shape of hydrangeas by pruning when flowering is done. The blooms next season, like these of* Hydrangea macrophylla *'Enziandom', are then better displayed.*

ABOVE Hydrangea macrophylla *'Hatfield Rose' is a popular choice in gardens because of its delicate lilac-pink flowerheads and its neat rounded shape.*

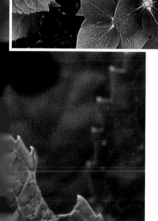

RIGHT *A large, vigorous, upright shrub,* Hydrangea paniculata *produces small, cream, fertile flowers and large, pinkish white, sterile florets that usually darken as they age. Prune the stems in late winter or early spring.*

RIGHT *With unusual, cup-shaped, pale lilac flowers, Hydrangea macrophylla 'Ayesha' is valued both in garden settings and as a potted indoor specimen.*
BELOW *Hydrangea arborescens 'Annabelle' bears rounded heads of small, mostly sterile, white flowers. The dark green leaves are equally attractive.*

ABOVE *Small, mauve-purple, fertile flowers with pinked edges, and white sterile florets turning pink as they age are produced in broad heads on Hydrangea serrata 'Grayswood'.*
RIGHT *Coming into bloom a little later than most other hydrangeas, Hydrangea paniculata 'Tardiva' is valued for its elegant spikes of white flowers and large dark green leaves.*
FAR RIGHT *Hydrangea macrophylla 'Mariesii Perfecta' shows off its gorgeous, purple, sterile florets and central, yellow and purple, fertile flowers during summer. Remove dead flowerheads.*

BELOW *A distinctive garden variety, crimson-flowered Hydrangea macrophylla 'Konigin Wilhelmina' gets its beautiful color from the alkaline soil.*

LEFT Iberis sempervirens, a spreading evergreen sub-shrub, bears pretty white flowers in dense heads. After flowering, trim the shrub to maintain its shape.

IBERIS

Popular for the bold effect of their massed heads of white, pink, mauve, or purple flowers, the 30-odd annuals, perennials, and subshrubs in this cabbage family (Brassicaceae) genus occur naturally in western and southern Europe and western Asia. They generally have simple, small, narrow leaves, and when not in flower form a rounded bush. The flowerheads open in spring or summer and are borne on short stems that hold them clear of the foliage. Both the genus and common name refer to the home of these plants: *Iberis* is derived from *Iberia*, the Roman name for Spain, while candy-tuft means "the tufted plant from Candia," the former name for Crete.

CULTIVATION

Plant in a sunny position in light, moist, well-drained soil. Deadhead regularly to encourage continuous blooming. *Iberis* plants appreciate a light dressing of dolomite lime. They are useful as ground covers, in rock gardens, and in massed displays. Propagate annuals from seed, and the perennials and subshrubs from seed or small cuttings.

ABOVE Iberis sempervirens 'Weisser Zwerg' is a compact version of the species, bearing white blooms with contrasting brown centers in spring and early summer.

RIGHT Iberis umbellata 'Flash Mixed' is valued for its attractive flowerheads that come in a variety of bright colors, and have a very pleasing scent.

Favorites

	Flower Color	Blooming Season	Flower Fragrance	Plant Height	Plant Width	Hardiness Zone	Frost Tolerance
Iberis amara	white, purplish white	summer	yes	12 in (30 cm)	6 in (15 cm)	7–11	yes
Iberis gibraltarica	pink, white with red tinges	summer	no	12 in (30 cm)	12 in (30 cm)	7–11	yes
Iberis saxatalis	white with purple tinges	summer	no	6 in (15 cm)	12 in (30 cm)	7–9	yes
Iberis sempervirens	white	spring to early summer	no	6–12 in (15–30 cm)	18 in (45 cm)	4–11	yes
Iberis sempervirens 'Weisser Zwerg'	white	spring to early summer	no	6 in (15 cm)	18 in (45 cm)	4–11	yes
Iberis umbellata	white, pink, lilac, red, purple	spring to early summer	yes	6–12 in (15–30 cm)	8 in (20 cm)	7–11	yes

RIGHT *The flattened lilac-pink flowers of* Iberis gibraltarica *are tinged white and appear in summer. This is a suitable plant for borders and rock gardens.*

Top Tip

Iberis species make great cut flowers, and because the flowerheads are showy and sometimes fragrant, they are also a popular choice for floral arrangements.

IMPATIENS

Variously known as balsam, busy lizzie, or water fuchsia, this genus of around 850 species of annuals, perennials, and sub-shrubs is widely distributed throughout the subtropics and tropics of Asia and Africa. They are generally soft-stemmed plants with simple, pointed, lance-shaped leaves that often have toothed edges. The flowers occur in many different colors, appear throughout the year in mild areas, and have 5 petals—an upper standard and the lower 4 fused into 2 pairs. The sepals are also partly fused to form a spur. The flowers are followed by seed pods that, when ripe, explosively eject their contents at the slightest touch. This memorable feature has given rise to the genus name *Impatiens*, which is Latin for impatient.

ABOVE Impatiens, *New Guinea Group, 'Tagula' has deep green pointed leaves, and flowers that are pale pink with a darker center. This cultivar makes an excellent cut flower.*

CULTIVATION

The annuals are grown as summer plants in cooler climates; the perennials are fairly tender and need mild winters. Shade from hot sun and plant in deep, cool, moist, humus-rich soil. Water and feed well. Propagate annuals from seed and perennials from cuttings. Some species self-sow and may be invasive.

RIGHT Impatiens, *New Guinea Group, 'Satchi' has cerise flowers. This perennial is often treated as an annual in cooler regions.*

Top Tip

Most *Impatiens* species make great indoor specimens, either in pots or hanging baskets. Keep the soil moist and tip prune to encourage more compact growth.

ABOVE *The pale lilac single flowers of* Impatiens sodenii *are borne on long stalks, and the lance-shaped leaves have toothed edges. It is best grown in frost-free areas.*

RIGHT Impatiens, *New Guinea Group, 'Celebration Hot Pink' is well-named, as the plant bears a profusion of festive pink flowers over quite a long period.*

Favorites

	Flower Color	Blooming Season	Flower Fragrance	Plant Height	Plant Width	Hardiness Zone	Frost Tolerance
Impatiens balsamina	pink, red, purple, white	summer to early autumn	no	12–30 in (30–75 cm)	18 in (45 cm)	9–12	no
Impatiens, **New Guinea Group**	pink, cerise, red, orange, white	summer	no	8–24 in (20–60 cm)	24–36 in (60–90 cm)	10–12	no
Impatiens niamniamensis	purple, pink, red, yellow	most of the year	no	24–36 in (60–90 cm)	24–36 in (60–90 cm)	10–12	no
Impatiens omeiana	yellow	early autumn	no	12 in (30 cm)	36 in (90 cm)	8–10	no
Impatiens sodenii	lilac, pink, white	summer	no	4–8 ft (1.2–2.4 m)	4 ft (1.2 m)	10–12	no
Impatiens walleriana	red, pink, white, orange, purple	most of the year	no	8–24 in (20–60 cm)	24 in (60 cm)	9–12	no

BELOW Impatiens, *New Guinea Group, 'Garden Leader Fuchsia'* is valued for the gorgeous color of the blooms. It is an ideal courtyard specimen.

ABOVE Impatiens walleriana *'Super Elfin Blush'* is a bushy fast-growing perennial that benefits from a light trim after flowering.
TOP Impatiens, *New Guinea Group, 'Celebration Light Lavender'* needs moist well-drained soil to produce its best blooms.

BELOW *Vibrant red flowers are what makes* Impatiens, *New Guinea Group, 'Timor' a welcome addition to the garden. The rich green leaves are also eye-catching.*

ABOVE Impatiens niamniamensis *is one of the more striking species in this genus. The color, which may vary from plant to plant, changes along the length of the flower.*

BELOW Impatiens, *New Guinea Group, 'Fiesta Salmon Sunshine' bears pinkish orange rose-like flowers for a long period over summer. In good conditions it will self-seed readily.*

Ipomoea

More than half of the 500-odd species of twining climbers, annual or perennial herbs, shrubs, and small trees in this large and variable genus originated in the Americas. Commonly known as morning glory, they are widely cultivated in tropical to warm-temperate areas for their showy flowers and vigorous growth. The genus is notable for easy culture, quick growth, and beautiful bell-shaped to tubular flowers appearing in colors ranging from purple through red to blue, white, or yellow. Individual flowers can be short lived but may open in succession in heads or on stalks. Some species, including the sweet potato (*Ipomoea batatas*), have tuberous roots that are edible.

Cultivation

These plants prefer full sun and plenty of water in the growing season, but will make the best of most conditions. Some species are propagated from softwood or half-hardened cuttings. Seeds are better started under glass. Germination may be improved by cutting a notch in the seed or soaking in warm water.

ABOVE Ipomoea carnea *is valued for its gorgeous, funnel-shaped, pinkish purple blooms that become dark purple at the base.*

RIGHT *The tubular scarlet flowers of* Ipomoea lobata *fade to orange and then to pale yellow; this color change is the reason why this plant is popular in temperate gardens.*

BELOW LEFT Ipomoea tricolor *'Tie Dye' has twining stems and attractive heart-shaped leaves displaying white and purple patterns.*

Favorites	Flower Color	Blooming Season	Flow Fragra
Ipomoea batatas	white to pale purple	summer	nc
Ipomoea carnea	pink to pinkish purple	spring to summer	nc
Ipomoea horsfalliae	rose purple, rose pink	summer to winter	ne
Ipomoea lobata	red, fading to orange and cream	late summer to late autumn	ne
Ipomoea nil	blue	summer to early autumn	n
Ipomoea tricolor	bright blue to purple	summer to early autumn	n

Top Tip

The climbing *Ipomoea* species, such as *I. nil* or *I. horsfalliae*, can be trained over arches, pergolas, fences, and trellises or over a cliff or steep grade.

BELOW Ipomoea horsfalliae *has rose purple blooms that are the color of a cardinal's robes, which is why this is also called cardinal creeper. It needs warm conditions.*

Plant Height	Plant Width	Hardiness Zone	Frost Tolerance
1–6 ft (0.3–1.8 m)	10 ft (3 m)	9–12	no
4–8 ft (1.2–2.4 m)	3–6 ft (0.9–1.8 m)	9–12	no
10 ft (3 m)	3–6 ft (0.9–1.8 m)	11–12	no
6–15 ft (1.8–4.5 m)	3–6 ft (0.9–1.8 m)	8–12	no
10–15 ft (3–4.5 m)	2–6 ft (0.6–1.8 m)	9–12	no
10 ft (3 m)	5 ft (1.5 m)	8–12	no

IRIS

There are 300-odd species of irises scattered over the northern temperate zones, occurring in bulbous- and rhizomatous-rooted forms. Those with very fine stolonlike rhizomes are sometimes called fibrous rooted. *Iris*, the type genus for the family Iridaceae, is named for the Greek goddess of the rainbow. Extremely popular, irises have been cultivated since the time of the Egyptian pharaoh Thutmosis I, around 1500 B.C. The leaves, often arranged in fans, are sword-shaped and sometimes variegated. The flowers come in all colors and have 6 petals, usually in the typical fleur-de-lis pattern of 3 upright standards and 3 downward-curving falls. Tennessee claims *Iris germanica* as its floral emblem.

ABOVE Iris sibirica *'Tropic Night' bears flowers with velvety petals of deep blue-violet. The falls have contrasting yellowish white markings at the petal base.*

Top Tip

With their impressive flowers held high on slender stems, irises will perform best in a location with plenty of sun, but with protection from buffeting winds.

BELOW *Sky blue flowers, colored yellow at the petal base, are the drawcard of* Iris sibirica *'Perry's Blue'. Summer-flowering, this is an old plant that is still popular with gardeners today.*

CULTIVATION

There are 4 categories: bog irises need a sunny position near pond margins or in damp soil; woodland irises thrive in dappled sunlight in moist well-drained soil; bearded irises should be dried off after flowering; and rockery irises require moist, well-drained, gritty soil. Propagation is usually by division when dormant, less commonly from seed.

LEFT *Blooming from late spring to early summer,* Iris *'Echo de France' is a Tall Bearded iris with creamy white standards and clear yellow falls. This cultivar can reach a height of 36 in (90 cm).*

Favorites

	Flower Color	Blooming Season	Flower Fragrance	Plant Height	Plant Width	Hardiness Zone	Frost Tolerance
Iris, Arilbred Hybrids	white, blue, red, yellow, brown	mid-spring to early summer	no	12–30 in (30–75 cm)	8–18 in (20–45 cm)	5–9	yes
Iris, Dutch Hybrids	blue to violet, yellow, orange	spring to early summer	no	10–36 in (25–90 cm)	6 in (15 cm)	7–9	yes
Iris, Dwarf Bearded	various	late spring	no	8–15 in (20–38 cm)	12–24 in (30–60 cm)	5–10	yes
Iris ensata	white, purple, lavender	late spring to early summer	no	36 in (90 cm)	12 in (30 cm)	4–10	yes
Iris germanica	blue-purple	spring	no	2–4 ft (0.6–1.2 m)	12–24 in (30–60 cm)	4–10	yes
Iris, Intermediate Bearded	various	late spring	no	15–24 in (38–60 cm)	12–24 in (30–60 cm)	5–10	yes
Iris, Louisiana Hybrids	various	mid-spring to early summer	no	36 in (90 cm)	36 in (90 cm)	7–11	yes
Iris, Pacific Coast Hybrids	various	mid- to late spring	no	12–24 in (30–60 cm)	12–24 in (30–60 cm)	8–10	yes
Iris sibirica	blue, purple, white	late spring to early summer	no	2–4 ft (0.6–1.2 m)	12–18 in (30–45 cm)	5–10	yes
Iris, Spuria Hybrids	various	late spring to early summer	no	2–4 ft (0.6–1.2 m)	18–24 in (45–60 cm)	4–9	yes
Iris, Tall Bearded	various	late spring	no	30–36 in (75–90 cm)	12–24 in (30–60 cm)	5–10	yes
Iris unguicularis	light to dark violet	autumn to spring	no	12 in (30 cm)	24 in (60 cm)	7–10	yes

ABOVE *Larger than the species type, the flowers of* Iris sibirica *'Anniversary' have lovely pristine white petals accented by yellow markings at the base.*

ABOVE *Clear yellow standards, yellow and red-brown falls, and a gold beard combine to make* Iris, Intermediate Bearded, 'Eye Magic' *a particularly attractive cultivar. This easy-care plant will flourish in a sunny spot in the garden.*
RIGHT *The ruffled petals of* Iris, Tall Bearded, *'Stepping Out' are edged in deep blue-purple. A white to pale blue beard adds the finishing touch to this lovely flower.*

LEFT *Ruffled petals in soft pastel colors are the eye-catching feature of* Iris, Tall Bearded, *'Celebration Song with the apricot-pink standards sitting atop the falls lilac-blue. The flowers are up to 6 in (15 cm) across.*

ABOVE *Extensive violet veining marks the lighter colored petals of* Iris ensata *'Flying Tiger'. This beautiful award-winning cultivar is ideal for container planting.*

RIGHT *A delicate picotee edging of silver adds a glamorous touch to the ruffled rich mid-blue petals of the aptly named* Iris sibirica *'Silver Edge'.*

LEFT *With a preference for moist soil, Iris sibirica 'White Swirl' produces bushy foliage and pure white, rounded, flared petals, tinged with yellow at the base.*
RIGHT *Reaching up to 30 in (75 cm) high, Iris, Tall Bearded, 'Pink Taffeta' has lovely, ruffled, pink petals.*

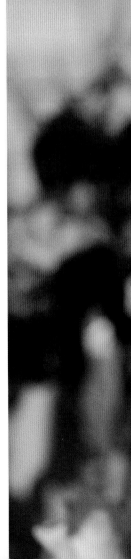

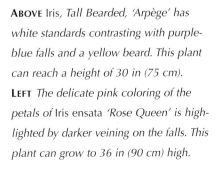

ABOVE *Iris, Tall Bearded, 'Arpège' has white standards contrasting with purple-blue falls and a yellow beard. This plant can reach a height of 30 in (75 cm).*
LEFT *The delicate pink coloring of the petals of Iris ensata 'Rose Queen' is high-lighted by darker veining on the falls. This plant can grow to 36 in (90 cm) high.*

RIGHT *Creating a dramatic impact in the garden,* Iris, *Tall Bearded,* 'Black Flag' *has standards of dark violet, surrounded by even deeper colored falls.*
BELOW *One of the Tall Bearded irises,* Iris 'Thornbird' *has creamy ecru standards and golden brown falls, which are highlighted with purplish veining.*

Ixia

Commonly known as corn lilies or wand flowers, this South African iris family (Iridaceae) genus contains some 50 species of corms with fine grassy foliage that is usually quite short in comparison to the tall, wiry, often arching flower stems. The flowers are simple 5- or 6-petalled structures, often star-shaped, and are borne massed in spikes at the stem tips. There are many cultivars, which are often brightly colored or may be pale with brighter markings. They also occur in some unusual shades, such as pale blue-green. It is a pity that the name of such beautiful flowers has rather an unpleasant origin: *ixia* is a Greek word for bird droppings, apparently a reference to the sticky sap.

Cultivation

Easily grown in a sunny position, *Ixia* species pre-fer a light well-drained soil. In hot areas the flowers will last longer in shade. Water well in spring but allow to dry off after flowering. Propa-gation is usually from off-sets or by division of the corms, less commonly from seed. Plant bulbs 2–3 in (5–8 cm) apart.

RIGHT Ixia maculata *has orange to yellow starry flowers, marked brown at the center, often with reddish undersides. The clusters of flowers appear on thin 18 in (45 cm) high stems.*

Top Tip

In a sunny spot, *Ixia* plants will flat-ten out their cup-shaped flowers to soak up the sun. In cooler climates they do best in a green-house environment.

LEFT *Ivory or pale lemon flowers, often with nuances of pink, top the slender stems of Ixia paniculata from spring to summer.*
BELOW *Ixia curta bears its lovely flowers in spring. The orange petals have darker markings at the base, and are often deeper colored on the undersides.*

Favorites	Flower Color	Blooming Season	Flower Fragrance	Plant Height	Plant Width	Hardiness Zone	Frost Tolerance
Ixia curta	orange with brownish blotch	spring	no	12–18 in (30–45 cm)	6 in (15 cm)	9–10	no
Ixia dubia	orange, yellow; brown center	spring to summer	no	8–18 in (20–45 cm)	6 in (15 cm)	9–10	no
Ixia maculata	orange, yellow; brown center	spring to early summer	no	15 in (38 cm)	6 in (15 cm)	9–10	no
Ixia monadelpha	white, pink, blue, mauve, purple	spring to early summer	no	12–18 in (30–45 cm)	6 in (15 cm)	10–11	no
Ixia paniculata	cream, yellow; tinged pink	late spring to early summer	no	12–24 in (30–60 cm)	10 in (25 cm)	9–10	no
Ixia viridiflora	pale green with purple center	spring to early summer	no	24–36 in (60–90 cm)	8 in (20 cm)	9–10	no

JASMINUM

amed for the fragrance of its flowers, this genus from Africa and Asia (with a lone American species) includes some 200 species of deciduous, semi-deciduous, and evergreen shrubs and woody-stemmed climbers. Both shrubs and climbers flower generously, though the foliage, which varies greatly in color and texture, will also add interest to a trellis or rock garden. The flowers, which are borne in clusters at the branch tips and leaf axils, are tubular with 5 widely flared lobes. They are most commonly white, white flushed pink, or yellow, and can be scentless to almost overpoweringly fragrant. Many properties are attributed to the plant's perfume, which is widely regarded to be an aphrodisiac.

CULTIVATION

Jasmines vary in hardiness depending on their origins, though few will tolerate repeated severe frosts. They are averse to drought, preferring moist, humus-rich, well-drained soil, and a position in full sun or partial shade. In suitable climates most species grow rapidly and some can become rather invasive. Propagate from seed, cuttings, or layers.

Top Tip

Popular in cottage gardens and a useful companion plant, jasmines can be kept neat and tidy if pinched back and pruned in spring before new growth occurs.

LEFT The yellow flowers of Jasminum nudiflorum, commonly known as winter jasmine, appear in the colder months before the leaves.
BELOW If supported during its early establishment, the yellow-flowered species Jasminum mesnyi can be trained to take a graceful cascading form.

Favorites

	Flower Color	Blooming Season	Flower Fragrance	Plant Height	Plant Width	Hardiness Zone	Frost Tolerance
Jasminum humile	bright yellow	spring to autumn	yes	8 ft (2.4 m)	10 ft (3 m)	8–11	yes
Jasminum mesnyi	bright yellow	late winter to early summer	no	10 ft (3 m)	10–15 ft (3–4.5 m)	8–11	yes
Jasminum nudiflorum	bright yellow	late winter to early spring	no	5–10 ft (1.5–3 m)	10 ft (3 m)	6–9	yes
Jasminum officinale	white	summer to early autumn	yes	8 ft (2.4 m)	8 ft (2.4 m)	6–10	yes
Jasminum sambac	white	continuously	yes	5–10 ft (1.5–3 m)	6 ft (1.8 m)	10–11	no
Jasminum × stephanense	pale pink	summer	yes	3–10 ft (0.9–3 m)	5–10 ft (1.5–3 m)	7–11	yes

FAR LEFT *The lovely, bright yellow, fragrant flowers and large, matt, dark green leaves of* Jasminum humile *'Revolutum' are both larger than those of the species.*

ABOVE *The abundant, tiny, white flowers of* Jasminum sambac *fill the air with their heady fragrance throughout the plant's long flowering season.*

KALANCHOE

This genus contains about 125 species of succulent shrubs, herbs, and climbers distributed mainly throughout tropical regions of Africa and Madagascar as well as parts of Asia. They are usually grown for their interesting foliage forms although a few bear vibrantly colored tubular flowers, including flaming Katie *(Kalanchoe blossfeldiana)*, which make them popular house plants. Growth habits range from low sprawling subshrubs to tall treelike plants, with a similarly wide variation in leaves, from small to large, glossy to felted, and gray-frosted to dark green. The genus has been extensively hybridized and, though the original species bore bright red flowers, the choice now includes white-, yellow-, pink-, and purple-flowering forms.

CULTIVATION

In all but the warmest climates these plants require indoor or greenhouse cultivation and should be grown in a moderately fertile gritty potting mix. If grown outdoors, they need a sunny sheltered position in humus-rich well-drained soil and should be kept reasonably dry in winter. Propagation is commonly by stem or leaf cuttings, or from seed sown in spring.

Favorites	Flower Color	Blooming Season	Flower Fragrance	Plant Height	Plant Width	Hardiness Zone	Frost Tolerance
Kalanchoe blossfeldiana	deep red	early spring	no	15 in (38 cm)	15 in (38 cm)	10–12	no
Kalanchoe daigremontiana	grayish violet	winter	no	3 ft (0.9 m)	12 in (30 cm)	9–12	no
Kalanchoe flammea	bright red	late spring to summer	no	10–12 in (25–30 cm)	6 in (15 cm)	10–11	no
Kalanchoe pumila	pink with purple markings	spring	no	8 in (20 cm)	18 in (45 cm)	11–12	no
Kalanchoe thyrsiflora	yellow	spring	yes	24 in (60 cm)	12 in (30 cm)	11–12	no
Kalanchoe tomentosa	yellow-green tinged purple	early spring	no	3 ft (0.9 m)	8 in (20 cm)	11–12	no

LEFT Kalanchoe flammea *is a succulent subshrub that produces tubular, vibrant red, 4-petalled blooms from the end of spring.*

BELOW *A small erect shrub,* Kalanchoe tomentosa *bears dense rosettes of thick, sometimes concave, oblong gray-green leaves that are heavily felted and have neat reddish brown markings near the tips. It produces small yellowish green flowers, but these are of secondary importance to the attractive foliage.*

Top Tip

These plants are ideal for indoor and balcony use. Prune after flowering has finished to ensure good future blooms; repotting can be done at this time as well.

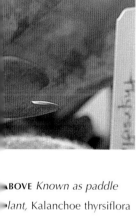

ABOVE *Known as paddle plant,* Kalanchoe thyrsiflora *is admired for its foliage: the young leaves are bright red, then turn pale green while retaining a reddish glow.*

RIGHT Kalanchoe pumila *is a small spreading subshrub. Its bed of frosted gray-green leaves is dotted with violet-pink flowers in spring.*

ABOVE AND BELOW Kalmia latifolia *bears highly distinctive flowers: the buds are crimped round the edges and open to reveal pink flowers. Numerous pretty cultivars have been developed, such as 'Olympic Fire', above, with deep red buds opening to large pink flowers, and 'Carousel', below, which has white flowers delicately flushed rosy pink.*

KALMIA

This genus of 7 species of shrubs in the family Ericaceae was named for Dr. Pehr Kalm, a botanist and explorer of the east coast of North America in the 1770s. Most species are evergreen and native to northeastern U.S.A., with a single species occurring in Cuba. They are grown for their attractive foliage and showy flowers, which range in color from pale pink to deep red. The leaves are smooth, opposite or alternate, deep green on the upper surface but paler on the underside, and occasionally stalkless. The attention-seeking flowers are bowl- or saucer-shaped and are generally borne in dense clusters, held well clear of the foliage. All make ideal border plants.

CULTIVATION

Kalmia species are at home in slightly acid peaty soil. Dappled shade under tall deciduous trees in a cool moist climate is ideal. Little pruning is necessary apart from the removal of spent flower clusters. Propagate from seed, which should be collected as soon as ripe and sown the following spring.

Favorites

	Flower Color	Blooming Season	Flower Fragrance	Plant Height	Plant Width	Hardiness Zone	Frost Tolerance
Kalmia angustifolia	reddish pink	early summer	no	3 ft (0.9 m)	4 ft (1.2 m)	2–9	yes
Kalmia latifolia	pale to dark pink	late spring to summer	no	5–8 ft (1.5–2.4 m)	6 ft (1.8 m)	3–9	yes
Kalmia latifolia 'Carousel'	white and pink	late spring	no	5–8 ft (1.5–2.4 m)	6 ft (1.8 m)	3–9	yes
Kalmia latifolia 'Olympic Fire'	pink	late spring	no	5–8 ft (1.5–2.4 m)	6 ft (1.8 m)	3–9	yes
Kalmia latifolia 'Pink Charm'	pink	late spring	no	5–8 ft (1.5–2.4 m)	6 ft (1.8 m)	3–9	yes
Kalmia polifolia	pinkish purple	spring	no	24 in (60 cm)	36 in (90 cm)	3–9	yes

LEFT *Deriving from north-eastern U.S.A., the dwarf shrub Kalmia angustifolia has smooth leaves and rosy pink flowers.*
BELOW Kalmia latifolia *is found from eastern Canada to the Gulf of Mexico, and is the state flower for Connecticut and Pennsylvania. Popular due to its soft pink flowers, it grows to 20 ft (6 m) in the wild.*

Top Tip

These plants are best suited to low-maintenance and informal garden schemes, where they can grow to their natural size and blooms can be best appreciated.

KNIPHOFIA

RIGHT *The elegant spikes of Kniphofia 'Primrose Beauty' bear pale yellow tubular flowers above clumps of sword-like leaves.*

BELOW *Truly dazzling from top to bottom,* Kniphofia caulescens *produces large rosettes of evergreen leaves and copper stems bearing flowers in rainbow shades of coral red to yellow.*

Most of the nearly 70 species in this aloe family (Aloeaceae) genus are native to South Africa. They are clump-forming perennials with grassy to sword-shaped, often evergreen foliage that emerges from vigorous rhizomes. From summer to autumn, bold spikes of intensely colored flowers are borne in bottlebrush heads at the top of strong, tall, upright stems, giving rise to the common names of red-hot poker and torch lily. Many hybrids and cultivars have been raised in a variety of sizes and flower colors; apart from the original yellows and oranges, white and red flowers are now also available. *Kniphofia* plants, named for the German professor Johann Hieronymus Kniphof (1704–1763), make excellent cut flowers.

CULTIVATION

Hardiness varies, though none will tolerate repeated heavy frosts. They are best planted in an open sunny position with moist, humus-rich, well-drained soil. Water and feed well when in active growth. The bulk will tolerate salt winds and thrive near the coast. Propagation is usually by division after flowering, or from seed.

Favorites	Flower Color	Blooming Season	Flo Fragr
Kniphofia caulescens	coral red, fading to yellow	late summer to mid-autumn	n
Kniphofia citrina	pale greenish yellow	summer to autumn	n
Kniphofia ensifolia	greenish yellow, dull pink buds	late summer to mid-autumn	n
Kniphofia northiae	pale yellow	summer	n
***Kniphofia* 'Primrose Beauty'**	light yellow	summer	n
Kniphofia rooperi	orange-red to orange-yellow	late summer to autumn	

Top Tip

Choose a mixture of the original yellow and orange flowering species, with their old-fashioned charm, and the newer cultivars, which delight with their bolder colors.

LEFT Kniphofia northiae *is of interest for its foliage as well as its flowers. Leaves are arching, broad, and blue-green. Orange buds open to pale yellow flowers.*

RIGHT *The robust* Kniphofia rooperi *is a magnificent late-flowerer, with orange-red blooms turning yellow. The spike is rounded rather than typically poker-like.*

Plant Height	Plant Width	Hardiness Zone	Frost Tolerance
4 ft (1.2 m)	24 in (60 cm)	7–10	yes
3 ft (0.9 m)	2–4 ft (0.6–1.2 m)	7–10	yes
2–4 ft (.6–1.2 m)	24 in (60 cm)	8–10	yes
4–6 ft (.2–1.8 m)	36 in (90 cm)	6–10	yes
3 ft (0.9 m)	3 ft (0.9 m)	7–10	yes
4 ft (1.2 m)	24 in (60 cm)	8–10	yes

LAELIA

This genus consists of around 50 species of mostly epiphytic orchids, occurring naturally from Central America to Brazil and Argentina. They are a popular group, appreciated for their easily grown, showy, and colorful flowers. Most have elongated bulblike stems, which bear 1, sometimes 2, thick semi-rigid leaves. Rather beautiful flowers are borne from the apex, or tip, of the stem, and they can vary greatly in size and color. Shades of white, pink, purple, and yellow are common, though with the introduction of the *Laeliacattleya* hybrids, which are a result of interbreeding between the *Laelia* and *Cattleya* genera, there are now even more colors to choose from.

CULTIVATION

Most *Laelia* species require bright, warm, and moist conditions while the plants are in active growth during the summer months; cool dry conditions are best during winter, when most species are dormant. Cultivated plants must have drainage that is unimpeded, and they can be mounted or grown in pots using a coarse bark-based medium.

ABOVE Laelia purpurata 'Carnea' *is popular because of its well-formed, beautifully colored salmon lip, and its temperature tolerance.*
BELOW *A relatively small plant,* Laelia milleri *has become a favorite in the last 20 years due to the intensity of its red to red-orange flowers. It requires warmth and bright light.*

Top Tip

In general, *Laelia* plants do not like being disturbed. They need bright light, and will withstand long periods of drought. Apply a nitrogen fertilizer in summer.

BELOW Laelia *Canariensis is an old hybrid that requires a dry period of dormancy so it can flower at its best.*

ABOVE *The flowers of 'Fort Caroline' are distinguished by their striking purple-blue lip. This plant is a cultivar of* Laelia anceps, *a Mexican species that can be grown indoors.*

Favorites

	Flower Color	Blooming Season	Flower Fragrance	Plant Height	Plant Width	Hardiness Zone	Frost Tolerance
Laelia anceps	lavender-pink; darker lip	winter	yes	18–24 in (45–60 cm)	12 in (30 cm)	10–12	no
Laelia autumnalis	rose pink; darker lip	autumn	yes	12–36 in (30–90 cm)	12 in (30 cm)	10–12	no
Laelia Canariensis	golden yellow	autumn	yes	18–24 in (45–60 cm)	12 in (30 cm)	10–12	no
Laelia crispa	white; purple and yellow lip	summer	yes	18–24 in (45–60 cm)	12 in (30 cm)	10–12	no
Laelia milleri	red to orange-red; yellow at throat	summer	no	12–18 in (30–45 cm)	12 in (30 cm)	10–12	no
Laelia purpurata	white; white and purple lip	spring to summer	yes	18 in (45 cm)	12 in (30 cm)	11–12	no

LAGERSTROEMIA

This genus belongs to the Lythraceae family and consists of about 53 species of mostly small evergreen or deciduous trees, occurring naturally from tropical Asia to Australia. A few species are widely bred, with many cultivars. They generally have simple variable leaves that are usually opposite, and capsular fruits. Their showy flowers have crinkled petals, somewhat crepelike in texture, and appear in differing shades of pink, mauve, and white. *Lagerstroemia* species make superb landscape subjects, valuable not only for their brightly colored flowers, but also for their attractive, often peeling, smooth bark, and colored autumn foliage. Some species have provided timber for furniture, bridges, and railway sleepers.

CULTIVATION

These trees are mostly easy to grow, and can cope with a wide variety of soils. They grow best in full sun in well-drained soil and are tolerant of light frosts. Propagate from seed or half-hardened cuttings in summer, or from hardwood cuttings in early winter.

Top Tip

Powdery mildew can be a problem with *Lagerstroemia* species, but cultivars such as the modern American hybrid *L.* 'Natchez' offer better disease resistance.

LEFT *'Andre de Martis' is one of the many popular flowering cultivars of* Lagerstroemia indica. *It bears bright pink flowers.*

ABOVE Lagerstroemia fauriei *is a fast-growing deciduous tree from Japan. Famed for its red-brown peeling bark, it bears small white flowers.*

ABOVE *Naturally found in China,* Lagerstroemia indica *is a multi-stemmed deciduous tree, with a wide-spreading, flat-topped, open habit when mature.*

RIGHT Lagerstroemia *'Natchez' is a wonderful landscape subject; it grows to 25 ft (8 m) high and has white flowers. The green leaves turn orange-red before falling in autumn.*

Favorites

	Flower Color	Blooming Season	Flower Fragrance	Plant Height	Plant Width	Hardiness Zone	Frost Tolerance
Lagerstroemia fauriei	white	summer	no	25 ft (8 m)	15–25 ft (4.5–8 m)	6–10	yes
Lagerstroemia floribunda	lavender-pink	spring to summer	no	15–30 ft (4.5–9 m)	15–25 ft (4.5–8 m)	10–12	no
Lagerstroemia indica	white, pink to dark red, purple	mid-summer to autumn	no	25 ft (8 m)	25 ft (8 m)	7–11	yes
Lagerstroemia 'Natchez'	white	summer to autumn	no	25 ft (8 m)	25 ft (8 m)	6–10	yes
Lagerstroemia speciosa	white, pink, purple	summer to autumn	no	25–50 ft (8–15 m)	15–30 ft (4.5–9 m)	10–12	no
Lagerstroemia subcostata	white tinged yellow	summer	no	15–40 ft (4.5–12 m)	15–25 ft (4.5–8 m)	7–9	yes

LAMPRANTHUS

This genus of 225-odd species from South Africa and Namibia contains many popular succulent garden plants, justifiably loved for their masses of colorful flowers, which are produced year-round, and especially in spring and summer. Most forms are low-growing mats or short shrubs, with pairs of short, waxy, cylindrical to triangular, yellow-green to blue-green leaves. The lustrous flowers open in the morning and close in the late afternoon, and are produced in such profusion that they usually obscure the entire plant body. Colors include pure white, red, yellow, orange, pink, and intermediate shades including bicolored forms. Curiously called pig face in Australia, the genus name is more complimentary; it comes from the Greek words *lampros* (bright) and *anthos* (flower).

CULTIVATION

Lampranthus species and their cultivars are reasonably easy to grow, though gardeners must remember not to over-water them. They are somewhat frost tender plants; however, they can withstand periods of drought. Grow either from cuttings or from seed.

ABOVE *Known as the mid-day flower,* Lampranthus amoenus *is a shrubby succulent perennial that needs full sun and good drainage.* **BELOW** Lampranthus auriantiacus *'Gold Nugget' has yellow-centered bright orange flowers. In summer, the foliage is hidden by a spectacular blanket of color.*

Top Tip

These hardy plants are ideal choices for gardeners who want attractive but low-maintenance plants. They are useful in rockeries, flowerbeds, banks, and borders.

ABOVE Lampranthus glaucus *is particularly recommended for the garden. It is characterized by its canary yellow daisylike flowers and rough-spotted leaves.*
RIGHT Lampranthus aurantiacus *has a spreading shrubby habit, and bears a profusion of yellow and orange flowers.*

Favorites	Flower Color	Blooming Season	Flower Fragrance	Plant Height	Plant Width	Hardiness Zone	Frost Tolerance
Lampranthus amoenus	rose purple	spring to summer	no	2–3 ft (0.6–0.9 m)	3–4 ft (0.9–1.2 m)	9–11	no
Lampranthus aurantiacus	orange and yellow	summer	no	18 in (45 cm)	30 in (75 cm)	9–11	no
Lampranthus aurantiacus 'Gold Nugget'	orange	summer	no	18 in (45 cm)	30 in (75 cm)	9–11	no
Lampranthus filicaulis	pale pink	early spring	no	3 in (8 cm)	36 in (90 cm)	9–11	no
Lampranthus glaucus	yellow	late spring	no	12 in (30 cm)	2–4 ft (0.6–1.2 m)	9–11	no
Lampranthus spectabilis	purple, pink, red	spring to summer	no	6–12 in (15–30 cm)	18–36 in (45–90 cm)	9–11	no

LATHYRUS

A member of the pea family (Fabaceae), this genus has far more than just the old-fashioned sweet pea to offer from among its 110 species of annuals and perennials. Found in Eurasia, North America, temperate South America, and the mountains of eastern Africa, many are climbers, others are low spreading plants, and some are shrubby. The climbers support themselves with tendrils found at the tips of the pinnate leaves, where the terminal leaflet would normally be. The eye-catching flowers occur in many colors, can be scented, and may be solitary or borne in clusters. The genus has long been popular with gardeners, including Thomas Jefferson, who planted *Lathyrus latifolius* at both his birthplace, Shadwell, and at his Virginia home, Monticello.

CULTIVATION

Non-climbing perennials require part-shade but otherwise keep the conditions sunny and well-ventilated to lessen the risk of mildew and botrytis. Plant in moist well-drained soil and provide stakes or wires for climbers. Propagation is from seed for the annuals and by division when dormant for the perennials.

ABOVE RIGHT *A compact bushy plant,* Lathyrus vernus 'Rosenelfe' *produces delicate pale pink and white flowers.*

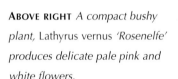

ABOVE Lathyrus grandiflorus *is a charming old garden perennial climber. It has mid-green leaves and bears deep magenta-pink flowers. As its common name, everlasting pea, suggests, it does not die easily once established.*

Favorites	Flower Color	Blooming Season	Flower Fragrance	Plant Height	Plant Width	Hardiness Zone	Frost Tolerance
Lathyrus grandiflorus	purple-pink	summer	no	6 ft (1.8 m)	6 ft (1.8 m)	6–9	yes
Lathyrus latifolius	red-purple, pink, white	summer	no	6 ft (1.8 m)	6–12 ft (1.8–3.5 m)	5–10	yes
Lathyrus nervosus	purple-blue	summer	yes	5 ft (1.5 m)	5 ft (1.5 m)	8–10	yes
Lathyrus odoratus	various	late winter to early summer	yes	6 ft (1.8 m)	24–36 in (60–90 cm)	4–10	yes
Lathyrus splendens	pink to purple-red	spring	no	6–10 ft (1.8–3 m)	6 ft (1.8 m)	8–10	yes
Lathyrus vernus	purple-blue	winter to spring	no	24 in (60 cm)	18 in (45 cm)	5–9	yes

RIGHT Lathyrus odoratus *is the most widely cultivated of all* Lathyrus *species, and cultivars have increased the color choice and number of flowers. 'All But Blue', right, has pure white flowers, edged with pale purple.*

LEFT Lathyrus odoratus *'Our Harry' bears magnificent deep purple-blue flowers, with frilled petal edges. It makes a stunning garden specimen on its own, or can be planted in beds with* L. odoratus *cultivars of contrasting hues for a breathtaking display of color.*

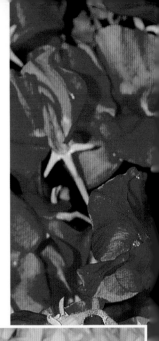

Top Tip

Many of these plants are excellent for cut flowers. Regular cutting for indoor use will encourage the further development of flowers, as will deadheading.

ABOVE Lathyrus vernus *forms clumps of mid-green foliage sprinkled with heads of tiny purple flowers. This is a good border plant as blooms appear early in winter and continue right through spring.*

ABOVE *The large, frilly, soft white flowers of* Lathyrus odoratus *'Anniversary' have ensured its instant success. A hardy annual climber, it deserves a prominent spot in the garden. The rose pink picotee edge to the blooms adds to its beauty.*
LEFT *The flowers of* Lathyrus odoratus *'Wiltshire Ripple' are a superb bi-colored mix of white flushed with claret. This is a prolific flowerer with a rich scent.*

ABOVE AND LEFT *The commercial cultivation of* Lathyrus odoratus *has produced plants with a number of attractions: height and vigor, a profusion of blooms, improved disease resistance, and gloriously colored flowers. 'Winner', above, has scarlet flowers with an orange tint, and 'Lisbeth', left, a relative newcomer, has award-winning pink blooms.*

RIGHT Lathyrus odoratus 'Apricot Queen' has wavy pale orange-pink blooms.

LAVANDULA

The 28 species of evergreen aromatic shrubs that belong to this genus are distributed from northern Africa and the Mediterranean to western Asia, India, and the Canary and Cape Verde Islands. Although their natural habitat is dry, sunny, and exposed rocky areas, lavender plants are at home in the garden, and their distinctive spikes of fragrant purple flowers and gray-green foliage can provide color for much of the year. Cultivated species belong to 3 groups: the hardy Spica (English lavender) Group, which produces the best oil; the slightly tender Stoechas Group, with fatter flower spikes topped by petallike bracts; and the tender Pterostoechas Group, with flowers that lack the true lavender fragrance. *Lavandula* is part of the large mint family, which includes herbs such as sage and rosemary.

CULTIVATION

Lavender plants are excellent for containers, hedges, and positions where they can be brushed against to release their aroma. They grow in a wide range of soils that must be well drained, particularly in winter. Hardy species should be pruned after flowering. Lavenders are usually propagated from tip cuttings in spring or half-hardened cuttings in autumn.

Favorites

	Flower Color	Blooming Season	Flower Fragrance	Plant Height	Plant Width	Hardiness Zone	Frost Tolerance
Lavandula angustifolia	purple	summer to early autumn	yes	3 ft (0.9 m)	30 in (75 cm)	6–10	yes
Lavandula dentata	mauve-blue	spring to summer	yes	3–4 ft (0.9–1.2 m)	5 ft (1.5 m)	8–10	yes
Lavandula × intermedia	purple	summer	yes	3 ft (0.9 m)	12–20 in (30–50 cm)	6–10	yes
Lavandula lanata	purple	mid- to late summer	yes	30 in (75 cm)	36 in (90 cm)	8–9	yes
Lavandula 'Sawyers'	purple	summer	yes	18 in (45 m)	30 in (75 cm)	6–10	yes
Lavandula stoechas	purple	summer to early autumn	yes	18–30 in (45–75 cm)	18–30 in (45–75 cm)	7–10	yes

LEFT Lavandula angustifolia *'Folgate' is an evergreen cultivar with a broad habit. It has violet flowers that are strongly scented, and gray-green foliage.*

BELOW CENTER *The scented* Lavandula stoechas *'Kew Red' makes a perfect small hedge or container plant. Its deep pink-purple flowers are topped with pale pink bracts.*

BELOW Lavandula angustifolia *'Royal Purple' is admired for its elegantly shaped flowers, which are bright violet-blue fading to dark lavender-blue.*

ABOVE *A low-growing shrub,* Lavandula *'Sawyers' has silvery leaves and bears purple flowers on tall slender stems. This is an attractive summer flowerer.*

Top Tip

Not only is the aroma of lavender known to relieve stress and nausea, it is also a natural insect repellant. Use the fragrant flower buds in place of mothballs.

RIGHT *A popular perennial, Lavandula angustifolia 'Lodden Blue' is an excellent ornamental lavender. It is also common in potpourri.*
BELOW *Lavandula stoechas is a variable species that is lower growing than many others. It bears many plump flowering spikes of deep purple topped by eye-catching petallike bracts.*

ABOVE *A member of the hardy Spica Group,* Lavandula angustifolia *is a good shrub for the garden. 'Hidcote', above, produces densely packed spikes of purple flowers.*

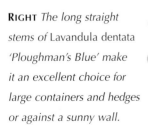

RIGHT *The long straight stems of* Lavandula dentata *'Ploughman's Blue' make it an excellent choice for large containers and hedges or against a sunny wall.*

BELOW *Native to the Mediterranean,* Lavandula stoechas *subsp.* aurantica *has gray-green leaves and plump flower spikes with prominent petallike bracts.*

LEPTOSPERMUM

This genus is made up of around 80 species of evergreen shrubs or small trees that have narrow leaves that are often aromatic, or occasionally lemon-scented, when crushed. All are Australian, apart from 1 species widespread in New Zealand and 2 found in Southeast Asia. They are collectively known as tea-trees because the leaves of some species were used as a tea substitute by Captain James Cook's crew and early settlers to Australia. The small open flowers with 5 petals are mostly white and pink or occasionally red, and are usually produced in profusion during the flowering season. The small woody capsules often persist for a long period. As a group, they are very popular in cultivation, and many are in great demand as cut flowers.

CULTIVATION

Good growers, most plants will tolerate an occasional light frost. They are best suited to well-drained soil in full sun, but some species can cope with wet conditions and nearly full shade. Regular pruning from an early age and each year after flowering is recommended to retain bushiness. Cultivars must be propagated from cuttings to maintain their characteristics.

Top Tip

These graceful screening plants will adapt to a variety of soil types and conditions; a light feeding with slow-release fertilizer in spring is beneficial.

RIGHT Leptospermum poly-galifolium *may vary in size from shrub to bushy tree. It has narrow aromatic leaves and bears masses of white flowers along the branches. The new growth is often a coppery red shade.*
BELOW LEFT *A medium-sized shrub,* Leptospermum scoparium *has small leaves and bears charming pink and white flowers.*

Favorites

	Flower Color	Blooming Season	Flov Fragr
Leptospermum javanicum	white	spring to autumn	ne
Leptospermum lanigerum	white	late spring to summer	n
Leptospermum polygalifolium	white, cream	late spring to summer	n
Leptospermum rupestre	white	late spring to summer	n
Leptospermum scoparium	white, pink, red	late spring to summer	n
Leptospermum scoparium 'Kiwi'	deep pink	late spring to summer	n

ABOVE AND BELOW *The erect shrub* Leptospermum scoparium *has produced many wonderful cultivars, displaying a large range of flower color and size. 'Big Red', above, lives up to its name with its covering of red flowers, and the deep pink blooms of 'Helene Strybing', below, make it a popular choice.*

Plant Height	Plant Width	Hardiness Zone	Frost Tolerance
10–25 ft (3–8 m)	8–12 ft (2.4–3.5 m)	10–11	no
8–15 ft (.4–4.5 m)	5–10 ft (1.5–3 m)	8–10	yes
6–20 ft (.8–6 m)	3–10 ft (0.9–3 m)	9–12	no
3–5 ft (9–1.5 m)	3–6 ft (0.9–1.8 m)	7–10	yes
5–10 ft (.5–3 m)	3–6 ft (0.9–1.8 m)	8–10	yes
3 ft (0.9 m)	3 ft (0.9 m)	8–10	yes

ABOVE Leptospermum scoparium *'Pink Cascades' has an attractive weeping form with pale pink flowers.*
BELOW *Fairly common in cultivation,* Leptospermum lanigerum *forms an erect bushy shrub. The new growth is covered in woolly hairs and leaves are silvery gray to dark green. Flowers are white, occasionally pink-tinged.*

RIGHT *This stunning floral display is by* Leptospermum scoparium *'Kiwi', a dwarf form that produces single dark pink flowers in late spring and early summer.*

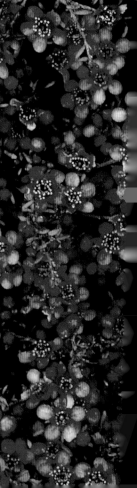

LEFT *The dark green lance-shaped leaves of Lepto-spermum scoparium 'Ray Williams' provide a good background for the small delicate pale pink flowers.*

ABOVE *Leptospermum scoparium 'Nanum Kea' is notable for its large pink-red flowers. It is suitable for container use and will thrive in a sunny position.*

LEUCANTHEMUM

Rather pragmatically named from the Greek *leukos* (white) and *anthemon* (flower), most of the 25 species of annual and perennial daisies in this Eurasian genus do indeed have flowers with white ray florets, usually around a central golden disc floret. Species often form quite large clumps of foliage with simple, bright to deep green, linear to spatula-shaped leaves. Stalks bearing their cheerful flowers appear among the foliage from summer to autumn, depending on the species. Hybridization has produced a wider range of flower form and color, including pompon-centered flowers, and of much interest to gardeners are the *Leucanthemum* × *superbum* hybrids. These robust clump-forming plants are commonly known as Shasta daisies, and are excellent in mixed borders and as cut flowers.

CULTIVATION

Leucanthemum plants are very easily grown in any sunny position with moist well-drained soil. Feeding and watering will result in more luxuriant plants but not necessarily more flowers. Tall varieties may need staking. The species are usually propagated from seed, while the cultivars and hybrids are propagated by division or from basal cuttings.

LEFT *The splendid* Leucanthemum × superbum *hybrid cultivars were first developed by Luther Burbank in 1890 at his garden near Mt. Shasta in northern California. Flowers are typically crisp white blooms with yellow centers borne on sturdy stems above glossy green foliage. 'T. E. Killin', left, is a large, flat, double-flowered example.*

BELOW LEFT Leucanthemum × superbum *'Snowcap' is a dwarf form that bears masses of long-lasting flowers, which are quite large for its size.*

Top Tip

Place these trouble-free plants at the front of borders or in containers for maximum effect. They also make great ground covers in a sunny part of the garden.

Favorites	Flower Color	Blooming Season	Flower Fragrance	Plant Height	Plant Width	Hardiness Zone	Frost Tolerance
Leucanthemum × superbum	white	summer to early autumn	no	24–36 in (60–90 cm)	24–36 in (60–90 cm)	5–10	yes
Leucanthemum × superbum 'Aglaia'	white	summer to early autumn	no	24 in (60 cm)	24–36 in (60–90 cm)	5–10	yes
Leucanthemum × superbum 'Esther Read'	white	summer to early autumn	no	18–24 in (45–60 cm)	24 in (60 cm)	5–10	yes
Leucanthemum × superbum 'Snowcap'	white	summer to early autumn	no	18 in (45 cm)	18 in (45 cm)	5–10	yes
Leucanthemum × superbum 'T. E. Killin'	white	summer to early autumn	no	30 in (75 cm)	24–36 in (60–90 cm)	5–10	yes
Leucanthemum vulgare	white	summer	no	12–30 in (30–75 cm)	12–24 in (30–60 cm)	3–10	yes

ABOVE *Naturally occurring in Europe and areas of Asia, Leucanthemum vulgare can be highly invasive in some places including parts of the U.S.A.*

RIGHT *The distinctive fringed semi-double flowers of Leucanthemum × superbum 'Aglaia' last throughout summer. Deadheading will prolong flowering.*

ABOVE Lewisia longipetala 'Little Plum' is an attractive easy-growing plant. Short stems bear intense rosy purple flowers tinged with orange above fleshy leaves.

BELOW Veined pale pink flowers are held above the dark green leaves of Lewisia columbiana. This compact evergreen can be found in the Columbia River Gorge.

LEWISIA

This genus consists of around 19 species of exquisite, semi-succulent, evergreen and deciduous, alpine and subalpine perennials of the portulaca family (Portulacaceae). They are found in the Rocky Mountains from New Mexico in the U.S.A. to southern Canada and usually form rosettes or tufts of fleshy, linear, lance- or spatula-shaped leaves. Their starry many-petalled flowers may be solitary or clustered and are borne at the end of short wiry stems. Yellow, apricot, and pink shades predominate. Hardy plants, they provide interest in rock gardens or even against a wall. The genus is named for North American explorer Captain Meriwether Lewis (1774–1809) of the famed Lewis and Clark expedition of 1804–07. *Lewisia rediviva* is the state flower of Montana.

CULTIVATION

Most species have deep taproots and prefer a gritty, humus-rich, free-draining soil that remains moist in the growing season but is otherwise dry. Plant in full or half sun and use gravel mulch around the crown to prevent rotting. The deciduous species generally only reproduce from seed, but evergreen plants can be propagated from seed or offsets.

Favorites	Flower Color	Blooming Season	Flow Fragra
Lewisia **columbiana**	white to pale pink	spring to summer	nc
Lewisia **cotyledon**	white to pale pink	spring to summer	nc
Lewisia, **Cotyledon Hybrids**	various	late spring to summer	ne
Lewisia **longipetala**	white, sometimes flushed pink	late spring to early summer	ne
Lewisia **rediviva**	white, pink	spring to summer	ne
Lewisia **tweedyi**	white to peach-pink	spring to summer	n

Top Tip

These Rocky
Mountain natives
are wonderfully
hardy. They are
able to take root
in rocky banks and
gardens, as well as
in the crevices of
a retaining wall.

Plant Height	Plant Width	Hardiness Zone	Frost Tolerance
6 in (15 cm)	8 in (20 cm)	5–9	yes
12 in (30 cm)	10 in (25 cm)	6–10	yes
6–12 in 5–30 cm)	8–15 in (20–38 cm)	6–8	yes
4 in (10 cm)	4 in (10 cm)	4–7	yes
2 in (5 cm)	4 in (10 cm)	4–10	yes
8 in (20 cm)	12 in (30 cm)	5–9	yes

TOP Lewisia cotyledon *has produced a number of hybrids, each exhibiting funnel-shaped flowers and rosettes of thick, toothed, dark green leaves. 'White Splendour', seen here, has pure white flowers, but shades of pink, orange, and yellow are also possible.*

ABOVE *From spring through to summer,* Lewisia tweedyi *produces these attractive, open funnel-shaped, many-petalled flowers in shades of creamy white with a soft flush of pink.*

BELOW *Shorter than the species, the* Liatris spicata *'Floristan' strain comes in 2 colors—purple-flowered 'Floristan Violett' and white-flowered 'Floristan Weiss'.*

LIATRIS

This genus of 35 perennials from the daisy family (Asteraceae) is native to eastern North America. It makes a bold splash of color in summer and couldn't be easier to grow. Developing from corms or modified flattened roots, the plants form foliage clumps with simple linear to lance-shaped leaves that are sometimes finely hairy. Tall stems emerge from the clump, developing at their top numerous long, quite un-daisylike, bottlebrush spikes of filamentous purple-pink flowers. Bees and butterflies are attracted to the fluffy flower spikes. As well as being suitable for borders, *Liatris* plants are ideal as cut flowers. Native Americans used the roots medicinally, and early settlers found that the dried roots were effective for repelling moths. Common names include blazing star and gayfeather.

CULTIVATION

Most are very frost resistant. Wild plants are usually found along watercourses; cultivated plants are easily grown in any sunny position with moist, humus-rich, well-drained soil. Locate at the back of borders to disguise the foliage clump and make use of the flower stem's height. Propagate by division or from seed.

Favorites	Flower Color	Blooming Season	Flower Fragrance	Plant Height	Plant Width	Hardiness Zone	Frost Tolerance
Liatris ligulistylis	purple	autumn	no	24 in (60 cm)	12 in (30 cm)	3–10	yes
Liatris pycnostachya	red-purple to purple	mid-summer to early autumn	no	5 ft (1.5 m)	18 in (45 cm)	4–9	yes
Liatris spicata	pink-purple	summer to early autumn	no	2–4 ft (0.6–1.2 m)	18 in (45 cm)	3–10	yes
Liatris spicata **'Callilepsis Purple'**	purple-pink	summer to early autumn	no	24–36 in (60–90 cm)	18 in (45 cm)	3–10	yes
Liatris spicata **'Kobold'**	pink-purple	summer to early autumn	no	15 in (38 cm)	12 in (30 cm)	3–10	yes
Liatris tenuifolia	purple-pink	summer to early autumn	no	36 in (90 cm)	12 in (30 cm)	7–10	yes

LEFT *A native of southeastern U.S.A., and known as the Kansas gayfeather, the natural habitat of* Liatris pycnostachya *is open woodland and prairie.*

BELOW LEFT Liatris spicata *has given rise to a host of cultivars. Pictured here is 'Callilepsis Purple', with elegant tall spires of rich purple flowers, which can be used to good effect in border situations or wildflower gardens.*

BELOW *Reaching just 15 in (38 cm) high,* Liatris spicata *'Kobold' is a dwarf cultivar which bears bright purple flowers from summer to early autumn.*

Top Tip

Liatris species will perform best in well-drained soil. This will also reduce the possibility of tubers becoming over-wet in winter.

LIGULARIA

While some of the popular species in this temperate Eurasian daisy family genus have been reclassified, including the one which has given the genus its common name of leopard plant, there are still some 180-odd species of perennials in *Ligularia*. They are vigorous plants that soon develop in spring into clumps of large broad leaves, usually kidney- to heart-shaped, with toothed edges. In summer and autumn, upright flower stems appear and may grow to some height, depending on the species. The stems bear eye-catching, large, golden yellow, daisylike flowers for around half their length. The plants have long been used in herbal cough remedies, and today extracts of the roots are being investigated for their cancer-fighting properties.

CULTIVATION

Ligularia species are mainly very hardy and easily grown in full or half sun. The soil needs to be fertile, humus-rich, and deep. Also, it should remain moist throughout the year. Cut back when the flowers and foliage fade. Propagate by division when dormant or raise from seed.

LEFT *Tall spires of yellow flowers appear on purplish stems above the large, up to 12 in (30 cm) wide, dark green leaves of* Ligularia przewalskii.

Favorites	Flower Color	Blooming Season	Flo Frag
Ligularia dentata	orange-yellow	mid-summer to early autumn	
Ligularia przewalskii	yellow	mid- to late summer	
Ligularia stenocephala	yellow	summer	
Ligularia 'The Rocket'	yellow	summer	
Ligularia veitchiana	yellow	mid- to late summer	
Ligularia wilsoniana	yellow	summer	

Top Tip

With ornamental foliage and flowers, *Ligularia* species are well suited to border planting. The taller varieties will add height, depth, and interest when in flower.

BELOW *Dark flower stems hold golden yellow flowers up to 6 ft (1.8 m) above the large toothed leaves* of Ligularia *'The Rocket', an award-winning cultivar.*

ABOVE *The sunny, orange-yellow, daisylike blooms of* Ligularia dentata *are held on tall stems above the large heart-shaped leaves.*
LEFT *Hailing from China and Japan,* Ligularia stenocephala *bears tall spikes of bright yellow flowers above its long triangular leaves.*

Plant Height	Plant Width	Hardiness Zone	Frost Tolerance
4 ft (1.2 m)	3 ft (0.9 m)	4–9	yes
6 ft (1.8 m)	3 ft (0.9 m)	4–9	yes
5 ft (1.5 m)	3 ft (0.9 m)	5–10	yes
6 ft (1.8 m)	5 ft (1.5 m)	5–10	yes
6 ft (1.8 m)	4 ft (1.2 m)	4–9	yes
6 ft (1.8 m)	4 ft (1.2 m)	5–9	yes

RIGHT *Like most of the Oriental Hybrids, Lilium 'Barbaresco' is a real show-stopper: it is highly fragrant with large warm pink flowers.*

BELOW *Summer sees the glorious tiger lily, Lilium lancifolium, live up to its name with the production of numerous orange flowers dotted in purple-black; its anthers are similarly colored.*

BOTTOM *Asiatic Hybrids are available in colors ranging from gentle pastels to fiery reds and oranges such as the glorious open-flowered Lilium 'Avignon'. They look magnificent in massed floral arrangements.*

LILIUM

Cultivated for over 5000 years, lilies are undeniably beautiful and with around 100 species of these bulbs spread over the northern temperate zone there are plenty to choose from. They are strongly upright plants with narrow leaves, and heads of cup-shaped, bell-shaped, or sometimes very large trumpet-shaped flowers occurring in a wide array of colors and patterns. According to folklore, plant hunter E. H. Wilson so prized his newly discovered Regal Lilies, that after an avalanche broke his leg, during an expedition in China in 1910, he carried on rather than abandon them, and when confronted with an approaching donkey train on the narrow trail he lay down and let the donkeys step over him one by one. Thus he preserved his prize but was left with a permanent "lily limp."

CULTIVATION

Lilies flower best with full sun for at least half a day. They need moist soil that is humus-rich, fertile, and well-drained. To guard against damage and moisture loss, do not store the bulbs dry, but in moist sawdust or shredded paper. Propagate from offsets, by scaling the bulbs, from leaf axil bulbils, or from seed.

Top Tip

When planting lilies in the garden, allow for a depth of around three times the height of the bulb. Once established, lilies can be left undisturbed for years.

Favorites

	Flower Color	Blooming Season	Flower Fragrance	Plant Height	Plant Width	Hardiness Zone	Frost Tolerance
Lilium, American Hybrids	pink, yellow, red, darker spotted	summer	no	4–6 ft (1.2–1.8 m)	12 in (30 cm)	5–10	yes
Lilium, Asiatic Hybrids	yellow, orange, red, mostly spotted	summer	no	18 in–4 ft (45 cm–1.2 m)	12–18 in (30–45 cm)	5–10	yes
Lilium, Candidum Hybrids	white, pink to orange-red	summer	no	2–4 ft (0.6–1.2 m)	12–18 in (30–45 cm)	6–9	yes
Lilium lancifolium	orange-red, spotted with black	mid- to late summer	no	4 ft (1.2 m)	5 ft (1.5 m)	4–10	yes
Lilium lankongense	green and pink	summer	yes	4 ft (1.2 m)	12 in (30 cm)	6–9	yes
Lilium, Longiflorum Hybrids	white	late spring to summer	yes	36 in (90 cm)	24 in (60 cm)	5–10	yes
Lilium martagon	white to purple	early to mid-summer	yes	6 ft (1.8 m)	12 in (30 cm)	4–9	yes
Lilium, Martagon Hybrids	cream, pink, gold, dull red	mid-summer	yes	5–6 ft (1.5–1.8 m)	12–18 in (30–45 cm)	5–9	yes
Lilium nepalense	yellow-green; maroon markings	summer	no	24–36 in (60–90 cm)	12 in (30 cm)	7–9	yes
Lilium, Oriental Hybrids	white, pink, red, yellow stripe	summer to early autumn	yes	4–7 ft (1.2–2 m)	15–24 in (38–60 cm)	6–9	yes
Lilium regale	white; maroon outside	summer	yes	6 ft (1.8 m)	18 in (45 cm)	5–9	yes
Lilium, Trumpet and Aurelian Hybrids	white, gold, pink, deep red, greenish	summer	no	3–6 ft (0.9–1.8 m)	12–18 in (30–45 cm)	5–9	yes

BELOW *This Oriental Hybrid, Lilium 'Sorbonne', bears the distinctive recurved petals, elegant long stamens, and attractive center markings typical of this group.*

RIGHT *The Asiatic Hybrid lilies are known for their straight stems, abundance of flowers—which may be up to 5 per stem—and their appealing color range. For these reasons, cultivars such as 'Vivaldi', right, with its pastel pink flowers, are very popular as cut flowers.*

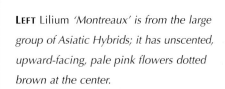

LEFT *Lilium 'Montreaux' is from the large group of Asiatic Hybrids; it has unscented, upward-facing, pale pink flowers dotted brown at the center.*

BELOW *The large, trumpet-shaped, fragrant Lilium, Longiflorum Hybrid, 'Casa Rosa' bears pink flowers with a darker center.*

LEFT *A popular Oriental Hybrid, Lilium 'Star Gazer' has large, upward-facing, reddish pink flowers, with darker freckles. Blooms are unscented and appear in mid-summer.*

ABOVE Lilium, *Oriental Hybrid, 'Acapulco' has large dark pink blooms enhanced with crimson spotting at the throat and ruffled edges. Leaves are a glossy green.*
LEFT *The flowers of* Lilium nepalense *are striking for their darker color palette. Funnel-shaped pale green flowers curve back to reveal a maroon-red center.*

LIMONIUM

This genus of around 150 species of mainly summer-flowering annuals, perennials, and small shrubs of the leadwort family (Plumbaginaceae) is widely distributed in the warm-temperate and subtropical zones. Most species form low-growing mounds of foliage rosettes. The leaves vary in size and tend to be lance-shaped or spatula-shaped. The individual flowers are minute but make a great display because they are borne in billowing sprays held well clear of the foliage on branching wiry stems. White, cream, and purple shades are common. *Limonium*, which comes from a Greek word meaning meadow, is still widely sold as *Statice*, the name under which it was formerly classified.

CULTIVATION

Many species are rather frost tender, thriving in coastal conditions, with a preference for sheltered sunny locations with light, well-drained, yet moist soil. Propagate from seed, root cuttings, or by division, depending on the plant type.

BELOW LEFT Limonium sinuatum, *with its small, papery, white and purple flowers, is often grown as an annual. There are several strains in a range of colors.*
BELOW *Summer-flowering* Limonium perezii, *with its shrubby habit, is suitable for a mixed border. It will tolerate coastal conditions and prefers full sun.*

Top Tip

Limonium species make good dried flowers. As soon as the flowers open, they should be cut and hung upside down to dry in a cool spot with good ventilation.

ABOVE Limonium bourgaei is easily grown from seed. The flowering stems and branches are covered in a fine growth of hairs, and the flowers are violet and white.

RIGHT The flowers of Limonium brassicifolium are tubular, rising from thick woody stems. A light fertilizer should be applied in spring to encourage growth.

Favorites

	Flower Color	Blooming Season	Flower Fragrance	Plant Height	Plant Width	Hardiness Zone	Frost Tolerance
Limonium bourgaei	purple; white corolla	spring to summer	no	15 in (38 cm)	18 in (45 cm)	9–11	no
Limonium brassicifolium	purple; white corolla	summer to autumn	no	8–15 in (20–38 cm)	18 in (45 cm)	9–11	no
Limonium gmelinii	lilac	summer	no	24 in (60 cm)	24 in (60 cm)	4–10	yes
Limonium latifolium	white, bluish lavender	summer	no	24 in (60 cm)	18 in (45 cm)	5–10	yes
Limonium perezii	blue-mauve; white corolla	summer	no	24 in (60 cm)	24 in (60 cm)	9–11	no
Limonium sinuatum	pink, purple-blue; white corolla	summer to early autumn	no	18 in (45 cm)	12 in (30 cm)	8–10	yes

LOBELIA

While the small mounding annuals often seen decorating flower borders are well-known, *Lobelia* is a large, enormously variable, and widespread genus that belongs to the bell-flower family (Campanulaceae). It includes over 350 species of annuals, perennials, and shrubs, including some amazing megaherbs from the mountains of East Africa. Other than the annuals, with their massed summer display of blue, white, or pink flowers, the cultivated forms are mainly perennials from the Americas, most of which form a basal clump of simple foliage from which emerge upright flower stems bearing spikes of brightly colored, tubular, 5-lobed flowers, the lower 3 of which are enlarged. *Lobelia* species were used medicinally by Native Americans; the Cherokee of the eighteenth century reputedly had an infallible lobelia-based syphilis cure.

ABOVE *The scarlet flowers of* Lobelia cardinalis *are held aloft on 15 in (38 cm) tall stems. They tower over the glossy, dark green, sometimes bronze-tinged foliage.*

Top Tip

Whether it is for adding a decorative touch to the garden border, for hanging basket culture, or for waterside planting—there's a lobelia for almost every purpose.

CULTIVATION

Requirements vary widely but most are at home in a sunny position with moist well-drained soil. Tall types may need staking. Propagation is from seed for annuals and perennials, the latter also by division or basal cuttings.

RIGHT Lobelia laxiflora *places few demands on the gardener. It will produce its pretty orange-red flowers over a long period, despite neglect and poor soils.*

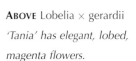

ABOVE Lobelia × gerardii *'Tania' has elegant, lobed, magenta flowers.*
LEFT Lobelia erinus *has given rise to a number of cultivars, such as the violet specimen pictured here.*

Favorites

	Flower Color	Blooming Season	Flower Fragrance	Plant Height	Plant Width	Hardiness Zone	Frost Tolerance
Lobelia cardinalis	scarlet	summer to early autumn	no	3 ft (0.9 m)	12 in (30 cm)	3–10	yes
Lobelia erinus	blue, purple, red, pink, white	spring to early autumn	no	3–6 in (8–15 cm)	18 in (45 cm)	7–11	no
Lobelia × gerardii 'Tania'	magenta	summer to early autumn	no	24–36 in (60–90 cm)	12 in (30 cm)	4–10	yes
Lobelia laxiflora	red and yellow	summer	no	3 ft (0.9 m)	3–6 ft (0.9–1.8 m)	9–11	yes
Lobelia siphilitica	blue	late summer to autumn	no	24–36 in (60–90 cm)	12 in (30 cm)	5–10	yes
Lobelia tupa	scarlet to red-purple	late summer to autumn	no	3–6 ft (0.9–1.8 m)	36 in (90 cm)	8–10	yes

LOBULARIA

Still widely and confusingly known as alyssum, after the genus in which it was originally included, this group of 5 species of annuals and perennials in the cabbage family (Brassicaceae) occurs naturally in the northern temperate zone and especially around the Mediterranean and Canary Islands. They are small mounding plants with simple linear to lance-shaped leaves, sometimes with fine silvery hairs. Their flowers, which appear over the warmer months, are tiny, often sweetly scented, and are borne in rounded heads. Garden forms occur in white and shades of primrose, apricot, mauve, and purple, and make pretty additions to a bedding scheme. The genus name comes from the Latin *lobulus* (a pod) and refers to the small seed capsules.

CULTIVATION

These plants are hardy and very easily grown in any sunny position with light free-draining soil. Watering will encourage heavier flowering but the plants are often more compact and less inclined to fall apart from the center if kept rather dry. Propagate from seed, which may be carefully sown or simply broadcast. *Lobularia* plants often self-sow.

BELOW LEFT *A popular, fast-growing, compact annual,* Lobularia maritima *has dull green leaves enlivened by masses of tiny, scented, white blooms.*

BELOW *The* Lobularia maritima *Easter Bonnet Series features a range of colors, including white, pink, and the rich purple of 'Easter Bonnet Lavender', below.*

Top Tip

These uniform and compact plants with their heavy blooming and sweet scent are great as fillers in summer beds, as well as along walls and paths.

LEFT Lobularia maritima *'Easter Bonnet Deep Rose'* is enjoyed for its rosy red blooms and lush foliage. **BELOW** Lobularia maritima *'Snow Crystals'* is a half-hardy, mound-forming, compact plant. White flowers smother the plant throughout spring and summer.

Favorites	Flower Color	Blooming Season	Flower Fragrance	Plant Height	Plant Width	Hardiness Zone	Frost Tolerance
Lobularia maritima	white	spring to early autumn	yes	3–12 in (8–30 cm)	8–12 in (20–30 cm)	7–10	yes
Lobularia maritima 'Carpet of Snow'	white	spring to early autumn	yes	4 in (10 cm)	8–12 in (20–30 cm)	7–10	yes
Lobularia maritima 'Easter Bonnet Deep Rose'	deep red	spring to early autumn	yes	3–4 in (8–10 cm)	8–12 in (20–30 cm)	7–10	yes
Lobularia maritima 'Easter Bonnet Lavender'	purple-pink	spring to early autumn	yes	3–4 in (8–10 cm)	8–12 in (20–30 cm)	7–10	yes
Lobularia maritima 'Rosie O'Day'	lavender-pink	spring to early autumn	yes	2–4 in (5–10 cm)	8–12 in (20–30 cm)	7–10	yes
Lobularia maritima 'Snow Crystals'	white	spring to early autumn	yes	10 in (25 cm)	8–12 in (20–30 cm)	7–10	yes

LONICERA

Honeysuckles are often regarded as slightly weedy second-class climbers, but in the right place they are among the easiest and most rewarding of plants. The 180-odd species in the genus are widely distributed in the Northern Hemisphere and include climbers, ground covers, and shrubs, both evergreen and deciduous, most of them very hardy. The foliage usually consists of opposite pairs of leathery leaves that vary in size from very small to quite long. The honeysuckle flowers can range in size as well, though most are tubular and are usually cream inside, with the outer colors featuring most shades except blue. The flowers are sometimes fragrant and are often followed by ornamental berries that are relished by birds and bees. The fruits are usually partially enclosed by bract-like calyces that may color slightly.

CULTIVATION

Although honeysuckles are tough adaptable plants that thrive in most conditions, they are generally best grown in rich, moist, humus-enriched, well-drained soil in either full sun or partial shade. They can be raised from seed, though most are easily grown from layers or half-hardened cuttings.

ABOVE *Masses of trumpet-shaped white or pink flower decorate the dark green leaves of* Lonicera tatarica, *a deciduous bushy shrub.*
LEFT *These truly outstandir flowers of* Lonicera heckrc tii *'Gold Flame' are initiall bold pink, softening as the blooms open to reveal the bright yellow inside. It is a vigorous grower with glos green leaves.*

Top Tip

In informal or wild gardens, climbers need little maintenance other than the occasional hard pruning to keep them in bounds. Trim hedges twice during summer.

ABOVE *This gorgeous coral honeysuckle,* Lonicera sempervirens, *bears long-tubed flowers that are red-orange on the outside and yellow inside. Bright red fruits follow.*

RIGHT *The long, tubular, red flowers of* Lonicera × brownii *'Dropmore Scarlet' provide color over a long period from spring.*

Favorites

	Flower Color	Blooming Season	Flower Fragrance	Plant Height	Plant Width	Hardiness Zone	Frost Tolerance
Lonicera × brownii	orange to red	spring to summer	no	10 ft (3 m)	4 ft (1.2 m)	4–10	yes
Lonicera × heckrottii	pink; yellow interior	late spring to summer	yes	15 ft (4.5 m)	5 ft (1.5 m)	5–10	yes
Lonicera nitida	creamy white	spring	no	4–8 ft (1.2–2.4 m)	4–8 ft (1.2–2.4 m)	6–10	yes
Lonicera periclymenum	white and pale yellow	summer	yes	8–20 ft (2.4–6 m)	5–10 ft (1.5–3 m)	4–10	yes
Lonicera sempervirens	orange-red; yellow interior	spring to autumn	no	10–20 ft (3–6 m)	5–10 ft (1.5–3 m)	4–10	yes
Lonicera tatarica	white, pink to dark red	late spring to early summer	no	12 ft (3.5 m)	10 ft (3 m)	2–9	yes

LUPINUS

There are about 200 species of annuals, perennials, and evergreen shrubs in this genus, which belongs to the legume family. They are found in North and South America, southern Europe, and northern Africa, usually in dry habitats. The leaves are palmate with lance-shaped leaflets, and the stems are often covered in fine soft down. Many have highly ornamental flowers borne in showy terminal racemes or spikes. The pealike flowers appear mainly throughout summer in many colors, including bicolors. A number of species are grown for horticultural purposes such as nitrogen fixing and stock fodder, and the seeds of some are processed in various ways for human consumption.

CULTIVATION

Lupinus species are best grown in full sun in moderately fertile well-drained soil. Shrubby species can be used in shrubberies or mixed borders, and *Lupinus arboreus* can be used for naturalizing rough areas. Deadhead spent spikes to ensure strong plants. Propagation is from seed or cuttings. The seedlings should be planted out when small, as these plants dislike root disturbance.

Favorites	Flower Color	Blooming Season	Flower Fragrance	Plant Height	Plant Width	Hardiness Zone	Frost Tolerance
Lupinus arboreus	yellow	spring to summer	yes	8 ft (2.4 m)	5–8 ft (1.5–2.4 m)	8–10	yes
Lupinus 'Bishop's Tipple'	purple-pink, white flecks	late spring to early summer	no	36 in (90 cm)	24 in (60 cm)	7–10	yes
Lupinus nanus	blue, white-spotted purple	spring to summer	no	20 in (50 cm)	8–12 in (20–30 cm)	7–11	yes
Lupinus 'Pagoda Prince'	magenta and white	spring to early summer	no	36 in (90 cm)	24 in (60 cm)	7–10	yes
Lupinus polyphyllus	blue, purple, red, white	summer	no	5 ft (1.5 m)	24–30 in (60–75 cm)	3–9	yes
Lupinus, Russell Hybrids	various	late spring to summer	yes	3 ft (0.9 m)	2–4 ft (0.6–1.2 m)	3–9	yes

Far Left Lupinus 'Pagoda Prince' is a stunning, tall-stemmed, bicolored hybrid. Mid-green leaves grow in a dense clump at its base.

Above Known as the Russell Hybrids, this famous group of Lupinus hybrids was developed by gardener George Russell in the early 1930s. They are strong-growing with long spikes of flowers appearing in many vibrant shades.

Left Lupinus 'Bishop's Tipple' is a tall hybrid with rich mauve blooms flecked with white. Leaflets are arranged in an attractive palmate pattern.

Right Naturally occurring in California, the evergreen Lupinus arboreus bears hairy gray-green leaves and yellow, sometimes blue, fragrant flowers.

Top Tip

Lupinus arboreus is an aggressive seeder and should be planted where it can be controlled; Lupinus, Russell Hybrids may self-sow, resulting in a variety of colors.

LEFT AND BELOW Lychnis *coronaria is an upright, clump-forming, short-lived perennial appreciated for its silvery foliage and colorful blooms borne on tall many-branching stems. 'Atro-sanguinea', left, has vivid red flowers, and 'Alba', below, is an attractive white-flowering cultivar.*

LYCHNIS

Found in the northern temperate and arctic zones, the 20-odd species of biennials and perennials in this genus belong to the carnation family (Caryophyllaceae). They are quite a variable lot and include erect or spreading forms, large clump-forming plants—sometimes with silver-gray leaves—and small alpine species. The flowers are simple 5-petalled structures, but are very brightly colored and showy, occurring in heads that are usually held well clear of the foliage to maximize the color effect. *Lychnis* or *lukhnis* is a Greek word meaning lamp; the name was given to the genus by Theophrastus in the third century B.C., presumably in reference to its vivid flowerheads. Lychnis is allied to the *Silene* genus.

CULTIVATION

Lychnis species are mostly very hardy and easily grown in any sunny position with moist well-drained soil. The silvery *Lychnis coronaria* prefers fairly dry conditions but most others can be given routine watering. Deadhead frequently to encourage continuous flowering. Propagate from seed, from basal cuttings, or by division, depending on the growth form.

Favorites

	Flower Color	Blooming Season	Flower Fragrance	Plant Height	Plant Width	Hardiness Zone	Frost Tolerance
Lychnis alpina	purple-pink	summer	no	6 in (15 cm)	6 in (15 cm)	2–8	yes
Lychnis × arkwrightii	orange-red	summer	no	10–18 in (25–45 cm)	12 in (30 cm)	6–9	yes
Lychnis chalcedonica	scarlet	early summer	no	4 ft (1.2 m)	12 in (30 cm)	4–10	yes
Lychnis coronaria	purple to purple-red	summer	no	30 in (75 cm)	18 in (45 cm)	4–10	yes
Lychnis flos-jovis	pink, scarlet, white	summer	no	24 in (60 cm)	18 in (45 cm)	5–9	yes
Lychnis viscaria	purple-pink	summer	no	18 in (45 cm)	18 in (45 cm)	4–9	yes

RIGHT *An alpine carpet-forming plant,* Lychnis viscaria *is commonly known as sticky catchfly due to its bronze sticky stems. Purple-pink flowers are borne in clusters of 5 to 6.*
BELOW *These twinkling orange-red flowers of* Lychnis × arkwrightii *'Vesuvius' grow to 1¹⁄₂ in (35 mm) across. Foliage is a mix of purple and green, especially on younger plants.*

Top Tip

Plant smaller alpine species like *Lychnis viscaria* in shaded rock gardens, and taller perennials such as *L. coronaria* in borders or informal massed clumps.

LYSIMACHIA

The name *Lysimachia* has a long history: it was given by Dioscorides, a physician in Nero's army of the first century A.D. for King Lysimachus of Thrace. Today's genus, part of the primrose family (Primulaceae) with around 150 species of perennials and subshrubs, is found not only in Thrace (northern Greece) but also over much of Europe and Asia as well as North America and South Africa. A few species are low spreading plants but most are clump-forming perennials with narrow, lance-shaped, often hairy leaves and upright spikes of small 5-petalled flowers, often in yellow shades, very rarely white or purple-pink. The flowers appear from early summer to autumn: when they appear en masse, they can create quite a dramatic feature in a garden.

CULTIVATION

Some species prefer the damp soil of pond margins or stream banks, others thrive in rockeries, but most are perfectly happy in full or half sun with moist well-drained garden soil. Propagate by division, from basal cuttings, or from layers, depending on the growth type.

Top Tip

In colder climates, plants that are not fully hardy will benefit from being overwintered in a greenhouse. Mulch can also be applied around the roots as extra protection.

ABOVE RIGHT *A spreading perennial,* Lysimachia clethroides *has pointed leaves and tapering flowering spikes that are pendent at first, becoming erect as the white blooms mature.*
RIGHT *Yellow-green leaves are almost lost among the dense profusion of deep yellow flowers of* Lysimachia nummularia *'Aurea'.*

Favorites	Flower Color	Blooming Season	Flower Fragrance	Plant Height	Plant Width	Hardiness Zone	Frost Tolerance
Lysimachia **'Aztec Sunset'**	golden yellow	summer	no	36 in (90 cm)	24 in (60 cm)	5–10	yes
Lysimachia ciliata	yellow	summer	no	4 ft (1.2 m)	24 in (60 cm)	4–10	yes
Lysimachia clethroides	white	summer	no	36 in (90 cm)	24 in (60 cm)	4–10	yes
Lysimachia ephemerum	white	summer	no	36 in (90 cm)	12 in (30 cm)	6–10	yes
Lysimachia nummularia	yellow	summer	no	4–8 in (10–20 cm)	24 in (60 cm)	4–10	yes
Lysimachia punctata	yellow	summer	no	36 in (90 cm)	24 in (60 cm)	5–10	yes

RIGHT *Cup-shaped yellow flowers grow among the broad green leaves of* Lysimachia punctata, *an erect perennial known as golden loosestrife.*

BELOW *The outstanding slow-growing* Lysimachia punctata *'Alexander' bears variegated sage green and cream leaves with masses of cup-shaped yellow blooms.*

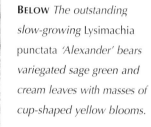

LEFT Magnolia × loebneri *is a prolifically flowering deciduous small tree or large shrub, adaptable to a wide range of soils.*

BELOW *The state flower of Louisiana and Mississippi, the magnificent blooms of* Magnolia grandiflora *are large, creamy white, saucer-shaped, fragrant, and appear in early summer.*

MAGNOLIA

A member of the Magnoliaeceae family, this large and varied genus consists of around 100 species of deciduous and evergreen trees as well as countless cultivars, and occurs naturally throughout Asia and North America. The leaves are usually large, oval, and smooth edged. The handsome flowers are generally large, fragrant, and solitary and vary in shape from almost flat and saucer-like to a narrow goblet shape. They occur in shades of white, yellow, pink, or purple. The flowers are primitive, pollinated largely by beetles, and their simplicity, often seen to advantage on bare limbs before the foliage appears, contributes to their appeal. The fruits that follow are often pink or red, conelike, showy clusters, with colorful seeds. *Magnolia* takes its name from the French botanist Pierre Magnol (1638-1715).

CULTIVATION

Generally fast growing, magnolias prefer light shade and sheltered spots in the garden away from the wind and late frosts. Although some species are lime tolerant, most prefer well-drained acid soils that are rich in humus. Propagate from cuttings in summer, by sowing seed in autumn, or by grafting in winter.

BELOW LEFT *Size and brightness of bloom are key attributes of* Magnolia *hybrids and 'Yellow Lantern', with its stunning lemon yellow tulip-shaped flowers, is no exception.*

ABOVE Magnolia stellata *'Royal Star' is a large deciduous shrub valued for its abundant clusters of double snow white flowers that appear in late winter.*

Favorites	Flower Color	Blooming Season	Flower Fragrance	Plant Height	Plant Width	Hardiness Zone	Frost Tolerance
Magnolia 'Apollo'	deep rose to violet	early to mid-spring	yes	35 ft (10 m)	20 ft (6 m)	5–9	yes
Magnolia 'Betty'	deep pink outside, white inside	mid-spring	yes	12 ft (3.5 m)	12 ft (3.5 m)	6–9	yes
Magnolia 'Elizabeth'	soft yellow	mid- to late spring	yes	30 ft (9 m)	20 ft (6 m)	6–9	yes
Magnolia grandiflora	white to creamy white	summer to autumn	yes	30–80 ft (9–24 m)	20–60 ft (6–18 m)	6–11	yes
Magnolia 'Iolanthe'	soft pink	early to mid-spring	yes	25 ft (8 m)	25 ft (8 m)	6–9	yes
Magnolia kobus	white	early to mid-spring	yes	15–40 ft (4.5–12 m)	20 ft (6 m)	5–9	yes
Magnolia × loebneri	white to pink	mid-spring	yes	20–30 ft (6–9 m)	25 ft (8 m)	5–9	yes
Magnolia × soulangeana	white, pink to purple-pink	late winter to mid-spring	yes	25 ft (8 m)	15 ft (4.5 m)	5–10	yes
Magnolia stellata	white, sometimes flushed pink	late winter to early spring	yes	10 ft (3 m)	10 ft (3 m)	5–9	yes
Magnolia virginiana	creamy white	summer	yes	30 ft (9 m)	20 ft (6 m)	5–10	yes
Magnolia wilsonii	white	late spring to early summer	yes	20 ft (6 m)	20 ft (6 m)	7–10	yes
Magnolia 'Yellow Lantern'	yellow	mid-spring	yes	25–50 ft (8–15 m)	15–25 ft (4.5–8 m)	5–10	yes

Top Tip

Wind and late frosts can damage the large magnolia flowers, so a sheltered spot is best for these plants.

RIGHT *Magnolia 'Betty' is part of the Eight Little Girls series of bright-blooming hybrids developed by De Vos & Kosar of the U.S.A.*
BELOW *The flowers of Magnolia × soulangeana appear before the foliage, even on young trees.*

ABOVE Magnolia 'Iolanthe' is an award-winning large-flowered hybrid. Its goblet-shaped blooms are rose-purple outside, and the palest of shell pinks inside.

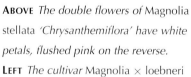

ABOVE The double flowers of Magnolia stellata 'Chrysanthemiflora' have white petals, flushed pink on the reverse.

LEFT The cultivar Magnolia × loebneri 'Leonard Messel' is especially valued for its abundant winter deep rose-lilac buds and pink narrow-petalled flowers, which are white on the inside.

RIGHT Magnolia × soulangeana is a deciduous, low-branched, hardy tree that has produced a number of worthy culti-vars. 'Verbanica', right, is fast growing, with white flowers tinged with pink.

LEFT *A lovely garden shrub,* Magnolia × soulangeana *'Burgundy' is a deep crim-son-flowered form, which flowers earlier than most hybrid cultivars.*

ABOVE AND RIGHT *These decorative, many-petalled, white-flowered cultivars, 'Star Bright', above, and the award-winning fragrant 'Merrill', right, are both derived from* Magnolia × loebneri, *itself the result of crossing between* M. kobus *and* M. stellata.
LEFT *This developing seed pod of* Magnolia virginiana *emerges from the cream or white, lemon-scented, cup-shaped flowers. Glossy leaves are silvery beneath. This tree is from coastal swampy areas in the U.S.A.*

RIGHT *These delicate buds of* Magnolia stellata, *a large deciduous shrub, will develop into fragrant ivory white flowers with straplike curved and reflexed petals.*

LEFT Magnolia kobus *is native to the forests of Japan and Korea and has dark green, smooth, oval leaves. Flowers are lightly fragrant, white, and often streaked pale pink at the base.*

ABOVE Mahonia aquifolium *'Compacta' is a dwarf form, with spiny-edged leaves and yellow flowers followed by edible berries. M. aquifolium is the state flower of Oregon.* **BELOW** *The widely cultivated* Mahonia lomariifolia *develops into a clump of strongly upright stems with bronze, later green, leaves and soft yellow flowers.*

MAHONIA

This genus of some 70 species of evergreen shrubs is found in Asia and North America with a few species extending into Central America. The leaves grow alternately on the stems or in whorls at the top of the stem, and are often very spiny. The foliage frequently passes through several color changes as it matures: light green or red-tinted in spring when new, deep green in summer, and red- or orange-tinted in winter. Sprays of small yellow flowers, sometimes scented, are clustered at the branch tips and appear in spring, summer, or autumn to early winter depending on the species. *Mahonia* is also known as holly grapes which the berries resemble.

CULTIVATION

Most *Mahonia* species are temperate-zone plants that tolerate moderate to hard frosts. For lush foliage, plant in moist well-drained soil that is fertile and humus-rich and protect from the hottest summer sun. Propagate from cuttings or from the rooted suckers that grow at the base of established plants.

Favorites

	Flower Color	Blooming Season	Flower Fragrance	Plant Height	Plant Width	Hardiness Zone	Frost Tolerance
Mahonia aquifolium	yellow	spring	no	6 ft (1.8 m)	5–8 ft (1.5–2.4 m)	5–10	yes
Mahonia fremontii	yellow	late spring to summer	no	12 ft (3.5 m)	6 ft (1.8 m)	8–11	yes
Mahonia lomariifolia	yellow	spring	no	10–12 ft (3–3.5 m)	6–10 ft (1.8–3 m)	7–10	yes
Mahonia × *media*	yellow	autumn to winter	yes	15 ft (4.5 m)	12 ft (3.5 m)	6–10	yes
Mahonia nevinii	yellow	spring	no	6 ft (1.8 m)	6 ft (1.8 m)	8–11	yes
Mahonia repens	deep yellow	spring	yes	12 in (30 cm)	36 in (90 cm)	6–9	yes

RIGHT Mahonia × media *was originally bred to combine lush foliage with hardiness. The cultivar 'Arthur Menzies', right, is notable for its long flowering spikes and blue-black berries.*

BELOW *Native to California,* Mahonia nevinii *is a tall shrub with grayish blue-green leaves. Small open racemes of light yellow flowers are borne in spring, followed by tiny red berries.*

MALUS

The apples and crabapples comprise a large genus of 35 species of deciduous flowering and fruiting trees. They belong to the rose family and are widely cultivated throughout the temperate regions of the world. The leaves are soft "apple" green and are generally simple and tooth-edged. The flowers grow in clusters that vary in color from white to deep rose pink and bold reddish purple. The cultivated apple is one of the most widely grown of all edible fruits and historical evidence shows that the Egyptians grew them as early as 1300 B.C. While not all crabapples are edible—some being too bitter—the species and cultivars are greatly appreciated as ornamental trees.

CULTIVATION

Very frost hardy, *Malus* trees prefer a cool moist climate and full sun, protection from strong winds, and fertile, well-drained, loamy soil. Cultivated apples need pruning in winter and regular spraying to protect against a variety of pests and diseases. Propagation is by budding in summer or grafting in winter.

Favorites	Flower Color	Blooming Season	Flo Frag
Malus × *domestica*	white, often tinged pink	spring	r
Malus floribunda	pale pink	mid- to late spring	y
Malus 'Harvest Gold'	white	mid- to late spring	r
Malus hupehensis	white	mid- to late spring	y
Malus 'Indian Summer'	rosy pink	mid- to late spring	
Malus ioensis	white, pink on the outside	late spring	y

BELOW LEFT *An ornamental crabapple,* Malus *'Indian Summer' is a deserved favorite with its rosy pink flowers, persistent red fruit, and good disease resistance.*

BELOW *The edible apple,* Malus × domestica *featur a range of forms, flowers, and fruits. 'Shakespeare', below, bears pink-flushed blooms that are paler insid*

Plant Height	Plant Width	Hardiness Zone	Frost Tolerance
20–30 ft (6–9 m)	15–25 ft (4.5–8 m)	3–9	yes
25 ft (8 m)	30 ft (9 m)	4–9	yes
30 ft (9 m)	15 ft (4.5 m)	4–9	yes
15–20 ft (4.5–6 m)	25 ft (8 m)	4–10	yes
20 ft (6 m)	20 ft (6 m)	4–9	yes
20 ft (6 m)	25 ft (8 m)	2–9	yes

ABOVE *Cultivars of* Malus × domestica, *the common eating apple, have come and gone over the years. 'Jonagold' has firm, juicy, full-flavored fruit that is red striped with yellow. Fruits ripen mid-season.*

ABOVE LEFT *The hybrid cultivar* Malus *'Harvest Gold' is an upright crabapple tree with single white flowers and golden fruit. It is very disease resistant.*

ABOVE Malus hupehensis *is a spreading crabapple tree, with pink buds opening to white fragrant flowers. Fruits are green-yellow, with a red cheek.*

RIGHT *One of the oldest cultivated crabapples,* Malus floribunda *is a spreading tree with dark pink buds, light pink blooms, and red and yellow fruits.*

LEFT Malus × domestica *'Granny Smith' from Australia is a winter apple, with a tart crisp taste.*

Top Tip

Apples and crabapples flower in spring, and the fruit follows in clusters of 3 to 5. Some thinning may be necessary for a maximum crop.

BELOW *One of the most beautiful crabapples, Malus ioensis is native to midwest U.S.A., occurring in woodlands and thickets. In late spring it is covered with pale pink flowers that gradually fade to white.*

LEFT *The upright spreading Malus ioensis 'Prairifire' blooms later than most crabapples, but is worth the wait for its appealing dark purple branches, red foliage, and deep red-pink flowers.*

MANDEVILLA

This large genus from Central and South America consists of around 120 species of mainly tuberous-rooted twining vines, and some perennials and subshrubs. Rather beautiful fast-growing climbers, they have large, deep green, elliptical to lance-shaped leaves with prominent drip-tips. They produce large numbers of showy trumpet-shaped flowers throughout the warmer months, which makes them popular plants for the garden trellis or arch. The 5-lobed flowers grow singly on long stems, and are often large, fragrant in some species, and occur in white to cream and various shades of pink. The genus *Mandevilla* was named for the nineteenth-century British diplomat and gardener, Henry Mandeville.

CULTIVATION

Only a few species will tolerate frost, the majority generally preferring a mild to warm climate, dappled sunlight, and moist, humus-rich, well-drained soil. Occasional feeding will produce lush foliage but will lead to rampant growth. Propagate from seed in spring or from cuttings in spring or summer.

Favorites	Flower Color	Blooming Season	Flo Frag
Mandevilla × amabilis	pink, darker at center	mid- to late spring	r
Mandevilla × amabilis 'Alice Du Pont'	deep pink	summer	
Mandevilla boliviensis	white with yellow throat	mid- to late summer	
Mandevilla laxa	white, creamy white	summer	
Mandevilla sanderi	rose pink	summer to autumn	
Mandevilla splendens	pink with yellow throat	late spring to early summer	

Top Tip

Mandevilla species should be watered regularly during the growth period and blooming season. Reduce watering during autumn, and keep to a bare minimum during winter.

LEFT *With a prolonged flowering season in warmer climates,* Mandevilla sanderi *'Scarlet Pimpernel' bears gorgeous, yellow-throated, scarlet-pink blooms.*

BELOW *The lustrous, dark green, pointed leaves of* Mandevilla boliviensis *are a perfect foil for the funnel-shaped, golden-throated, white flowers.*

Plant Height	Plant Width	Hardiness Zone	Frost Tolerance
12 ft (3.5 m)	6 ft (1.8 m)	10–12	no
20–30 ft (6–9 m)	6 ft (1.8 m)	10–12	no
12 ft (3.5 m)	4 ft (1.2 m)	10–12	no
15 ft (4.5 m)	15 ft (4.5 m)	9–11	no
3–10 ft (0.9–3 m)	24 in (60 cm)	10–12	no
10–20 ft (3–6 m)	6 ft (1.8 m)	10–12	no

MATTHIOLA

Famous for its sweet scent, this genus of 55 species of bushy erect annuals, perennials, and subshrubs is a member of the cabbage family (Brassicaceae). The species are native to Europe, central and southwestern Asia, and North Africa. The leaves are simple, often gray-green, and are sometimes toothed. The flowers, appearing from spring through to summer, are 4-petalled and grow on upright, often branching stems. They range in color from pink to mauve and purple, and some species can make lovely cut flowers as well as being suitable for garden bedding. Also known as stock or gillyflower, these plants get their genus name from the Italian botanist Pierandrea Mattioli (1501–1577), who grew these plants for "matters of love and lust."

CULTIVATION

Plant in full sun with moist well-drained soil and a light dressing of lime. Taller species need staking and shelter from wind. Propagated from seed, *Matthiola* plants can provide continuous flowering over spring and summer.

ABOVE AND LEFT Matthiola incana *is a woody-based upright perennial or subshrub with very fragrant brightly colored flowers. Many cultivars have been developed, and it is these that are most often used for garden purposes. 'Vintage Burgundy', above, and 'Vintage Lavender', left, are just two examples of the pretty color range available*

Top Tip

Cultivars of *Matthiola incana* are well-loved as bedding plants and as cut flowers. Plant in 3 in (8 cm) pots for a pretty window display.

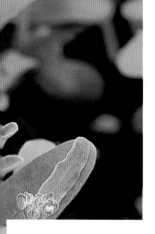

BELOW Matthiola incana *'Cinderella Rose' bears many double purple-pink flowers; forms with dark purple, pink, and softer shades of lavender-blue blooms are also available.*

ABOVE *'Cinderella White' belongs to the Cinderella group* of Matthiola incana *cultivars, and bears double snow white flowers in tall racemes.*

Favorites

	Flower Color	Blooming Season	Flower Fragrance	Plant Height	Plant Width	Hardiness Zone	Frost Tolerance
Matthiola incana	various	spring to summer	yes	24 in (60 cm)	12 in (30 cm)	6–10	yes
Matthiola incana **'Cinderella Rose'**	rose pink	late spring to summer	yes	10 in (25 cm)	12 in (30 cm)	6–10	yes
Matthiola incana **'Cinderella White'**	pure white	late spring to summer	yes	10 in (25 cm)	12 in (30 cm)	6–10	yes
Matthiola incana **'Vintage Burgundy'**	burgundy	late spring to summer	yes	12–18 in (30–45 cm)	18 in (45 cm)	6–10	yes
Matthiola incana **'Vintage Lavender'**	purple-pink	late spring to summer	yes	12–18 in (30–45 cm)	18 in (45 cm)	6–10	yes
Matthiola longipetala	green, yellow, pink	spring	yes	10–20 in (25–50 cm)	12 in (30 cm)	8–10	yes

LEFT *Easy-care, and tolerant of poor soils, Meconopsis cambrica var. aurantiaca has stunning orange flowers and mid-green leaves.*
BELOW *Occurring in shades of pink, red, and purple, the somewhat nodding flowers of Meconopsis napaulensis have a central mass of golden yellow stamens.*

MECONOPSIS

Found mainly in the Himalayan region, this genus of more than 40 species is a member of the Papaveraceae family and includes annuals, biennials, and short-lived perennials. Compact mounding plants, they have coarse hairy leaves that are simple, round or lobed, and deeply toothed. The attractive saucer- to cup-shaped flowers usually grow singly on short or tall stems, open in spring or summer, and have papery petals with a central cluster of stamens. *Meconopsis* is well known for its blue flowers, but some more easily grown species bloom in the traditional poppy shades of yellow, pink, or red. The name comes from the Greek *mecon* (poppy) and *opsis* (to see or looks like), a reference to their resemblance to the poppy.

CULTIVATION

Most species grow best in woodland conditions in a cool-temperate climate with reliable rainfall. Plant in a sheltered and partly shaded position with moist, deep, humus-rich, well-drained soil, and water well in spring and early summer. Propagate from seed.

FAR LEFT *Its likeness to the true poppy and its striking blue, crinkled, papery petals have earned Meconopsis betonicifolia the common name of the blue poppy.*

Favorites	Flower Color	Blooming Season	Flower Fragrance	Plant Height	Plant Width	Hardiness Zone	Frost Tolerance
Meconopsis betonicifolia	sky blue	late spring to early summer	no	5 ft (1.5 m)	18 in (45 cm)	7–9	yes
Meconopsis cambrica	yellow to orange	mid-spring to mid-autumn	no	18 in (45 cm)	12 in (30 cm)	6–10	yes
Meconopsis grandis	rich blue	early summer	no	4 ft (1.2 m)	24 in (60 cm)	5–9	yes
Meconopsis horridula	light to dark blue	early to mid-summer	no	36 in (90 cm)	18 in (45 cm)	6–9	yes
Meconopsis napaulensis	pink, red, purple to blue	late spring to mid-summer	no	8 ft (2.4 m)	36 in (90 cm)	8–9	yes
Meconopsis × sheldonii	blue	late spring to early summer	no	5 ft (1.5 m)	24 in (60 cm)	6–9	yes

Top Tip

Allow time to establish *Meconopsis* species as they can take 3–4 years to flower. Though they usually die off after flowering, they are self-seeding, ensuring further displays.

RIGHT *Flowering just once before dying (monocarpic),* Meconopsis horridula *was named for the many "horrid" spines found on the leaves, stems, and buds.*

MILTONIOPSIS

This pretty genus is commonly known as pansy orchid and contains around 5 species, primarily from Colombia and Ecuador. They are low-growing clump-forming plants with pale green strap-like leaves that grow from a fleshy bulblike stem. The flowers grow in small clusters and generally appear in late spring. The large, flat, almost circular flowers have vivid markings reminiscent of pansies and are extremely colorful, blooming in shades of bright yellow, white, red, and pink, often with gold, purple, or brown blotches or streaks. A number of decorative hybrids have been cultivated for garden use and can look spectacular when grown in small pots.

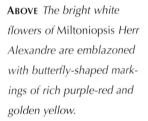

ABOVE *The bright white flowers of* Miltoniopsis *Herr Alexandre are emblazoned with butterfly-shaped markings of rich purple-red and golden yellow.*

BELOW RIGHT *The eye-catching purple-pink flowers of* Miltoniopsis *Jean Carlson are accented with white and bright orange-red markings at the base of the lip.*

CULTIVATION

The plants do best in open compost and light shade. They can grow outdoors in tropical and subtropical climates but need to be kept in a greenhouse if the climate is cooler. Pot-grown *Miltoniopsis* plants will grow well in sphagnum moss. Propagate by division after flowering.

Top Tip

These gorgeous plants will reward with flowers in dazzling strong colors, with some flowering twice in a season. They dislike direct sunlight, preferring shady humid conditions.

LEFT Miltoniopsis *Hudson Bay* has white petals boldly colored with rich purple-red. The markings are strongest on the upper petals, with softer markings delicately etched on the lower lip. **BELOW** *Flowering from late spring to autumn, the pretty soft yellow blooms of* Miltoniopsis *Zorro 'Yellow Delight' are highlighted by red and gold markings.*

Favorites

	Flower Color	Blooming Season	Flower Fragrance	Plant Height	Plant Width	Hardiness Zone	Frost Tolerance
Miltoniopsis **Herr Alexandre**	white, deep rose, yellow spots	late spring to summer	no	12 in (30 cm)	12 in (30 cm)	9–11	no
Miltoniopsis **Hudson Bay**	white, maroon blotch and stripes	summer to autumn	no	12 in (30 cm)	12 in (30 cm)	9–11	no
Miltoniopsis **Jean Carlson**	magenta with vermilion center	late spring to autumn	no	12 in (30 cm)	12 in (30 cm)	9–11	no
Miltoniopsis **Rouge 'California Plum'**	maroon and deep rose, edged white	late spring to autumn	no	12 in (30 cm)	12 in (30 cm)	9–11	no
Miltoniopsis **Saint Helier 'Pink Delight'**	mauve-pink, maroon, and white	late spring to early summer	no	12 in (30 cm)	12 in (30 cm)	9–11	no
Miltoniopsis **Zorro 'Yellow Delight'**	pale lemon with red blotch	late spring to autumn	no	12 in (30 cm)	12 in (30 cm)	9–11	no

LEFT Mimulus 'Malibu' comes in a range of colors including vivid red, bright orange, and cream. It is an ideal candidate for pot-plant culture.
BELOW A native of California, Mimulus bifidus bears white-throated flowers in a range of shades from pale yellow to dull orange.

MIMULUS

While it is best known for its annuals and perennials, this mostly North and South American genus of some 180 species also includes a few shrubs and fast-growing upright plants. The leaves are generally deep to light green, sharply toothed, hairy, and slightly sticky. The stems are also covered in fine hairs and have sticky glands. The tubular flowers have flared mouths and come in a wide range of colors, including brown, orange, yellow, red, pink, and crimson. The spotting and mottling on the flowers has been likened to grinning monkey faces, which has resulted in the common name of monkey flower. The genus is also known as musk.

CULTIVATION

In mild climates, shrubby *Mimulus* plants are easy to grow provided they are given full sun and a well-drained soil that remains moist through summer. They are quick growing and become untidy unless routinely pinched back. They tend to be short-lived but are readily raised from seed or half-hardened cuttings.

Top Tip

To add color in a hurry, plant *Mimulus* species in a border, window box, or container. Many of these cute plants also adapt well to wet or damp conditions.

Favorites

	Flower Color	Blooming Season	Flower Fragrance	Plant Height	Plant Width	Hardiness Zone	Frost Tolerance
Mimulus aurantiacus	yellow, orange, crimson	spring to summer	no	36 in (90 cm)	36 in (90 cm)	8–10	yes
Mimulus bifidus	pale orange-yellow to white	spring to summer	no	15–30 in (38–75 cm)	18–36 in (45–90 cm)	8–11	yes
Mimulus cardinalis	scarlet with yellow throat	summer	no	18–36 in (45–90 cm)	18 in (45 cm)	7–11	yes
Mimulus guttatus	yellow with red-marked throat	summer	no	1–4 ft (0.3–1.2 m)	6–18 in (15–45 cm)	6–10	yes
Mimulus 'Highland Red'	deep scarlet	summer	no	8 in (20 cm)	12 in (30 cm)	7–10	yes
Mimulus 'Malibu'	scarlet, orange, yellow, cream	summer	no	6–10 in (15–25 cm)	6–10 in (15–25 cm)	9–11	no

RIGHT Mimulus cardinalis *is happiest when situated near the water's edge. This pretty scarlet-flowered plant is often found on the banks of streams and ponds.*

BELOW *Though short-lived, the award-winning hybrid cultivar Mimulus 'Highland Red' provides a colorful summer display of large deep red flowers coupled with mid-green leaves.*

MONARDA

This genus of 16 species of perennials and annuals from North America is a member of the mint family (Lamiaceae). These plants form large clumps, dying away completely in winter but recovering quickly in spring to form thickets of angled stems with lance-shaped aromatic leaves that are often red-tinted and hairy, with serrated edges. In summer the top of each stem carries several whorls of tubular flowers backed by leafy bracts. These plants are much loved by bees, which is reflected in the common name of bee balm. Other common names for *Monarda* are bergamot and horsemint. The genus name *Monarda* honors Nicholas Monardes, a fourteenth-century Spanish botanist.

CULTIVATION

Monarda species are very hardy and easily grown in any open sunny position with moist well-drained soil. Mildew is often a problem in late summer, so good ventilation is important. Propagation is by division when dormant or from cuttings taken from the base of the plant.

RIGHT *Sturdy stems hold the feathery flowers of* Monarda *'Ruby Glow' above the red-tinged mid-green leaves. This attractive plant grows to 30 in (75 cm) high.*

ABOVE *In its native habitat,* Monarda didyma *will send out fleshy stems underground to quickly populate an area. In the garden, these stems should be kept under control to minimize spread.*

Top Tip

With aromatic leaves and nectar-rich flowers, not only will the air be deliciously scented, but bees and hummingbirds will be regular visitors to the garden where *Monarda* plants are featured.

Favorites	Flower Color	Blooming Season	Flower Fragrance	Plant Height	Plant Width	Hardiness Zone	Frost Tolerance
Monarda **'Cambridge Scarlet'**	scarlet	mid-summer to early autumn	no	36 in (90 cm)	18 in (45 cm)	4–9	yes
Monarda didyma	white, pink, red	mid- to late summer	no	36 in (90 cm)	18 in (45 cm)	4–10	yes
Monarda didyma **'Violet Queen'**	lavender	mid- to late summer	no	36 in (90 cm)	18 in (45 cm)	4–10	yes
Monarda fistulosa	lavender to pale pink	late summer to early autumn	no	4 ft (1.2 m)	18 in (45 cm)	4–10	yes
Monarda **'Ruby Glow'**	pinkish red	summer to early autumn	no	24–30 in (60–75 cm)	12–18 in (30–45 cm)	4–9	yes
Monarda **'Vintage Wine'**	red-purple	mid-summer to early autumn	no	36 in (90 cm)	18 in (45 cm)	4–9	yes

BELOW *Flowering from mid-summer to early autumn,* Monarda *'Vintage Wine' has aromatic leaves and impressive, 2-lipped, purple-red flowers encircled by brown-green bracts.*

RIGHT *Known as wild bergamot, the purple-tinged whitish bracts of* Monarda fistulosa *carry flowers of lavender to pink. This plant is well suited to a wildflower or cottage garden.*

ABOVE *Myosotis alpestris, known as alpine forget-me-not, bears minute, dainty, blue flowers with a yellow eye. This pretty flower is the floral emblem of Alaska.*

MYOSOTIS

This is a genus of around 50 species of annuals, biennials, and perennials of the borage family (Boraginaceae), with the centers of distribution in Europe, Asia, the Americas, and New Zealand. Most are small tufted plants with simple, blunt, lance-shaped leaves that are sometimes grayish and often covered in fine hairs. Their 5-petalled flowers are tiny but quite showy as they are usually borne in sprays on short branching stems. Most bloom in spring and early summer, and flowers are usually white, cream, pink, or various shades of blue and mauve. A German legend attributes the common name of forget-me-not to a lover who, while gathering the flowers, fell into a river and cried "forget-me-not" as he drowned.

Top Tip

Relatively trouble-free, *Myosotis* species thrive in a cool, damp environment, and are especially suitable for woodland gardens or water-side planting.

CULTIVATION

These plants are very easily grown in any position, sunny or shady, as long as it remains moist during summer. Alpine species benefit from a gritty free-draining soil but the others aren't fussy. The perennials may be propagated from seed or by careful division in late winter, the annuals from seed sown in spring.

RIGHT *Throughout spring, Myosotis sylvatica, known as the garden forget-me-not, is covered in tiny, yellow-eyed, blue flowers. This European native has given rise to a large number of popular cultivars.*

ABOVE *Ideal as a ground cover,* Myosotis sylvatica *'Music' is smothered in clusters of deep blue, yellow-eyed flowers from spring to early summer.*
LEFT *Low-growing,* Myosotis alpestris *'Alba' is well suited to rockery planting, producing a carpet of dainty white flowers in the spring and summer months.*

Favorites

	Flower Color	Blooming Season	Flower Fragrance	Plant Height	Plant Width	Hardiness Zone	Frost Tolerance
Myosotis alpestris	bright blue with yellow eyes	spring to early summer	no	4–6 in (10–15 cm)	4–6 in (10–15 cm)	4–10	yes
Myosotis explanata	white	early summer	no	8 in (20 cm)	6 in (15 cm)	8–9	yes
Myosotis scorpioides	blue with yellow, white, or pink eye	summer	no	12 in (30 cm)	12 in (30 cm)	5–10	yes
Myosotis sylvatica	lavender-blue with yellow eyes	spring to early summer	no	10–18 in (25–45 cm)	12 in (30 cm)	5–10	yes
Myosotis sylvatica **'Blue Ball'**	bright blue	spring to early summer	no	4–8 in (10–20 cm)	8 in (20 cm)	5–10	yes
Myosotis sylvatica **'Music'**	deep blue with yellow eye	spring to early summer	no	10 in (25 cm)	12 in (30 cm)	5–10	yes

NARCISSUS

Commonly known as daffodil and jonquil, *Narcissus* is part of the amaryllis family (Amaryllidaceae) and includes around 50 species of mainly spring-flowering bulbs found from Europe and North Africa to Japan. Leaves are grassy to straplike, and the flowers almost always have the characteristic cup- or trumpet-shaped corona backed by 6 petals (the perianth). Their appeal is such that thousands of garden forms are now available. Horticulturalists have divided them according to flower type into 12 divisions. The genus name comes from the Greek mythological tale of the youth Narcissus who fell in love with his reflection in a pool. Unable to pull himself away, he eventually wasted away to become a flower.

CULTIVATION

Narcissus plants are generally very hardy and quite adaptable, growing in borders, pots, or in drifts across lawns. They prefer full or half sun when in growth and do well under deciduous trees. Good drainage is important. Propagate by breaking up established clumps.

LEFT Narcissus *'Palmares'* belongs to the Split-corona group of cultivars, and its cups are indeed split for about half their length into 2 or more segments. The frilled edges appear to bend back toward the petals.

BELOW *The plants of the* Narcissus, *Triandrus group bear 2 or more flowers per stem. 'Thalia', below, has elegant white blooms with slightly swept back petals borne on sturdy stems.* **BELOW LEFT** Narcissus, *Tazetta, 'Silver Chimes' bears up to 10 sweetly scented creamy white flowers per plant. It is commonly known as pheasant's eye narcissus.*

Favorites

	Flower Color	Blooming Season	Flower Fragrance	Plant Height	Plant Width	Hardiness Zone	Frost Tolerance
Narcissus, Bulbocodium	pale to deep yellow	spring	no	4–8 in (10–20 cm)	6 in (15 cm)	6–9	yes
Narcissus, Cyclamineus	pale to deep yellow, orange	early to mid-spring	no	6–12 in (15–30 cm)	3 in (8 cm)	6–9	yes
Narcissus, Double-flowered	white to deep yellow	mid-spring	no	12–18 in (30–45 cm)	6 in (15 cm)	4–10	yes
Narcissus, Jonquilla and Apodanthus	pale to deep yellow	mid- to late spring	yes	8–15 in (20–38 cm)	6 in (15 cm)	4–9	yes
Narcissus, Large-cupped	white, yellow, orange, pink	mid-spring	no	12–18 in (30–45 cm)	6 in (15 cm)	4–10	yes
Narcissus, Poeticus	white, with orange-scarlet center	late spring to early summer	yes	6–18 in (15–45 cm)	6 in (15 cm)	4–9	yes
Narcissus, Small-cupped	white, yellow, orange, pink	early to mid-spring	no	12–18 in (30–45 cm)	6 in (15 cm)	4–10	yes
Narcissus, Split-corona	white, yellow, orange, pink	spring	no	12–18 in (30–45 cm)	6 in (15 cm)	4–10	yes
Narcissus, Tazetta	white to yellow, orange center	autumn to spring	yes	15–18 in (38–45 cm)	8 in (20 cm)	8–10	yes
Narcissus, 'Tête-à-Tête'	golden yellow	early spring	no	6 in (15 cm)	3 in (8 cm)	5–9	yes
Narcissus, Triandrus	pale to deep yellow	mid- to late spring	no	6–12 in (15–30 cm)	4 in (10 cm)	4–9	yes
Narcissus, Trumpet	white, yellow, orange, pink	spring	no	12–18 in (30–45 cm)	6 in (15 cm)	4–10	yes

BELOW *A classic member of the Trumpet group,* Narcissus *'Mount Hood' was first introduced in the 1930s. It has long-lasting blooms with an ivory cup as long as the petals.*

Top Tip

Daffodils make excellent cut flowers and are best picked when the buds are almost ready to open. Change the water daily or use a good cut flower additive.

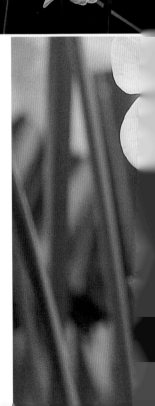

ABOVE *'Actaea' is an award-winning* Narcissus *from the Poeticus group. As is typical with flowers from that group, it bears a single pure white flower per stem with a small yellow cup, edged in scarlet.*

RIGHT *Double-flowered* Narcissus *plants have twice as many petals or cups—or both—than other cultivar groups. 'Cheerfulness' has an old-fashioned charm with its ruffled creamy petals.*

LEFT *The vividly colored* Narcissus, *Small-cupped, 'Barrett Browning' will brighten up any rock garden, as it has white petals with a yellow base and a deep orange cup.*

RIGHT *The early bloom-ing Cyclamineus hybrids are valued for their under-stated elegance. Narcissus, Cyclamineus, 'Jack Snipe' has white petals and a long yellow cup, and can reach 8 in (20 cm) high.*

BELOW *Narcissus, Jonquilla and Apodanthus, 'Trevithian' usually bears 2 or more blooms per stem, typically with small, shallow, wide orange cups and lemon yellow petals. They are enjoyed for their fragrance.*

Nemesia

Confined to South Africa, this figwort family (Scrophulariaceae) genus includes around 65 species of annuals, perennials, and subshrubs. They form small mounds of foliage with toothed, linear, or lance-shaped leaves. Their flowers, which grow in clusters on short stems, are trumpet-shaped and 2-lipped; the upper lip is 4-lobed, the lower lip 1- or 2-lobed, often in a contrasting color. The annuals are popular short-lived bedding plants occurring in a wide range of bright colors. While less vividly colored, the perennials live longer, are sometimes mildly scented, and are useful plants for borders, rockeries, or pots. The genus is named for Nemesis, the goddess of retribution, though the reason why these inoffensive little plants should bear such a name is intriguingly unclear.

Cultivation

Plant in a sunny position with light free-draining soil that can be kept moist. Pinch back leaf tips when plants are young to keep the compact shape. Annuals should be sown in succession for continuous bloom. The perennials tolerate light frosts and grow from the cuttings of non-flowering stems.

Top Tip

Nemesia species flower for only a short time but it is possible to prolong the flowering period by cutting the plants back hard when the blooms have finished.

Right *Due to its often bicolored flowers,* Nemesia strumosa *is a favorite in the garden. It is a small fast-growing plant that is ideal for beds or in pots.*

Below *An evergreen plant,* Nemesia caerulea *'Innocence' bears an abundance of tiny clear white flowers with yellow centers from summer to autumn.*

Left Nemesia denticulata *is the sort of plant every gardener cherishes. Its only requirement is a sunny spot to produce masses of soft lilac blooms. As an added extra, its perfume permeates the air on a warm day.*

RIGHT Nemesia caerulea *'Hubbird', formerly called N. fruticosa 'Blue Bird', makes a bright splash of purple-blue color in any garden. Rockeries and borders are ideally suited to its semi-trailing habit.*

Favorites	Flower Color	Blooming Season	Flower Fragrance	Plant Height	Plant Width	Hardiness Zone	Frost Tolerance
Nemesia caerulea	pink, lavender, blue	summer to autumn	no	15–24 in (38–60 cm)	12 in (30 cm)	8–10	yes
Nemesia caerulea 'Hubbird'	violet-blue	summer to autumn	no	15 in (38 cm)	18 in (45 cm)	8–10	yes
Nemesia caerulea 'Innocence'	white, yellow centered	summer to autumn	no	15 in (38 cm)	18 in (45 cm)	8–10	yes
Nemesia denticulata	lilac-mauve	late spring to early autumn	yes	15 in (38 cm)	24–36 in (60–90 cm)	7–10	yes
Nemesia strumosa	various	summer to autumn	no	8–12 in (20–30 cm)	12 in (30 cm)	9–11	no
Nemesia versicolor	various	summer to autumn	no	10–18 in (25–45 cm)	8–12 in (20–30 cm)	9–11	no

ABOVE Nepeta racemosa 'Walker's Low' has finely hairy gray-green leaves and long-blooming lavender-blue flowers.
BELOW Dense spikes of purple-blue (occasionally yellow) flowers are borne on the sturdy stems of Nepeta nervosa. The deeply veined leaves grow to a length of 4 in (10 cm).

NEPETA

A member of the mint family (Lamiaceae), this genus of around 250 mainly aromatic perennials is native to a wide area of Eurasia, North Africa, and the mountains of tropical Africa. They are mainly low-growing plants, rather sprawling in habit, with small, toothed, often aromatic leaves. In summer the gray-green foliage disappears under upright spikes bearing many tiny flowers along their length. The 2-lipped flowers range in color from white to mauve-blue to deep purple. *Nepeta* hybrids make exceptional garden plants and are ideal for herbaceous borders, for edgings, or as ground covers. The common names of catnip and catmint refer to the fondness that cats have for playing and lying in this plant.

CULTIVATION

Best grown in full sun, *Nepeta* species prefer light free-draining soil. Pinch back in spring to encourage compact growth and water well. Cutting back the plants each year will maintain their shape and keep them tidy. Propagation is by division, from cuttings taken during late spring or summer, or from seed.

LEFT *A vigorous grower,* Nepeta racemosa *is suitable for growing in a herbaceous border. Cutting the short-blooming flowers back will usually result in rebloom.* BELOW Nepeta × faassenii *'Six Hills Giant' is wonderful as an edging plant. It tolerates damp conditions better than other cultivars.*

Top Tip

Nepeta species self-seed very freely and can become invasive. To prevent this, give the plants a light trim in the growing season and cut back the old growth in spring.

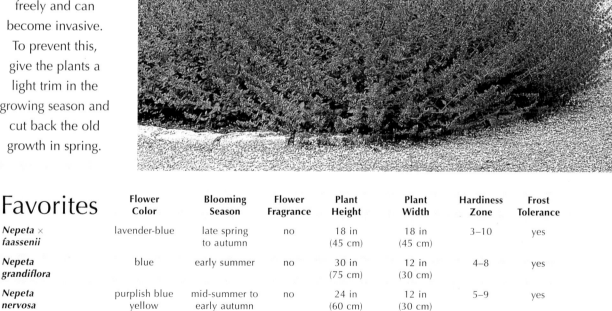

Favorites

	Flower Color	Blooming Season	Flower Fragrance	Plant Height	Plant Width	Hardiness Zone	Frost Tolerance
Nepeta × faassenii	lavender-blue	late spring to autumn	no	18 in (45 cm)	18 in (45 cm)	3–10	yes
Nepeta grandiflora	blue	early summer	no	30 in (75 cm)	12 in (30 cm)	4–8	yes
Nepeta nervosa	purplish blue yellow	mid-summer to early autumn	no	24 in (60 cm)	12 in (30 cm)	5–9	yes
Nepeta racemosa	lavender-blue	summer	no	12 in (30 cm)	18 in (45 cm)	3–10	yes
Nepeta sibirica	blue to violet-blue	mid- to late summer	no	12 in (30 cm)	18 in (45 cm)	3–8	yes
Nepeta tuberosa	violet-purple, pinkish bracts	summer	no	12–30 in (30–75 cm)	18 in (45 cm)	8–10	yes

NERINE

Commonly known as the spider lily or Guernsey lily, this genus is an autumn-flowering member of the amaryllis family and includes around 30 species of bulbs that often resemble smaller versions of *Amaryllis*. Native to southern Africa, these plants may be evergreen or die down in summer. The deep to bright green leaves vary from grassy to straplike and surround upright flower stems carrying many-flowered heads of long-tubed funnel-shaped blooms each with 6 widely flared, narrow petals. Flower color ranges from pink and red to scarlet and white. A story, probably apocryphal, says the Guernsey lily was so-named because *Nerine* was introduced to Europe when a bulb washed up on the island of Guernsey.

LEFT Nerine *masoniorum bears clusters of rose pink flowers, the petals of which have a central stripe of deeper pink.*
RIGHT *The large pink flowers of* Nerine *bowdenii are held aloft on tall, 24 in (60 cm) high, leafless stems.*

CULTIVATION

Plant, with the neck of the bulb exposed, in half or full sun in well-drained, humus-rich, sandy soil. Grow in pots in areas of severe frosts. Water well during the growth period but keep dry when dormant; the watering program should be maintained for evergreen species. Propagate by division, from shoots growing at the base of the plant, or from seed.

Favorites

	Flower Color	Blooming Season	Flower Fragrance	Plant Height	Plant Width	Hardiness Zone	Frost Tolerance
Nerine bowdenii	pink with darker central rib	autumn	yes	24 in (60 cm)	12 in (30 cm)	8–10	yes
Nerine filifolia	white, rosy pink to red	autumn	no	10 in (25 cm)	6 in (15 cm)	9–10	no
Nerine flexuosa	pink with darker central rib	late autumn	no	12–24 in (30–60 cm)	12 in (30 cm)	8–10	yes
Nerine flexuosa 'Alba'	white	late autumn	no	12–18 in (30–45 cm)	12 in (30 cm)	8–10	yes
Nerine masoniorum	pink with darker central rib	autumn	no	8 in (20 cm)	4 in (10 cm)	8–10	yes
Nerine sarniensis	bright red to orange-red	early autumn	no	18–24 in (45–60 cm)	3 in (8 cm)	9–11	no

ABOVE *Spectacular in both color and form, the brilliant red flowers of* Nerine sarniensis *are enhanced by long red stamens with golden yellow tips.*

BELOW *Nerine sarniensis var. curvifolia f. fothergillii 'Major' is an early-flowering variety, which bears clusters of vivid red flowers with prominent stamens.*

Top Tip

In cooler climates, containers of *Nerine* species can be brought indoors, where the long-lasting statuesque flowers will create a dramatic effect.

NERIUM

This small genus belongs to the dogbane family and consists of only 2 species of long-flowering evergreen shrubs native to the area from southwestern Asia across to China. The leaves are simple, smooth-edged, narrow, and lance-shaped, providing a background for the attractive flowers that range in color from white and pale pink to red. The numerous cultivars further broaden the color spectrum. Appearing in clusters, the flowers are made up of 5 broad petals that are fused into a narrow tube at one end and flare open at the other into a disc or a shallow cup. *Nerium* plants are very beautiful garden subjects but are also extremely poisonous; care is needed when working with them in the garden.

CULTIVATION

Plant in almost any type of soil, except wet, in full sun. They will tolerate light frosts if grown in a sheltered position. Well-established plants may be pruned quite severely in winter, about once every 3 years, to maintain their shape. Propagate from half-hardened cuttings taken in autumn or from seed in spring.

ABOVE LEFT Nerium oleander *'Petite Salmon', as its name suggests, bears blooms of a delicate salmon pink shade on an attractive dwarf bush. It is suitable as a hedging plant.*
ABOVE *Bearing single pink blooms,* Nerium oleander *'Docteur Golfin' is a popular landscaping plant in warm climates. Once established, it needs very little watering.*
RIGHT Nerium oleander *comes in a variety of colors and sizes. It is a long-lived plant and is often grown as an informal hedge, in a shrub border, or in a large container.*

Favorites	Flower Color	Blooming Season	Flow Fragra
Nerium oleander	white, yellow, pink, red	spring to early autumn	n
Nerium oleander 'Album'	white; creamy white at center	spring to early autumn	n
Nerium oleander 'Docteur Golfin'	bright pink	spring to early autumn	n
Nerium oleander 'Petite Salmon'	salmon pink	spring to early autumn	n
Nerium oleander 'Splendens'	rosy pink	spring to early autumn	n
Nerium oleander 'Splendens Variegatum'	rosy pink	spring to early autumn	n

Top Tip

Although they are
extremely hardy
plants in mild
climates, in cooler
areas *Nerium
oleander* and its
cultivars need to
be overwintered
indoors as they are
not cold-hardy.

BELOW *The attractive foliage
is the first thing that catches
the eye on* Nerium oleander
*'Splendens Variegatum'. The
leaves contrast with the stunning double pink flowers.*

Plant Height	Plant Width	Hardiness Zone	Frost Tolerance
8–15 ft (.4–4.5 m)	6–12 ft (1.8–3.5 m)	8–11	yes
8–15 ft (.4–4.5 m)	6–12 ft (1.8–3.5 m)	8–11	yes
8–15 ft (.4–4.5 m)	6–12 ft (1.8–3.5 m)	8–11	yes
2–4 ft (.6–1.2 m)	2–4 ft (0.6–1.2 m)	8–11	yes
6–15 ft (.8–4.5 m)	6–12 ft (1.8–3.5 m)	8–11	yes
6–15 ft (.8–4.5 m)	6–12 ft (1.8–3.5 m)	8–11	yes

NICOTIANA

As the genus name indicates, this is the well-known source of tobacco leaf. There are over 65 species in this genus, the bulk of which are annuals and perennials native to tropical and subtropical America, as well as Australia. Most species are tall and treelike but a few species grow as shrubs, though they tend to be softwooded and short-lived. Their leaves are usually deep green, very large, and covered with fine hairs. They are sticky to the touch, and may exude a fragrance when crushed. The attractive flowers are tubular or bell-shaped; mostly white or in pastel shades of green, pale yellow, pink, or soft red; and usually open only in the early evening or at night. If the blooms are fragrant, the scent is also often released at night.

CULTIVATION

Most tobacco species are marginally frost hardy to frost tender. They grow best in warm humid climates with ample summer rainfall in full sun or partial shade. They require soil that is moist, well-drained, and reasonably fertile. Most *Nicotiana* species are propagated from seed sown in the spring, though some will grow from cuttings.

ABOVE *The leaves of* Nicotiana tabacum *have long been used to make tobacco products, but this plant also produces pretty little pink flowers.*
RIGHT *Nicotiana alata 'Nicky' is often grown as an annual and produces clusters of scented crimson flowers. It is a good choice for borders.*

Favorites	Flower Color	Blooming Season	Flower Fragrance	Plant Height	Plant Width	Hardiness Zone	Frost Tolerance
Nicotiana alata	greenish white and white	summer to early autumn	yes	2–4 ft (0.6–1.2 m)	18 in (45 cm)	7–11	no
Nicotiana 'Avalon Bright Pink'	pink	summer to autumn	no	8–12 in (20–30 cm)	8–12 in (20–30 cm)	8–11	no
Nicotiana langsdorffii	green	summer	no	2–5 ft (0.6–1.5 m)	18–30 in (45–75 cm)	9–11	no
Nicotiana 'Saratoga Mixed'	white, greenish white, pink, red	summer to autumn	no	10–12 in (25–30 cm)	10–12 in (25–30 cm)	8–11	no
Nicotiana sylvestris	white	summer	yes	5 ft (1.5 m)	24 in (60 cm)	8–11	no
Nicotiana tabacum	greenish white to dull pink	summer	yes	4–6 ft (1.2–1.8 m)	3 ft (0.9 m)	9–11	no

ABOVE Nicotiana sylvestris bears long tubular to trumpet-shaped white flowers and is often planted near doors and windows in order to enjoy the evening scent.

BELOW If planted in full sun, the white, pale pink, cerise, and ruby red flowers of Nicotiana 'Saratoga Mixed' will open for some time during the day.

Top Tip

Many *Nicotiana* species are happy in large containers. Use a multi-purpose compost and add a slow-release fertilizer to the soil before planting.

OENOTHERA

Commonly referred to as evening primrose, this genus contains over 120 species of annuals, biennials, and perennials of the willow herb family (Onagraceae). Species are found in the temperate zones of the Americas and may vary considerably: some have taproots and tend to grow upright; others have fibrous roots; and certain species have a sprawling growth habit. The foliage varies from clump-forming with soft, hairy, toothed- or lance-shaped leaves to large rough leaves growing on erect stems. The cup-shaped flowers make a lovely display over summer in bright shades of yellow, or less commonly, pink, red, or white. Evening primrose oil is extracted from the plant's tiny seeds and is used in a range of homeopathic remedies.

ABOVE *A clump-forming perennial,* Oenothera *'Crown Imperial' produces a breathtaking display of large bright yellow blooms in summer. It has rich green leaves, and the flowers age to orange-re*

LEFT Oenothera *'Lemon Sunset', as its name suggest: bears large lemon yellow blooms that fade to pink as they age.*

CULTIVATION

Mostly very hardy, these tough adaptable plants prefer full sun and light, gritty, free-draining soil. Summer watering produces stronger growth but they will also tolerate drought conditions. Fibrous-rooted species can be divided when dormant, otherwise propagate from seed or from cuttings taken from the base of the plant.

Favorites

	Flower Color	Blooming Season	Flower Fragrance	Plant Height	Plant Width	Hardiness Zone	Frost Tolerance
Oenothera caespitosa	white, ageing to pink	summer	yes	6 in (15 cm)	8 in (20 cm)	5–9	yes
Oenothera 'Crown Imperial'	yellow	early summer	no	18 in (45 cm)	24 in (60 cm)	5–9	yes
Oenothera fruticosa	deep yellow	late spring to summer	no	18–36 in (45–90 cm)	12 in (30 cm)	4–10	yes
Oenothera 'Lemon Sunset'	cream, yellow center ageing to pink	summer to early autumn	no	24–36 in (60–90 cm)	12 in (30 cm)	5–9	yes
Oenothera macrocarpa	yellow	late spring to early autumn	yes	6–12 in (15–30 cm)	24 in (60 cm)	5–9	yes
Oenothera speciosa	white, ageing to pink	spring to early autumn	yes	18–24 in (45–60 cm)	24 in (60 cm)	5–10	yes

LEFT *Although potentially invasive, Oenothera speciosa 'Siskiyou' is valued for the delicate pink shade of its shallow saucer-shaped flowers, as well as its long blooming season.*

BELOW *Oenothera speciosa 'Alba' bears yellow-centered, pure white, fragrant flowers that open during the day. Its simple charm makes it a cottage garden favorite.*

Top Tip

These plants have both culinary and medicinal uses. Evening primrose oil from the seeds is said to be highly therapeutic, and the leaves can be eaten in salads or used to make tea.

ORNITHOGALUM

Top Tip

Although popular in rock gardens, *Ornithogalum* species also do well in containers. Use a loam-based potting mix and water sufficiently for moist but not damp soil.

This large genus belongs to the hyacinth family (Hyacinthaceae) and contains around 80 species of bulbs native to South Africa and the Mediterranean region. They quickly form large clumps of grassy to strap-like leaves, sometimes with a rib down the middle of them. In spring or summer, depending on the species, upright conical spikes of white to cream flowers appear. Often called chincherinchee or the star-of-Bethlehem, the flowers are sometimes mildly scented. They are usually starry or cup-shaped and have 6 petals in 2 whorls of 3. The botanical name comes from the Greek *ornis* (a bird) and *gala* (milk), as the flowers resemble a white bird when they are spread out. They are striking additions to a rock garden or border.

CULTIVATION

Most of the European species tolerate moderate frosts whereas the South African species are frost tender and may need to be lifted for winter. Plant in a sunny open position with light well-drained soil. Water well when flowering, then dry off when the plants are dormant. Propagate by division.

BELOW *Standing well clear of the strappy foliage below, the funnel-shaped white flowers of* Ornithogalum reverchonii *make excellent border or cut flowers.*

LEFT Ornithogalum nutans *has distinctive starlike flowers with recurved white and green petals and a cluster of yellow-tipped stamens in the center.*

Favorites	Flower Color	Blooming Season	Flower Fragrance	Plant Height	Plant Width	Hardiness Zone	Frost Tolerance
Ornithogalum arabicum	white with black eye	early summer	yes	12–24 in (30–60 cm)	8 in (20 cm)	9–11	no
Ornithogalum dubium	orange, yellow, red, with black eye	winter to spring	yes	6–12 in (15–30 cm)	4 in (10 cm)	7–10	yes
Ornithogalum narbonense	white with black eye	late spring to early summer	no	12–36 in (30–90 cm)	8 in (20 cm)	7–10	yes
Ornithogalum nutans	white with green stripes	late spring to early summer	no	12–24 in (30–60 cm)	10 in (25 cm)	6–10	yes
Ornithogalum reverchonii	white	late spring to early summer	no	24 in (60 cm)	8 in (20 cm)	5–9	yes
Ornithogalum umbellatum	white with green stripes	early summer	no	12 in (30 cm)	4 in (10 cm)	5–10	yes

RIGHT *Bold yellow-orange blooms with a black eye attract gardeners to* Ornithogalum dubium. *When the leaves have finished, do not water until the foliage reappears.*

BELOW Ornithogalum arabicum *bears 6-petalled white flowers with a large shiny center. They do best in a warm sunny spot in the garden and require little water.*

OSTEOSPERMUM

ound mainly in southern Africa, this genus consists of some 70 species of annuals, perennials, and subshrubs of the daisy family (Asteraceae). The plants are generally low, spreading, or mounding in growth habit with simple, broadly toothed, elliptical to spatula-shaped leaves. *Osteospermum* plants are valued for the cheerful carpet of flowers they provide through the warmer months. The flowers are daisylike: a large outer ring of petallike ray florets, mainly pink, purple, or white, surrounds a central disc, often an unusual purple-blue color and sporting golden pollen-bearing anthers, which add to the plant's beauty. The genus name comes from the Greek words *osteon* (bone) and *sperma* (seed) and refers to the hard seeds.

ABOVE Osteospermum jucundum *produces striking solitary, mauve-pink, daisy-like blooms with a purple-blue center that fades to a yellow color as it ages. The flowers tend to close on overcast days.*

CULTIVATION

Most species will tolerate only light frosts and prefer a sunny position in light well-drained soil. Avoid over-watering as this can lead to straggly growth. Pinching back and deadheading keeps the plants compact. Propagate annuals from seed and perennials from tip cuttings.

Top Tip

Very hardy plants, *Osteospermum* species suit a range of garden situations including along paths, in borders, over embankments, or in rock gardens.

ABOVE Osteospermum 'Orange Symphony' bears light orange blooms with dark blue centers. It has a mounding habit so is often used for container growing. **LEFT** Osteospermum 'Nasinga Purple', part of the Nasinga Series, need to be grown en masse in order to fully appreciate the blue-centered purple flowers. **FAR LEFT** Lovely white petals surround the blue and yellow center of Osteospermum 'Sunny Gustav'. It has a prostrate habit and benefits from a trim when flowering has finished.

Favorites

	Flower Color	Blooming Season	Flower Fragrance	Plant Height	Plant Width	Hardiness Zone	Frost Tolerance
Osteospermum jucundum	purple-pink	autumn to spring	no	8–12 in (20–30 cm)	36 in (90 cm)	8–10	yes
Osteospermum, Nasinga Series	white, cream, pink, purple	spring to summer	no	12–18 in (30–45 cm)	24 in (60 cm)	8–10	yes
Osteospermum, Side Series	white, mauve-pink, purple-red	spring to summer	no	10–12 in (25–30 cm)	18 in (45 cm)	8–10	yes
Osteospermum 'Sunny Gustav'	white	spring to summer	no	12 in (30 cm)	18 in (45 cm)	8–10	yes
Osteospermum, Symphony Series	cream, yellow, orange, salmon	summer to autumn	no	10–15 in (25–38 cm)	18–24 in (45–60 cm)	8–10	yes
Osteospermum 'Whirligig'	white with gray-blue underside	late spring to autumn	no	18–24 in (45–60 cm)	24 in (60 cm)	8–10	yes

PAEONIA

There are 30 or so species in this genus of beautiful herbaceous perennials and deciduous shrubs, all native to temperate parts of the Northern Hemisphere. They have long-lived, rather woody rootstocks and stems, and bold foliage. Leaves are dark green to blue-green, usually toothed or lobed, and are sometimes maroon or red-tinged. The large flowers are usually erect and solitary, cup- or saucer-shaped, and have brightly colored petals surrounding a mass of short stamens. Petals may be white, yellow, or shades of pink, sometimes flushed red at the center, and stamens are mostly white or yellow. The genus name goes back to Ancient Greek times and refers to the supposed medicinal properties of the species.

CULTIVATION

Paeonia species can survive in cold climates as long as they have protection from early spring frosts, strong winds, and hot sun. They prefer full or slightly filtered sunlight with cool moist soil. Propagate from seed or by division.

ABOVE LEFT *The gorgeous, bright yellow, cup-shaped flowers of Paeonia lutea have a dramatic center of orange-yellow stamens, wonderfully set off by the green foliage.*
BELOW Paeonia anomala *var.* intermedia, *with its blood red blooms, is an excellent cut flower. Keep the flowers in a cool part of the home and change the water each day.*

LEFT *Perfect for a mixed or shrub border,* Paeonia tenuifolia *bears large, single, cup-shaped, deep red blooms complemented by a cluster of yellow stamens.*

ABOVE *Valued for its yellow flowers with a deep orange center,* Paeonia × lemoinei *'Roman Child' is an upright deciduous shrub with dark green divided leaves.*

Favorites

	Flower Color	Blooming Season	Flower Fragrance	Plant Height	Plant Width	Hardiness Zone	Frost Tolerance
Paeonia anomala	bright red	early summer	no	20–24 in (50–60 cm)	24 in (60 cm)	5–8	yes
Paeonia cambessedesii	deep pink	late spring	no	18 in (45 cm)	18–24 in (45–60 cm)	8–10	yes
Paeonia delavayi	dark red	summer	no	6 ft (1.8 m)	4 ft (1.2 m)	6–9	yes
Paeonia lactiflora	white, pink to deep red	late spring to mid-summer	yes	24 in (60 cm)	24 in (60 cm)	6–9	yes
Paeonia × lemoinei	yellow with red or orange marks	spring to early summer	no	6 ft (1.8 m)	5 ft (1.5 m)	6–9	yes
Paeonia lutea	bright yellow	spring to early summer	no	5 ft (1.5 m)	5 ft (1.5 m)	6–9	yes
Paeonia mascula	deep pink to red, sometimes white	summer	no	24–36 in (60–90 cm)	24–36 in (60–90 cm)	8–10	yes
Paeonia mlokosewitschii	pale to bright yellow	spring	no	30–36 in (75–90 cm)	30–36 in (75–90 cm)	6–9	yes
Paeonia officinalis	rose pink to purple, red	spring to mid-summer	no	24 in (60 cm)	24 in (60 cm)	8–10	yes
Paeonia suffruticosa	white, yellow, pink, red	spring	no	3–6 ft (0.9–1.8 m)	3–6 ft (0.9–1.8 m)	4–9	yes
Paeonia tenuifolia	deep red	late spring to early summer	no	20–27 in (50–70 cm)	20–27 in (50–70 cm)	5–8	yes
Paeonia veitchii	pale to bright magenta, white	late spring to early summer	no	20–24 in (50–60 cm)	20–24 in (50–60 cm)	6–8	yes

ABOVE *The maroon-veined dark green leaves of* Paeonia cambessedesii *are reddish purple underneath: the perfect foil for the deep pink flowers and showy yellow stamens.*

BELOW *All peonies benefit from the applicaton of a general fertilizer in spring and* Paeonia mascula *subsp.* arietina *is no exception, rewarding this effort with longer-lasting blooms.*

Top Tip

Paeonia plants are susceptible to gray mold, which rots leaf bases, stems, and buds. Spray affected plants with a fungicide and make sure the soil is well drained.

BELOW Paeonia veitchii *has deep green leaves and solitary, single, bowl-shaped blooms that are either white or a shade of pink.*

ABOVE *The glorious double white blooms of* Paeonia suffruticosa *'Mountain Treasure' have deep red markings at the center and a mass of golden stamens, making this plant a delight in any garden.*

LEFT Paeonia lactiflora *'Bowl of Beauty' is just one of numerous lovely cultivars, enjoyed by gardeners for their delicious scent and beautiful summer blooms. Indiana has taken the flower of* Paeonia lactiflora *as its state floral emblem.*

PAPAVER

Instantly recognized as the poppy, this wide-spread group of about 50 species of annuals and perennials belongs to the Papaveraceae family. Leaves grow from the base of the plant to form rosettes and are usually dark to light green, lobed, and covered in fine hairs. Upright flower stems covered in bristles grow out of the leaf rosettes and hold aloft the nodding bud that develops into the distinctive flower. These are usually 4-petalled, paper-textured, cup-shaped, and occur in shades of white, yellow, orange, pink, or red. The poppy is often associated with war remembrance days, a link attributed to Homer, the eighth-century B.C. Greek poet, who first associated the drooping poppy bud with the form of a dying soldier.

CULTIVATION

Poppies are frost hardy and prefer a sunny position with light, moist, and well-drained soil. Most species are propagated from seed although perennial poppy cultivars are propagated from root cuttings.

LEFT Rich red petals with dramatic black spots mak Papaver commutatum a spectacular poppy. The single flowers make their appearance in summer, h on furry gray stems above downy mid-green leaves.

Favorites	Flower Color	Blooming Season	Flower Fragrance	Plant Height	Plant Width	Hardiness Zone	Frost Tolerance
Papaver commutatum	bright red; black spot at petal base	summer	no	18–20 in (45–50 cm)	6 in (15 cm)	8–10	yes
Papaver miyabeanum	pale yellow	late spring to early summer	no	6 in (15 cm)	6 in (15 cm)	5–9	yes
Papaver nudicaule	white, yellow, orange, pink	winter to spring	yes	12–24 in (30–60 cm)	6–12 in (15–30 cm)	2–10	yes
Papaver orientale	pink to red; black spot at petal base	summer	no	18–36 in (45–90 cm)	24–36 in (60–90 cm)	3–9	yes
Papaver rupifragum	pale orange to scarlet	summer	no	18–24 in (45–60 cm)	12 in (30 cm)	6–9	yes
Papaver somniferum	white, pink, red, purple	summer	no	2–4 ft (0.6–1.2 m)	12 in (30 cm)	7–10	yes

LEFT Papaver nudicaule 'Meadhome's Strain' has bright orange and yellow flowers that add a uniquely cheerful atmosphere to any style of garden.

BELOW Oriental poppies, such as Papaver orientale 'Marcus Perry', are equally at home in a formal border or a wild garden. These coral blooms suit most situations.

Top Tip

Papaver nudicaule, the Iceland poppy, is the best species for cut flowers. Pick just as the buds are beginning to open, and singe the ends before placing in water.

LOW As with all Oriental ppies, Papaver orientale, liath Group, 'Beauty of ermere' self-seeds freely. has the characteristic ck spot on each petal.

LEFT *The rather beautiful blooms of* Paphiopedilum haynaldianum *blend shades of green, dusky pink, and brown to remarkable effect. Leaves are long and strap-shaped, with a neat habit.*

BELOW *The white flowers of* Paphiopedilum bellatulum *are marked with dramatic maroon-red spots. The gray-green leaves are long and strap-shaped.*

Top Tip

When growing *Paphiopedilum* species in pots, choose a potting mix that drains fast but retains some moisture. The plants like to be crowded, so a medium-sized pot should be used.

PAPHIOPEDILUM

This orchid genus of 80 or more species extends from India through to Southeast Asia, including southern China, and from the Philippines and Malaysia to New Guinea and the Solomon Islands. The plants grow mostly at moderate altitudes in dense shade on the rainforest floor, in leaf mold on rock faces, or occasionally on the trunk and leaves of other plants. They are usually compact, consisting of fleshy roots, a short stem, and a few large, often mottled, straplike leaves with a spray of one or a few highly exotic looking flowers. The flowers are large with a pouched lip and come in a wide range of shapes and colors, including striped, mottled, and spotted.

CULTIVATION

The growing requirements depend on the origin, habitat, and altitude of the particular species. *Paphiopedilum* species are best grown in part-shade, although some tolerate sunny positions. They are best grown in containers, with a well-drained bark-based potting mix. Propagate from seed or by division.

Favorites	Flower Color	Blooming Season	Flo Fragr
Paphiopedilum bellatulum	white or cream; spotted maroon	late spring to early summer	n
Paphiopedilum Darling	pink and lemon; spotted crimson	summer	r
Paphiopedilum haynaldianum	green and pink; spotted maroon	spring	r
Paphiopedilum hirsutissimum	green-brown and rose pink	late spring to early summer	r
Paphiopedilum insigne	yellow, green, and reddish brown	autumn to spring	r
Paphiopedilum villosum	green, brown; maroon markings	winter to spring	r

ABOVE *The greenish brown pouch of* Paphiopedilum hirsutissimum *is perfectly complemented by the dark pink petals, the greenish brown upper sepals, and the arching graceful leaves.*

RIGHT *Increasingly, hybrids are selected for their round flowers and vigorous nature, such as the pink-flowered* Paphiopedilum *Darling.*

BELOW *One of the most cold tolerant of the species,* Paphiopedilum insigne *bears its solitary yellow-brown flowers on erect, somewhat hairy stems, from autumn through to spring.*

Plant Height	Plant Width	Hardiness Zone	Frost Tolerance
5 in (12 cm)	8 in (20 cm)	11–12	no
15 in (38 cm)	10 in (25 cm)	11–12	no
18 in (45 cm)	12 in (30 cm)	11–12	no
6 in (15 cm)	8 in (20 cm)	11–12	no
12–18 in (30–45 cm)	12–18 in (30–45 cm)	10–12	no
6 in (15 cm)	6 in (15 cm)	11–12	no

PASSIFLORA

ABOVE *Passiflora violacea bears its amethyst-colored blooms in summer. Like all passion flowers, it is a vigorous climber and tolerates a range of soil types.*

BELOW *The magnificent Passiflora caerulea produces greenish white flowers and striking white and purple anthers that act as a beacon for the ovary and stamens.*

This genus of the family Passifloraceae contains over 500 species of mainly evergreen tendril-climbing vines from tropical America. They are known for their ornamental blossoms and their pulpy pale yellow to purple-black fruit, the passionfruit. The flowerheads are made up of a tubular casing at the base; 5 to 10 tepals that are spread out flat, arching, or bowl-shaped; a crown of anthers; and a single stalk in the center bearing the stamen and ovaries, often in a 3-pronged starlike formation. Colors range from pale yellow or pink to purple-red. The common name of passion flower comes from the Jesuit association of the flower structure with the crucifixion of Christ.

CULTIVATION

Most species are frost tender and like a warm climate in full or half sun with deep, moist, humus-rich, well-drained soil. Feed and water well. Trim and remove any frosted foliage in spring. Propagate from seed, layers, or cuttings

Favorites

	Flower Color	Blooming Season	Flower Fragrance	Plant Height	Plant Width	Hardiness Zone	Frost Tolerance
Passiflora caerulea	white to pale violet, purple corona	summer to autumn	no	10–30 ft (3–9 m)	10 ft (3 m)	7–11	yes
Passiflora incarnata	purple to white; purple and white corona	summer	yes	6 ft (1.8 m)	4 ft (1.2 m)	7–10	yes
Passiflora quadrangularis	dark red; white and purple corona	mid-summer to autumn	yes	15–30 ft (4.5–9 m)	10 ft (3 m)	10–12	no
Passiflora racemosa	red	summer to autumn	no	15 ft (4.5 m)	10 ft (3 m)	10–12	no
Passiflora violacea	purple and white	summer to autumn	no	10 ft (3 m)	4 ft (1.2 m)	10–12	no
Passiflora vitifolia	red; red and yellow corona	early summer to autumn	no	15 ft (4.5 m)	8 ft (2.4 m)	10–12	no

RIGHT *One of the hardiest of the passion flowers, Passiflora incarnata is also easy to grow from seed. The purple blooms can be up to 3 in (8 cm) across.*
BELOW *Passiflora racemosa produces bright red flowers with a creamy crown of anthers. It looks particularly effective when grown over a pergola or a garden fence.*

Top Tip

Hardy *Passiflora* species can be trained to grow over walls, arches, and trellises, but they will require pruning in late winter so they don't become congested.

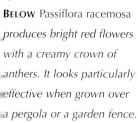

PELARGONIUM

Most of the 250 species of annuals, perennials, and subshrubs in this geranium family (Geraniaceae) genus come from South Africa, with a few from Australia, the Middle East, and other parts of Africa. The foliage is quite varied but is often light green, rounded or hand-shaped, with conspicuous lobes, fine hairs, and dark blotches. Some species have semi-succulent leaves. The flowers are simple and 5-petalled, often brightly colored, and sometimes grown in a mass of blooms, ranging in color from white and pink to mauve and purple. The genus name comes from the Greek word *pelargos* (a stork), referring to the shape of the seed pod, as does the genus's common name of storksbill.

CULTIVATION

These mostly frost-tender plants grow well in a mild climate and are suitable for garden beds and pots. Plant in full sun with fertile, light, well-drained soil. Once established, *Pelargonium* plants are drought tolerant. Propagate the annuals and species from seed and the perennials and shrubs from cuttings.

Favorites

	Flower Color	Blooming Season	Flower Fragrance	Plant Height	Plant Width	Hardiness Zone	Frost Tolerance
Pelargonium, Angel	pink, purple, red, white	spring to summer	no	10–18 in (25–45 cm)	12–18 in (30–45 cm)	9–11	no
Pelargonium crispum	pink	spring to summer	no	3 ft (0.9 m)	24 in (60 cm)	9–11	no
Pelargonium, Dwarf	white, pink, orange, red	spring to summer	no	8 in (20 cm)	8 in (20 cm)	9–11	no
Pelargonium echinatum	white, pink to purple-pink	spring to early summer	no	18 in (45 cm)	12 in (30 cm)	9–11	no
Pelargonium, Ivy-leafed	white, pink, red, purple	spring to autumn	no	8–36 in (20–90 cm)	12–36 in (30–90 cm)	9–11	no
Pelargonium, Miniature	white, pink, orange, red	spring to autumn	no	6 in (15 cm)	6 in (15 cm)	9–11	no
Pelargonium, Regal	white, purple, pink to red	late spring to summer	no	24 in (60 cm)	3–5 ft (0.9–1.5 m)	9–11	no
Pelargonium, Scented-leafed	white, pink, purple	spring to early summer	no	12–36 in (30–90 cm)	12–36 in (30–90 cm)	8–11	no
Pelargonium, Stellar	white, pink, orange, red	spring to summer	no	12–30 in (30–75 cm)	12–24 in (30–60 cm)	9–11	no
Pelargonium triste	yellow, green, pink	spring to summer	yes	8–12 in (20–30 cm)	12–18 in (30–45 cm)	9–11	no
Pelargonium, Unique	white, pink, red, purple, orange	spring to early summer	no	18 in (45 cm)	18 in (45 cm)	9–11	no
Pelargonium, Zonal	red, pink, white, orange, cream	spring to autumn	no	2–4 ft (0.6–1.2 m)	18–36 in (45–90 cm)	9–11	no

TOP LEFT *'Gemstone' is a Scented-leafed Pelargonium. These perennials are grown as much for their foliage, which releases a pleasant fragrance when crushed, as* for *their attractive flowers.*

LEFT *Pelargonium, Zonal, 'Sassa', with its compact habit, distinctively marked leaves, and abundance of mauve-pink flowers, makes an ideal bedding plant.*

RIGHT *Pelargoniums of the Angel type are recognized by their bushy habit, mid-green leaves, and masses of single flowers. 'Suffolk Garnet' bears rich crimson blooms with a white center.*

ABOVE Pelargonium, *Regal*, 'Askham Fringed Aztec' produces clusters of pretty pale pink fringed blooms with magenta lines radiating from the center.

INSET A vigorous shrub, Pelargonium 'Lara Starshine' is valued for its delicate, large, mauve-pink flowers and aromatic mid-green leaves. It is one of the Scented-leafed pelargoniums, whose potent essential oils are undergoing research to discover their properties.

RIGHT Pelargonium, *Unique*, 'Scarlet Unique' produces clusters of flared bright red blooms. The toothed leaves are also a feature: they emit a sharp musky scent when crushed or brushed against.

LEFT *With mid-green leaves edged pale yellow and pink starry flowers, Pelargonium, Miniature, 'Variegated Kleine Liebling' is a great choice for a hanging basket.*

RIGHT Pelargonium crispum 'Variegated Prince Rupert' *is often referred to as the lemon geranium, due to the fragrance released when the leaves are crushed.* **BELOW** *Pelargonium, Miniature/Stellar, 'Mrs Pat' bears interesting green-gold leaves with a broad brown band. Flowers are salmon pink, and growth is upright.*

PENSTEMON

This genus consists of around 250 species of deciduous, evergreen, or semi-evergreen subshrubs and perennials found from Alaska to Guatemala, as well as cool-temperate Asia. Some species are mat-forming, others are shrubby, but most form clumps of simple linear to lance-shaped leaves that grow in opposite pairs on the stem. The flowers appear mainly in summer, borne at the end of erect flower spikes; they are slightly hanging and tubular to bell-shaped, with 2 upper lobes and 3 larger lower lobes. They come in blues, reds, white, and bicolors. Many cultivars have been bred, selected for their generous numbers of flowers. Native Americans used parts of several species in herbal medicines, primarily for pain relief and to control bleeding.

CULTIVATION

These marginally to very frost-hardy plants do well in fertile well-drained soil and full sun. Cut plants back hard after flowering has finished. Certain species may need protection over winter with a layer of mulch. Propagate from seed in spring or autumn, by division in spring, or from cuttings in late summer.

Top Tip

It is easy to grow *Penstemon* species from seed. Before planting in spring, refrigerate the seeds for 3 weeks, as they need a cold period if they are to germinate.

ABOVE Penstemon eatonii *bears tubular scarlet flowers on tall spikes in summer. Because the blooms appear on one side of the stem, it is often called the fire-cracker penstemon.*
RIGHT *A popular plant for a rock garden,* Penstemon pinifolius *has short needle-like leaves and spikes of vibrant orange-red flowers.*

ABOVE *A cluster of showy purple-pink blooms with a white center sits atop the long spike of* Penstemon *'Stapleford Gem', one of a number of hardy cultivars.* **LEFT** Penstemon parryi *has long gray-green leaves and cerise-pink bell-shaped flowers. It self-seeds quite readily, growing best in temperate climates.*

Favorites	Flower Color	Blooming Season	Flower Fragrance	Plant Height	Plant Width	Hardiness Zone	Frost Tolerance
Penstemon barbatus	red	summer to early autumn	no	24–36 in (60–90 cm)	12–18 in (30–45 cm)	3–10	yes
Penstemon eatonii	scarlet	spring to summer	no	12–36 in (30–90 cm)	12–24 in (30–60 cm)	4–9	yes
Penstemon parryi	deep pink to magenta	spring	no	2–4 ft (0.6–1.2 m)	12–36 in (30–90 cm)	8–10	yes
Penstemon pinifolius	orange-red	late spring to mid-summer	no	6–10 in (15–25 cm)	18 in (45 cm)	8–11	yes
Penstemon rupicola	rose pink	late spring to summer	no	4 in (10 cm)	18 in (45 cm)	7–10	yes
Penstemon 'Stapleford Gem'	violet-pink	mid-summer to autumn	no	3–4 ft (0.9–1.2 m)	18 in (45 cm)	7–10	yes

PETUNIA

This tropical South American genus of the potato family (Solanaceae) includes some 35 species of annuals, perennials, and shrubs. Most species are low spreading plants with dark green, soft, downy, rounded leaves, and large trumpet-shaped flowers that have 5 fused lobes and range in color from white, pink, and red to blue and purple, often with a variety of multicolored markings. Cultivated varieties occur in virtually every color but lack the soft fragrance of some of the species. The genus is closely allied to tobacco *(Nicotiana),* and the leaves having a similar narcotic effect. The genus name comes from *petun,* a Brazilian Indian name for tobacco.

CULTIVATION

Plant in full sun with moist, humus-rich, well-drained soil. While the plants need watering, the flowers are easily damaged when sprayed too heavily with water. Modern strains of the plant are more resistant to this, as well as wet-weather damage. Propagate from seed or from cuttings.

ABOVE *The hot pink flowers of Petunia 'Pink Wave' measure about 3 in (8 cm) across. Its trailing habit makes it suitable for use as a colorful ground cover.*
LEFT *Petunia 'Superior Cascade Blue' bears deep blue-purple flared trumpet-shaped flowers all summer long. It does best in a spot sheltered from the wind.*

Favorites	Flower Color	Blooming Season	Flower Fragrance	Plant Height	Plant Width	Hardiness Zone	Frost Tolerance
Petunia, Daddy Series	pink to purple, darker-veined	late spring to late autumn	no	15 in (38 cm)	12–24 in (30–60 cm)	9–11	no
Petunia integrifolia	pink-purple, darker at throat	late spring to late autumn	no	18–24 in (45–60 cm)	24 in (60 cm)	9–11	no
Petunia 'Pink Wave'	deep pink	late spring to late autumn	no	8 in (20 cm)	30 in (75 cm)	9–11	no
Petunia 'Purple Wave'	magenta	late spring to late autumn	no	8 in (20 cm)	30 in (75 cm)	9–11	no
Petunia 'Superior Cascade Blue'	purple-blue	late spring to late autumn	no	8–12 in (20–30 cm)	24 in (60 cm)	9–11	no
Petunia, Surfinia Series, 'Surfinia Pink'	cerise	late spring to late autumn	no	4 in (10 cm)	24 in (60 cm)	9–11	no

Top Tip

Petunias will thrive if they are given a high-potassium fertilizer weekly during the growing season. If in a pot, add slow-release fertilizer to the potting mix.

BELOW Petunia *'Purple Wave'* bears dense masses of magenta flowers that are reasonably weather-resistant. This is a fast-growing plant with a spreading habit.

RIGHT Petunia, *Surfinia Series* is extremely popular, valued for its full range of flower colors—such as this glorious pink—its trailing habit, and abundant blooms.

PHALAENOPSIS

There are nearly 50 species of primarily
evergreen epiphytic orchids in this genus.
They are found throughout the tropical rainforests of Southeast Asia and grow on the
trunks and leaves of other plants. The plain
green or spotted fleshy leaves grow from the
rootstock, and the arching flower stems reach
above the broad straplike foliage. The stems
bear up to 20 often pendent flowers that are
made up of intricate petals and are most often
white but are sometimes pale pink. These
spectacular flowers appear at almost any time
of the year and look like fluttering butterflies,
giving the genus *Phalaenopsis* the common
name of moth orchid.

CULTIVATION

These orchids require warm,
humid, and damp conditions,
or a well-ventilated greenhouse, with filtered light, constant moisture, and rich but
well-drained compost. They are
generally best grown in pots
and, once established, should
be left undisturbed. Propagate
by division in spring.

ABOVE Phalaenopsis
Brother Little Spotty derives
from the Brother Orchid
Nursery in Taiwan, which is
famed among growers for
its successful breeding.
LEFT *Among hybrids, there*
are starry and reflexed type
or full and flat ones, in
yellow, pink, red, and pure
white shades, such as
Phalaenopsis *Chancellor.*

Favorites	Flower Color	Blooming Season	Flower Fragrance	Plant Height	Plant Width	Hardiness Zone	Frost Tolerance
Phalaenopsis Artemis	white; pink and orange center	most of the year	no	12 in (30 cm)	12 in (30 cm)	11–12	no
Phalaenopsis Brother John	white; heavily spotted pink	most of the year	no	12 in (30 cm)	12 in (30 cm)	11–12	no
Phalaenopsis Brother Little Spotty	white; lightly spotted purple	most of the year	no	12 in (30 cm)	12 in (30 cm)	11–12	no
Phalaenopsis Chancellor	white; yellow center	most of the year	no	12 in (30 cm)	12 in (30 cm)	11–12	no
Phalaenopsis lueddemanniana	white; pink lips, purple markings	summer	no	6 in (15 cm)	8 in (20 cm)	11–12	no
Phalaenopsis Taisuco Firebird	white; heavily veined purple-pink	most of the year	no	12 in (30 cm)	12 in (30 cm)	11–12	no

LEFT *The hybridization of* Phalaenopsis *has proved enormously popular, with ever-better shapes, sizes, and colors. P. Artemis bears lovely pink-flushed white blooms with an orange lip.* **BELOW** Phalaenopsis *make perfect house plants: in return for the warm shady environment they bear wonderful blooms such as these of P. Taisuco Firebird.*

Top Tip

Phalaenopsis plants can bloom at any time, and up to 3 times a year. When taking flowers, cut just above one of the little bracts on the stem, as this will encourage re-blooming.

PHILADELPHUS

This genus of 60 species is a member of the Hydrangeaceae/Philadelphaceae family and is made up of deciduous shrubs from the temperate regions of East Asia, the Himalayas, the Caucasus, and Central and North America. The plants generally have peeling bark and light green roughly elliptical leaves that are smooth; in some species, the leaves are slightly hairy on the undersides. They flower in spring and summer, mostly bearing 4-petalled white or cream flowers that grow in loose clusters at the end of the leaf stem. Blooms can be single, semi-double, or double. The scent of the flower is very similar to that of orange blossom, hence the common name of mock orange. *Phila-delphus lewisii* is the state flower of Idaho.

CULTIVATION

Philadelphus plants are easily grown in full sun, partial shade, or in deciduous open woodland in moist well-drained soil. Planting in full sun will increase the number of flowers. Propagate from softwood cuttings taken in summer or hardwood cuttings in autumn and winter.

ABOVE Philadelphus *'Manteau d'Hermine' is a popular dwarf variety of the mock orange. It bears superb clusters of double, vanilla-scented, creamy white flowers. This hardy deciduous plant makes an excellent ground cover.*
RIGHT *The single white blooms of* Philadelphus *'Rosace' often open in late spring, and can be useful for providing some simple elegance to shrub borders.*

Favorites	Flower Color	Blooming Season	Flo Frag
Philadelphus 'Belle Etoile'	white; small red blotch	late spring to early summer	y
Philadelphus coronarius	white	early summer	y
Philadelphus 'Manteau d'Hermine'	creamy white	summer	y
Philadelphus mexicanus	creamy white	summer	s
Philadelphus 'Rosace'	white	late spring to early summer	
Philadelphus subcanus	white	early summer	

RIGHT *Golden yellow foliage turning yellow-green in summer is the hallmark of* Philadelphus coronarius *'Aureus', which is an old garden favorite valued for its fragrant blooms.*

Top Tip

The delicious fragrance of *Philadelphus* flowers can be enjoyed indoors. Simply float fresh-cut flowerheads in a shallow bowl filled with water.

BELOW Philadelphus subcanus *var.* magdalenae *produces shallow bowl-shaped white blooms. Each year cut out the oldest wood at the base when the flowers have finished.*

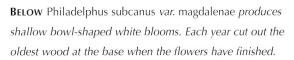

Plant Height	Plant Width	Hardiness Zone	Frost Tolerance
6 ft (1.8 m)	8 ft (2.4 m)	5–9	yes
10 ft (3 m)	5 ft (1.5 m)	2–9	yes
30 in 75 cm)	5 ft (1.5 m)	5–9	yes
0–20 ft 3–6 m)	6 ft (1.8 m)	9–10	no
5 ft 1.5 m)	4 ft (1.2 m)	5–9	yes
20 ft (6 m)	6–10 ft (1.8–3 m)	6–9	no

PHLOX

This genus contains 67 species of annuals and perennials and belongs to the phlox family, the Polemoniaceae. Annual phlox tend to be small mounding bushes; rock phlox closely hug the ground; trailing forms have long stems; and border phlox are upright and bushy. The leaves range from rounded and shiny to narrow and hairy, depending on the species. The small flowers are long-tubed, widely flared, bell-shaped, slightly fragrant, and grow in clusters of brightly colored floral sprays ranging from white and pale pink to bright pink, red, and purple. The genus name *Phlox* comes from the Greek word for flame. Use in bedding and border schemes.

CULTIVATION

Although all species prefer well-drained soil that can be kept moist, annual and rock phlox need full sun, while border and trailing forms will grow in part-shade. Border phlox need good ventilation to prevent mildew. Propagate from seed, by division, or from cuttings.

ABOVE *Annual phlox,* Phlox drummondii, *is grown for its rounded heads of flowers in pink, red, cream, and purple. Add compost or manure to the soil for best results.*

TOP *Phlox paniculata 'Prospero' bears pale lilac flowers charmingly edged with white. It needs good air circulation as it is susceptible to powdery mildew.*

Favorites

	Flower Color	Blooming Season	Flower Fragrance	Plant Height	Plant Width	Hardiness Zone	Frost Tolerance
Phlox divaricata	blue, lavender, white	spring	yes	15 in (38 cm)	20 in (50 cm)	4–9	yes
Phlox drummondii	pink, red, purple, cream	summer to autumn	yes	6–15 in (15–38 cm)	10 in (25 cm)	6–10	yes
Phlox maculata	white, pink, purple	mid-summer	yes	24–36 in (60–90 cm)	18 in (45 cm)	5–10	yes
Phlox paniculata	pink to red, purple, white	summer to autumn	yes	24–36 in (60–90 cm)	24–36 in (60–90 cm)	4–9	yes
Phlox stolonifera	lavender to deep purple	spring	no	3–6 in (8–15 cm)	18 in (45 cm)	3–9	yes
Phlox subulata	pink, lavender-blue, white	late spring to early summer	no	2–4 in (5–10 cm)	18–30 in (45–75 cm)	3–9	yes

Top Tip

Clumps of summer phlox should be divided every 3 to 4 years. Divide carefully using a clean sharp knife, making sure that each division has a good set of roots.

RIGHT Phlox paniculata *is also known as summer or perennial phlox. It is a wonderful choice for mass planting and makes an excellent cut flower.*

BELOW *Low-growing moss phlox or* Phlox subulata *'Emerald Blue' is perfect in a border or rock garden. Its pale mauve blooms appear in spring.*

PHYSOSTEGIA

This North American genus is a member of the mint family (Lamiaceae), and is made up of 2 species of perennials. Most form a clump of unbranched upright stems covered with dark green, toothed, narrow elliptical to lance-shaped leaves. From late summer to early autumn, flowerheads develop at the stem tips and are made up of clusters of 5-lobed, tubular to bell-shaped blooms, mainly in pink and purple shades. Though sometimes called false dragonhead, *Physostegia* species are more commonly known as the obedient plant, a reference to the way in which the flowers remain in place when twisted or moved.

CULTIVATION

These easy-growing hardy plants do best in any full or half sun position with moist well-drained soil. They spread by their fleshy roots and can become invasive. Propagate by division.

ABOVE *A graceful easy-growing plant,* Physostegia virginiana *'Alba' produces dense spikes of pure white tubular blooms in summer.*
RIGHT *The flowering spikes of* Physostegia virginiana *'Rose Queen' grow to 27 in (70 cm), and are covered in large rose pink blooms.*

LEFT *A constant favorite with gardeners,* Physostegia virginiana *'Rosea' produces spikes of large pale lilac-pink flowers in summer. This deciduous perennial has a spreading habit, and grows to little more than 3 ft (0.9 m) in height.*

Favorites	Flower Color	Blooming Season	Flov Fragr
Physostegia virginiana	blue-pink to magenta, white	late summer to early autumn	n
Physostegia virginiana 'Alba'	white	late summer to early autumn	r
Physostegia virginiana 'Crown of Snow'	white	late summer to early autumn	r
Physostegia virginiana 'Summer Snow'	white	late summer to early autumn	r
Physostegia virginiana 'Variegata'	purple-pink	late summer to early autumn	r
Physostegia virginiana 'Vivid'	rose pink	late summer to early autumn	r

Top Tip

Physostegia plants make excellent choices for the back of borders, as they offer height and color with their tall flowering spikes, and coverage with the foliage clumps.

BELOW *Position* Physostegia *virginiana 'Variegata' where both the soft purple-pink flowers and the interesting gray-green leaves, edged in cream, can be appreciated.*

Plant Height	Plant Width	Hardiness Zone	Frost Tolerance
2–4 ft (.6–1.2 m)	3 ft (0.9 m)	3–10	yes
2–4 ft (.6–1.2 m)	3 ft (0.9 m)	3–10	yes
2–4 ft (.6–1.2 m)	3 ft (0.9 m)	3–10	yes
4–30 in (0–75 cm)	24 in (60 cm)	3–10	yes
4–30 in (0–75 cm)	24 in (60 cm)	3–10	yes
24 in (60 cm)	24 in (60 cm)	3–10	yes

PIERIS

This Erica family genus consists of 7 species, mainly evergreen shrubs from the subtropical and temperate regions of the Himalayas and eastern Asia, as well as a vine and some shrubby species from eastern America and the West Indies. The species have been widely cultivated and extensively hybridized, and the best known are extremely popular evergreen shrubs for temperate gardens. Typically, the glossy green leaves are simple, pointed, and elliptical-shaped, often with serrated edges, and the flowers are bell-shaped, downward-facing, and are borne in panicles of white to pale pink clusters. The flowers usually open in spring and are sometimes scented.

CULTIVATION

Pieris plants will perform best in cool, moist, humus-rich, well-drained soil. A position in full sun yields more flowers, whereas light shade produces foliage that is more lush. They are naturally tidy plants, but a light trimming will help keep them that way. Propagate from half-hardened cuttings or by layering.

ABOVE Pieris japonica *'Mountain Fire' is grown for the bright red color of the new leaves (featured here) and its pretty, white, bell-shaped blooms that appear in spring.*
BELOW LEFT *The white blooms of* Pieris japonica *open from pinkish brown buds, and hang in drooping clusters early in spring. It needs protection from strong winds.*

Favorites

	Flower Color	Blooming Season	Flower Fragrance	Plant Height	Plant Width	Hardiness Zone	Frost Tolerance
Pieris **'Flaming Silver'**	white	early spring	no	4–10 ft (1.2–3 m)	4–8 ft (1.2–2.4 m)	6–9	yes
Pieris **'Forest Flame'**	white	mid-spring	no	12 ft (3.5 m)	8 ft (2.4 m)	6–9	yes
Pieris formosa	white; sometimes pink-tinged	mid-spring	no	10 ft (3 m)	12 ft (3.5 m)	6–9	yes
Pieris japonica	white	early spring	no	6–12 ft (1.8–3.5 m)	6–12 ft (1.8–3.5 m)	4–10	yes
Pieris japonica **'Scarlett O'Hara'**	creamy white; scarlet markings	early spring	no	6–12 ft (1.8–3.5 m)	6–12 ft (1.8–3.5 m)	4–10	yes
Pieris japonica **'Valley Valentine'**	pink to deep red	early spring	no	5–7 ft (1.5–2 m)	5–7 ft (1.5–2 m)	4–10	yes

BELOW *Dense clusters of creamy white flowers make Pieris japonica 'Scarlett O'Hara' a charming garden plant. As the flowers fade they should be removed.*

Top Tip

Pieris species make good companion plants for heath (*Erica* species), azaleas, and rhododendrons as they all enjoy an acid soil and warm, but not hot, summers.

ABOVE *The flowers of Pieris japonica 'Valley Valentine' start pink and turn a rich deep red as they age. Like other P. japonica varieties, the new leaves are red.*

PLATYCODON

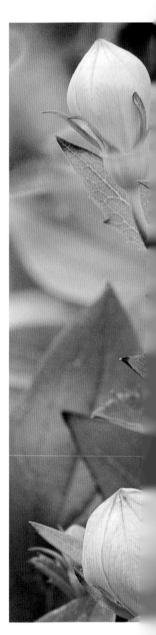

The sole species in this bellflower genus (Campanulaceae) is a perennial found in Japan and nearby parts of China. Also known as the Chinese bellflower, it is a fast-growing clump-forming plant with bold, lance-shaped, blue-green leaves with toothed edges. The flowers open from enlarged balloon-like buds, giving the plant the common name of balloon flower. Once opened, the flowers are cup- to bell-shaped, with 5 broad lobes; they are white, pink, or blue and, depending on the cultivar, come in double-flowered and dwarf forms. *Platycodon* root has long been used in traditional Chinese medicine and is now being studied for its gene mutating effects on tumors.

CULTIVATION

This perennial is best in distinctly seasonal temperate climates. Plant in sun or part-shade with moist, humus-rich, well-drained soil. While it may be slow to become established, it is long-lived and very hardy. Propagate from seed or by occasional division.

LEFT Platycodon grandiflorus 'Apoyama' has pretty violet-blue flowers, which are complemented by the attractive, blue-green, lance-shaped leaves.

ABOVE The blue flowers of Platycodon grandiflorus emerge from large balloon-shaped buds, which are a feature in themselves.

ABOVE LEFT Platycodon grandiflorus 'Fuji Blue' stands out in the crowd. It reaches up to 30 in (75 cm) in height, and has large deep blue flowers.

ABOVE *Cultivars in the Fuji Series are available in white, blue, and pink.* Platycodon grandiflorus *'Fuji White' is a tall plant with pure white flowers.*

Top Tip

The hardy versatile *Platycodon* plant is a good specimen for herbaceous borders or rock gardens. It also works as a cut flower.

Favorites	Flower Color	Blooming Season	Flower Fragrance	Plant Height	Plant Width	Hardiness Zone	Frost Tolerance
Platycodon grandiflorus	blue to purple-blue, white, pink	summer	no	24 in (60 cm)	12 in (30 cm)	4–10	yes
Platycodon grandiflorus **'Apoyama'**	deep violet-blue	summer	no	10–12 in (25–30 cm)	8 in (20 cm)	4–10	yes
Platycodon grandiflorus **'Fuji Blue'**	blue	summer	no	24–30 in (60–75 cm)	12 in (30 cm)	4–10	yes
Platycodon grandiflorus **'Fuji White'**	white	summer	no	24–30 in (60–75 cm)	12 in (30 cm)	4–10	yes
Platycodon grandiflorus **'Mariesii'**	deep blue	summer	no	12–18 in (30–45 cm)	12 in (30 cm)	4–10	yes
Platycodon grandiflorus **'Sentimental Blue'**	blue	summer	no	8–10 in (20–25 cm)	8 in (20 cm)	4–10	yes

PLEIONE

This is a small genus of about 20 mostly semi-alpine miniature orchids that are related to *Coelogyne*. The species occur at high altitudes in a wide variety of mountainous habitats from Nepal to China. They mostly grow in the ground or on mossy limbs of trees or fallen rotting logs. One or two deciduous oval-shaped leaves grow from a bulblike stem, known as a pseudobulb. The large and showy flowers are borne on short stems, appearing mostly in spring, though they can appear at various times of the year. The white, cream, purple and pale pink flowers are intriguingly shaped with an unusual frilled lower lip surrounded by 5 straplike petals.

CULTIVATION

These plants are easy to grow in mild cool climates with protection from the winter wet. They are usually grown in pots in rich well-drained orchid potting mix and like part-shade. Propagate by division.

ABOVE Pleione *Zeus Weinstein is the result of a cross between* P. formosana *and* P. forrestii. *It is a superb plant, its flowers combining soft pink petals with a creamy yellow frilled lip, marked in blood red.*

LEFT *A number of Pleione Alishan hybrids have been developed, including this lovely 'Soldier Blue'. All are easy to grow and usually produce 2 flowers per stalk. Color varies from white to pale and dark pink, with variable lip marking*

Top Tip

Pleione plants are relatively easy to grow and so are ideal for beginners or children. They can be kept in a greenhouse or on a cool windowsill.

BELOW Pleione formosana *is one of the more popular and hardy* Pleione *species in cultivation. The cultivar 'Clare', below, bears its solitary white flowers in spring.*

ABOVE Pleione *Britannia 'Doreen' produces purplepink blooms with orange markings on the lip. It is not fully hardy and may need care over winter.*

Favorites

	Flower Color	Blooming Season	Flower Fragrance	Plant Height	Plant Width	Hardiness Zone	Frost Tolerance
Pleione Alishan 'Soldier Blue'	creamy white; maroon markings	spring	no	6 in (15 cm)	12 in (30 cm)	8–10	yes
Pleione Britannia 'Doreen'	purple-pink, orange on lip	spring	no	6 in (15 cm)	12 in (30 cm)	8–10	yes
Pleione bulbocodioides	pink to purple, white and orange lip	early spring	no	6 in (15 cm)	12 in (30 cm)	8–10	yes
Pleione formosana	purple, pink, or white	spring	no	6 in (15 cm)	12 in (30 cm)	7–10	yes
Pleione Tongariro 'Jackdaw'	cerise; gold and red on lip	spring	no	8 in (20 cm)	12 in (30 cm)	8–10	yes
Pleione Zeus Weinstein	pink; lip cream spotted dark red	spring	no	6 in (15 cm)	12 in (30 cm)	8–10	yes

Favorites	Flower Color	Blooming Season	Flower Fragrance
Potentilla alba	white	spring to summer	no
Potentilla 'Flamenco'	scarlet	late spring to mid-summer	no
Potentilla fruticosa	white to yellow, orange, red	early summer to autumn	no
Potentilla megalantha	bright yellow	summer	no
Potentilla nepalensis	pink to light orange	summer	no
Potentilla recta	yellow	summer	no

ABOVE LEFT *A low-growing shrub,* Potentilla fruticosa *'Red Ace' bears vibrant orange-red flowers. Plant with other potentillas for a pretty hedge.*

BELOW *The fiery Spanish dance was obviously the inspiration behind* Potentilla *'Flamenco'. With its rich red blooms it evokes the passion of the dance.*

POTENTILLA

This is a large genus of some 500 species belonging to the rose family. While most are herbaceous perennials, the shrubby species can be extremely useful as small ornamental plants. They are indigenous to the Northern Hemisphere, occurring from temperate to arctic regions. The gray-green to dark green leaves are mostly made up of 5 small leaflets and can have the appearance of feathers. The pretty flowers resemble small single roses; they appear from spring to summer and sometimes autumn, in small colorful clusters of yellow, orange, pink, and blood red. Some species are used medicinally—the root bark of *Potentilla reptans* is said to stop nosebleeds and even internal bleeding.

CULTIVATION

These are hardy plants that grow in full sun or part-shade, preferring a fertile well-drained soil. Cultivars with orange, red, or pink flowers need to be carefully placed where they will receive some shade during the hottest part of the day. Propagation is from cuttings in summer or seed in autumn.

Plant Height	Plant Width	Hardiness Zone	Frost Tolerance
4 in (10 cm)	12 in (30 cm)	5–9	yes
18 in (45 cm)	24 in (60 cm)	5–8	yes
3 ft (0.9 m)	4 ft (1.2 m)	3–9	yes
6–12 in (15–30 cm)	12 in (30 cm)	5–9	yes
12–24 in (30–60 cm)	24 in (60 cm)	5–9	yes
18 in (45 cm)	18 in (45 cm)	4–9	yes

ABOVE RIGHT *The beautiful cerise-pink blooms with a darker pink center of 'Miss Willmott' make it one of the best-loved cultivars of* Potentilla nepalensis.

Top Tip

To make room for new growth, the oldest stems of *Potentilla* plants should be cut out every few years. This should be done only when flowering is over.

ABOVE *The lemony white blooms of* Potentilla fruticosa *'Ochroleuca' appear throughout the summer and autumn months. Grow this shrubby cultivar in full sun to obtain the best results.*

PRIMULA

This well-known genus of perennials is native to the Northern Hemisphere. The heavily veined, toothed, or scalloped-edged leaves are pale to dark green and form basal rosettes. Single blooms may be tucked in among the leaves or borne in clusters through-out spring. The tubular flowers open out into a funnel shape or flat disc; are made up of 5 or more petals, which are notched at their tips; and come in a variety of colors ranging from white, yellow, and pink to lilac and purple. Primulas are known variously as primrose, polyanthus, and cowslip, and some have been used medicinally for their astringent and mildly sedative properties.

CULTIVATION

Most species prefer the dappled shade of a woodland garden and like moist, humus-rich, well-drained soil. The so-called bog primroses prefer damper conditions and often naturalize along streamsides. Propagate from seed or by dividing established clumps when dormant.

ABOVE *English primrose,* Primula vulgaris, *is an old garden favorite that looks best in massed plantings. It forms tufts of green leaves with pale yellow flowers each held on its own stem above the foliage.*

ABOVE LEFT *The unusual and striking* Primula vialii, *known as Chinese pagoda primrose, bears violet-blue blooms on stout rocketlike flowering spikes.*

LEFT Primula japonica *is a classic candelabra-style o primula. Its deep rich pink flowers open in tiers on ta stems some way above th foliage. Grow in shady or streamside situations.*

ABOVE *Like other primroses,* Primula verticillata *grows in clumps that should be divided when they become crowded or are looking a little tired. Do this after flowering.*

Favorites	Flower Color	Blooming Season	Flower Fragrance	Plant Height	Plant Width	Hardiness Zone	Frost Tolerance
Primula auricula	various	spring to mid-summer	yes	3–8 in (8–20 cm)	8–12 in (20–30 cm)	3–9	yes
Primula bulleyana	bright yellow, fading to orange	summer	no	24 in (60 cm)	24 in (60 cm)	6–9	yes
Primula denticulata	pink to purple	early to mid-spring	no	12 in (30 cm)	12 in (30 cm)	6 9	yes
Primula florindae	bright yellow	late spring to summer	yes	36 in (90 cm)	24–36 in (60–90 cm)	6–9	yes
Primula forrestii	bright yellow	spring	no	24 in (60 cm)	18 in (45 cm)	6–9	yes
Primula japonica	pink to red-purple, white	late spring to early summer	no	18–24 in (45–60 cm)	18 in (45 cm)	5–10	yes
Primula, Juliana	various	early spring	no	4–6 in (10–15 cm)	8–12 in (20–30 cm)	5–9	yes
Primula pulverulenta	pale pink to red-purple	late spring to summer	no	36 in (90 cm)	24 in (60 cm)	6–9	yes
Primula sieboldii	white, pink, purple	spring to early summer	no	12 in (30 cm)	12 in (30 cm)	5–9	yes
Primula verticillata	yellow	spring	yes	8 in (20 cm)	8 in (20 cm)	8–10	yes
Primula vialii	purple	late spring to summer	yes	24 in (60 cm)	12 in (30 cm)	7–9	yes
Primula vulgaris	pale yellow	early to late spring	yes	8 in (20 cm)	12 in (30 cm)	6–9	yes

ABOVE Primula auricula 'Alicia' needs regular water to produce its glorious ruby red and creamy yellow blooms. It is often grown in pots for indoor decoration.

BELOW Primula bulleyana is a rosette-forming perennial that dies down over winter. Dark crimson buds open to yellow flowers, held in tiers on stout stems.

LEFT *The drumstick primrose,* Primula denticulata, *gets its common name from the rounded head of flowers that come in colors from pink to purple. Plant in a cool shady spot.*
BELOW *The attractive toothed leaves of* Primula sieboldii *'Mikado' usually die back not long after the plant has flowered. Like all primroses, it needs plenty of water.*

LEFT *Primula,* Juliana, *'Iris Mainwaring' bears an abundance of yellow-centered soft pink flowers above neat rosettes of light green leaves.*

Top Tip

Primulas can bring a burst of life to the garden. Easy to grow and readily available, they come in a wide array of different colours.

PRUNUS

Commonly known as cherry or cherry plum, *Prunus* includes both ornamental and fruiting species—cherries, plums, apricots, peaches, and nectarines—that are naturally widespread throughout the northern temperate regions and also have a toehold in South America. The genus also includes a wide range of shrubs and trees, many of them deciduous. Most bloom from late winter to early summer, producing flowers either singly or in clusters, in colors from white through to dark pink, followed by fleshy single-seeded fruit. The leaves are usually simple pointed ellipses, often with serrated edges, which sometimes develop brilliant autumn colors. *Prunus persica* is the state flower of Delaware.

CULTIVATION

Plant in moist, fertile, humus-rich, and well-drained soil in full sun. Provide some protection from strong wind. Propagate the fruiting plants by grafting, and the ornamental plants by grafts or in some cases by cuttings.

Top Tip

Correct pruning techniques are vital for fruiting varieties of *Prunus,* but less so for ornamentals. If silverleaf disease is present, cut back in summer rather than in winter.

Favorites

	Flower Color	Blooming Season	Flower Fragrance	Plant Height	Plant Width	Hardiness Zone	Frost Tolerance
Prunus × *blireana*	pink	spring	no	15 ft (4.5 m)	12 ft (3.5 m)	5–10	yes
Prunus cerasifera	white	spring	no	30 ft (9 m)	30 ft (9 m)	4–10	yes
Prunus maackii	creamy white	mid-spring	yes	30 ft (9 m)	25 ft (8 m)	2–9	yes
Prunus, Sato-zakura Group, 'Kanzan'	rose pink	mid- to late spring	no	30 ft (9 m)	30 ft (9 m)	5–9	yes
Prunus × *subhirtella*	white, pink	autumn to spring	no	50 ft (15 m)	25 ft (8 m)	5–9	yes
Prunus triloba	pink	spring	no	6–12 ft (1.8–3.5 m)	8–10 ft (2.4–3 m)	5–9	yes

RIGHT Prunus × blireana *is one of the best spring-flowering* Prunus *trees. Its foliage is purple when young, turning green as it matures. Branches are slender and arching.*
BELOW Prunus cerasifera *'Pissardii' is greatly admired for its striking purple-red leaves and pale pink flowers fading to white. It is very tolerant of dry conditions.*

PULSATILLA

This genus of about 30 Eurasian and North American deciduous perennials (family Ranunculaceae) forms clumps of ferny leaves, which in most species are made silver by a dense covering of fine hairs. Long-stemmed cup- or bell-shaped flowers are carried singly with 5 to 8 petals and a prominent golden cluster of stamens. The flowers are graceful and occur in shades of white and yellow to violet-blue. The common name of pasque flower is from the old French word *Pasque,* meaning Easter, which is around the time when the plants flower in the Northern Hemisphere. *Pulsatilla hirsutissima* is the state flower of South Dakota.

ABOVE Pulsatilla vulgaris *'Rubra' bears purple-red blooms with a golden center above dainty foliage. The good-sized flowers make this cultivar a great choice for mass planting.*

CULTIVATION

Pulsatilla plants flowers are hardy and need a seasonal temperate climate. They grow well in woodland conditions but are at their best with sun or part-shade and gritty, humus-rich, well-drained yet moist soil, such as that found in rocky crevices. Propagate by division when dormant or from seed.

Top Tip

Gardeners with sensitive skin should wear gloves when handling *Pulsatilla* plants, as both the leaves and the flowers may irritate the skin.

LEFT *The violet flowers of* Pulsatilla vulgaris *'Papagen are followed by attractive seed heads. When these fa it is time to cut back the plant and tidy the foliage.*

ABOVE Pulsatilla vulgaris *has long been a popular garden plant due to its stunning silky purple flowers, finely dissected leaves, and attractive spherical seed heads.*

RIGHT *The low-growing* Pulsatilla montana *makes a good rock-garden plant. Its bell-shaped purple-blue flowers nod gracefully from the top of 6 in (15 cm) stems.*

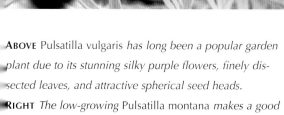

Favorites	Flower Color	Blooming Season	Flower Fragrance	Plant Height	Plant Width	Hardiness Zone	Frost Tolerance
Pulsatilla albana	yellow, blue-violet	early summer	no	2–8 in (5–20 cm)	8 in (20 cm)	5–9	yes
Pulsatilla hirsutissima	lavender	spring	no	4–6 in (10–15 cm)	8 in (20 cm)	4–9	yes
Pulsatilla montana	deep blue to purple	spring	no	4–8 in (10–20 cm)	8 in (20 cm)	6–9	yes
Pulsatilla patens	purple, yellow	late spring	no	4–6 in (10–15 cm)	4–8 in (10–20 cm)	4–9	yes
Pulsatilla pratensis	light to dark purple	spring to early summer	no	6–12 in (15–30 cm)	8 in (20 cm)	5–9	yes
Pulsatilla vulgaris	white, pink to red, purple	spring to early summer	no	4–10 in (10–25 cm)	10 in (25 cm)	5–9	yes

RANUNCULUS

The type genus for its family, the Ranunculaceae, this is a widespread group encompassing some 400 species of annuals, biennials, and perennials, many of which are cultivated, while others are admired in the wild, and some are despised as invasive weeds. The foliage varies markedly, though glossy, leathery, kidney-shaped leaves and deeply lobed leaves predominate. The flowers, too, are often glossy and they are borne singly or in small clusters through spring and summer. Most species have yellow flowers but cultivated forms occur in many colors, such as white, pink, and orange. *Ranunculus* is Latin for little frog, a name given by the Roman Pliny because of the wet conditions in which these plants are often found.

CULTIVATION

Commonly known as buttercups, these plants are very hardy and will grow in a wide range of conditions but they prefer to have their roots kept cool and moist. Many species have strong rhizomes that can be invasive if care is not taken to ensure that they are planted where they can be controlled. Propagate by division or from seed. Mildew can be a problem in autumn.

ABOVE *The dark leaves create a dramatic backdrop for the glistening golden yellow flowers of* Ranunculus ficaria *'Brazen Hussy'.*

Favorites	Flower Color	Blooming Season	Flower Fragrance
Ranunculus aconitifolius	white	spring to summer	no
Ranunculus asiaticus	white, pink, red, yellow, orange	spring to summer	no
Ranunculus constantinopolitanus	yellow	mid-spring to mid-summer	no
Ranunculus ficaria	golden yellow	spring	no
Ranunculus gramineus	yellow	late spring to early summer	no
Ranunculus lyallii	white	summer	no

RIGHT Ranunculus lyalli— *seen here in the wild in Mount Cook National Park, New Zealand—is known as the Mount Cook lily.*

Top Tip

Adaptable to most conditions and soil types, buttercups will bring sunny colors to borders or pond edges.

Plant Height	Plant Width	Hardiness Zone	Frost Tolerance
24 in (60 cm)	18 in (45 cm)	6–10	yes
8–18 in (20–45 cm)	8 in (20 cm)	8–10	yes
12–30 in (30–75 cm)	12 in (30 cm)	5–9	yes
2 in (5 cm)	12 in (30 cm)	5–10	yes
18 in (45 cm)	6 in (15 cm)	7–10	yes
36 in (90 cm)	15 in (38 cm)	7–9	yes

ABOVE *Native to the Mediterranean and Asia,* Ranunculus asiaticus *has given rise to many cultivars and hybrids.*
BELOW Ranunculus asiaticus, *Tecolote Hybrids produce lovely double blooms in a range of warm colors.*

RHODODENDRON

This very diverse genus of 800 or more species is widely distributed across the Northern Hemisphere, with the majority growing in temperate to cool regions. They range from tiny ground-hugging plants to small trees and even epiphytes, which grow in the branches of trees or on rock faces. Foliage comes in great diversity of form, and most rhododendrons bear "trusses" of up to 24 spectacular blooms, in colors ranging from white to pink, red, yellow, and mauve. Flowers are often multicolored, with spots, stripes, edging, or a single blotch of a different color in the throat of the flower. With the exception of some Vireya species and hybrids, fragrant rhododendrons are always white or very pale pink. Blooms vary in size and shape but are generally bell-shaped, appearing from early spring to early summer. The fruit is a many-seeded capsule, normally woody, and sometimes bearing wings or taillike appendages to aid transportation. *Rhododendron macrophyllum* is the state flower of Washington, while West Virginia claims *Rhododendron maximum* as its state flower.

CULTIVATION

All rhododendrons prefer acidic soils, high in organic matter and freely draining. While most prefer some protection from wind, sun, and frost, many others tolerate these conditions. Evergreen rhododendrons may be propagated by taking tip cuttings of the new growth in spring; deciduous azaleas are best grown from hardwood cuttings taken in winter.

BELOW Rhododendron, *Tender Hybrid, 'Countess of Haddington' is a tidy medium-sized shrub with hair-edged leaves and delicate white blooms tinged pink.*

BELOW Rhododendron *'Wattlebird' is one of the many eye-catching Vireya Hybrids most at home in a sheltered frost-free spot.*

RIGHT *The Vireya Hybrids, such as 'Pink Veitch', bear trumpet-shaped or bell-shaped flowers in heads of between 5 and 9 blooms.*

LEFT *The orange-red flowers of* Rhododendron, *Vireya Hybrid, 'Liberty Bar' are borne on a shrub that can reach to 6 ft (1.8 m). It has a straggly growth habit.*

Favorites

	Flower Color	Blooming Season	Flower Fragrance	Plant Height	Plant Width	Hardiness Zone	Frost Tolerance
Rhododendron, Azaleodendron Hybrids	mauve, pink, yellow, cream	late spring to early summer	yes	3–8 ft (0.9–2.4 m)	4–8 ft (1.2–2.4 m)	5–9	yes
Rhododendron, Ghent Azalea Hybrids	white, pink, red, orange, yellow	early summer	yes	6 ft (1.8 m)	4 ft (1.2 m)	5–9	yes
Rhododendron, Hardy Medium Hybrids	various	spring	varied	3–6 ft (0.9–1.8 m)	3–8 ft (0.9–2.4 m)	3–9	yes
Rhododendron, Hardy Small Hybrids	various	spring	varied	1–4 ft (0.3–1.2 m)	2–5 ft (0.6–1.5 m)	4–9	yes
Rhododendron, Hardy Tall Hybrids	various	spring	varied	7–20 ft (2–6 m)	7–15 ft (2–4.5 m)	4–9	yes
Rhododendron, Indica Azalea Hybrids	various	winter	no	3–6 ft (0.9–1.8 m)	3–8 ft (0.9–2.4 m)	8–11	yes
Rhododendron, Knap Hill and Exbury Azalea Hybrids	various	mid- to late spring	no	6–10 ft (1.8–3 m)	6 ft (1.8 m)	5–9	yes
Rhododendron, Kurume Azalea Hybrids	various	spring	no	3–5 ft (0.9–1.5 m)	3–5 ft (0.9–1.5 m)	7–10	yes
Rhododendron macrophyllum	purple-pink to white	late spring to early summer	no	15 ft (4.5 m)	15 ft (4.5 m)	6–9	yes
Rhododendron maximum	white to dark pink; green spots	summer	no	3–15 ft (0.9–4.5 m)	4–10 ft (1.2–3 m)	3–9	yes
Rhododendron, Mollis Azalea Hybrids	orange, red, yellow, cream	spring	no	6–8 ft (1.8–2.4 m)	3–6 ft (0.9–1.8 m)	5–9	yes
Rhododendron, Occidentale Azalea Hybrids	pink, white	summer	yes	8 ft (2.4 m)	7 ft (2 m)	6–9	yes
Rhododendron, Rustica Azalea Hybrids	yellow to red	late spring to early summer	yes	10 ft (3 m)	15 ft (4.5 m)	5–9	yes
Rhododendron, Satsuki Azalea Hybrids	white, pink, purple, red	late spring to early summer	no	20–36 in (50–90 cm)	36 in (90 cm)	7–11	yes
Rhododendron, Tender Hybrids	various	spring	varied	3–12 ft (0.9–3.5 m)	3–12 ft (0.9–3.5 m)	9–10	no
Rhododendron, Vireya Hybrids	various	throughout the year	varied	2–7 ft (0.6–2 m)	2–5 ft (0.6–1.5 m)	9–12	no
Rhododendron, Viscosum Azalea Hybrids	orange, red, yellow	late spring to early summer	yes	8 ft (2.4 m)	8 ft (2.4 m)	4–8	yes
Rhododendron, Yak Hybrids	white, pink	mid-spring	no	3–4 ft (0.9–1.2 m)	3–6 ft (0.9–1.8 m)	4–9	yes

CLASSIFICATION

Rhododendrons can be broadly divided into 5 groups: rhododendron species; rhododendron cultivars (including the "hardy" hybrids and the Vireya rhododendrons); deciduous azaleas; evergreen azaleas; and the azaleodendrons. Azaleas, which had originally been classified as a separate genus, are now regarded as botanically part of this genus and have contributed numerous cultivars and hybrids. Rhododendron leaves are usually mid- to deep green in color and broadly elliptical in shape. In evergreen azaleas, the new leaf shoots often form attractive perpendicular "candle-sticks," while the foliage of deciduous azaleas progresses from bright green shoots in spring to bronze in summer, followed by rich reds to yellows in autumn. Deciduous azaleas flower in spring on bare branches just before or at the same time as new leaf growth. Azaleodendrons are mostly semi-evergreen shrubs with yellow, pink, or mauve flowers. Rhododendrons and azaleas make excellent ornamental plants with their masses of colorful flowers. Many rhododendron species and hybrids also have year-round foliage, attractively textured bark, and a rich floral fragrance.

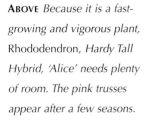

ABOVE *Because it is a fast-growing and vigorous plant,* Rhododendron, *Hardy Tall Hybrid, 'Alice' needs plenty of room. The pink trusses appear after a few seasons.*

BELOW Rhododendron *'Fastuosum Flore Pleno' is a free-flowering Hardy Tall Hybrid that tolerates both wind and sun, making it a desirable addition to a temperate garden.*

ABOVE *The bluish lavende[r] blooms of* Rhododendron, *Hardy Tall Hybrid, 'Susan[']* fade to white with maroo[n] spots. This plant has good disease resistance.*

Top Tip

Mulching is import-
ant for successful
rhododendrons. In
warm areas, mulch
keeps soil cool; in
cold areas, mulch
helps the soil retain
some warmth.

ABOVE *Named for the re-
nowned Australian soprano,
Rhododendron, Hardy Tall
Hybrid, 'Dame Nellie
Melba' needs protection
from the hot sun.*

RIGHT *Suitable for a container, Rhododendron, Yak
Hybrid, 'Percy Wiseman' is
a compact plant with shiny
leaves and pink blooms.*

LEFT Rhododendron
'Anah Kruschke' is a Hardy
Medium Hybrid boasting
lush dark leaves and trusses
of lavender to purple-red
flowers in late spring.

ABOVE Rhododendron, *Hardy Medium Hybrid,*
'Boule de Neige' has dark green elliptic leaves that
contrast strikingly with the white flowers.
BELOW *'President Roosevelt', a Hardy Medium*
Hybrid, is one of the most popular of all rhododen-
drons, and is distinguished by its variegated leaves.

RIGHT Rhododendron, *Hardy Small Hybrid, 'Jingle Bells'* bears orange and red flowers that fade to yellow. It is a low-growing plant with dense foliage.

ABOVE Rhododendron, *Hardy Small Hybrid, 'Blue Tit'* is a compact sun-tolerant plant that bears a profusion of mauve to gray-blue flowers. The new leaves are yellow.

LEFT *'Elizabeth'* is considered one of the best Hardy Small rhododendrons. Its pinkish red flowers are funnel shaped and appear in early to mid-spring, and again randomly in autumn.

RIGHT Rhododendron *'Gog'* has the strong coloring of a deciduous azalea. It is a Knap Hill and Exbury Azalea Hybrid developed by the Waterer family in England. **BELOW** Rhododendron, *Occidentale Azalea Hybrid, 'Coccinto Speciosa'* has dense rounded clusters of deep orange flowers that appear in mid-spring.

ABOVE *The Knap Hill and Exbury Azalea Hybrids form large bushy shrubs with trusses of blooms. Rhododendron 'Lady Roseberry' (above) has scarlet flowers.* **BELOW** Rhododendron, *Ghent Azalea Hybrid, 'Daviesii' has fragrant white flowers with a yellow blotch. Ghent Hybrids were bred in Belgium in the early 1800s.*

ABOVE Rhododendron, *Ghent Azalea Hybrid*, *'Pucella' has* *lovely pink flowers with a bright orange blotch. The Ghent* *Hybrids bear large trusses of relatively small flowers.*

ABOVE Rhododendron *'Arpège' is a Viscosum Azalea Hybrid* *that, like the French perfume for which it is named, has a* *gorgeous scent. The flowers are a delightful shade of yellow.*

ABOVE *The Rutherford Indica Azalea Hybrids are bred for their excellent flower quality. Rhododendron 'Purity' (pictured) has large snow white flowers.*

ABOVE Rhododendron *'Alphonse Anderson' is a Southern Indica Azalea Hybrid that flowers early and produces pink blooms with a darker blotch.*
BELOW Rhododendron, *Azaleodendron Hybrid, 'Hardijzer's Beauty' is a vigorous shrub with bright pink flowers and small glossy leaves.*

RIGHT Rhododendron *'Snow Prince', a Southern Indica Azalea Hybrid, becomes smothered in an abundance of pink-tinted white flowers quite early in the season. It is a vigorous and sun-tolerant shrub.*

BELOW Rhododendron *'Leopold Astrid' is a Belgian Indica Azalea Hybrid with large, frilled, double, white flowers edged in red. The Indicas are widely grown in temperate climates.*

ABOVE A delightful Azaleodendron Hybrid, Rhododendron 'Martine' produces funnel-shaped pink flowers with dark spots on the upper lobes.

ROSA

The genus *Rosa* is one of the most widely grown and best loved of all plant genera around the world. Since ancient times roses have been valued for their beauty and fragrance as well as for their medicinal, culinary, and cosmetic properties. There are between 100 and 150 species of rose, which range in habit from erect and arching shrubs to scramblers and climbers. The majority of species are deciduous and most have prickles or bristles. They are found in temperate and subtropical zones of the Northern Hemisphere. The leaves are usually comprised of 5 to 9 serrated-edged leaflets. Flowers, borne singly or in clusters, range from single, usually 5-petalled blooms to those with many closely packed petals. Many are intensely fragrant. Most species and old garden roses flower only once a year but many of the modern cultivars are repeat blooming. Rose fruits (hips or heps) are usually orangey red, but can be dark. Iowa and North Dakota have *Rosa arkansana* as their floral emblem, while *R. laevigata* is the state flower of Georgia.

ABOVE Rosa, *Large-flowered (Hybrid Tea), 'Blessings' is perfect in a bed or border. Modern roses are popular as they flower through the warmer months.*

BELOW Rosa, *Large-flowered (Hybrid Tea), 'Pristine' keeps its colors even in a range of climatic conditions, which would ordinarily result in color variations.*

CULTIVATION

Roses can be grown in formal and informal settings, in separate beds or mixed borders, as ground covers, climbing up arches and pergolas, as hedging, and in containers. Most roses require a sunny site and well-drained medium-loamy soil. Roses should be pruned to maintain strong healthy growth and a good shape. Except for the old Tea roses, most roses are very hardy. Propagation is from hardwood cuttings in autumn or softwood cuttings in summer.

LEFT *Grown for its rich red blooms and delightful fragrance, 'Crimson Glory', a Large-flowered (Hybrid Tea) rose, is a reliable repeat-flowering plant.*

RIGHT *Following the introduction of* Rosa, *Large-flowered (Hybrid Tea), 'Peace' in 1942, roses became more popular than ever.*

Favorites

	Flower Color	Blooming Season	Flower Fragrance	Plant Height	Plant Width	Hardiness Zone	Frost Tolerance
Rosa, Alba	white, pale pink	mid-summer	yes	6–8 ft (1.8–2.4 m)	4–6 ft (1.2–1.8 m)	4–10	yes
Rosa blanda	pink	spring	no	5 ft (1.5 m)	5 ft (1.5 m)	3–9	yes
Rosa, Bourbon	white, pink, red	summer to early autumn	yes	4–7 ft (1.2–2 m)	3–6 ft (0.9–1.8 m)	6–10	yes
Rosa, China	pink, red	summer to autumn	yes	3–6 ft (0.9–1.8 m)	3–6 ft (0.9–1.8 m)	7–11	yes
Rosa, Cluster-flowered (Floribunda)	various	summer to autumn	yes	3–5 ft (0.9–1.5 m)	2–4 ft (0.6–1.2 m)	5–11	yes
Rosa, Damask	white, pale pink	spring or summer	yes	3–7 ft (0.9–2 m)	3–5 ft (0.9–1.5 m)	5–10	yes
Rosa, Gallica	pink, red, pinkish purple	spring or summer	yes	4–6 ft (1.2–1.8 m)	3–5 ft (0.9–1.5 m)	5–10	yes
Rosa, Hybrid Perpetual	white, pink, red	spring to autumn	yes	4–7 ft (1.2–2 m)	3–5 ft (0.9–1.5 m)	5–10	yes
Rosa, Hybrid Rugosa	white, pink, yellow, red	summer to autumn	yes	3–7 ft (0.9–2 m)	3–7 ft (0.9–2 m)	3–10	yes
Rosa laevigata	white	late spring to summer	yes	15 ft (4.5 m)	5 ft (1.5 m)	4–11	yes
Rosa, Large-flowered (Hybrid Tea)	various	summer to autumn	yes	4–7 ft (1.2–2 m)	3–5 ft (0.9–1.5 m)	4–11	yes
Rosa, Miniature	various	summer to autumn	yes	8–30 in (20–75 cm)	8–18 in (20–45 cm)	5–11	yes
Rosa, Moss	white, pink, red	summer	yes	4–6 ft (1.2–1.8 m)	4–6 ft (1.2–1.8 m)	5–10	yes
Rosa, Patio (Dwarf Cluster-flowered)	various	summer to autumn	no	2 ft (0.6 m)	6 ft (1.8 m)	4–11	yes
Rosa, Polyantha	various	summer to autumn	no	2 ft (0.6 m)	18 in (45 cm)	3–10	yes
Rosa setigera	deep pink fading to white	early to late summer	yes	5 ft (1.5 m)	10 ft (3 m)	4–9	yes
Rosa, Shrub	various	summer to autumn	yes	4–10 ft (1.2–3 m)	3–8 ft (0.9–2.4 m)	4–11	yes
Rosa, Tea	cream, yellow, pink, red	summer to autumn	yes	4–7 ft (1.2–2 m)	3–5 ft (0.9–1.5 m)	7–11	yes

ROSE TYPES

Roses have been bred for centuries and are divided into groups. The old garden roses were originally bred from a handful of species and include the groups Gallica, Damask, Moss, Alba, China, Tea, Bourbon, and Hybrid Perpetual. In the late eighteenth century the repeat-flowering China rose *(Rosa chinensis)* arrived in Europe. The Tea roses, also repeat-flowering, followed in the nineteenth century, and 50 years later a Frenchman bred the first modern Large-flowered rose. Large-flowered (Hybrid Tea), Polyantha, Cluster-flowered (Floribunda), Shrub, Hybrid Rugosa, Miniature, and Patio (Dwarf Cluster-flowered) modern roses proliferated in the twentieth century. While most species and old roses are in shades of pink, red, and purple or white, modern rose-breeding programs have seen yellow and orange flowers appear.

LEFT *Most roses, such as Rosa, Large-flowered (Hybrid Tea), 'Double Delight', make perfect hedges because they have minimal water requirements.*

RIGHT *The most common diseases affecting roses are mildew, rust, and black spot. Rosa, Large-flowered (Hybrid Tea), 'Caribbean' is, however, disease-resistant.*

BELOW *Gorgeous, semi-double, red blooms* make Rosa, *Cluster-flowered (Floribunda),* 'Royal Occasion' *a must for the rose garden.*

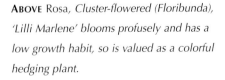

ABOVE Rosa, *Cluster-flowered (Floribunda),* 'Lilli Marlene' *blooms profusely and has a low growth habit, so is valued as a colorful hedging plant.*

LEFT *Modern roses can look stunning in mixed plantings. Rosa, Cluster-flowered (Floribunda), 'Wee Cracker' is a wonderful companion plant for tulips and daisies.*
RIGHT *'Amber Queen' is an award-winning Cluster-flowered (Floribunda) rose, well suited as a standard or as a bedding rose. A layer of mulch will keep it healthy.*

ABOVE *Although it may be affected by mildew, Rosa, Cluster-flowered (Floribunda), 'Mary Cave' is still valued for its bright yellow blooms and upright habit.*
LEFT *Rosa, Cluster-flowered (Floribunda), 'Remembrance' makes a great standard but needs to be trained when young. Standard roses add elegance to any garden.*

Top Tip

When growing roses in containers, place a layer of stones in the pot, use a soil-based potting mix, and be mindful of the growth habit when selecting the pot.

ABOVE Rosa, *Cluster-flowered (Floribunda)*, 'Pleasure' has an old-fashioned charm. Though often regarded as difficult plants, roses are essentially easy to cultivate.

ABOVE *Reaching 30 in (75 cm) high, Rosa, Cluster-flowered (Floribunda), 'Anna Livia' is an award-winning exhibition favorite.*

ABOVE *Because it is simple and easy to look after, Rosa Cluster-flowered (Floribunda), 'Simplicity' is often used as a landscaping plant. Remove old dead wood when flowering has finished.*

LEFT *Rosa, Cluster-flowered (Floribunda), 'Aberdeen Celebration' bears rich deep orange blooms. Cut flowers should be taken early in the morning.*

ABOVE *A very hardy Cluster-flowered (Floribunda) rose, 'Betty Prior' has an upright habit and bears masses of 5-petalled pink blooms that are paler at the center.*
LEFT *The popular 'Queen Elizabeth' is a Cluster-flowered (Floribunda) rose named for the mother of Britain's Queen Elizabeth II. It tolerates a hard cutting back every few years.*

BELOW *Blooming profusely from summer to autumn, Rosa, Polyantha, 'Mevrouw Nathalie Nypels' is a tidy shrub useful in borders or beds. Its compact habit also makes it ideal for containers.*

ABOVE *Hybrid Rugosa roses, such as 'Fimbriata', are re-markable for their hardiness. They are perfect as hedges, as the fringed wrinkly leaves are a landscaping feature.*
RIGHT *The yellow-pink blooms of Rosa, Hybrid Rugosa, 'Dr Eckener' are usually followed by attrac-tive orange-red hips that are a feature in themselves.*
FAR RIGHT *Like all the shrub roses, Rosa, Shrub, 'Golden Celebration' is very vigorous and easy to grow. It rewards the grower with scented yellow blooms.*

BELOW *A popular container-grown rose because of its small size, Rosa, Shrub, 'Country Dancer' is valued for its graceful deep pink blooms and its glossy foliage.*

ABOVE

'Happy Child' is a Shrub rose often classified as an English rose. It has a tidy habit and reaches an average height, making it a good border plant.

ABOVE Rosa, *China, 'Old Blush' dates from the mid-1700s. Many advances have been made in repeat-flowering rose cultivation since its introduction.*

ABOVE *The Bourbon roses are so named for the Ile de Bourbon where they were first raised. Rosa 'Louise Odier', above, has an arching growth habit.*

LEFT Rosa, Hybrid Perpetual, 'Ferdinand Pichard' produces glorious, red-striped, pink blooms that change color as they age. It is a very disease-resistant rose.

BELOW Large, round, pink flowers make Rosa, Hybrid Perpetual, 'Comtesse Cécile de Chabrillant' a striking garden plant, although it can be hard to find.

RIGHT Pure old-style elegance, dark green foliage, and large, velvety, crimson-purple blooms make Rosa, Gallica, 'Charles de Mills' one of the best of the Old roses. The Gallicas flower once in spring or summer.

LEFT China roses, such as 'Fabvier', like a sheltered spot in the garden where they can bear their beautiful blooms without fuss. The semi-double blooms of 'Fabvier' make long-lasting cut flowers.

ROSMARINUS

This genus is part of the large mint family, which includes many familiar culinary and medicinal herbs. Rosemary itself has been cultivated for centuries, being grown for the aromatic oil distilled from the shoots and leaves, and for use as a culinary herb. The genus contains just 2 species of evergreen shrubs from the Mediterranean region, and includes upright and prostrate varieties. They have short linear leaves and their small 2-lipped flowers are usually pale blue and borne along the branches, which can become quite woody with age. Apart from its culinary uses, rosemary has been credited with many properties throughout its long cultivation: in ancient Greece, students wore sprigs of fresh rosemary in their hair believing the invigorating aroma would serve as an aid to mental clarity. This benefit has also been recognized by modern-day practitioners of aromatherapy.

CULTIVATION

Rosemary likes a hot dry position and will grow in all sorts of well-drained soils; it will not tolerate wet winter conditions. It should be pruned after flowering to maintain a bushy compact habit, and is suitable for use as a hedging plant. Propagation is usually from softwood or half-hardened cuttings taken in summer.

Favorites	Flower Color	Blooming Season	Flower Fragrance
Rosmarinus officinalis	purple-blue	late autumn to early summer	no
Rosmarinus officinalis 'Arp'	dark blue	late autumn to early summer	no
Rosmarinus officinalis 'Joyce de Baggio'	blue	late autumn to early summer	no
Rosmarinus officinalis 'Majorca Pink'	lilac-pink	late autumn to early summer	no
Rosmarinus officinalis 'Prostratus'	blue	late autumn to early summer	no
Rosmarinus officinalis 'Tuscan Blue'	dark blue	late autumn to early summer	no

ABOVE Rosmarinus officinalis *var.* albiflorus *is a tall, hardy, semi-upright, white-flowered plant that can reach up to 6 ft (1.8 m) in both height and width.*
LEFT *The seed crop of* Rosmarinus officinalis *'Majorca Pink' is heavy, and can bend and distort the shape of this upright pink-flowered plant.*

Plant Height	Plant Width	Hardiness Zone	Frost Tolerance
3–5 ft (0.9–1.5 m)	5 ft (1.5 m)	6–11	yes
4–5 ft (1.2–1.5 m)	3 ft (0.9 m)	6–11	yes
3 ft (0.9 m)	5 ft (1.5 m)	6–11	yes
3 ft (0.9 m)	5 ft (1.5 m)	6–11	yes
6 in (15 cm)	3 ft (0.9 m)	6–11	yes
5 ft (1.5 m)	5 ft (1.5 m)	6–11	yes

BELOW *As its name indicates, Rosmarinus officinalis 'Prostratus' is a prostrate form that is suitable for use as a ground cover or in rock gardens and hanging baskets.*

ABOVE *Rosmarinus officinalis 'Blue Lagoon' has deep purple-blue flowers. Native to the Mediterranean coastline, the species grows well in seaside conditions.*

Top Tip

Rosemary is an ideal plant for a mixed border, a hedge, or against a sunny wall. The flowers are edible, as well as decorative, and can be used in salads.

RUDBECKIA

This North American genus belonging to the daisy family (Asteraceae) consists of 15 species of perennials. It is very popular in gardens because of the plants's great hardiness, ease of cultivation, and valuable late season flowering. Most are fairly bulky plants, with branched or unbranched stems, and often have lance-shaped deeply veined leaves. From late summer they carry masses of large golden yellow daisies, usually with dark brown to black disc florets. Dwarf, double-flowered, and variously colored forms are available. They flower until cut back by frost. *Rudbeckia* was named by Linnaeus for a professor at the University of Uppsala, Olaus Rudbeck (1660–1740), who employed the young Linnaeus as a tutor for his children, of which he had 24!

CULTIVATION

Plant in a sunny open position with moist well-drained soil. Deadhead or use as a cut flower to encourage continued blooming. Mildew can occur but usually only late in the season. Propagate by division, from basal cuttings, or from seed.

Top Tip

Because *Rudbeckia* plants bloom late in summer, they bring welcome color to borders and beds when the blooms of other plants have faded.

ABOVE *Informal yellow blooms with drooping petals make* Rudbeckia laciniata *an interesting long-lasting cut flower.*
BELOW Rudbeckia fulgida *var.* sullivantii *'Goldsturm' is an old garden favorite with large cheerful flowerheads.*

BELOW *Black-eyed Susan,* Rudbeckia fulgida, *is a vigorous grower in the garden, but may need an application of liquid fertilizer when cultivated in pots.*

LEFT *The floral emblem of Maryland,* Rudbeckia hirta *is highly valued for its bright yellow daisylike flowers featuring a dark brown-purple central disc.*

Favorites	Flower Color	Blooming Season	Flower Fragrance	Plant Height	Plant Width	Hardiness Zone	Frost Tolerance
Rudbeckia fulgida	orange-yellow; brown center	late summer to mid-autumn	no	36 in (90 cm)	24 in (60 cm)	3–10	yes
Rudbeckia fulgida var. sullivantii 'Goldsturm'	orange-yellow; brown center	late summer to mid-autumn	no	24 in (60 cm)	24 in (60 cm)	3–10	yes
Rudbeckia hirta	yellow; brown-purple center	summer to early autumn	no	12–36 in (30–90 cm)	12–24 in (30–60 cm)	3–10	yes
Rudbeckia hirta 'Irish Eyes'	yellow; green center	summer to early autumn	no	24–30 in (60–75 cm)	24 in (60 cm)	3–10	yes
Rudbeckia laciniata	yellow; greenish center	mid-summer to mid-autumn	no	4–6 ft (1.2–1.8 m)	3–5 ft (0.9–1.5 m)	3–10	yes
Rudbeckia nitida	yellow; green center	late summer to early autumn	no	4–6 ft (1.2–1.8 m)	3 ft (0.9 m)	3–10	yes

SALVIA

Containing about 900 species of annuals, perennials, and softwooded evergreen shrubs, this genus is the largest in the mint family. They are found in temperate and subtropical regions throughout the world, with the exception of Australasia, and grow in a wide range of habitats, from coastal to alpine. A number of *Salvia* species are used for culinary and medicinal purposes, and the genus name is derived from the Latin *salvare*, meaning to heal or save. Most species are hairy to some extent and many have foliage that is aromatic when crushed or rubbed. The flowers are tubular with the petals split into 2 lips, which may be straight or flaring. The flowers vary greatly in size, and the color range moves through shades of blue to purple, and pink to red, as well as white and some yellows.

ABOVE LEFT *A native of central Mexico, summer-flowering* Salvia patens *has bright green foliage and clear blue flowers.*
BELOW Salvia officinalis, *or common sage, is the traditional herb used in cooking and for its medicinal properties.*

CULTIVATION

Most are best grown in full sun and all require a well-drained situation; generally, the shrubby plants dislike heavy wet soils. Propagation of most shrubby species is very easy from softwood cuttings taken throughout the growing season. Seed of all species is sown in spring.

ABOVE *Emerging from felty purple buds, the purple and white flowers of* Salvia leucantha *are produced on long spikes over a lengthy flowering period.*

LEFT *Persistent reddish purple bracts hold the violet flowers of* Salvia nemorosa *'Lubecca'. Rosettes of gray-green leaves encircle the base of the flowering stems.*

Favorites	Flower Color	Blooming Season	Flower Fragrance	Plant Height	Plant Width	Hardiness Zone	Frost Tolerance
Salvia coccinea	scarlet	early summer to late autumn	no	24–30 in (60–75 cm)	12–24 in (30–60 cm)	9–11	no
Salvia elegans	bright red	late summer to autumn	no	4–6 ft (1.2–1.8 m)	4–6 ft (1.2–1.8 m)	9–11	no
Salvia farinacea	violet-blue	summer to autumn	no	24 in (60 cm)	12 in (30 cm)	9–11	no
Salvia × jamensis	red, orange, pink, creamy yellow	summer to autumn	no	20–36 in (50–90 cm)	20–36 in (50–90 cm)	8–11	yes
Salvia leucantha	purple and white	winter to spring	no	24–36 in (60–90 cm)	2–5 ft (0.6–1.5 m)	9–11	no
Salvia nemorosa	purple, violet, white to pink	mid-summer to mid-autumn	no	3 ft (0.9 m)	24 in (60 cm)	5–10	yes
Salvia officinalis	lilac-blue	summer	no	18–30 in (45–75 cm)	24–36 in (60–90 cm)	5–10	yes
Salvia patens	blue	mid-summer to mid-autumn	no	18–24 in (45–60 cm)	18 in (45 cm)	8–10	yes
Salvia splendens	bright red	summer to autumn	no	15 in–8 ft (38 cm–2.4 m)	12 in–8 ft (30 cm–2.4 m)	9–12	no
Salvia × superba	violet, purple	mid-summer to early autumn	no	24–36 in (60–90 cm)	18–24 in (45–60 cm)	5–10	yes
Salvia uliginosa	sky blue	late summer to mid-autumn	no	3–6 ft (0.9–1.8 m)	3 ft (0.9 m)	8–10	yes
Salvia verticillata	lilac-blue, violet, rarely white	summer	no	3 ft (0.9 m)	18 in (45 cm)	6–10	yes

Top Tip

While many *Salvia* or sage plants are tolerant of considerable dryness, most benefit from an occasional deep watering.

LEFT *Reaching 18–20 in (45–50 cm) high, Salvia farinacea 'Victoria' is an award-winning cultivar with deep violet-blue flowers.*

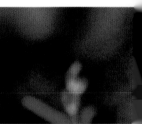

RIGHT *Known as the bog sage,* Salvia uliginosa *can quickly spread in its favored conditions of moist soil and full sun.*
BELOW *Hailing from Mexico,* Salvia × jamensis *is a drought-tolerant evergreen species with a bushy habit.*

RIGHT Salvia elegans *is usually grown for its lovely pineapple-scented leaves, popular for flavoring drinks or used as a garnish for fruit salads and desserts.*

ABOVE *The spectacular scarlet flowers of* Salvia splendens *are held on tall stems above the light to dark green leaves.*
LEFT Salvia nemorosa *will provide a display of purple, pink, or white flowers from summer through to autumn.*

Favorites	Flower Color	Blooming Season	Flower Fragrance
Saponaria 'Bressingham'	deep pink	summer	no
Saponaria lutea	pale yellow	early summer	no
Saponaria ocymoides	pink to red	summer	no
Saponaria officinalis	white, pink, red	summer to autumn	no
Saponaria × olivana	pale pink	summer	no
Saponaria pumilio	purple-pink, rarely white	summer	no

LEFT *When in bloom, the hairy dark green leaves of* Saponaria ocymoides *are almost entirely hidden by the masses of small, pink, starry flowers.*

TOP RIGHT *Long stamens protrude from the pale yellow flowers of* Saponaria lutea. *This perennial species has linear mid-green leaves.*

Top Tip

Making a soft carpet of starry flowers, *Saponaria* species are most at home spilling over banks, in rockeries, or placed in sunny perennial borders.

SAPONARIA

This genus belongs to the carnation family (Caryophyllaceae), and features around 20 species of Eurasian annuals and perennials containing saponin, a glucoside that forms a soapy solution when mixed with water. The roots in particular were once used as soap, and the extract is present in detergents and foaming agents—hence the common name of soapwort. That use aside, these are pretty little plants that are well worth growing for their beauty alone. They are mainly low growing and range from tufted mounds to quite wide-spreading ground covers. They have blue-green linear to spatula-shaped leaves, sometimes toothed, and in summer are smothered in heads of small, starry, 5-petalled flowers.

CULTIVATION

Mainly very hardy and easily grown, they do best in gritty, moist, humus-rich, free-draining soil. They will also take slightly alkaline soil. Propagate by cuttings, from layers, or from seed.

ABOVE *Carried above the foliage on tall stems, the flowers of* Saponaria officinalis *occur in shades of red, pink, or white.*

RIGHT *With its double pink flowers and dark green foliage,* Saponaria officinalis *'Rosea Plena' is a favorite in gardens.*

Plant Height	Plant Width	Hardiness Zone	Frost Tolerance
3 in (8 cm)	12 in (30 cm)	5–10	yes
2–4 in (5–10 cm)	12–18 in (30–45 cm)	5–8	yes
6–10 in (15–25 cm)	18 in (45 cm)	4–9	yes
24 in (60 cm)	20 in (50 cm)	5–10	yes
2 in (5 cm)	6 in (15 cm)	5–9	yes
2 in (5 cm)	12 in (30 cm)	4–8	yes

SCABIOSA

An unpleasant sounding name, *Scabiosa* is derived from *scabies*, a Latin word for scurf or mange, the itchiness of which was said to be relieved by rubbing the affected area with the leaves of these plants. The genus, a member of the teasel family (Dipsacaceae), is composed of around 80 species of annuals and perennials found from Europe and North Africa to Japan. Most species form a spreading basal clump of light green to gray-green, rounded to lance-shaped leaves, with deeply incised notches or lobes. A few species have an erect or branching habit. The flowers are individually tiny but occur in rounded to flattened composite heads on stems that hold them clear of the foliage. White, pale yellow, soft pink, blue, and mauve are the usual colors.

ABOVE Scabiosa atropurpurea *'Chile Black' has a gorgeous dark red to black flowerhead that resembles a pincushion. Regular deadheading will prolong the flowering season into the autumn months.*

CULTIVATION

The plants are hardy and easily grown in any sunny position with moderately fertile, moist, free-draining, slightly alkaline soil. Deadhead to prolong flowering. The annuals are raised from seed, and the perennials can be propagated from seed, from basal cuttings, or by division.

RIGHT Scabiosa colum-*baria var. ochroleuca bears lemon yellow blooms on long stalks. Cuttings can be taken in summer, or the plant can be divided in early spring.*

Favorites	Flower Color	Blooming Season	Flower Fragrance	Plant Height	Plant Width	Hardiness Zone	Frost Tolerance
Scabiosa atropurpurea	purple, pink, rose, white	summer	no	24–36 in (60–90 cm)	10 in (25 cm)	7–11	yes
Scabiosa caucasica	lavender, pale blue	summer	no	24 in (60 cm)	24 in (60 cm)	4–10	yes
Scabiosa caucasica 'Alba'	white	summer	no	24 in (60 cm)	24 in (60 cm)	4–10	yes
Scabiosa caucasica 'Fama'	blue, lavender	summer	no	24–36 in (60–90 cm)	24 in (60 cm)	4–10	yes
Scabiosa columbaria	lilac-blue to reddish purple	summer to early autumn	no	20–27 in (50–70 cm)	3 ft (0.9 m)	6–10	yes
Scabiosa farinosa	mauve	spring to summer	no	12–18 in (30–45 cm)	12–24 in (30–60 cm)	6–10	yes

BELOW Scabiosa caucasica 'Fama' is a clump-forming perennial that produces blue flowerheads in summer. This picture shows the flowerhead in the budding stage.

RIGHT Scabiosa caucasica 'Alba' has a dense center that resembles a pincushion, from which the pure white flowers radiate. It also makes a very good cut flower.

Top Tip

To attract butterflies and bees to the garden, *Scabiosa* species can be planted in borders and rock gardens. The long-flowering species make good container plants.

SCHIZANTHUS

This Chilean genus of 12 species of annuals and biennials is in the potato family (Solanaceae), though that relationship is not obvious. The cultivated species are small upright plants with soft green ferny foliage, often with a covering of fine hairs. Their flowers, which appear from spring to autumn, are borne in branching panicles held above the foliage. They are beautifully marked and shaped, with a prominent lower lip, hence the common name of poor man's orchid. Modern strains are available in a wide range of colors and sizes. The genus name comes from the Greek *schizo* (divide) and *anthos* (a flower), referring to the deeply divided corolla.

ABOVE *Many garden strains originate from* Schizanthus × wisetonensis. *This cheerful hybrid comes in an array of colors, all with speckled yellow throats.*

CULTIVATION

Schizanthus plants are tender, but easily grown as annuals where the summer temperatures are warm and even. Elsewhere treat as greenhouse pot plants. Plant in a bright position with fertile, moist, well-drained soil. Raise from seed, with several sowings to ensure continued flowering. Pinch out the growing tips when young to encourage bushiness.

LEFT *This dramatic form of* Schizanthus × wisetonensis *has deep pink flowers with a black center and speckled yellow throat.*

Top Tip

Schizanthus plants are a bit fragile, but are worth the time spent providing care and protection. They don't like heavy rain or temperature extremes.

ABOVE Schizanthus *is also known as butterfly flower. This S.* × wisetonensis *variety has rich red flowers, which are nicely complemented by ferny foliage.*
LEFT *The plants in the Dwarf Bouquet Mix come in lively shades of amber, pink, and red. There are also pretty bicolored forms, such as that seen here.*

Favorites	Flower Color	Blooming Season	Flower Fragrance	Plant Height	Plant Width	Hardiness Zone	Frost Tolerance
Schizanthus, Angel Wings Mix	pink, red, purple	spring to autumn	no	12–18 in (30–45 cm)	8–12 in (20–30 cm)	9–11	no
Schizanthus, Disco Mix	crimson, pink	spring to autumn	no	8–10 in (20–25 cm)	8–10 in (20–25 cm)	9–11	no
Schizanthus, Dwarf Bouquet Mix	amber, red, pink	spring to autumn	no	12–15 in (30–38 cm)	8–10 in (20–25 cm)	9–11	no
Schizanthus, Star Parade Mix	various	spring to autumn	no	8 in (20 cm)	8 in (20 cm)	9–11	no
Schizanthus 'Sweet Lips'	pink and red, red and white	spring to autumn	no	12–15 in (30–38 cm)	10–12 in (25–30 cm)	9–11	no
Schizanthus × *wisetonensis*	white, blue, pink red-brown	spring to summer	no	8–18 in (20–45 cm)	8–12 in (20–30 cm)	9–11	no

SEDUM

This genus of over 300 species of succulent annuals, perennials, and subshrubs is found in the northern temperate regions and the mountains of the tropics. Members of the crassula family (Crassulaceae), species differ greatly in foliage and form. Some are shrubby, with flattened, oval, gray-green leaves, others trail and have succulent, rounded, "jelly bean" leaves, and some form very compact mats. Most produce small heads of tiny, 5-petalled, bright yellow flowers in summer and autumn. The genus name dates from Roman times and was used for several succulent plants. It is derived from the Latin *sedo* (to sit), referring to their low spreading habit. Some species have been used medicinally and as salad vegetables.

CULTIVATION

Plant in full sun with gritty well-drained soil. Most *Sedum* species appreciate water at flowering time but are otherwise drought tolerant. Propagate by division, from cuttings, or from seed, depending on the growth type.

Top Tip

The partnership of plump fleshy leaves and dainty starry flowers seen in *Sedum* species can be used to great effect in the garden to add textural and tonal contrasts.

ABOVE *It is the attractive foliage of* Sedum spurium *'Variegatum' that sets it apart from the species, with leaf margins delicately edged in cream and pink.*
LEFT *From the mountainous regions of central and western Europe,* Sedum rupestre *is a resilient, mat-forming, perennial species.*

ABOVE Sedum spathulifolium 'Cape Blanco' produces starry yellow flowers. The distinctive leaves form fleshy silvery green rosettes around the stems of the summer blooms.
RIGHT With impressive flowerheads of mauve-pink through to red, Sedum spectabile 'Brilliant' is a popular garden plant. When in flower, this award-winning cultivar will attract butterflies and bees to the garden.

Favorites

	Flower Color	Blooming Season	Flower Fragrance	Plant Height	Plant Width	Hardiness Zone	Frost Tolerance
Sedum album	white	summer	no	2–6 in (5–15 cm)	12–24 in (30–60 cm)	6–11	yes
Sedum kamtschaticum	golden yellow	summer	no	4–8 in (10–20 cm)	10 in (25 cm)	7–10	yes
Sedum rupestre	yellow	summer	no	4 in (10 cm)	24 in (60 cm)	7–10	yes
Sedum spathulifolium	yellow	summer	no	4 in (10 cm)	24 in (60 cm)	7–10	yes
Sedum spectabile	pink	late summer to autumn	no	18 in (45 cm)	18 in (45 cm)	5–10	yes
Sedum spurium	white, pink, purple	late summer	no	4 in (10 cm)	24 in (60 cm)	7–10	yes

SINNINGIA

Named for Wilhelm Sinning (1792–1874), a horticulturalist and botanist at the University of Bonn, this African violet family (Gesneriaceae) genus is made up of about 40 species of tuberous perennials and small shrubs distributed from Mexico to Argentina. The commonly cultivated species are perennials with large lance- to heart-shaped leaves made velvety by a dense covering of fine hairs. The well-known florist's gloxinia (*Sinningia speciosa*) has large, upward-facing, bell-shaped flowers, although other species have tubular flowers and are sometimes scented. Their vivid showy flowers make the plants ideal for the house or greenhouse, as well as being lovely summer annuals or year-round plants in subtropical to tropical areas.

ABOVE *A native of Brazil,* Sinningia cardinalis *is also known as the cardinal flower. It has large ovate leaves and bears clusters of bright red tubular flowers.*

Top Tip

As indoor pot plants, *Sinningia* species will benefit from half-strength high-potash fertilizer applied every few weeks during the growing season.

CULTIVATION

They prefer warm humid conditions with a bright but not overly sunny exposure. The soil should be well-drained, moist, and humus-rich. Propagate by lifting and dividing after the foliage has died back, from seed, or by leaf-petiole cuttings. The tubers may be stored dry.

RIGHT Sinningia aggregata *is an interesting-looking plant with red or orange tube-shaped flowers that are solitary or arranged in pairs.*
ABOVE RIGHT Sinningia speciosa, Lawn Hybrid, *'Sunset' has velvety flowers of rich red that are delicately edged with white.*

Favorites

	Flower Color	Blooming Season	Flower Fragrance	Plant Height	Plant Width	Hardiness Zone	Frost Tolerance
Sinningia aggregata	red, orange	summer	no	15–30 in (38–75 cm)	12–24 in (30–60 cm)	10–12	no
Sinningia canescens	red, pink, orange	late spring to early summer	no	12 in (30 cm)	8–12 in (20–30 cm)	10–12	no
Sinningia cardinalis	purple, pink, red, white	late summer to autumn	no	12 in (30 cm)	12 in (30 cm)	10–12	no
Sinningia pusilla	lilac	summer	no	2 in (5 cm)	2 in (5 cm)	11–12	no
Sinningia speciosa	white, red, purple, blue	summer	no	12 in (30 cm)	12 in (30 cm)	11–12	no
Sinningia tubiflora	white	summer	yes	24 in (60 cm)	18 in (45 cm)	10–12	no

SOLANUM

Famous for the humble potato *(Solanum tuberosum)* in its myriad forms, this genus includes some 1,400 species of often tuberous-rooted herbs, vines, shrubs, and trees that have a cosmopolitan distribution, with many from tropical America. The trees and shrubs may be evergreen or deciduous and many are armed with thorns. They are a variable lot but their flowers are all remarkably similar, being simple, small, 5-petalled structures carried singly or in clusters with a central cone of yellow stamens. Fleshy berries follow the flowers and are often the most brightly colored part of the plant. Some species have spherical fruit, while others have elongated fruit shaped like chilies. The berries are usually somewhat poisonous and, because of their conspicuous color, may be attractive to children.

CULTIVATION

These plants vary in hardiness, though few are really frost tolerant and most are quite tender. They are generally easily grown in any well-aerated well-drained soil. Most species prefer sun or partial shade. Propagate from seed or cuttings, or in a few cases by division.

Top Tip

The climbing *Solanum* species can be trained to grow over tall trees, pergolas, and eaves, or against a sunny wall.

BELOW Solanum aviculare *is a fast-growing species native to Australia and New Zealand. It has smooth, deep green, lance-shaped leaves; purple flowers; and scarlet fruit.*

ABOVE *Also known as Costa Rican nightshade or giant potato creeper,* Solanum wendlandii *is a climber that bears hanging clusters of lilac-blue flowerheads in summer.*

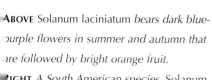

ABOVE Solanum laciniatum *bears dark blue-purple flowers in summer and autumn that are followed by bright orange fruit.*

RIGHT *A South American species,* Solanum rantonnetii *can be grown as a shrub, a vine, or a ground cover.*

Favorites

	Flower Color	Blooming Season	Flower Fragrance	Plant Height	Plant Width	Hardiness Zone	Frost Tolerance
Solanum aviculare	purple	spring to summer	no	6–12 ft (1.8–3.5 m)	5–8 ft (1.5–2.4 m)	9–11	no
Solanum crispum	lilac-blue	summer	no	10–20 ft (3–6 m)	8 ft (2.4 m)	8–11	yes
Solanum laciniatum	dark blue-purple	summer to autumn	no	6 ft (1.8 m)	5 ft (1.5 m)	9–11	no
Solanum quitoense	white	summer	no	4–6 ft (1.2–1.8 m)	3 ft (0.9 m)	9–12	no
Solanum rantonnetii	violet-blue	summer	no	4–8 ft (1.2–2.4 m)	3–6 ft (0.9–1.8 m)	9–11	no
Solanum wendlandii	lilac-blue	summer	no	8–20 ft (2.4–6 m)	6 ft (1.8 m)	10–12	no

LEFT Solidago californica *is a deciduous goldenrod native to Mexico and south-western U.S.A. Its showy flowers are attractive to bees and butterflies.*

SOLIDAGO

Although a few species are dotted in other temperate regions, this daisy family (Asteraceae) genus of around 100 species of perennials is primarily North American. They form clumps of upright, sometimes branching stems, the upper half of which bear panicles of tiny golden yellow flowers; these have earned the plant the common name of goldenrod. The leaves may be lance-shaped, linear, or a pointed oval shape, and often have toothed edges. By the time flowering starts in late summer many of the lower leaves have withered somewhat. Native Americans used this late-flowering habit as a guide to when the corn would ripen. *Solidago altissima* is the state flower of Kentucky, and *S. gigantea* is the state flower of Nebraska.

CULTIVATION

Solidago plants are hardy and easily grown in full or half sun in any position with reasonably fertile, moist, well-drained soil. They will grow in poor soil and withstand drought but will not flower well or reach their maximum size with such conditions. Propagate by division, or from seed or basal cuttings. They may self-sow.

Favorites	Flower Color	Blooming Season	Flower Fragrance	Plant Height	Plant Width	Hardiness Zone	Frost Tolerance
Solidago altissima	yellow	autumn	no	5–7 ft (1.5–2 m)	3 ft (0.9 m)	4–10	yes
Solidago californica	yellow	autumn	no	18 in–4 ft (45 cm–1.2 m)	3 ft (0.9 m)	6–10	yes
Solidago canadensis	yellow	mid-summer to autumn	no	2–5 ft (0.6–1.5 m)	5–8 ft (1.5–2.4 m)	3–10	yes
Solidago 'Crown of Rays'	yellow	mid- to late summer	no	24 in (60 cm)	18 in (45 cm)	5–9	yes
Solidago gigantea	yellow	mid-summer to autumn	no	3–8 ft (0.9–2.4 m)	3 ft (0.9 m)	3–10	yes
Solidago sphacelata	yellow	late summer to autumn	no	24–36 in (60–90 cm)	24 in (60 cm)	4–9	yes

LEFT Solidago *'Crown of Rays' is similar to several wild North American species. Its bright yellow flowers appear in summer.*
BELOW *The Canadian goldenrod* (Solidago canadensis) *bears plumelike sprays of bright yellow flowers in summer and autumn. Dead stalks should be cut down in winter.*

Top Tip

Sparaxis species
are suitable for the
front of borders or
in raised beds. In
cold areas they may
need to be placed
in a greenhouse, or
planted against a
sunny wall, pro-
tected from wind.

RIGHT *Sparaxis grandiflora
usually has flowers that are
purple-red, but there is also
a delightful white-flowered
form. Each bloom has a
stunning yellow throat.*
BELOW *The summer garden
will certainly be enlivened
by the presence of* Sparaxis
tricolor *flowers, as their hot-
colored petals are accen-
tuated by a yellow center
lined with black.*

SPARAXIS

A South African genus of 6 species of
corms of the iris family (Iridaceae),
Sparaxis plants will naturalize and form
large drifts of brightly colored flowers
under suitable conditions. The leaves
are grassy to sword-shaped, with prominent ribbing, and develop quickly from
late winter. They are soon followed by wiry
spikes carrying anywhere from just a few
blooms to fanlike sprays of funnel-shaped
6-petalled flowers. The flowers may
be white, yellow, or shades of pink to
orange and red, usually with a yellow
center and contrasting dark colors in
the throat. The genus name comes
from the Greek word *sparasso* (to tear),
referring to the lacerated bracts at the
base of the flowers.

CULTIVATION

These plants are not hardy where the
soil freezes but are otherwise easily
grown in full sun with fertile, moist,
well-drained soil. In cold areas they
can be lifted in autumn and replanted
in early spring for a later flower show.
Propagate from seed or by division.

Favorites	Flower Color	Blooming Season	Flower Fragrance	Plant Height	Plant Width	Hardiness Zone	Frost Tolerance
Sparaxis elegans	various	spring to summer	no	4–12 in (10–30 cm)	4 in (10 cm)	9–10	no
Sparaxis fragrans	various	spring	yes	4–10 in (10–25 cm)	4 in (10 cm)	9–10	no
Sparaxis grandiflora	purple-red; yellow tubes	spring	no	4–15 in (10–38 cm)	6 in (15 cm)	9–10	no
Sparaxis pillansii	rose pink, red; yellow center	spring	no	12–24 in (30–60 cm)	6 in (15 cm)	9–10	no
Sparaxis tricolor	pink to orange; yellow and black	spring to summer	no	4–15 in (10–38 cm)	4 in (10 cm)	9–10	no
Sparaxis variegata	purple	spring	no	6–12 in (15–30 cm)	4 in (10 cm)	9–10	no

BELOW Sparaxis fragrans *subsp.* acutiloba *is taller than the species, growing to 18 in (45 cm). The flowers are purple or yellow, occasionally with black markings.*

SPIRAEA

This genus consists of about 70 species of mainly deciduous, but sometimes semi-evergreen, flowering shrubs from the rose family (Rosaceae). They are found in many northern temperate areas, mainly in eastern and southeastern Asia, as well as in North America. Plants are highly appreciated for their flowering and foliage qualities. Leaves are simple and alternate, variously toothed and lobed, and may have gray or blue-gray downy undersides. Many species have attractive golden, orange, or bronze foliage over autumn. Flowers are borne in dense profusions in clusters, on terminal panicles, or along

ABOVE Spiraea thunbergii *is a Chinese native that grows to 5 ft (1.5 m) tall. It produces small clusters of white flowers in late spring; its leaves are narrow with toothed margins.*
BELOW LEFT Spiraea × vanhouttei *is a robust shrub that produces dense umbels of white flowers in mid-summer.*

branch tips in spring or summer. The color range is generally white, yellow, pink, or crimson. The genus *Spiraea* is commonly known as bridal wreath.

CULTIVATION

They thrive in most soils, though some grow poorly on chalk, and prefer a sunny position and cool moist conditions. For pruning purposes, these plants fall into 2 groups: those that flower on the current year's growth, which can be hard pruned in spring, and those that flower on the previous year's growth, which should have old flowering shoots removed just after flowering. Propagation is from soft-tip or half-hardened cuttings in summer.

Favorites	Flower Color	Blooming Season	Flower Fragrance	Plant Height	Plant Width	Hardiness Zone	Frost Tolerance
Spiraea fritschiana	white and pink	summer	no	3 ft (0.9 m)	3 ft (0.9 m)	4–9	yes
Spiraea japonica	rose pink	late spring to summer	no	2–6 ft (0.6–1.8 m)	2–6 ft (0.6–1.8 m)	3–10	yes
Spiraea nipponica	white	summer	no	3–6 ft (0.9–1.8 m)	3–6 ft (0.9–1.8 m)	5–10	yes
Spiraea prunifolia	white	mid- to late spring	no	6 ft (1.8 m)	6 ft (1.8 m)	4–10	yes
Spiraea thunbergii	white	late spring to summer	no	5 ft (1.5 m)	6 ft (1.8 m)	4–10	yes
Spiraea × vanhouttei	white	summer	no	6 ft (1.8 m)	5 ft (1.5 m)	4–10	yes

ABOVE A Korean mounding shrub, Spiraea fritschiana produces large clusters of white and pink flowers in summer, and purple-tinted foliage in autumn.

RIGHT Spiraea japonica 'Crispa' is valued for its bright pink flower clusters and feathery, rich green, toothed leaves.

Top Tip

A second bloom will occur if spent flower clusters are removed after the first flowering. However, the second bloom will be less profuse.

LEFT *'Mary Gregory' is one of the most delightful* Stokesia laevis *cultivars. Its fringed lemon yellow flowers will add color and interest to a herbaceous border.*
BELOW Stokesia laevis *'Purple Parasols' is known for its ability to change color—from pale blue to indigo and purple, then becoming magenta-pink. In warm climates it can flower for most of the year.*

STOKESIA

Although there is just 1 species in this daisy family (Asteraceae) genus, it has been extensively developed in cultivation and is now available in a wide range of plant sizes, flower colors, and forms. A summer- to autumn-flowering perennial from the southeastern U.S.A., *Stokesia*—or Stokes' aster—was named for Dr. Jonathan Stokes (1755-1831), English doctor and botanist. It arrived in England in 1766 and was in vogue in Victorian times, especially as a cut flower. It later languished but is now popular again. *Stokesia* is an upright plant with simple evergreen leaves borne in basal rosettes and large cornflowerlike heads of white, yellow, or mauve to deep purple-blue flowers. *Stokesia* plants are well suited to herbaceous borders.

CULTIVATION

Plant in full or half sun in light free-draining soil. Water and feed well. Watch for mildew in late summer. Propagate by division near the end of the dormant period, or raise from seed.

Favorites	Flower Color	Blooming Season	Flower Fragrance	Plant Height	Plant Width	Hardiness Zone	Frost Tolerance
Stokesia laevis	lilac-blue, pink, white	mid-summer to early autumn	no	12–24 in (30–60 cm)	18 in (45 cm)	6–10	yes
Stokesia laevis 'Blue Danube'	dark blue	mid-summer to early autumn	no	15 in (38 cm)	18 in (45 cm)	6–10	yes
Stokesia laevis 'Bluestone'	blue	mid-summer to early autumn	no	10–12 in (25–30 cm)	15 in (38 cm)	6–10	yes
Stokesia laevis 'Mary Gregory'	lemon yellow	mid-summer to early autumn	no	15–18 in (38–45 cm)	18 in (45 cm)	6–10	yes
Stokesia laevis 'Silver Moon'	whitish silver	mid-summer to early autumn	no	18 in (45 cm)	18 in (45 cm)	6–10	yes
Stokesia laevis 'Wyoming'	dark blue	mid-summer to early autumn	no	18–24 in (45–60 cm)	18 in (45 cm)	6–10	yes

Top Tip

To prolong the *Stokesia* flowering season, remove the spent flower stems immediately. This cornflower look-alike is ideal for cutting and drying.

BELOW *As well as the pretty flowers, the leaves are also a feature of* Stokesia laevis. *They are lance-shaped with a paler midrib, and persist throughout winter.*

STREPTOCARPUS

Although widespread in the African and Asian tropics and subtropics, most of the cultivated plants in this African violet family (Gesneriaceae) genus of around 130 species of annuals and perennials are natives of southern Africa. They are a very diverse group, ranging from tiny rosette-forming plants to others that produce just a single huge leaf. But despite this variation of form they share some features, especially among their flowers. The leaves are velvety, heavily veined, and slightly crinkled. The flowers are long-tubed, primroselike, and usually have 5 petals; they occur in heads on short upright stems. The genus name is of Greek origin, derived from *streptos* (twisted) and *karpos* (a fruit), referring to the unusual form of the spirally twisted fruits.

ABOVE Streptocarpus *'Tina'* *is one of several hybrids widely available. It forms rosettes of duo-toned pink flowers.*

CULTIVATION

Cold tolerance varies, though none withstand more than the lightest frost. Plant in a bright but not sunny position that is warm and draft free. The soil should be fertile, moist, humus-rich, and well-drained. Propagate by division, from leaf-petiole cuttings, or from seed.

Favorites	Flower Color	Blooming Season	Flower Fragrance	Plant Height	Plant Width	Hardiness Zone	Frost Tolerance
Streptocarpus baudertii	white to mauve; yellow throat	summer	no	12 in (30 cm)	18 in (45 cm)	9–12	no
Streptocarpus candidus	white with violet and yellow	summer	yes	12 in (30 cm)	24 in (60 cm)	9–12	no
Streptocarpus 'Chorus Line'	white, veined mauve	spring to autumn	no	12 in (30 cm)	18 in (45 cm)	10–12	no
Streptocarpus 'Crystal Ice'	white and lilac	most of the year	no	12 in (30 cm)	18 in (45 cm)	10–12	no
Streptocarpus cyaneus	white, pink, lilac; yellow markings	spring to summer	no	10 in (25 cm)	15 in (38 cm)	9–12	no
Streptocarpus 'Heidi'	lilac-blue; purple center	spring to autumn	no	10 in (25 cm)	18 in (45 cm)	10–12	no
Streptocarpus johannis	white to mauve	spring	no	12 in (30 cm)	18 in (45 cm)	9–12	no
Streptocarpus 'Kim'	purple	spring to summer	no	8 in (20 cm)	15 in (38 cm)	10–12	no
Streptocarpus primulifolius	mauve and violet	spring to summer	no	10 in (25 cm)	18 in (45 cm)	9–12	no
Streptocarpus 'Ruby'	rose red	spring to autumn	no	12 in (30 cm)	15 in (38 cm)	10–12	no
Streptocarpus saxorum	lilac and white	most of the year	no	6 in (15 cm)	24 in (60 cm)	10–12	no
Streptocarpus 'Tina'	pink and magenta	spring to autumn	no	12 in (30 cm)	15 in (38 cm)	10–12	no

Top Tip

Treat *Streptocarpus* plants similarly to *Saintpaulia* when grown indoors. Use an African violet potting mix and place in a bright but not too sunny spot.

LEFT *White flowers with purple blotches make* Streptocarpus *'Crystal Ice' an eye-catching pot plant. It needs a warm position.* **BELOW** Streptocarpus *'Chorus Line' has white trumpet-shaped blooms blotched mauve all over.*

LEFT Streptocarpus cyaneus *subsp.* polackii *has deep green semi-upright leaves and funnel-shaped purple-blue flowers. In cool areas it needs the protection of a greenhouse.*

ABOVE Streptocarpus 'Ruby' bears rich red flowers perfectly complemented by the deep green leaves.

LEFT Streptocarpus saxorum produces enchanting pale mauve-blue flowers on long slender stems.

RIGHT Streptocarpus 'Kim' is prized for its production of abundant dark purple flowers and contrasting mid-green leaves.

LEFT Streptocarpus primulifolius, with its funnel-shaped mauve-blue blooms, is a popular container plant that needs lots of water in the growing season.
RIGHT Its delicate mauve flowers and hairy, semi-erect leaves make Streptocarpus johannis an attractive plant.

BELOW The prostrate leaves of Streptocarpus baudertii are arranged in a pretty rosette, from which the pale mauve flowers with yellow centers appear. This species needs to be given fertilizer monthly during the growing season, and like all Streptocarpus plants it should be repotted each spring.

SYRINGA

Pity the tropical gardener who has never breathed the scent of lilacs in the spring. This olive family (Oleaceae) genus is made up of only around 20 species but was so greatly developed by Lemoine and later hybridizers that the selection is now huge. *Syringa*, or lilac, species are mainly deciduous shrubs and trees, and naturally occur from southeastern Europe to Japan. They have simple, pointed, elliptical or heart-shaped leaves and in spring produce upright panicles of small 4-petalled flowers with an overpowering fragrance. Flowers may be white or shades of pink, red, purple, and blue. The genus name comes from the Greek *syrinx* (a pipe), which refers to the hollow stems, and is also the origin of the word syringe.

CULTIVATION

Mostly hardy, *Syringa* plants prefer full or half sun and fertile, moist, humus-rich, well-drained soil. The roots can be invasive, and continually removing suckers can weary even the most ardent lilac lover. Propagate species by seed or cuttings, and cultivars by cuttings or grafting.

Favorites

	Flower Color	Blooming Season	Flower Fragrance	Plant Height	Plant Width	Hardiness Zone	Frost Tolerance
Syringa × *chinensis*	lilac-purple	late spring	yes	12 ft (3.5 m)	12 ft (3.5 m)	5–9	yes
Syringa × *hyacinthiflora*	white, pink blue, lilac, purple	mid- to late spring	yes	15 ft (4.5 m)	10–15 ft (3–4.5 m)	4–9	yes
Syringa × *josiflexa*	lavender-pink	early summer	yes	10 ft (3 m)	6 ft (1.8 m)	5–9	yes
Syringa komarowii	pink	late spring to early summer	yes	10–15 ft (3–4.5 m)	10 ft (3 m)	5–9	yes
Syringa × *laciniata*	lilac	late spring	yes	6 ft (1.8 m)	10 ft (3 m)	5–9	yes
Syringa meyeri	purple-mauve	spring to summer	yes	6 ft (1.8 m)	4 ft (1.2 m)	4–9	yes
Syringa oblata	lilac	spring	yes	8–12 ft (2.4–3.5 m)	8 ft (2.4 m)	5–9	yes
Syringa × *prestoniae*	white, pink, blue, lavender, purple	early summer	yes	12 ft (3.5 m)	12 ft (3.5 m)	4–9	yes
Syringa pubescens	lilac-purple	spring to early summer	yes	12 ft (3.5 m)	12 ft (3.5 m)	5–9	yes
Syringa reticulata	creamy white	summer	yes	15–30 ft (4.5–9 m)	10–20 ft (3–6 m)	3–9	yes
Syringa × *swegiflexa*	pink	late spring to early summer	yes	12 ft (3.5 m)	8 ft (2.5 m)	5–9	yes
Syringa vulgaris	lilac, purple, pink, blue, white	late spring to early summer	yes	8–20 ft (2.4–6 m)	6–10 ft (1.8–3 m)	4–9	yes

LEFT *A very early flowering lilac,* Syringa oblata *bears delightful pale lilac blooms in dense heads. It is also valued for the lovely autumn color of the foliage.*

BELOW *Syringa* komarowii *grows quickly to 10 ft (3 m) tall, and can eventually exceed 15 ft (4.5 m) in height.*

Top Tip

Because most lilacs bloom on the previous year's wood, pruning should be done immediately after the flowers have finished. To encourage new growth, the old stems should be cut out each year.

ABOVE *Lilacs are among the most popular of all cool-climate shrubs. Syringa* × prestoniae *is popular for its slightly drooping heads of soft pink to light purple flowers.* **BELOW** *'William Robinson' is one of the cultivars of Syringa* vulgaris *and bears light pink to purple double blooms. Spent flowers should be removed immediately after the petals fade.*

ABOVE Syringa × hyacinthi-flora *'Laurentian' bears pinkish purple flowers, and is a strong-growing plant.* **RIGHT** Syringa vulgaris *'Président Grévy' performs best in areas that have cold winters, but it does not like strong winds.*

BELOW *For pure old-fashioned elegance, it's hard to beat Syringa vulgaris 'Ann Tighe', with its purple-red blooms.*

ABOVE *'Vestale' is a pure white-flowered form of* Syringa vulgaris *that can be grown in a shrub border in full sun.*

TAGETES

A lthough the commonly grown marigolds are often known as African or French, in fact, all but one of the 50-odd species of this daisy family (Asteraceae) genus originate in the American tropics and subtropics. They are mainly upright annuals or perennials with dark green, sometimes aromatic, pinnate leaves that have toothed edges. Their flowers, usually a vibrant golden yellow or orange, are often typically daisylike, with obvious ray and disc florets, but in some forms the disc florets are largely hidden. The genus name comes from *Tages*, an Etruscan deity, grandson of Jupiter, who sprang from the ploughed earth. This is a reference to the marigold's habit of just pop-ping up from seed.

CULTIVATION

Tagetes plants prefer a warm sunny position with light well-drained soil. Water well and feed if the foliage is at all yellow. Deadhead frequently to ensure continuous blooming. Propagate from seed, which is usually started indoors in early spring.

Favorites	Flower Color	Blooming Season	Flov Fragr
Tagetes erecta, Antigua Series	yellow, gold, orange	late spring to autumn	n
Tagetes lemmonii	golden yellow	spring to autumn	n
Tagetes patula	yellow, orange, red	late spring to autumn	n
Tagetes patula, Bonanza Series	orange, gold, reddish brown	late spring to autumn	r
Tagetes, Safari Series	yellow, red, orange	late spring to early autumn	r
Tagetes tenuifolia	yellow	late summer to autumn	

ABOVE Tagetes, *Safari Series, 'Safari Yellow'* bears heads of broad-petalled bright yellow flowers that are suitable in a mixed border or in a sunny window box.

Top Tip

African marigolds, such as *Tagetes,* Antigua Series, are excellent for cutting because the dense pomponlike flowerheads last for a long time in fresh water.

LEFT *Signet marigolds are profuse flowerers so are perfect for quick outdoor decoration. Tagetes tenuifolia 'Starfire', with its neat habit, is ideal for edges.*
BELOW *The Bonanza Series of* Tagetes patula *includes robust plants producing dense flowerheads in yellow and orange tones, as shown by 'Bonanza Bolero'.*

Plant Height	Plant Width	Hardiness Zone	Frost Tolerance
10–12 in (25–30 cm)	12–18 in (30–45 cm)	9–12	no
3–5 ft (0.9–1.5 m)	3–5 ft (0.9–1.5 m)	9–12	no
12 in (30 cm)	12 in (30 cm)	9–12	no
8–10 in (20–25 cm)	8 in (20 cm)	9–12	no
8–12 in (20–30 cm)	8 in (20 cm)	9–12	no
2–24 in (20–60 cm)	8–12 in (20–30 cm)	9–12	no

Thalictrum

A buttercup family (Ranunculaceae) genus of around 130 species of tuberous or rhizome-rooted perennials, *Thalictrum* is found mainly in the northern temperate zone, with a few species straying south of the equator into the tropics. They are upright plants with lacy, pinnate, blue-green leaves reminiscent of aquilegia or maidenhair fern foliage. Tall elegant flower stems grow well above the foliage, and from late spring to autumn, depending on the species, the stems bear clusters of small fluffy flowers. Occurring mainly in pink and mauve, but also in white and yellow, the petalless flowers may sometimes gain color from the 4 to 5 petallike sepals. Also known as meadow rue, *Thalictrum* plants were significant in the herbal lore and medicine of ancient Rome.

Cultivation

These plants are mostly hardy and easily grown in a temperate climate in full or half sun. The soil should be fertile, humus-rich, and well-drained. It is usually propagated by division, as cultivated plants are mainly selected forms.

Favorites	Flower Color	Blooming Season	Flower Fragrance
Thalictrum aquilegifolium	pink, lilac, white	summer	no
Thalictrum delavayi	lilac with yellow stamens	mid-summer to late autumn	no
Thalictrum flavum	yellow	summer	no
Thalictrum kiusianum	mauve-purple	summer	no
Thalictrum orientale	white, pink, lilac	late spring to early summer	no
Thalictrum rochebrunianum	pale lilac	summer	no

Left Thalictrum rochebrunianum, *native to Japan, puts on a beautiful display of summer color with its lilac flowers featuring prominent yellow-tipped stamens*

Plant Height	Plant Width	Hardiness Zone	Frost Tolerance
3 ft (0.9 m)	18 in (45 cm)	6–10	yes
4 ft (1.2 m)	24 in (60 cm)	7–10	yes
3 ft (0.9 m)	18 in (45 cm)	6–9	yes
4 in (10 cm)	12 in (30 cm)	8–10	yes
12 in (30 cm)	12 in (30 cm)	5–9	yes
36 in (90 cm)	12 in (30 cm)	8–10	yes

ABOVE Thalictrum orientale *is slow growing, but will reward the patient gardener with attractive deep green leaves and delicate flowers.* **LEFT** Thalictrum delavayi *from China takes its name from French botanist Jean Marie Delavay (1834-1895), who introduced many Asian plants to the West.*

Top Tip

Thalictrum species are useful plants in woodland gardens, borders, or rock gardens. The ferny foliage is an effective backdrop in floral arrangements.

RIGHT Thalictrum delavayi *'Hewitt's Double' needs to be replanted every few years to maintain its vitality. It is a sterile cultivar, propagated only by division.*

THUNBERGIA

This Old World tropical genus consists of around 100 species of annuals, perennials, and shrubs of the acanthus family. Many are vigorous twining climbers, while others are shrubby in habit. They are an enormously varied group, usually with pointed oval to heart-shaped leaves, sometimes lobed or toothed. The flowers occur in a wide color range: mostly yellow, orange, and purple-blue shades. They may be borne singly or in racemes and are mostly long-tubed trumpets with 5 large lobes. The genus was named for Carl Peter Thunberg (1743–1828), a Swedish physician and botanist employed by the Dutch East India Company. He was the first Western botanist to visit Japan in over 100 years, and brought back to Europe flora that was previously largely unknown.

CULTIVATION

Thunbergia species are frost tender or tolerant of very light frosts. Plant in a warm sheltered position with moist, humus-rich, well-drained soil. Many species are drought tolerant; most perform best with frequent watering and feeding. Propagate from cuttings or seed.

ABOVE *The spectacular maroon and yellow flowers of* Thunbergia mysorensis *may bloom all year round in areas with mild winters. Its sweet nectar attracts hummingbirds.*
RIGHT *The very versatile* Thunbergia gregorii, *known as orange clock vine, can be used as a ground cover or twining climber for a wall or fence.*

Favorites

	Flower Color	Blooming Season	Flower Fragrance	Plant Height	Plant Width	Hardiness Zone	Frost Tolerance
Thunbergia alata	orange with black center	summer to autumn	no	5–10 ft (1.5–3 m)	10 ft (3 m)	9–11	no
Thunbergia erecta	creamy yellow; purple lobes	summer	no	4–6 ft (1.2–1.8 m)	2–4 ft (0.6–1.2 m)	10–12	no
Thunbergia grandiflora	sky blue to dark blue	summer	no	15–30 ft (4.5–9 m)	10 ft (3 m)	10–12	no
Thunbergia gregorii	orange	summer	no	6 ft (1.8 m)	6 ft (1.8 m)	9–11	no
Thunbergia mysorensis	yellow and maroon	spring	no	10–20 ft (3–6 m)	10–15 ft (3–4.5 m)	10–12	no
Thunbergia togoensis	violet-blue; yellow center	summer	no	10 ft (3 m)	6 ft (1.8 m)	10–12	no

Top Tip

For an eye-catching effect in the garden, train *Thunbergia* species up through other annuals, such as sunflowers, or around and through the branches of a small tree.

RIGHT Thunbergia togoensis *is a semi-climbing shrub that bears purple blooms; they should be deadheaded as necessary. They are not suitable as cut flowers.*
BELOW *There's no mistaking* Thunbergia alata, *or black-eyed Susan, with its distinctive dark center. It blooms over a long season, making it lovely in hanging baskets.*

TRADESCANTIA

ABOVE Tradescantia *'Little Doll'*, from the Andersoniana Group, is an easy-going long-blooming perennial. It bears mauve flowers with contrasting bright yellow stamens.
BELOW The flowers of Tradescantia, Andersoniana Group, *'Bilberry Ice'* have 3 white petals each with a lilac streak. This plant can be cut back quite severely in late autumn.

Introduced to cultivation in 1637 by John Tradescant the Younger and named for him by Linnaeus, this dayflower family (Commelinaceae) genus of around 70 species of annuals and perennials from the Americas includes a few that, while attractive as garden plants, have become serious pests in some areas. Tuberous or fibrous rooted and often evergreen, they have rather succulent stems and fleshy, pointed elliptical, lance-shaped, or narrow leaves. Attractive variegated and colored foliage forms are common. Clusters of small 3-petalled flowers subtended by bracts appear over the warmer months and are sometimes very bright magenta, though white, soft pink, and blue to mauve colors predominate.

CULTIVATION

Most species are tolerant of light to moderate frosts. Some prefer a sunny aspect and are drought tolerant, but most are happier with part-shade and moist well-drained soil. Propagate by division, from tip cuttings, or from seed, depending on the growth form.

LEFT Tradescantia *Andersoniana Group, 'Blue and Gold'* is suitable for a range of garden uses—from mixed borders and ground covers to hanging baskets.
BELOW Tradescantia virginiana *bears 3-petalled purple flowers that last for just a day, but as the plant is rarely out of bloom, summer color is assured. It self-sows quickly.*

Top Tip

Very hardy in mild climates, *Trade-scantia*, or spider-wort, plants may need to be grown in a greenhouse in cooler areas. A general fertilizer can be of benefit in early spring.

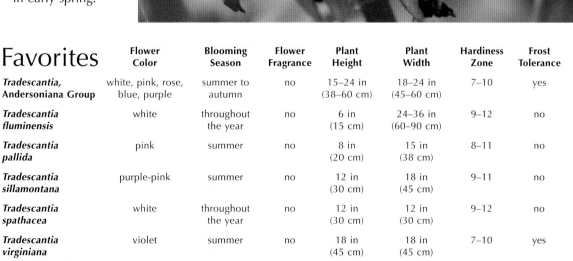

Favorites	Flower Color	Blooming Season	Flower Fragrance	Plant Height	Plant Width	Hardiness Zone	Frost Tolerance
Tradescantia, **Andersoniana Group**	white, pink, rose, blue, purple	summer to autumn	no	15–24 in (38–60 cm)	18–24 in (45–60 cm)	7–10	yes
Tradescantia **fluminensis**	white	throughout the year	no	6 in (15 cm)	24–36 in (60–90 cm)	9–12	no
Tradescantia **pallida**	pink	summer	no	8 in (20 cm)	15 in (38 cm)	8–11	no
Tradescantia **sillamontana**	purple-pink	summer	no	12 in (30 cm)	18 in (45 cm)	9–11	no
Tradescantia **spathacea**	white	throughout the year	no	12 in (30 cm)	12 in (30 cm)	9–12	no
Tradescantia **virginiana**	violet	summer	no	18 in (45 cm)	18 in (45 cm)	7–10	yes

TRIFOLIUM

*T*rifolium, or clover, is so well-known that
the leaf shape is not just a description
in itself, but a symbol, too. Associated with
Ireland ever since St. Patrick used it to describe
the Christian Trinity, the cloverleaf and the
4-leafed shamrock are today primarily associated with good luck and have been adopted
by countries, football teams, and casinos.
Clover is also a vitally important component
in the world's pastures while at the same time
being far less welcome in its lawns. Found
naturally throughout the temperate and subtropical zones except Australasia, *Trifolium*
is a genus of around 230 species of annuals,
biennials, and perennials of the pea family
(Fabaceae). Leaves are typically trifoliate and
bright green, and are sometimes darkly marked.
Examined closely, the individual flowers are
very much like pea-flowers. They are borne in
rounded heads or terminal racemes. *Trifolium
pratense* is the state flower of Vermont.

CULTIVATION

Trifolium species are usually hardy and easily
grown. Plant in full or half sun with moist
well-drained soil. The plants may be divided,
but they usually self-sow.

Top Tip

When growing
clover in pots, use
a potting mix that
contains equal pro-
portions of loam,
sand, and leafmold.
While growing,
keep moist during
the winter months.

ABOVE *A bushy, vigorous,
upright perennial,* Trifoliu
pannonicum *produces
creamy white to yellow
flowers that last well whe
cut for indoor decoration*
BELOW RIGHT *Trifolium
repens is invasive and no
normally grown in garder
Some cultivars are more
suitable, however, such a
'Pentaphyllum' (pictured)*

Favorites	Flower Color	Blooming Season	Flower Fragrance	Plant Height	Plant Width	Hardiness Zone	Frost Tolerance
Trifolium pannonicum	cream, ageing to rusty red	spring to early summer	no	12–18 in (30–45 cm)	12–24 in (30–60 cm)	5–9	yes
Trifolium repens	white	spring to autumn	no	3–12 in (8–30 cm)	24–36 in (60–90 cm)	4–10	yes
Trifolium repens 'Green Ice'	white	spring to autumn	no	3–8 in (8–20 cm)	24–36 in (60–90 cm)	4–10	yes
Trifolium repens 'Pentaphyllum'	white	spring to autumn	no	6–12 in (15–30 cm)	18–24 in (45–60 cm)	4–10	yes
Trifolium rubens	reddish purple	spring to early summer	no	12–18 in (30–45 cm)	18 in (45 cm)	7–9	yes
Trifolium uniflorum	creamy white to purple-pink	spring to autumn	no	1–2 in (2.5–5 cm)	12–18 in (30–45 cm)	6–9	yes

ABOVE RIGHT *Suitable for a large rock garden,* Trifolium uniflorum *is grown for its abundance of yellow-white trumpet-shaped flowers. It can quickly cover a bank or tumble over a wall.*
RIGHT *It's not hard to see why* Trifolium rubens *is the most popular garden clover. Allow it sufficient space to display its superb blooms.*

TRILLIUM

This striking group of 30 rhizome-rooted, spring-flowering, woodland perennials from North America and temperate Asia is the type genus for its family, the Trilliaceae. The genus name is derived from *tri-lilium*, 3-part lily, because the leaf and floral parts are grouped in 3s. Although ranging from the tiny *Trillium rivale* at just a couple of inches high through to species that are 24 in (60 cm) tall in flower, the genus is remarkably consistent in form. The leaflets are bright green, often silver- or purple-mottled, and usually broadly oval, tapering to a point. At the center of the 3-leaf cluster is a simple 3-petalled flower that may be white, cream, pink, or deep maroon.

CULTIVATION

Plant *Trillium* species in part- or full shade in cool, moist, humus-rich, well-drained soil. All species die away completely in autumn but quickly return to growth in early spring, often flowering before the equinox. The common name of wake robin comes from this early flowering habit—it is supposedly the plant that wakes the robin in spring. Propagate by division of the rhizomes after flowering, or from seed.

Favorites

	Flower Color	Blooming Season	Flower Fragrance	Plant Height	Plant Width	Hardiness Zone	Frost Tolerance
Trillium albidum	white with pink tinges	spring	yes	12–20 in (30–50 cm)	12 in (30 cm)	6–9	yes
Trillium chloropetalum	white, yellow, pink, maroon	spring	yes	8–15 in (20–38 cm)	8–15 in (20–38 cm)	6–9	yes
Trillium erectum	pale green with red-purple tinges	late spring	no	8–20 in (20–50 cm)	12 in (30 cm)	4–9	yes
Trillium grandiflorum	white, fading to pink	late spring	no	10–15 in (25–38 cm)	12 in (30 cm)	3–9	yes
Trillium ovatum	white with yellow center	spring	no	8–20 in (20–50 cm)	8 in (20 cm)	5–8	yes
Trillium pusillum	white, ageing pink to purple	spring	no	6 in (15 cm)	4 in (10 cm)	5–8	yes

Top Tip

Trillium species are best planted under trees and large shrubs where the conditions match their native habitat. Once established, they require very little attention.

ABOVE RIGHT *Endangered in its native habitat,* Trillium pusillum *var.* pusillum *bears bright white flowers that age to pale pink.*

RIGHT *The stalkless maroon flowers of the robust perennial* Trillium chloropetalum *var.* giganteum *sit among lush green foliage.*

TROPAEOLUM

Found from Mexico to the southern tip of South America, this genus contains about 80 species of annuals and perennials commonly known as nasturtiums. Many are climbers, using their twining leaf-stalks to scramble and cling. Though variable, the foliage is often shield-shaped and tinted blue-green. All species have long-spurred 5-petalled flowers, which occur in a wide range of mainly warm shades. The degree of development of petals and spurs varies, leading to a range of flower shapes and sizes. The genus name comes from the Greek *tropaion* (trophy), a term used for the tree trunks on which were hung the shields and helmets of defeated enemies. *Tropaeolum* leaves (shields) and flowers (helmets) reminded Linnaeus of this Greek tradition, and he named the genus accordingly.

ABOVE *'Red Wonder' is one of the many cultivars of* Tropaeolum majus. *It is a fast-growing annual climber that will often twine itself through garden shrubs.*

BELOW *The scarlet flowers of the trailing* Tropaeolum majus *'Empress of India' contrast with the dark green leaves. The flowers make a spicy addition to salads.*

CULTIVATION

Plant in full or half sun with moist well-drained soil. Plants may need trimming back and support for climbing stems. Propagate by division from basal cuttings, or from seed.

RIGHT *Leaves and flowers of* Tropaeolum majus *cultivars such as 'Whirlibird Cherry Rose' (pictured) can be used in summer salads, adding color and taste.*

BELOW *Trailing* Tropaeolum polyphyllum *bears attractive blue-green leaves and bold yellow flowers all summer. All nasturtiums self-seed very readily, so thin out the plant when necessary.*

Top Tip

Tropaeolum seeds should not be sown until after the last frosts. Feeding is often not required and some species, such as *Tropaeolum majus*, actually prefer poor soil.

Favorites	Flower Color	Blooming Season	Flower Fragrance	Plant Height	Plant Width	Hardiness Zone	Frost Tolerance
Tropaeolum majus	yellow, orange, red	summer to autumn	no	8–24 in (20–60 cm)	3 ft (0.9 m)	8–11	no
Tropaeolum majus 'Empress of India'	scarlet	summer to autumn	no	8–24 in (20–60 cm)	3 ft (0.9 m)	8–11	no
Tropaeolum majus 'Hermine Grashoff'	orange-red	summer to autumn	no	8–24 in (20–60 cm)	3 ft (0.9 m)	8–11	no
Tropaeolum polyphyllum	yellow to orange	summer	no	2–3 in (5–8 cm)	3 ft (0.9 m)	8–11	yes
Tropaeolum speciosum	deep red	summer to autumn	no	4–10 ft (1.2–3 m)	5 ft (1.5 m)	8–10	yes
Tropaeolum tuberosum	orange-red, yellow, and brown	summer to autumn	no	6–12 ft (1.8–3.5 m)	3 ft (0.9 m)	8–10	no

TULIPA

Occurring naturally in the northern temperate regions, especially central Asia, the genus *Tulipa* contains around 100 species of bulbs. They have been cultivated for at least 3,000 years and reached Europe from Turkey in 1554. They quickly became a garden favorite but it was not until the Dutch "tulipomania" of the 1630s that tulips became established in our folklore as well as our gardens. Tulip leaves are gray-green to blue-green and may be grassy or quite broad, with contrasting markings. The flowers vary widely between the species, and so many hybrids and cultivars exist that they are often divided into 15 groups based primarily on parentage and flower type. The blooms are unfailingly delightful, especially if planted as a massed bedding of a single type.

ABOVE *The Lily-flowered Group of tulips, such as 'Queen of Sheba', bring a formal note to gardens with their elegant goblet-shaped blooms and pointed petals.*
BELOW LEFT *Most tulips sold as cut flowers are from the Darwin Hybrid Group, which includes* Tulipa *'Olympic Flame' (pictured).*

CULTIVATION

Tulips need a temperate climate and winter chilling. They do best in a sunny position that does not bake in summer. Plant fairly deeply in autumn, around 6 in (15 cm) deep, and water well once the foliage appears. Propagate hybrids and cultivars from offsets; the species can be propagated from seed.

Favorites	Flower Color	Blooming Season	Flow Fragra
Tulipa, Darwin Hybrid Group	yellow, orange, red, pink	spring	no
Tulipa, Double Late Group	various	late spring	no
Tulipa, Greigii Group	yellow to red	early to mid-spring	ne
Tulipa hageri	yellow-green and red	early to mid-spring	n
Tulipa, Lily-flowered Group	various	late spring	n
Tulipa, Parrot Group	various	late spring	n
Tulipa, Single Early Group	white to deep purple	early to mid-spring	n
Tulipa, Single Late Group	various	late spring	
Tulipa, Triumph Group	various	mid- to late spring	
Tulipa urumiensis	yellow with reddish brown tints	early spring	
Tulipa, Viridiflora Group	various	late spring	
Tulipa vvedenskyi	various	spring	

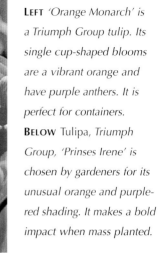

LEFT *'Orange Monarch' is a Triumph Group tulip. Its single cup-shaped blooms are a vibrant orange and have purple anthers. It is perfect for containers.*
BELOW Tulipa, *Triumph Group, 'Prinses Irene' is chosen by gardeners for its unusual orange and purple-red shading. It makes a bold impact when mass planted.*

Plant Height	Plant Width	Hardiness Zone	Frost Tolerance
20–26 in (50–65 cm)	6 in (15 cm)	5–9	yes
15–24 in (38–60 cm)	6 in (15 cm)	5–9	yes
6–12 in (15–30 cm)	8 in (20 cm)	5–9	yes
15 in (38 cm)	6 in (15 cm)	5–9	yes
18–26 in (45–65 cm)	6 in (15 cm)	5–9	yes
20–26 in (50–65 cm)	6 in (15 cm)	5–9	yes
6–18 in (15–45 cm)	6 in (15 cm)	5–9	yes
18–30 in (45–75 cm)	6 in (15 cm)	5–9	yes
15–24 in (38–60 cm)	6 in (15 cm)	5–9	yes
5 in (12 cm)	6 in (15 cm)	5–9	yes
15–22 in (38–55 cm)	6 in (15 cm)	5–9	yes
20 in (50 cm)	6 in (15 cm)	5–9	yes

RIGHT *Irregular frilled petals are the distinguishing feature of the Parrot Group. The stunning Tulipa 'Blue Parrot' looks wonderful potted-up.*

Top Tip

When cutting tulips for indoor decoration, select flowers that have not yet opened and cut them early in the morning while the day is still cool.

RIGHT *The stunning Tulipa, Lily-flowered Group, 'Ballerina' almost glows in the sunlight. It has pointed arching petals that are sunset orange.*

BELOW *The creamy yellow and green flowers of Tulipa, Viridiflora Group, 'Spring Green' go superbly with green-colored plants such as hostas.*

LEFT *The Single Late Group of tulips is valued for its late-flowering long-stemmed blooms. Colors range from white, pink, and red to this superb dark purple of the stately 'Queen of Night'.*

RIGHT *Members of the Greigii Group of tulips often have somewhat mottled leaves. 'Toronto' (pictured) has pinkish red flowers and a bright yellow base. It does well in a rock garden.*

RIGHT Tulipa hageri *bears pretty yellow to red-orange blooms on long thin stems. It is perfect for naturalizing: for best results, plant the bulbs in well-drained soil, and take care not to over-water them.*

VANDA

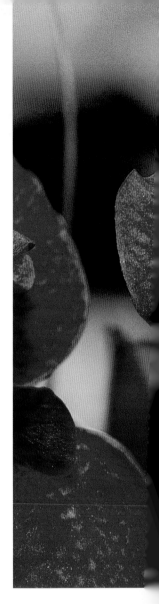

This is a group of about 50 species of sturdy single-stemmed orchids with representatives from Sri Lanka and India, across Southeast Asia to New Guinea and northeastern Australia. They are erect growing, with straplike semi-rigid leaves in 2 ranks. Larger plants may branch at the base, and have numerous, very thick, cordlike roots. The flowers appear from the stem at the base of the leaf. They have showy long-lasting blooms, which come in a range of colors, often with delicate markings. This is one of the most important genera of plants for cut-flower production in Thailand and Singapore. A large export industry has developed using a handful of species in an extensive hybridizing program, both within *Vanda* and in combination with related genera.

ABOVE Vanda *is a recently evolved genus with many hybrids, which often display the best of the genus's features, such as this superb speckling on the flowers of Pranerm Prai.*

CULTIVATION

Vanda plants are easy to grow in wooden baskets, with most thriving in bright, humid, and warm to intermediate conditions. During the warmer months they require liberal watering; reduce this over winter. Plants are mostly frost tender.

ABOVE *These magnificent flat-faced flowers of* Vanda Lumpini Red 'AM' *have hot pink patterning against a paler pink background. A healthy plant may flower 2 to 3 times a year.*

LEFT Vanda *Marlie Dolera, like most plants in the genus, thrives on sunlight. The pink blooms appear almost inquisitive on their slightly arching stems. Pla in a wooden basket, wher it can stay for years.*

Top Tip

Vanda plants need a coarse growing medium, so add charcoal or bark chips to the potting mix. Humidity is also important— regularly spray the leaves with a fine mist of water.

RIGHT Vanda *Iailor Blue has rich violet checkering on a white background. All Vanda plants are superb in hanging baskets or attached to the trunk of a water-tolerant plant.*

Favorites	Flower Color	Blooming Season	Flower Fragrance	Plant Height	Plant Width	Hardiness Zone	Frost Tolerance
Vanda Lumpini Red 'AM'	rose pink and cerise	most of the year	no	24–36 in (60–90 cm)	24 in (60 cm)	11–12	no
Vanda Marlie Dolera	deep rose and cerise	most of the year	no	3–6 ft (0.9–1.8 m)	18 in (45 cm)	11–12	no
Vanda Pranerm Prai	pale yellow with red markings	most of the year	no	24–36 in (60–90 cm)	24 in (60 cm)	11–12	no
Vanda Rothschildiana	violet-blue, dark-veined	most of the year	no	24 in (60 cm)	18 in (45 cm)	11–12	no
Vanda sanderiana var. *albata*	white and pale yellow-green	autumn	no	18–36 in (45–90 cm)	24 in (60 cm)	11–12	no
Vanda Tailor Blue	violet and white	most of the year	no	24–36 in (60–90 cm)	24 in (60 cm)	11–12	no

VERBASCUM

BELOW Verbascum chaixii *'Mont Blanc' is a tall sturdy plant clothed in downy gray-green leaves. Slender unbranched stems bear tightly packed pure white flowers with yellow centers.*

This figwort family (Scrophulariaceae) genus of some 300 species of annuals, biennials, perennials, and subshrubs includes cultivated plants and many that have become weeds outside their natural Eurasian and North African range. The commonly cultivated species usually form basal rosettes of large elliptical leaves, often quite heavily veined and sometimes felted. Tall upright flower spikes emerge from the rosettes carrying massed, small, 5-petalled flowers, usually in white, yellow, or pink to lavender shades. The Roman Pliny described *Verbascum,* noting that they attracted moths and thus called them moth mulleins, and in Greek legends the plant featured as a protection against evil and was used as an everyday medicinal plant to treat a variety of illnesses.

CULTIVATION

Hardiness varies with the species. Most prefer a sunny position with light, gritty, free-draining soil. They can tolerate summer drought but need moisture until flowering has ended. Propagate by division or from seed, depending on the growth form.

Top Tip

You can encourage the production of fresh flowering spikes by cutting off the spikes with spent flowers just below the bottommost flower.

ABOVE Verbascum acaule *is a rosette-forming perennial with toothed veined leaves. Bright yellow flowers are lifted above the foliage on slender stems.*

LEFT *The attractive copper-pink purple-centered flowers of* Verbascum chaixii *'Cotswold Beauty' emerge from big rosettes of crinkly gray-green leaves.*

RIGHT *The award-winning* Verbascum *'Helen Johnson' is a robust hardy perennial that performs well in a variety of conditions, including seaside gardens.*

Favorites

	Flower Color	Blooming Season	Flower Fragrance	Plant Height	Plant Width	Hardiness Zone	Frost Tolerance
Verbascum acaule	yellow	mid-summer	no	2 in (5 cm)	6 in (15 cm)	6–9	yes
Verbascum bombyciferum	yellow	summer	no	6 ft (1.8 m)	24 in (60 cm)	6–10	yes
Verbascum chaixii	yellow	summer	no	36 in (90 cm)	24 in (60 cm)	5–10	yes
Verbascum dumulosum	bright yellow	late spring to early summer	no	6–12 in (15–30 cm)	18 in (45 cm)	8–10	yes
Verbascum 'Helen Johnson'	deep apricot	late spring to early autumn	no	36 in (90 cm)	12 in (30 cm)	7–10	yes
Verbascum 'Jackie'	pinkish yellow	late spring to early autumn	no	18–24 in (45–60 cm)	18 in (45 cm)	7–10	yes

LEFT *An excellent ground cover, Veronica peduncularis 'Georgia Blue' bears wonderfully hued blooms against dark green foliage.* RIGHT *The delicate airy spires of Veronica 'Pink Damask' carry soft pink flowers above clumps of deep green foliage.*

Top Tip

These mostly hardy plants are not fussy, managing in any reasonable soil. Protect plants with downy leaves from winter wet.

FAR RIGHT *Veronica spicata 'Heidekind' is a mat-forming plant with silver-gray foliage and raspberry pink blooms.* BELOW *Though the blooms of Veronica austriaca subsp. teucrium are small, their abundance and strong clear blue color make a fabulous display in the garden.*

VERONICA

A figwort family (Scrophulariaceae) genus of 250 species of annuals and perennials, it is widespread in the northern temperate zones. Most species are creeping mat-forming plants that sometimes strike root as they spread. Their leaves tend to be small, oval to lance-shaped, often shallowly toothed, and rarely pinnately lobed. A few species have solitary flowers but more often upright spikes bearing many flowers develop in spring and summer. The color range is mainly in the white and pink to rich purple-blue shades, including some striking deep blue flowers. The genus is probably named in honor of St. Veronica, perhaps because the floral markings of some species are said to resemble the marks left on Veronica's sacred veil, with which she wiped Christ's face as he carried the cross.

CULTIVATION

Mostly hardy and easily grown in full or half sun with moist well-drained soil, some are great rockery plants, while others are suited to borders. Propagate from cuttings, self-rooted layers, division, or seed.

Favorites

	Flower Color	Blooming Season	Flower Fragrance	Plant Height	Plant Width	Hardiness Zone	Frost Tolerance
Veronica alpina	blue, white	late spring to early autumn	no	4–8 in (10–20 cm)	12 in (30 cm)	5–9	yes
Veronica austriaca	blue	late spring to early summer	no	8–18 in (20–45 cm)	12 in (30 cm)	5–10	yes
Veronica gentianoides	pale blue, sometimes white	late spring	no	12–24 in (30–60 cm)	12–24 in (30–60 cm)	4–9	yes
Veronica peduncularis	blue, white, pink; with pink veining	late spring to early summer	no	4 in (10 cm)	24 in (60 cm)	6–9	yes
Veronica 'Pink Damask'	soft pink	summer to autumn	no	36 in (90 cm)	18 in (45 cm)	5–9	yes
Veronica spicata	blue	summer	no	24 in (60 cm)	36 in (90 cm)	3–9	yes

Top Tip

Bring interest to the winter garden with late-flowering species such as *Viburnum tinus,* and with species such as *V. opulus,* whose leaves turn red in autumn.

VIBURNUM

This genus consists of 150 easily grown; cool-climate; deciduous, semi-evergreen, or evergreen; shrubby plants that are grown for their flowers, autumnal leaf color, and berries. Most have erect branching stems, paired leaves, and a spread about two-thirds their height. Small, sometimes fragrant, white flowers are displayed in dense clusters. In certain species the flowers somewhat resemble lacecap hydrangeas; like them, they bear sterile ray florets that surround a center of small fertile flowers. The buds and petals, particularly in cultivars, may be softly colored in tints of pink, yellow, and green. The berries are vividly colored, often red, blue, or black.

CULTIVATION

Light open positions and light well-drained soils are preferred. Many are drought tender. Prune the evergreens by clipping in late spring and the deciduous species by removing entire old stems after flowering. For a good berry display, grow several shrubs in the same area. Propagation is from cuttings taken in summer, or from seed in autumn.

BELOW *The large, snowball-like, creamy white flower clusters of* Viburnum opulus *'Roseum'—with pale rosy pink markings on some of the petals—usually appear in mid-spring with the leaves. This lovely form is thought to have appeared sometime in the sixteenth century.*

BELOW *Viburnum 'Eskimo' is an attractive dwarf shrub with a mounding form and semi-evergreen, glossy, dark green leaves. Many small white flowers, opening from pink-tinted buds, are borne in rounded heads in spring.*

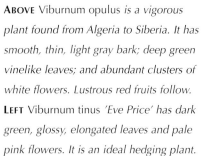

ABOVE Viburnum opulus *is a vigorous plant found from Algeria to Siberia. It has smooth, thin, light gray bark; deep green vinelike leaves; and abundant clusters of white flowers. Lustrous red fruits follow.* **LEFT** Viburnum tinus *'Eve Price' has dark green, glossy, elongated leaves and pale pink flowers. It is an ideal hedging plant.*

Favorites	Flower Color	Blooming Season	Flower Fragrance	Plant Height	Plant Width	Hardiness Zone	Frost Tolerance
Viburnum × bodnantense	deep pink to white-pink	autumn to early spring	yes	10 ft (3 m)	6 ft (1.8 m)	5–9	yes
Viburnum carlesii	white, sometimes flushed pink	spring	yes	4–8 ft (1.2–2.4 m)	4–8 ft (1.2–2.4 m)	5–9	yes
Viburnum 'Eskimo'	white	late spring	no	5–7 ft (1.5–2 m)	8–10 ft (2.4–3 m)	5–9	yes
Viburnum farreri	white to pink	late autumn to spring	yes	10 ft (3 m)	8 ft (2.4 m)	6–9	yes
Viburnum lantana	white	late spring to early summer	no	7–15 ft (2–4.5 m)	6–12 ft (1.8–3.5 m)	3–10	yes
Viburnum nudum	white to lemon yellow	summer	no	5–8 ft (1.5–2.4 m)	5–8 ft (1.5–2.4 m)	6–9	yes
Viburnum opulus	white	spring	no	8–15 ft (2.4–4.5 m)	6–12 ft (1.8–3.5 m)	3–9	yes
Viburnum plicatum	white	late spring to early summer	no	8–10 ft (2.4–3 m)	10–12 ft (3–3.5 m)	4–9	yes
Viburnum rhytidophyllum	white, yellowish to pinkish white	spring to early summer	no	15 ft (4.5 m)	12 ft (3.5 m)	6–10	yes
Viburnum sieboldii	creamy white	late spring to early summer	no	10–20 ft (3–6 m)	10 ft (3 m)	4–10	yes
Viburnum tinus	white to pink	autumn to spring	yes	8–12 ft (2.4–3.5 m)	5–8 ft (1.5–2.4 m)	7–10	yes
Viburnum trilobum	white	early summer	no	10–15 ft (3–4.5 m)	6–12 ft (1.8–3.5 m)	2–9	yes

LEFT Viburnum sieboldii *'Seneca' reaches up to 30 ft (9 m) in height. It has clusters of white flowers followed by persistent red fruits that mature to almost black.*
BELOW *This popular cultivar,* Viburnum plicatum *'Grandiflorum', is a selection of the wild parent form. It has large white flower clusters that turn pink over time.*

LEFT *From late spring to early summer, Viburnum plicatum bears numerous small, cream, fertile flowers surrounded by larger, pure white, sterile flowers.*

BELOW *Viburnum trilobum 'Wentworth' is popular with gardeners for its glorious crop of brightly colored long-lasting fruits and for its tolerance of damp soils.*

ABOVE *Viburnum lantana is a robust deciduous shrub that is notable for its new shoots, which have a silvery hairy appearance. Flower clusters are followed by red fruits.*

BELOW *The horizontal overlapping branches of Viburnum plicatum 'Mariesii' add interest to its spreading habit. Flat heads of mainly sterile flowers appear among the leaves.*

VIOLA

The type genus for the family Violaceae, *Viola* includes some 500 species of annuals, perennials, and subshrubs found in the world's temperate zones, ranging from the subarctic to the mountains of New Zealand. The majority are small clump-forming plants with lobed, kidney-shaped, or heart-shaped leaves. All violas have similarly shaped 5-petalled flowers, with the lower petal often carrying dark markings. White, yellow, and purple predominate but the flowers occur in every color, at least among the garden forms—often referred to as violets or pansies. The genus was named for a lover of the god Zeus, and *Viola tricolor* was used as a symbol of Athens. *V. palmata* is the floral emblem of Rhode Island, while both New Jersey and Wisconsin have adopted *V. sororia* as their state flower.

ABOVE Viola × wittrockiana *'Crystal Bowl Orange' is a member of the Crystal Bowl Series, which is appreciated for both compact form and abundant brightly colored flowers produced through-out summer.*

CULTIVATION

These plants are mostly very hardy and easily grown in sun or shade. The woodland species pre-fer humus-rich soil, while the rockery types require something grittier, but most are fine in any moist well-drained soil. Propa-gate by division, or from seed or basal cuttings.

RIGHT *A popular modern yellow Cornuta Hybrid, 'Pat Kavanagh' is a strong clump-forming viola.*

ABOVE *The neat yellow-eyed flowers of* Viola tricolor *'Bowles' Black' appear almost velvety, such is their rich black color.* **LEFT** *Viola × wittrockiana 'Norah Leigh', a Viola cultivar, makes a pleasing display with its clear purple flowers.*

Favorites	Flower Color	Blooming Season	Flower Fragrance	Plant Height	Plant Width	Hardiness Zone	Frost Tolerance
Viola adunca	lavender-blue, violet	spring	yes	2–4 in (5–10 cm)	4 in (10 cm)	4–9	yes
Viola, **Cornuta Hybrids**	white, purple, blue mauve, yellow	summer	no	6–12 in (15–30 cm)	3–6 in (8–15 cm)	4–10	yes
Viola obliqua	violet, white	spring to summer	no	3 in (8 cm)	10 in (25 cm)	8–9	yes
Viola odorata	violet, pink, white	late winter to spring	yes	3–12 in (8–30 cm)	2–4 ft (0.6–1.2 m)	4–10	yes
Viola pedata	violet	early spring to early summer	no	2 in (5 cm)	4 in (10 cm)	4–9	yes
Viola riviniana	pale purple	spring	no	2–4 in (5–10 cm)	8–15 in (20–38 cm)	5–10	yes
Viola sororia	white with violet-blue markings	spring to early summer	no	4–6 in (10–15 cm)	8 in (20 cm)	4–10	yes
Viola tricolor	purple, blue, yellow, white	spring to early autumn	no	6 in (15 cm)	6 in (15 cm)	4–10	yes
Viola, **Violettas**	blue, violet, mauve, yellow, white	spring to summer	yes	4–6 in (10–15 cm)	6–8 in (15–20 cm)	4–10	yes
Viola × **wittrockiana**	various	early spring to summer	no	8 in (20 cm)	8 in (20 cm)	5–10	yes
Viola × wittrockiana, **Fancy Pansies**	various	late autumn to early summer	no	4–8 in (10–20 cm)	6–10 in (15–25 cm)	7–10	yes
Viola × wittrockiana, **Violas**	white, black, blue, purple, yellow	winter to early summer	yes	3–8 in (8–20 cm)	6–12 in (15–30 cm)	7–10	yes

LEFT *As with all cultivars in the Fama Series,* Viola × wittrockiana *'Fama Blue Angel' bears large flowers over winter and spring. The flowers can be single-colored or a mixture of colors, as seen here.*

RIGHT Viola × wittrockiana *'Delta Pure Rose' has large boldly colored flowers and a compact form. Other cultivars in the Delta Series may have marked flowers.*

BELOW *The long-lasting* Viola × wittrockiana *'Molly Sanderson', a Viola cultivar, is notable for its gold center in an otherwise black flower.*

Top Tip

Plant garden pansies, violas, and violettas in window boxes, containers, and borders, or beneath taller shrubs for a splash of bold color.

ABOVE *An evergreen short-lived perennial, Viola × wittrockiana 'Irish Molly' is a favorite old Viola cultivar. Its smooth-textured flowers are orange-gold.*

ABOVE RIGHT *As its name attests, the small white flowers of the remarkable Viola sororia 'Freckles' are decorated with violet dots.*

RIGHT *Violetta cultivars are more compact than violas, and their oval flowers are splashed with yellow in the center, seen here on Viola 'Melinda'.*

WEIGELA

The 10 or 12 species of this genus within the Caprifoliaceae family are deciduous long-lived shrubs with opposite oblong to elliptic leaves. Their natural habitat is scrubland and the edges of woods in eastern Asia. Cultivated for their bell- or funnel-shaped flowers that are produced in late spring and early summer, they have pink, red, white, or sometimes yellow blooms, which grow on the previous year's wood. The leaves make a subtle background to the colorful flowers; mostly dark green, some hybrids have yellow-green, golden yellow, or variegated leaves.

CULTIVATION

Weigela shrubs need moist but well-drained fertile soil in sun or partial shade. Propagate by sowing seed in autumn in an area protected from winter frosts or from half-hardened cuttings in summer. Seed may not come true, as they hybridize freely.

Top Tip

These neat shrubs make excellent border plants and ornamentals. There are a great many hybrids, offering a choice of plant size and flower color.

LEFT Weigela 'Newport Red' is a widely grown hybrid, appreciated for its height, very hardy nature, and dark red flowers.

ABOVE *The vivid green leaves of* Weigela middendorfiana *surround pretty, pale yellow, bell-shaped flowers, marked at the throat with orange or red.*

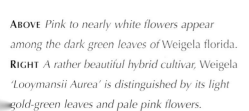

ABOVE *Pink to nearly white flowers appear among the dark green leaves of* Weigela florida. **RIGHT** *A rather beautiful hybrid cultivar,* Weigela *'Looymansii Aurea' is distinguished by its light gold-green leaves and pale pink flowers.*

Favorites	Flower Color	Blooming Season	Flower Fragrance	Plant Height	Plant Width	Hardiness Zone	Frost Tolerance
Weigela 'Bristol Ruby'	dark red	late spring to early summer	no	6 ft (1.8 m)	6 ft (1.8 m)	5–10	yes
Weigela florida	pink	late spring to early summer	no	8 ft (2.4 m)	8 ft (2.4 m)	5–10	yes
Weigela 'Looymansii Aurea'	pink	late spring to early summer	no	5 ft (1.5 m)	5 ft (1.5 m)	5–10	yes
Weigela middendorfiana	yellow, with red or orange throat	mid-spring to mid-summer	no	6 ft (1.8 m)	6 ft (1.8 m)	4–10	yes
Weigela 'Newport Red'	red	spring	no	6 ft (1.8 m)	6 ft (1.8 m)	5–10	yes
Weigela praecox	pink	late spring to early summer	no	8 ft (2.4 m)	6 ft (1.8 m)	5–10	yes

Top Tip

Wisterias can be trained against walls, up trees, and over arbors. They can also be treated as free-standing plants—just as long as they have strong support.

WISTERIA

Often seen luxuriously covering porches and verandahs and capable of spreading a considerable distance, the 10 species of twining deciduous vines of the genus *Wisteria* belong in the pea family (Fabaceae). When young, the pinnate leaves are a soft bronze-green shade but turn light green when mature. The flowers, primarily mauve in the species, occur in long racemes and start to open as the leaves expand. Cultivated forms occur in white and a range of pink to purple tones. The English botanist Thomas Nuttall named the genus for Caspar Wistar (1761–1818), a professor of anatomy at the University of Pennsylvania, though the reason for the change in spelling of his last name remains unclear.

CULTIVATION

Like *Clematis*, wisterias prefer to have their tops in the sun and their roots in cool, moist, humus-rich, well-drained soil. They are hardy, heavy-wooded, vigorous climbers that need sturdy support and routine trimming. Propagate from cuttings, layers, grafts, or seed.

LEFT *Wisteria* × *formosa* *'Yae-kokuryû' has pendent clusters of lavender-pink flowers. The sweet scent of the flowers is reminiscent of candies.*

Favorites	Flower Color	Blooming Season	Flower Fragrance	Plant Height	Plant Width	Hardiness Zone	Frost Tolerance
Wisteria brachybotrys 'Shiro-kapitan'	white to pale violet	late spring to early summer	yes	15–30 ft (4.5–9 m)	10–30 ft (3–9 m)	6–10	yes
Wisteria 'Caroline'	grayish purple	spring	yes	15–35 ft (4.5–10 m)	10–30 ft (3–9 m)	5–10	yes
Wisteria floribunda	white, pink, violet	late spring to early summer	yes	15–30 ft (4.5–9 m)	10–30 ft (3–9 m)	5–10	yes
Wisteria × *formosa*	violet	late spring to early summer	yes	15–30 ft (4.5–9 m)	10–30 ft (3–9 m)	6–10	yes
Wisteria frutescens	light purple to violet	late spring	yes	10–30 ft (3–9 m)	10–30 ft (3–9 m)	5–9	yes
Wisteria sinensis	white, pink	mid-spring to early summer	yes	15–35 ft (4.5–10 m)	10–30 ft (3–9 m)	5–10	yes

LEFT AND BELOW Wisteria floribunda, *native to Japan, is a vigorous climber, and is ideally suited to a pergola or arch. The species (left) and cultivars such as 'Alba' (below) have long drooping stems covered with fragrant blooms. Color varies from blue, lilac, and purple to white and pink.*

BOVE *Known as silky wisteria due to its softly hairy leaves, 'isteria brachybotrys 'Shiro-kapitan' bears heavy clusters of :hly scented white flowers. This is a good shrubby climber.*

YUCCA

Native to hot dry regions stretching from North to Central America and the West Indies, there are about 40 species in this genus within the Agavaceae family, including evergreen herbaceous perennials, trees, and shrubs. They have a strong bold form with strap- to lance-shaped leaves arranged in rosettes. Bell- to cup-shaped flowers are held on mostly erect panicles. Flowers are usually white or cream, though they may be tinged with purple. *Yucca whipplei* holds the record for the fastest plant growth; its flowering spike emerges and grows to 12 ft (3.5 m) in just 14 days. *Yucca glauca* is the state flower of New Mexico.

CULTIVATION

Yucca species grow best in loamy soil with good drainage, but will tolerate poor sandy soil. They range from frost hardy to frost tender. In colder areas it is advisable to grow the tender species in large pots in loam-based potting compost and overwinter indoors. If grown outdoors they need good light in summer, a monthly feed, and careful watering. Propagation is by sowing seed in spring, although seed may take some time to germinate. Take root cuttings in winter, or remove suckers in spring.

Top Tip

With their dramatic foliage and form, these are not plants for crowded corners. As in their native environment—deserts and sand dunes— a sparse setting suits them best.

Favorites	Flower Color	Blooming Season	Flower Fragrance
Yucca elata	creamy white	summer	yes
Yucca filamentosa	white	summer	no
Yucca gloriosa	white with pinkish tints	late summer to autumn	no
Yucca recurvifolia	cream	late summer to autumn	no
Yucca rostrata	white	autumn	no
Yucca whipplei	white	summer	no

RIGHT *The flowering stalk of* Yucca elata *grows to 6 ft (1.8 m) tall with creamy white flowers, sometimes tinted pink or green. The new green leaves are edged with fine hairs.*

RIGHT *Found from North Carolina to Florida, U.S.A.,* Yucca gloriosa *has stiff, thin, lance-shaped, blue-green leaves that turn dark green with age. Its pendent bell-shaped flowers are white, occasionally tinged pink.*

Plant Height	Plant Width	Hardiness Zone	Frost Tolerance
10–30 ft (3–9 m)	4–8 ft (1.2–2.4 m)	7–11	yes
4–12 ft (1.2–3.5 m)	5–8 ft (1.5–2.4 m)	4–10	yes
6–15 ft (1.8–4.5 m)	6–12 ft (1.8–3.5 m)	7–10	yes
5–8 ft (1.5–2.4 m)	4–8 ft (1.2–2.4 m)	7–11	yes
8–15 ft (2.4–4.5 m)	4–8 ft (1.2–2.4 m)	7–11	yes
6–12 ft (1.8–3.5 m)	3–6 ft (0.9–1.8 m)	7–11	yes

ABOVE *The remarkable* Yucca whipplei *subsp.* parishii *may grow to 7–20 ft (2–6 m) tall, and the purple-tinged flower-head, consisting of many flowers, averages 6 ft (1.8 m) tall.*
BELOW Yucca filamentosa *'Bright Edge' is a dwarf cultivar that produces multiple, long, yellow-edged leaves, and a number of flower stems bearing pendulous creamy blooms.*

ZANTEDESCHIA

The large calla lily (*Zantedeschia aethiopica*) is a plant that polarizes opinions. Some gardeners love it, while others can't abide its funereal associations. Named for Italian botanist Giovanni Zantedeschi (1773–1846), this arum family (Araceae) genus comprises 6 species of rhizome-rooted perennials from southern Africa. They have large, elongated, upward-facing, heart-shaped leaves that taper to long drip-tips and are sometimes speckled with translucent spots. The flower spathe is funnel-shaped and also tapers to a drip-tip. The spikelike spadix may be enclosed within the spathe or protrude slightly. Although the white calla is the best known, modern hybrids cover a wide color range. Both the leaves and the flowers are supported by strong stalks.

CULTIVATION

Cultivated *Zantedeschia* species may withstand moderate frosts. They lose their leaves in cold winters but may retain some in milder conditions. Some prefer damp, almost boggy conditions but most will grow in full or half sun in any garden soil that does not dry out. Propagate by division, or from basal offsets or seed.

ABOVE LEFT Zantedeschia 'Scarlet Pimpernel' makes a dramatic impact in the garden with its rich tones of red-orange and deep green. The flowers grow among, rather than above, the lush foliage.

RIGHT The large flowers of Zantedeschia aethiopica 'Green Goddess' differ from those of its parent species by the attractive splashes of green on the spathes, which are normally pure white.

Top Tip

These wonderful house plants will perform well if placed near a window and given some protection against the midday sun. They are also superb in cut-flower arrangements.

Plant Height	Plant Width	Hardiness Zone	Frost Tolerance
3 ft (0.9 m)	2 ft (0.6 m)	8–11	yes
12–18 in (30–45 cm)	10 in (25 cm)	9–11	no
18 in (45 cm)	12 in (30 cm)	9–10	no
24–36 in (60–90 cm)	8 in (20 cm)	9–10	no
18–24 in (45–60 cm)	12 in (30 cm)	9–10	no
18–36 in (45–90 cm)	12–24 in (30–60 cm)	9–10	no

ABOVE The summer blooming Zantedeschia 'Flame' produces yellow flowers, flecked with red, that turn a deeper orange-red with age.
LEFT The beautiful white spathe of Zantedeschia aethiopica surrounds a bright yellow spadix. The large flowers are borne from spring to autumn.

ZINNIA

This daisy family (Asteraceae) genus of around 20 species of annuals, perennials, and small shrubs occurs naturally from the south-central U.S.A. to Argentina, with its center in Mexico. They have soft light green leaves that range from linear to broadly spatula-shaped, depending on the species. While the flowers of the wild species are typically daisy-like with conspicuous ray and disc florets, modern seed strains are mainly doubles with the central disc florets mostly hidden or absent. The color range is extensive, though mostly confined to the warm tones: yellow, pink, orange, and red to mahogany. The genus is named for Johann Gottfried Zinn (1727–1759), a botany professor at Gottingen University.

ABOVE AND RIGHT Native to Mexico, the sturdy bushy Zinnia elegans *has produced many lovely cultivars. 'Dreamland Scarlet', above, is a compact dwarf variety with orange-red blooms, and 'Mammoth Exhibition', right, has large flowers in a range of colors.*

CULTIVATION

The cultivated plants are mostly frost tender summer annuals that should be grown in a sunny position sheltered from drafts. Moist well-drained soil is ideal, though they can withstand dry periods. Frequent deadheading is needed to prolong flowering. Propagate from seed.

LEFT The majority of cultivars derived from Zinnia elegans *have semi-double or double flowers, such as these lime green blooms of 'Envy'.*
RIGHT Zinnia haageana *'Stargold' produces small but densely clustered, dainty, star-shaped, golden flowers above dark green narrow leaves.*

Favorites	Flower Color	Blooming Season	Flower Fragrance	Plant Height	Plant Width	Hardiness Zone	Frost Tolerance
Zinnia elegans	various	summer to autumn	no	10–30 in (25–75 cm)	12 in (30 cm)	8–11	no
Zinnia elegans 'Envy'	pale yellow-green	summer to autumn	no	24 in (60 cm)	12 in (30 cm)	8–11	no
Zinnia haageana	orange, yellow, bronze	summer to early autumn	no	24 in (60 cm)	8 in (20 cm)	8–11	no
Zinnia peruviana	yellow, red	summer to early autumn	no	24–36 in (60–90 cm)	12 in (30 cm)	8–11	no
Zinnia 'Pink Splendor'	bright pink	summer to autumn	no	18–24 in (45–60 cm)	12–18 in (30–45 cm)	8–11	no
Zinnia 'Profusion Cherry'	dark red	late spring to mid-autumn	no	12 in (30 cm)	12 in (30 cm)	8–11	no

RIGHT *A deservedly popular cultivar, Zinnia 'Profusion Cherry' lives up to its name each flowering season with a mass of warm cherry red blooms with yellow centers providing continuous color over a number of months.*

Top Tip

Most cultivars
are derived from
Zinnia elegans and
Z. haageana. Use
dwarf forms to edge
paths, and taller
types at the back
of flowerbeds.

RIGHT *Justifiably popular
with gardeners,* Zinnia
haageana *'Crystal White' is
a trouble-free plant that will
produce white blooms over
a long flowering period.*
BELOW *The Splendor series
makes excellent cut flowers.
It includes the vibrant 'Pink
Splendor', below, as well
as red and yellow forms.*

GLOSSARY

Acid (of soils) Having a pH below about 6. The more strongly acid soils are mostly high in organic materials such as peat; lime (calcium carbonate) is completely absent from them. Acid soils dominate in regions of higher rainfall.

Adventitious (of roots or buds) Arising at various points along a stem rather than at the base or apex, or another such specific part of the plant.

Aerial (of plant parts) Arising anywhere above the ground.

Alkaline (of soils) Having a pH above about 8. Alkaline soils usually contain lime in the form of calcium carbonate or calcium hydroxide. They occur naturally in regions of lower rainfall.

Alpine (of plants) Those adapted to high mountain environments where they are usually blanketed in snow during winter; they may be damaged by heavy frost if not protected by snow, and in cold climates are therefore grown in "alpine houses" under glass. Alpine vegetation is the low herbs and shrubs growing above the treeline on high mountains.

Alternate (of the arrangement of leaves on a stem) Arising one from each node in a staggered formation. Many alternate leaf arrangements are also spiral, their points of attachment forming a spiral around the stem; others are alternate and distichous, forming 2 rows more or less in a single plane.

Angiosperm The flowering plants, defined by possession of true flowers and seeds fully enclosed in fruit. The vast majority of the world's larger land plant species are angiosperms, the main exceptions being the conifers, cycads, and ferns.

Annual A plant species or variety with a life span of 1 year or less, within which time it both flowers and fruits. All annuals depend entirely on seeds for reproduction.

Anther The pollen-containing organ of a stamen, the other part being the filament (stalk).

Aquatic A plant species that grows in water for at least the greater part of its life cycle. Aquatics are divided into submerged, emergent, and floating.

Axil The inner angle between an organ such as a leaf and the organ that supports it, usually a stem.

Axillary (of buds, flowers, inflorescences) Arising from a leaf axil.

Basal At or near the base of a plant's trunk, stem, leaf, etc.

Biennial A plant that completes its life cycle within 2 years and then dies. It may flower and fruit in each of the 2 years, or only in the second year.

Botanical name The internationally recognized name of a plant species, genus, family, etc., usually derived from Latin or Latinized Greek elements, and published in conformity with the *International Code of Botanical Nomenclature.*

Bract A modified leaf associated with a flower or an inflorescence; not to be confused with a sepal, though in some plants bracts may mimic sepals.

Bud The early stage of a flower or group of flowers, or of a leafy shoot (vegetative bud), before expanding or elongating.

Bulb Storage organ of herbaceous perennials consisting of expanded fleshy leaf bases arranged in concentric layers. A bulb is tunicate if the leaf bases are all encircling, as in an onion, or scaly if they are narrower but with overlapping edges, as in a lily.

Bulbil A small bulb, emerging from the axil of a leaf. Distinct to a bulblet, which is produced at the base of a parent bulb and referred to as an "offset."

Calyx The lowest or outermost of the layers attached to the receptacle of a flower. The calyx consists of sepals, that may be separate or partly or fully fused to one another and which are commonly green in contrast to the more colorful petals.

Carpel The fundamental unit of a flower's female organ, usually differentiated into an ovary containing ovules (embryonic seeds) and a narrower style tipped by a stigma that receives pollen. Carpels may be single or multiple in the 1 flower, and multiple carpels are often fused together.

Columnar (of growth habit) Shaped more or less like a column or cylinder.

Common name The name of a plant species that is not its botanical or scientific name and has no scientific status. Common names are generally in the language of the country where the plant is growing. A species may have many common names, or if obscure may never have acquired any.

Conservatory An attachment to a house, glass-roofed or at least with glass external walls, in which cold-tender plants may be grown.

Corm A swollen stem modified for the purpose of food storage and annual renewal, usually underground and upright, with a new corm or section of corm added above each growing season and an old one withering below.

Corolla Collective term for the petals of a flower, which may be separate or wholly or partly fused into a tube, bell, or disc.

Corona A crownlike part of a flower, consisting of a ring of fused outgrowths from either the petals or stamens. Species of *Narcissus* have a prominent corona arising from the petals.

Corymb An inflorescence with the stalks of the lower flowers elongated to bring them to the same level as the upper flowers.

Cross A less formal term for hybrid, also applicable to plants resulting from cross-pollination of different races or cultivars within a species.

Cross-pollination Transmission of pollen from one plant to another plant that is not part of the same clone/cultivar, with resulting fertilization of its flowers.

Cultivar A cultivated variety that has been given a distinguishing name. A cultivar is assumed to be constant in its horticultural qualities and able to be propagated with those qualities unaltered. Modern cultivars must be given names of non-Latin form. Their names are enclosed in single quotes and are capitalized, e.g. 'Golden Delicious'.

Cultivar group A group of cultivars that share a common character or origin, e.g. *Prunus*, Sato-zakura Group.

Cultivated (of a plant species) Established in cultivation with its requirements known to gardeners.

Cutting A piece of plant stem (more rarely of leaf, root, or rhizome) cut off the parent plant for the purposes of propagation; its lower end is inserted in soil or a sterile medium such as sand until roots form and a new plant is obtained.

Deciduous (of a plant species) Losing all leaves at a certain season of the year, usually winter in the case of cool-climate species, usually the dry season in the case of tropical species.

Disease Any kind of ill health or disfigurement of a plant caused by micro-organisms such as viruses, bacteria, or fungi, or by deficiency or excess of a particular nutrient element. Distinct from pests, which is a term applied to more visible insects or other fauna that attack the plant.

Disc floret One of the individual small flowers that make up the central disc of a daisy flower (family Asteraceae), when these are different from the outer circle of longer-petalled ray florets, as in a sunflower.

Dormant State of suspended growth of a plant, usually during winter or other adverse season and usually in a leafless state.

Double (of garden flowers) Having more than the regular number of petals occurring in the wild form, found mainly in cultivars.

Elliptic (of leaves, petals, etc.) In the shape of an ellipse but commonly with both ends more or less pointed, with the widest part of the structure at the midpoint of the length.

Endemic (of a species, genus, etc.) Occurring in the wild only in a single readily defined geographical region, e.g. *Franklinia* endemic to Georgia, U.S.A.; *Sorb anglica* is a British endemic.

Entire (of margins of leaves, leaflets, petals, etc.) Smooth, without indentations or projections such as teeth or lobes.

Epiphyte (of a plant species) One that habitually grows in the wild on the branches or trunk of a tree, well above the ground. Epiphytes do not feed on the living tissue of their host but on dead bark, leaf litter, and dust, often using a symbiotic fungus to extract nutrients from these. Most cultivated orchids are epiphytes.

Evergreen (of a plant species) Maintaining its foliage through all seasons, although old leaves may be shed in larger numbers in certain seasons.

Family The next major category above genus within plant classification. A family may contain a single genus (e.g. Cercidiphyllaceae) or many genera (e.g. Fabaceae, with around 650 genera). In modern systems all family names end in -aceae. A family name is grammatically a plural.

Fertile (of soil) Having adequate amounts of the major and minor mineral nutrients for plant growth; (of plants or flowers) bearing viable sexual organs.

Fertilize (in gardening) To add nutrients to soil; (in botany) to bring pollen to a stigma and effectively pollinate it so that the pollen nucleus combines with the egg nucleus in the ovule.

Filament The stalk of a stamen, bearing the anther at its tip.

Floret Any one of the small flowers in a dense inflorescence such as a flowerhead.

Flower The reproductive organ of all members of the flowering plants (angiosperms) consisting typically of a perianth, which is often differentiated into calyx and corolla, a group of stamens that release pollen, and one or more carpels containing ovules that on fertilization develop into seeds. Many flowers are reduced in structure with some of these parts missing.

Flowerhead Any dense cluster of flowers that is more or less regular in size.

Forma A level in botanical classification below species, subspecies, and variety, normally applied to a variation in a single character that may recur in wild stands. Abbreviated as f., and referred to as "form" in English.

Frost hardy (of plant species, varieties, or cultivars) Able to withstand exposure to frost without damage to foliage, stems, or whatever parts normally persist through winter. Frost hardiness is entirely relative to climate, for example *Abutilon megapotamicum* survives the light frosts in the hills of southeastern Australia (Zone 8) but will not survive outdoors in the interior of Britain (Zone 7); and while *Araucaria araucana* tolerates winters in most parts of Britain, it is killed outright by winter frost in northeastern U.S.A. (Zone 5).

Fruit (in botany) The seed-containing organ of any of the flowering plants, whether fleshy or dry in texture. Normally a single fruit is developed from a single flower.

Genus (plural genera) The next level of botanical classification above species. The genus name can stand by itself, e.g. *Erysimum* (the wallflower genus), but it also forms the first part of a species name, e.g. *Erysimum asperum* (the Western wallflower).

Growth habit The overall form or shape of a plant.

Habitat (of a species) The sum of geographical locations, soil, topography, and vegetation type in which a species is found wild.

Hair Any fine hairlike outgrowth from the surface of a plant part. If it is noticeably flattened it is usually termed a scale.

Hardy (of a species or cultivar) Ability to survive and thrive in a hostile environment; gardeners in cold climates have generally narrowed its meaning to frost hardy.

Hemisphere One half of the earth's surface, most commonly the Northern or Southern Hemisphere, divided by the equator, although historically Eastern and Western Hemispheres were just as important, the latter centered on the Americas.

Herb (in botany) A plant with non-woody stems; (in gardening and cookery) an edible plant that adds flavor rather than bulk to a cooked dish or salad.

Herbaceous (in gardening) usually taken to refer to perennials that die back each winter to a rootstock, rhizome, or tuber.

Horticulture The practice of growing plants, and other aspects of gardening. Commercial horticulture embraces the fruit, nut, and cut-flower industries as well as the nursery and landscape industries.

Humus The organic matter in soil, derived in nature from leaf and twig litter, dead roots, and decayed tree trunks; in gardens it can be added in the form of compost, manure, or peat. Humus greatly improves soil by retaining moisture and mineral nutrients, keeping the soil open and well aerated.

Hybrid The progeny resulting from fertilization of a species by a different species, combining the genetic makeup of both. The progeny of hybrids continue to be hybrids.

Incurved (of leaves, petals) With margins curved both upwards and inwards.

Inflorescence Specialized flower-bearing branch of a plant, together with the flowers on it.

Introduced (of plant species) Not native (indigenous) to the country or region in question; usually implying deliberate introduction by humans.

Invasive (of a species or cultivar) Tending to spread well beyond the place where it was planted in the garden, whether by seeds or rhizomes, etc., and thereby becoming a nuisance.

Leaflet One of the leaflike parts that make up a compound leaf.

Lime Mineral component of or additive to soil, always a form of the element calcium. There are various forms of lime, such as quicklime; all are alkaline or at least neutralize acidity in soils, making certain nutrients more available to plants, others less so.

Loam A soil in which the proportions of clay, sand, and silt are fairly evenly balanced and the humus content is adequate. A clay loam is one with a higher clay content, a sandy loam is one with more sand.

Lobe (of leaves) A large projection of the margin, generally one that measures at least a quarter of the distance from the leaf's main central vein (the midrib) to its outer edge.

Mulch (in gardening) Any material that can be spread over the soil surface for the purposes of preventing water loss, insulating against cold or heat, and suppressing weed growth. Mulches may consist of gravel, pebbles, plastic film, newspapers, straw, wood or bark chips, dead leaves, grass clippings, or compost, to name the most common.

Native (of a species) Forming part of the original wild flora of the country or region under consideration.

Naturalized (of a species) Not originally native to the country or region under consideration but now established, reproducing itself freely and spreading into new areas without human aid. In gardening, naturalizing sometimes means letting a particular plant multiply and spread over successive seasons, with no need for cultivation.

Nectary A gland found at the base of flowers that secretes nectar, the sugary liquid that is collected by bees.

Neutral (of soils) Having a pH of 7 or very close to 7 (on a scale of 0–14), that is, neither acid (below 7) nor alkaline (above 7).

Nutrient (of plants) The mineral elements that the plant absorbs from the soil or growing medium through its roots, in the form of salts dissolved in the water taken up. They are divided into the major or essential elements nitrogen, phosphorus, potassium, sulfur, calcium, and magnesium; and the minor or trace elements iron, manganese, copper, zinc, boron, and molybdenum.

Opposite (of leaves) Attached to the stem in pairs, on opposite sides of a node.

Organic (of substances) Being composed of molecules that originated in living things.

Ornamental A plant grown primarily for ornamental purposes, as opposed to food, timber, fiber, drugs, and the like.

Ovary (in flowers) The swollen part of the female organ containing the ovules.

Panicle In the looser sense, any inflorescence that is repeatedly branched, though more strictly it is a branched raceme.

Pedicel The stalk of an individual flower.

Peduncle The common stalk of a group of flowers or of a whole inflorescence.

Perennial (of a species) In botanical usage, a plant that has an indefinite life span, or at least 3 years's life span. By this criterion all trees and shrubs are perennials. But gardeners tend to use the term to mean a herbaceous perennial, in contrast to trees and shrubs.

Perianth The parts of a flower that enclose the sexual organs in bud, normally the combined petals (corolla) and sepals (calyx).

Pests (in gardening) Mostly insects or other small fauna that feed on plants, either weakening them or disfiguring them.

Petal The inner layer of the 2 layers of organs that enclose the sexual organs of a flower, the outer being the sepals. Petals are often thin and brightly colored or white, and are seldom green like sepals. The petals of a single flower are collectively termed the corolla. They may be fused into a tube, bell, or funnel, or may be absent.

Petiole The stalk of an individual leaf.

pH (in chemistry) The scale by which acidity and alkalinity are measured, applicable to soils, potting media, and water for irrigation. It runs from 0 (extreme acidity) to 14 (extreme alkalinity) with the midpoint 7 regarded as neutral.

Picotee Fine colored edging on petals, producing a lacy effect, such as on the flowers of certain *Dianthus* cultivars.

Pinnate (of compound leaves) Having the leaflets attached in 2 rows, on either side of a center stalk, in the manner of a feather.

Pod Any fruit that is hollow inside and eventually splits open to reveal its seeds.

Pollen The dustlike material produced by the male organs of flowering plants, each tiny grain containing a male nucleus that combines with a female nucleus in an ovule to prduce a seed. In flowering plants a pollen grain is received on the stigma and "germinates," producing an extremely fine tube that grows down through the style and into an ovule, the nucleus descending through this tube.

Pollination The mechanism by which pollen is transferred from stamens to stigma, whether in the same flower or different flowers, or to different plants. Agents of pollination include wind, insects, and birds; pollen can be deliberately transferred by humans.

Propagation The practice of multiplying plants artificially, whether by seed, cuttings, layers, grafts, divisions, or tissue culture.

Prostrate (of plants) With the branches lying flat on the ground.

Pubescence The coating of hairs on plant parts such as the calyx.

Raceme An unbranched inflorescence that consists of an elongated stem bearing a succession of stalked flowers, the youngest located at the tip.

Ray floret (in members of the daisy family, Asteraceae or Compositae) The outer ring of florets in a head, when these are distinct from the inner ones or disc florets. They usually have longer petals that are fused together side by side to form a flat strap.

Receptacle That part of a flower, at the apex of its stalk, to which all the other parts (the sepals, petals, stamens, and carpels) are attached.

Recurved (of leaves, stalks, petals, or sepals) Curved downward; (of a leaf margin) curved gently downward but not rolled.

Reflexed Like recurved but more sharply bent rather than curved.

Rhizome A stem that runs horizontally along or below the soil surface, putting out roots along its length and sending up erect shoots at intervals; it may be swollen and behave as a storage or overwintering organ.

Root The organ of absorption of water and mineral nutrients, as well as of anchorage to the soil, in the higher plants. Roots are distinguished from underground stems (such as rhizomes) by their anatomical structure.

Rootstock The base of a stem, from which the roots emerge. The underground overwintering stem bases of many herbaceous perennials are termed rootstocks. In grafting, the rootstock is the stem, usually grown from a seedling, onto which the scion is grafted.

Rosette Any group of plant organs such as leaves that radiate out from a central point on a stem, e.g. the "stemless" yuccas or the short shoots of *Cedrus*.

Scion The subject of propagation, usually a cut piece of branch or twig of the desired cultivar, which is grafted on to the rootstock.

Seed Organ of reproduction and dispersal of flowering plants, which develops inside the fruit. A seed consists of a plant embryo, food storage tissue, and a protective seed coat. A seed may remain dormant for a long period before its germination is initiated by moisture and warmth.

Semi-double (of cultivars) Having flowers with more than the normal number of petals of the wild species, and usually forming more than 1 row, but with stamens still visible in the flower's center.

Sepal A single segment of the calyx of a flower. Sepals are normally green in contrast to the colored petals; they may be fused to one another, at least toward their bases.

Series (of cultivars) A group of cultivars with a common ancestry and often sold under the one name but with mixed colors; this is most usually encountered in annuals.

Simple (of leaves) Individual leaves without discrete leaflets.

Single (of cultivars) Having flowers with much the same number of petals as the wild species of the genus to which they belong, or at least having the petals forming a single row.

Solitary (of flowers) Borne singly, not grouped in an inflorescence. A flower may be solitary and terminal, borne at the tip of a branch, or solitary and axillary, borne in a leaf axil.

Spadix A spike or dense panicle of flowers. This is a somewhat obsolete term among botanists except for its use for the specialized inflorescence of members of the arum family.

Spathe A large bract that encloses a whole inflorescence in bud. Like spadix, this term is now most commonly used for the inflorescence of members of the arum family.

Species (abbreviation sp., plural spp.) The basic unit of plant classification, usually consisting of a population of individuals that are fairly uniform in character and breed freely with one another over many generations without obvious change in their progeny. If a species breeds with another species, the resulting progeny do not remain constant or do not produce viable seed.

The scientific name of a species consists of the name of the genus to which it belongs, followed by a name referred to as the specific epithet, somewhat like a person's given name— e.g. *Magnolia stellata*.

Spur A backward projection from a petal or sepal in the shape of a spur or horn, usually hollow and containing nectar.

Stalk The part of a leaf that attaches to the plant stem, at least when it is distinct from the leaf blade; likewise the organ that supports an individual flower, or that supports a whole inflorescence.

Stamen The male reproductive organ in a flower, consisting typically of a slender stalk and a pollen-sac, which opens by either a slit or pore to release pollen. The stamens form the third row of organs from the outside of a flower, inside the sepals and petals.

Stem The organ of a plant that supports the leaves and flowers, and to which the roots are attached; in the broadest sense, any shoot, trunk, branch, or twig is a stem.

Stigma The part of a carpel that is receptive to pollen, which is often separated from the ovary by a slender style.

Subshrub A low-growing shrub that is not very woody at the base, and hence is somewhat intermediate between a shrub and a herbaceous perennial.

Subspecies A major division of a species, above variety and forma, though used by some botanists instead of variety. A subspecies may be thought of as a species still in the process of evolving but not yet reproductively isolated from its related subspecies except by geography. Abbreviated to subsp. or ssp.

Taproot A thick central root that goes vertically down into the soil; a carrot is an extreme example.

Temperate (of climates) Those of lands lying between the Tropic of Cancer and the Arctic Circle, or between the Tropic of Capricorn and the Antarctic Circle. Temperate climates may also be found at high altitudes in the tropics.

Tepals Where the sepals and petals are virtually indistinguishable, as is the case with certain tulips and lilies.

Terminal (of flowers) Positioned at the apex of a stem or inflorescence branch and terminating its growth.

Terrestrial (of a species) Normally found in the ground and on dry land, as opposed to epiphytic or aquatic.

Tessellated (of corolla) Distinctive checkered pattern against a contrasting background.

Throat (of a flower) The inside of the tube of a funnel-shaped or trumpet-shaped flower.

Tropical (of climates, species) Occurring in the lands between the Tropic of Cancer and Tropic of Capricorn.

Tuber (adjective tuberous) A stem modified into a storage organ, either underground or at the soil surface. A potato is the archetypal tuber.

Umbel An inflorescence in which the individual flower stalks radiate from the end of the common stalk.

Variegated (of leaves) Mottled, streaked, edged, or striped with colors (mostly white to yellow) other than the normal green of wild plants. They are mostly found in ornamental cultivars.

Variety (in plant classification) A subdivision of a species, of lower rank than subspecies but higher than forma. In a looser sense variety may refer to a cultivar.

Whorled (of leaves) Arranged in groups of 3 or more at a single node, distributed equally around each particular node.

KEYS

The following lists are keys to the Seasonal Calendars and Cultivation Guidelines that follow. The Seasonal Calendars are divided into summer, autumn, winter, and spring; the page numbers given under the main plant group headings in these keys will take you to the first entry for that plant group in each particular season.

The Cultivation Guidelines are easy to follow. If, for example, you wish to find out how to propagate *Convolvulus tricolor*, you simply locate it in the keys below (Annuals, low-growing, summer–autumn-flowering), find that group in the Cultivation Guidelines, then move across the columns until you reach the one headed "Propagation."

For ease of reference, each of the plants listed here is also listed in the Index to Plants, with page numbers referring to where it occurs in the text and where it occurs in these keys.

ANNUALS AND PERENNIALS

Summer page 602   Autumn page 616
Winter page 630   Spring page 644

The cultivation of annual and perennial plants is rewarding, as a large variety of flowering plants can be grown to bloom throughout the year. To grow the more unusual annual flowers from seed requires patience, as germination can be erratic, and constant attention, as seedlings need an even light source and must never be allowed to dry out. In other words, their best chance of healthy development requires daily care.

Perennials, on the other hand, are not called hardy for nothing. Different perennials can be found for cold mountainous climates, for salt-spray coastal gardens, and for excessively dry, wet, or shady positions. Simple maintenance practices such as removing spent flowers, checking under leaves for pests, and a tidy up during winter are all they need. Regular mulching and fertilizing during the growing and flowering seasons helps maintain their vigor, and before long there will be excess plants to give away to friends.

Annuals, low-growing, summer–autumn-flowering
Begonia, Semperflorens-
    cultorum Group
Calceolaria, Herbeohybrida
    Group
Calceolaria, Herbeohybrida
    Group, 'Sunset Red'
Convolvulus tricolor
Eschscholzia caespitosa
Eschscholzia caespitosa 'Sundew'
Iberis amara
Mimulus 'Highland Red'
Mimulus 'Malibu'
Nemesia strumosa
Nemesia versicolor
Nicotiana 'Avalon Bright Pink'
Nicotiana 'Saratoga Mixed'
Phlox drummondii
Tagetes erecta, Antigua Series
Tagetes patula
Tagetes patula, Bonanza Series
Tagetes, Safari Series
Zinnia 'Profusion Cherry'

Annuals, low-growing, spring–summer-flowering
Dianthus, Annual Pinks
Eschscholzia californica
Eschscholzia californica 'Purple
    Gleam'
Eschscholzia lobbii
Iberis umbellata
Lobelia erinus
Lobularia maritima
Lobularia maritima 'Carpet
    of Snow'
Lobularia maritima 'Easter
    Bonnet Deep Rose'
Lobularia maritima 'Easter
    Bonnet Lavender'

Lobularia maritima 'Rosie O'Day'

Lobularia maritima 'Snow
    Crystals'

Petunia 'Pink Wave'

Petunia 'Purple Wave'

Petunia 'Superior Cascade Blue'

Petunia, Surfinia Series, 'Surfinia
    Pink'

Schizanthus, Angel Wings Mix

Schizanthus, Disco Mix

Schizanthus, Dwarf Bouquet Mix

Schizanthus, Star Parade Mix

Schizanthus 'Sweet Lips'

Schizanthus × wisetonensis

Viola tricolor

Viola, Violettas

Viola × wittrockiana

Viola × wittrockiana, Fancy
    Pansies

Viola × wittrockiana, Violas

Annuals, low-growing,
winter–spring-flowering

Eschscholzia mexicana

Felicia bergeriana

Annuals, medium-growing,
summer-flowering

Antirrhinum majus

Antirrhinum majus, Sonnet Series

Catharanthus roseus

Catharanthus roseus 'Albus'

Catharanthus roseus 'Blue Pearl'

Catharanthus roseus 'Cooler
    Blush'

Catharanthus roseus, Pacifica
    Series

Catharanthus roseus, Victory
    Series

Celosia argentea, Plumosa Group

Celosia argentea, Plumosa
    Group, 'Castle Mix'

Celosia argentea, Plumosa
    Group, 'Forest Fire'

Celosia spicata

Celosia 'Startrek Lilac'

Celosia 'Venezuela'

Clarkia unguiculata

Consolida regalis 'Blue Cloud'

Coreopsis tinctoria

Cosmos bipinnatus, Sonata Series

Cosmos sulphureus

Echium vulgare

Eustoma grandiflorum

Eustoma grandiflorum 'Echo
    Blue'

Eustoma grandiflorum 'Echo
    White'

Eustoma grandiflorum 'Echo
    Yellow'

Eustoma grandiflorum 'Forever
    Blue'

Eustoma grandiflorum 'Lilac Rose'

Gaillardia pulchella

Gaillardia pulchella, Plume Series

Gypsophila elegans

Impatiens balsamina

Impatiens walleriana

Limonium sinuatum

Mimulus guttatus

Nicotiana langsdorffii

Papaver commutatum

Papaver somniferum

Petunia, Daddy Series

Petunia integrifolia

Rudbeckia hirta

Rudbeckia hirta 'Irish Eyes'

Scabiosa atropurpurea

Tagetes tenuifolia

Tropaeolum majus

Tropaeolum majus 'Empress
    of India'

Tropaeolum majus 'Hermine
    Grashoff'

Zinnia elegans

Zinnia elegans 'Envy'

Zinnia haageana

Zinnia peruviana

Zinnia 'Pink Splendor'

Annuals, medium-growing,
spring–summer-flowering

Calendula officinalis

Calendula officinalis 'Bon Bon'

Calendula officinalis 'Fiesta
    Gitana'

Calendula officinalis 'Greenheart
    Orange'

Calendula officinalis 'Indian
    Prince'

Calendula officinalis, Pacific
    Beauty Series

Centaurea cyanus

Clarkia amoena

Clarkia amoena, Grace Series

Clarkia amoena, Satin Series

Clarkia concinna

Clarkia pulchella

Consolida ajacis

Consolida 'Frosted Skies'

Consolida, Giant Imperial Series

Consolida, Giant Imperial Series,
    'Miss California'

Consolida, Giant Imperial Series,
    'Rosalie'

Dianthus barbatus

Echium plantagineum

Lupinus nanus

Matthiola incana

Matthiola incana 'Cinderella Rose'

Matthiola incana 'Cinderella
    White'

Matthiola incana 'Vintage
    Burgundy'

Matthiola incana 'Vintage
    Lavender'

Matthiola longipetala
Papaver nudicaule

Annuals, tall-growing, spring–summer-flowering

Lathyrus odoratus

Annuals, tall-growing, summer-flowering

Amaranthus caudatus
Amaranthus caudatus 'Green Tails'
Amaranthus cruentus
Amaranthus hypochondriacus
Amaranthus tricolor
Amaranthus tricolor 'Joseph's Coat'
Cosmos bipinnatus
Cosmos bipinnatus 'Sea Shells'
Cosmos bipinnatus, Sensation Series
Digitalis purpurea
Echium pininana
Echium wildpretii
Euphorbia marginata
Helianthus annuus
Helianthus annuus 'Ring of Fire'
Helianthus annuus 'Ruby Eclipse'
Nicotiana alata
Nicotiana sylvestris
Nicotiana tabacum
Verbascum bombyciferum

Perennials, spring– early summer-flowering

Anemone sylvestris
Anigozanthos, Bush Gems Series, 'Bush Haze'
Anigozanthos, Bush Gems Series, 'Bush Nugget'
Anigozanthos, Bush Gems Series, 'Bush Ruby'

Anigozanthos flavidus
Anigozanthos 'Pink Joey'
Armeria 'Bee's Ruby'
Armeria girardii
Armeria juniperifolia
Armeria maritima
Armeria 'Westacre Beauty'
Artemisia alba
Asclepias linaria
Centaurea dealbata
Centaurea montana
Clivia caulescens
Clivia miniata
Clivia miniata 'Flame'
Clivia miniata 'Kirstenbosch Yellow'
Clivia miniata 'Striata'
Coreopsis grandiflora
Coreopsis lanceolata
Coreopsis 'Sunray'
Dianthus, Malmaison Carnations
Dianthus, Perpetual-flowering Carnations
Dianthus, Pinks
Dicentra 'Bacchanal'
Dicentra formosa
Dicentra 'Langtrees'
Dicentra spectabilis
Euphorbia amygdaloides
Euphorbia cyparissias
Euphorbia × *martinii*
Euphorbia nicaeensis
Geranium cinereum
Geranium 'Patricia'
Geranium phaeum
Geranium 'Sue Crûg'
Geranium sylvaticum
Geranium tuberosum
Gypsophila paniculata
Gypsophila paniculata 'Bristol Fairy'

Lathyrus splendens
Limonium bourgaei
Lupinus 'Bishop's Tipple'
Lupinus 'Pagoda Prince'
Lupinus, Russell Hybrids
Meconopsis cambrica
Meconopsis napaulensis
Meconopsis × *sheldonii*
Oenothera fruticosa
Osteospermum, Nasinga Series
Osteospermum, Side Series
Osteospermum 'Sunny Gustav'
Paeonia cambessedesii
Paeonia lactiflora
Paeonia mlokosewitschii
Paeonia officinalis
Paeonia tenuifolia
Paeonia veitchii
Penstemon eatonii
Penstemon parryi
Phlox divaricata
Potentilla 'Flamenco'
Ranunculus aconitifolius
Ranunculus constantinopolitanus
Ranunculus gramineus
Scabiosa farinosa
Trifolium pannonicum
Trifolium rubens
Trillium albidum
Trillium chloropetalum
Trillium erectum
Trillium grandiflorum
Trillium ovatum
Trillium pusillum
Veronica austriaca
Veronica gentianoides

Perennials, spring– early summer-flowering, short-lived

Anigozanthos manglesii
Aquilegia caerulea

Aquilegia canadensis
Aquilegia 'Crimson Star'
Aquilegia, Songbird Series
Aquilegia vulgaris
Delphinium nudicaule
Dianthus, Border Carnations
Digitalis ciliata
Erysimum 'Gold Shot'
Erysimum 'Wenlock Beauty'
Gaillardia 'Kobold'
Meconopsis betonicifolia
Myosotis sylvatica
Myosotis sylvatica 'Blue Ball'
Myosotis sylvatica 'Music'
Viola, Cornuta Hybrids

Perennials, summer-flowering, sun

Achillea ageratifolia
Achillea 'Coronation Gold'
Achillea millefolium
Achillea 'Terracotta'
Achillea tomentosa
Achillea umbellata
Agapanthus africanus
Agapanthus campanulatus
Agapanthus inapertus
Agapanthus 'Lilliput'
Agapanthus praecox
Agapanthus 'Rancho White'
Agastache aurantica 'Apricot
    Sunrise'
Agastache 'Blue Fortune'
Agastache cana
Agastache foeniculum
Agastache rupestris
Agastache 'Tutti Frutti'
Alstroemeria 'Apollo'
Alstroemeria aurea
Alstroemeria, Dr Salter's Hybrids
Alstroemeria, Dutch Hybrids
Alstroemeria, Ligtu Hybrids

Alstroemeria pelegrina
Antirrhinum grosii
Antirrhinum hispanicum
Antirrhinum molle
Antirrhinum sempervirens
Aquilegia flabellata
Armeria alliacea
Artemisia lactiflora
Artemisia ludoviciana
Asclepias speciosa
Asclepias subulata
Asclepias tuberosa
Aster radula
Campanula lactiflora
Centaurea macrocephala
Delphinium, Belladonna Group
Delphinium grandiflorum
Delphinium 'Michael Ayres'
Delphinium, Pacific Hybrids
Dianthus caryophyllus
Diascia integerrima
Digitalis grandiflora
Digitalis parviflora
Echinacea angustifolia
Echinacea pallida
Echinacea purpurea
Echinacea purpurea 'Magnus'
Echinacea purpurea 'White
    Lustre'
Echinacea purpurea 'White Swan'
Echinops bannaticus
Echinops bannaticus 'Taplow
    Blue'
Echinops ritro
Echinops ritro 'Blue Glow'
Echinops sphaerocephalus
Echinops sphaerocephalus 'Arctic
    Glow'
Eryngium amethystinum
Eryngium giganteum
Eryngium 'Jos Eijking'
Eryngium planum

Eryngium variifolium
Euphorbia griffithii
Gaillardia 'Burgunder'
Gaillardia 'Dazzler'
Gentiana makinoi
Helenium bigelovii
Helenium hoopesii
Hemerocallis lilioasphodelus
Hemerocallis 'Stella de Oro'
Iberis gibraltarica
Kniphofia northiae
Kniphofia 'Primrose Beauty'
Lathyrus grandiflorus
Lathyrus nervosus
Leucanthemum vulgare
Ligularia przewalskii
Ligularia stenocephala
Ligularia 'The Rocket'
Ligularia veitchiana
Ligularia wilsoniana
Limonium gmelinii
Limonium latifolium
Lupinus polyphyllus
Lychnis × arkwrightii
Lychnis chalcedonica
Lychnis coronaria
Lychnis flos-jovis
Lychnis viscaria
Lysimachia 'Aztec Sunset'
Lysimachia ciliata
Lysimachia clethroides
Lysimachia ephemerum
Lysimachia punctata
Mimulus cardinalis
Monarda didyma
Monarda didyma 'Violet Queen'
Nepeta grandiflora
Nepeta racemosa
Nepeta sibirica
Nepeta tuberosa
Oenothera 'Crown Imperial'
Oenothera speciosa

Paeonia mascula
Papaver orientale
Papaver rupifragum
Phlox maculata
Platycodon grandiflorus
Platycodon grandiflorus 'Apoyama'
Platycodon grandiflorus 'Fuji Blue'
Platycodon grandiflorus 'Fuji White'
Platycodon grandiflorus 'Mariesii'
Platycodon grandiflorus 'Sentimental Blue'
Potentilla megalantha
Potentilla nepalensis
Potentilla recta
Ranunculus lyallii
Salvia verticillata
Scabiosa caucasica
Scabiosa caucasica 'Alba'
Scabiosa caucasica 'Fama'
Solidago 'Crown of Rays'
Thalictrum aquilegifolium
Thalictrum flavum
Thalictrum rochebrunianum
Verbascum chaixii
Veronica spicata
Yucca filamentosa

Perennials, summer-flowering, shade to part-shade

Anemone multifida
Astilbe × arendsii
Astilbe chinensis
Astilbe japonica
Astilbe koreana
Astilbe simplicifolia
Astilbe thunbergii
Astrantia carniolica
Astrantia carniolica 'Rubra'
Astrantia major
Astrantia major 'Ruby Wedding'
Astrantia major subsp. involucrata 'Moira Reid'
Astrantia maxima
Calceolaria biflora
Calceolaria 'John Innes'
Campanula punctata
Campanula takesimana
Clivia × cyrtanthiflora
Dicentra scandens
Digitalis ferruginea
Geranium pratense
Geranium renardii
Geranium sanguineum
Geranium sessiliflorum
Meconopsis grandis
Meconopsis horridula
Myosotis scorpioides
Paeonia anomala

Perennials, winter–early summer-flowering

Bergenia 'Abendglut'
Bergenia ciliata
Bergenia cordifolia
Bergenia crassifolia
Bergenia emeiensis
Bergenia × schmidtii
Erysimum 'Bowles' Mauve'
Geranium maderense
Helleborus argutifolius
Helleborus foetidus
Helleborus 'Halliwell Purple'
Helleborus lividus
Helleborus niger
Helleborus orientalis
Lathyrus vernus
Osteospermum jucundum

Perennials, summer–autumn-flowering

Aconitum altissimum
Aconitum carmichaelii
Aconitum lycoctonum
Aconitum napellus
Aconitum 'Spark's Variety'
Aconitum 'Stainless Steel'
Anemone hupehensis
Anemone × hybrida
Artemisia vulgaris
Asclepias curassavica
Asclepias incarnata
Aster amellus
Aster × frikartii
Aster novae-angliae
Aster novi-belgii
Canna 'Erebus'
Canna 'Intrigue'
Canna iridiflora
Canna 'Phasion'
Canna 'Pretoria'
Canna 'Wyoming'
Centaurea rothrockii
Chrysanthemum, Anemone-centered
Chrysanthemum, Incurved
Chrysanthemum, Pompon
Chrysanthemum, Quill-shaped
Chrysanthemum, Reflexed
Chrysanthemum, Single
Chrysanthemum, Spider-form
Chrysanthemum, Spoon-shaped
Chrysanthemum, Spray
Chrysanthemum weyrichii
Chrysanthemum yezoense
Chrysanthemum zawadskii
Coreopsis rosea
Coreopsis verticillata
Cosmos atrosanguineus
Dahlia, Anemone-flowered
Dahlia, Ball
Dahlia, Cactus
Dahlia coccinea
Dahlia, Collarette
Dahlia, Decorative

Dahlia imperialis

Dahlia merckii

Dahlia, Pompon

Dahlia, Semi-cactus

Dahlia, Single

Dahlia, Waterlily

Delphinium, Elatum Group

Diascia fetcaniensis

Diascia 'Langthorn's
   Lavender'

Diascia 'Little Dancer'

Diascia 'Twinkle'

Diascia vigilis

Dicentra eximia

Eryngium alpinum

Gaillardia × grandiflora

Gentiana asclepiadea

Geranium 'Ann Folkard'

Helenium autumnale

Helenium 'Blopip'

Helenium 'Waldtraut'

Helenium 'Wyndley'

Helianthus maximiliani

Helianthus × multiflorus

Helianthus salicifolius

Hemerocallis 'Buzz Bomb'

Hemerocallis fulva

Hemerocallis 'Green Flutter'

Hemerocallis 'Prairie Blue Eyes'

Hibiscus moscheutos

Impatiens omeiana

Kniphofia caulescens

Kniphofia citrina

Kniphofia ensifolia

Kniphofia rooperi

Leucanthemum × superbum

Leucanthemum × superbum
   'Aglaia'

Leucanthemum × superbum
   'Esther Read'

Leucanthemum × superbum
   'Snowcap'

Leucanthemum × superbum
   'T. E. Killin'

Liatris ligulistylis

Liatris pycnostachya

Liatris spicata

Liatris spicata 'Callilepsis Purple'

Liatris spicata 'Kobold'

Liatris tenuifolia

Ligularia dentata

Limonium brassicifolium

Lobelia cardinalis

Lobelia × gerardii 'Tania'

Lobelia siphilitica

Monarda 'Cambridge Scarlet'

Monarda fistulosa

Monarda 'Ruby Glow'

Monarda 'Vintage Wine'

Nemesia caerulea

Nemesia caerulea 'Hubbird'

Nemesia caerulea 'Innocence'

Nemesia denticulata

Nepeta × faassenii

Nepeta nervosa

Oenothera 'Lemon Sunset'

Osteospermum, Symphony Series

Penstemon barbatus

Penstemon 'Stapleford Gem'

Phlox paniculata

Physostegia virginiana

Physostegia virginiana 'Alba'

Physostegia virginiana 'Crown
   of Snow'

Physostegia virginiana 'Summer
   Snow'

Physostegia virginiana 'Variegata'

Physostegia virginiana 'Vivid'

Rudbeckia fulgida

Rudbeckia fulgida var. sullivantii
   'Goldsturm'

Rudbeckia laciniata

Rudbeckia nitida

Salvia farinacea

Salvia nemorosa

Salvia patens

Salvia × superba

Salvia uliginosa

Saponaria officinalis

Scabiosa columbaria

Sedum spectabile

Solidago altissima

Solidago californica

Solidago canadensis

Solidago gigantea

Solidago sphacelata

Stokesia laevis

Stokesia laevis 'Blue Danube'

Stokesia laevis 'Bluestone'

Stokesia laevis 'Mary Gregory'

Stokesia laevis 'Silver Moon'

Stokesia laevis 'Wyoming'

Thalictrum delavayi

Tradescantia, Andersoniana
   Group

Tradescantia virginiana

Verbascum 'Helen Johnson'

Verbascum 'Jackie'

Veronica 'Pink Damask'

Yucca gloriosa

Yucca recurvifolia

Perennials, ground covers and rock plants, mild climate

Arctotis acaulis

Arctotis fastuosa

Arctotis, Harlequin Hybrids

Arctotis, Harlequin Hybrids
   'Flame'

Arctotis, Harlequin Hybrids
   'Red Devil'

Arctotis venusta

Convolvulus althaeoides

Convolvulus sabatius

Echium amoenum

Fuchsia procumbens
Gazania 'Blackberry Ripple'
Gazania, Chansonette Series
Gazania 'Christopher Lloyd'
Gazania linearis
Gazania rigens
Gazania rigens 'Variegata'
Limonium perezii
Tradescantia fluminensis
Tradescantia pallida
Tradescantia sillamontana

Perennials, alpines, ground covers, and rock plants, cool climate

Calceolaria uniflora var. darwinii
Campanula carpatica
Campanula cochleariifolia
Campanula garganica
Centaurea simplicicaulis
Convolvulus boissieri
Convolvulus lineatus
Cornus canadensis
Dianthus alpinus
Dianthus carthusianorum
Dianthus deltoides
Dianthus gratianopolitanus
Dianthus pavonius
Epimedium acuminatum
Epimedium grandiflorum
Epimedium × perralchicum
Epimedium pinnatum
Epimedium platypetalum
Epimedium × versicolor
Erysimum bonannianum
Erysimum kotschyanum
Erysimum 'Sunlight'
Euphorbia myrsinites
Euphorbia myrsinites subsp. pontica
Gentiana acaulis
Gentiana clusii

Gentiana septemfida
Gentiana ternifolia
Gypsophila cerastoides
Gypsophila muralis
Gypsophila repens
Iberis saxatalis
Iberis sempervirens
Iberis sempervirens 'Weisser Zwerg'
Lewisia columbiana
Lewisia cotyledon
Lewisia, Cotyledon Hybrids
Lewisia longipetala
Lewisia rediviva
Lewisia tweedyi
Lychnis alpina
Lysimachia nummularia
Myosotis alpestris
Myosotis explanata
Oenothera caespitosa
Oenothera macrocarpa
Papaver miyabeanum
Penstemon rupicola
Phlox stolonifera
Phlox subulata
Potentilla alba
Pulsatilla albana
Pulsatilla hirsutissima
Pulsatilla montana
Pulsatilla patens
Pulsatilla pratensis
Pulsatilla vulgaris
Ranunculus ficaria
Saponaria 'Bressingham'
Saponaria lutea
Saponaria ocymoides
Saponaria × olivana
Saponaria pumilio
Sedum kamtschaticum
Sedum rupestre
Sedum spathulifolium
Sedum spurium

Thalictrum kiusianum
Thalictrum orientale
Trifolium repens
Trifolium repens 'Green Ice'
Trifolium repens 'Pentaphyllum'
Trifolium uniflorum
Tropaeolum polyphyllum
Verbascum acaule
Verbascum dumulosum
Veronica alpina
Veronica peduncularis
Viola adunca
Viola obliqua
Viola odorata
Viola pedata
Viola riviniana
Viola sororia

Perennials, subshrubs, sun

Argyranthemum 'Butterfly'
Argyranthemum 'Donnington Hero'
Argyranthemum frutescens
Argyranthemum gracile
Argyranthemum maderense
Argyranthemum 'Petite Pink'
Artemisia 'Powis Castle'
Convolvulus cneorum
Digitalis obscura
Echium candicans
Euphorbia characias
Felicia amelloides
Felicia amelloides 'Variegata'
Felicia filifolia
Felicia fruticosa
Felicia 'Spring Melchen'
Lavandula angustifolia
Lavandula × intermedia
Lavandula lanata
Lavandula 'Sawyers'
Lavandula stoechas
Lobelia laxiflora

Mimulus aurantiacus

Mimulus bifidus

Osteospermum 'Whirligig'

Penstemon pinifolius

Ranunculus asiaticus

Salvia coccinea

Salvia elegans

Salvia × *jamensis*

Salvia leucantha

Salvia splendens

Tagetes lemmonii

Perennials, subshrubs, shade to part-shade

Lobelia tupa

Perennials, water-garden plants

Zantedeschia aethiopica

Perennials, for tropical effect

Hedychium coccineum

Hedychium coronarium

Hedychium densiflorum

Hedychium gardnerianum

Hedychium greenei

Hedychium spicatum

Impatiens, New Guinea Group

Impatiens niamniamensis

Impatiens sodenii

Tradescantia spathacea

Perennials, irises

Iris, Arilbred Hybrids

Iris, Dwarf Bearded

Iris ensata

Iris germanica

Iris, Intermediate Bearded

Iris, Louisiana Hybrids

Iris, Pacific Coast Hybrids

Iris sibirica

Iris, Spuria Hybrids

Iris, Tall Bearded

Iris unguicularis

Perennials, pelargoniums

Pelargonium, Angel

Pelargonium crispum

Pelargonium, Dwarf

Pelargonium echinatum

Pelargonium, Ivy-leafed

Pelargonium, Miniature

Pelargonium, Regal

Pelargonium, Scented-leafed

Pelargonium, Stellar

Pelargonium triste

Pelargonium, Unique

Pelargonium, Zonal

Perennials, primulas

Primula auricula

Primula bulleyana

Primula denticulata

Primula florindae

Primula forrestii

Primula japonica

Primula, Juliana

Primula pulverulenta

Primula sieboldii

Primula verticillata

Primula vialii

Primula vulgaris

SHRUBS

Summer page 606   Autumn page 620
Winter page 634   Spring page 648

The cultivation of shrubs will only be successful if they are correctly located. A sun-loving shrub will never flower brilliantly in a dark damp corner; instead, it will sulk for years

and produce only a few flowers if any at all.

Always provide adequate water during dry spells as water stress often leaves shrubs vulnerable to insect attack. Using plenty of mulch around plants will help to conserve water. Conversely, planting in waterlogged soils may result in shrubs suffering root rot or fungal diseases, so an even balance needs to be found.

Regular controlled pruning after flowering will result in healthy well-formed shrubs. Deciduous shrubs should not be cut back when the leaves drop off as the next season's flowers may be inadvertently removed as well. If you don't have the time for regular pruning, plant the same shrub in groups of 3 or 5, as this will look much better than a single straggly individual. Also, lightly fertilize every few months rather than in a big hit; avoid heaping animal manure up around plants's main stems.

Wander through a botanic garden to see shrubs growing well. At the same time you can discover which shrubs might be suitable for your garden.

Low-growing, frost-hardy, evergreen

Daphne × *burkwoodii*

Daphne cneorum

Daphne × *napolitana*

Daphne odora

Kalmia angustifolia
Kalmia polifolia
Mahonia repens
Rosmarinus officinalis
Rosmarinus officinalis 'Arp'
Rosmarinus officinalis 'Joyce
de Baggio'
Rosmarinus officinalis 'Majorca
Pink'
Rosmarinus officinalis
'Prostratus'
Rosmarinus officinalis 'Tuscan
Blue'

Low-growing, frost-tender, evergreen

Abutilon megapotamicum
Calceolaria integrifolia

Low-growing, frost-hardy, deciduous

Ceanothus americanus
Chaenomeles japonica
Cytisus × *kewensis*
Cytisus × *praecox*
Cytisus purgans
Daphne genkwa
Deutzia gracilis
Forsythia 'Arnold Dwarf'
Potentilla fruticosa

Medium- to tall-growing, frost-hardy, evergreen

Ceanothus 'Dark Star'
Ceanothus × *delileanus* 'Gloire
de Versailles'
Ceanothus griseus
Ceanothus incanus
Ceanothus thyrsiflorus
Fremontodendron 'California
Glory'
Fremontodendron californicum

Fremontodendron decumbens
Fremontodendron 'Ken Taylor'
Fremontodendron 'Pacific
Sunset'
Jasminum humile
Jasminum mesnyi
Kalmia latifolia
Kalmia latifolia 'Carousel'
Kalmia latifolia 'Olympic Fire'
Kalmia latifolia 'Pink Charm'
Lonicera nitida
Lupinus arboreus
Mahonia aquifolium
Mahonia fremontii
Mahonia lomariifolia
Mahonia × *media*
Mahonia nevinii
Pieris 'Flaming Silver'
Pieris 'Forest Flame'
Pieris formosa
Pieris japonica
Pieris japonica 'Scarlett O'Hara'
Pieris japonica 'Valley Valentine'

Medium- to tall-growing, frost-tender, evergreen

Abutilon × *hybridum* 'Ashford
Red'
Abutilon × *hybridum* 'Canary
Bird'
Abutilon × *hybridum* 'Souvenir
de Bonn'
Abutilon pictum
Brugmansia aurea
Brugmansia × *candida*
Brugmansia 'Charles Grimaldi'
Brugmansia 'Inca Queen'
Brugmansia sanguinea
Brugmansia suaveolens
Cytisus supranubius
Fremontodendron mexicanum
Solanum aviculare

Solanum laciniatum
Solanum rantonnetii
Thunbergia erecta

Medium- to tall-growing, frost-hardy, deciduous

Abutilon × *suntense*
Amelanchier alnifolia
Amelanchier denticulata
Amelanchier spicata
Chaenomeles × *californica*
Chaenomeles cathayensis
Chaenomeles speciosa
Chaenomeles × *superba*
Chaenomeles × *superba*
'Rowallane'
Cornus alba
Cornus officinalis
Cornus sanguinea
Cornus stolonifera
Cytisus battandieri
Cytisus scoparius
Daphne caucasica
Deutzia compacta
Deutzia crenata
Deutzia × *hybrida*
Deutzia × *magnifica*
Deutzia setchuenensis
Forsythia × *intermedia*
Forsythia 'Northern Gold'
Forsythia 'Northern Sun'
Forsythia ovata
Forsythia suspensa
Jasminum nudiflorum
Jasminum officinale
Lonicera tatarica
Magnolia 'Betty'
Magnolia stellata
Paeonia delavayi
Paeonia × *lemoinei*
Paeonia lutea
Paeonia suffruticosa

Acacia

Acacia farnesiana

Acacia longifolia

Acacia paradoxa

Acacia pravissima

Banksia

Banksia ericifolia

Banksia marginata

Banksia speciosa

Banksia spinulosa

Buddleja

Buddleja alternifolia

Buddleja davidii

Buddleja fallowiana

Buddleja globosa

Buddleja salviifolia

Buddleja × weyeriana

Callistemon

Callistemon citrinus

Callistemon citrinus 'Splendens'

Callistemon 'Mauve Mist'

Callistemon polandii

Callistemon rigidus

Callistemon viridiflorus

Camellia

Camellia hiemalis

Camellia hiemalis 'Chansonette'

Camellia japonica

Camellia japonica 'Nuccio's Gem'

Camellia lutchuensis

Camellia 'Night Rider'

Camellia nitidissima

Camellia pitardii

Camellia reticulata

Camellia reticulata 'Captain
  Rawes'

Camellia saluensis

Camellia sasanqua

Camellia sasanqua 'Shishigashira'

Camellia sinensis

Camellia tsaii

Camellia × williamsii

Camellia × williamsii 'Bow Bells'

Camellia × williamsii 'Donation'

Cistus

Cistus × aguilarii

Cistus creticus

Cistus ladanifer

Cistus × pulverulentus

Cistus × purpureus

Cistus salviifolius

Erica

Erica canaliculata

Erica carnea

Erica cinerea

Erica × darleyensis

Erica lusitanica

Erica vagans

Euphorbia

Euphorbia pulcherrima

Fuchsia

Fuchsia arborescens

Fuchsia boliviana

Fuchsia denticulata

Fuchsia 'Eva Boerg'

Fuchsia magellanica

Fuchsia 'Mrs Popple'

Fuchsia 'Orange Flare'

Fuchsia paniculata

Fuchsia 'Swingtime'

Fuchsia thymifolia

Fuchsia triphylla

Gardenia

Gardenia augusta

Gardenia augusta 'Kleim's Hardy'

Gardenia augusta 'Mystery'

Gardenia augusta 'Radicans'

Gardenia augusta 'Veitchii'

Gardenia thunbergia

Hebe

Hebe 'Blue Clouds'

Hebe 'Caledonia'

Hebe 'Great Orme'

Hebe 'Nicola's Blush'

Hebe ochracea

Hebe pinguifolia

Hibiscus

Hibiscus brackenridgei

Hibiscus mutabilis

Hibiscus rosa-sinensis

Hibiscus schizopetalus

Hibiscus syriacus

Hydrangea

Hydrangea arborescens

Hydrangea involucrata

Hydrangea macrophylla

Hydrangea paniculata

Hydrangea quercifolia

Hydrangea serrata

Lavandula

Lavandula dentata

Leptospermum

Leptospermum javanicum

Leptospermum lanigerum

Leptospermum polygalifolium

Leptospermum rupestre

Leptospermum scoparium

Leptospermum scoparium 'Kiwi'

Nerium

Nerium oleander

Nerium oleander 'Album'

Nerium oleander 'Docteur Golfin'
Nerium oleander 'Petite Salmon'
Nerium oleander 'Splendens'
Nerium oleander 'Splendens
    Variegatum'

Philadelphus

Philadelphus 'Belle Etoile'
Philadelphus coronarius
Philadelphus 'Manteau
    d'Hermine'
Philadelphus mexicanus
Philadelphus 'Rosace'
Philadelphus subcanus

Rhododendron

Rhododendron, Azaleodendron
    Hybrids
Rhododendron, Ghent Azalea
    Hybrids
Rhododendron, Hardy Medium
    Hybrids
Rhododendron, Hardy Small
    Hybrids
Rhododendron, Hardy Tall
    Hybrids
Rhododendron, Indica Azalea
    Hybrids
Rhododendron, Knap Hill and
    Exbury Azalea Hybrids
Rhododendron, Kurume Azalea
    Hybrids
Rhododendron macrophyllum
Rhododendron maximum
Rhododendron, Mollis Azalea
    Hybrids
Rhododendron, Occidentale
    Azalea Hybrids
Rhododendron, Rustica Azalea
    Hybrids
Rhododendron, Satsuki Azalea
    Hybrids

Rhododendron, Tender Hybrids
Rhododendron, Vireya Hybrids
Rhododendron, Viscosum Azalea
    Hybrids
Rhododendron, Yak Hybrids

Rosa

Rosa, Alba
Rosa blanda
Rosa, Bourbon
Rosa, China
Rosa, Cluster-flowered
    (Floribunda)
Rosa, Damask
Rosa, Gallica
Rosa, Hybrid Perpetual
Rosa, Hybrid Rugosa
Rosa, Large-flowered (Hybrid
    Tea)
Rosa, Miniature
Rosa, Moss
Rosa, Patio (Dwarf Cluster-
    flowered)
Rosa, Polyantha
Rosa setigera
Rosa, Shrub
Rosa, Tea

Spiraea

Spiraea fritschiana
Spiraea japonica
Spiraea nipponica
Spiraea prunifolia
Spiraea thunbergii
Spiraea × vanhouttei

Syringa

Syringa × chinensis
Syringa × hyacinthiflora
Syringa × josiflexa
Syringa komarowii
Syringa × laciniata

Syringa meyeri
Syringa oblata
Syringa × prestoniae
Syringa pubescens
Syringa reticulata
Syringa × swegiflexa
Syringa vulgaris

Viburnum

Viburnum × bodnantense
Viburnum carlesii
Viburnum 'Eskimo'
Viburnum farreri
Viburnum lantana
Viburnum nudum
Viburnum opulus
Viburnum plicatum
Viburnum rhytidophyllum
Viburnum sieboldii
Viburnum tinus
Viburnum trilobum

Weigela

Weigela 'Bristol Ruby'
Weigela florida
Weigela 'Looymansii Aurea'
Weigela middendorfiana
Weigela 'Newport Red'
Weigela praecox

TREES

Summer page 610   Autumn page 624
Winter page 638   Spring page 654

Choosing the right tree for a
location requires careful consideration—the tiny seedling
tree you admire in a pot may
grow to overwhelm a small gar
den or cause major problems t
building foundations and unde
ground pipes. Always check th

mature height of a tree before purchase and allow plenty of room for it to fully develop. Visit an arboretum to see trees growing at their best when choosing one for your garden.

At planting time dig a hole at least 3 times the root volume and add compost and a complete fertilizer. To help the tree get off to a good start, cut off any coiled or damaged roots, plant firmly, and leave a slight depression around the main stem to allow rainwater to collect. Although many trees are drought-tolerant, they still require a good supply of water for growth. As the tree grows, avoid root disturbance at all times and remove any crossing or rubbing branches. Fertilize to the dripline of trees during rainy weather.

When pruning mature trees always cut flush to a branch or trunk, leaving no stubs—these look unsightly and give insect pests and diseases an easy entry into the tree. Seasonal checks for insect pests may be necessary. Small holes or sawdust on the trunk can indicate the presence of borers.

Evergreen

Acacia baileyana
Acacia dealbata
Banksia integrifolia
Banksia serrata
Cornus capitata
Magnolia grandiflora

Deciduous, taller than 35 ft (10 m)

Cornus controversa
Crataegus punctata
Crataegus viridis
Magnolia 'Apollo'
Magnolia virginiana
Magnolia 'Yellow
  Lantern'

Deciduous, 35 ft (10 m) or shorter

Amelanchier arborea
Amelanchier × grandiflora
Amelanchier laevis
Cercis canadensis
Cercis canadensis 'Forest
  Pansy'
Cercis chinensis
Cercis griffithii
Cercis occidentalis
Cercis siliquastrum
Cornus alternifolia
Cornus florida
Cornus kousa
Cornus mas
Cornus × rutgersiensis
Crataegus laevigata
Crataegus × lavallei
Crataegus monogyna
Crataegus persimilis 'Prunifolia
  Splendens'
Lagerstroemia fauriei
Lagerstroemia indica
Lagerstroemia 'Natchez'
Lagerstroemia subcostata
Magnolia 'Elizabeth'
Magnolia 'Iolanthe'
Magnolia kobus
Magnolia × loebneri
Magnolia × soulangeana
Magnolia wilsonii

Ornamental, blossom and/or fruit

Malus floribunda
Malus 'Harvest Gold'
Malus hupehensis
Malus 'Indian Summer'
Malus ioensis
Prunus × blireana
Prunus cerasifera
Prunus maackii
Prunus, Sato-zakura Group,
  'Kanzan'
Prunus × subhirtella
Prunus triloba

Tropical and subtropical

Lagerstroemia floribunda
Lagerstroemia speciosa

Eucalyptus

Eucalyptus cinerea
Eucalyptus gunnii
Eucalyptus leucoxylon
Eucalyptus microcorys
Eucalyptus pauciflora
Eucalyptus woodwardii

BULBS, CORMS, AND TUBERS

Summer page 610   Autumn page 626
Winter page 640   Spring page 654

Bulbs are one of the easiest groups of plants to grow, as they are adaptable to a wide range of climates and growing conditions. Select firm healthy bulbs when buying and check around the surface or under the outer papery casing for any sign of insects or grubs. Soft damp spots or gray mold may indicate damage from a fungus. Many popular bulbs in or near flowering time are now available ready-planted in pots.

If you live in a warm climate and wish to grow cold-climate bulbs, you may have to give the bulbs an artificial winter in the refrigerator crisper for around 6 weeks before planting. In a cold climate, lift frost-tender bulbs over winter, grow them in pots, and plant them out in spring when the danger of frost has passed.

Certain bulbs are known as "garden escapees." Many of these bulbs in lawns or on roadsides in spring are popular with everyone, however, other bulbs appearing in prime country pasture cause heartache for farmers. Check with a reputable dealer if in doubt about the suitability of any bulb.

Summer-flowering, sun

Crinum 'Ellen Bosanquet'
Crocosmia × crocosmiiflora
Crocosmia 'Emily McKenzie'
Crocosmia 'Lucifer'
Crocosmia masoniorum
Crocosmia pottsii
Crocosmia 'Rowallane Yellow'
Eucomis bicolor
Eucomis 'Sparkling Burgundy'
Eucomis pallidiflora
Eucomis zambesiaca
Ornithogalum arabicum
Ornithogalum umbellatum
Zantedeschia 'Flame'
Zantedeschia pentlandii

Summer-flowering, part-shade

Cyclamen purpurascens

Autumn-flowering

Colchicum agrippinum
Colchicum autumnale
Colchicum cilicicum
Colchicum parnassicum
Colchicum speciosum
Colchicum speciosum 'Album'
Crocus serotinus
Crocus speciosus
Cyclamen hederifolium
Nerine bowdenii
Nerine filifolia
Nerine flexuosa
Nerine flexuosa 'Alba'
Nerine masoniorum
Nerine sarniensis

Winter-flowering

Cyclamen persicum
Galanthus ikarae
Galanthus nivalis
Galanthus nivalis 'Flore Pleno'

Winter–spring-flowering

Crocus chrysanthus
Crocus sieberi
Crocus tomasinianus
Cyclamen cilicium
Cyclamen coum
Galanthus elwesii
Galanthus plicatus
Galanthus 'S. Arnott'
Hippeastrum 'Christmas Star'
Hippeastrum × johnsonii
Hippeastrum 'Pamela'
Hippeastrum 'Picotee'
Hippeastrum 'Royal Velvet'
Ornithogalum dubium

Spring-flowering, sun

Crinum bulbispermum
Ixia curta
Sparaxis fragrans
Sparaxis grandiflora
Sparaxis pillansii
Sparaxis variegata
Zantedeschia rehmannii

Spring-flowering, shade to part-shade

Anemone blanda
Arisaema amurense
Cyclamen repandum
Hyacinthus orientalis
Hyacinthus orientalis 'Blue Jacket'
Hyacinthus orientalis 'Carnegie'
Hyacinthus orientalis 'City of Haarlem'
Hyacinthus orientalis 'Jan Bos'
Hyacinthus orientalis 'Pink Pearl'

Summer–autumn-flowering

Camassia scilloides
Crinum americanum
Crinum erubescens
Crinum moorei
Crinum × powellii
Eucomis autumnalis
Eucomis comosa

Spring–summer-flowering, sun

Calochortus albus
Calochortus luteus
Calochortus monophyllus
Calochortus nuttallii
Calochortus splendens
Calochortus tolmiei
Camassia cusickii
Camassia leichtlinii

Camassia leichtlinii 'Semiplena'

Camassia leichtlinii subsp. suksdorfii

Camassia quamash

Hippeastrum papilio

Iris, Dutch Hybrids

Ixia dubia

Ixia maculata

Ixia monadelpha

Ixia paniculata

Ixia viridiflora

Ornithogalum narbonense

Ornithogalum nutans

Ornithogalum reverchonii

Sparaxis elegans

Sparaxis tricolor

Zantedeschia albomaculata

Zantedeschia 'Scarlet Pimpernel'

Spring–summer-flowering, shade

Anemone nemorosa

Arisaema concinnum

Arisaema kishidae

Arisaema limbatum

Arisaema ringens

Arisaema sikokianum

Convallaria majalis

Convallaria majalis 'Aureomarginata'

Convallaria majalis 'Hardwick Hall'

Convallaria majalis 'Prolificans'

Convallaria majalis var. rosea

Convallaria majalis 'Variegata'

Crocus vernus

Allium

Allium cristophii

Allium karataviense

Allium moly

Allium paradoxum

Allium porrum

Allium sphaerocephalon

Begonia

Begonia, Tuberhybrida Group

Fritillaria

Fritillaria camschatcensis

Fritillaria imperialis

Fritillaria meleagris

Fritillaria michailovskyi

Fritillaria pallidiflora

Fritillaria persica

Gladiolus

Gladiolus callianthus

Gladiolus communis

Gladiolus 'Green Woodpecker'

Gladiolus 'Red Beauty'

Gladiolus tristis

Gladiolus viridiflorus

Lilium

Lilium, American Hybrids

Lilium, Asiatic Hybrids

Lilium, Candidum Hybrids

Lilium lancifolium

Lilium lankongense

Lilium, Longiflorum Hybrids

Lilium martagon

Lilium, Martagon Hybrids

Lilium nepalense

Lilium, Oriental Hybrids

Lilium regale

Lilium, Trumpet and Aurelian Hybrids

Narcissus

Narcissus, Bulbocodium

Narcissus, Cyclamineus

Narcissus, Double-flowered

Narcissus, Jonquilla and Apodanthus

Narcissus, Large-cupped

Narcissus, Poeticus

Narcissus, Small-cupped

Narcissus, Split-corona

Narcissus, Tazetta

Narcissus 'Tête-à-Tête'

Narcissus, Triandrus

Narcissus, Trumpet

Tulipa

Tulipa, Darwin Hybrid Group

Tulipa, Double Late Group

Tulipa, Greigii Group

Tulipa hageri

Tulipa, Lily-flowered Group

Tulipa, Parrot Group

Tulipa, Single Early Group

Tulipa, Single Late Group

Tulipa, Triumph Group

Tulipa urumiensis

Tulipa, Viridiflora Group

Tulipa vvedenskyi

HERBS

Summer page 614   Autumn page 628
Winter page 642   Spring page 658

Herbs are ideally suited to cultivation in cool-temperate climates where summers may be hot but not humid. They can tolerate a range of growing conditions within a garden, from dry, gravelly, limy positions in full sun to cool, moist, partly shaded positions.

Herbs don't need a special garden of their own although this is often more convenient. Prepare the garden position by adding plenty of compost and a light application of fertilizer, or else grow in pots with a good-quality potting mix and some slow-release fertilizer.

Annual herbs grown from seed need to be sown regularly to ensure a constant supply for the kitchen. They tend to bolt to seed when fluctuations of temperature occur. Perennial herbs should be tip pruned regularly for compact growth, checked occasionally for invasions of leaf-eating insects or snails, and tidied up in late winter before spring growth starts.

Cuttings strike readily during spring and summer, or herbs can be divided during the cooler months. Frost-tender herbs may need to be moved to a sheltered position during winter in cold climates. Otherwise, their demands are few.

Herbs make good companion plants and mix happily with flowers, vegetables, and fruit or they can be used as ground covers among shrubs.

Artemisia dracunculus
Rosmarinus officinalis
Salvia officinalis

FRUIT TREES

Summer page 614   Autumn page 630
Winter page 642   Spring page 658

The basic requirement for fruit trees is a good, deep, fertile soil that is well-drained. Have your soil tested in a laboratory to see if it is deficient in certain elements; this will save a lot of problems later on after planting. As well, check with a reputable dealer for varieties suitable for your area and for the pollination requirements.

Remember to always choose virus-free or organically grown fruit trees. Prune to allow light and air into the tree and to encourage continuous cropping. Keep the area around trees free of weeds, and mulch and fertilize regularly.

Pest and disease problems may be numerous, so always seek expert advice on the safest way of dealing with them. Plant companion plants that are beneficial for insect control and fruit production. Do not attempt to grow cool-temperate fruits in warm climates. If you follow these simple procedures you will soon be able to enjoy the "fruits" of your labor.

Tropical to subtropical
Solanum quitoense

Cool-temperate
Malus × *domestica*

Citrus
Citrus × *aurantium*
Citrus glauca
Citrus ichangensis
Citrus limon
Citrus reticulata
Citrus sinensis

INDOOR PLANTS

Cultivation of indoor plants is simple if they are given positions with reasonable light and warmth, are kept evenly moist (but slightly drier during the winter months), and have regular weak doses of liquid fertilizer. Check regularly for pests such as mealy bugs, scale insects, and mites on the stems and undersides of leaves, as these bugs thrive in warm enclosed conditions. Also, take plants outside occasionally to wash the dust from the leaves, never allowing them to sit in the sun as they will quickly burn.

If you live in a warm climate, don't be tempted to plant indoor plants in the garden if they have become too big—they may grow even bigger outside and cause real problems.

Propagation is fairly easy, particularly from stem or leaf cuttings during the warmer months. Clump-forming types can be divided once they have outgrown their pots. Seasonal flowering plants such as cyclamen are best discarded after they flower, as they rarely perform as well the next year.

Indoor flowering and foliage plants
Aechmea fasciata
Aechmea fulgens
Aechmea miniata var. *discolor*
Aechmea ornata var. *hoehneana*
Aechmea recurvata

Aechmea weilbachii

Anthurium andraeanum

Anthurium crystallinum

Anthurium scandens

Anthurium scherzerianum

Anthurium umbrosum

Anthurium veitchii

Begonia boliviensis

Begonia bowerae

Begonia, Cane-stemmed

Begonia, Rex-cultorum Group

Billbergia distachia

Billbergia nutans

Billbergia pyramidalis

Billbergia sanderiana

Billbergia venezuelana

Billbergia zebrina

Columnea arguta

Columnea 'Early Bird'

Columnea gloriosa

Columnea microphylla

Columnea scandens

Columnea schiedeana

Impatiens, New Guinea Group

Sinningia aggregata

Sinningia canescens

Sinningia cardinalis

Sinningia pusilla

Sinningia speciosa

Sinningia tubiflora

Streptocarpus baudertii

Streptocarpus candidus

Streptocarpus 'Chorus Line'

Streptocarpus 'Crystal Ice'

Streptocarpus cyaneus

Streptocarpus 'Heidi'

Streptocarpus johannis

Streptocarpus 'Kim'

Streptocarpus primulifolius

Streptocarpus 'Ruby'

Streptocarpus saxorum

Streptocarpus 'Tina'

CACTI AND SUCCULENTS

Summer page 614   Autumn page 630
Winter page 644   Spring page 658

Most of these weirdly decorative and fascinating plants are native to arid regions of the world and their cultivation requirements are fairly simple: that is, a warm dry atmosphere and protection from too much moisture. The misconception arising from this, unfortunately, is that they should all be planted in the hottest, most desolate site in a garden or be allowed to languish in pots without any attention. This simply is not true.

Species such as *Kalanchoe* prefer shade and more fertile soil, and they will tolerate humidity. As a general rule, water well only during the growing or flowering periods, then give them a rest.

Propagation is from seed or cuttings in spring and summer. The stored moisture inside leaves and stems is mucilaginous, or jelly-like, and should be allowed to dry out slightly before propagation. Wear thick gloves when handling cacti with sharp spines and protect your eyes. Watch for pests such as scale insects, mealy bugs, and aphids, which tend to hide between cacti spines or in the closely packed rosette leaves of succulents.

Cacti and succulents are fun to collect, so join a cacti and succulent society to obtain the more unusual ones or visit a specialist nursery.

Delosperma congestum

Delosperma cooperi

Delosperma lehmannii

Delosperma nubigenum

Delosperma sphalmanthoides

Delosperma sutherlandii

Echinocereus coccineus

Echinocereus engelmannii

Echinocereus reichenbachii

Echinocereus rigidissimus

Echinocereus triglochidiatus

Echinocereus viridiflorus

Euphorbia keithii

Euphorbia milii

Kalanchoe blossfeldiana

Kalanchoe daigremontiana

Kalanchoe flammea

Kalanchoe pumila

Kalanchoe thyrsiflora

Kalanchoe tomentosa

Lampranthus amoenus

Lampranthus aurantiacus

Lampranthus aurantiacus 'Gold Nugget'

Lampranthus filicaulis

Lampranthus glaucus

Lampranthus spectabilis

Sedum album

Yucca elata

Yucca rostrata

Yucca whipplei

ORCHIDS

Summer page 614   Autumn page 630
Winter page 644   Spring page 660

There is a large selection of orchids for warm-temperate

climates, or cooler climates if extra protection is given over winter. You don't need a special greenhouse to cultivate orchids as they can be successfully grown outdoors in pots, in garden beds, or on the trunks and branches of trees.

There is no great mystery to growing orchids, as their requirements are similar to other groups of plants. The correct temperature is the most important factor, although lighting, atmosphere, water supply, and food should also be taken into consideration. Propagation is usually carried out in spring by division of well-established clumps. The method of division depends on the species.

Terrestrial orchids grown in gardens or pots need good drainage and plenty of leaf mold and well-rotted cow manure at planting time. Epiphytes can be grown in pots or on trees; if planting on a tree make sure it is one with rough, fibrous bark that does not shed. Pests and diseases will be kept to a minimum if plants are well fertilized, well watered, and there is good air circulation around them. Look out for the dendrobium beetle, though, as it is well known for causing havoc.

If you want to include orchids in your garden, try just a few different types first before considering a large and expensive collection.

Cattleya aurantiaca
Cattleya bicolor
Cattleya, Bifoliate Hybrids
Cattleya loddigesii
Cattleya skinneri
Cattleya, Unifoliate Hybrids
Cymbidium Alexfrida 'The Queen'
Cymbidium erythrostylum
Cymbidium goeringii
Cymbidium lowianum
Cymbidium sinense
Cymbidium tracyanum
Dendrobium bigibbum
Dendrobium binoculare
Dendrobium kingianum
Dendrobium Thanaid Stripes
Dendrobium wardianum
Dendrobium White Fairy
Laelia anceps
Laelia autumnalis
Laelia Canariensis
Laelia crispa
Laelia milleri
Laelia purpurata
Miltoniopsis Herr Alexandre
Miltoniopsis Hudson Bay
Miltoniopsis Jean Carlson
Miltoniopsis Rouge 'California Plum'
Miltoniopsis Saint Helier 'Pink Delight'
Miltoniopsis Zorro 'Yellow Delight'
Paphiopedilum bellatulum
Paphiopedilum Darling
Paphiopedilum haynaldianum
Paphiopedilum hirsutissimum
Paphiopedilum insigne
Paphiopedilum villosum
Phalaenopsis Artemis
Phalaenopsis Brother John
Phalaenopsis Brother Little Spotty
Phalaenopsis Chancellor
Phalaenopsis lueddemanniana
Phalaenopsis Taisuco Firebird
Pleione Alishan 'Soldier Blue'
Pleione Britannia 'Doreen'
Pleione bulbocodioides
Pleione formosana
Pleione Tongariro 'Jackdaw'
Pleione Zeus Weinstein
Vanda Lumpini Red 'AM'
Vanda Marlie Dolera
Vanda Pranerm Prai
Vanda Rothschildiana
Vanda sanderiana var. *albata*
Vanda Tailor Blue

CLIMBERS AND CREEPERS

**Summer page 616   Autumn page 630
Winter page 644   Spring page 660**

Both climbers and creepers are adaptable to a wide range of climates, and even exotic-looking subtropical ones may adapt to cold frosty areas. They will look ragged, tattered, or even leafless over winter, but will spring back into growth once the weather warms up.

Be prepared to work hard to look after climbing and creeping plants, pruning, training, and tying them up to shape them the way you want; even self-clinging types will wander if they are not strictly controlled. Be careful not to leave training for too long, as brittle stems will break.

Carefully prepare the soil before planting climbers and creepers by digging in plenty of compost and a complete fertilizer to ensure healthy results. Adequate water during the growing season and mulching are also essential practices. Check the Cultivation Guidelines table for information on propagation plus pest and disease problems.

Warm-temperate to cool-temperate

Aristolochia californica
Aristolochia clematitis
Aristolochia macrophylla
Aristolochia tomentosa
Campsis grandiflora
Campsis grandiflora 'Morning Charm'
Campsis radicans
Campsis radicans f. *flava*
Campsis × *tagliabuana*
Campsis × *tagliabuana* 'Madame Galen'
Clematis armandii
Clematis cirrhosa
Clematis, Diversifolia Group
Clematis, Florida Group
Clematis, Forsteri Group
Clematis integrifolia
Clematis, Jackmanii Group
Clematis, Lanuginosa Group
Clematis macropetala
Clematis, Patens Group
Clematis, Texensis Group
Clematis, Viticella Group
Jasminum × *stephanense*
Lathyrus latifolius
Lonicera × *brownii*
Lonicera × *heckrottii*
Lonicera periclymenum
Lonicera sempervirens
Mandevilla laxa
Passiflora caerulea
Passiflora incarnata
Rosa laevigata
Solanum crispum
Thunbergia alata
Thunbergia gregorii
Tropaeolum speciosum
Tropaeolum tuberosum
Wisteria brachybotrys 'Shiro-kapitan'
Wisteria 'Caroline'
Wisteria floribunda
Wisteria × *formosa*
Wisteria frutescens
Wisteria sinensis

Tropical to subtropical

Aristolochia fimbriata
Aristolochia littoralis
Bougainvillea 'Barbara Karst'
Bougainvillea × *buttiana*
Bougainvillea glabra
Bougainvillea 'Miss Manila'
Bougainvillea 'Scarlett O'Hara'
Bougainvillea 'Sundance'
Ipomoea batatas
Ipomoea carnea
Ipomoea horsfalliae
Ipomoea lobata
Ipomoea nil
Ipomoea tricolor
Jasminum sambac
Mandevilla × *amabilis*
Mandevilla × *amabilis* 'Alice du Pont'
Mandevilla boliviensis
Mandevilla sanderi
Mandevilla splendens
Passiflora quadrangularis
Passiflora racemosa
Passiflora violacea
Passiflora vitifolia
Solanum wendlandii
Thunbergia grandiflora
Thunbergia mysorensis
Thunbergia togoensis

SEASONAL CALENDARS

PLANT	EARLY SUMMER
ANNUALS AND PERENNIALS	
Annuals, low-growing, summer–autumn-flowering	Mulch plants to conserve water • Peak flowering time
Annuals, low-growing, spring–summer-flowering	Add spent plants to compost • Practice crop rotation
Annuals, low-growing, winter–spring-flowering	Sharpen and oil garden tools
Annuals, medium-growing, summer-flowering	Water and liquid fertilize regularly • Compost to conserve water, suppress weeds, and keep roots cool
Annuals, medium-growing, spring–summer-flowering	*Clarkia* in flower by summer solstice
Annuals, tall-growing, spring–summer-flowering	Remove spent flowers • Spray rust and powdery mildew with a fungicide or wettable sulfur • Break down organic matter with liquid fertilizer
Annuals, tall-growing, summer-flowering	Mulch garden • Liquid fertilize • Spray black aphids with pyrethrum • Spray leaf spot with a fungicide
Perennials, spring–early summer-flowering	Prune dead flower stems of *Anigozanthos* and liquid fertilize
Perennials, spring–early summer-flowering, short-lived	Plants can be allowed to seed—scatter seed to produce new plants
Perennials, summer-flowering, sun	Flowering begins • Liquid fertilize regularly

MID-SUMMER	LATE SUMMER
Compost spent flowers • Watch for aphids, white fly; spray with pyrethrum • Peak flowering time • Store saved seed in dry place	Check for nematodes • Cut back straggly growth or replant with fresh seedlings • Spray powdery mildew with a fungicide or wettable sulfur
Add spent plants to compost • Practice crop rotation	Add spent plants to compost • Practice crop rotation
Look for seed suppliers in garden magazines	Sow seed in a seed-raising mix in a well-lit sheltered position
Remove spent flowers regularly to prolong flowering • Pick zinnia flowers regularly to prolong flowering • Protect *Impatiens* from afternoon sun	Spray powdery mildew with a fungicide
Clarkia continues to flower	Sow seed • As seedlings emerge, drench soil with a fungicide to prevent damping off
Remove spent plants and add to compost heap • Practice crop rotation	Sow seed in seed-raising mix • Protect seedlings from damping off using a fungicide
Add spent blooms to compost heap • Spray mildew with a fungicide or wettable sulfur • Ensure adequate water for optimum flowering	Cut back overgrown plants to continue flowering • Store saved seed in dry location • Add summer weeds to compost before seed sets
Water *Anigozanthos* well during hot dry periods to prolong flowering period	Water *Anigozanthos* sparingly in humid weather to prevent root rot • Collar rot may occur in *Dianthus* • Gravel mulch
Provide a mulch of compost but keep away from plant stems	Provide gravel mulch for those plants that need sharp drainage
Remove spent flowers and add to compost • Ensure adequate water • Soak plants once a week if dry	Tidy up plants, removing old foliage • Liquid fertilize to encourage continuous blooming

PLANT	EARLY SUMMER
ANNUALS AND PERENNIALS (cont.)	
Perennials, summer-flowering, shade to part-shade	Protect plants from hot drying winds • Ensure plentiful supply of water • Pick flowering stems to encourage more blooms
Perennials, winter– early summer-flowering	Ensure adequate water • Provide a leaf compost and light dressing of blood and bone fertilizer • Protect plants from hot winds
Perennials, summer– autumn-flowering	Mulch around plants to conserve water and suppress weeds • Watch for snails and slugs
Perennials, ground covers and rock plants, mild climate	Mulch plants with compost; side dress with blood and bone fertilizer • Remove spent flowers • Cut back hard plants that overgrow others
Perennials, alpines, ground covers, and rock plants, cool climate	Cut back spring-flowering plants
Perennials, subshrubs, sun	Mulch plants with compost; side dress with blood and bone • Cuttings may be planted out
Perennials, subshrubs, shade to part-shade	Flowering season • Ensure adequate water during summer • Apply liquid fertilizer regularly
Perennials, water-garden plants	Feed water plants with slow-release fertilizer
Perennials, for tropical effect	Mulch with compost and ensure adequate water for summer flowering
Perennials, irises	Fertilize and mulch
Perennials, pelargoniums	Mulch around plants to conserve water • Water only during very dry spells
Perennials, primulas	Liquid fertilize regularly • Remove old leaves from around base of plants

MID-SUMMER	LATE SUMMER
Liquid fertilize regularly • Check plants for snail or slug damage	Remove old flowers
Ensure adequate water • Provide a leaf compost and light dressing of blood and bone fertilizer • Protect plants from hot winds	Ensure adequate water • Provide a leaf compost and light dressing of blood and bone fertilizer • Protect plants from hot winds
Liquid fertilize regularly • Flowering stems appear	Flowering • Provide stakes for tall flower stems
Ensure adequate water for plants	Provide gravel mulch in humid conditions to prevent root rot diseases of *Gazania* and *Arctotis* • Take half-hardened cuttings
Take half-hardened cuttings • Provide shade and extra water if required • Remove dead sections from rosette plants	Take half-hardened cuttings • Provide shade and extra water if required • Remove dead sections from rosette plants
Spray leaf miner on *Argyranthemum* with an insecticide • Ensure adequate water in dry weather	Cut back *Argyranthemum* to promote new growth
Flowering season • Ensure adequate water during summer • Apply liquid fertilizer regularly	*Lobelia tupa* begins flowering; flower stems may need staking
Cut back plants which crowd out others • Take softwood cuttings	Collect ripe seed from water plants • Sow and keep covered
Spray stem borer on *Hedychium* with an insecticide	Spray stem borer on *Hedychium* with an insecticide
Divide and replant bearded irises	Divide and replant bearded irises
Spray bud caterpillars on flowers with an insecticide • Water early morning to discourage black stem rot • Treat soil with a fungicide	Spray rust on plants with a fungicide or wettable sulfur
Keep plants moist during summer • Shelter from hot winds	Remove plants after 3 years if flowering diminishes • Spray two-spotted mite with insecticide

PLANT	EARLY SUMMER
SHRUBS	
Low-growing, frost-hardy, evergreen	Provide adequate water during dry spells • Prune after flowering • Mulch and fertilize
Low-growing, frost-tender, evergreen	Check for summer pests • Provide adequate water during dry spells
Low-growing, frost-hardy, deciduous	Take softwood cuttings • Mulch and fertilize • Check for summer insect pests
Medium- to tall-growing, frost-hardy, evergreen	Provide adequate water during dry spells • Prune after flowering • Mulch and fertilize
Medium- to tall-growing, frost-tender, evergreen	Check for summer pests • Provide adequate water during dry spells
Medium- to tall-growing, frost-hardy, deciduous	Take softwood cuttings • Mulch and fertilize • Check for summer insect pests
Acacia	Check older plants for signs of borer, sawdust, or small holes in trunk
Banksia	Apply a leaf mulch of gum leaves
Buddleja	*B. globosa* in flower
Callistemon	Take cuttings of half-hardened wood • Apply mulch around plants • Fertilize lightly with complete or slow-release plant food
Camellia	Sunburn may cause brown patches on leaves; move plant to cooler location
Cistus	Apply gravel mulch to imitate natural habitat
Erica	*E. cinerea* in flower • Lightly prune after flowering

MID-SUMMER	LATE SUMMER
Take half-hardened cuttings • Tip prune regularly	Check for insect pests • Prune after flowering • Mulch and fertilize
Mulch • Fertilize	Ensure good drainage in hot humid weather
Provide adequate water during dry spells • Mulch	Prune after flowering • Mulch and fertilize
Take half-hardened cuttings • Tip prune regularly	Check for insect pests • Prune after flowering • Mulch and fertilize
Mulch • Fertilize	Ensure good drainage in hot humid weather
Ensure adequate water during dry spells • Mulch	Prune after flowering • Mulch and fertilize
Ensure adequate water during dry spells • Remove galls if they appear at end of stems	Lightly prune to shape
Ensure adequate water during dry spells	Plants may suffer root rot disease in very humid weather
Prune spent flowers regularly to encourage continuous blooming	Ensure adequate water during dry spells, although all are drought-tolerant
Ensure adequate water during dry spells • Mulch well • Tip bug may cause wilting and death of young shoots	Check for pests; sawfly larvae may defoliate shrubs, thrip damage may cause deformed leaves
Check for aphids, thrips, and mealy bugs • Cut out variegated leaves	Check for aphids, thrips, and mealy bugs • Cut out variegated leaves
Ensure adequate water during dry spells, although *Cistus* is drought-tolerant	*Cistus* resents humid weather • Ensure soil is well-drained • Allow free air movement around plants
Take half-hardened cuttings	Take half-hardened cuttings

PLANT	EARLY SUMMER
SHRUBS (cont.)	
Euphorbia	Take cuttings of half-hardened wood • Ensure adequate water
Fuchsia	Liquid fertilize regularly to promote continuous flowering
Gardenia	If growth is stunted, dig up plants and check roots for nematode infestation; treat soil with a nematicide or plant marigolds
Hebe	Ensure adequate water during dry spells, although most are drought-tolerant
Hibiscus	Check for insect pests but spray only when necessary
Hydrangea	Protect from hot dry winds, as foliage and flowers may burn
Lavandula	Take half-hardened cuttings • Provide gravel mulch
Leptospermum	Take half-hardened cuttings
Nerium	Take half-hardened cuttings • Striped orange caterpillars may be present; leave to watch turn into butterflies
Philadelphus	Take softwood cuttings
Rhododendron	Apply compost or leaf litter around plants • Supply adequate water • Do not dig around plants as root system may be damaged
Rosa	Soak plants heavily once a week • Spray scale insects on stems with white oil plus an insecticide

MID-SUMMER	LATE SUMMER
Ensure adequate water	Ensure adequate water
Provide adequate water during dry spells	Cuttings may be taken • Check leaves for spider mite damage
Ensure adequate water during dry spells or buds may drop • Check for scale insects and mealy bugs on leaves and stems	Some leaves will turn yellow and drop off • If foliage is yellow or pale green, add iron or magnesium
Check for damage by scale insects or leaf miner	Downy mildew may occur in humid weather; spray with a fungicide
Hibiscus spray will control aphids, caterpillars	Do not apply mulch around stem or collar rot may occur
Provide adequate water and mulch well • Two-spotted mite may cause silvery leaves	Powdery mildew may occur in humid weather; spray with a fungicide • Take cuttings
Ensure good drainage and air flow around plants • Fertilize lightly	Stems may blacken and die in humid weather • Prune out dead wood
Watch out for scale insects, which may result in sooty mold on stems	Web-spinning moth larvae may cause damage; remove affected branches
Nerium plants are drought-tolerant, but provide them with adequate water for good flowering	Prune as flowers fade • Spray wax or brown scale on stems with white oil
Provide some shade in warm districts	Ensure adequate water • Mulch • Lightly fertilize
Protect plants from hot afternoon sun • Propagation may be carried out by layering	Remove unsprayed plants that have been badly damaged by insect attack • Check for mildew during humid weather; spray with a fungicide
Spray rust spores with sulfur; remove affected leaves • Prune back sucker growth from base rootstocks • Propagate by budding	Mildew may be a problem • Spray black spot at 2-week intervals • Allow good air movement

PLANT	EARLY SUMMER
SHRUBS *(cont.)*	
Spiraea	Provide adequate water during dry spells • Take softwood cuttings
Syringa	Mulch around plants and keep moist during dry spells
Viburnum	Take softwood cuttings of deciduous plants • Take half-hardened cuttings of evergreens • Prune old flower stems • Mulch and fertilize
Weigela	Take softwood cuttings • Prune after flowering
TREES	
Evergreen	Take half-hardened cuttings
Deciduous, all heights	Mulch and lightly fertilize
Ornamental, blossom and/or fruit	Provide cool moist conditions over summer • Mulch and fertilize
Tropical and subtropical	Prune young trees to shape • Mulch
Eucalyptus	Provide adequate water during dry spells
BULBS, CORMS, AND TUBERS	
Summer-flowering, sun	Provide adequate water during summer months while plants are in active growth and producing flowers
Summer-flowering, part-shade	Flowering
Autumn-flowering	Allow summer sun to bake bulbs in the ground

Mid-Summer	Late Summer
Provide adequate water during dry spells • Take softwood cuttings	Provide adequate water during dry spells • Take softwood cuttings
Take softwood cuttings or buy grafted specimens for greater hardiness	Lightly prune to shape
Ensure adequate water during dry spells • Mulch and fertilize	Two-spotted mite may cause silvering on leaves of *V. tinus*; control may be difficult
Ensure adequate water during dry spells • Mulch • Lightly fertilize	Ensure adequate water during dry spells
Watch for summer insect pests	Watch for summer insect pests
Watch for summer insect pests	Watch for summer insect pests
Prune back suckers near ground level • Watch for insect pests during warm weather	Watch for insect pests during warm weather
Mulch to conserve water	Watch for summer insect pests
Watch for summer insect pests • Prune young trees of unwanted branches	Watch for summer insect pests • Ensure soil is well-drained or root rot diseases may occur
Flowering • Provide adequate water	Flowering • Provide adequate water
Flowering	Allow *Cyclamen* plants to dry out
Plant bulbs • Prepare soil with plenty of compost and slow-release fertilizer for bulbs • Select *Colchicum* for a cool climate	Foliage dies down • Reduce watering • Plant bulbs just below ground in hot districts or with neck exposed in cool districts

PLANT	EARLY SUMMER
BULBS, CORMS, AND TUBERS (cont.)	
Winter-flowering	—
Winter–spring-flowering	Dormancy
Spring-flowering, sun	Dry off over summer • Bulbs may be lifted and stored in a cool dry place or left to naturalize
Spring-flowering, shade to part-shade	—
Summer–autumn-flowering	Maintain adequate water during dry spells
Spring–summer-flowering, sun	Allow bulbs to dry off during summer • A hot dry summer will help bulbs mature
Spring–summer-flowering, shade	Ensure plenty of shade so foliage and flowers do not burn or wilt
Allium	*A. moly* in flower through summer
Begonia	Liquid fertilize regularly • Do not water foliage if possible, just fine spray occasionally • Support flowering stems with thin wire stakes
Fritillaria	Store bulbs in a cool dry place
Gladiolus	Leave 3 or 4 leaves when flowers are cut

MID-SUMMER	LATE SUMMER
—	Order bulbs from a reputable grower • Sow seed of *Cyclamen* in compost seed-raising mix • Pot on when large enough
Plant out *Hippeastrum* with top at ground level in humus-rich soil	Dig in plenty of compost and well-rotted cow manure • Make sure soil is well-drained or bulbs may rot • Order bulbs
Dry off (bake) bulbs in ground	Add light dressing of lime/dolomite compost and blood and bone fertilizer to soil
—	Sow *Anemone* seed in sandy loam or seed-raising mix • Add compost, leaf mold, and a low-nitrogen fertilizer to soil
Bulbs begin main flowering season and continue to autumn	Keep *Crinum* plants well watered during the growing season
Allow bulbs to dry off during summer • A hot dry summer will help bulbs mature	Allow bulbs to dry off during summer • A hot dry summer will help bulbs mature
Ensure plenty of shade so foliage and flowers do not burn or wilt	Add plenty of compost and fertilizer to soil
Leave foliage to die down • Pick flowers for indoor decoration	Divide plants of *A. cristophii*
Plan a visit to begonia festivals	Plan a visit to begonia festivals
Store bulbs in a cool dry place	In cold climates prepare part-shaded moist sites with compost, cocopeat, and leaf mold • *Fritillaria* plants tolerate slightly limy soil
Lift when foliage starts to fade • Cut off stems when dry	Add compost and complete fertilizer • Dig sandy loam into heavy soils • *G. callianthus* in flower

PLANT	EARLY SUMMER
BULBS, CORMS, AND TUBERS (cont.)	
Lilium	Mulch with compost and fertilizer • Cut flower stems for decoration • Remove seed capsules as flowers fade
Narcissus	Cut down yellow foliage • Lift bulbs and store in cool dry place in warm climates
Tulipa	Check stored bulbs for any insect damage • Keep only large healthy bulbs • Use insecticide granules to control insect attack
HERBS	Harvest and dry leaf herbs • Place paper bag over annual herbs to collect seed
FRUIT TREES	
Tropical to subtropical	Establish plants during or after good summer rain • Add plenty of compost and complete fertilizer to soil
Cool-temperate	Practice fruit thinning so that branches are able to support crop • Mulch well to inhibit summer weeds
Citrus	Check for pests • If leaves are discolored, check for signs of deficiency in soil
CACTI AND SUCCULENTS	Check for pests on spines or under leaves
ORCHIDS	Mist spray daily • Water daily as required in late afternoon • Fertilize weekly with weak solution of orchid food

MID-SUMMER	LATE SUMMER
L., Longiflorum Hybrids reliable in warm climates • *L. regale* and *L. martagon* in flower • Take scales from flowering plants for propagation	Plant bulbs in a sunny spot in well-drained, rich, neutral soil • Allow plants to die down naturally after flowering
Order bulbs from catalog of reputable grower	Planting may start in cool districts • Lightly dress soil with dolomite/lime and/or add compost, well-rotted manure, and small amount of complete fertilizer
Order bulbs from reputable grower • Plan a garden display keeping same variety together for mass planting	In warm climates store bulbs in refrigerator before planting • Lightly dress soil with dolomite/lime and/or add compost and well-rotted manure
Mulch garden to conserve water	Take cuttings of all perennial herbs
Fertilize established plants • Buy virus-free stock, or from an organic grower	Check for seasonal pests • Identify common problems and treat with safe methods
Use trickle irrigation in dry spells • Summer prune where appropriate to encourage fruit • Bud graft tree fruits onto suitable rootstocks	Bud graft tree fruits onto suitable rootstocks • Check for branches rubbing against stakes
Leaf miner a common problem; cut off damaged section or spray weekly with an insecticide in cool of day	Mulch and fertilize
Protect tender specimens from really hot sun	Root rot diseases occur in humid weather • Top up gravel mulch and ensure good drainage
Control pests and diseases as noticed • Allow air circulation around pots • Fertilize weekly with weak solution of orchid food	Ensure plants are dry before watering • Check for fungal diseases in humid weather

PLANT	EARLY SUMMER
CLIMBERS AND CREEPERS	
Warm-temperate to cool-temperate	Mulch around climbers as weather heats up • Ensure adequate water during dry spells • Frequent wilting indicates dryness
Tropical to subtropical	Plant evergreen climbers during or after rain periods • Check foliage for damage by caterpillars; spray with a pesticide

PLANT	EARLY AUTUMN
ANNUALS AND PERENNIALS	
Annuals, low-growing, summer–autumn-flowering	Liquid fertilizer at 2-week intervals • Peak flowering time • Watch out for snails and caterpillars
Annuals, low-growing, spring–summer-flowering	Sow seed • Mix seed with sand for even coverage • Dress soil with dolomite/lime and/or add compost and complete or slow-release fertilizer
Annuals, low-growing, winter–spring-flowering	Protect seedlings with a fungicide • Dress garden beds with compost, complete fertilizer, or slow-release fertilizer • Sow seed direct
Annuals, medium-growing, summer-flowering	Sow seed of *Eustoma;* keep moist until germination
Annuals, medium-growing, spring–summer-flowering	Plant lupins with a minimum of fertilizer to encourage flowers • Plant seedlings • Apply lime when planting out *Matthiola*
Annuals, tall-growing, spring–summer-flowering	Sow seed • Protect from damping off using a fungicide • Lightly apply dolomite/lime to soil and/or add compost and slow-release fertilizer

MID-SUMMER

Cut overgrowth back drastically • Fertilize, mulch, and water well and growth should recommence • Spray caterpillars on large-leafed climbers with a pesticide

Mulch around plants

LATE SUMMER

Prune back early summer-flowering climbers • Lightly apply complete fertilizer • If soil is badly drained, root rot diseases may occur

Prune back excess or rampant growth regularly

MID-AUTUMN

Add spent flowers to compost • Peak flowering time • Store saved seed in dry place

Sow large seed direct

Protect young seedlings from snails

Cut back *Catharanthus;* treat as biennial • Add spent annuals to compost heap

Plant seedlings • Plant *Dianthus* with the crown above soil level to avoid phytophthora collar rot

Plant seedlings • Give weak solution of liquid fertilizer once established • Protect from snails

LATE AUTUMN

Practice crop rotation • Use green manure crops • Wear safety equipment if you plan to spray

Protect seedlings from transplant shock by drenching soil with liquid fertilizer

Liquid fertilize with weak solution of fertilizer

Sow seed • Keep sheltered • For hard-to-get seeds contact a reputable seed supply company

Thin seedlings to avoid overcrowding and diseases • Plant seedlings

Plant seedlings • Give weak solution of liquid fertilizer once established

PLANT	EARLY AUTUMN
ANNUALS AND PERENNIALS (cont.)	
Annuals, tall-growing, summer-flowering	Add compost or waste from worm farm • Store saved seeds in dry location
Perennials, spring– early summer-flowering	Divide *Anigozanthos* • Take cuttings of *Dianthus* • Sow seed of *Potentilla*
Perennials, spring–early summer-flowering, short-lived	Cut back old foliage of *Aquilegia* and mulch with compost • Liquid fertilize to encourage new growth
Perennials, summer-flowering, sun	Collect seed from flower stems and store in cool dry place
Perennials, summer-flowering, shade to part-shade	Prepare soil with generous amount of compost, leaf mold, cocopeat • Order new plants • Collect seed and store in cool dry place
Perennials, winter– early summer-flowering	*Bergenia* produces colored foliage
Perennials, summer– autumn-flowering	Peak flowering • Cut flower stems for indoor decoration
Perennials, ground covers and rock plants, mild climate	Take cuttings of gazanias and place in peat/sand mix in warm position • Second flush of flowers as weather cools
Perennials, alpines, ground covers, and rock plants, cool climate	Take cuttings now • Sow seed and keep moist until germination
Perennials, subshrubs, sun	Plant seed collected during summer; keep moist until germination • Light pruning of plants

Mid-Autumn	**Late Autumn**
Add spent plants to compost heap • Practice crop rotation • Remove autumn weeds as they appear	Investigate companion planting to reduce spraying with chemicals
Plant *Lupinus*, Russell Hybrids now but only in a cold climate • Plants begin winter dormancy • Plants may be divided now	Dig in compost and complete fertilizer • Apply low-phosphorus fertilizer to native plants • Divide *Lupinus*, Russell Hybrids every 3 to 5 years
Prepare a cool site for *Aquilegia* and *Myosotis*; apply compost and a complete fertilizer	Prepare a cool site for *Aquilegia* and *Myosotis*; apply compost and a complete fertilizer
Order new plants for summer flowering • Check heights and spreads • Organize a color scheme	Cut down old flower stems to ground level • Plants may be divided now • Prepare soil as for early spring
Divide established plants	Tidy up plants of old flowering stems • Allow leaves from deciduous trees to gently cover established plants
Divide plants • Prepare soil with good quantity of compost and complete fertilizer	Prune any old remaining leaves from deciduous *Helleborus* plants when the flower buds appear
Peak flowering	Flowering may continue until frosts • Cut down spent flower stems to ground level • Divide established plants
Plants may be divided • Liquid fertilize plants in warm districts	Reset stones in rock gardens to protect plants during winter
Divide mat- and clump-forming plants	Protect plants from winter wet if necessary • Plan a raised bed to display alpine plants
Spot flowering occurs on some plants	Spot flowering occurs on some plants

PLANT	EARLY AUTUMN
ANNUALS AND PERENNIALS (cont.)	
Perennials, subshrubs, shade to part-shade	Some plants still producing flowers in warmer areas
Perennials, water-garden plants	Divide established clumps of waterside plants
Perennials, for tropical effect	Add plenty of manure and compost to soil • Establish plants in pots then plant in spring
Perennials, irises	Sow seed and keep moist until germination
Perennials, pelargoniums	Take cuttings from overgrown summer growth; strike in sand • Keep cuttings in warm dry location
Perennials, primulas	Apply blood and bone to existing plants • Remove plants that flower poorly
SHRUBS	
Low-growing, frost-hardy, evergreen	Choose right shrub for right location • Prepare planting site with compost and complete fertilizer
Low-growing, frost-tender, evergreen	Lightly prune • Mulch • Lightly fertilize
Low-growing, frost-hardy, deciduous	Mulch • Lightly fertilize for winter hardiness
Medium- to tall-growing, frost-hardy, evergreen	Choose right shrub for right location • Prepare planting site with compost and complete fertilizer
Medium- to tall-growing, frost-tender, evergreen	Mulch • Lightly prune • Lightly fertilize
Medium- to tall-growing, frost-hardy, deciduous	Mulch • Lightly fertilize for winter hardiness

MID-AUTUMN	LATE AUTUMN
Plants may be divided now	Allow leaves from deciduous trees to protect plants over winter
Remove all dead or dying foliage from submerged plants	Cover ponds to keep out leaves from deciduous trees • Move frost-tender plants to warm position
Cut down flowering stems of *Hedychium* after they have finished flowering • Tidy up plants	Cut down flowering stems of *Hedychium* after they have finished flowering • Tidy up plants
Divide overcrowded clumps • Do not damage rhizomes when digging up • Cut foliage down before replanting	Divide overcrowded clumps • Do not damage rhizomes when digging up • Cut foliage down before replanting
Remove spent flowers	Remove old foliage and tidy up plants
Prepare garden site with compost and old manure • Select site with heavy or clay soil	Set out new plants • Divide old plants; trim old roots and excess foliage
Water well until established • Mulch	Water well until established
Add compost and complete fertilizer at planting time	Add compost and complete fertilizer at planting time
Autumn color on some plants	Autumn color on some plants
Water well until established • Mulch	Water well until established
Add compost and complete fertilizer at planting time	Add compost and complete fertilizer at planting time
Autumn color on some plants	Autumn color on some plants

PLANT	EARLY AUTUMN
SHRUBS (cont.)	
Acacia	Top up mulch around plants • Lightly fertilize with blood and bone • Ensure soil is moist before applying fertilizer
Banksia	Ensure soil is well-drained before planting
Buddleja	Prune old flowers • Apply compost around plants
Callistemon	Sow seed collected from previous season; keep moist until germination • Lightly fertilize with blood and bone
Camellia	Lightly fertilize; water well before and after • Apply compost mulch around plants; keep away from main stem
Cistus	Prune lightly • Tip prune
Erica	Provide well-drained soil for planting • Check soil pH
Euphorbia	Mulch around plants and fertilize
Fuchsia	Plant in sites sheltered from strong wind • Apply compost and complete fertilizer before planting • Lightly fertilize established plants
Gardenia	Tip prune regularly • Lightly fertilize with blood and bone
Hebe	Mulch • Lightly fertilize with complete fertilizer
Hibiscus	Select a warm location for planting • Ensure good drainage • Dig in compost • Fertilize once established
Hydrangea	Flowering

MID-AUTUMN	LATE AUTUMN
Plant new specimens • Prepare soil by digging in compost and slow-release fertilizer	Plant new specimens • Prepare soil by digging in compost and slow-release fertilizer
Use a low-phosphorus plant food for banksias	Flowers appear on *B. ericifolia*
Prune lightly	Prune lightly
Mulch well and check again for insect pests	Watch for web worm in dry districts
Debud large flowering varieties to encourage better size and color • *C. sasanqua* in flower • Established plants may be moved	Debud
Cistus tolerates coastal conditions	*Cistus* tolerates coastal conditions
Cut old flowering stems and lightly prune to shape	——
Mulch around plants and fertilize	Leaves fall from *E. pulcherrima* as flowers form
Flowering continues in warm districts	Flowering may continue in warm districts
Second flush of flowers may occur	Second flush of flowers may occur
Some species flowering	Some species flowering
Flowering continues	Flowering continues
Remove spent flowerheads	Remove spent flowers • Prune out dead wood

PLANT	EARLY AUTUMN
SHRUBS *(cont.)*	
Lavandula	Some species still flowering
Leptospermum	Top up mulch • Lightly fertilize
Nerium	Prune old or faded flowers
Philadelphus	—
Rhododendron	Apply light application of fertilizer, and water in well • Take cuttings of half-hardened wood • Pot on layer-grown plants
Rosa	Lightly dress soil with dolomite/lime and/or dig in compost or well-rotted manure, especially in sandy soil • Improve drainage in heavy soil
Spiraea	Prune lightly to shape
Syringa	Mulch around established plants with compost
Viburnum	Mulch and fertilize lightly
Weigela	—
TREES	
Evergreen	Plant new trees in areas of autumn rains • Lightly fertilize established trees
Deciduous, all heights	Prepare planting site 2 months ahead if planting bare-rooted young trees
Ornamental, blossom and/or fruit	Prepare planting site 2 months ahead for bare-rooted trees

MID-AUTUMN	LATE AUTUMN
Some species still flowering	Prune off dead flowers to encourage continuous blooming of *L. dentata*
Tip prune regularly	——
——	——
——	Some species may be deciduous over winter
Apply mulch of compost or well-rotted animal manure	Spot flowering occurs
Pick rose hip stems for decoration • Check rose catalogs for varieties suitable for your area	Do not prune old-fashioned roses • Clip annually; shorten back flowering canes • Take cuttings
In cold districts autumn leaf color may occur	In cold districts autumn leaf color may occur
Mulch around established plants with compost	Prepare soil for planting with light application of dolomite/lime and/or compost • Ensure good drainage
Autumn leaf color may occur in deciduous species • Berries may remain on some species	Autumn leaf color may occur in deciduous species
Plants begin to lose leaves	Plants continue to lose leaves
Plant new trees in areas of autumn rains • Lightly fertilize established trees	Plant new trees in areas of autumn rains • Lightly fertilize established trees
Dig in plenty of compost and complete fertilizer	Transplant established trees
Dig in plenty of compost and complete fertilizer	Ornamental fruits appear on *Malus* • Leave on tree for winter or until fallen

PLANT	EARLY AUTUMN
TREES *(cont.)*	
Tropical and subtropical	Mulch and lightly fertilize
Eucalyptus	Plant if autumn rains occur
BULBS, CORMS, AND TUBERS	
Summer-flowering, sun	Plant *Eucomis* bulbs just below soil surface • Plant *Ornithogalum* 3 in (8 cm) deep, 6 in (15 cm) apart
Summer-flowering, part-shade	Do not divide bulbs
Autumn-flowering	Flowering • Top dress areas of naturalized bulbs with compost • Liquid fertilize regularly
Winter-flowering	Select a cool, moist, part-shaded site under deciduous trees or shrubs • Add compost, leaf mold, and slow-release fertilizer • Plant bulbs 2 in (5 cm) deep
Winter–spring-flowering	Plant *Crocus* under deciduous trees in cold climates • In warm areas plant in pots of bulb fiber
Spring-flowering, sun	Bulb planting time • Keep moist during growing season
Spring-flowering, shade to part-shade	Choose a cool moist spot for *Cyclamen*
Summer–autumn-flowering	Choose a sunny spot and well-drained soil enriched with compost and low-nitrogen bulb fertilizer for bulb planting
Spring–summer-flowering, sun	Sow bulb seed in seed-raising mix

MID-AUTUMN	LATE AUTUMN
Prune out dead or diseased limbs • Plant new trees during rainy weather	Prune out dead or diseased limbs • Plant new trees during rainy weather
Plant if autumn rains occur	Plant if autumn rains occur
Plant *Crinum* bulbs in warm climates or divide clumps and plant offsets • Plant just below soil surface	In frost-prone regions, lift *Crocosmia* bulbs and store dry over winter
Propagate *Cyclamen* from seed	Mulch planting area with compost or allow leaves from deciduous trees to gently cover bulbs
Flowering • Divide established clumps • Replant healthiest bulbs • Plant *Nerine filifolia* in a rock garden	Flowering • Fertilize bulbs as foliage begins to die down • *Nerine* foliage appears after flowering
Select a cool, moist, part-shaded site under deciduous trees or shrubs • Add compost, leaf mold, and slow-release fertilizer • Plant bulbs 2 in (5 cm) deep	——
Crocus species in flower • Water *Galanthus* well during the growing period	*Crocus* species in flower • Water *Galanthus* well during the growing period
Bulb planting time • Plant *Sparaxis*	Bulb planting time
Plants left in ground may be divided • Plant *Anemone* and *Cyclamen*	Spot flowering of *Anemone* occurs if plants have been left in ground • Allow deciduous leaves to fall over bulb planting area
Water bulbs well once foliage appears • Liquid fertilize when flower buds appear • Protect from snails	The end of the flowering season for most *Crinum* species • Store dormant *Eucomis* bulbs indoors in frost-prone areas
Plant bulbs of *Ixia* 3 in (8 cm) deep • Lightly apply compost, but average soil is tolerated	——

PLANT	EARLY AUTUMN
BULBS, CORMS, AND TUBERS (cont.)	
Spring–summer-flowering, shade	Plan a woodland garden in a part-shaded site with plenty of leaf compost
Allium	Plant all seed varieties; sow in seed-raising mix and pot when ready • Top dress with blood and bone as flowering dies down
Begonia	Plan a visit to begonia festivals
Fritillaria	In cold climates only, plant *Fritillaria* 4 in (10 cm) deep, 8 in (20 cm) apart • Choose *F. persica* for warmer climates
Gladiolus	Start planting spring-flowering plants; plant below freezing depth
Lilium	Sow seed in seed-raising mix mulched with organic matter • Raise in pots • Divide and plant new bulbs in conditioned soil
Narcissus	Plant *N.*, Bulbocodium and *N.*, Cyclamineus in rock gardens or pots 2 in (5 cm) deep, $1\frac{1}{4}$ in (3 cm) apart • Plant others 3 in (8 cm) deep, 4 in (10 cm) apart
Tulipa	Planting time • Overplant with violas or forget-me-nots • Plant same varieties en masse • Add slow-release bulb fertilizer
HERBS	Continue to take cuttings • Harvest ripening seed

MID-AUTUMN	LATE AUTUMN
Main bulb planting time	Main bulb planting time
Plant bulbs of all varieties when available	Plant bulbs of all varieties when available
Lift tubers and allow to dry off in a cool position • Do not remove soil from around tuber until dry	Greenhouse-grown plants are available for indoor use most of the year • Store dry tubers in sand or dry peat moss
—	—
Plant spring-flowering corms below freezing depth	Corms can be planted in subtropical or warm climates • Plant at intervals to flower over a long period
Plant bulbs immediately; do not store	Avoid using garden forks as bulbs damage easily • Greenhouse-grown plants available in flower • After flowering, plant out in spring
Lightly fertilize bulbs with blood and bone if naturalized in garden position	Overwatering bulbs may cause bulb rot • Watch for aphids when buds form • Otherwise few problems
Planting time	Planting time
Harvest and dry last of summer herbs • Remove spent annual herbs and add to compost heap	Cut back overgrown plants • Shelter over winter

PLANT	EARLY AUTUMN
FRUIT TREES	
Tropical to subtropical	Prune to allow light into tree, or shape for good fruiting
Cool-temperate	Prepare ground for planting bare-rooted trees and soft-fruit canes • Dig in compost or well-rotted manure • Check soil pH; the ideal level is 6–6.5
Citrus	Mulch and fertilize
CACTI AND SUCCULENTS	Root rot diseases occur in humid weather • Ensure perfect drainage
ORCHIDS	Provide a well-lit position but not direct sunlight
CLIMBERS AND CREEPERS	
Warm-temperate to cool-temperate	Check undersides of leaves for snails • Spray scale insects with white oil • Ants climbing up stems indicates presence of scale insects
Tropical to subtropical	Summer-flowering species continue to flower in warm districts

PLANT	EARLY WINTER
ANNUALS AND PERENNIALS	
Annuals, low-growing, summer–autumn-flowering	Sow seed in hot districts • Sharpen and oil garden tools

MID-AUTUMN

Mulch • Fertilize lightly

Check pollination requirements of new plants •
Provide stakes or trellis support where appropriate
• Take hardwood cuttings from established plants

Ensure adequate water at all times

Remove old dry leaves around succulents •
Repot crowded specimens

Protect flower spikes from insect damage

Deciduous climbers show autumn color •
Prune after all leaves have dropped or growth
may recommence while weather is still warm

Second flush of flowers for spring-flowering
species

LATE AUTUMN

Mulch • Fertilize lightly

Check pollination requirements of new plants
• Take hardwood cuttings from established
plants

Ensure adequate water at all times

Tidy up plants and move to a sunny location •
Give weak solution of liquid fertilizer for those
with flower buds

Reduce watering in deciduous species

Dig plenty of compost and a complete fertilizer into soil • Allow adequate space and
strong support • Ensure soil is well-drained

Mulch well around plants and ensure adequate
water during dry spells

MID-WINTER

Join a garden club to discuss your success with
others

LATE WINTER

Sow seed • Lightly apply dolomite/lime to soil
and/or add compost and apply complete or
slow-release fertilizer • In shaded positions add
extra cocopeat

PLANT	EARLY WINTER
ANNUALS AND PERENNIALS *(cont.)*	
Annuals, low-growing, spring–summer-flowering	In frosty areas protect plants with loose straw or sow seed in protected position then plant when frost is over
Annuals, low-growing, winter-spring-flowering	Protect plants with loose straw in frosty areas
Annuals, medium-growing, summer-flowering	Protect plants in frosty areas
Annuals, medium-growing, spring–summer-flowering	Use loose straw to protect against frost, or plant seedlings in spring • Sow seed in hot districts • Protect seedlings from wind
Annuals, tall-growing, spring–summer-flowering	Protect seedlings from frost in cold districts or plant out when danger of frost is over
Annuals, tall-growing, summer-flowering	Look for seed suppliers in garden magazines • Sow seed in hot districts
Perennials, spring–early summer-flowering	Protect plants over winter with loose straw
Perennials, spring–early summer-flowering, short-lived	Protect frost-tender plants from early frost with a layer of loose straw
Perennials, summer-flowering, sun	Protect plants with loose straw in frosty areas
Perennials, summer-flowering, shade to part-shade	Winter dormancy
Perennials, winter–early summer-flowering	*Bergenia* plants develop red-tinted foliage

MID-WINTER	LATE WINTER
In frosty areas protect plants with loose straw or sow seed in protected position then plant when frost is over	In frosty areas protect plants with loose straw or sow seed in protected position then plant when frost is over
Flowering begins in warm districts	Spray with pyrethrum if aphids appear • Check underside of leaves
Sow seed in warm districts • Plant a children's summer garden • Do not use sprays in gardens where children play	Sow seed in warm districts • Plant a children's summer garden • Do not use sprays in gardens where children play
Use loose straw to protect against frost, or plant seedlings in spring • Sow seed in hot districts • Protect seedlings from wind	Use loose straw to protect against frost, or plant seedlings in spring • Sow seed in hot districts • Protect seedlings from wind
Apply loose straw around plants to help protect from cold	Protect plants from cold winds • Give weak solution of liquid fertilizer
Start a worm farm for valuable humus and summer fishing	Sow seed ensuring good light and even moisture • Lightly apply dolomite/lime to soil and/or add compost and complete or slow-release fertilizer
Protect plants over winter with loose straw	Protect plants over winter with loose straw
Protect plants in frosty areas with loose straw	Protect plants in frosty areas with loose straw • Propagate *Myosotis* by division
Take root cuttings of *Echinops, Eryngium, Gaillardia, Verbascum*	Take root cuttings of *Echinops, Eryngium, Gaillardia, Verbascum*
Winter dormancy	Winter dormancy
New foliage begins to appear • *Helleborus* in flower	New foliage begins to appear • Some plants may start to flower • Apply a weak solution of liquid fertilizer

PLANT	EARLY WINTER
ANNUALS AND PERENNIALS *(cont.)*	
Perennials, summer–autumn-flowering	Winter dormancy
Perennials, ground covers and rock plants, mild climate	Protect plants with loose straw in frosty areas • Provide minimum water over winter
Perennials, alpines, ground covers, and rock plants, cool climate	Protect plants from winter wet if necessary • Plan a raised bed to display alpine plants
Perennials, subshrubs, sun	Protect plants in areas of severe frost
Perennials, subshrubs, shade to part-shade	Allow leaves from deciduous trees to protect plants over winter
Perennials, water-garden plants	Cover ponds to keep out leaves from deciduous trees • Move frost-tender plants to warm position
Perennials, for tropical effect	Reduce watering and allow plants to rest
Perennials, irises	Divide overcrowded clumps, if necessary
Perennials, pelargoniums	Protect plants in frosty areas • Move to warm location over winter • *P. echinatum* loses leaves—keep dry over winter
Perennials, primulas	Take root cuttings of *P. denticulata* in 2 in (5 cm) pieces; propagate in sharp sand
SHRUBS	
Low-growing, frost-hardy, evergreen	Protect young plants in frosty areas
Low-growing, frost-tender, evergreen	Provide some winter protection if growing in cold districts
Low-growing, frost-hardy, deciduous	Take hardwood cuttings

Mid-Winter	Late Winter
Winter dormancy	Protect emerging foliage from snail damage
Protect plants with loose straw in frosty areas • Provide minimum water over winter	Prepare soil for spring planting with compost and general-purpose fertilizer • Prepare heavy soil with gypsum and drainage material
Apply loamy soil, cocopeat, and sharp sand • Provide extra cocopeat for acid-loving plants such as *Gentiana*	Apply loamy soil, cocopeat, and sharp sand • Provide extra cocopeat for acid-loving plants such as *Gentiana*
Protect plants in areas of severe frost	Protect plants in areas of severe frost
Allow leaves from deciduous trees to protect plants over winter	Allow leaves from deciduous trees to protect plants over winter
Cover ponds to keep out leaves from deciduous trees • Move frost-tender plants to warm position	Clean and drain pond or water garden in preparation for spring planting
Supply a well-drained position	Supply a well-drained position
Divide overcrowded clumps, if necessary	Divide overcrowded clumps, if necessary
Prepare soil for summer display • Dig in compost and complete fertilizer • Ensure good drainage	Protect plants from strong winds • *P. echinatum* in flower
Propagate dormant plants by dividing established clumps	Move plants outdoors as weather warms up
Protect young plants in frosty areas	Protect young plants in frosty areas
Provide some winter protection if growing in cold districts	Prune after flowering in warm districts • Mulch and fertilize
Flowering may begin in warm districts	Flowering may begin

PLANT	EARLY WINTER
SHRUBS (cont.)	
Medium- to tall-growing, frost-hardy, evergreen	Protect young plants in frosty areas
Medium- to tall-growing, frost-tender, evergreen	Provide some winter protection if growing in cold districts
Medium- to tall-growing, frost-hardy, deciduous	Take hardwood cuttings
Acacia	Flowering begins
Banksia	Provide a gravel mulch around plants in very cold districts
Buddleja	Plants may be deciduous in very cold districts
Callistemon	Watch for web worm in dry districts
Camellia	Select camellias while in flower • Sun may damage flowers in the morning if they are wet with dew
Cistus	Protect from very cold winds
Erica	——
Euphorbia	Protect flowering stems from strong winds
Fuchsia	Provide some shelter from cold winter winds
Gardenia	Provide shelter from cold winds • Move plants in pots to warm location in frosty areas
Hebe	Some species flowering

MID-WINTER	LATE WINTER
Protect young plants in frosty areas	Protect young plants in frosty areas
Provide some winter protection if growing in cold districts	Prune after flowering in warm districts • Mulch and fertilize
Remove dead wood • Flowering may begin in warm districts	Flowering may begin
Flowering	Flowering
Provide a gravel mulch around plants in very cold districts	Provide a gravel mulch around plants in very cold districts
B. salviifolia in flower in warm districts	Cut out old or woody stems
——	——
Prepare planting site • Dig in plenty of compost • Add cocopeat • Ensure soil is well-drained to deter root rot	Prune while blooming to remove dead, diseased, or straggling branches
Protect from very cold winds	Protect from very cold winds
E. carnea in flower • Tolerates a position with some lime	*E. darleyensis* in flower
Protect flowering stems from strong winds	Protect flowering stems from strong winds
Frost may damage some stems but growth will recommence in spring	Frost may damage some stems but growth will recommence in spring
Provide shelter from cold winds • Move plants in pots to warm location in frosty areas	Provide shelter from cold winds • Move plants in pots to warm location in frosty areas
Some species flowering	Some species flowering

PLANT	EARLY WINTER
SHRUBS *(cont.)*	
Hibiscus	In warm districts cut back by half deciduous hibiscus, *H. mutabilis* and *H. syriacus* • After pruning, mulch and fertilize with complete fertilizer
Hydrangea	Frost may cause some damage in cold districts; wait until spring to prune
Lavandula	*L. dentata* produces purple bracts with its flowers
Leptospermum	——
Nerium	Give some protection to young plants in frosty areas
Philadelphus	Protect *P. mexicanus* from frost; grow in pot and move to sheltered location
Rhododendron	Protect young plants in frosty areas • Move vireyas into warm sheltered position if in pots
Rosa	Main pruning time for Large-flowered (Hybrid Tea) and Cluster-flowered (Floribunda) roses • Prune back dead, weak, or spindly growth • Prune to outward pointing bud
Spiraea	——
Syringa	Select grafted, bare-rooted, healthy specimens for planting
Viburnum	*V. tinus* begins to flower
Weigela	Deciduous
TREES	
Evergreen	Mulch around young trees with gravel to protect from frost, or cover with hessian overnight

MID-WINTER	LATE WINTER
As for early winter in cooler districts • Use prunings for cutting material	——
Prune *H. macrophylla* in warm climates; prune to flowering buds	Prune *H. macrophylla* in warm climates; prune to flowering buds
L. dentata produces purple bracts with its flowers	*L. dentata* produces purple bracts with its flowers
——	——
Give some protection to young plants in frosty areas	Give some protection to young plants in frosty areas
Protect *P. mexicanus* from frost; grow in pot and move to sheltered location	Some species may be deciduous
Ensure adequate water if cold dry winds occur	Flowering in warm districts
Pruning continues • Bare-rooted roses may be purchased • Water well after planting • When planting, do not allow roots to be bent	Spray scale insects with a white oil and water mix • To exhibit roses, join a horticultural society
——	——
Prune out dead or weak shoots on established plants	Some species may flower again
V. tinus flowering	*V. tinus* flowering
Deciduous	Deciduous
Mulch around young trees with gravel to protect from frost, or cover with hessian overnight	Mulch around young trees with gravel to protect from frost, or cover with hessian overnight

PLANT	EARLY WINTER
TREES *(cont.)*	
Deciduous, all heights	Protect young trees with gravel mulch in frosty areas
Ornamental, blossom and/or fruit	Purchase bare-rooted trees • Do not let roots turn up when planting • Prune branches lightly after planting
Tropical and subtropical	Protect trees from cold wind if growing in cooler climates
Eucalyptus	Protect young trees with gravel mulch in frosty areas
BULBS, CORMS, AND TUBERS	
Summer-flowering, sun	Bulbs are hardy but give some protection in areas of severe frost with mulch of loose straw or dry leaves
Summer-flowering, part-shade	Keep in pots over winter
Autumn-flowering	Flowers die down • Allow leaves from deciduous trees to cover areas of naturalized bulbs
Winter-flowering	Main flowering period
Winter–spring-flowering	Protect *Hippeastrum* bulbs in frosty areas with mulch of loose straw • Bulb flowering time from now until mid-spring
Spring-flowering, sun	Provide shelter from cold winds • Protect bulbs in frosty areas with mulch of loose straw or dry leaves
Spring-flowering, shade to part-shade	Protect *Anemone* in frosty areas with mulch of loose straw
Summer–autumn-flowering	Dormant months • Protect tender plants from frost

MID-WINTER	LATE WINTER
Take hardwood cuttings	Remove old or dead branches • Shape trees if not flowering species
Water well until established, but not excessively	Water well until established, but not excessively
Protect trees from cold wind if growing in cooler climates	Protect trees from cold wind if growing in cooler climates
Protect young trees with gravel mulch in frosty areas	Protect young trees with gravel mulch in frosty areas
Bulbs are hardy but give some protection in areas of severe frost with mulch of loose straw or dry leaves	Bulbs are hardy but give some protection in areas of severe frost with mulch of loose straw or dry leaves
Keep in pots over winter	Keep in pots over winter
Protect bulbs with loose straw in areas of severe frost	Protect bulbs with loose straw in areas of severe frost
Main flowering period • Do not allow to seed as plants may escape to areas of native vegetation	Leave bulbs to naturalize
Protect *Hippeastrum* bulbs in frosty areas with mulch of loose straw	Protect *Hippeastrum* flower buds from snails • Liquid fertilize regularly • Plant in pots for indoor decoration
Provide shelter from cold winds • Protect bulbs in frosty areas with mulch of loose straw or dry leaves	Flowering may start in warm climates • Pick naturalized flowers from roadsides and areas of native vegetation
Do not water *Hyacinthus* unless it is an extremely dry winter	Ensure adequate moisture if cold dry winds occur
Dormant months • Protect tender plants from frost	Dormant months • Protect tender plants from frost

PLANT	EARLY WINTER
BULBS, CORMS, AND TUBERS (cont.)	
Spring–summer-flowering, sun	In frost-prone areas grow potted bulbs in sheltered positions; plant out in spring • If left in ground, protect with straw
Spring–summer-flowering, shade	Protect plants from frost in cold districts; keep in a dry sheltered position
Allium	——
Begonia	Turn potted specimens on their sides to dry off
Fritillaria	Watch for winter weeds
Gladiolus	Lift bulbs in cold areas or wet areas • Dust bulbs with sulfur fungicide and store in a cool dry place
Lilium	Do not water bulbs over winter
Narcissus	Protect plants from strong wind • Odd flowers of *N.*, Jonquilla and Apodanthus may appear in warm climates
Tulipa	Watch for winter weeds
HERBS	*Artemisia* goes dormant
FRUIT TREES	
Tropical to subtropical	Protect plants from cold winds if growing in warm-temperate climates

MID-WINTER	LATE WINTER
In frost-prone areas grow potted bulbs in sheltered positions; plant out in spring • If left in ground, protect with straw	In frost-prone areas grow potted bulbs in sheltered positions; plant out in spring • If left in ground, protect with straw
Protect plants from frost in cold districts; keep in a dry sheltered position	Liquid fertilize as buds start to develop in late winter and early spring
——	——
Prepare a soil mix for begonias with equal parts loamy soil, leaf mold or cocopeat, cow manure, and blood and bone	Tubers available until late spring; begin in pots of sand/peat before transferring to garden • Ensure tubers are firm
Watch for winter weeds	Watch for winter weeds
Store bulbs in a cool dry place	Store bulbs in a cool dry place
Frost-hardy over winter	Frost-hardy over winter
Liquid fertilize as flower stems appear • *N.*, Tazetta in flower	*N.*, Cyclamineus and *N.*, Jonquilla and Apodanthus in flower
Watch for winter weeds	——
Mulch plants with loose straw over winter	Sow annual seeds either under glass or in a well-protected position • Lightly apply dolomite/lime to soil and/or dig in compost and complete fertilizer
Protect plants from cold winds if growing in warm-temperate climates	Protect plants from cold winds if growing in warm-temperate climates

PLANT	EARLY WINTER
FRUIT TREES *(cont.)*	
Cool-temperate	Soak bare-rooted plants well, before planting out; do not plant below graft level • Protect young plants from severe frost with hessian tent • Prune established plants to maintain high yields
Citrus	Choose citrus species by cold tolerance; some are frost-tender
CACTI AND SUCCULENTS	Some are frost-hardy but most will require protection over winter • Move pots to sheltered location
ORCHIDS	Maintain warmth during winter months where appropriate • Reduce watering
CLIMBERS AND CREEPERS	
Warm-temperate to cool-temperate	Add gypsum to badly drained heavy soil or use gravel at bottom of planting hole • Protect frost-tender species with hessian
Tropical to subtropical	Mulch well around plants and ensure adequate water during dry spells • Protect with hessian blanket if growing in cold districts

PLANT	EARLY SPRING
ANNUALS AND PERENNIALS	
Annuals, low-growing, summer–autumn-flowering	Sow seed or plant seedlings • Water regularly • Protect from snails • Apply liquid fertilizer to increase humus level and prevent transplant shock

MID-WINTER

Protect young plants from severe frost with hessian tent • Prune established plants to maintain high yields • Prune to open structure to allow light to reach ripening fruit

Cold winds and frost can cause foliage to curl up

Reduce watering for all except those in flower

Maintain warmth during winter months where appropriate • Reduce watering

Planting time for deciduous climbers • Prune climbing roses • Prune *Wisteria* to flowering buds

Frost may kill tropical species or damage sub-tropical ones • Growth may recommence from base in spring

LATE WINTER

Protect young plants from severe frost with hessian tent • Prune established plants to maintain high yields • Prune to open structure to allow light to reach ripening fruit

Fertilize and mulch

Bring potted specimens indoors for brief periods and place in a well-lit location

Maintain warmth during winter months where appropriate • Reduce watering

Wait until all frost danger is passed before cutting back damaged climbers

In warm districts, prune back stems that have been damaged by cold weather or wind • Side dress established plants with blood and bone or complete fertilizer

MID-SPRING

Thin seedlings if too close • Plant seedlings in cold districts • Protect seedlings from damping off with a fungicide

LATE SPRING

Collect rainwater to water garden • Tip prune • Liquid fertilize buds at 2-week intervals

PLANT	EARLY SPRING
ANNUALS AND PERENNIALS *(cont.)*	
Annuals, low-growing, spring– summer-flowering	Pinch out growing tips to encourage bushy growth • Liquid fertilize • Spray leaf spot with a fungicide • Plant seedlings in cool districts
Annuals, low-growing, winter– spring-flowering	Remove spent flowers to encourage more blooms • Liquid fertilize at 2-week intervals
Annuals, medium-growing, summer-flowering	Plant seed in cold areas after frost has passed • Cultivate soil for direct sowing and add sand
Annuals, medium-growing, spring– summer-flowering	Sow seed in cold districts
Annuals, tall-growing, spring– summer-flowering	Provide support for flower stems using light-weight stakes • Liquid fertilize regularly • Plant seedlings in cold districts
Annuals, tall-growing, summer-flowering	Sow seed direct or plant out seedlings when frost is over • Protect from snails • Apply liquid fertilizer when transplanting seedlings
Perennials, spring– early summer-flowering	Main flowering season begins
Perennials, spring–early summer-flowering, short-lived	Main flowering period • Deadhead flowers to encourage continuous blooming • Fresh seed may be sown
Perennials, summer-flowering, sun	Take stem cuttings • Divide plants • Lightly dress soil with lime; dig in compost, complete fertilizer, or slow-release fertilizer for perennials
Perennials, summer-flowering, shade to part-shade	Plant seed and keep moist until germination in warm sheltered place
Perennials, winter– early summer-flowering	Plants in flower

MID-SPRING	LATE SPRING
Spray caterpillars with a pesticide • Check undersides of leaves	Flowering continues • If growth is poor, check soil for nematode activity
Flowering continues	Flowering continues
Protect young seedlings from snails and slugs • Practice crop rotation	As flower buds form, liquid fertilize at 2-week intervals
As buds appear, liquid fertilize at 2-week intervals	Spray rust on foliage underside with a fungicide • Spray budworm on *Dianthus* buds with an insecticide • Pick flowers for indoor decoration
Spray pests with pyrethrum or use biological control • Liquid fertilize to promote flowering	Remove spent flowers • Spray rust and powdery mildew with a fungicide or wettable sulfur • Mulch • Break down organic matter with liquid fertilizer
Thin out seedlings and support with stakes or tripods • Spray caterpillars with an insecticide • Liquid fertilize regularly	Spray cutworms with an insecticide • Control weeds to reduce cutworm population • Sow extra seed to fill in gaps of planting
Spray budworm on *Dianthus* with an insecticide	Collect seed as it matures
Main flowering period • Deadhead flowers to encourage continuous blooming • Fresh seed may be sown	Cut back plants after flowering • Use for cuttings
Protect new foliage from snails and slugs • Take stem cuttings from established plants	Mulch around plants to conserve water and suppress weeds • Add water-storing granules in dry areas • Side dress plants with blood and bone
Side dress with blood and bone as weather warms up	Mulch garden and compost around plants
Collect and sow seed as it ripens • Stake tall-flowering stems	Pot on self-sown seedlings

PLANT	EARLY SPRING
ANNUALS AND PERENNIALS *(cont.)*	
Perennials, summer–autumn-flowering	Divide plants • Take root cuttings of *Verbascum* • Take care in handling *Aconitum* as it is very poisonous
Perennials, ground covers and rock plants, mild climate	Flowering • Take stem cuttings
Perennials, alpines, ground covers, and rock plants, cool climate	Plant out rock-garden plants • Fertilize lightly with complete plant food or slow-release fertilizer
Perennials, subshrubs, sun	Liquid fertilize as plants come into bud • For planting out choose a sunny, well-drained, light soil
Perennials, subshrubs, shade to part-shade	Divide overgrown clumps • Replant with addition of compost
Perennials, water-garden plants	Prepare planting site • Use compost and well-rotted cow manure • Plant marginal, shallow, deep water plants
Perennials, for tropical effect	Divide established clumps of *Hedychium*
Perennials, irises	Fertilize and mulch
Perennials, pelargoniums	Flowering • Remove dead flowers
Perennials, primulas	Sow seed in seed-raising mix • *P. vulgaris* in flower
SHRUBS	
Low-growing, frost-hardy, evergreen	Prune after flowering

MID-SPRING	LATE SPRING
Add compost around plants • Side dress established plants with blood and bone	Side dress plants with blood and bone
Flowering • Remove spent blooms regularly	Flowering • Plants may be divided or cut back after flowering • Liquid fertilize regularly to prolong flowering into summer
Plants begin to flower and continue into summer • Plants may be divided now	Flowering continues • Plants may be divided
Main flowering period through to late summer • Take cuttings and strike in sand/peat mix	Flowering • Prune after flowering to maintain good shape
Place flat rocks near plants to keep roots cool and for plants to grow over	Mulch around plants with leaf mold compost; side dress with blood and bone
Divide overcrowded plants • Plant water plants in heavy loam with compost and slow-release fertilizer	Provide gravel mulch over water plants if fish are active
Divide established clumps of *Hedychium*	Liquid fertilize *Impatiens* to produce good flowers
Visit a specialist grower to choose correct iris for your garden • Apply generous compost • Check soil pH before planting	Check plants for any sign of pests and disease, especially discolored or streaked foliage • Iris may suffer from fungus disease
Tip prune regularly • Plant *P. crispum* near a path so it releases fragrance when brushed against	Liquid fertilize regularly to encourage flowers
Treat gray mold botrytis with a fungicide • *P. vialii* in flower	Mulch around plants • Remove spent flowers • *P. florindae* in flower
Sow seed and keep moist until germination	Take half-hardened cuttings • Mulch • Lightly fertilize

PLANT	EARLY SPRING
SHRUBS (cont.)	
Low-growing, frost-tender, evergreen	Fertilize established shrubs • Add compost and complete fertilizer at planting time
Low-growing, frost-hardy, deciduous	Flowering
Medium- to tall-growing, frost-hardy, evergreen	Prune after flowering • Mulch and fertilize
Medium- to tall-growing, frost-tender, evergreen	Fertilize established shrubs • Add compost and complete fertilizer at planting time
Medium- to tall-growing, frost-hardy, deciduous	Flowering
Acacia	Flowering
Banksia	Flowering
Buddleja	Cut back plants • Add compost and complete fertilizer
Callistemon	Flowering period
Camellia	Test soil pH if growth is unsatisfactory
Cistus	Ensure perfect drainage when planting • Dig in compost and slow-release fertilizer
Erica	Dig in plenty of compost and complete fertilizer before planting
Euphorbia	Choose a warm sunny location for planting • Prune as flowers fade
Fuchsia	Prune • Fertilize with complete fertilizer

MID-SPRING	LATE SPRING
Add compost and complete fertilizer at planting time	Take half-hardened cuttings • Mulch
Prune after flowering • Mulch and fertilize	Prune after flowering • Mulch and fertilize
Prune after flowering • Mulch and fertilize • Sow seed and keep moist until germination	Take half-hardened cuttings • Mulch • Lightly fertilize
Add compost and complete fertilizer at planting time	Mulch • Take half-hardened cuttings
Prune after flowering • Mulch and fertilize	Prune after flowering • Mulch and fertilize
Collect ripe seed as covering turns brown • Treat with boiling water before sowing	Lightly prune • Apply mulch • Side dress with slow-release fertilizer
Apply iron chelate for banksias with yellow leaf tips and margins	Treat seed cones with heat to release seed • Lightly prune to shape
Give plenty of space when planting	*B. davidii* begins to flower
Flowering period	Prune off all spent flowers; retain some for seed collection
Prune long or straggly growth • Lightly fertilize with azalea/camellia food	Mulch around plants as weather warms up • Spray scale insect attack with white oil
Flowering • Prune lightly after flowering	Take cuttings • Apply light application of fertilizer
Sow seed; keep moist until germination	Fertilize and mulch
Mulch and fertilize • Prune as flowers fade	Ensure adequate water, although most are drought-tolerant
Tip prune young plants for good shape	Mulch around plants with compost

PLANT	EARLY SPRING
SHRUBS (cont.)	
Gardenia	Dig in plenty of compost and complete or slow-release fertilizer • Check soil pH; it should be slightly acid
Hebe	Some species flowering
Hibiscus	In warm districts prune *H. rosa-sinensis* • Prune by a third; use for cuttings • Mulch and fertilize after pruning
Hydrangea	Prune *H. paniculata* and *H. quercifolia* by a half • Mulch and fertilize well
Lavandula	When planting, add light application of dolomite/lime to soil and/or compost and complete fertilizer
Leptospermum	Sow seed; keep moist until germination
Nerium	Leaves and flowers are poisonous • Sow seed; keep moist until germination • Prune to shape • Mulch and fertilize
Philadelphus	Prepare planting site • Dig in compost and complete fertilizer
Rhododendron	Main flowering period • Apply compost or well-rotted animal manure and a complete plant food for rhododendrons • Water well before planting
Rosa	Protect new foliage from wind damage • In warmer districts some roses begin to flower • Choose roses by perfume
Spiraea	Cut out old or dead wood

MID-SPRING	LATE SPRING
Prune old or woody plants hard • Fertilize and mulch	Remove spent flowers regularly
Prune back old flowering stems • Fertilize and water well	Mulch around plants • Take half-hardened cuttings
In warm districts prune *H. rosa-sinensis* • Prune by a third; use for cuttings • Mulch and fertilize after pruning	Flowering season late spring to late autumn • Fertilize regularly with a high-potassium fertilizer • Mulch well but keep away from stem
Select a cool moist location for planting • Dig in plenty of compost and complete fertilizer • Take cuttings	Liquid fertilize as buds develop • Take cuttings
Tip prune young plants to ensure compact habit	Prune lightly after or during flowering
Ensure good drainage • Fertilize and mulch	Tip prune regularly or use hedge shears over plants
Tip prune young plants to promote compact growth or train as a standard	Old plants may be cut back hard
Provide part-shade in hot districts	Prune after flowering, especially older shoots • Mulch and fertilize
Main flowering period • Do not water directly onto flowers • Spray petal blight with a fungicide • Take cuttings 6 weeks after flowering	Prune lightly after flowering • If growth is poor, check soil pH • Use a systemic insecticide regularly to combat insect damage on leaves
Use commercial preparations on insect pests and diseases, or plant garlic or onion chives and encourage birds • Prune after flowering	Mulch thickly with straw or old cow manure; keep mulch away from plant stems • Lightly apply fertilizer every 6 weeks
Prune after flowering • Cut out old or dead wood	Fertilize and mulch well

PLANT	EARLY SPRING
SHRUBS (cont.)	
Syringa	—
Viburnum	Prepare planting site • Dig in plenty of compost and complete fertilizer
Weigela	Hard prune overgrown or straggly specimens • Mulch and fertilize
TREES	
Evergreen	Sow tree seed and keep moist until germination
Deciduous, all heights	Plant container specimens
Ornamental, blossom and/or fruit	Cut flowering branches for indoor decoration
Tropical and subtropical	Mulch and fertilize • Plant seed and keep moist until germination
Eucalyptus	Prepare ground for planting; dig large hole and incorporate compost and fertilizer suitable for Eucalyptus
BULBS, CORMS, AND TUBERS	
Summer-flowering, sun	Plant Eucomis bulbs just below soil surface • Add compost and blood and bone fertilizer
Summer-flowering, part-shade	Liquid fertilize as weather warms up and plants emerge or grow
Autumn-flowering	Divide bulbs if overcrowded • Sow seed from previous autumn flowering

MID-SPRING	LATE SPRING
Fertilize young plants with complete fertilizer once established	Prune old flowers; prune to shape after flowering
Ensure adequate water as flower buds develop	Prune out any old or dead wood • Pick flowering branches for indoor decoration
Prepare planting site • Dig in plenty of compost and complete fertilizer	Tip prune young plants regularly
Mulch well as weather warms up • Fertilize during periods of good rain	Mulch well as weather warms up • Fertilize during periods of good rain
Prune blossom trees after flowering • Mulch and fertilize	Ensure adequate water during dry spells
Mulch and fertilize well	Prune after flowering except *Prunus × blireana* and *P. cerasifera;* shorten interior branches only
Prune established trees after flowering • Take cuttings	Prepare planting site if good rains have fallen • Dig in compost and complete fertilizer
Planting continues if rain is present	Fertilize young trees with slow-release fertilizer • Mulch
Plant *Crinum* bulbs or seed in cool climates; plants grown from seed may take several years to flower • Protect plants from snails and slugs	Mulch bulbs with compost and liquid fertilize regularly • Give *Crinum* plants plenty of room to grow
Liquid fertilize as weather warms up and plants emerge or grow	Keep soil evenly moist over summer
Plant fresh bulbs	Provide adequate water while foliage is growing; reduce watering once foliage has died down

PLANT	EARLY SPRING
BULBS, CORMS, AND TUBERS (cont.)	
Winter-flowering	Allow bulbs to dry off after flowering • Mulch area with compost • Bulbs may be divided
Winter–spring-flowering	Water well while in flower
Spring-flowering, sun	Main flowering period • Pick flowers regularly for indoor decoration
Spring-flowering, shade to part-shade	Bulbs in full flower • Pick flowers for indoor decoration
Summer–autumn-flowering	Sow seed of bulbs in pots until planted out • Divide large clumps of bulbs if overcrowded
Spring–summer-flowering, sun	Water bulbs well during the growing and flowering season
Spring–summer-flowering, shade	Flowering time begins and continues to early summer
Allium	*A. cristophii* in flower
Begonia	Sow seed with fine sand for even distribution; sow in moist fine compost and cover with thin layer of sand
Fritillaria	Flowering in cold climates
Gladiolus	Plant bulbs in cool climates • Add compost and lightly apply blood and bone fertilizer • Discard insect-damaged bulbs

MID-SPRING	LATE SPRING
—	—
Sprinkle blood and bone fertilizer over bulbs as they die down	Dormancy
Main flowering period	Cut off flower stems after flowering • Collect seed for autumn sowing • Destroy surplus bulbs if growing close to areas of native vegetation
Flowering continues • When flowering finishes lift *Anemone* and store in a cool dry place	Leave bulbs in ground to die off • Mulch with compost
Sow seed of bulbs in pots until planted out • Divide large clumps of bulbs if overcrowded • Give away excess bulbs	Maintain adequate water during dry spells
Main flowering period begins • Water bulbs well during the growing and flowering season	Water bulbs well during the growing and flowering season
Pick flowers regularly for indoor decoration	Pick flowers regularly for indoor decoration
Divide clumps of *A. moly*	Provide adequate water for summer-flowering species
Pot seedlings in sand/peat; mix 50:50 with slow-release fertilizer • Don't overpot • Keep in greenhouse or warm position	If planting out, acclimatize plants gradually • Prepare position with well-rotted cow manure and compost
Flowering	Lift bulbs from areas with high summer rain or bulbs may rot • Store in cool dry place
Gladiolus hybrids flowering in warm climates • *G. tristis* in flower	Thrips may cause silver streaks on leaves and deformed flowers • Spray with an insecticide • Stake flowering stems in windy sites

PLANT	EARLY SPRING
BULBS, CORMS, AND TUBERS (cont.)	
Lilium	Avoid overwatering as bulbs may rot • Mulch soil with compost and water infrequently • Apply a liquid fertilizer once growth starts
Narcissus	N., Bulbocodium in flower • Pick flower stems just before they open
Tulipa	Save seed of species tulips for sowing
HERBS	Lightly apply dolomite/lime and/or dig in compost and fertilize with complete or slow-release fertilizer • Prune dead wood • Sow seed of annuals in seed-raising mix
FRUIT TREES	
Tropical to subtropical	Provide adequate water during dry spells • Mulch well
Cool-temperate	Plant out container-grown fruits; choose healthy sturdy plants, less than 2 years old • Spread a balanced fertilizer just beyond where branches grow • Check weekly for signs of pest or disease problems
Citrus	Choose a sheltered position for planting • Prepare site with compost and a complete fertilizer • Ensure good drainage
CACTI AND SUCCULENTS	Sow seed or take cuttings • In garden, build up soil to allow good drainage; add sand, gravel, and slow-release fertilizer

MID-SPRING	LATE SPRING
L., Candidum Hybrids in flower • Protect flower stems from snail damage • Stake tall flower stems	*L.,* Longiflorum Hybrids and *L. lancifolium* in flower • Cucumber mosaic virus may cause reflexing and streaking of leaves; destroy affected plants
Main flowering period for hybrids	Liquid fertilize as bulbs die down • Tie up untidy foliage • Divide bulbs every 2 to 3 years • Reduce watering
Spray any aphid infestation with an insecticide • Spray tulip fire botrytis with a fungicide • Do not water tulip plants from overhead • Practice crop rotation	Remove spent flowers and let bulbs die down naturally • Lift bulbs and store in cool dry place
Plant out established plants in pots • Harvest young fresh leaves • Apply a weak solution of liquid fertilizer	Tip prune plants regularly to ensure compact growth
Ensure good pollination of flowers	Apply mulch • Suppress weeds • Plant companion plants
Mulch established plants with compost and manure • Check for leaf discoloration as a nutrient deficiency may be present • Protect buds and developing fruit from birds	Spread a balanced fertilizer just beyond where branches grow • Check weekly for signs of pest or disease problems • Protect buds and developing fruit from birds
Mulch and fertilize • Keep mulch away from main trunk	Keep trunk free from weeds
Divide established clumps and repot or replant • Give weak solution of liquid fertilizer	Cut off old flowering stems • Watch for snails—they enjoy the fleshy leaves

PLANT	EARLY SPRING
ORCHIDS	Repot overcrowded specimens • Trim dead or damaged roots from plants if repotting
CLIMBERS AND CREEPERS	
Warm-temperate to cool-temperate	Prepare evergreen climbers; planting position as for late autumn • Spring climbers in flower • Cut back frost-damaged shoots and leaves on tender plants
Tropical to subtropical	Sow fresh seed in seed-raising mix • Prune summer–autumn-flowering climbers • Apply blood and bone or complete fertilizer

Mid-Spring

Water regularly during growing period • Fertilize regularly • Divide established plants

Plant evergreen climbers • Prune established climbers after flowering • Side dress with blood and bone • Sow fresh climber seed in seed-raising mix

Dig plenty of compost and a complete fertilizer into soil • Ensure strong support for holding growth • Tip prune regularly

Late Spring

Apply extra leaf mold and well-rotted cow manure on garden specimens

Tie new growth into growing position • Spray aphids with pyrethrum • Take half-hardened cuttings from vigorous plants • Strike in coarse sand/peat mix 3:1

Take half-hardened cuttings from vigorous young plants • Train climbers where you want them to grow • Tie up with soft material

CULTIVATION GUIDELINES

PLANT	ORIGIN	LIGHT	SOIL PREPARATION
ANNUALS AND PERENNIALS			
Annuals, low-growing, summer–autumn-flowering	Warm to cool-temperate	Sun or part-shade in all districts	Light application of dolomite/lime and/or add compost and fertilizer
Annuals, low-growing, spring–summer-flowering	Temperate	Sun; part-shade in hot districts	Dolomite/lime and/or compost and fertilizer
Annuals, low-growing, winter–spring-flowering	Temperate	Sun; part-shade in hot districts	Light application of dolomite/lime and/or compost and fertilizer
Annuals, medium-growing, summer-flowering	Cool to warm-temperate	Sun or part-shade	Light application of dolomite/lime and/or compost and fertilizer
Annuals, medium-growing, spring–summer-flowering	Cool-temperate to warm-temperate	Sun; part-shade in hot districts	Light application of dolomite/lime and/or compost and fertilizer
Annuals, tall-growing, spring–summer-flowering	Temperate	Sun; part-shade in hot districts	Light application of dolomite/lime and/or compost and fertilizer
Annuals, tall-growing, summer-flowering	Cool-temperate to warm-temperate	Sun or part-shade in all districts	Light application of dolomite/lime and/or compost and fertilizer
Perennials, spring–early summer-flowering	Temperate	Sun	Compost • Fertilizer • Drainage material
Perennials, spring–early summer-flowering, short-lived	Warm-temperate	Part-shade	Compost • Fertilizer • Sharp sand or grit for drainage

MAINTENANCE	PLANT PROTECTION	PROPAGATION
Water by trickle irrigation • Tip prune to encourage compact habit • Liquid fertilize to prolong flowering	Snails, slugs, mildew, nematodes, aphids, white flies	Seed, seedlings
Pick flowers to encourage more blooms • Liquid fertilize regularly • Mulch	Aphids, caterpillars, snails, slugs, damping off, leaf spot, root rot	Seed, seedlings
Protect with loose straw in cold districts • Remove spent flowers • Liquid fertilize regularly • Mulch	Snails, aphids, damping off, mildew	Seed, seedlings
Pick flowers to encourage continuous blooming • Liquid fertilize regularly • Mulch	Snails, mildew, caterpillars, aphids	Seed, seedlings
Shelter from strong winds • Pick flowers regularly to encourage continuous flowering • Liquid fertilize regularly • Mulch	Rust, aphids, snails, mites, budworms, leaf miners	Seed, seedlings
Provide tripods if necessary or stakes • Remove spent flowers • Liquid fertilize at regular intervals • Mulch	Rust, mildew, aphids, snails, two-spotted mites	Seed, seedlings
Provide tripods if necessary • Shelter from wind • Remove spent flowers • Liquid fertilize regularly • Mulch	Mildew, aphids, leaf-eating insects, snails, cutworms, leaf spot	Seed, seedlings
Remove spent flowers	Few problems	Division, seed, cuttings
Remove plants after several seasons or allow to self-seed	Root rot diseases	Cuttings, seed, root cuttings

PLANT	ORIGIN	LIGHT	SOIL PREPARATION
ANNUALS AND PERENNIALS (cont.)			
Perennials, summer-flowering, sun	Temperate	Sun; part-shade in hot districts	Dolomite/lime and/or compost and complete fertilizer • Well-drained soil
Perennials, summer-flowering, shade to part-shade	Cool-temperate	Part-shade to shade in all districts	Moist humus-rich soil
Perennials, winter–early summer-flowering	Temperate	Part-shade to shade	Moist humus-rich soil
Perennials, summer–autumn-flowering	Temperate	Sun or part-shade	Compost • Fertilizer
Perennials, ground covers and rock plants, mild climate	Cool-temperate to warm	Sun	Tolerant of average well-drained soil conditions
Perennials, alpines, ground covers, and rock plants, cool climate	Cold-temperate	Sun or part-shade	Garden loam with a little compost and sharp sand in a 3:2:1 ratio • Fertilizer
Perennials, subshrubs, sun	Cool to warm-temperate	Sun	Average garden soil enriched with compost and a complete fertilizer
Perennials, subshrubs, shade to part-shade	Temperate	Part-shade to shade	Humus-rich, cool, moist soil
Perennials, water-garden plants	Cool to warm-temperate	Sun or part-shade	Moist or wet conditions as recommended
Perennials, for tropical effect	Tropical to subtropical	Sun or part-shade	Moist humus-rich soil

MAINTENANCE	PLANT PROTECTION	PROPAGATION
Stake tall-flowering plants • Deadhead old flowers	Snails, slugs, few problems	Division, seed, root cuttings, stem cuttings
Divide every few years	Snails, slugs	Division, seed, stem cuttings
Divide every few years	Snails, slugs, wilt disease	Division, seed, root cuttings
Remove spent flowers • Divide every few years	Snails, slugs, few problems	Division, seed, root cuttings
Prune overgrown plants	Few problems	Cuttings, division
Winter protection from wet	Few problems	Seed, cuttings
Remove spent flowers • Prune to shape	Few problems, leaf miners on *Argyranthemum*	Cuttings, seed
Cut back overgrown plants	Mildew, root rot	Division, cuttings
Divide every 3 to 5 years	Few problems	Division, seed
Remove spent flower stems	Stem borers, snails	Division, cuttings, seed

PLANT	ORIGIN	LIGHT	SOIL PREPARATION
ANNUALS AND PERENNIALS (cont.)			
Perennials, irises	Cool-temperate	Sun, part-shade, or shade	Soil requirements as specified in genus entry
Perennials, pelargoniums	Warm-temperate	Sun or part-shade	Average garden soil enriched with compost and complete fertilizer
Perennials, primulas	Temperate	Part-shade	Moisture-retaining humus-rich soil
SHRUBS			
Low-growing, frost-hardy, evergreen	Warm-temperate to cool-temperate	Sun or part-shade	Well-drained humus-rich soil, pH adjustment likely
Low-growing, frost-tender, evergreen	Subtropical to warm-temperate	Sun or part-shade	Average, fertile, humus-rich soil
Low-growing, frost-hardy, deciduous	Cool-temperate	Sun or part-shade	Well-drained, fertile, humus-rich soil
Medium- to tall-growing, frost-hardy, evergreen	Warm-temperate to cool-temperate	Sun, part-shade, or shade	Well-drained, fertile, humus-rich soil
Medium- to tall-growing, frost-tender, evergreen	Subtropical to warm-temperate	Sun or part-shade	Average, fertile, humus-rich soil
Medium- to tall-growing, frost-hardy, deciduous	Temperate	Sun or part-shade	Compost • Complete fertilizer • Well-drained soil
Acacia	Temperate	Sun or part-shade	Average, well-drained soil

MAINTENANCE	PLANT PROTECTION	PROPAGATION
Remove spent flowers • Divide when overcrowded	Mosaic virus, rust, collar rot	Division in autumn to spring, seed in autumn
Regular pruning	Caterpillars, rust, stem rot	Cuttings, seed
Frequent liquid fertilizer • Cool site required • Mulch	Snails, mold, mites	Division, seed, root cuttings for *P. denticulata*
Mulch regularly • Prune regularly • Some protection for young specimens in very cold conditions	Occasional insect damage; less in fertile well-drained soils	Seed, cuttings, layering
Prune to shape or after flowering • Mulch	Occasional insect damage; less in fertile well-drained soils	Seed, cuttings
Mulch regularly • Prune regularly	Occasional insect damage; less in fertile soils	Seed, cuttings
Mulch regularly • Prune regularly • Some are able to withstand dry periods	Occasional insect damage; less in fertile soils	Seed, cuttings
Prune to shape or after flowering • Mulch	Occasional insect damage; less in fertile well-drained soils	Seed, cuttings
Prune regularly • Mulch	Occasional pest damage; less in fertile soils	Cuttings, grafting
Tip prune regularly • Leaf mulch	Borers, galls	Seed, cuttings

PLANT	ORIGIN	LIGHT	SOIL PREPARATION
SHRUBS (cont.)			
Banksia	Cool-temperate to warm-temperate	Sun or part-shade	Well-drained soil, low pH
Buddleja	Temperate	Sun	Average soil
Callistemon	Temperate	Sun	Compost • Complete fertilizer • Moisture-retaining soil
Camellia	Temperate	Sun or part-shade	Moist, well-drained, humus-rich soil
Cistus	Warm-temperate	Sun	Well-drained light soil
Erica	Temperate	Sun	Acid well-drained soil
Euphorbia	Warm-temperate to subtropical	Sun	Average well-drained soil
Fuchsia	Temperate	Part-shade	Moist, well-drained, humus-rich soil
Gardenia	Warm-temperate	Sun or part-shade	Moist, well-drained, humus-rich soil, acid pH
Hebe	Temperate	Sun	Average soil
Hibiscus	Warm-temperate to subtropical	Sun	Well-drained fertile soil
Hydrangea	Temperate	Part-shade	Cool, moist, humus-rich soil

MAINTENANCE	PLANT PROTECTION	PROPAGATION
Fertilize with low-phosphorus fertilizer • Leaf mulch	Phytophthora root rot	Seed
Prune	Few problems	Cuttings
Prune after flowering	Sawflies, tip bugs, thrips, borers	Seed, cuttings
Provide shelter from weather extremes • Debud	Scale insects, mites	Cuttings
Prune after flowering	Few problems	Cuttings
Prune after flowering	Few problems	Cuttings
Prune regularly	Few problems	Cuttings
Protect from strong winds	Thrips, mites, mealy bugs	Cuttings
Prune and fertilize regularly • Correct iron or magnesium deficiency	Mealy bugs, scale insects, nematodes	Cuttings
Prune regularly	Scale insects, leaf miners, downy mildew	Cuttings
Prune regularly	Aphids, scale insects, mealy bugs, hibiscus beetles, collar rot	Cuttings
Prune regularly	Mildew, two-spotted mites	Cuttings

PLANT	ORIGIN	LIGHT	SOIL PREPARATION
SHRUBS (cont.)			
Lavandula	Temperate	Sun	Well-drained fertile soil
Leptospermum	Temperate	Sun	Light well-drained soil
Nerium	Warm-temperate	Sun	Average soil
Philadelphus	Temperate	Sun or part-shade	Moist humus-rich soil
Rhododendron	Temperate	Sun, part-shade, or shade	Well-drained humus-rich soil, acid pH
Rosa	Temperate	Sun	Well-drained, organic, humus-rich soil
Spiraea	Temperate	Sun	Average soil
Syringa	Cool-temperate	Sun	Alkaline, rich, cool soil
Viburnum	Temperate	Sun or part-shade	Fertile humus-rich soil
Weigela	Temperate	Sun	Fertile humus-rich soil
TREES			
Evergreen	Subtropical to cool-temperate	Sun to part-shade	Well-drained, humus-rich, fertile soil
Deciduous, taller than 35 ft (10 m)	Temperate	Sun to part-shade	Well-drained, humus-rich, fertile soil

MAINTENANCE	PLANT PROTECTION	PROPAGATION
Tip prune regularly	Few problems	Cuttings
Tip prune regularly	Web moths, borers, manuka blight	Seed, cuttings
Prune after flowering	Scale insects	Cuttings
Prune hard after spring flowering	Few problems	Cuttings
Water regularly • Mulch	Two-spotted mites, lace bugs, thrips, caterpillars, leaf miners, petal blight, mildew	Layering, cuttings
Water regularly • Lightly apply fertilizer • Remove dead or unproductive branches • Mulch with straw or old animal manure • Allow good air circulation	Thrips, aphids, scale insects, mildew, rust, blackspot, caterpillars	Buds, cuttings
Prune straggly growth to shape	Few problems	Cuttings
Remove sucker growth	Keep under cool conditions	Graft on *Privet* rootstock
Prune after flowering	Two-spotted mites, thrips	Cuttings
Prune older branches	Few problems	Cuttings
Regular pruning when young to shape • Mulch • Fertilize on drip line	Seasonal insect pests, root rot diseases on poorly drained soils	Seed, cuttings, grafting
Regular pruning when young to shape • Mulch • Fertilize on drip line	Seasonal insect pests, root rot diseases on poorly drained soils	Seed, cuttings, grafting

PLANT	ORIGIN	LIGHT	SOIL PREPARATION
TREES *(cont.)*			
Deciduous, 35 ft (10 m) or shorter	Temperate	Sun to part-shade	Well-drained, humus-rich, fertile soil
Ornamental, blossom and/or fruit	Temperate	Sun	Well-drained, humus-rich, deep soil
Tropical and subtropical	Tropical to subtropical	Sun to part-shade	Well-drained, humus-rich, fertile soil
Eucalyptus	Warm-temperate to cool-temperate	Sun	Well-drained, humus-rich, fertile to average soil
BULBS, CORMS, AND TUBERS			
Summer-flowering, sun	Warm-temperate to cool-temperate	Sun or part-shade	Rich, organic, well-drained soil
Summer-flowering, part-shade	Cool-temperate	Part-shade	Cool, moist, humus-rich soil
Autumn-flowering	Temperate	Sun or part-shade	Well-drained humus-rich soil • Add compost, fertilizer, or bulb food
Winter-flowering	Temperate	Sun or part-shade	Humus-rich soil with compost
Winter–spring-flowering	Cool-temperate	Sun or part-shade in warm districts	Prepare soil with compost and complete fertilizer • Soil should be well-drained
Spring-flowering, sun	Warm-temperate	Sun	Average well-drained soil • Add compost before planting and complete fertilizer or bulb food

MAINTENANCE	PLANT PROTECTION	PROPAGATION
Regular pruning when young to shape • Mulch • Fertilize on drip line	Seasonal insect pests, root rot diseases on poorly drained soils	Seed, cuttings, grafting
Prune after flowering to shape • Mulch • Fertilizer	Shot hole, rust, leaf curl, pear and cherry slugs, aphids	Cuttings, grafting
Regular pruning when young to shape • Mulch • Fertilize on drip line	Seasonal insect pests, root rot diseases on poorly drained soils	Seed, cuttings
Prune to shape when young • Gum-leaf mulch	Various insect pests, root rot diseases	Seed
Provide adequate water during growing season • Protect plants with loose straw in frosty areas	Few problems	Seed, division, offsets
Mulch with compost once or twice a year	Few problems	Seed, division
Leave to naturalize or lift and store when dormant	Aphids, snails, bacterial rot	Seed, division
Leave to naturalize	Few problems	Division
Remove spent flowers • Lift and divide every 3 to 5 years	Snails	Seed in autumn, or offsets; divide clumps
Keep moist during growing season; dry off in summer • Protect with loose straw in frosty areas	Few problems	Seed, division, offsets

PLANT	ORIGIN	LIGHT	SOIL PREPARATION
BULBS, CORMS, AND TUBERS (cont.)			
Spring-flowering, shade to part-shade	Temperate to cool-temperate	Part-shade to shade	Moist humus-rich soil • Add compost and complete fertilizer or bulb food
Summer–autumn-flowering	Temperate	Sun or part-shade	Average garden soil enriched with compost and complete fertilizer or bulb food
Spring–summer-flowering, sun	Warm-temperate to cool-temperate	Sun or part-shade in all districts	Average well-drained soil enriched with compost or bulb food
Spring–summer-flowering, shade	Temperate	Sun, but most prefer cool shade	Well-drained fertile soil enriched with compost and bulb food
Allium	Temperate	Sun	Well-drained fertile soil
Begonia	Subtropical	Part-shade	Moist gritty compost in pots or garden • Position not overwet
Fritillaria	Cold-temperate	Sun or part-shade	Lime/dolomite • Deep, rich, well-drained soil
Gladiolus	Warm-temperate	Sun	Well-drained, light, sandy loam
Lilium	Temperate	Sun or, preferably, part-shade	Well-drained fertile soil; neutral pH
Narcissus	Temperate	Sun or part-shade	Well-drained soil • Dolomite/lime and/or compost and low-nitrogen fertilizer

MAINTENANCE	PLANT PROTECTION	PROPAGATION
Annual compost	Few problems	Seed, division
Water during growing season • Allow to dry out when dormant	Snails	Seed, division
Protect bulbs with straw in frosty areas • Lift and store in areas with wet humid summers	Few problems	Seed, offsets
Naturalize or replant each year • Protect bulbs with loose straw in frosty areas	Few problems	Seed, bulbs, tuber-claw
Remove spent flowers	Few problems	Seed, division
Keep dry over winter • Liquid fertilize regularly	Damping off, bulb rot	Seed or tubers in spring
Summer moisture	Bulb rot	Seed, offsets
Lift and divide every few years	Thrips	Corms, cormlets
Minimal disturbance of established plants • Mulch in spring/summer • Allow stems to die down before removal	Bulb rot, cucumber mosaic virus	Seed, offsets, bulb scales
Provide shelter from strong winds • Lift and divide in warm climates	Bulb rot, aphids	Offsets

PLANT	ORIGIN	LIGHT	SOIL PREPARATION
BULBS, CORMS, AND TUBERS (cont.)			
Tulipa	Temperate	Sun	Well-drained • Lightly apply dolomite/lime and/or add compost and blood and bone fertilizer • Add coarse sand in heavy soils
HERBS	Warm-temperate to cool-temperate	Sun or part-shade	Dolomite/lime and/or compost and fertilizer
FRUIT TREES			
Tropical to subtropical	Tropical to subtropical	Full sun	Topsoil at least 24 in (60 cm) deep • Compost • Fertilizer
Cool-temperate	Temperate	Sun	Well-drained humus-rich soil
Citrus	Warm-temperate to cool-temperate	Sun	Humus-rich well-drained soil
INDOOR PLANTS			
Indoor flowering and foliage plants	Subtropical to warm-temperate	Good light to part-shade	Humus-rich soil
CACTI AND SUCCULENTS	Tropical to subtropical	Sun or part-shade	Light gritty soil • Sharp drainage essential

Maintenance	Plant Protection	Propagation
Disease control in spring	Tulip fire botrytis, mosaic virus, aphids	Seed, division
Tip prune regularly • Harvest spring and summer	Few problems	Cuttings, seed, division
Training • Pruning • Fertilizing • Shelter	Seasonal pest problems, root rot diseases	Seed, cuttings, grafting
Regular pruning for maximum fruit production • Mulch • Fertilizer • Weed control • Check pollination requirements	Root rot diseases, insects, various bacteria canker	Grafting, budding, cuttings
Regular fertilizer • Mulch • Prune	Scale insects, leaf miners, aphids, caterpillars	Grafting, *trifoliata* or *citronelle* root stocks
Keep soil evenly moist • Dry in winter • Warm conditions • Remove dead flowers/foliage	Mealy bugs, mites, scale insects	Seed, cuttings
Water during flowering, then rest	Root rot diseases, mealy bugs, scale insects, aphids	Seed, cuttings

PLANT	ORIGIN	LIGHT	SOIL PREPARATION
ORCHIDS	Tropical to subtropical, temperate	Part-shade	Open free-draining soil containing bark/ leaf litter/charcoal peatmoss mixture for epiphytes and terrestrials
CLIMBERS AND CREEPERS			
Warm-temperate to cool-temperate	Warm-temperate to cool-temperate	Sun or part-shade	Compost • Complete fertilizer
Tropical to subtropical	Tropical to subtropical	Sun or part-shade	Compost • Complete fertilizer

MAINTENANCE	PLANT PROTECTION	PROPAGATION
Regular fertilizer when not in flower • Maintain high humidity where appropriate • Good air circulation	Aphids, scale, mealy bugs, beetles, bulb rot	Seed, seedlings, division
Regular pruning • Mulch	Few problems	Seed, cuttings
Regular pruning • Mulch	Few problems	Seed, cuttings

INDEX TO PLANTS

Photography

Chris Bell, Rob Blakers, Lorraine Blyth, Ken Brass, Geoff Bryant,
Derek Butcher, Claver Carroll, Leigh Clapp, Grant Dixon, e-garden Ltd,
Katie Fallows, Richard Francis, Bill Grant, Denise Greig, Barry Grossman,
Gil Hanly, Ivy Hansen, Dennis Harding, Jack Hobbs, Neil Holmes,
Paul Huntley, Richard I'Anson, David Keith Jones, Ionas Kaltenbach,
Willie Kempen, Robert M. Knight, Carol Knoll, Albert Kuhnigk,
Mike Langford, Gary Lewis, Geoff Longford, Stirling Macoboy,
John McCann, David McGonigal, Richard McKenna, Ron Moon,
Eberhard Morell, Connall Oosterbrock, Larry Pitt, Craig Potton,
Janet Price, Geof Prigge, Nick Rains, Howard Rice, Jamie Robertson,
Tony Rodd, Rolf Ulrich Roesler, Don Skirrow, Raoul Slater, Peter Solness,
Ken Stepnell, Oliver Strewe, J. Peter Thoeming, David Titmuss,
Wayne Turville, Sharyn Vanderhorst, Vic Widman, Brent Wilson,
Grant Young, James Young

Produced by Global Book Publishing Pty Ltd
1/181 High Street, Willoughby, NSW Australia 2068
Phone 61 2 9967 3100   Fax 61 2 9967 5891
Email globalpub@ozemail.com.au

the house in the twentieth century

the house in the twentieth century

RICHARD WESTON

LAURENCE KING PUBLISHING

LAURENCE KING

Published 2002 by
Laurence King Publishing Ltd
71 Great Russell Street
London WC1B 3BP
Tel: +44 20 7430 8850
Fax: +44 20 7430 8880
E-mail: enquiries@laurenceking.co.uk
www.laurenceking.co.uk

A catalogue record for this book is
available from the British Library.

ISBN 1 85669 219 1

Picture research by Mary-Jane Gibson

Design by Keith Lovegrove

Printed in Hong Kong

contents

introduction

Throughout the twentieth century the house has commended itself as the most appropriate and responsive vehicle for testing ideas and expressing an architectural position in built form. A history of the twentieth-century house is also, therefore, to some extent a history of the leading ideas of the century's architecture: the scope is enormous, and this book is intended to be inclusive but not comprehensive. Despite the global approach it was decided at the outset not to include Japan because it would be impossible to do justice to the diversity and depth of the designs produced there. But to every rule there must be an exception and ours is Tadao Ando. His work is of such international importance that to omit it would be to impoverish any account of the house during the last quarter of the century. I trust that most readers will discover many if not all of their favourite houses here, as well as some unexpected delights, and those less familiar with the subject matter will, I hope, find sufficient contextual information to situate the houses in the wider currents of architectural development.

The book is organized thematically rather than strictly chronologically. The first chapter begins where many histories of modern architecture begin, in the middle of the nineteenth century, and then moves on to the *fin de siècle*, where ideas belonging to the dying century culminate and mingle with premonitions of things to come. The second chapter deals with the larger incarnations of the classic Modern (with a capital 'M') house, and the third with the smaller 'machines for living in' advanced as solutions to the housing problem. The latter includes Le Corbusier's Unité d'Habitation at Marseilles, because of its pivotal role in his development and the trajectory of post-war architecture, and also a tiny block of apartments in Israel which vividly illustrates many of the ideas and deserves to be better known. Otherwise, I have stuck to the principle that this is a book about houses, not apartments or housing (although one or two seminal housing developments have been allowed in).

The fourth chapter follows the dissemination and adaptation of modern architecture in diverse places, climates and cultures. To capture the variety of approaches it ranges across five continents and decades, but excludes the USA and Scandinavia to which the next two chapters are devoted. The seventh chapter examines the episode of stylistic Post-Modernism in the 1960s and 1970s and the broader post-modern critique, with particular reference to the issues of 'place' and 'dwelling'; in a book of this scope it seemed wise not to tread too deeply into the murky waters of post-modern theory. The final chapter reviews houses built primarily during the last quarter of the century: the selection attempts to illustrate the bewildering diversity of approaches and forms that characterize our own *fin de siècle*, but makes no claims to being definitive.

The house remains the basic building-block of the man-made environment and in the West, at least, is still closely identified with the nuclear family, even when that unit in its traditional form accounts for less than half of the households in many countries. Other histories of the twentieth-century house could and will focus on issues of psychology, family structure and the changing roles of women and developments in biulding technology – such as frame construction and central heating, which made the open plan possible. This book makes no attempt to address these issues, or to examine the domain of mass house-builders, whose products remained largely untouched by modern architectural thought.

Opposite Koshino House, Ashiya, Japan, 1982, Tadao Ando. Built as a 'bastion of resistance' against the consumerism that was sweeping Japan, the Koshino House is closed to its suburban neighbours but open to nature.

the house as a work of art

1859 may seem an unlikely point to begin a history of the twentieth-century house. And at first sight Red House, completed that year in Bexleyheath, Kent, by the young English architect Philip Webb, does not appear especially innovative, its brick walls, steep-pitched tiled roofs and gothic arches looking more medieval than modern. But to Hermann Muthesius, who came to London in 1896 as cultural attaché at the German embassy and eight years later published an influential account of English domestic architecture entitled *Das englische Haus*, it exhibited 'independence and originality' in every aspect of its design. These sentiments were echoed forty years later by Nikolaus Pevsner in his seminal 1936 book, *Pioneers of the Modern Movement* (better known by its later title, *Pioneers of Modern Design*): 'a building of surprisingly independent character,' he declared, 'solid and spacious looking and yet not in the least pretentious.'

Red House Bexleyheath, England, 1859, Philip Webb

To its many admirers, Red House represented a key moment in the development of architecture. Nineteenth-century architects, bemused by the possibilities of new, industrially produced materials such as cast iron and large sheets of glass, and confronted by unprecedented building types like factories and railway stations, which engineers seemed better equipped to tackle, were obsessed by the issue of style. The authority of Classical architecture, largely unquestioned since the Renaissance, was challenged and a host of styles revived – Egyptian, Greek, Romanesque, Gothic. Many designers flourished amid the spirit of eclecticism, but to others the new freedom seemed more like licence. What they sought was not a confusing multiplicity of styles, but a new style to capture the 'spirit of the age' – an elusive concept for which German has a special word, *Zeitgeist*.

Red House stood for the rejection of easy stylistic eclecticism and gratuitous ornament. It embraced simplicity and sought to ground architectural expression in the nature of building materials and construction. Unlike most middle-class villas of its day, it did not imitate grander – typically Italian – architecture, but was content to draw on the English vernacular. It was not without stylistic features, nor stylistically consistent – the roofs and arches are gothic, sash-windows Queen Anne, and the picturesque arrangement looks back to monastic architecture – but the ensemble was novel and, internally, bolder and more original.

But what made Red House so important had as much to do with its owner as the undoubted virtues of its design. Like many of the houses we will explore, it was a manifesto in bricks and mortar, space and light; not just a house, but the embodiment of a vision for a new way of living. Webb's client was William Morris, a young designer and propagandist who became one of the most influential figures of his day, and his house was intended to exemplify the values of the Arts and Crafts movement he led. Disgusted at the vulgar eclecticism of Victorian architecture and design, Morris became an implacable enemy of industrialization and the sham products that poured relentlessly from its factories which, to compound the folly, made slaves of their workers. He valued the intrinsic qualities of materials and workmanship, and believed all true art was rooted in craftsmanship and 'joy in making'. These ideas helped to redefine the way we look at buildings and objects, and Morris's example established the house as a vehicle for personal artistic expression.

We have become so accustomed to the idea that an original designer of talent such as Philip Webb has the right – even duty – to break with tradition, to reject outmoded styles and to design freely in response to his client's requirements, that it is difficult to realize just how revolutionary a proposition it was at the time. And it is in this sense, above all, that Red House embodies the spirit imbuing the houses discussed in this book: for the first time in the history of architecture, the private house – as opposed to the mansion or palace – became the focus of the most advanced ideas of the day.

The idea of the house as a work of art, promoted by magazines like *The Studio*, caught on like wildfire towards the end of the nineteenth century and domestic commissions from enlightened patrons frequently offered architects the greatest opportunities for innovation. The most original English Arts and Crafts architect, C. F. A. Voysey, was born just two years before Red House was built. Perrycroft, completed in the Malvern Hills in 1894, is typical of his early work. Its white pebble-dashed walls, broad slate roofs peppered with tall chimneys, small-paned windows grouped into horizontal bands, and battered piers owed more to vernacular buildings than recognized architectural styles. Markedly simple by the standards of the day, these features led historians and critics of teleological inclination such as Pevsner to see it as 'anticipating' the whitewashed surfaces of the 1920s, an idea Voysey himself never understood. Internally, Perrycroft remained a fairly traditional composition of individual rooms, albeit functional and progressive in its arrangements – the servants' rooms, he said, should be 'cheerful, not shabby and dark'. Later, in the double-height halls and studied asymmetry and informality of the principal rooms of houses such as Broadleys of 1898, built on a magnificent site overlooking Lake Windermere, Voysey began to open up the internal spaces in a way that was taken further in the work of his younger contemporary, M. H. Baillie Scott.

The medieval-looking, half-timbered hall and pargeted plaster frieze in the drawing room of a house such as Blackwell – sited, like Broadleys, overlooking Windermere and completed by Baillie Scott in 1900 – are misleading. They do not strike the modern viewer as especially progressive, but the consistent attention to detail and the determination to give each space a distinctive character have a hitherto unmatched consistency. This yields an organic quality which led Muthesius to hail Baillie Scott as 'the first to have realized the new idea of the interior as a work of art'. This integrating vision was quickly extended to the outdoors, and turn-of-the-century English houses are notable for their use of pergolas, sunken areas and artful steps to achieve a fusion of house and garden, an interplay raised to exceptional heights in the partnership of Edwin Lutyens and the doyenne of Edwardian gardeners, Gertrude Jekyll.

In Britain, by far the most original realization of the ideal of the house as a work of art came in Scotland in the work of Charles Rennie Mackintosh. His masterpiece, the Glasgow School of Art, was won in competition in 1896 in the name of his employers Honeyman and Keppie. It took several years to complete and he burst onto the international scene in 1900 by winning a special prize – no first was given, and Baillie Scott won second – in the competition to design a 'House for an Art Lover' organized by the magazine *Zeitschrift für Innendekoration*. The contrast between the two designs could hardly have been greater: Baillie Scott's, a fantasy of turrets, gables, chimneys and proliferating

Overleaf Red House, Bexleyheath, England, 1859, Philip Webb. Built for the young William Morris, who later wrote, 'If I were asked to say what is at once the most important production of Art and the thing most to be longed for, I should answer A BEAUTIFUL HOUSE.' Red House stood for the rejection of stylistic eclecticism and belief in truth to materials which were central to the Arts and Crafts movement.

11

rooms, assembled with artfully contrived inconsistencies; Mackintosh's, a bold massing of clear volumes which doubtless owed something to Voysey but whose impact was wholly original and, unlike most Arts and Crafts houses, thoroughly urban. Internally, it showed the openness and complexity beloved of Baillie Scott, but under altogether tighter control.

The House for an Art Lover was not built – or at least not for ninety years, when a posthumous version was completed in Glasgow as a commercial venture – but two years later the publisher Walter Blackie commissioned a house at Helensburgh, west of Glasgow on a site overlooking the Firth of Clyde, which gave Mackintosh the opportunity to put theory into practice.

The Hill House Helensburgh, Scotland, 1902, Charles Rennie Mackintosh

Externally, The Hill House is overtly Scottish – the debt to the Scottish Baronial style is more conspicuous than that to Voysey – and characterized by Mackintosh's remarkable talent for giving order and tension to a seemingly disparate collection of windows, which on analysis turn out to be both functionally placed and organized into a complex series of dynamic or partial symmetries.

Internally, the same organizational talent is set to work on the individual rooms. In the drawing room, for example, Mackintosh projects a light-filled bay beyond the main volume of the house. It has an enticing built-in seat and two doors leading out into the garden, and to complement this openness the 'winter end' of the room is intimate, gathered around the fireplace and lit by a single, small window. A large recess, designed to house a piano or act as an informal stage for the children's theatrical performances, shares the same ceiling height as the window bay. Both are defined by the continuous shallow cornice that runs around the interior: below it, the colours are white or pale; above it, darkness reigns.

The main bedroom exhibits the same attention to use, and even greater formal control. The pervading atmosphere is unmistakably feminine. This is an intimate realm that the husband entered only after changing in a separate dressing room, from where a door led directly into the square alcove housing the bed, above which is a shallow barrel-vaulted ceiling. At its end the bed is elaborated with an abstract flower motif and adjacent to it a small cupboard of drawers sits below a tiny, shuttered window in a curved bay, slightly shallower than a semi-circle, echoing the ceiling. The washstand is built-in, and backed by decoration that could almost be an adaptation of Mondrian's mature style of the 1920s. In fact, it is underpinned by a complex modular arrangement that echoes the plan of the house and is integrated with a rose motif.

Mackintosh's motifs were generally rooted in nature, flowers in particular, and transformed into artistic form by the use of geometry. In the inner hall and staircase we see him at the height of his powers. The double-layered structure of beams and joists is fully exposed and stained black, and a series of full-height timber slats enclose the stair and are echoed on the walls as a kind of wainscoting, framing a three-dimensional volume as lines and planes in a way that seems unmistakably modern. Each slat tapers slightly, like a plant stem, and at their tops they divide into two branches around an inset of pink glass; on the wall a decorative frieze, half-geometric, half-organic, suggests flowering plants.

The abstraction and geometric control that pervade Mackintosh's work were seen as alien and exotic by many in Britain, but found numerous admirers on the

Above Blackwell, Windermere, England, 1900, M. H. Baillie Scott. The medieval-looking hall is the focus of a house which exemplified the new ideal of the interior as a work of art in which each room has a distinctive character suited to its purpose.

Opposite Perrycroft, Colwall, England, 1894, C. F. A. Voysey. Spectacularly sited in the Malvern Hills, Perrycroft's exterior is typical of Voysey's combination of broadly treated surfaces and idiosyncratic details, whilst inside a new openness in planning was becoming apparent.

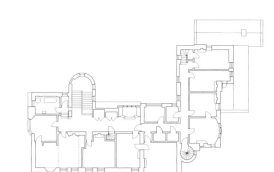

10m
30ft

N

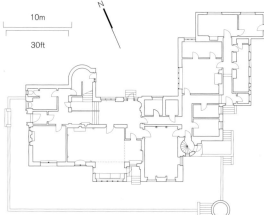

Above and opposite The Hill House, Helensburgh, Scotland, 1902, Charles Rennie Mackintosh. Picturesquely planned around a masterfully orchestrated circulation route, externally the house evokes memories of Scottish Baronial architecture. Internally, however, geometry and abstraction from nature rule, as seen in the light-filled bay projected from the living room.

Continent, above all in Vienna. In The Hill House he was given control over every detail and the cumulative effect of this synthesis of space, light, decoration and furniture is overwhelming. The decorative elaboration can easily blind us to the imagination and discipline with which Mackintosh's ideas were grounded in responses to patterns of use, and proved an embarrassment to later critics. Eager to claim him as a pioneer of the more austerely functional virtues of the International style of the 1930s, they attributed the decorative qualities, wholly without foundation, to the influence of his wife, the talented artist Margaret Macdonald.

In continental Europe the search for new forms culminated in the Art Nouveau style that flourished for little more than a decade either side of 1900. In architecture, the first breakthrough came in Brussels with Victor Horta's Hôtel Tassel of 1892–3. The Kingdom of Belgium had been established as recently as 1830, in the wake of Napoleon's defeat. By the 1890s, when the country was thriving economically, Brussels had a reputation as an emancipated city that played host to a lively cultural avant-garde and was a home to many innovators before they were accepted in their countries of origin. Like London, but unlike other major continental cities, its expansion was based on terraced houses – the larger being known as *hôtels* – rather than apartment buildings.

Hôtel Tassel Brussels, Belgium, 1892–3, Victor Horta

The façade of Horta's *hôtel* gives little away. The bowed front and restrained use of stone are notably elegant but only the exposure of a single iron beam below the cornice declares the originality of what lies within. Once inside you enter a dark lobby, where the only daylight enters surprisingly and somewhat mysteriously from *within* the house. A day-lit cloakroom leads to an octagonal vestibule, positioned a metre (3 feet) lower than the floor, a stage from which to view the interior that opens on several different levels. Seven steps rise into a light-well bay, which functions almost as a tiny *cour d'honneur*. Its internal façade is framed by steel piers – at the time a daring breach with domestic decorum; to one side is the roof-lit winter garden, an exotic world of curvilinear metalwork, bamboo chairs and tropical plants, and to the other, mirroring it in plan, the main stair – a design of great geometric complexity which must have delighted Horta's client, who was a Professor of Descriptive Geometry. On the floor, serpentine decorative motifs writhe out into the adjacent spaces, while overhead arching steel beams are supported by a cast-iron column whose capital blossoms into thin iron tendrils, which seem designed to hold down rather than support the stair floating above.

Spatially, the Hôtel Tassel was unusually intricately worked, and Horta took the openness further in later designs such as the Hôtel Solvay, where the three principal rooms were divided by folding doors which could open to form a continuous, differentiated space. The 'honest' exposure of metal structure, derived from French Rationalists such as Viollet-le-Duc, and the determination to look to nature rather than to previous styles for inspiration in the design of the tendril-like ornaments were equally remarkable. In this Horta's work appears remarkably modern, but in other respects it was very much a product of its time, and nowhere can this be better grasped than in the small salon of the Hôtel Tassel. Isolated from the street and garden by the entrance spaces and dining room, and

5m

15ft

Opposite Hôtel Tassel, Brussels, Belgium, 1893, Victor Horta. The serpentine motifs which swarm across the plan and walls of the Hôtel Tassel are quintessentially Art Nouveau, but architecturally the house's greatest innovation lies in the use of structural iron. This permitted a spatial openness which Horta took further in the Hôtel Solvay, **above**, completed nearby in 1900.

Below Castel Orgeval, Villemoisson, France, 1905, Hector Guimard. Medieval fantasies combine with typical Art Nouveau curvilinear forms to create an organic whole which seems to grow from the site.

looking into the light-well through obscured glass, it presented a private, inner world in which every element, functional and decorative, was integrated into a symphonic whole. For all the use of nature as a source of inspiration, the artificiality of the result is striking. Like the Symbolist poets and painters by whose ideas he was influenced, Horta was trying to create a synthetic paradise through which art could challenge the assumptions of a society increasingly committed to the blind pursuit of technological progress.

Shortly after the completion of the Hôtel Tassel Horta's fellow countryman, Henry van de Velde, built a house for himself at Uccle outside Brussels, replete with organically inspired furniture. It brought him an invitation to design four rooms for the Salon de l'Art Nouveau opened by Samuel Bing in Paris in 1895, the shop that gave the new style its name and was intended, according to Bing, to be a 'meeting ground for all young spirits anxious to manifest the modernness of their tendencies'. Art Nouveau found most of its patrons among the *nouveaux riches*, anxious to display their wealth through an art as distinctive and individual as their lifestyles.

Notable among the 'young spirits' whom Bing influenced was Hector Guimard, best known as the designer of the celebrated Paris Métro entrances but also architect of several outstanding houses. Among these the demolished Castel Henriette (1899–1900) in Sèvres and Castel Orgeval at Villemoisson near Paris were outstanding. Both combined suave Art Nouveau details with wilfully rustic vernacular stonework, suggesting an almost medieval character. Castel Orgeval seems to grow spontaneously from its site, while Castel Henriette was notable for an extraordinary plan in which two orthogonal systems crash obliquely together. This leads a functionally expressive sequence of volumes to explode into a hybrid of load-bearing masonry and structural frames surmounted by picturesque roofs, terraces, balconies, chimneys and, to crown the composition, a campanile-like look-out tower. Superficially, Hôtel Guimard, the house and studio Guimard completed for himself in Paris in 1912, has little in common with these precocious works. But the plan, which melds oval volumes with diagonal axes, reveals a similar, if less violent, fascination with colliding geometries, and the exterior, with its swelling, bulbous forms so redolent of organic growth, looks back, ultimately, to medieval precedents.

In the German-speaking world the new style was christened Jugendstil, and its greatest flowering came in Austria, among the group of artists and architects known as the Secessionists. In architecture their mentor was Otto Wagner, a fervent advocate of building as the basis of design, who believed that a modern style was being forged by engineers who were the masters of the new materials. The young Secessionists, led by the painter Gustav Klimt, seceded in 1897 from the same Academy at which Wagner taught, in protest at its conservatism, and much to his colleagues' astonishment and outrage he joined them two years later. In his lectures Wagner argued for bright, well-ventilated houses with simple furnishings. His influence was enormous: he was an exemplar for Josef Olbrich and his students included Josef Hoffmann and Rudolf Schindler, who later left Vienna to work for Frank Lloyd Wright.

The rectilinear style of Art Nouveau that characterizes the work of the Viennese was developed by Olbrich and Hoffmann in the late 1890s, and taken

Above Hôtel Guimard, Paris, France, 1909–12, Hector Guimard. Stone and brick seem to flow and congeal into drapery-like curves of suave sophistication.

Opposite Olbrich House, Darmstadt, Germany, 1900, Josef Maria Olbrich. Part of the artists' colony which flourished under the patronage of the Grand Duke of Hesse, Olbrich's house combined vernacular German forms with typical Secessionist refinement and decorative motifs of Vienna.

to Germany in 1899 when Olbrich accepted an invitation to join the artists' colony established by the Grand Duke of Hesse on the Mathildenhöhe in Darmstadt. It was the most extravagant piece of artistic patronage in Europe and until his premature death in his early forties Olbrich flourished in the new surroundings, completing not only the central education and exhibition buildings, with their celebrated 'Wedding Tower', but also a string of large private villas around the park. One of the first, built in 1900, was his own house and studio. The exterior, with its distinctive gambrel roof, recalls rural German vernacular houses – a popular allusion at the time among practitioners of National Romanticism – while internally the planning, organized like most of his houses in Darmstadt around an open, multi-purpose living hall, was clearly indebted to Baillie Scott.

The synthesis was Olbrich's alone, however, and on closer examination nothing is as simple as it might appear. The roof, for example, is asymmetrical, with a hanging 'flower gallery' balancing the lower eaves opposite. The fenestration is similarly artfully balanced, with windows positioned in response to the spaces within and bound together by a horizontal frieze of blue and white tiles arranged chequerboard fashion – a trademark of the Secession style that may well have reflected the influence of Charles Rennie Mackintosh, whose work the Viennese greatly admired.

In 1903 Hoffmann and the artist Koloman Moser formed the studios and workshops known as the Wiener Werkstätte. In the spirit of William Morris their programme stated, 'We consider it our most noble duty to regain for the workers a joy in work and an existence worthy of a human being.' This faith in art to bring about, as Olbrich put it at the dedication ceremony of the Darmstadt colony, an 'increase in prosperity' and an 'equalization in social conditions' may seem naïve, but was widely held at the time. In practice, however, Hoffmann was more interested in artistic than social or political questions. He did not believe that it was 'possible to convert the masses' to an appreciation of art and was happy to satisfy 'the few' who could appreciate his refined, abstract style of geometrically pure forms. Two years after the foundation of the Werkstätte he was given the opportunity to create a *Gesamtkunstwerk* – total work of art – in Brussels. The clients were Adolphe Stoclet, a Belgian financier who had lived in Vienna, and his wife Suzanne, a beautiful Parisienne whom he had married against his family's wishes. Their brief was to create a house in which to exhibit their ever-growing collection of art and to entertain the artistic élite of Europe – the guest book (designed by Hoffmann, naturally) contains the names of Diaghilev, Paderewski, Stravinsky, Cocteau and Anatole France.

The site was ideal, situated almost on the edge of the built-up area on the Avenue de Tervueren, a continuation of the prestigious Rue de la Loi. It enjoyed fine views south over woods and parkland and to take maximum advantage of these Hoffmann arranged the extensive accommodation as an axially composed sequence of en-suite rooms forming a linear block facing the road. The major reception spaces, such as the hall and dining and music rooms were expressed as boldly projecting bays, establishing a subtle interplay of crossing axes that extended out into the garden. The planning was highly accomplished but not especially innovative, still rooted in classical principles – unlike Mackintosh's

House for an Art Lover, which may have influenced the massing. What makes Palais Stoclet one of the most remarkable achievements of the pre-war years is Hoffmann's handling of surfaces and the unrivalled sophistication and completeness of the interior decoration.

Palais Stoclet Brussels, Belgium, 1905–11, Josef Hoffmann

Palais Stoclet was built of brick and clad in large, thin slabs of stone, a perfect example of the 'slablike treatment of the surface' that Hoffmann's teacher Otto Wagner had proposed as a leitmotif of a genuinely modern architecture. The size of the slabs alone showed that they must be a thin veneer, not an ashlar wall, but like Wagner, who had famously used exposed fixings like 'nails' on his Vienna Postal Savings Bank, Hoffmann was at pains to emphasize that this was cladding, not solid masonry. He did so by marking corners and framing openings with thin metal profiles, like tautly stretched ropes which seem to spill down from the tower that forms the culmination of the massing. The result is striking, even disconcerting, completely undermining the expressed interaction of load and support that underpinned most previous architecture. In Palais Stoclet the windows are no longer holes in a wall but rectangular surfaces on – and in some cases, actually in front of – the wall. The volumes read as compositions of planes, emphasizing the geometric purity of the design, and the effect is so light as to feel almost unreal – after all, stone, even thin stone, is a heavy material. Hoffmann exploits the planar quality to dramatic effect in details such as the covered seating area carved out of the garden elevation, where the languorously sagging soffit and façade seem, thanks to the doubling of the mouldings, almost ready to slide down like a giant gate.

The interiors were designed collaboratively with his Secession colleagues, the individual artists and craftsmen being given exceptional freedom to develop themes and ideas of their own choosing within Hoffmann's framework. Every means at their disposal was deployed – changes of shape, proportion and volume; varied combinations of natural and artificial light; luxurious surface treatments and colour. In lesser hands the opulence could have been oppressive, but the refinement and control were masterly. Consider the dining room for example. The walls are recessed in three stages: dark Portovenere marble and macassar wood cabinets project furthest, recessed above them is a band of light Paonozzo marble, and above and slightly behind that, appear mosaic decorations by Klimt, also articulated by projecting and receding materials – the subtlety of which quite escapes the camera. Less opulent but no less remarkable was the ample main bathroom, with its walls of pale marble inlaid with strips of black marble and malachite, and furnishings and silver toilet articles purpose-made by the Wiener Werkstätte; it even opened onto a generous exercise balcony, reflecting the fitness cults that anticipated the obsession with health and exercise in the 1920s.

More completely than any other house, perhaps, Palais Stoclet exemplified the European ideal of the aestheticization of life, over which the architect and artist assumed a god-like control, transforming the dwelling from a setting for normal, everyday life into a higher realm consecrated by art. Early visitors reported that the Stoclets lived out this vision, achieving perfect harmony with their surroundings. Nothing was left to chance: in his obituary, their friend E. De Bruyn recalled that the flowers were always of one colour, and even M. Stoclet's cravat

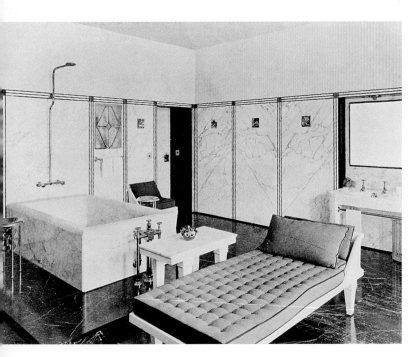

Above Palais Stoclet, Brussels, Belgium, 1905–11, Josef Hoffmann. Like every space in this ultimate *Gesamtkunstwerk*, the bathroom was designed down to the last detail to create an ambience of luxurious cleanliness.

Above, left and below Palais
Stoclet, Brussels, Belgium, 1905–11,
Josef Hoffmann. The axially controlled
planning was stylistically conservative,
but the stone revetment of the
exterior transformed the building mass
into a radically new interplay of
volumes and planes. The supremely
refined interiors, such as the dining
room seen here, combine exquisite
materials with decorations by Gustav
Klimt and Wiener Werkstälte fittings
and furniture.

10m

30ft

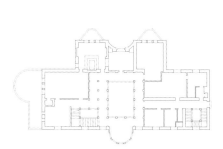

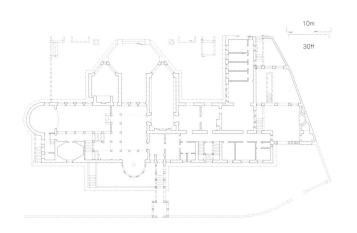

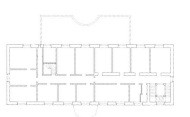

Above Kalela, Lake Ruovesi, Finland, 1895, Akseli Gallen-Kallela. The 'studio in the wilds' became a favoured model throughout Scandinavia at the turn of the century, nowhere better seen than in the painter Gallen-Kallela's home, which he modelled on a Finnish farmhouse and built himself.

Below Hvitträsk, Lake Vitträsk, Finland, 1901, Gesellius, Lindgren, Saarinen. The log-walls, exposed beams, giant fireplace (glimpsed on the right) and *ryijy* rug transform the living room into a fantasy of an ideal Finnish past.

Hvitträsk Lake Vitträsk, Finland, 1901, Gesellius, Lindgren, Saarinen

was chosen to harmonize with his wife's *toilette*. Eduard Sekler, author of the definitive account of Hoffmann's work, has suggested that Palais Stoclet embodies the 'ambiguity and uncertainty' that his contemporary Hugo von Hoffmannsthal believed characterized their epoch. The preciousness and exclusivity of the way of life it celebrated were destined to be swept away by the impending world war, but as we shall see in the next chapter its aesthetic premises were challenged well before then by one of the most incisive critical minds of the day, that of the architect Adolf Loos.

Nowhere, arguably, beyond its places of origin, did the ideal of the house as a work of art fall on more fertile ground than in Scandinavia, where the search for national identity – common throughout central Europe, Germany and the Nordic countries following the era of state formation in the nineteenth century – was especially keenly felt. Throughout Scandinavia the new ideal was the 'studio in the wilds' and artists led the way in showing how to live an authentic life away from the temptations of urban society. Artistically, the most compelling results came in Finland where progressive artists were struggling to assert cultural independence from Russian rule. The pioneer was the painter Axel Gallén, who changed his Swedish name to the Finnish Akseli Gallen-Kallela in 1906. In 1895 he completed a log-built studio home modelled on farmhouses from the remote region of Karelia, which he thought was free of Russian taint (erroneously, as later scholarship revealed).

Gallen-Kallela's example was followed by several leading Finnish artists, including the composer Sibelius and the architects Hermann Gesellius, Armas Lindgren and Eliel Saarinen, who came to fame as designers of the much admired Finnish Pavilion at the 1900 Paris World Fair. The following year Saarinen, with help from his partners, built a house and studio for the practice on a site at Lake Vitträsk, some 30 kilometres (19 miles) west of Helsinki – at that time still 'in the wilds', but close enough to the capital to enable them to pursue their work. The accommodation was organized in three wings around a courtyard. The earliest was modelled on the log and plank buildings of Karelia, and almost immediately acquired a rustic stone entrance tower; that to the south, with its logs, stone base, and steep tiled roofs seems to grow out of the dramatic site and has often been compared to English Arts and Crafts houses, but in fact was based largely on Finnish examples; finally, to the north and originally occupied by Lindgren, was another timber wing with a beguiling fantasy of a tower based on Finnish wooden churches which was destroyed by fire in 1922.

All too predictably the ideal of harmonious living in Hvitträsk – as the house was named – proved less durable than the architecture. Following realignments of the marital arrangements, Gesellius and Lindgren departed and the house was occupied by Saarinen and his wife Louise ('Loja') Gesellius, who enriched it with furniture, rugs and textiles. In keeping with Jugendstil practice, each room acquired its own character and ambience. The one-and-a-half storey high living room, with its exposed logs and beams, *ryijy* rug draped over a built-in bench, and giant fireplace, was modelled on the multi-purpose room known as the *tupa* of regional Karelian farmhouses. In other rooms the national tone was transformed by derivations from architects whom the Saarinens admired. The children's bedroom, for example, was a *petit-*

Above, left and below 'Lilla Hyttnäs' (Larsson House), Sundborn, Sweden, 1893–1919, Carl and Karin Larsson. The Larssons' widely influential vision of a relaxed domestic life, centred around children and celebrated in bright colours, natural materials, folksy details and unconfining clothes, was disseminated through Carl's paintings and books.

hommage to Charles Rennie Mackintosh, while elsewhere Viennese influence can be discerned.

Sweden produced nothing to match Hvitträsk architecturally, but the house the artist Carl Larsson created with his artist-wife Karin Bergöö became the inspiration for idealized images of domestic life whose influence were to ripple through the twentieth century. It all began modestly enough in 1893, with a small log house inherited from Karin's aunt. They added a studio two years later, made it their year-round home in 1901, named it Lilla Hyttnäs, and continued to expand the property so that the old building was all but engulfed in new construction. 'A home is not dead but living,' said Carl Larsson, 'and like all living things must obey the laws of nature by constantly changing.' In 1897 Larsson exhibited his watercolours of the house and in 1899, with an additional four images, they were published as the book *Ett hem* (A Home), which was immediately translated into German and went through several editions. Other books followed, all depicting an unprecedentedly relaxed family life, with children at its centre, lived close to the land and filled with sunlight and smiling faces. German translations emphasized the importance of light – titles included 'The House in the Sun' and 'Let the Light in!' – and notable visitors such as Diaghilev, Strindberg and the royal painter Prince Eugen helped spread the Larssons' fame.

Karin designed several pieces of furniture for Lilla Hyttnäs, made woven textiles and, influenced by the movement to reform women's clothes, developed a new style of dress, flowing and unconfined, for herself and her daughters. Larsson's globetrotting lifestyle was hardly in keeping with the homely life among the 'people of my own kind' whom he portrayed in his paintings and autobiography, but the images were compelling. The Larssons' vision made an immediate impact on numerous contemporaries, not least on Friedrich Alfred Krupp, founder of the industrial giant that bears his name and enthusiastic builder of housing for workers modelled on the Garden City ideal of the English reformer Ebenezer Howard. And it anticipated a vision of modern living that ultimately spread far from its Scandinavian origins. It was not simply national sentiment that led IKEA to sponsor the exhibition 'Carl and Karin Larsson: Creator of the Swedish Style' held at London's Victoria & Albert Museum in 1998, but also recognition of the debt the world's most successful furniture company owed to the aesthetic and lifestyle they pioneered.

Across the Atlantic the vision of a new form of house for new ways of living crystallized in the 1880s on the East Coast of the United States in what the historian Vincent Scully later christened the Shingle style. It drew on earlier Colonial architecture and a way of building Scully termed the Stick style. These native traditions were combined with the picturesque manner of the prolific English architect Richard Norman Shaw and the open, framed spaces and pierced screens of Japanese architecture, which had made a huge impression when a complete house was exhibited at the Philadelphia Centennial Exposition in 1876. Many of the new houses were built as vacation homes, several of the best in the fashionable Rhode Island resort of Newport (for example the Isaac Bell house, illustrated overleaf). Their architects, among whom the young New York firm of McKim, Mead and White were pre-eminent, exploited the more relaxed social requirements to open the interior to an unprecedented degree.

Opposite Isaac Bell House, Newport, Rhode Island, 1882–3, McKim, Mead and White. The light, shingled mass, large windows and generous porches exemplify the airiness of the so-called Shingle Style made possible by timber construction.
Below Winslow House, River Forest, Illinois, USA, 1893, Frank Lloyd Wright. The cruciform plan, with a great hearth at its centre, anticipates the organization and spatial continuity of Wright's Prairie Houses.

Winslow House River Forest, Illinois, USA, 1893, Frank Lloyd Wright

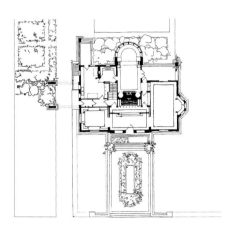

Their typical plan-type placed an English-style living hall at its heart and expanded the spaces horizontally into generous bay windows and porches. Vincent Scully's description cannot be bettered: 'Inside the variety was like that of a nineteenth-century landscape painting, where gradations of light – partly in full flood, partly shielded by porches; sometimes golden, sometimes thunderous – defined flickering interior landscapes at various levels, broader and more extensive than any that America had known before and flowing on to the outside through wide doors and echoing porches.'

The Japanese influence on American architecture was reinforced with the publication in 1886 of Edward Sylvester Morse's classic book *Japanese Homes and Their Surroundings*. It received a further boost with the exhibition of the Ho-o-Den temple at the 1893 World's Columbian Exposition in Chicago, where it was seen by a twenty-five-year-old architect of genius at the moment he was poised to launch his solo career. His name, needless to say, was Frank Lloyd Wright, and in the same year as the Exposition he designed a house and stables that anticipated by almost ten years his revolutionary Prairie Style. The client was William Herman Winslow, president of a highly successful ornamental ironwork firm and keen amateur typographer.

The site is on a large suburban lot in River Forest near Chicago, and the street elevation is divided into three horizontal bands: a brick base, which sits on a clearly defined stone foundation and rises beyond the first floor, terminating in a white cornice; a narrower, dark band made of strongly textured terracotta panels, punctuated by three windows which fill its height; and a deeply overhanging hipped roof. By separating the elements in this way Wright effected a radical simplification, further enhanced by binding together the entrance door and adjacent windows in a rectangular stone panel. The composition, however, is still strictly symmetrical – a public face guarding the private world within – and sits uneasily against the asymmetrical spaces that unfold behind. At their centre is a strongly emphasized fireplace: a 'fire burning deep in the solid masonry of the house' was, for Wright, the abiding symbol of home and here it greets the visitor immediately on entry. Placed three steps up on its own podium and set behind an arcaded screen, which Noris Kelly Smith has interpreted as a rood screen, it has the formality of a chancel with the hearth as its altar, an interpretation wholly in keeping, as we shall see, with Wright's religious view of the home. The principal rooms unfold around the fireplace, and you move through them along their edges, not centres. Traces of the Beaux-Arts planning that still characterized a house like Palais Stoclet are present, but at no point are you allowed to enter a space axially.

The Winslow House is impressive, but in the stables Wright built behind it we find something far more original. The upper level plan is cruciform, generated by two interpenetrating volumes, and the elevations are composed of continuous horizontal layers – anticipated in the house, but without any suggestion of the boxiness of traditional buildings. Each layer is free to assume whatever shape and dimensions the pressure of the spaces inside might dictate. For Wright 'letting the room within come through' was the key to what he called natural, 'organic' architecture and here, in the Winslow stables, the architectural means to realize that idea seem to have sprung to life fully formed. Spatially, it made

everything done in Europe before the Great War seem old fashioned, and it would take Wright himself several years to assimilate its possibilities.

Three years after completing the Winslow House Wright began a collaboration with his client on a book entitled *The House Beautiful*. The text was a popular sermon, distributed the previous year as a pamphlet, by the famous Unitarian minister William C. Gannett, a long-time friend of Wright's uncle. The book took three years of part-time work to produce, and ninety copies were finally printed on a press housed in Winslow's stables. Gannett's text, scattered with quotations from poetry and the Bible, was typical of the day, ornate in style and, to modern ears, cloyingly pious and sentimental. In keeping with the thought of his time, Gannett ascribed moral and religious value to the home, and throughout his long life Wright himself regarded it as both an almost sacred institution and the basis of American democracy. 'The ideal of beauty is simplicity and repose' was the book's central message, to be followed not only in the design and furnishing of the home but equally in the lifestyles of its occupants. The text was preceded by twelve exquisite photogravures of wildflowers taken by Wright, who was a keen photographer, and framed by elaborate but highly abstract graphic designs based on natural forms, in which the influence of the Viennese, Art Nouveau, the English and American Arts and Crafts movements and even Wright's love of Oriental rugs can all be discerned. But as with his architecture, Wright's ability to absorb and abstract yielded results that seem at the same time intensely personal and universal.

The influence of the Arts and Crafts movement and of Japan were just as keenly felt on the American West Coast where, above all in California, the challenge of developing completely new lifestyles for a culture still untainted by industrialization, in a climate that encouraged outdoor living, remained full of promise. This vision of California as a second Eden, ripe for innovation, would run right through the twentieth century and yield some of its outstanding houses. First among these were the so-called 'California bungalows', of which the recognized masters were the brothers Charles and Henry Greene. Born and schooled in the mid-West, where they received early encouragement to work with timber, they assimilated the lessons of the French Beaux-Arts system as students at the Massachusetts Institute of Technology in Cambridge. They moved to California in 1893, opened an office the following year, and in 1907 began work on their masterpiece, the Gamble House in their adopted town of Pasadena, now part of greater Los Angeles. The client was wealthy – a son of one of the founders of Procter and Gamble, the soap-makers – and his house large yet surprisingly intimate.

Gamble House Pasadena, California, USA, 1907–8, Greene and Greene

The Gamble House stands on a rustic rubble-stone plinth and was built entirely of timber: redwood framing externally, much teak internally. The plan, with its principal rooms organized axially around fireplaces, shows the influence of Wright, but is looser and more rambling, dissolving around the perimeter into generous balconies and sleeping porches from which vegetation spills out of large planting boxes. The open timber framing recalls earlier East Coast Stick style houses, but nowhere had the widely espoused ideal of natural living been so vividly achieved. The handling of the wooden structure shows a keen knowledge of Japanese practice, and as in

Above and opposite Gamble House, Pasadena, California, USA, 1907–8, Greene and Greene. With its integral terraces and sleeping-balconies the Gamble House exemplifies the relaxed way of life made possible by the equable Californian climate. The interior, a masterpiece of exposed timber structure and construction, is at its most compelling in the stair-hall.

Japan the construction was designed to move, to cope with tremors from the notorious San Andreas Fault. The pegged joints and metal straps – which bind the members together like thongs but enable them to slide when required – are marvellously refined and ornamental in effect, and all the structural elements are subtly tapered and rounded. The architects, who were also skilled carpenters, perfected many of the details on site and the craftsmanship and attention to detail are awesome.

The exterior quality is fully matched in the interior. A Live Oak rendered in stained glass fills the entrance doors and screen, and the living room, made entirely of teak, is a masterpiece of expressed structure and construction. Open trusses with sinuous corbelled brackets frame alcoves around the perimeter, and everything is exquisitely detailed down to the exposed fixings and art-glass lamps. Clouds drift across the bookcase glass and the tendrils of a vine climb up the fireplace tiles, displacing any possible doubts about the pervasive debt to Japan. Most inventive and memorable of all, however, is the main stair. A miracle of interlocking pieces of Burmese teak, it is almost animate in the way it seems to climb between floors. Dovetailed joints like interlocking fingers greet you beside the lowest steps, while above, the handrail zigzags its way up with muscular, animal grace. Each of the three sections of rail was carved from a single piece of wood, lending the whole a rare combination of constructive and sculptural power and marking it out as one of the supreme achievements of the Arts and Crafts movements on either side of the Atlantic.

The Gamble House was the most luxurious flower of a determination in California to develop bungalows and furniture appropriate to the new frontier. Its chief propagandist was Gustav Stickley, whose magazine *The Craftsman*, distributed from 1901 to 1916, was widely influential, and its most original talent was Bernard Maybeck, whose work fell into obscurity until its rediscovery in the 1970s. Although trained in the 1880s in that still mighty bastion of Classicism, the Ecole des Beaux-Arts in Paris, Maybeck developed a highly eclectic personal manner that drew on twelfth-century Gothic as freely as modern steel construction. Many of his early houses around San Francisco were inspired by the Swiss-chalet style, but he quickly stamped his own ideas on the type, tailoring each house to its site and owners, and endeavouring to make it embody an individual way of life. Interviewed in 1927 he said that, 'the thing to do is to make the home fit the family…. I never plan a home for a man until I have asked him a lot of questions. "What sort of woman is your wife? What kind of clothes do you both wear? What do you most like to read? Do you enjoy music?"'

Maybeck's chalet-style culminated in 1914 with the Guy Hyde Chick House in Berkeley's Chabot canyon. Framed in timber and clad in a mixture of vertical redwood boards, grey-green stained shingles and sand-finished plaster, it blends superbly with the native Live Oaks and the Japanese-inspired garden that threads among them. Large sliding doors connect the reception rooms to each other and, on every elevation, to outdoor paths and shallow terraces. Maybeck once defined architecture as 'landscape gardening around a few rooms'; the integration of house and garden here surpassed anything attempted by Greene and Greene and rivalled, in a more informal mode, the mature Prairie Style houses of Wright. The rooms were by no

Guy Hyde Chick House Berkeley, California, USA, 1914, Bernard Maybeck means as casually arranged as Maybeck's description might suggest, and on the upper floor three of the bedrooms have a strikingly novel feature: wardrobes that project beyond the volume of the house. They were not so much built-in as 'built-out', an idea Charles Moore later referred to as 'saddlebags' and were used to house kitchens, bathrooms and other service spaces. True to Maybeck's principles, the rooms reflected the life they were to accommodate. Most of the walls were plastered, but the living room was more refined, covered in dull gold velvet and trimmed in redwood, while in total contrast the boys' room upstairs, anticipating rougher treatment, was a timber world of board and batten walls and exposed beams and rafters.

Designed as war was breaking out in Europe, Maybeck's Chick House was but one of many built in the early 1900s in which we can see the culmination of ideas that had been maturing for half a century alongside hints of more radical innovations to come. The openness of its planning and effortless integration with the site anticipated ways of living that would not be widely adopted for several decades, but like all the houses we have explored in this chapter it looked back to the ideals of the Arts and Crafts movement with which the story of the twentieth-century house begins, more than forward to the possibilities of industrial production. Ideas and techniques that would ultimately transform the conception of the house from a handmade work of art into a 'machine for living in' had been developing throughout the nineteenth century, and it is to their consequences that we now turn.

Right and opposite Guy Hyde Chick House, Berkeley, California, USA, 1914, Bernard Maybeck. Combining native Californian timber-building traditions with Japanese influence, Maybeck fused house and garden, opening the principal rooms freely into each other and to the surrounding landscape.

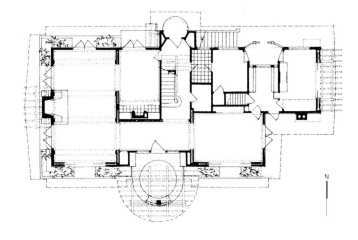

the modern house

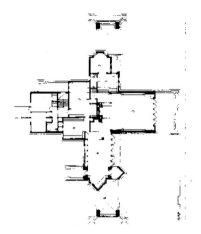

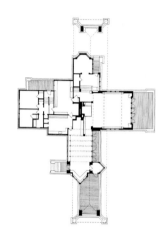

The Modern house with a capital 'M' was born on the continent of Europe in the 1920s and quickly disseminated around the world. Externally, its walls were plain and unornamented, with large areas of glass, while internally separate rooms were replaced by a continuum of space made possible by a structural frame. The resulting 'open plan' reflected a new openness in living, the gradual breakdown of old social hierarchies, and a reduced dependence on servants. The first houses we could call modern with a small 'm', however, were built in the United States by Frank Lloyd Wright shortly after the earliest recorded use of the word 'modern' as a description of architecture. It occurred in the title – 'Moderne Architektur' – of Otto Wagner's inaugural lecture as professor at the Vienna Academy, given in 1895 and published the following year as a book. 'It may be regarded as proved,' Wagner said, 'that art and artists always represent their own epoch…. New forms originate from new construction, new materials, new human tasks and ideas.' Therefore 'all modern forms must correspond to new materials and the new requirements of our time, if they are to fit modern mankind.'

The search for a 'modern' style had been a preoccupation throughout the nineteenth century, underpinning the ideals of those who rejected the machine, like the exponents of the Arts and Crafts movement, as much as those who urged architects to embrace it, like Wagner. The engineer was widely seen as *l'homme moderne par excellence*, as a pupil of Emmanuel Viollet-le-Duc wrote in a paean of praise for the Eiffel Tower in 1889, and as early as the 1840s the American sculptor Horatio Greenough declared that 'form follows function' and compared steamships to the Parthenon. His assertion was popularized by Frank Lloyd Wright's mentor, Louis Sullivan, and Wright in turn quickly moved on from his Arts and Crafts roots to become a leading advocate of 'The Art and Craft of the Machine', as he entitled an important lecture given in Chicago in 1901. 'In the machine lies the only future of art and craft,' Wright declared, 'as I believe, a glorious future.' In the same year he designed the Ward Willits House in Highland Park, on the outskirts of Chicago: it is often called the 'first Prairie Style house' and in it Wright crystallized the ideas of form and space implicit in the Winslow House stables (see page 27).

The plan of the Willits House is cruciform, and on the ground floor the major rooms have open corners which interlock to form a continuous space that pinwheels around the central fireplace. The external form, horizontally layered and with low-pitched, deeply overhanging roofs which cantilever out to shelter porches and verandas, is a direct expression of this inner organization, and a response to the prairie landscape of the region. Only the vertical framing of the living room breaks the horizontal continuity, marking the double-height volume behind. Wright built the house using the standard American 'balloon frame' system, in which two-storey-high walls are framed in 10 x 5 centimetre (4 x 2 inch) timbers, sheathed and covered in stucco. Frames, trims and cover strips were all plain rectangular sections – he complained how difficult it was to get them without mouldings and so remain true to the simplicity he wanted to represent the 'art and craft of the machine'.

The clarity achieved in the Willits House was hard-won, the result of several years of experimentation, and Wright went on to exploit his innovations in a series of houses, many of them located in the Chicago suburb of Oak Park. Several of his clients were young engineers who shared his progressive ideals and had become managers of successful manufacturing companies. The thirty-year-old Frederick Robie was typical: an inventor who made bicycles and car parts in his father's firm.

Unusually, Robie found an urban corner site in south Chicago, near the University. It was tighter than Wright was used to working with and brought out what he considered to be the most extreme and conclusive expression of the Prairie House type. The Robie House has three floors, but at first sight it looks like a single, elevated level with a small addition emerging from the overhanging roofs; in fact there is also an almost invisible ground floor, like a basement above ground – Wright hated the ubiquitous American basement, believing it unhygienic. The house hugs the ground, yet the elevated brick walls and deeply undercut roofs appear almost to defy gravity: Wright's advocacy of building 'in the nature of materials' did not preclude the use, as here, of hidden steelwork to achieve the effects he was after. He was always sceptical of other architects' commitment to the 'honest' exposure of structure – 'I call it *indecent exposure*,' he said with characteristically caustic wit.

The horizontality is boldly reinforced by the stone foundation and lines of copings, and more subtly by the choice of a long Roman brick which is laid in thick, plain mortar beds but has narrower vertical joints pointed in coloured mortar to match the brick. Wright's attention to detail was total, and his specifications called for any exposed screw-heads to have their slots set horizontally: nothing was allowed to contradict the broad horizontals, the 'strong earth-line' which for Wright was always a vital expression of home and freedom in the open American landscape.

The Robie House plan has traces of the classic cruciform type, but to fit the site it was transformed into a long room with a vestigial cross-axis marked by the entrance, located out of sight around the back to ensure privacy, avoid breaking up the street frontage and heighten the sense of arrival. The fireplace, as we have come to expect, is at the heart of the house, sunk into the floor to suggest vertical continuity and opened above to allow an almost uninterrupted horizontal flow of space from living to dining room. Both ends of the main volume terminate in pointed prows framed by staggered piers, and the perimeter is enclosed by a ribbon of floor-to-ceiling doors and waist-high windows, all glazed with leaded lights of Wright's design. The composite effect is the dissolution of solid enclosure and the framing of space by folding planes – what Wright would later call the 'destruction of the box'. Artificial lighting, heating and ventilation are integrated seamlessly into the design: pierced wooden grilles above the windows conceal lamps which cast a gentle dappled light onto the floor, like sunlight through foliage, while the small globes suspended by the oak strips that weave their way back and forth across the ceiling reinforce the feeling of a folded plane floating above you.

Contemporary observers nicknamed the Robie House a 'ship of the prairie' and Neil Levine, the most thought-provoking recent interpreter of Wright's work, has likened his achievement here to the exactly contemporary Analytical Cubism of Picasso and Braque. Just as they fragmented figures into intersecting,

Robie House Oak Park, Illinois, USA, 1909, Frank Lloyd Wright

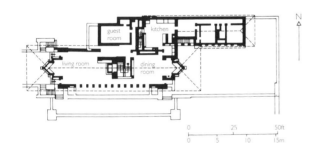

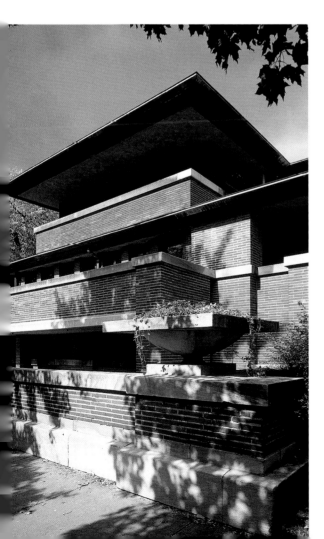

overlapping planes, Wright subjected the traditional image of the house – still secure in the Winslow design – to a series of transformations. He reinvented the dwelling as abstract planes that defined shifting geometric shapes in which traditional distinctions between wall and window, inside and out, cease to be valid. The real prairie may have been physically distant from Wright's Prairie houses, but he re-created its openness for their occupants through the abstraction of spatial continuity and horizontally stretched forms. This process reached its highpoint in the Robie House, which has a strong claim to be called the first fully modern house in which space itself is the prime medium of composition and the external forms are a direct expression of the habitable volumes within.

The same could almost be said of the extraordinary Torre de la Creu which stands just outside Barcelona. It was designed by Josep Maria Jujol, a talented former assistant of Antoni Gaudí now thought to be responsible for some of his finest ironwork and other details. The Torre contains a pair of houses and the plan is composed of six intersecting circles which rise as cylinders to various heights. Within the three larger, interpenetrating circles the rooms are subdivided orthogonally – a simple but clever move – and conventional horizontal circulation is replaced by the spiral stairs that occupy two of the smaller circles and bring light down into the interior. Everything flows from this singular plan which, as Le Corbusier would later declare, should be the 'generator' of the massing and surfaces. Torre de la Creu hardly conforms to our expectations of a 'modern' house – the formal elaboration seems vaguely Islamic, and it might well have been inspired by circular Romanesque churches in the region – but it is unique and utterly original, the forms ultimately Jujol's alone. In 1913, when he built it, only Frank Lloyd Wright had surpassed this level of spatial and formal innovation.

Torre de la Creu was destined to remain unknown, however: Jujol never rivalled its originality and had no impact on mainstream developments. Frank Lloyd Wright, on the other hand, had already produced a substantial body of work and would continue to build for another half century. His buildings may have been far away across the Atlantic and physically inaccessible to most, but increasingly architectural ideas would be promulgated in print. Two folios of Wright's work were published by Ernst Wasmuth of Berlin in 1910 and 1911 and they staggered the emerging European avant-garde. There, fully-formed, were compelling examples of that modern spatial art for which they were still searching. Wright's influence was clear as early as 1916 in the first concrete-framed house in Europe, a villa at Huis ter Heide designed by Robert van't Hoff, one of the few to see his work at first hand. Writing in 1918 another Dutchman J. J. P. Oud was in no doubt that Wright had 'advanced on the way towards the machine aesthetic' and 'laid the basis of a new plasticism in architecture'.

Closest among the Europeans to a comparable breakthrough, arguably, was the Viennese Adolf Loos; he was also the most acerbic critic of Art Nouveau. Loos launched his attacks as early as 1898 in Vienna's leading newspaper, writing about such ordinary things as underwear, men's hats and plumbing. Left to their own devices, he argued, the crafts unselfconsciously produced a 'modern' style, but they were being corrupted by style-mongers like the Secessionists. Loos thought these self-styled arbiters of 'taste' had no right to impose their

Torre de la Creu Barcelona, Spain, 1913, Josep Maria Jujol

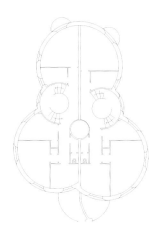

Above and right Torre de la Creu, Barcelona, Spain, 1913, Josep Maria Jujol. The spaces and external forms of this artfully asymmetrical pair of houses flow directly from the plan in a way which is thoroughly modern – despite the inventive but traditional-looking exterior.

Opposite Villa at Huis ter Heide, The Netherlands, 1916, Robert van't Hoff. The first concrete framed house in Europe, the villa was also first to have assimilated the lessons of Wright's Prairie Style.

values on others – in your flat, he said, 'it is you who are always right' – and he composed a story in which a 'poor rich man' commissioned an interior makeover (to borrow the term beloved of popular television home decorating programmes) by a thinly disguised Josef Hoffmann. He invited the master to see the completed interior, only for him to be horrified by the sight of the owner's embroidered slippers: "'But Mr Architect! have you already forgotten? You yourself designed them!" "Of course," thundered the architect, "but for the bedroom! They completely disrupt the mood here with these two impossible spots of colour. Can't you see that?"'

Loos famously inveighed against gratuitous ornament. His most celebrated essay was entitled *Ornament and Crime* (1908), often misquoted as 'ornament is crime', in which he argued that the 'evolution of culture marches with the elimination of ornament from useful objects'. In place of stylistic fripperies he advised his readers to study the everyday products of crafts and modern engineering: 'Behold the bicycle!' he urged, 'does not the spirit of Periclean Athens permeate its forms?' For Loos the Greeks still epitomized the ability to choose the 'one right form' and their modern counterparts were 'the English as a people, the engineers as a profession'.

Unlike many talented critics, Loos could match deed to word and the Steiner House he designed in Vienna in 1910 was the most austerely simple anywhere, its exterior relying solely on well proportioned, white rendered surfaces and large plate-glass windows. Two years later he completed the Scheu and Horner Houses. In 1934 the British journal *The Architectural Review* declared the former was the 'first in the world of which we can say without any sort of mental reservation that it is "modern" in our own specific sense of the word.' The *Review* was guilty of judging by appearances, however, as spatially the interiors were relatively traditional: arrangements of rooms, not compositions of space. In both there was also a radical disjunction between the austere exterior – a response to the anonymity of the modern city – and the intimate, private world of the interior with its panelled walls and exposed oak beams. This contrast was central to Loos's vision of the house as a shelter to the psyche as well as to the body and would persist in his work throughout the 1920s.

Around the period of 1912 to 1913 Loos began to have the germs of a spatial idea that blossomed after the war: 'This is the great revolution in architecture,' he declared, 'the planning of a building in volume.' He called his 'plan of volumes' a *Raumplan*, and viewed the building cube as a void to be filled freely with rooms of different volume, scaled in section as well as plan to fit the activities they contain. We first see the *Raumplan* fully at work in the Rufer House, built in Vienna in 1922. The exterior is almost completely cubic, broken only by a veranda and a roof terrace cut into the volume, and the windows are scattered, apparently at random, across the rendered surfaces. In fact, of course, they are positioned to suit the rooms within, and adjusted to achieve a dynamic balance externally. The plan revolves around a central column, which doubles as a central-heating flue, and the principal rooms – named music and dining – open around it on different levels. 'Floors', in their familiar guise, were beginning to disappear, something he took further in several subsequent designs, culminating with the Müller House of 1930 in Prague.

Above Horner House, Vienna, Austria, 1912, Adolf Loos. The idiosyncratic placement of the windows directly reflects the organization of the rooms and staircase within. The austere exterior was Loos's response to the anonymity of the modern city, in striking contrast to the inner life of rich materials to be discovered in the privacy of the dwelling.

Müller House Prague, Czech Republic, 1930, Adolf Loos

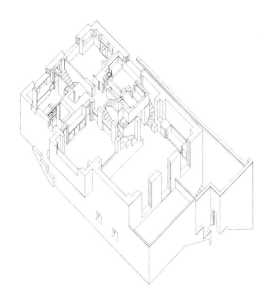

Schröder House Utrecht, the Netherlands, 1924, Gerrit Rietveld

On paper we can see that, in principle, the plan of the Müller House is organized on multiple levels around a central stair. But this stair is only reached after passing through an anteroom, turning left up seven risers onto a landing before the main hall, and then turning right and rising another half-level to reach the core. The interior verges on the labyrinthine: few rooms share the same 'floor' and the identity of each is reinforced by varied proportions and unique surface treatments. The latter were grounded in Loos's commitment to the theory of cladding articulated by Gottfried Semper in the mid-nineteenth century, and based on a radical division between structure and enclosure. Semper traced this idea back to animal skins or carpets hung from a timber framework. To emphasize that his finishes were (almost literally) only skin deep, Loos favoured veneers of highly figured stone and wood, deploying them both to assert the uniqueness of each room and, by allowing the material of one space to invade the next, to ensure a degree of ambiguity and continuity.

Although Loos's writings were widely admired – several essays were reproduced in the magazine *L'Esprit nouveau* founded in 1920 by Amedée Ozenfant and Charles-Edouard Jeanneret (who soon restyled himself Le Corbusier) – his work had little impact on mainstream developments. His way of composing was, in some respects, more fully three-dimensional than the 'open plan' which, by the mid 1920s, came to define the Modern house. But he still thought in terms of rooms, and the truly radical innovation of European Modernism, anticipated by Wright, was to reinvent the house as a continuous spatial field. The first time we see that idea fully realized is in the Schröder House in Utrecht, a collaboration between the client, Truus Schröder-Schräder, and Gerrit Rietveld, who studied architecture in the evenings after training as a furniture-maker. In this capacity, from 1917 to 1918, he created one of the first and most unforgettable icons of modern design, the 'Red and Blue' chair.

Truus Schröder-Schräder was married to a lawyer but preferred to socialize with the avant-garde and immerse herself in books on philosophy, art and architecture. She tried, often against her husband's wishes, to implement progressive educational ideas for her three children and when he died young in 1923 decided to make a new start in a new home. She found a small plot at the end of a terrace facing open country (now, sadly, occupied by an elevated motorway and, beyond it, more housing, including some designed by Rietveld). Rietveld had previously worked on the Schröder's flat, and other small conversions, but had never designed a new building. He brought a strong personal vision about form and space to the task, but few preconceptions about what a house should be, and so the design evolved in response to the liberated life Truus wanted to live. Architect and client became – possibly already were – lovers, but although Rietveld kept an office in the house, he only moved in after the death of his wife in 1958.

Mrs Schröder-Schräder decided to live at first floor level, to enjoy the views, and wanted to be in close contact with her children whom she thought should be educated by mixing with the artists and intellectuals she entertained. To circumvent building regulations, the ground floor was designed with relatively

Above Müller House, Prague, Czech
Republic, 1930, Adolf Loos. The cubic
form belies the complex sequence of
rooms organised on many levels within,
where the materials and colours are
chosen to create an appropriate
atmosphere – as seen in the contrast
between the children's suite (**right**)
and the formality and luxury of the
principal reception room (**below**).

Above Schröder House, Utrecht,
The Netherlands, 1924, Gerrit Rietveld.
The ground floor plan (**below**) was
conventional, the upper floor (**top,
centre and right**), which Mrs
Schröder-Schräder occupied,
unprecedented in its openness.
The space can be transformed by
sliding and folding partitions and
furniture, and is articulated by coloured
planes: 'the destruction of the box'
announced by Wright was complete.

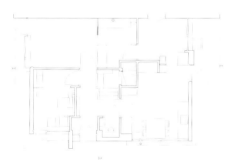

conventional rooms, including a built-in garage – novel at the time, especially as she didn't have a car – and the first floor was left open and called simply 'attic'. It proved to be the most important attic in the history of architecture. Near its centre Rietveld placed a tight, winding staircase, lit through the flat roof by a cubic skylight. In the rear corner, tucked against the party wall, was Truus's room, which could open into the living area via a folding door. The rest of the space could be completely open, or subdivided by thin sliding partitions into living space, a room for her two girls, and one for her boy.

With a craftsman's eye for detail Rietveld redesigned everything in the house in light of the aesthetic principles explored in his furniture. The windows, framed by differently coloured strips of wood, could be either closed or secured fully open at 90 degrees to the façade so as not to introduce a jarring diagonal (there were several sizes of opening to allow for different rates of ventilation). Broad sills were provided for ornaments and plants – very Dutch, like the bench beside the entrance – and all the furniture was either built-in or of Rietveld's design.

Every detail reflected the organizing principle of the house: the definition, but not containment, of space by sticks and planes. To emphasize their autonomy they were variously coloured, and either freestanding or slipped past one another to avoid conventional corners. To open the interior to the garden and countryside, columns retreated from the corners, which could be completely dissolved by opening the windows. The result was a complete *Gesamtkunstwerk*, like the Palais Stoclet, but free of inner tensions between the modernity of the surfaces and a classical plan. And whereas the houses we considered in the last chapter all too easily, as Adolf Loos realized, became aesthetic tyrannies, Rietveld's masterpiece was liberating and receptive to ordinary living: Truus Schröder-Schräder dwelt there happily until her death in 1985.

The Schröder House was the first building to match the widely shared post-war dream of a new world, rebuilt from the ground up on new aesthetic, social and political principles. In the Schröder House, as in all the greatest modern houses, the architectural means were developed and deployed in the service of a new vision for living. To Rietveld and his client, clarity and simplicity were articles of faith as much as artistic means. Truus Schröder-Schräder's ideas about the family, the role of women in society, and the shared responsibilities of individuals were central to the making of her house, and Rietveld's unsurpassed achievement was to create an environment in which simple acts like closing partitions or raising and lowering a table assumed ritual significance as part of a conscious celebration of daily life.

In the absence of evidence to the contrary, it might be tempting to suppose that the Schröder House was an inhabitable version of a Mondrian painting. Rietveld, like Mondrian, was embraced by Theo van Doesburg, leader of the Dutch De Stijl movement, but he arrived at his key ideas largely independently and never fully subscribed to theirs. He worked by instinct rather than theory and in this respect was an unusual figure among the pioneers of modern architecture, with whom ideas frequently ran ahead of the ability – or opportunities – to realize them. This was the case with Le Corbusier who began promoting his revolutionary vision in earnest in *L'Esprit Nouveau* in 1920, and then in 1923 assembled the articles to form the book *Vers une architecture*. It was translated into English in 1927 and published, slightly misleadingly, under the title *Towards a New Architecture*. It proved to be one of the most influential books on architecture ever written.

Like Loos in Vienna, Le Corbusier began by attacking his *bêtes noires* – the overblown, worn-out Classicism of the Ecole des Beaux-Arts and the, to him, absurd idea that architecture could be reduced to a superficial question of 'style'. After reminding his fellow architects of the timeless means of their art – the control of mass, surface and plan (which, as we noted above, he called the 'generator'), and the use of geometrically ordered 'regulating lines' to control proportions of the locations and sizes of openings – he went on to explain, for 'eyes which do not see', the aesthetic virtues of engineering structures and machines. He illustrated his arguments with American grain silos (pictures of which were in circulation in Europe before the war) and other engineering works, comparing in a famous pairing of images a 1907 Humber with the early Greek temple at Paestum, and a racy 'Grand-Sport' Delage of 1921 with the Parthenon. His message was that whereas it had taken over a century and a half to achieve the refinement of the Greek temples, it took only fourteen years to move from the 'primitive' to the 'classic' phase in car design. This progress, he argued, was driven by a process he called 'mechanical selection', a Darwinian view of industry which he believed resulted in functionally perfect *objets-types.* The comparisons were persuasive but like much propaganda, at times devious: the Delage was a handcrafted product, not mass-produced like the famous Model T Ford.

Vers une architecture culminated in a call for mass-produced houses to meet the housing shortage afflicting Europe in the wake of war, a call later summed up by a phrase that has entered the language: 'the house is a machine for living in' (although 'a machine for living' might have been more accurate). To confound any narrowly mechanistic interpretation, Le Corbusier defined beauty and a sense of proportion as key features of this 'machine'. The design of compact houses for low-paid working families preoccupied many leading architects in the 1920s, not least those at the Bauhaus, the most influential art and design school of the century, and will be considered in detail in the next chapter. Here we will concentrate on the spatial ideas that were more fully realized in larger, private commissions.

Le Corbusier's new vision of space was made possible by replacing load-bearing walls with structural frames. It was implicit in the Dom-Ino house he developed in 1914 in response to the early devastation of the war in Flanders, but it took him a decade, he later explained, to realize its architectural possibilities. These he duly published at the Weissenhof Exhibition of new housing in Stuttgart as the 'Five Points of a New Architecture':

1. Columns (he called them *pilotis*) to raise the house in the air, freeing the ground for the movement of people and vehicles.
2. A *roof garden* on the *flat roof*, to replace the ground lost by development.
3. Extending the *pilotis* through as a structural frame to free the external walls and partitions, enabling the latter to be freely arranged to suit the planning requirements – which he termed the *plan libre*, or free plan.
4. Disposing windows and terraces as required by the interior to create what he called a *free façade.*
5. Long horizontal windows – *fenêtres en longueur* or ribbon windows – to give an even, generous distribution of light.

As principles go these are an odd mixture of construction, functional organization and aesthetic preference. Ribbon windows certainly do not give the light distribution he claimed, but they do differ radically from the upright stance of conventional windows, which is what he needed to express the continuous, 'flowing' space within. They were all seen for the first time in the modestly sized Cook House built on the outskirts of Paris in 1926, on a site overlooking the Bois de Boulogne. To emphasize its machine-like modernity the entrance, with its curved front and narrow band of windows, recalls the cockpit of the 'Goliath' biplane illustrated in *Vers une architecture*, while the wing-like roof canopy is supported by columns as slender as those holding the plane's wings together. Internally, the compact form did not allow much room to demonstrate the virtues of the *plan libre* – even after, to his client's cost and annoyance, Le Corbusier 'stole' an extra half metre (1.5 feet) from the neighbouring property – but three-quarters of the main level is a continuous open space, with the living room itself occupying a double-height volume. On the bedroom floor the partitions demonstrate their freedom by artfully evading the columns and wrapping sinuously around a wash-basin and built-in table.

In the vastly larger villa at Garches, begun the same year and completed in 1928, Le Corbusier exploited the new possibilities to the full, carving terraces at various levels out of the broad rectangular block and interlinking and interpenetrating spaces vertically and horizontally to form a continuous whole of great complexity. The clients could hardly have been more exciting: the Stein family – the legendary Gertrude, Leo, Michael and his wife Sarah, one of Matisse's most important patrons – wished to share it with their friend Gabrielle Colaço-Osorio de Monzie and her daughter. Michael Stein was a classic example of the 'new man' whose virtues were extolled in *L'Esprit Nouveau* and described by Le Corbusier's colleague Charlotte Perriand as the 'type of individual who keeps pace with scientific thought, who understands his age and lives it: the Aeroplane, the Ocean Liner and the Motor are at his service; Sport gives him health; his house is his resting place'. And like Madame de Monzie, who owned several châteaux in the South of France, he was also passionate about art and rich enough to build on the grand scale.

Villa Stein Garches, France, 1926–8, Le Corbusier

The freedom of the *plan libre* came into its own in accommodating the clients' intricate living arrangements and they in turn fell in love with their new house and garden, nicknaming it Les Terrasses. They disappointed Le Corbusier by insisting on furnishing it with their heavy antiques, and he conspicuously omitted all furniture, save for some casually placed white Parisian chairs on the terrace, from the photographs in the first volume of his *Oeuvre complète*.

Like several of Le Corbusier's larger houses of the 1920s, that at Garches seems to engage in a dialogue with the master of the Classical villa, Andrea Palladio. The column grid alternates between wide and narrow bays, and the spaces are similarly layered in contrasting zones from front to back. Centrality, a hallmark of Classicism, is asserted and then denied: the ribbon windows force the eye to the edges, and incidents are scattered around the perimeter of the plan. The front elevation is a masterpiece of subverted symmetries, geometrically controlled by hidden regulating lines: ribbon window balances garage door;

Above Cook House, Paris, France, 1926, Le Corbusier. Raised on *pilotis*, freely planned behind a continuous ribbon window, which expresses the spatial continuity within, and culminating in a small roof garden, we see here the first built expression of Le Corbusier's 'Five Points of a New Architecture'.

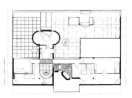

Above and left Villa Stein, Garches, France, 1926–8, Le Corbusier. Artfully asymmetrical and layered in plan and elevation, the Villa Stein was a sophisticated re-working of the compositional norms of the Classical villa, designed to accommodate the clients' unusually complicated domestic requirements.

principal entrance and cantilevered canopy assert their primacy over the matching servant's entrance, lowered beneath a projecting balcony tucked behind the main stair on the *piano nobile*. By comparison the garden front is calm, inviting and permeable. This disjunctive mode of composition is reminiscent of the post-Cubist style of painting that Ozenfant and Le Corbusier called Purism. At no point can the visitor grasp the whole organization. Instead it unfolds fragmentarily and sequentially in what Le Corbusier called a *promenade architecturale*, an idea inspired by the ascent to the Acropolis in Athens, which he brought to a peak of perfection in the house with which this phase of his work culminated, the Villa Savoye in Poissy.

Villa Savoye Poissy, France, 1928-30, Le Corbusier

The site for the villa is now hemmed in by trees which screen a large school, but it was originally open and enjoyed fine views over the Seine valley. So, like Palladio in his Villa Rotunda, Le Corbusier opted for a square plan to address the four horizons. But in place of the central room with its dome, he placed a ramp around which the promenade through space unfolds. In fact things are not quite so simple: the square is defined by a classically incorrect four-by-four bay system ('incorrect' because there is a column, not a visually restful open bay, at the centre) and extended by cantilevers along the direction of approach to imply an understated major axis, along which the ramp, in turn, is displaced off-centre. The visitor is greeted by a true 'elevation', a flat plane which touches the ground, but all the other sides are undercut at ground level by a curving screen of glass and metal whose radius was defined by the turning circle of a Voisin car, to be driven in the gap between the columns into the three-bay garage – M. Savoye, another New Man, also liked his cars.

You enter the house on axis at the centre of the curved screen and are greeted immediately by the ramp and, to its left, a freestanding pedestal wash-basin, an industrially produced *objet-type* that almost inevitably brings to mind Marcel Duchamp's notorious urinal 'fountain'. As the ramp gently rises and turns to ascend to the first floor, views open invitingly to the right – where the sculptural stair, bathed in sunlight, corkscrews up and out of sight – and then to the left, enabling you to see through a triangle of glass, across the open terrace, through the corner of the living room and out to the landscape framed by the ribbon window. The living room, glimpsed during your ascent, opens to the terrace via almost 10 metres (32 feet) of full-height glazing, half of which can slide open courtesy of a hand-crank. The terrace retreats beneath the roof slab into an outdoor room from where, in one of the defining views of the new ideal of interpenetrating spaces, you can see directly out through the glassless ribbon window, back through the living room to the landscape, and up to the roof garden and sky.

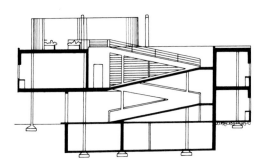

The ramp obligingly appears outside on the terrace to continue the promenade that culminates on the roof. You arrive, on axis with an opening framing a view towards the Seine, in a 'solarium' defined by a freestanding wall – originally painted pink and blue – whose plan recalls a guitar in a Cubist painting. The roof is planted with low shrubs and paved, partly with slabs like the terrace, partly with gravel like the driveway framed below, but despite these landscape materials it feels more like the deck of a ship, an image Le Corbusier prompts with the funnel-like enclosure of the stair and white-painted, nautical steel-tube handrails. What he wants us to experience here, beneath the sun and surrounded by pure form, is

This page and opposite

Villa Savoye, Poissy, France, 1928–30, Le Corbusier. Floating like an ocean liner in a meadow outside Paris, this weekend house marks the culmination of Le Corbusier's 1920s villas. Organized as a winding 'architectural promenade' around the ramp (**opposite, centre and bottom**), which leads to the roof-top solarium and (originally) open views over the Seine valley. The full-height glazing to the living room (**left and above**) can slide away to unite interior and terrace; the small planters frame a roof-light in the garage below, which further opens the house vertically.

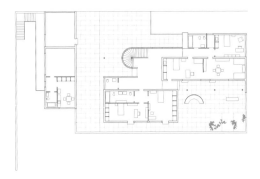

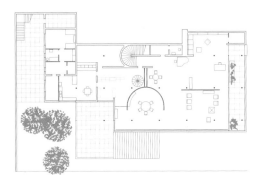

Above, below, opposite and overleaf Tugendhat House, Brno, Czech Republic, 1928–30, Mies van der Rohe. Like all Mies's buildings, this exceptionally large house is organized as spatially independent layers. The open-plan living floor sits below the bedrooms and is articulated by free-standing planes of luxurious materials; the entire south-facing glazed wall can disappear into the basement, transforming the interior into an open belvedere with splendid views of distant parkland.

what he called 'architecture's purest gift, mathematical lyricism'.

The Villa Savoye is a work of consummate artistry in which freedom and order coexist in subtle and ever-shifting tension. The architectural order, posited by the column grid and latent symmetries, recalls the disciplines of Classicism but is everywhere responsive to patterns of use and to the presence of the observer. One notices, for example, how the ramp is framed by two rows of columns, not divided by them as the grid would require, and that these are then doubled to mark a rectangular place of arrival. Elsewhere, individual columns step aside to free a room – there are none in the generous garage – or move slightly to engage with a partition: freestanding columns are always round, engaged ones square. Space is designed to be experienced, not as a formal end in itself, and the experience is inseparable from movement, upwards and outwards, towards the landscape and sky, towards nature.

Le Corbusier described the house as 'a place that gives birth to happiness' and architecture as 'a floor bathed in light', and in houses like the Villa Savoye the 'natural joys' of *soleil, espace et verdure* ('sun, space and greenery') are framed and represented in heightened form. The main bathroom, for example, is en suite with the master bedroom and internal, but opens to the sky through a roof light which unexpectedly fills it with sun. For all the rhetoric about machines and an engineer's aesthetic, these houses are profoundly humane, designed to reconnect us to nature and to elevate the dwelling to the status of a temple to the family. They bring to mind Baudelaire's desire for '*luxe, calme et volupté*' ('luxury, calm and voluptuous') a phrase used as the title of a celebrated painting by Matisse – and achieve this feeling using the purest of architectural means, 'volumes brought together in light', to use part of a famous definition in *Vers une architecture*. In this respect Le Corbusier differs significantly from the only European to rival him in talent, the German Mies van der Rohe. The son of a stonemason and heir to the German tradition of *Baukunst*, the 'art of building', Mies always retained a love of craftsmanship and fine materials. Echoing Hegel's belief in the *Zeitgeist* he defined architecture as 'the will of an epoch translated into space; living, changing, new'. He aimed to free architecture from 'problems of form' and return it to 'problems of building'.

Between 1919 and 1924 Mies exhibited a series of seminal projects, each based on a specific material. By reducing architecture to its structural essentials he anticipated its trajectory over the next few decades – variations on his Glass Tower and Concrete Office Building would be built worldwide in the 1950s and 1960s. The 1923 project for a Brick Country House was composed solely of straight and L-shaped brick walls and planes of glass. Mies was certainly familiar with the innovations of Frank Lloyd Wright and De Stijl – the pinwheeling pattern recalls some of Wright's plans, and more directly a 1917 painting, *Rhythms of a Russian Dance*, by Theo van Doesburg – and his idealized house combined the abstract quality of the Dutch exemplars with a determination to stay close to the 'nature of materials': the drawings show every brick, laid in Flemish bond. Mies built several fine brick houses during the 1920s, but none had the spatial freedom of this early project. The breakthrough came with the German Pavilion at the Barcelona Exhibition of 1929 and the Tugendhat House in Brno completed the following year, when Mies also took over as director of the Bauhaus.

Brno became an important industrial centre in the late nineteenth century, the population reaching 100,000 at the turn of the century. New suburbs blossomed, including Cerná Pole where, as part of his wife Greta Weiss's dowry, Fritz Tugendhat acquired a large sloping plot, facing south over parkland towards the city. They married in 1928 after putting in hand the construction of their house, which they entrusted to Mies on the basis of the initial design for the German Pavilion seen on a visit to Berlin the previous year. Tugendhat was a successful cloth manufacturer and the couple's combined resources were considerable: the first thing to be said about the Tugendhat House is that, at 2,000 square metres (21,000 square feet), including a generous basement, it is very large indeed – something not always grasped in photographs and drawings.

Tugendhat House Brno, Czech Republic, 1928-30, Mies van der Rohe

The house occupies a sloping site and is entered at the upper level, between two pavilions containing the bedrooms. Thanks to the travertine floor, full-height translucent glass and dark, palisander-veneered doors and wall panelling, the atmosphere is calm, inward-looking, and quietly opulent. You descend via a broad dog-leg stair and emerge into the vast living space. Directly ahead, filling the short side, is a winter garden bursting with exotic plants. To your right, glimpsed between the straight plane of pale onyx that screens the library and a semi-circle of highly figured red- and brown-streaked macassar enclosing the dining alcove, is a wall of cast glass which not only runs the full 24-metre (79-foot) length of the space but can disappear, as if by magic, into the basement, transforming the entire living area into an open belvedere overlooking the garden. All the furniture was designed by Mies, some of it, like the 'Brno Chair', especially for the house, and the materials – emerald green leather, ruby velvet and white vellum – are luxurious and colourful. Each piece had its appointed place, where it was meant to remain, frozen in time – an aesthetic vision very different from that of Le Corbusier's *plan libre*.

Believing that a 'clear structure is the basis of the free plan', Mies maintained the regularity of the grid throughout most of the interior; a few columns are replaced by walls, but for the most part the grid reads clearly as a counterpoint to the freestanding partitions and furniture. The columns are cruciform, made of eight steel angles clad in polished, highly reflective chrome: slender and shiny, they hardly appear capable of bearing the load. The floor is finished in ivory-coloured linoleum – a modern material par excellence in the 1930s – which by day assumes an almost identical tone to the white ceiling. At 3 metres (10 feet) the ceiling height is sufficiently generous for the space not to appear cramped, and the space is contrived to ensure that your eye level is poised halfway between the floor and ceiling planes. As Robin Evans has pointed out, in the similarly dimensioned German Pavilion at Barcelona the classical symmetries banished from the plan reappear in section in a way that reinforces the feeling of a 'floating world' of reflective surfaces and luxurious materials transfigured by light. It was perhaps this which inspired a contemporary critic to remark that Mies here showed how to 'elevate oneself above purely rational and functional thinking . . . into the realm of the spiritual.'

The Tugendhats, who were Jewish, fled their house in 1938. It was eventually taken over by the Communist authorities and during the 1960s the living room

was used as a gymnasium to help rehabilitate disabled children – many of the interior details survived, but the floor was painted bright red. It was restored, minus the original furniture and many of the fittings, in the late 1980s.

Maison de Verre Paris, France, 1928–32, Pierre Chareau

The Maison de Verre in Paris by Pierre Chareau, assisted by the Dutchman Bernard Bijvoet, suffered a different sort of neglect: forgotten by all but a few cognoscenti until the 1960s. But by the 1980s it had achieved cult status and was acclaimed by some, rather extravagantly, as the 'greatest house of the century'. Realized between 1928 and 1932 and designed down to the last detail, here was a very different vision of the 'machine for living in', singular and grand.

The house was wedged in between and under surrounding apartments and both elevations were made almost entirely of glass bricks of the type normally found in public lavatories: laid in four-brick-wide panels, they established the 91-centimetre (36-inch) module that runs throughout the design. Industrial steel sections were riveted together to form the main structure – they look as if they might have escaped from a factory – and the interior bristles with endlessly inventive details: bookcase balustrades, a lift-out-of-the-way ship's stair and warm-air filled hollow steel floors. The bathrooms, which eventually found many imitators, are screened by curving panels of finely perforated aluminium, and duralumin was used to make sleekly efficient wardrobes and drawers. It seems an unlikely home and office for a gynaecologist, although Chareau's attention to the hygienic virtues of clear air, natural light and durable materials was exemplary, offering a different vision of architectural modernity to that of Le Corbusier, who was a regular visitor during construction. In place of the classical disciplines of form, proportion and space modelled by light, Chareau – an interior and furniture designer by training – toiled in his workshop producing what he described as 'a model executed by craftsmen with the aim of industrial standardization': virtues calculated to appeal to new generations of designers after 1945.

From its inception, the pioneers of the new architecture had seen it as international in spirit and scope. The first Bauhaus book, published in 1925, was dedicated to 'International Architecture', and lecturing in Buenos Aires four years later Le Corbusier looked forward to an improbable utopia when rooms everywhere could be conditioned to a standardized 18°C (64°F). This faith was grounded in the widely felt need to transcend the national differences that had led to war and to build a new world order based on rational, supposedly universal, values. Modern art and architecture could be as international as modern science and technology because it was believed that, 'all men react unanimously to broad daylight or full night, or red or black, or love or death', to quote *Foundations of Modern Art* by Le Corbusier's former colleague Ozenfant.

In light of such beliefs, the new architecture was designed to appear universal, independent of specific materials, sites or cultural traditions. Despite its proponents' belief that their ideas transcended traditional ideas of style, it was almost inevitable that sooner or later someone would christen it the 'International Style'. It happened in 1932, at New York's Museum of Modern Art (the first such in the world), courtesy of Henry-Russell Hitchcock and Philip Johnson who used it as the title of a book published to accompany an exhibition of almost a hundred buildings from sixteen countries. The exhibition travelled to eleven other cities in America but

Above and opposite Maison de Verre, Paris, France, 1928–32, Pierre Chareau. Enclosed by glass brick panels framed in steel, the house was conceived as a cage of light, wedged into a tight Parisian courtyard. Internally the planning is intricate and the detailing endlessly surprising and inventive – riveted factory-style columns, book-case balustrades and warm-air filled floors.

3m
10ft

Lovell Health House Los Angeles, California, USA, 1927–9, Richard Neutra

Above Lovell Beach House, Los Angeles, California, USA, 1926, Rudolf Schindler. Behind the boldly exposed frame the planning reflects the influence of Adolf Loos, whose work Schindler knew before leaving Vienna to work for Frank Lloyd Wright.

made little impact; the book, on the other hand, travelled the world and did.

Hitchcock and Johnson defined the new style by three features: the treatment of a building as a *volume* defined by surfaces, not as a mass; *formal regularity*, resulting from proportional control and orderly structure; and the *avoidance of applied decoration* – superficial, stylistic criteria that missed the spatial essence of the new 'style'. Frank Lloyd Wright figured in the exhibition – which had the less exclusive title 'Modern Architecture: International Exhibition' – but not the book; his former assistant Rudolf Schindler, whom we met in the last chapter as a student of Otto Wagner, was not in either. He probably ruined his chances by explaining with his submission, 'I am not a stylist, not a functionalist, nor any other sloganist.'

Schindler was, however, an exceedingly good architect and his Lovell Beach House, completed in 1926 in Los Angeles, flaunted a gymnastic structural frame containing cleverly worked spaces that owed something to Loos's *Raumplan*. It was one of the most inventive houses of the decade and, although far from orthodox, certainly met all of Hitchcock and Johnson's rather woolly criteria. The house ran slightly over budget and Schindler lost his client to his supposed friend and fellow Austrian emigré, Richard Neutra. Lovell, a fanatical advocate of natural remedies, vegetarianism, exercise and nude sunbathing, and author of a column entitled 'Care of the Body' for the *Los Angeles Times*, commissioned a house in the Hollywood Hills from Neutra; it eventually cost more than twice the estimate on its completion in 1929. The design was steel-framed, relaxed and rambling, in a way that Californian houses tend to be, and featured inventive details such as suspended aluminium light troughs and a Model T Ford headlamp to light the staircase. Lovell promoted his house vigorously, opening it regularly to an amazed public: 15,000 came, making the 'Health House', as it was soon known, an instant star and ensuring its inclusion in Hitchcock and Johnson's canon.

In the same year that the Health House opened in Los Angeles, in Copenhagen Arne Jacobsen exhibited a project for a circular 'House of the Future', complete with a helicopter on its roof terrace. He also moved into his own house of white-painted brick: like many, it looked thoroughly modern, thanks to large areas of glass and corner windows, but the plan was still relatively conventional. In 1930 the Stockholm Exhibition, co-ordinated by Gunnar Asplund, disseminated the new ideas widely in Scandinavia, while in Italy Figini and Pollini showed their Electric House at an exhibition of decorative art in Monza. In the same year, the Swede Sven Markelius demonstrated his mastery of modernity in his own house in Nockeby, and Amyas Connell built 'High and Over' in Amersham, England. This was the first British house to look authentically modern, although the Corbusian motifs could not disguise Connell's abiding love of Classicism, plain for all to see in the symmetrical Y-shaped plan extending into a formal garden.

Although it accounted for a tiny proportion of new buildings, the International style proved attractive to clients worldwide who were eager to assert their modernity. In Norway Arne Korsmo became an inventive exponent, as witnessed by houses like Villa Damman of 1934, and the same year in New York William Lescaze built his own house, adapting the new style to the constraints of a

Above and overleaf Lovell Health House, Los Angeles, California, USA, 1927–9, Richard Neutra. The Health House was built in the Hollywood Hills for the same client as Schindler's Beach House. A well known journalist and advocate of healthy living, Lovell promoted his Health House assiduously, helping to make it the best known emblem of the new architecture in the USA.

Above House of the Future
(exhibition project), Copenhagen,
Denmark, 1929, Arne Jacobsen.
Replete with roof-top helicopter
pad, the house offered a playful
interpretation of the radical new
spirit of modernity.
Below Stockholm Exhibition,
Stockholm, Sweden, 1930, Gunnar
Asplund *et al*. Arguably the best of
many staged to promote the new
ideas, the Stockholm Exhibition
marked the official arrival of modern
architecture in Scandinavia, where it
flourished in the social-democratic
political climate.

narrow mid-terrace plot. By 1932 Spain and Mexico could boast fine examples, such as Josep Lluis Sert's Galobart House and Juan O'Gorman's studio and apartment for Frances Toor in Mexico City. With its deep blue walls and Venetian red stair the latter clearly referred to the Mexican vernacular – but also to the 'machines for living in' that Le Corbusier had designed at Pessac. The mid-1930s saw the completion of several fine houses in Italy. Notable among them were Luigi Figini's own house in the Villagio dei Giornalisti in Milan in 1935, an essay in the Corbusian manner raised high on square *pilotis* and capturing a tree in its courtyard, and the richly layered Villa Bianca in Seveso, completed in 1937 by Giuseppe Terragni, one of the most formidable talents of his generation.

Modern architecture spread extensively through Eastern Europe, where private houses, such as Jozsef Fischer's Villa Hoffmann in Hungary, were outnumbered by dwellings and flats for workers, and it was taken to Palestine by Jews fleeing the Nazis. The most notable among them was Erich Mendelsohn, but again flats rather than private houses predominated, so much so that Tel Aviv can probably boast more 'Bauhaus' buildings than any other city. A group of talented young modernists led by Rex Martienssen flourished in South Africa and were honoured with a dedication by Le Corbusier in the 1936 edition of the first volume of his *Oeuvre complète*. Most of the houses built around the world were competent essays in the new manner rather than notably innovative, however, and during the 1930s the most far-reaching developments came from reinterpretations of the new ideas in light of local traditions, cultures and climates, which we will examine in Chapter 4.

The European examples we have so far considered are 'modern' in a particular sense of the word: they exemplify a set of ideas about spatial continuity and functional organization, and exhibit a marked preference, as Hitchcock and Johnson spotted, for simple volumes, regularity, and the avoidance of applied decoration. These aspects of the modern style were interrelated, but by no means always interdependent, and a significant competing set of ideas, sometimes described by the misleading term 'Expressionist', was largely banished from the official canon of the International style because of its love of what the mainstream saw as arbitrary irregularity. The leading theorist of this strand of thought was Hugo Häring, and its most gifted practitioner Hans Scharoun.

Häring rejected aesthetic dogma and set himself the task of challenging Le Corbusier, whom he saw as a representative of 'Latin Classicism', determined to impose geometric forms on life. Nature was Häring's model, and he believed that after centuries of oppression by arbitrary geometry, 'light constructions, with elastic and supple materials' offered the freedom to respond organically to building programmes. He illustrated his ideas in 1923 with a 'house shaped by use and movement'. Although conceived independently, it might have been intended as a direct, organically functional response to Mies's Brick Country House exhibited that same year. Where Mies's design was a differentiated field of space which left the viewer to speculate how it might be inhabited, Häring's showed every piece of furniture to illustrate how completely the walls wrapped themselves around the life to be lived – in places quite literally, around specific tables and chairs. By the 1940s Häring would go so far as to show coat hooks and a pair of gloves left on the hall table placed to receive them.

Above Villa Damman, Oslo, Norway, 1934, Arne Korsmo. The villa is organized around a double-height living room, which was running the full length of the house high, blank walls to display pictures.

Below Lescaze House, New York, USA, 1934, William Lescaze. Dispensing with a sub-basement, the house steps boldly forward of its terraced neighbours.

Above 'High and Over', Amersham, England, 1930, Amyas Connell. Modernist surfaces and volumetric composition are deployed around a classically symmetrical plan.

Left Figini House, Milan, Italy, 1935, Luigi Figini. Le Corbusier's 'Five Points' are reinterpreted in the light of Italian Rationalism. The long, narrow volume is entered from below via an external staircase.

Right Villa Bianca, Seveso, Italy, 1937, Giuseppe Terragni. The house is a richly layered composition of volumes and planes by the most gifted Italian architect of his generation.

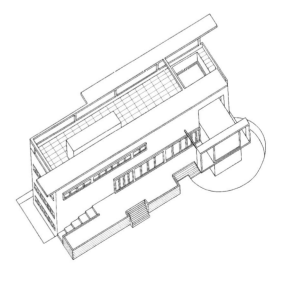

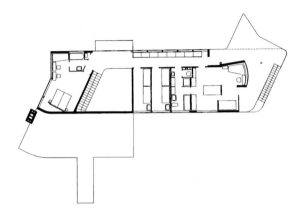

Schminke House Löbau, Germany, 1932–3, Hans Scharoun

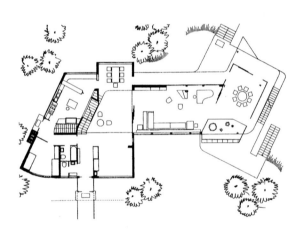

Melnikov House and Studio Moscow, Russia, 1927, Konstantin Melnikov

Hans Scharoun was deeply influenced by Häring's ideas, but by no means unresponsive to the visual power of Le Corbusier's work. Even in the absence of other evidence one might surmise as much from an early perspective sketch of his finest house, which shows the owner's car sweeping under a boldly projecting terrace, suggesting a likely debt to the Villa Savoye. The house was built from 1932 to 1933 for the wealthy industrialist Fritz Schminke, on a site in Löbau near the Czech border, and in most other respects is in total contrast to the Villa Savoye. Where Le Corbusier was generic and enjoyed exploiting the tension between a complex programme and a regular form, Scharoun was specific and allowed the exterior to expand and contract in response to spatial and functional pressures within.

The site for the Schminke House was challenging. Entered from the south, it enjoyed a spectacular distant view to the north-east – never an easy combination to resolve. In response these conditions Scharoun placed the main body of the house facing south, but turned the east and west ends to align with the site boundary. In the process the solarium at the eastern end was neatly aligned to the view – Scharoun labelled it *Blickachse* (view axis) on some of the plans. This in turn prompted him to align the main staircase on this same diagonal, creating a powerful dynamic element at the heart of the plan, greatly enriching the pattern of movement through the house, and establishing the shifted geometry as a second orthogonal system, in counterpoint to the dominant east-west alignment.

The planning is functionally zoned, and while the spaces flow together in the modern manner, they are also clearly identified as well defined territories designed for specific patterns of use. Bays push or swell out to accommodate activities. A free-standing fireplace is placed to give focus to the living room, around whose perimeter long, immovable ranges of seating define places to sit. Lighting specific to each area is provided – ceiling light for the dining table; place-lamps for the piano, hearth and sofa; spotlights for bookshelves and flowers. The composition culminates in the fully glazed solarium and winter garden, below which the ground falls away dramatically, leaving the house and terraces to soar over the landscape. The views here, seen across an interior bathed in light, are as beguiling a celebration of the virtues of sun, space, outdoor life and greenery as Le Corbusier's roof gardens.

Although he pursued ideas that differed radically from the mainstream, Scharoun is not difficult to accommodate in the narrative of the Modern house. But as we noted in the case of Jujol's Torre de la Creu, some houses refuse to conform to convenient classifications. One such is the extraordinary home and studio built for himself by Konstantin Melnikov, one of the most original architects of the post-Revolutionary period in Russia.

Radical new ideas flourished for a decade after the 1917 Revolution but private houses, needless to say, did not: Melnikov's is the only one to become widely known. Even within the very different Soviet context, his design was singular and generated, like the Torre de la Creu, from intersecting circles – in this case two of equal size. The reasons continue to intrigue scholars. The cylinder was a favourite motif, and the work of Claude-Nicholas Ledoux, Russian Orthodox churches and the American grain silos beloved of European modernists have all

Above, top and opposite
Schminke House, Löbau, Germany,
1932–3, Hans Scharoun. The formal
language of the International Style is
here made responsive to the nuances
of site and programme – note how the
plan cranks to address a view and
variously swells to make places to eat
and sit, alone or in groups.

Right Melnikov House and Studio,
Moscow, Russia, 1927, Konstantin
Melnikov. Two intersecting cylinders
and a mysterious grid of hexagonal
windows contain and light a suite of
vertically interlocking rooms.

E.1027 Roquebrune, France, 1926–9, Eileen Gray

been suggested as possible inspirations: the result certainly has something of the monumentality of a silo.

The monumentality is reinforced by making the entrance part of a glazed slot running through the full four-storey height, while to the rear the rendered surface of the other cylinder is peppered with hexagonal windows, some with horizontal glazing bars, others with diagonals. This unique fenestration provides an extraordinary light in the double-height studio, and was achieved by replacing the brick walls with a network of diagonal columns, enabling Melnikov to make openings or carve out niches at will. The studio interlocks with the similarly double-height drawing room – the juxtaposition in section recalls Le Corbusier's project for a house in Carthage, made the following year. Finally, as if to confound any easy interpretation, Melnikov chose to furnish his revolutionary house with heavy, traditional pieces, providing an almost surreal contrast to the modernity of the architecture and making it all the more difficult to relate to contemporary developments elsewhere.

At first sight the design with which we conclude our exploration of the Modern House appears to belong comfortably in the mainstream, but for many years, if it was remembered at all, it was regarded as of only marginal interest. The site at Roquebrune, Cap-Martin, overlooking the Mediterranean, was remote and singular, but the house was well published and visited by leading Modernists – Le Corbusier took Rex Martienssen from South Africa there. It did not help that the owner and designer was a woman, Eileen Gray, still less that she was well known for her Art Deco furniture and interiors. The house was completed in 1929 and given the laconic name E.1027, not, Gray said, as a mark of machine-age anonymity but as a secret tribute to her confidant Jean Badovici, whose initials were the tenth and second letters of the alphabet – hence E. J.B.G.

Romanian-born and Paris-trained, Badovici was editor of *L'Architecture vivante*: launched in 1923, it was one of the main vehicles for disseminating modern architecture, but less polemical than a partisan journal like *L'Esprit nouveau*. Badovici provided technical advice, but the house was essentially Gray's own work. Le Corbusier, a close friend of Badovici, stayed there in 1938 and after his visit wrote a letter to Gray praising the 'rare spirit which has given the modern furniture and installations such a dignified, charming and witty shape.' And then, later that year, in an act whose motives have been the subject of much psychological speculation, he defaced it with a series of exclamatory and completely unsolicited murals.

The two-storey house was small – 160 square metres (1,722 square feet), twelve would fit comfortably inside the Tugendhat – and exquisitely adapted to the different levels of its rocky, coastal site, which Gray in turn adapted to create a seaside garden: the modernist living-machine and wild nature rarely achieved such a poetic and habitable fusion. The plan lacks Le Corbusier's rigour, but is intricately functional, and benefited from a furniture designer's eye applied to every detail. The house is filled with inventive, often witty furniture and while there are traces of Art Deco stylization (which Le Corbusier perhaps hinted at in his letter) everything springs from a rich imagination responding to the patterns of living. The plans feel almost like diagrams of frozen movement, with partitions poised to slide, doors to swing, and furniture ready to transform itself by folding away or opening out to serve some unexpected purpose.

Gray's classic circular side tables adjust in height to sit by a sofa or over a bed, and around her own bed she made special places for books and even for a hot-water bottle – Häring would surely have approved! Blue night-lights recalled the romance of sleepless hours on trains speeding to distant climes; the canvas balustrade to the terrace could be removed to allow the low sun to warm her legs in winter; the kitchen could open completely to the courtyard via folding glass panels, enabling her maid to prepare food outside in the summer 'like peasant women'. Everywhere you look, every nuance of daily life seems to have been imagined and celebrated, and in this it recalls that other lyrical and intensely personal hymn to the art of living, the Schröder House.

Badovici devoted a whole issue of *L'Architecture vivante* to E.1027 and cast the preface in the form of an interview between a rationalist interrogator and Eileen Gray: 'We had to get rid of the old oppression,' she says, 'in order to be conscious again of freedom. But the intellectual coldness that ensued, and which corresponds all too well to the harsh laws of modern machinery, can only be a transition. It is necessary to rediscover once more the human being in the plastic form, the human will under the material appearance, and the pathos of modern life.' Her sentiments would find numerous echoes in the decades to come, as criticisms grew of what many came to perceive as the excessive rationalism of modern architecture, exemplified by some of the widely misunderstood 'machines for living in' of the next chapter.

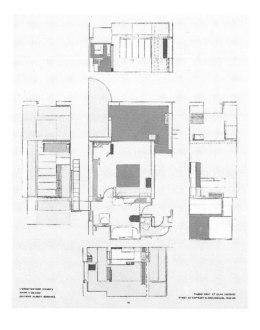

machines for living in

'We must create the mass-production spirit. The spirit of constructing mass-production houses. The spirit of living in mass-production houses. The spirit of conceiving mass-production houses.' With these typically stirring words Le Corbusier launched the penultimate chapter of *Vers une architecture*. While later critics and historians, like Hitchcock and Johnson with their 'International' style, tended to focus on the aesthetic implications of the new 'House-Machine', Le Corbusier left no doubt that what was at issue was a technical and social revolution, of which a new 'machine aesthetic' would be an expression, not an end in itself. A house for the 'common man' was, he concluded his polemic, 'the problem of the epoch. The balance of society comes down to a question of building…. Architecture or Revolution?'

In France, the context of this challenge was the Loucheur Act with its call for 500,000 new dwellings to be built well and cheaply to help restore the stock lost in the First World War. Le Corbusier was convinced industry was a sleeping giant waiting to be stirred into action and many of the building products required, he pointed out, were already being industrially produced - cements, steel girders, sanitary fittings, ironmongery, and so on. What was needed was the vision ('mass-production spirit') to change the way buildings were conceived, as well as industrialized building contractors and a system of national standardization to co-ordinate the disparate producers.

As predictions about the future of construction, these ideas proved prescient – dimensional co-ordination, rapid advances in building services, massive contracting firms and so forth have all become familiar realities – but the contention that 'a house will no longer be this solidly-built thing which sets out to defy time and decay… an expensive luxury by which wealth can be shown', but rather, 'a tool as the motor-car is becoming a tool' proved more problematic. The house, as Adolf Loos observed, is by nature conservative and despite being transformed by industrially produced components and ceasing to be a product of craft traditions, most prospective inhabitants, where they had a choice, proved stubbornly resistant to the aesthetic representations of modernity.

In *Vers une architecture* Le Corbusier illustrated various ideas for houses, including two basic types to which he returned throughout his life. The first, designed in 1919, he called the Monol. It was intended to exploit mass-produced asbestos panels. These were to be used to frame walls, which were then filled with rubble found locally, and covered in corrugated sheeting to form permanent shuttering for shallow concrete vaults. New materials like Eternit were widely exhibited in France in the 1920s as part of conventional-looking prefabricated houses designed to meet the same housing crisis, but most architects regarded them as unsuited to the Fine Art of architecture. The construction of Monol was inventive, and the forms it generated would be echoed in other materials by numerous modern architects; Le Corbusier himself reinterpreted them in the small weekend house and the Jaoul Houses we discuss in the next chapter. The second, designed in 1921–2, he called 'Citrohan' – a punning reference to the car manufacturer. This was a compact version of a Dom-Ino design like the Cook House. It had hollow concrete cross-walls in place of columns and a double-height living space with an open dining room and kitchen tucked under a mezzanine floor for bedrooms: he said the basic idea dawned on him in a Paris

Right Citrohan House, project, 1921–2, Le Corbusier. This prototype was intended to be mass-produced, hence the punning reference to the French car-maker. Although it never went into production, the organization around a double-height living space established a spatial type to which Le Corbusier frequently returned.

Above Monol House, project, 1919, Le Corbusier. Designed for rapid construction using industrially produced materials – corrugated sheeting on the roof, asbestos panels for the walls – the Monol was a response to the massive housing shortages in France in the wake of the First World War

café with a similar arrangement. The ground floor was given over to the garage and 'servants well cared for' – this was no compact worker's house – and two further bedrooms were provided overlooking the roof-top solarium.

Le Corbusier was convinced he would find a major car manufacturer to build his mass-production houses, but the call finally came from the owner of a sugar refinery in Bordeaux, Henry Frugès. He wrote to Le Corbusier in November 1923 to commission a small group of workers' houses for his new sawmill in Lège. The basic unit was a smaller version of the Citrohan type. Despite numerous technical difficulties with the sprayed concrete construction and local ridicule for the

Les Quartiers Modernes Frugès Pessac, France, 1924–6, Le Corbusier

'Frugès cubes', the client decided to press on with a larger development in the fast-expanding rural suburb of Pessac. It became known as Les Quartiers Modernes Frugès.

The layout was based on garden-city principles, including an impressive gateway marked by a six-storey apartment block, but in other ways it was radically innovative. In one sector the open space formed a continuous realm in which traditional distinctions between front, back and side, public and private, were eliminated in favour of a continuous shared realm. In another the street was deliberately asymmetrical, with narrow, so-called 'skyscraper' *(gratte-ciel)* units framing open spaces at intervals along the street, across which was a more conventional two-storey terrace. Four standard house types were developed, all evolving from a spatial core 5 metres (16.5 feet) wide and planned around a single-flight transverse stair. The 'skyscraper' was the flagship, a free-standing back-to-back pair of houses extending vertically rather than horizontally and culminating in a roof garden accessible via an external stair, with a canopy and 'nautical' handrails to help evoke the image of a ship sailing through space.

Pessac was completed in 1926 and almost immediately favoured with a visit by M. de Monzie, the minister of public works. Three years later when M. Loucheur, the employment minister, came it was still empty, having fallen foul of local bureaucracy and outraged influential citizens. When it was finally inhabited the development soon fell into neglect, and pitched roofs, window shutters, stuck-on stone, scalloped window-boxes and a host of other details appeared to make the buildings look more like 'proper' houses. The biggest single source of outrage was the vivid polychromy. Henry Frugès later claimed that the colour schemes were implemented at his initiative but there is no doubt about Le Corbusier's enthusiasm for the idea. 'Architectural polychromy', he exclaimed, 'takes possession of the entire wall and splashes it with pulsating blood, or clothes it in the fresh hues of a prairie, the bright luminosity of the sun, or the deep tones of the sky and sea. What power!' The colour was applied to ameliorate the drab grey of the concrete walls, but it also permitted the further manipulation of space and form, making one wall appear to recede, another to advance, shattering symmetry and destroying boxiness and the feeling of enclosure.

The reasons for the scheme's social failure are more complex than simple rejection of its unfamiliar aesthetic and layout. A tradition of workers' housing in Bordeaux was well established before the First World War. Its funding and management were geared to ensuring that the workers were financially tied to their properties through a savings scheme, and then encouraged to busy themselves in productive gardening and work around the house: with revolution

Above, below and opposite Les Quartiers Modernes Frugès, Pessac, France, 1924–6. This estate of workers' housing was the nearest Le Corbusier came to building 'mass-production houses'. The units were all planned using standard 5-metre- (6-foot-6-inch-) square units, the grandest being the tall 'skyscraper' double-houses (**opposite**).

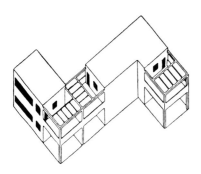

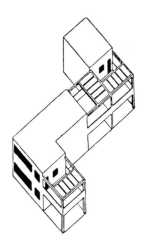

brewing in Russia and an active left wing in France, it was considered a social imperative to occupy workers' spare hours. Frugès and Le Corbusier, with boundless, ill-placed optimism, opted for a different funding system and believed that functionally planned, well ventilated and light-filled dwellings would not only create a healthy environment but also help free time for leisure pursuits and the arts. Their optimism proved ill founded, but when the houses were eventually restored in the 1980s they became sought-after as distinctive homes for middle-class families and urban professionals.

Weimar Germany, with its liberal democratic constitution and determination to break with the outmoded values that had led to war, provided a more favourable climate for experimentation than conservative France, where the dominant voices were calling for a return to the Classical tradition. There was already a strong housing reform movement, which was taken up after the war by the burgeoning women's movement. After five years of increasingly rampant inflation the economy began to stabilize in 1924 with the implementation of the Dawes Plan. US dollars were vital in the short term, but the acceptance of American ways of organizing workers and production methods was of more far-reaching significance. The enormous popularity of Henry Ford's autobiography, *My Life and Work*, which arrived in Germany in 1923, was seminal in spreading the message. It explained in euphoric prose the success of his production-line methods for making the Model T and was, incidentally, just as popular in Communist Russia, where Ford became an unlikely folk hero.

Against this background it comes as no surprise to hear the architect Bruno Taut argue that the 'problem of house-building today must be tackled along lines that are valid in industry for the production of machines, cars and similar objects. The success of Henry Ford in car production is in part based on the fact that he selects his raw materials in the best possible way…. Exactly the same can be applied to house-building.' What is slightly surprising is that these words came from the man who, in the immediate aftermath of the war, had dreamt of a chain of glass structures across the Alps as a symbol of the New World to be built out of the ashes of the Old. The road from visionary to advocate of industrialized building was not as long as it might appear, given the exalted language in which industry was frequently praised, and institutionally exactly the same path was trodden by the Bauhaus.

The industrialization of house building along Fordist lines meant the use of large-scale plant and machinery, efficient programming, centralization to form large efficient sites, and mobile building systems. And in order to have standardized dwellings like the Model T – *a Wohnford* (or 'living-Ford') as Sigfried Giedion, secretary of CIAM (Congrés Internationaux d'Architecture Moderne), called it in discussion with the Dutchman J. J. P. Oud – scientific methods had to be applied to both the building process and the design of the house or flat. Leaders of the women's movement persuaded the government to sponsor research in housing to help raise standards in the subsidized workers' accommodation being built across Germany. As a result of this and other pressures the RfG *(Reichsforschungsgesellschaft)* was established in 1926 to study all aspects of the design, construction and management of housing. It subsidized the use of prefabricated building systems on various projects, such as the Dessau-Törten estate designed under the direction of Walter Gropius, founder of the Bauhaus, and promoted experimentation in everything from housing layout to kitchen design.

The major focus for innovation in housing was Frankfurt where, in 1925, Ernst May, a native of the city, was appointed city planner and head of the department of buildings. May had trained as an architect in Darmstadt, where he was stimulated by contact with Olbrich, and then went to Munich to study city planning under the celebrated Theodor Fischer. He knew the pre-war innovations of Krupp in Essen and the small houses of Heinrich Tessenow, which later became sullied through identification with the goals of National Socialism. And he had met leaders of the avant-garde at an international conference on city planning held in Amsterdam in 1924, when he also saw the celebrated South Amsterdam expansion planned by Berlage and the work of Oud in Rotterdam. Out of these experiences he formed a clear vision for a New City and a New Home. It would become internationally known as *Das Neue Frankfurt* – the title of a magazine launched to publicize and celebrate the achievements – and the city would soon have to employ three guides for the people who flocked to see the acclaimed Römerstadt and other developments.

Tuberculosis and rickets were still familiar urban ills in Frankfurt, as in so many dense European cities (Le Corbusier's controversial planning ideas developed in part as a response to what he called 'tubercular Paris') and May waged reform under the slogan 'Light, Air, and Sun, a healthy life for all people'. He set about developing standards – the *Frankfurter Normen* – which included plywood doors with steel frames, unornamented hardware, a compact sit-up bathtub to save space and water and, most famously of all, the Frankfurt Kitchen. Intended to be tailormade for 'modern women with little time for domestic cares', the new kitchen was seen as central to the new home. It was the work of Grete Lihotzky who came to work in Frankfurt from Vienna, where she had assisted Adolf Loos and amassed five years' experience designing kitchens for small apartments.

Frankfurt Kitchen Frankfurt, Germany, 1926, Grete Lihotzky

The original ideas for new kitchens came from America, where the social worker Catherine Beacher had analyzed, as models for small homes, the compact types made for Mississippi steamers and the ideas patented by Pullman in 1869 for use in his trains. In 1923, at an exhibition to promote the work of the Bauhaus, visitors to the Haus am Horn built specially for the show could see a kitchen by the brilliant Hungarian student Marcel Breuer, who soon went on to design several classic pieces of bent-metal furniture. His kitchen was the first in Germany to have a continuous run of work surfaces and wall cupboards.

Lihotzky said her models were the pharmacy and the laboratory, and her design method was derived from Christine Frederick's 1912 American classic, *The New Housekeeping. Efficiency Studies in Home Management*, which became the bible of household reform. Frederick analyzed domestic tasks using the work-study principles developed in America by Frederick W. Taylor to speed-up factory production, and Lihotzky in turn studied kitchen tasks to ensure that everything was within easy reach and efficiently placed: all aspects of a kitchen were examined functionally from first principles. The countless innovations, small and large, included storing crockery behind glass doors, keeping pans on sloping,

Right Frankfurt Kitchen, Frankfurt Germany, 1926, Grete Lihotzky. Designed after exhaustive analysis of the practical requirements, the kitchen was eventually installed in some 10,000 workers' apartments and houses. Many features that we now take for granted – continuous work-surfaces, wall cupboards, specialized storage units – were developed in the 1920s.

Above and opposite
Weissenhofsiedlung, Stuttgart,
Germany, 1927, Mies van der Rohe
(master-planner). Intended to
introduce the new architecture to the
wider German public, the Weissenhof
presented designs by many of
Europe's leading Modernists, and was
occupied as permanent housing
following the exhibition. The smaller of
the two houses designed by Le
Corbusier (**top**) was architecturally
outstanding, whilst a terrace of five
workers' houses by the Dutchman J. J.
P. Oud (**above**) was particularly
praised in the German press.

slatted shelves, a fold-away ironing board, and a bank of eighteen specially made aluminium containers. Known as *Schütte* when they went into production, these containers housed all kinds of dry goods and came complete with a tapering end for pouring.

The new kitchen was a small room (6.5 square metres, 70 square feet), separated for reasons of hygiene from the living area, from which it could be shut off, if required, by a sliding door. Ten thousand were eventually installed in workers' housing in Frankfurt, and the decision to replace the familiar kitchen-living room with the new arrangement had far-reaching implications, becoming the norm for several decades. Adolf Loos thought the trend misguided and in 1926, the year his former employee's design was completed, he defended the traditional living-kitchen for reasons that were social, not narrowly functional and hygienic. Cooking near the table was a sign of a high-quality restaurant – why should the working class not enjoy this pleasure, he asked? After all, the kitchen was the traditional gathering place for a family, and children love to be in it, near the fire, which heated the whole house and provided its natural centre; and moreover the arrangement did not cut off the housewife from her family while cooking. As we shall see, these sentiments would be echoed twenty years later, in almost exactly the same terms, by Le Corbusier in explaining the design of his Unité d'Habitation in Marseilles.

The early Frankfurt estates, based on industrially built two-storey houses of 60 to 70 square metres (645 to 753 square feet), still proved beyond the budget of factory workers to rent, let alone buy – even using the specially developed *Hauszinssteuer* mortgages, partly paid for by an unpopular tax on the city's better-off residents. The floor area had to be reduced still further, and houses changed for flats: they became known as *Existenzminimum* dwellings, and were made the subject of the 1929 CIAM congress (Congrés Internationaux d'Architecture Moderne) held in Frankfurt. One hundred and twenty delegates attended from eighteen countries – politicians, sociologists, psychologists, representatives of women's organizations and others, as well as architects – and just how minimal workers' housing could be, as well as the balance to be sought between individual and more collective forms, were fiercely debated.

In Frankfurt, housing with what May regarded as the 'absolute minimum' of 32 square metres (344 square feet) had been built the previous year, in a transit settlement for refugees. It quickly became permanent housing and was copied elsewhere, but after the stock market crash of 1929 and the ensuing economic chaos even this *Ration Wohnung* (Ration Flat) would prove impossible to provide for the many. By the time CIAM met there, Frankfurt's heyday as a centre of innovation was over. Responding to the darkening economic and political climate – the inexorable rise of National Socialism was by then all too obvious – May accepted an appointment as an advisor on industrial cities in the Soviet Union. When he left in 1930, 11 percent of the city's population had been housed in sanitary new accommodation but the *Hauszinssteuer* had dried up.

New approaches to living – *die neue Wohnkultur* – were a subject of wide interest in Germany and among the exhibitions held on the theme, one came to be seen as marking the moment at which the New Architecture reached maturity: the Weissenhofsiedlung in Stuttgart. It was organized by the Deutscher

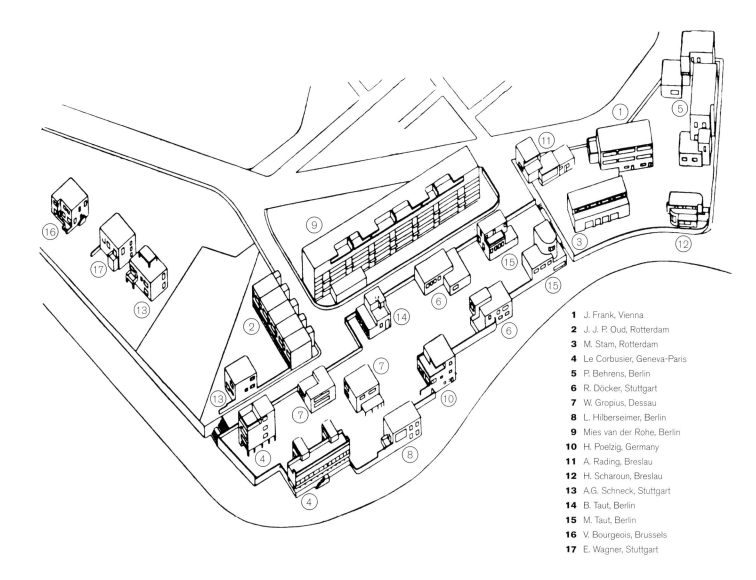

1 J. Frank, Vienna
2 J. J. P. Oud, Rotterdam
3 M. Stam, Rotterdam
4 Le Corbusier, Geneva-Paris
5 P. Behrens, Berlin
6 R. Döcker, Stuttgart
7 W. Gropius, Dessau
8 L. Hilberseimer, Berlin
9 Mies van der Rohe, Berlin
10 H. Poelzig, Germany
11 A. Rading, Breslau
12 H. Scharoun, Breslau
13 A.G. Schneck, Stuttgart
14 B. Taut, Berlin
15 M. Taut, Berlin
16 V. Bourgeois, Brussels
17 E. Wagner, Stuttgart

Werkbund, an association formed in 1907 to promote progressive ideas on art and design. It held several exhibitions before the war, and another in 1924 entitled 'Die Form', dedicated to promoting, as the invitation to participants stated, 'the extraordinary wealth of expression that can be embodied in pure form without the addition of any ornament'. A policy paper for the Stuttgart exhibition entitled 'Housing for a New Age' made it clear that they wanted projects geared to the city's pressing needs, not 'exhibition buildings or luxury homes' which, though 'technically irreproachable and architecturally strong and forward-looking', would be unsuited to everyday life.

Weissenhofsiedlung Exhibition Stuttgart, Germany, 1927

The overall planning of the exhibition, which was to become a habitable development, was entrusted to Mies van der Rohe, but his first proposal was not what the organizers anticipated: formalistic, uneconomic, overly complicated, unrelated to the city expansion plan – these were just some of the criticisms. Where his critics asked for 'evolution, not innovation', Mies explained that 'a New Home will extend beyond four walls. This is not a matter of producing to a layout as a pattern, in the old way; here, as also in the buildings, I want to break new ground.' He revised his design, but still managed to produce an innovative layout that shared an interest in the interplay of volumes similar to that of Le Corbusier at Pessac.

The choice of architects for the various buildings proved as problematic as their arrangement. It had more to do with political compromise between the different interest-groups involved than with producing the seamless demonstration of the New Architecture that Mies, if not the organizers, hoped for. Henry van de Velde was rejected because of his forthright attacks on Germany during the war, and Adolf Loos, who dearly wanted to be included, was eliminated because of his characteristically vigorous pre-war attacks on the Werkbund, which began life in the penumbra of Jugendstil as much as at the dawn of modernity. Mies thought that only left-wing architects should be appointed, Hugo Häring, who shared an office with Mies, argued that their intellectual rather than political views were more important. In the event twenty-one structures were commissioned from seventeen architects, with interiors by a further fifty-five designers. To accompany the model housing, a large exhibition entitled *Die Wohnung* (The Dwelling) was held in the city centre, and in his opening speech the mayor, Dr Lautenschlage, caught the ambition of both perfectly:

This exhibition departs markedly from outworn tradition. The idea behind it has sprung from the urgent needs of the present day: it is intended to serve immediate practical ends, and to show through drawings, models, furnishings, everyday utensils, and completed, permanent buildings, how by using simple means and taking up a minimum of space a comfortable, practical home can be achieved, satisfying every need and how, in particular, the harassed housewife can maintain her home with ease in the absence of unnecessary ornament, trinkets, and cumbersome furnishings.

I have quoted these remarks at length, because you almost have to pinch yourself to realize that they are the words of a politician, and spoken in 1927. In his introductory speech, Mies took the opportunity to set out the problem of the

New Home as being 'rooted in the altered material, social, and mental structure of our time' which was, he said, 'a problem of the new mind' and part of the 'great struggle for new forms of living'. His contribution to the exhibition took the form of a linear block of flats with flexible internal plans designed to emphasize the benefits of new construction techniques. Although externally, with its plain white surfaces and long strips of glazing, it looked radically new, the flexibility did not differ significantly from the contemporary plan studies of Alexander Klein, who preferred traditional exteriors. Walter Gropius contributed two houses designed to demonstrate the virtues of factory production. The first used conventional materials assembled as prefabricated panels, while the second was more radical, using an I-section steel frame infilled with cork insulation panels and clad with asbestos sheeting externally and Celotex-Lignat panels internally. The new construction, which did little more than translate timber-frame methods into steel, proved expensive. Visually, too, the results were far from appealing and they were widely criticized for looking 'like temporary barracks'.

Le Corbusier was asked to design for the 'educated middle class' and contributed two projects. The first was a gem based on the Citrohan house type, elevated on *pilotis*, which Mies called the 'most beautiful and best thing at the Weissenhof'. The second was a double villa, with planning, he said, like a sleeping car – by day it could be completely open, and then at night the small 'sleeping compartments' could be closed for privacy. Probably anticipating general puzzlement, Le Corbusier explained that it represented 'a way of living perhaps not common in Germany but which presents great advantages for the Parisian'. The professional and women's press were critical of both designs, but saved their most stinging remarks for the double villa. It might suit Parisians, they said, but it was irrelevant to the German search for a new culture of living and to the theme of the exhibition, which was widely assumed to be specifically housing for workers (which was not, of course, Le Corbusier's brief).

The designs that received the greatest approval were by Bruno Taut – whose vivid red, blue and yellow walls were the first realization of his 1919 'Call for Colourful Building' – and, widely singled out for praise, a small terrace by J. J. P. Oud, the city architect of Rotterdam from 1918 to 1933. To Erna Meyer, whose book *Der rationelle Haushalt* (The Rational Household) was a bestseller, Oud's row of five compact houses was wholly appropriate to German needs and skilfully designed to assist the housewife in her work. Oud's description stressed the practical features of his house-type: the serving-hatch – a key innovation of Functionalism – which made for easy contact between the living room and kitchen, which itself was large enough to eat in using a fold-down table; a separate utility room for washing and ironing; warm-air heating; and small holes in the doors to see where any lights had been left on and prevent wastage of artificial light.

Whatever the merits or failings of the individual designs, there is no doubt that the Weissenhof succeeded in bringing the new architecture to a much wider public, even if it was not the unified and unqualified triumph acclaimed by later, partisan accounts of the Modern Movement. Many, inevitably, were bemused. The hard Left dubbed the architects Salon Marxists, more interested in New Form for its own sake than in New Life; whereas to the burgeoning National Socialists they were Bolshevik Builders – the Nazis circulated a postcard in which the white buildings were transformed into an Arab settlement. But for the racist motivation it would have been rather amusing.

The new ideas on workers' housing diffused throughout the Continent and found fertile ground in the Netherlands where, following the Housing Act of 1901 and an increase in the Dutch population before the war, council-built workers' housing was in great demand. Oud's pioneering scheme in Rotterdam's Tussendijken district of 1920 was widely admired and at the time of the Weissenhof in 1927 he was at work on what proved to be his masterpiece, the

Kiefhoek Housing Development Rotterdam, the Netherlands, 1927, J. J. P. Oud

Kiefhoek development, also in Rotterdam. It was planned to minimum specifications for large families – two parents and six children – and each house had to be built for £213: 'All this,' said Oud, 'led me to look for a type, which one could think of as a Ford dwelling' – a concept that he had once discussed with Sigfried Giedion, secretary of CIAM. Despite the budgetary constraints he managed to achieve a dignified layout in which, as the English architects Alison and Peter Smithson later wrote, 'each change of road width, every set-back is made to speak of use'.

The majority of blocks in the Kiefhoek were aligned north-east/south-west, regarded as optimal at the time, but the layout was not dominated by rational lighting requirements, as happened so often in Germany, but based on a network of well-defined open spaces. Low brick walls accentuate the individuality of the dwellings, while the red doors and grey window frames reflected Oud's time as a member of De Stijl. Although he was skilled in meeting the demands of *Existenzminimum* accommodation, Oud never subscribed to the view that housing could be satisfactorily reduced to a narrowly defined 'functional' problem. In 1925 in his contribution to a collection of writings on architecture and the machine he wrote: 'I'm longing for a dwelling which satisfies all the demands of my love of comfort, but a house is more to me than a machine-for-living-in.'

During the 1930s, as we noted in the last chapter, the International Style found particularly fertile ground in Eastern Europe and Palestine, following the arrival of several German architects, including some trained at the Bauhaus. It was there, in the Upper Hadar district of Haifa – recently christened 'The Bauhaus on the Carmel' – that one of the most extraordinary expressions of the dwelling as a machine for living in of which I am aware was completed in 1940 by Theodor Menkes, who immigrated to Palestine from Vienna in 1934. Named the 'Glass House' after the all-glass enclosure of its stairs (subsequently removed, perhaps because of over-heating), it is a small, U-shaped block of one-room flats, originally built for bachelor British army officers and now occupied as social housing. The *Existenzminimum* dwellings occupy two sides of the U and the main stair the third; access to each of the four storeys is via open decks – the longer originally enjoying a clear view to the Mediterranean – along whose edges, at handrail level, are continuous plant boxes which were watered by pipes built into the soffit of the floor above.

The units are all identical and entered between a tiny bathroom and kitchen, which shows Frankfurt-like attention to detail. The square living room has a bed alcove placed behind the bathroom, and beyond it a door leads out to the recessed half of a two-metre- (6.5-foot-) square balcony, half of which also

Below 'Glass House', Haifa, Israel, 1940, Theodor Menkes. Designed as minimal bachelor housing for British army officers, this small block epitomized the Modernist vision of healthy, efficient living – there was originally a caged-in tennis court on the roof and a swimming pool in the courtyard.

Above and left Kiefhoek Housing Development, Rotterdam, The Netherlands, 1927, J. J. P. Oud. As City Architect of Rotterdam, Oud produced several outstanding workers' housing estates. Although his plans reflect the concern with 'rational' daylighting and serial production, Oud's projects never succumbed to the numbing repetition this frequently produced.

projects beyond the façade – an arrangement similar to that of the student hostel at the Bauhaus designed by Walter Gropius. The external walls of the bathrooms were originally made entirely of glass bricks, and the entrance doors are framed by the cast-iron drainage pipes. The kitchen and bathroom ceilings are both lower than the living room, enabling a bulkhead to be formed to allow cross ventilation. The communal facilities included a kitchen with dumb-waiter to bring meals to each level; a swimming pool in the courtyard, now sadly filled in but originally providing both recreation and evaporative cooling; and finally, and most striking, a steel-mesh cage housing a tennis court on the roof, reached via a steep stair of distinctly nautical provenance. Rarely can such modest resources have yielded such inspiring results. The building is currently in parlous condition, but if restored would make superb student housing. Almost unknown, it deserves recognition as an outstanding realization of the dream of the New Life.

Unité d'Habitation Marseilles,, France, 1947–52, Le Corbusier

It is a considerable leap to Le Corbusier's Unité d'Habitation in Marseilles, and I hesitated before including it in what is, after all, an account of the house rather than housing. But the Unité looms so large, in every sense, that to omit it seemed almost unthinkable. Its apartments were intended to have many of the qualities we associate with 'house' as opposed to apartment, and it marks, within the work of the century's most influential architect, the culmination of the strand of thinking we have been discussing. The Unité was realized from 1947–52 and remains Le Corbusier's grandest vision of a 'machine for living in', while at the same time marking his emphatic rejection of the machine aesthetic in which that vision was first cast.

Like the Dom-Ino, Citrohan, Monol and other would-be mass-production houses the Unité was promoted as a response to the demands of reconstruction after the devastation of war. Le Corbusier called it a 'vertical garden city' and said that, as in nature, its design began with the living cell. And that in turn revolved around 'the fire, the hearth', where the family should eat together – in his mind, modern 'fire' came down pipes or through wires. In the absence of servants, he argued, '*the living-room must be a kitchen, the kitchen a living-room*' – italicized for emphasis in the book about the project he published in 1953. We are back with Loos's criticism of the separate, Frankfurt-style kitchen: Le Corbusier also thought it essential that this age-old tradition of civilization 'be rehabilitated lest the modern family fall to pieces'. The key to preventing the family's dissolution, he thought, lay in efficiently planned and serviced homes. Privacy must be ensured by isolating the family from potentially noisy neighbours, and a range of support facilities should be close at hand.

The Unité was designed as an independent structural framework into which the individual apartments could be slotted – like wine-bottles in a rack, Le Corbusier said. In theory, they could have been mass-produced off-site, and a perfectly workable, prototype steel-framed unit was developed by Jean Prouvé, who specialized in industrialized construction methods. In practice, traditional on-site methods were eventually adopted – Prouvé said he never understood why – including the double-skin construction to ensure acoustic privacy (it actually proved too quiet for some, who felt isolated). The apartments were designed on two floors, like a house, and locked together in an ingenious cross-over section which gave each family a frontage and private balcony on both sides of the

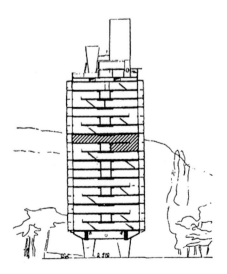

Below and opposite and overleaf Unité d'Habitation, Marseilles, France, 1947–52, Le Corbusier. This vast block, riding the landscape like an ocean liner, contains 337 apartments, a small hotel and a range of communal facilities, and is crowned by the grandest of Le Corbusier's roof-gardens, dedicated to play, fitness, and the contemplation of sky and distant mountains.

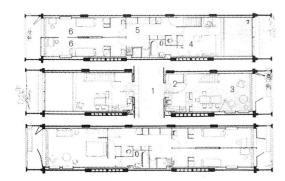

Above Unité d'Habitation, Marseilles, France, 1947–52, Le Corbusier. Typical floor-plans of two, two-storey apartments, organized around the shared 'internal street'.

building and enabled one broad corridor – he called them 'interior streets' – to serve three stories of accommodation. The living room was double-height, with the kitchen either under or on the mezzanine floor, as in the original Citrohan type. The parents had an en-suite bathroom, the children their own shower, and light reached the heart of the rooms thanks to full-height glazing protected by a concrete sunscreen or *brise-soleil*.

Twenty-three variants of the basic flat were designed, and the eighteen-storey block contained 337 apartments in all. On the roof – one of Le Corbusier's truly heroic spaces, addressing the coastal mountains – were a swimming pool, covered and open gymnasia, and, echoing the famous roof top test track of the Fiat factory near Turin, a running track. On the two floors below were a crèche and nursery, and half the seventh and eighth floors were occupied by other communal facilities – a co-operative store, smaller shops, restaurant, and an eighteen-room hotel.

The closest analogy to the Unité both in scale - it is 135 metres long (443 feet) – and contents is one of Le Corbusier's favourite 'machines', the ocean liner. But whereas the occupants of a liner are temporary and when at sea have no alternative to the on-board facilities, the Unité was permanently moored outside Marseilles and the residents preferred to go out for most of their shopping and recreation. The internal commercial and residential 'streets' were destined to remain no more than broad corridors, devoid of anything resembling the bustle of urban life. It was a magnificent yet flawed vision, a fragment of a larger proposal for the radical restructuring of the modern city to ensure the 'essential joys' of *soleil, espace et verdure*. These, however, mattered less to the residents than the traditional pleasures of urban life they sought outside. Well managed from the outset, unlike several late Unités, the Marseilles block was always popular and like Pessac is now inhabited predominantly by middle-class families.

Aesthetically, the Unité marked a radical break with Le Corbusier's work of the 1920s, where the geometric forms and sleek surfaces he believed would result from industrial production had either been simulated using blockwork and plaster, as in the Villa Savoye, or had to be painted over, as at Pessac, when sprayed concrete failed to live up to expectations. The abstract language of planes, smooth surfaces and slender columns was abandoned in favour of a delight in muscular, sculptural forms, and the roughness of raw concrete struck from grainy, timber-boarded shutters, which he christened *béton brut*. Stylistically, it would prove hugely influential for more than a decade to come.

The dream of machine-made houses manifested itself in other guises outside the architectural mainstream. To a visionary like the American Richard Buckminster Fuller the Europeans had not begun to come to terms with the real potential of new materials and mass-production. To do so he argued, the world's resources and means of production had to be looked at holistically, outmoded economic systems based on memories of scarcity and isolation replaced, and problems like housing stripped of their cultural baggage and seen, like a military operation, as a problem of logistics. His solution was to mass-produce houses as autonomous units and airlift them to anywhere in the world. The house would be designed to exhibit maximum strength at minimum weight, and like an aeroplane it would separate out compression and tension members and maximize the use of the latter. He called his first house 4D and published the designs in 1928; the following year it was given the name by which it became generally known – the Dymaxion House – by the Marshall Field store in Chicago, who used a mock-up as a futuristic stage-set for new furniture.

Dymaxion House Prototype 1928, Richard Buckminster Fuller

The Dymaxion House was a literal rather than metaphoric 'machine for living in'. The living areas were housed in a hexagonal, glazed enclosure hung, like a wire-wheel, from a central mast containing all the services. It was to be fully air-conditioned and cleaned using central compressed air and vacuum systems; laundry would be automatically washed, dried, pressed and placed in storage containers; clothes and food storage was based on revolving shelves. It was designed to be relatively independent of mains water: the atomizer bath would need only two pints of water, which would be filtered, sterilized and re-circulated after use, and the toilets would operate without water at all. And so it went on…. Much of the technology Fuller envisaged was not immediately to hand, but most of it now is – some, not surprisingly, developed to enable astronauts to survive in space.

Below Dymaxion House, prototype, 1928, Richard Buckminster Fuller. Intended to be airlifted to anywhere in the world, this visionary prototype for an autonomous house used aircraft construction materials and techniques for lightness and envisaged a range of new technologies, some of which became a reality with the development of space travel.

Fuller was fond of rhetorical questions like 'Madam, how much does your house weigh?' to get people to think about the resources they used. The smart answer was, 'It doesn't matter, because it doesn't have to fly', but regardless of whether or not they were to be air-lifted, Fuller considered heavy compression materials like brick and stone hopelessly outmoded and priced his designs by the pound. He estimated the Dymaxion House could be mass-produced for 25 US cents per pound, only slightly more than Fords and Chevrolets in 1928.

Fuller provocatively offered the patents on his design to the American Institute of Architects, whose vice-president at the time was his father-in-law. They declined the offer, and passed a motion stating their opposition to all 'peas-in-a-pod-like repeatable designs'. He pressed on, designing the Dymaxion Bathroom from 1938 to 1940, which anticipated the industrially produced all-in-one units now available, and then, in 1944, the circular, metal-clad Dymaxion Dwelling Machine designed to exploit aeronautical techniques – unlike the earlier Dymaxion it got as far as a habitable prototype. Fuller's ideas took the Modernist dream of a universal industrial culture to a logical – in his own technocratic terms – conclusion, but to most his logic was fatally flawed by the absolute refusal to address housing as a cultural as well as a technical challenge. His example, however, exerted a continuing appeal to dreamers of technological utopias, such as the British Archigram group of the 1960s, and to High Tech architects fascinated by the idea of 'technology transfer' from more advanced fields such as aeronautics and sailing. The house-building system developed in 1985 by the British architect Richard Horden, for instance, used aluminium yacht-components.

The European rhetoric about 'machines for living in' and the *Existenzminimum* generally fell on deaf ears in the USA, where the impact of the First World War was less directly felt and the traditional balloon-frame was, in effect, an early form of system-building. Not surprisingly, it fell to a European to produce the most machine-like house included in Hitchcock and Johnson's exhibition *The International Style*. The Aluminaire House was designed by the Swiss-born Albert Frey in partnership with A. Lawrence Kocher, managing editor of the magazine *Architectural Record*. Frey had previously worked on the Villa Savoye

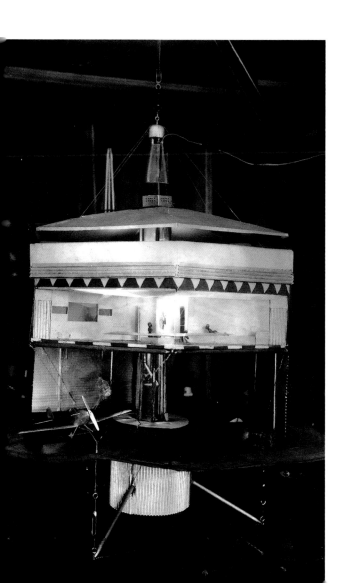

Opposite Dymaxion Dwelling Machine, prototype, Wichita, Kansas, USA, 1944, Richard Buckminster Fuller. More practical than the first Dymaxion, Fuller's later prototype was designed to use the spare capacity of the aeronautical industry following the end of the Second World War.

Above Aluminaire House, Syosset, New York, USA, 1931: Albert Frey and A. Lawrence Kocher. Made of aluminium and steel and prefabricated and erected in ten days, the design was based on the smaller of Le Corbusier's houses at the Weissenhof exhibition.

Left and below Yacht House, New Forest, England, 1985, Richard Horden. Incorporating aluminium yacht-building components, this housing system epitomized the idea of 'technology transfer', which continues to fascinate High Tech architects.

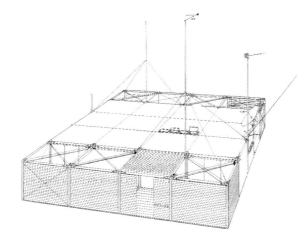

with Le Corbusier and greatly admired the freestanding house at the Weissenhof, which he took as a model for his, built in an exhibition hall in New York in 1931. The name was meant to conjure up aluminium, light and lightness, and the three-storey house was elevated on aluminium pipe-columns, fitted with steel-framed windows and doors, and clad in ribbed aluminium sheets. It was prefabricated and erected in ten days. Later it was dismantled in six hours and re-sited on Long Island, where it was altered and extended almost beyond recognition.

The architect who came closest to building a bridge between the technocratic utopia of Fuller and mainstream architecture was Jean Prouvé. During the 1930s he was preoccupied with exploring the architectural implications of new methods of construction. He developed factory-based techniques for manufacturing new components and for the off-site assembly of complete or sectional buildings which found fulfilment in the design of emergency dwellings during the Second World War, when 1200 six-metre-square (64.5-foot-square) units were ordered. They continued to be occupied during peacetime, proving their versatility by changing locations as well as occupants. Eight-metre-square (86-foot-square) versions were considered by the French government for large-scale use during reconstruction after the war, but only twenty-five trial houses were eventually manufactured, in 1949. After bureaucratic bungling these ended up scattered through France – some even turned up in Algeria – with the largest group at Meudon from which they took their name.

'Meudon' Prefabricated Housing Meudon, France, 1949, Jean Prouvé

Staying true to his conviction that 'the individual dwelling must be light and dynamic' and 'an expression of large-scale production and therefore characteristic of industry', Prouvé continued to design prototypes. Among these are two which merit special mention: the all-metal aluminium and steel Tropical House of 1949 which, with its outrigged external blinds and exemplary response to the climate, proved an inspiration to High Tech architects such as Norman Foster; and the prefabricated, two-bedroom, 50-square-metre (538-square-foot) house designed for the Abbé Pierre who helped provoke a national outcry about the housing crisis. 'A house built in less than seven hours', declared a headline in the Nancy newspaper *Républicain*, beside a picture of a tiny kitchen being craned into place, complete with five saucepans hanging ready for action. Prouvé also completed several private houses, including his own, built in Nancy in 1954. This was a relaxed assemblage of factory-made components which he used as a test-bed for new materials, including aluminium panels punched with small 'porthole' windows and laminated board panels for the roof. 'Everything Prouvé touches and designs,' said Le Corbusier, 'immediately takes on an elegant plastic form, while at the same time he provides brilliant solutions to the problems concerning the strength of the materials and fabrication.'

Prouvé's buildings looked unashamedly factory made. In Britain similar attempts to marshal the defence industry's vastly enlarged manufacturing capacity to help meet the urgent need for housing were generally made to look as conventionally house-like as possible. The ARCON house, which the anonymously styled Architectural Consultants group developed in 1944, was an exception. It used a steel framework that gave flexibility in internal arrangement, and the rounded ridge and pressed steel cladding panels were expressive of

Above Tropical House, prototype, 1949, Jean Prouvé. This all-metal house demonstrated a concern with 'passive' climate control techniques which was well ahead of its time.
Opposite 'Meudon' prefabricated housing, Meudon, France, 1949, Jean Prouvé. Intended as a solution to the post-war housing shortages, only twenty-five of these eight-metre- (26.5-foot-) square houses were actually built, the largest group being in Meudon.

Right and below Prouvé House, Nancy, France, 1954, Jean Prouvé. The interior of his own house reflects Prouvé's relaxed yet thoroughly professional command of building technology. The plan opens to the south against an insulating, north-facing storage wall, and he used the fabric as a test-bed for new materials and components.

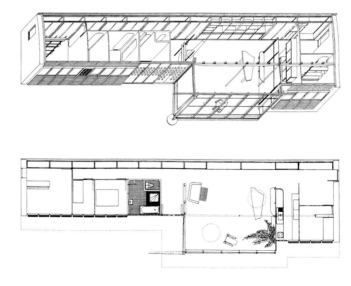

steel construction. Numerous factory-made, single-storey 'prefabs' – as they became known – were sited all over Britain in cities that had suffered serious bomb damage. They were meant to be temporary, but most long exceeded their projected life span, and some are still happily lived in over half a century later.

The humble British prefabs may not have looked much like the heroic 'machines for living in' espoused in the 1920s but the technology deployed in fabricating them was in fact highly sophisticated. Although they were genuine mass-production houses, in Britain, as in most parts of the world, the desire to live in houses that *looked* mass-produced did not exist, and the house-building industry quickly reverted to more traditional techniques. Behind the reassuringly familiar façades, however, the replacement of craft processes by industrial products gathered pace: the failure, if such it was, of the Modernist vision of the house as a 'machine for living in' was cultural more than technical.

Above ARCON permanent 'prefab' house, 1944, Architectural Consultants. Architecturally one of the most sophisticated of the prefabricated designs produced in Britain, this example is unusual for being a two-storey house.
Right British 'prefab' house, late 1940s. Although visually worlds apart from the visionary mass-production houses with which this chapter began, the British prefabs were genuinely mass-produced in large numbers using 'technology-transfer' from war-time industry – despite the reassuringly 'normal' exterior's attempt to suggest otherwise.

place, climate and culture

Above Villa de Mandrot, near Toulon, France, 1931, Le Corbusier. The raised courtyard framed by walls of local stone signals a departure from the abstraction and flowing spaces of his 1920s villas.
Below Weekend House, Paris, France, 1935, Le Corbusier. The vaulted Monol house type was here rendered in concrete, stone and turf – externally only the glass brick infill panels signal the house's modernity.

After moving to the USA in 1930 and establishing his credentials as an exponent of the new architecture with the Aluminaire house exhibited in New York the following year, the Swiss architect Albert Frey embarked on several trips across the country. He discovered a new wonderland of light, colours and materials and by 1940, when he decided to build his own, truly tiny house (32 square metres/344 square feet) in the desert near Palm Springs in California, his architectural aspirations had shifted decisively. The house was composed from planes of metal, plaster and glass, in the manner pioneered by Rietveld and Mies van der Rohe – it was from Mies, he said, that he learnt to extend a house into its site – but the colours and materials no longer represented the elusive spirit of the Machine Age, nor the universal truths of De Stijl, but were subtly attuned to the setting.

Aluminium, a shiny emblem of technology in the Aluminaire House, was now used to heighten by contrast and reflection our awareness of the colours and textures of the red-brown rocks of the Mojave Desert. Rose-red and sage-green walls echoed the flowers and foliage, midnight-blue curtains in the bedroom substituted for the night, while ceilings were a paler blue, like the daytime sky. Photographed in black and white, the colours of the International Style, Frey's house appeared orthodox. Comprehended in full colour, however, it represented an attitude that had begun to transform modern architecture in the 1930s and would become increasingly dominant as the century progressed. The spatial, formal and constructional innovations of the new architecture were to be inflected in response to specific places, climates and cultures, not deployed as a universal affirmation of modernity. In this chapter we will see this process at work over five decades in Europe and Central and South America, in India, South Africa and Australia. The United States, where so many significant private houses were produced, will be considered in the following chapter, followed by a briefer exploration of the most distinctive and influential tradition of house building to emerge in Europe following the Second World War, that of Scandinavia.

The first stirrings of the new attitude are to be found in a house Le Corbusier completed in 1931, immediately after the Villa Savoye. Designed for a rural site outside Toulon, the Villa de Mandrot has a U-shaped plan framing an elevated, south-facing courtyard, and is built with walls of local stone. The planning and use of reinforced concrete, Le Corbusier stressed in his description, demonstrated the 'ideas habitually exploited in our houses', but the change in attitude was clear, and confirmed four years later when he built the small Weekend House on the outskirts of Paris, not in the depths of rural France, using shallow barrel vaults and random rubble walls. Spatially, the design was a reinterpretation of the mass-production Monol type, but here the vault is closer to the peasant Catalan form rather than an attempt to exploit new materials. An understanding of the 'intrinsic qualities of materials' was, Le Corbusier still maintained, vital to advancing the cause of modern architecture, but those materials now included stone and turf – which covered the roof – as well as concrete and glass bricks.

In part the new attitude can be explained pragmatically, as a response to the technical problems afflicting his houses – the Villa Savoye, in particular, was plagued by leaks. Although some designers, most notably Mies van der Rohe,

Above Frey House I, Palm Springs, California, USA, 1940, Albert Frey. In black and white this tiny house looks like an orthodox exercise in planar modern architecture, but seen in colour it is revealed as a vivid response to the plants and rocks of the desert.

Right This adaptation to place is taken much further in the second house Frey built on the site between 1964 and 1971.

Villa Mairea Noormarkku, Finland, 1937–40, Alvar Aalto

Above Aalto House and Studio, Helsinki, Finland, 1935, Alvar Aalto. The L-shaped plan and use of timber boarding anticipate Aalto's Villa Mairea, whilst the volumetric composition suggests a debt to Walter Gropius's houses for the Bauhaus Masters in Dessau.

remained true to the vision of a universal modern style, the move towards an architecture more responsive to locality quickly gathered strength. One of the earliest and most influential critiques of 'an international, rootless modern architecture' began in Finland in the mid 1930s: the words are those of the country's finest architect, Alvar Aalto.

Aalto came to worldwide prominence as the designer of one of the major buildings of the International Style, the Tuberculosis Sanatorium at Paimio (1928–33), but he quickly became dissatisfied with what he saw as the one-sided rationalism of orthodox modern architecture. In a 1935 lecture entitled 'Rationalism and Man' he put forward nature as a model – 'formally rich and luxuriant' – and argued that supposedly rational, functional architecture had become just another style, 'a pleasant compôte of chromed tubes, glass tops, cubistic forms, and astounding colour combinations'. And even when 'rational', he argued, its rationality did not go far enough, applying only to aspects of the object, with results that lacked 'human qualities'. In the same year he gave this lecture Aalto demonstrated what he meant in his own house and studio in the outskirts of Helsinki at Munkkiniemi. The L-shaped form, wrapped around a roof garden and projecting over a ground-floor terrace, recalls the Masters' Houses designed by Walter Gropius for the Bauhaus staff in Dessau. But in place of crisp plaster surfaces we are confronted by lime-washed brickwork, weather-boarding, and bamboo-like poles for climbing plants.

The sources of his inspiration are not hard to guess: the International Style was being reinterpreted in the light of Mediterranean vernacular houses and Finnish timber buildings, lightened by contact with Japan. Any doubts on this score are quickly dispelled by the Villa Mairea, one of the century's great houses, completed in 1940. Aalto began work on the project in late 1937 and the clients, as so often with major modern houses, were wealthy industrialists, Harry and Maire Gullichsen. Maire had studied painting in Paris in the 1920s and owned an important collection of modern art; she was also heir to the vast Ahlström timber and paper company of which Harry, following their marriage, became managing director.

In the wake of liberation from Russia in 1917 the Finns were acutely conscious of their native traditions and in the 1930s the 'birch bark' culture, as it was deprecatingly known by the modernizers, was still in the ascendant. Industrialists like the Gullichsens, on the other hand, eager to establish Finland's place in the wider world and build export markets, were sympathetic to the progressive ideas emanating from the Continent. Their brief to Aalto was to design them a large summer house both modern and Finnish, on their estate at Noormarkku outside Pori on the west coast. Aalto's friend Gustav Strengell used to refer to the Munkkiniemi house and studio as the 'modern Niemelä', the name of a re-created farmstead in the nearby folk museum on Seurasaari island. It needed insight to see Niemelä there, but with the Villa Mairea the inspiration came out into the open: it was conceived less as a single structure than as a collection of buildings, earth mounds and planting framing a courtyard, a perennial form of settlement in much of Finland.

Historically, the first building a peasant farmer would erect was the sauna, and in the villa it can also be seen as the first, elemental component of a composition

Above, below and right Villa
Mairea, Noormarkku, Finland,
1937–40, Alvar Aalto. In this collage-
like composition Aalto combined
references to vernacular buildings,
orthodox modern architecture and
traditional Japanese houses into a
compelling synthesis which is
unmistakably modern and Finnish.

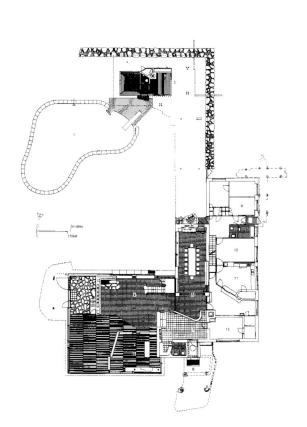

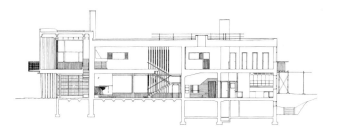

Above Villa Mairea, Noormarkku, Finland, 1937–40, Alvar Aalto. The interior unfolds as an abstraction of the Finnish pine forest, with black-painted steel columns wrapped in rattan or clad with birch strips, and the entrance area and main staircase screened by vertical poles.

that grows in scale and sophistication around the courtyard, to culminate in Maire's first floor studio. Like the sauna, the studio is clad in wood, but here the boards are subtly moulded, identical to those Aalto designed for the Finnish Pavilion at the 1935 Paris World Fair, intended perhaps as a reminder of Maire's student days in the city. With its grass roof and wooden walls, the sauna seems reassuringly traditional, but the roof is flat and the boards have the sophistication of a Japanese tea-house – Aalto was besotted with Japan, and used to appear in the office in a kimono given him by the Japanese ambassador. Similar complexities occur all through the house. The covered dining terrace, for example recalls a single-storey fragment of a Dom-Ino house, but sports a grass roof on timber boarding and a wooden gutter hollowed from a log.

Internally, Aalto planned a continuous living space to meld modern open plan with the traditional *tupa* emulated by Gallen-Kallela and Saarinen. In the *tupa*, spaces were differentiated by poles at ceiling level, but in the Villa Mairea Aalto used a change of level to separate the entrance area. Also, the floor finishes become progressively more domestic and intimate – from stone through tiles, to timber boarding and rugs. As in a traditional house the focus is the fireplace, which greets you across a long diagonal vista. Where it meets the glass, the white-plastered block is hollowed out by a sinuous curve – nicknamed 'Aalto's ear' in the office – which recalls the sculpted forms of wind-driven snow, visible outside for several weeks in most years.

A regular grid of columns runs through the living space, but the black-painted circular steel columns are rendered unique by being variously doubled or trebled, wrapped with rattan singly or in pairs, clad with birch-wood strips or – in the library – made of concrete instead. His aim, Aalto said, was 'to avoid all artificial architectural rhythms', and in place of the 'clear structure' of Mies we are presented with a system that refuses to be seen as a grid. The presiding metaphor is the forest, emblem of Finnish identity and freedom, and it is reinforced by the detailed articulation. The rattan-wrapped columns, for example, are abstract representations of pine trees, whose dark bark peels to reveal a golden core. The library is separated from the living space by an undulating glazed screen in which glass alternates with solid, curved panels: with low sun or artificial light spilling through, it reminds you of sunlight through trees. And, to add another subtlety, the twin-sectioned white column supporting the studio can be seen as a metaphoric birch tree at the edge of the 'pine-forest' within – the inclined half is structurally redundant, and was only included at Maire's insistence after the engineer asked for it to be omitted.

In the Villa Mairea, Aalto collaged together fragments designed to bring to mind traditional Finnish buildings, memories of nature and more exotic sources. Japan is the most obvious, but also his beloved Italy – the white surfaces are again lime-washed brickwork, not render – and even Hollywood in the racily modern swimming pool. The spaces are all designed with the human subject as their centre: the main living area no longer has a dominant structure of its own, but seems to open and close, restructuring itself around you as you move through the space. It was a brilliant response to his clients' demand for a house both Finnish and modern, and nothing produced in Europe before the war came close to rivalling its inventive transformation of modern architecture to respond to specific cultural traditions. When, after the war, he came to embody his personal vision of life close to nature Aalto again turned to collage-like techniques to conjure up a slightly different set of associations.

Aalto's summer house was built in 1953 as a gift for his new wife Elissa (he had lost his first wife, Aino, to cancer in 1949), on land given to him by the grateful client for his recently completed masterpiece, Säynätsalo Town Hall. The site was on the nearby island of Muuratsalo, at that time accessible only by boat, and the L-shaped house frames a small square courtyard, from whose corner a slender tail of timber buildings and fenced enclosures runs into the forest, each element angling and adjusting itself to the site – the foundations are made of logs positioned according to the rocks. The courtyard is the set-piece. At its centre is a square barbecue pit – square within square within square – and facing the living room the wall breaks completely to open a long view down the lake. In the other wall, at high level, a large opening is screened by white timber slats that rhyme with the trees. The walls themselves are a richly textured patchwork of bricks, tiles and climbing plants. Aalto described them as 'experimental' and said it was vital for him to test materials in the harsh northern climate before imposing them on his clients.

The 'experiments' were part of an unsuccessful ruse to avoid tax by claiming the house as a business expense, but the real innovation was aesthetic, not technical, and again Aalto's intentions are revealed by the details. Next to the living room door is a blue-tiled 'window', complete with wooden lintel; elsewhere, patches of brickwork suggest openings that have been closed up. 'I always have a journey to Italy in mind', he once remarked, and here, beside a Finnish lake, Aalto created his own Italian fantasy, a private piazzetta, patched and pre-weathered to inscribe time and the elements into the place and to defy the shock of the new. It is difficult to imagine anything further in substance or spirit from the seamless surfaces of the International style.

The summer house has offered many Nordic architects a unique opportunity to escape not only the city but also the expectations of their day-to-day professional life. When he built his at Stennäs in 1937, Aalto's friend and mentor Gunnar Asplund turned resolutely towards the vernacular. Although at first glance it might appear simple to the point of being cottagey, it was in fact a deceptively refined design. One notes, for example, the asymmetry of the main roof, which subtly adjusts both to the site and to the needs of the spaces within, and the artful crank in plan that pivots around the cavernous fireplace to realign the main room in recognition of the view.

Few summer houses better express the widely felt Nordic ideal of retreating to nature for physical and spiritual refreshment than that built by the Norwegian Knut Knutsen. Although he never subscribed to the values of the new architecture, and was known for his commitment to the national traditions of building, Knutsen was a notably inventive designer. During the 1930s he became the focus of opposition to the circle of ardent young Modernists gathered around Arne Korsmo, so when he built his summer house in 1949 on a rocky coastal site at Portør, it came as no surprise that he chose to make it entirely of that most traditional of Norwegian building materials, wood. The result, however, was

Aalto Summer House Muuratsalo, Finland, 1953, Alvar Aalto

Below Summer House, Muuratsalo, Finland, 1953, Alvar Aalto. Built as a wedding gift for his second wife Elissa, Aalto used the summer house as an opportunity to experiment further with architectural collage. The presiding image is the time-worn walls of Italian streets and piazzas, with blue tiles here standing in for the southern sky seen through an empty window opening.

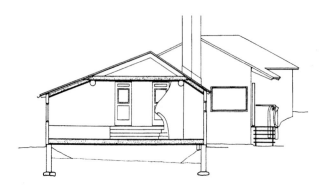

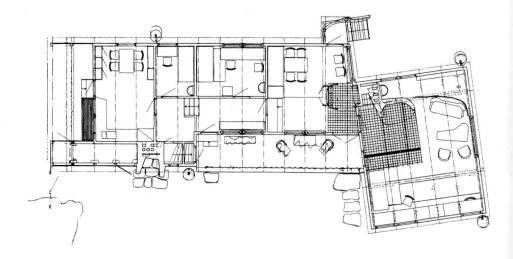

Right and opposite Asplund
Summer House, Stennäs, Sweden,
1937, Gunnar Asplund. The references
to the vernacular are more pervasive
here than in Aalto's Villa Mairea, but
the subtle adjustments to the
topography and views lift the design
far above a simple-minded exercise in
the neo-vernacular.

Above Knutsen Summer House,
Portør, Norway, 1949, Knut Knutsen.
The architect's sketch captures better
than a photograph the essence of his
design – folded planes of wood
emulating the rocky landscape of the
coastal site.

Below Ugalde House, near Barcelona,
Spain, 1951, Antonio Coderch.
Whitewashed stone walls, the smoothly
abstract surfaces of the International
Style and a site-adjusted plan combine
to create an architecture inseparable
from its Mediterranean context.

radical. From a distance the folded planes of the roof, clad in wide, overlapping
boards, are almost indistinguishable from the surrounding rocks. Close to, they
are revealed as wonderfully irregular, slipping and dipping to link house to
landscape, whose rooms in turn jut and deflect as they settle into the terrain.
Rediscovered in the 1980s by a new generation of architects, Knutsen's house
became an emblem of the burgeoning Norwegian 'green' movement.

Recourse to the vernacular became a favourite strategy for reconnecting the
rootless International style to local traditions. Gerrit Rietveld's cleverly
asymmetrical Verrijn Stuart summer house in Breukelerveen, The Netherlands, in
1941 projects a relaxed, timeless air, as does the Ugalde House, built by Antonio
Coderch on a coastal site at Caldes d'Estrac outside Barcelona in 1951. By
combining thick, whitewashed walls, modern transparency and a complex, site-
adjusted plan, Coderch achieved a serene power of expression that would
influence a new generation of Barcelona architects three decades hence. For
those Modernists who did not flee Nazi Germany the vernacular provided a safe
dress beneath which spatial adventures could be indulged in private. Thus, for
example, in 1937 we find Hugo Häring reinterpreting the Bavarian gabled
farmhouse in his Von Prittwitz House at Starnbergersee near Munich, and Hans
Scharoun wrapping the still impressively free interior of his house for the painter
Oscar Moll in Berlin Grünewald with a folksy exterior.

Flight from Hitler brought several leading Modernists to London in the mid-
1930s, among them Walter Gropius, Serge Chermayeff and Marcel Breuer.
Chermayeff stayed long enough to build himself a large country house near
Halland in Sussex. He submitted the design for planning permission in 1935 and
was refused, only to win – a familiar story in England – following an appeal and
public inquiry. The house was unmistakably modern, but made almost entirely of
timber in deference to its rural location. Far from turning to the vernacular
language of barns, however, Chermayeff discreetly but unmistakably evoked the
tradition of the English country house. The garden front, with its exposed
structure and layered façade is formal, even classical in spirit, while the entrance
court is far less self-conscious and given over largely to service rooms. There is a
generous, slightly raised terrace that just prevents the lawn lapping right up to
the house in the manner of Capability Brown, and from today's perspective the
scheme seems to resonate with tradition, whereas to the hapless planning
officials at the time it doubtless threatened an alien modernity. What could be
more English?

Climates and cultures radically different from those of its origins provoked
many of the most original adaptations and transformations of the International
style, but we cannot leave Europe without mentioning one of the most singular
houses in the world, that of Curzio Malaparte on Capri. A prolific writer in several
genres, war correspondent, magazine owner and film maker, Malaparte was also
at various times a Fascist, a Communist and a Maoist. He was exiled and
imprisoned for his varied but fanatically held convictions, and it was during one of
his island exiles that he resolved to build a house on the Bay of Naples. He
settled upon the site on Capri in 1937. The scenery, rediscovered by aristocratic
nature-lovers early in the century, was outstanding and there was the added
advantage that Mussolini's son-in-law, who was also the Italian foreign minister,

Above Chermayeff House, Halland,
England, 1935–7, Serge Chermayeff.
Modern Movement structure acquires an
appropriately classical air on the garden
front as the *emigré* Chermayeff
responds to the English country
house tradition.

Above and opposite Casa
Malaparte, Capri, Italy, 1937–40,
Curzio Malaparte. Spectacularly sited
on a headland on the island of Capri,
Malaparte's house is a platform and
frame for viewing the landscape. In
the sparsely furnished main salon the
fire in the hearth (seen on the right)
burns against a tiny window, uniting
interior and sea, fire and water.

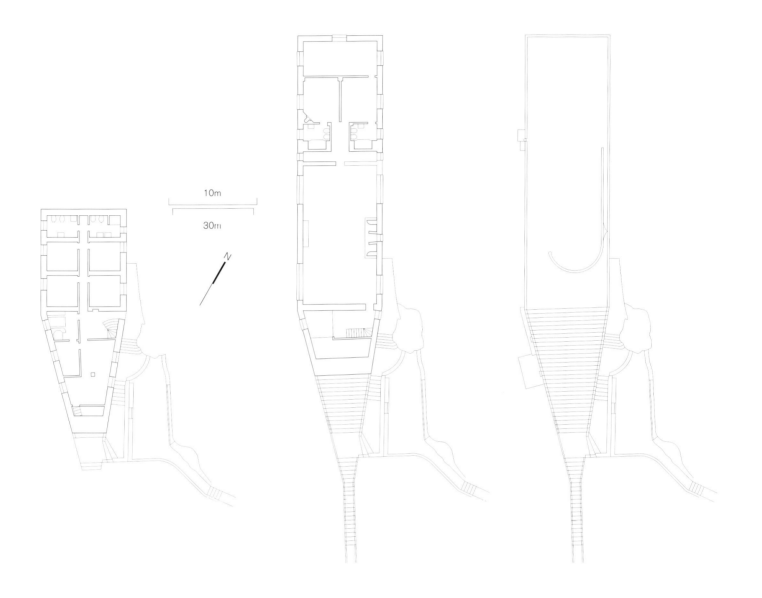

10m

30m

N

holidayed there – and promised to get him a building permit. The site must be among the most breathtaking in the world and to obtain permission to build there Malaparte commissioned a design from the Roman architect Adalberto Libera, to whom the house was attributed for many years. It is now clear that most of what was built was the work of Malaparte himself, supported by his master-mason Adolfo Amitrano.

Casa Malaparte Capri, Italy, 1937–40, Curzio Malaparte

The house grows directly out of the rocky headland, with its roof forming an outdoor terrace, approached via steps that widen as you ascend – they recall those by Michelangelo for the approach to the Campidoglio in Rome, but were modelled on the Church of the Annunciation in Lipari. Malaparte widened the foundations slightly to enable him to construct an axial sequence of rooms, rather than the single-banked corridor Libera envisaged: it seems likely that his model for the planning was the Hellenistic *domus*, examples of which were excavated during the 1930s. To reinforce the Classical atmosphere he formed the main entrance through the steps, modelled on the similarly formed *vomitorium* in a Greek theatre, but this was blocked up before completion, at the mason's insistence, because it risked flooding the interior. Malaparte then moved the entrance to the long flank, which explains, if not excuses, the modest, boxed-in staircase that leads rather inauspiciously to the 15-metre (49-foot) long salon above, leaving the stairs outside to serve only the roof.

The plan is rigorously orthogonal within the site-defined perimeter, neat and familiar so it does not obtrude on what really matters: the landscape, both built – the house as platform – and, supremely, natural. The breathtaking scenery becomes an endless performance to be viewed from the theatrical steps, and from inside every view is stunning, framed and viewed by the simplest of rectangular windows cut in the massive 80-centimetre- (30-inch-) thick walls. 'I didn't construct the house,' Malaparte claimed to have told Field Marshal Rommel, 'but I did construct the landscape'. The only overtly artful touch comes in the main salon, with the small glazed opening in the hearth through which you can see flames flickering in the Mediterranean, fire and water combining in a moment of sublime artistry.

Malaparte furnished the huge salon with white-covered sofas which look almost ethereal beside the slabs of wood on massive, fluted stone or timber columns that he used for tables. The means are minimal and the effect surreal, like a De Chirico painting – Malaparte explained it as an expression of his 'nostalgia' for the prison in which he was confined on Lipari. The house lay empty and sealed for twenty years following its owner's death in 1957. It seems likely that he wanted it to be his personal mausoleum, like the 'flaming red pyramid' of a Roman tomb Amedeo Maiuri claimed, in his *Breviario di Capri* of 1937, to have seen on the Anatolian coast. Whatever its meaning for the creator and owner, Casa Malaparte stands outside time and any conventional narrative of architectural development. The sensibility behind it is, however, unmistakably modern, even if the romantic, rebellious intellectual who created it was dreaming of the confinement of prison and the idealized freedom of the Classical world.

Leaving Europe for Brazil we return to the mainstream, and then quickly swerve into new territory as the genius of the place asserted itself. Modern architecture arrived there in earnest in 1936 when Le Corbusier was enlisted by

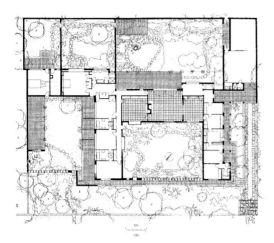

Lúcio Costa to help his team of recent graduates with the design of the new Ministry of Education building. Another European arrival was Bernard Rudofsky, who was born and trained in Austria before leaving for South America in 1937. He later achieved fame as the advocate of 'architecture without architects'. In 1941 Rudofsky completed an unassumingly modern house in São Paulo in which, predictably in view of his later interests, he turned to the patio-type as a response to the climate – although, due to local regulations, the form was not popular in the city. The house was laid out around a sequence of outdoor living spaces and, seen in plan, inside and outside appear almost interchangeable. The courtyards were heavily planted to provide shade, and deep overhangs supported on slender steel columns created large covered terraces and porches. The planning is modern, with a suite of interconnected living spaces, but spatially unremarkable. What marks the house out is its avoidance of stylistic affectation and wholehearted adaptation to the climate.

Le Corbusier's presence, needless to say, was galvanizing to local architects, above all to Oscar Niemeyer, the most gifted of Costa's team. When Niemeyer designed his own house in Rio de Janeiro in 1942 it was unashamedly conceived as a homage to Le Corbusier. The plot was small so he raised the accommodation on *pilotis* to preserve the continuity of the ground. With reflected light from the brilliant, high sun, the space below the building was credible as a continuation of the garden in a way that was rare in Europe. The house itself was organized around a ramp, which began its journey in the covered garden and ended, somewhat unceremoniously, in a narrow landing outside the bedrooms. The design was more than competent, but gave few hints of the explosive talent already evident in another project Niemeyer designed the same year. This was the Casino, the first of a group of recreational buildings at Pampulha in which the freedom of planning and dynamism of form made Le Corbusier's first moves in that direction look tentative.

The so-called 'Glass House', designed from 1950 to 1951 (and also lived in) by Lina Bo Bardi on a site outside São Paulo, became the social focus of modern architecture in Brazil and a mandatory visit for foreign artists and intellectuals – the architect-visitors included Max Bill, Gio Ponti and Aldo van Eyck. Italian by birth, Lina Bo edited the influential magazine *Domus* during the war before marrying the scholar Pietro Maria Bardi and settling in Brazil. Their house was Miesian in inspiration, perched dramatically above a reserve of Brazilian forest on impossibly slender tubular columns – the great engineer Pier Luigi Nervi assured them it would not have been allowed in Europe (and would not now in Brazil). The vast living room, fully-glazed on three sides, backed up against the bedrooms, which looked into a private court against the blank wall of the servants' wing. At first sight it seems an orthodox International style building, but the atmosphere is subtly different, softened by the sky-blue flooring and columns, the curtains which replace walls, the gentle curve of the roof, and the relaxed cohabitation of antique and modern furniture. Seen in the embrace of the surrounding forest, with its exotic birds and croaking frogs, it strikes visitors as organic, unmistakably feminine and quintessentially Brazilian.

In 1953 Oscar Niemeyer decided to build a new house for himself on a dramatic site in Rio de Janeiro occupying high ground between two towering

Above Courtyard House, São Paulo, Brazil, 1941, Bernard Rudofsky. Although not popular in the city due to local regulations, the courtyard form was ideally adapted to a climate which demanded shady interiors and invited outdoor-living.

Overleaf Glass House, near São Paulo, Brazil, 1950–51, Lina Bo Bardi. Lina Bo's house became both an emblem of the new architecture in Brazil and a social focus of progressive culture. The blue colouring and gently curved roof create sufficient distance from International Style norms to suggest something subtly adapted to the Brazilian context.

Niemeyer House Rio de Janeiro, Brazil, 1953, Oscar Niemeyer

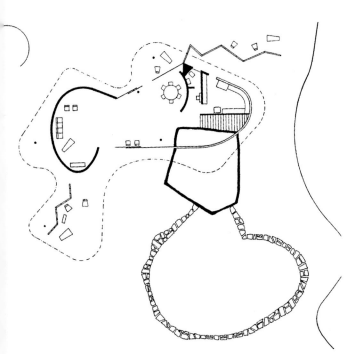

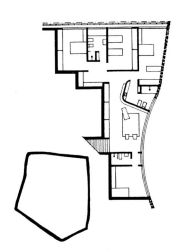

hills, with spectacular views down-slope which he wanted to preserve by ensuring visual continuity through the interior. This suggested large areas of glass shaded by an overhanging roof to ensure transparency and minimal internal divisions, so he consigned the four bedrooms and a sitting space to a lower level, cut into the hill. Its roof was treated as new ground, across which the living spaces and an open terrace were freely disposed — more freely, perhaps, than in any other house that has been considered here.

At first sight the main plan resembles an abstract painting more than a building. A continuous broken line, signifying the roof, meanders apparently at random around some freely arranged curved and straight planes; a shallow arc makes a place for the dining table, evoking memories of Mies's Tugendhat House, and then breaks free to zigzag its way into the landscape (its echo is found on the covered terrace, where a zigzag screen shelters outdoor seating); an irregular pentagon drawn with a thick black line represents a massive, immovable boulder which juts into the free-form swimming pool. Beyond the house, more wriggling lines describe tropical plants — or are they abstract sculptures? — of which the roof, suddenly, seems like a massive enlargement. 'It is not the right angle that attracts me,' Niemeyer explained, 'nor the straight line, hard and inflexible, created by man. What attracts me is the free and sensual curve — the curve that I find in the mountains of my country, in the sinuous course of its rivers, in the body of the beloved woman'.

Niemeyer's house offended some of its earliest European visitors, who found the relationship between the two floors incoherent, and the intensely personal quality arbitrary. But, by rejecting the formal consistency of orthodox modern architecture and responding directly to the site, Niemeyer achieved an unsurpassed integration with the setting. House and garden were unified visually and formally, and the latter was designed by his friend Roberto Burle Marx, a master of the art. All the forms can be read as abstractions of vegetation or rocks, and the large preserved rock outcrop became the pivot of the composition. It links pool to house, supports a roof column, marks the tapering edge of the stairs, and dominates views of the house. As in a Japanese garden, it also stands as a miniature of the hills to either side, which in turn are integrated into the space like living murals — the abstract spatial continuity of early modern architecture here became palpable and intensely habitable. Niemeyer pushed the *plan libre* to new extremes of freedom, but for all its suave sophistication his house also conjures up the atmosphere of a primitive shelter: as a vision of an earthly paradise it has few rivals.

A similar vision was realized, using very different architectural means, by the Mexican Luis Barragán, who was renowned almost as much for his gardens as for his buildings. Born in Guadalajara in 1902, he trained as an engineer but almost immediately made the move into architecture, completing a couple of dozen Spanish Colonial style projects in his native city over the next decade. He travelled to Europe in 1931 and 1932, where he met Le Corbusier and assimilated the ideas espoused in *L'Esprit Nouveau*. Eager to practise the new architecture on his return, he moved to Mexico City, where he rapidly completed some thirty projects in an accomplished and markedly anonymous version of the

Above, right and opposite.
Niemeyer House, Rio de Janeiro,
Brazil, 1953, Oscar Niemeyer. By
radically separating the lower,
bedroom, floor from the living level,
Niemeyer achieved an unprecedented
freedom of planning and a total
integration of house, garden
(designed by Roberto Burle Marx)
and landscape.

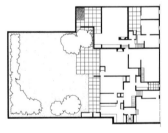

Above, right and opposite
Barragán House and Studio, Mexico
City, Mexico, 1947, Luis Barragán.
Designed as a refuge from the tumult
of the city, Barragán's house deploys
simple architectural means – cubic
volumes, planes of colour, stone floors
– to elemental effect, not least in the
almost surreal roof-garden.

International Style. Then, in 1940, he informed his clients and friends that he was retiring from commercial practice, acquired a large estate and developed a house for himself. Externally it still bore the marks of the International style, however the organization was based not on an open plan but on rooms inside and, just as important, outside, in the interlinked walled gardens. Seven years later, he built a second house on a site nearby, which he continued to work on throughout his life. It became his living laboratory, and in the process grew into one of the century's great dwellings.

Barragán House and Studio Mexico City, Mexico, 1947, Luis Barragán

Externally the Barragán House and Studio are stark and unremarkable, an anonymous presence in its unpretentious neighbourhood. But as soon as you open the door the ambience is unique. It owes something to Spanish Colonial architecture, much more to the vivid colours of traditional Mexican building and, in the preference for geometric clarity, to the International Style. But the whole is new and timeless. The walls are framed in concrete and filled with concrete blocks; most are roughly plastered and brilliantly coloured, their intensity and rough textures enhanced by indirect lighting. The only other materials you see are large pine beams, wide floorboards and volcanic rock paving and steps. The living room faces a main garden contained by ivy-clad walls, like a captive slice of jungle intended to bring the pleasures of wild nature into the house. You look into the garden through a vast sheet of glass divided by a thin cruciform mullion. This religious note is entirely deliberate, adding a mystical quality to the boundary between interior and garden, where nature was allowed free rein – Barragán chose to introduce no objects, nor to interfere in the processes of growth and decay.

From the hall a granite staircase supported by a yellow wall connects to the bedrooms, and from the upper floor a small staircase leads up to the roof garden – an abstract world now open only to the sky (he raised the walls higher in 1954 to block out Mexico City's growing skyline). It clearly owed something to Le Corbusier, and is contained by vividly coloured walls – cream and terracotta, scarlet and purple – of varying heights, interspersed with tall blocks of plain cement render. In a light less intense than Mexico's it would easily turn to kitsch and in photographs it can look slightly lurid, but this is misleading. According to the Portuguese architect Alvaro Siza: 'The photographs show vivid, pure colours – the colours one finds in any Mexico City street, or in a Mayan ruin – but of my visit to Barragán's house, the colour I remember is gold.'

Octavio Paz, the Nobel Prize-winning novelist, has written that the 'Mexican searches for the silence of closed worlds', and in what has become the world's most populous city Barragán's house was designed as a defence. 'The walls create silence', he said, and sheltered by them he could face life. Deeply Catholic, Barragán believed beauty has a redemptive quality and that a stoical acceptance of solitude was part of our fate. His house was also inextricably bound up with ideas on time: with the luxury of 'wasting' time in contemplative inaction; with surfaces that register the passage of time through the development of patina – unlike those of the International Style, unchanging and timeless; and finally with the ability of the house to evolve through time in response to his needs – the cross of redemption in the window, for example, was one of his last interventions. A bastion against the tumult of modern life, Barragán's house was more like a life

Below and opposite Jaoul Houses, Neuilly-sur-Seine, France, 1954, Le Corbusier. Like the *béton brut* of the Marseilles Unité, the exterior of the Jaoul Houses signalled the new, tougher sensibility of Le Corbusier's post-war work. Internally, however, they are marvellously inviting: punctuated by sculptural built-in furniture and bursts of brilliant colour, the spaces unfold freely along and across the shallow vaults.

Top Villa Sarabhai, Ahmedabad, India, 1951–6, Le Corbusier. The vaulted Monol-type was combined with materials such as handmade bricks to create a modern Indian vernacular.

Jaoul Houses Neuilly-sur-Seine, France, 1954, Le Corbusier

lived than a design: it offers a compelling critique of the belief that a true dwelling can be reduced to either an industrial product or an unchanging work of art.

Le Corbusier's post-war houses continued the move towards rougher, natural materials and the muscular, sculpturally expressive forms of the Unité at Marseilles. In 1951, in a pair of houses at Neuilly-sur-Seine on the edge of Paris – close to the Cook and Stein houses – he returned to the vaulted structure of the Weekend House of 1935. The Jaoul Houses, as they were called, were composed of a narrow and a wide band of space, with shallow Catalan vaults of rough concrete forming the suspended floors and roofs. Internally and externally, the finishes were deliberately crude and tough – roughly pointed brickwork, tiles, board-marked concrete – but the spaces were rendered enticingly habitable by a revetment of plaster and timber.

On their completion in 1954 the Jaoul Houses divided even Le Corbusier's most fervent admirers, some of whom seemed to have forgotten the Weekend House and must have ignored or not taken seriously the eulogies of peasant building that peppered his writings of the 1940s. They provoked a celebrated debate in England. Peter Smithson thought they were perfectly poised 'on the knife edge of peasantism', whereas James Stirling, in an influential article for *The Architectural Review* entitled 'From Garches to Jaoul', criticized them as a dangerous retreat from the polemical vigour of what the Smithsons later christened the 'Heroic Period' of the 1920s. But when, in the same year that his article appeared, Stirling came to design a group of flats at Ham Common the influence of the Jaoul Houses was obvious, as it was in many buildings of the late 1950s and 1960s.

Following an invitation in 1951 to plan Chandigarh, the new capital of the Punjab, Le Corbusier received several private commissions in India. They included two for houses in Ahmedabad, centre of the textile industry. In them he brought the Monol and Citrohan/Dom-Ino types to a new peak of spatial refinement. Handmade sun-dried bricks and rough concrete were the modern vernacular of India and for the first of the houses, for Manorama Sarabhai, his wife and their extended family, Le Corbusier opted for the vaulted Monol type. The main body of the house is ten bays wide, and the interior expands laterally through large gaps in the supporting brick walls to form a deep, freely spreading space. Rectangular and free-form timber boxes, housing bathrooms and other service spaces, sit below the concrete beams, frequently bridging the spatial units to establish a counterpoint to the dominant grain.

The open ends of the house are oriented towards the prevailing winds to ventilate the interior naturally, with the glazing and infill panels set well back to provide shading and form generous covered porches. The roof, accessible from a small upper storey, was grassed and planted to become, Le Corbusier said, 'a magnificent garden of lawn and charming flowers'. To cope with the heavy storms brought by the monsoon winds it was provided with a system of concrete channels: water from the first floor disgorges through large gargoyles, while that from the upper level plunges dramatically down an enormous chute, like a children's slide, into a pool. To the Indian architect Charles Correa, the Sarabhai House was a masterly response to the needs of an extended family, 'as complex, as amorphous, and as open-ended as a Banyan tree'.

Above Villa Shodhan, Ahmedabad, India, 1952–6, Le Corbusier. Adapted to the Indian climate, the vision of the modern house as a continuous, three-dimensional field of space shielded by *brises-soleil* found a compelling new form.

Halfway House Transvaal, South Africa, 1976, Stanley Saitowitz

At first sight the Villa Shodhan, the second house, forms a complete contrast: upright, four-square and permeable, it is a descendant of the Dom-Ino type explored at length in the 1920s. In keeping with his new, robust manner and in response to the climate, concrete piers have replaced spindly *pilotis*, large areas of solid wall alternate with deep *brises-soleil* and porches, and the roof garden has given way to a shady parasol. The composition exploits the freedom of the *plan libre*, although the majority of the spatial divisions follow the lines of the structural grid. In this respect it resembles the Sarabhai House, but whereas there the space expands only horizontally, here it is fully three-dimensional. Alan Colquhoun has remarked that the Corbusian free plan was won at the expense of a paralysis of the section, with space sandwiched between the floor slabs. Here we see Le Corbusier attempting to free the section through the complex interlocking of single-, double- and triple-height spaces to create an interior through which both the eye and the air can move freely.

Like the Unité at Marseilles, Le Corbusier's post-war houses make clear that his belief in a machine-age utopia had given way to a concern for a timeless, elemental relationship with nature. Deeply moved by the experience of India, he wrote about the 'possibility of getting in touch with the essential joys of Hindu principles: a brotherhood of relationships between the cosmos and all living things'. Although they were not always cast in such heroic terms, architectural expressions of affinity with nature have been a recurring theme in modern architecture, as they were two decades later for a young and then unknown South African architect, Stanley Saitowitz.

We noted in Chapter 2 that a strong group of young Modernists flourished in South Africa. They built several fine houses in a post-Corbusian style but the most talented among them, Rex Martienssen, died tragically young in 1942 and after the war the impetus was lost. The darkening political climate was not conducive to further development but in the 1970s Saitowitz – who now works in San Francisco – designed a house that beautifully illustrates the meeting of global and local cultures we have been exploring. It is located, somewhat confusingly, at Halfway House (which I will use as its name), on six acres of savannah on the high veld in the Transvaal.

Saitowitz's ideas – which he characterizes as 'geological architecture' – were informed by studying the homes of the native N'debele people. Made from the earth on which they stand, the houses are loosely gathered to form a settlement defined by walls and thresholds. Freshly painted, the mud walls bloom in the spring, only to erode in the summer rains, and then be remade by the occupants each winter: their architecture, like their agriculture, is inseparable from the natural rhythms of the seasons, and their houses are more like a process than a product.

Halfway House is sited in the shelter of a cluster of rocks, against which a circle was marked on the ground; within it, the contours were heightened by terracing and planted with alternating strains of grass. Close to the rocks the terraces sweep up to form a series of arched roofs, which are then staggered to allow light to pour in at high level through the gaps. Echoing the roofs, the straight, parallel terrace walls turn into semi-circles which ripple out from the bathroom, growing in scale, to celebrate – Saitowitz explained – the curves of the

Above and right Halfway House,
Transvaal, South Africa, 1976 Stanley
Saitowitz. Lightweight, seemingly
improvised, the design is a response
to the rocky outcrops and towering
clouds of the high veld and creates
a richly habitable place in the
open landscape.

115

body within the geometric system; in the process they define specific 'places' within the spatial field. Both the language and strategy owe a debt to the Dutch architect Aldo van Eyck, who was the first to use the word 'place' in the 1950s as a counter to the abstraction of Modernist 'space', and whose temporary Sonsbeek sculpture pavilion used a similar geometry of parallel walls broken by circular enclosures. The living space flows freely across changes of level within the billowing enclosure. It is closed at one end by the box-like kitchen and at the other by the bathroom, and opens onto an 'oasis' and lawn within the dry landscape through continuous runs of sliding-folding doors. With its artfully layered geometries, Halfway House uses the disciplines of the free plan to create architectural counterpoint of considerable sophistication.

The spatial complexity is matched by the layers of association created by the forms. From a distance, the house appears to be all roof, and like Knut Knutsen's summer house, almost as much an outcrop as the rocks beside which it has settled. But the roofs are light and delicate, earth-bound abstractions of the towering clouds of the high veld. Seen from inside, the tapering gaps burst the space dramatically open and frame views of the sky. When the torrential rains come, water cascades down the stepped roof surfaces and fills a narrow channel – a 'moat' Saitowitz calls it – which unerringly marks in the ground the undulating profile of the roofs, cutting, like a stream in a flash flood, unexpectedly across the paved surfaces. As symbols of rocks and clouds the roofs relate the house to earth and sky, yet they also evoke almost subliminal echoes of the traditional huts of the N'debele, with their thatched roofs draped over stone walls like giant hats.

With its bow trusses and apparently casually juxtaposed roof sections, Halfway House looks almost improvised, like a slightly more refined version of a shelter you might assemble out of the bits and pieces of an old barn. This apparent casualness is a significant part of its artistry, and something of the same spirit is apparent in the Nicholas House (1977–80) by the Australian architect Glenn Murcutt. Here vernacular materials and details – such as corrugated iron roofs, water butts and pivoting ventilation shutters of agricultural provenance – are melded with the planning and tectonic disciplines of Mies van der Rohe and the California School that we explore in the next chapter. First and foremost, however, Murcutt's houses are a response to the landscape, above all to the Australian light. Their delicate, at times fragile, forms are designed to exploit a light so intense that trees like the eucalyptus turn the edges rather than faces of their leaves to the sun. In moister climes the atmosphere unites near and far, but in Australia the dazzling light fragments the landscape, isolating rather than connecting things.

Externally, Murcutt exploits the unforgiving light to emphasize the individual elements of structure and the passage of time. Members project and slide past each other to cast shadows, the roof is reduced to a rippling plane of metal supported by slender steel purlins, the play of shadows on the corrugated walls records the movement of the high sun. Internally, the light is filtered and reflected, permeating the house to create a uniformly luminous whole: colours are homogeneous, textures less pronounced, and partitions meet the roof as transparent planes of glass to ensure continuity of vision and inter-reflection of light.

Opposite Nicholas House, Mount Irvine, New South Wales, Australia, 1977–80, Glenn Murcutt. The shed-like front of the house echoes the agricultural buildings of the region, whilst to the rear the same profiled-steel roof is bent into artful curves.

Magney House Bingi Point, Australia, 1984, Glenn Murcutt

Magney House, completed in 1984 on Bingi Point, New South Wales, represents a lyrical peak in the development of Murcutt's favourite house-type, a long metal pavilion with, ideally, an en-suite sequence of rooms. It sits on 33 hectares (82 acres) of bare, almost tree-less coastal land, where the clients had camped regularly and wanted a house that would preserve a sense of relaxation. The linear plan is oriented east-west and organized around central living and dining areas, with the parents' bedroom at one end, and two for children or visitors at the other. Along the southern (sunless) frontage is a narrow band of service spaces – kitchens, toilets, showers, and so on – and next to them a longitudinal open passage which turns into a closed corridor only where needed to separate the children's/guest bedrooms.

The section, with its sinuous, asymmetrical gull-wing roof, directly echoes the plan and was developed in response to the prevailing winds and solar penetration. The southerly elevation is solid brick up to 2.1 metres (7 feet), above which a sloping glass clerestory is cantilevered out with pivoting wooden slats, in the horizontal gap between wall and glass, to allow for cross-ventilation in summer. The north elevation is fully glazed, with continuous external louvres in front of sliding doors and a roof overhang – restrained by elegant diagonal ties – to exclude high sun from the clerestory. Louvres and doors can all open to give the occupants the feeling of sitting outdoors. Seen from close to, the house is an exquisitely made object; at a distance, it is reduced to an evanescent silver slash in the landscape, as if to obey the Aboriginal injunction to 'touch this earth lightly'.

The love of clarity of construction evident in Murcutt's houses has been a recurring theme in English architecture. William Morris, we may recall, ascribed ethical value to 'truth to materials' and his favourite building was a medieval tithe barn at Great Coxwell, Gloucestershire, a majestic work of pure construction. A similar commitment informs the work of Edward Cullinan, who traces many of his architectural values back to the Arts and Crafts movement. Cullinan's love of how buildings are made manifested itself in a desire to build as well as design. This led, as he observed, to 'a mode of construction and expression that uses a severely limited range of available materials, puts a stress on "placed together" joints and junctions, has materials mastering and oversailing one another and avoids the partial sophistication of "flushness" and hidden detailing.' In his own house, built in 1963 in a mews in London's Camden Town, Cullinan turned these principles into a language of great subtlety and power. Built between two party walls, two-storeys high to the north, one-storey to the south, the house has a cave-like base of London stock bricks containing bedrooms and a bathroom, above which an open-plan, timber-framed eyrie is layered over and between concrete columns and beams. To the rear of the tiny plot a single garage was somehow squeezed in. Its roof became a terrace, accessible from the inside via a timber deck and steps from the living room, and from the outside by narrow steps and an ingenious ramp which wrapped up and around the back of the garage under the foliage of a sycamore tree – a miniature but authentic *promenade architecturale*.

In the work of the German architect Walter Segal, who settled in London in 1936, an interest in self-building led to the development of a readily assembled timber-building system based on the American balloon-frame. He tried it out on

Below and opposite Magney House, Bingi Point, New South Wales, Australia, 1984, Glenn Murcutt. Combining his favourite linear plan-type with a suavely curvilinear roof, Murcutt creates a statement of great elegance and clarity, its under-stated formality a perfect foil to the relaxed life of holidays by the sea.

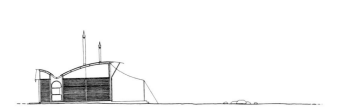

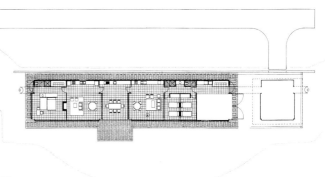

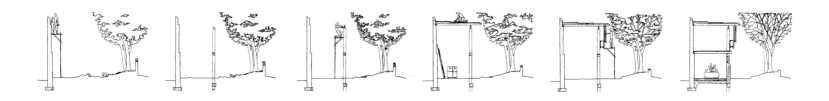

Creek Vean Pill Creek, Cornwall, England, 1966, Team 4

himself in 1963, building the 'Little House' in his back garden. Then, eventually, after many false dawns, in 1976 the council of the London borough of Lewisham approved – by one vote – a proposal to set up a self-build housing scheme for people on their housing waiting list. It took almost three more years for work to begin on site, and by mid-1980 fourteen unique council houses were ready for occupation. 'He taught us to think for ourselves', said one of the builder-residents, 'and gave us such confidence when we finished our houses we felt we could go on to do anything we set our minds to – he literally changed our lives'. In *Eupalinos or the Architect* the poet Paul Valéry has his architect observe that, 'By dint of constructing. . . I truly believe that I have constructed myself'. The houses and lives of Cullinan and Segal testify to the power of this belief.

The love of clear construction was combined with a passion for landscape in arguably the finest English house built in the 1960s, Creek Vean by Norman Foster and Richard Rogers, then practising with their wives Wendy and Sue as Team 4. Hugging the contours of a Cornish headland and opening to the views through splayed rooms, the plan is spilt into two wings by a grass-covered staircase. Inspired by Aalto's example at Säynätsalo Town Hall, its straight steps appear organically curved in perspective, like natural contours, due to the irregular geometry. Cornwall had long been a favourite haunt of English Modernists and a colony of artists had flourished in St Ives since the 1930s. The house contained many examples of their work – by Ben Nicholson, Barbara Hepworth and Patrick Heron, among others – which evoked the spirit of modernity and place that drew artists to this unique peninsula. Externally, the bare concrete-block surfaces are softened by vegetation spilling down from the roofs. Inside, the crisply geometric spaces unfold like an inner landscape beneath a sinuous roof, epitomizing a liberating functionalism which, by reducing things to essentials and inscribing itself into the landscape, heightens our awareness of the ever-changing nuances of a local light of unsurpassed clarity.

As an expression of a new machine for civilization, the International Style aspired to a global relevance predicated on unending economic growth. Culturally, as we have seen, these ideals were being questioned as early as the 1930s, but in the commercial sphere they went unchallenged and by the 1960s Miesian steel-and-glass towers were the dominant emblem of multinational corporate power. It took the oil crisis of the 1970s to make businesses look seriously at the energy consequences of large areas of glass, which were often unsuited to the climate and necessitated air-conditioning for comfort. But in most of the houses we have examined in this chapter efforts were made to respond to the climate, and in some – those by Barragán and Murcutt, for example – it was a major determinant of their design. In the work of the English architect Ralph Erskine, who has lived in Sweden all his professional life, climatic considerations were of overwhelming importance well before worries about global warming forced them into every architect's consciousness.

Erskine's convictions were partly born out of necessity when he built a tiny house near Stockholm – known as 'The Box' – for himself and his wife in 1942. It consisted of only two spaces, kitchen and living room, in which the bed doubled as a sofa and could be lifted up to the ceiling to free the space for work. The

Above Walters Way Self-build Housing, Lewisham, England, 1976–85, Walter Segal. This group of fourteen houses was built by their residents using the 'Segal System' of timber construction. Ecologically ahead of its time, it allowed for the possibility of the houses being taken apart and their components re-used.
Opposite and below Cullinan House, London, England, 1963, Edward Cullinan. This self-built house is organized as a timber 'nest' of living space above a brick 'cave' of bedrooms, and detailed to simplify and celebrate the process of construction.

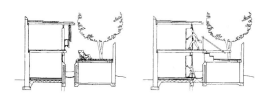

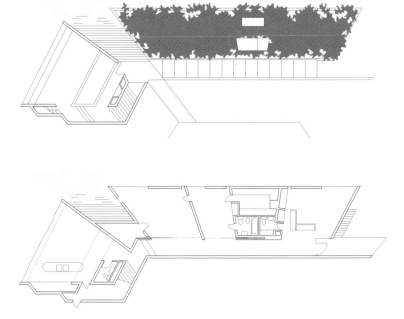

Above right and opposite Creek
Vean, Pill Creek, Cornwall, England,
1966, Team 4. Tucked tightly into a
steep headland and engulfed in plants,
the house makes the most of the
Cornish landscape and light by opening
to the views and sky through splayed
reflecting walls and a linear roof-light.

only water was from a well, the only heat from a log fire. Along the north elevation Erskine placed a hollowed-out 'thick wall' for storage, from which his desk folded down and against which, under cover outside, logs were stacked to increase the insulation. To the south, the living room's full-height glazing captured winter sun, but was saved from overheating in summer by the oversailing roof.

Erskine's fascination with climate assumed more dramatic form in the Villa Ström, built near Stockholm in 1961. The house sits on a steep slope and is entered at high level, from where the spaces spiral down, around the central fireplace, growing in volume in a manner reminiscent of Adolf Loos's *Raumplan* as much as modern 'flowing space'. The form is cubic, to minimize the external envelope, and the balconies are freestanding structures to prevent thermal transmission through their exposed surfaces. On the roof, angled plates reflect the low sun into the heart of the house through roof lights, the light spilling down over the hearth. Energy from sun, fire and wind was central to Erskine's conception of a building, and as we shall see, in the era of global warming many of the 'passive' energy-control ideas he pioneered have become part of the language of architecture.

Can Lis Porto Petro, Majorca, Spain, 1973, Jørn Utzon

No house better sums up the issues we have considered in this chapter than Can Lis, the home Jørn Utzon built for himself and his wife Lis on Majorca in 1973. As befits its Mediterranean setting, Can Lis has classical roots – 'crystal clear forms on a site-adjusted base', as Utzon puts it. But the architect's openness to the possibilities of the site, the use of locally available materials, and the creative collaboration with the masons who built it, lend the composition a suppleness and ease that are more often to be found in a vernacular building. Sited on a long strip of land running between a narrow, pine-roofed road and a precipitous 20-metre- (66-foot-) high cliff, it consists of a series of small buildings and walled patios. Each is adjusted to the site and to the horizon, and there are tapering gaps between them to allow glimpses through to the sea. You enter via a generous covered porch beneath which, in a gesture of welcome as much symbolic as practical, stands a tiled bench. Open the plain wooden door and you are greeted by a crescent moon-shaped opening through which you glimpse the slender, twisted trunk of a young pine silhouetted against the blazing light – the moon was inspired by nothing more exotic than the name of the road, Media Luna, Half Moon.

After this magical moment of arrival you are drawn into the golden light of a nine-square plan, colonnaded court, from where you face the sea on a stone platform which steps down towards a low wall. It feels timeless, ancient as the ruins of a Greek *stoa*. The kitchen and dining room line the rear wall, and under one of the colonnades is another stone bench and a table over which is draped a tiled 'cloth'. Retracing your steps you pass under cover into a small court and from there into the living room. As high as it is deep and receding upwards into shade, it is articulated by a free-standing column into a square sitting space and narrow, L-shaped passage. Roughly at the centre of the square Utzon put three unequal tables – sectors of an implied polygon – and around them an almost semi-circular couch, also of stone with blue tiled nosings and white cushions. Large enough to gather the whole family in its embrace before the spectacle of Nature, the couch is a permanent emblem of the values he holds most dear.

Above Erskine House ('The Box'), Lissma, Sweden, 1942, Ralph Erskine. With its concern for the minutiae of living, fully-glazed south-facing living space and solid north wall insulated by storage inside and stacked logs outside, this tiny house exemplifies the principles which inform Erskine's later work.

Opposite Villa Ström, near Stockholm, Sweden, 1961, Ralph Erskine. Minimizing heat losses and maximizing exposure to sun and daylight generated the cubic form, light reflectors and free-standing balconies of this climate-responsive house.

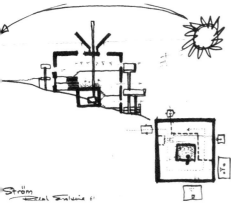

Ström
Ralal Erskine 6?

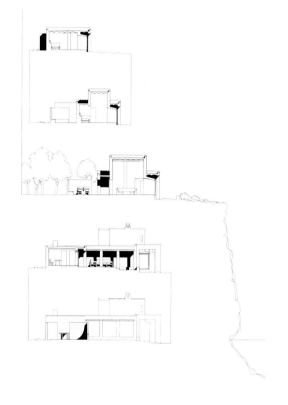

From the seat you view the world through windows large enough to stand in, with deep reveals and soffits angled inwards and downwards to direct your gaze towards the meeting of sea and sky. In mid-afternoon a slice of sun, so distinct you feel you could pick it up, falls on the floor to the left, through a small glazed opening – too rudimentary to call a 'window' – placed high in the west wall. Minutes later, a diagonal slash of wall above the windows is dusted with light, intensifying for a few precious minutes into a stone-dissolving shaft only to recede, leaving a glowing patch of light to linger in the opening as a reminder of the sun's daily visit.

If the Villa Savoye remains, after almost three-quarters of a century, the most compelling vision of the early Modernist dream of a new way of living, serviced by machines and detached from the particularities of place, Can Lis represents a high point of that other face of Modernism, pioneered by Le Corbusier in the wake of a second world war, which sought to renew a declining Western civilization through recourse to the primordial. It is a measure of the architect's artistry that Can Lis feels as natural as the sun, stone and sea whose intercourse it celebrates.

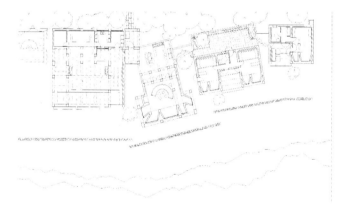

Above and opposite Can Lis, Porto Petro, Majorca, Spain, 1973, Jørn Utzon. Built on a dramatic cliff-top site Utzon's vacation/retirement home uses the readily available building materials of Majorca to create a house imbued with the spirit of the Mediterranean, ancient as Mycenae yet unmistakably modern in its abstraction and acute sensitivity to place.

the american dream

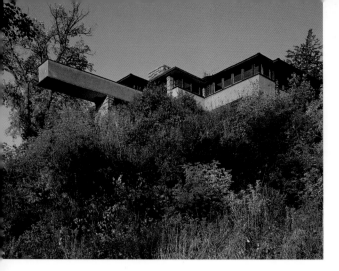

Taliesin East Spring Green, Wisconsin, USA, 1911, Frank Lloyd Wright

Above and opposite Taliesin East, Spring Green, Wisconsin, USA, 1911, Frank Lloyd Wright. Intended to be 'of, not on, the hill', Wright's home and studio was designed to grow out of the landscape as naturally as the rock strata it emulated.

America's greatest monuments are the work of Nature, not Man, and the canonical American houses are all rural, not urban – the southern plantation house, Jefferson's Monticello, Thoreau's hut by Walden Pond, Frank Lloyd Wright's Fallingwater. When asked to explain his approach to architecture Wright said, 'I was born an American child of the ground and of space'. To Wright, as to many Americans, the family house occupying its own plot of land was an emblem of freedom and the basis of American democracy, for which he invented the word Usonia. The frontier might no longer be there in reality, but the frontier spirit, determined to push ever-outwards into open space and virgin land, was still alive in the imagination, finding its ultimate expression in the twentieth century in putting men on the moon. Asked by clients how far out of the city they should look for land, Wright advised them to go 'ten times as far as you think you ought to go' because the future, he was convinced, lay in decentralization and re-establishing contact with the earth. And when he said a natural house should 'grow out of the ground' on which it stood, he meant it quite literally: all Wright's great houses were driven by his desire to derive their architecture from the land.

The Prairie houses were Wright's first attempt to design a natural house, although as we have seen their relationship to the landscape was abstract rather than direct. Their influence is still very much apparent in Taliesin East, the home and studio Wright built for himself in 1911 in Wisconsin, but there the buildings are inseparable from the terrain. The siting was critical: the house is wrapped around a hill, of which it becomes the brow – Wright had Welsh ancestry and Taliesin is an old Welsh word meaning 'shining brow'. The house is no longer 'on the hill', he said, but 'of the hill', and after studying the rock strata visible in the landscape he took the 'outcropping ledges in the façades of the hills' as the model for his stonework. All traces of ornament were expunged, leaving Nature to provide the decoration – 'icicles by invitation might beautify the eaves', he suggested; the 'sweeping, soft air of the rain' would make 'music on the roofs'; and entire walls of glazed doors could 'open to the breezes of summer and become like an open camp'.

Wright's aspirations were rooted in the Romantic tradition that figured so strongly in nineteenth-century American thought, and as such are hardly new. What was new, and so radically new that it takes some effort to see through its seeming naturalness, is the way he gave formal expression to the idea of uniting architecture and nature. The richly layered timbers and rubble stone walls of Greene and Greene's Gamble House shared a similar ambition, but are still eminently recognizable as a 'house' and a 'terrace', whereas in Taliesin, as Neil Levine has suggested, 'the piers and parapets of stone, the planes of plaster, and the lines of shingled roof are experienced primarily as . . . shapes disengaged from any figurative role'. By collapsing the familiar image of a house Wright was able to rid himself of all traces of traditional styles, freeing his architecture to take Nature as its model. Traditional houses might be articulated to link to their sites, but Wright's would now appear to grow out of the site, as he put it, 'like the rocks and trees'. The walls of Taliesin were not calculated to *look like* an outcrop, but *made as if they were* outcrops, seemingly as natural as strata exposed by millennia of erosion.

The aspirations first realized at Taliesin informed all Wright's later work, to a

Above La Miniatura (Millard House), Pasadena, California, USA, 1922–3, Frank Lloyd Wright. Built of specially designed concrete 'textile blocks', La Miniatura was Wright's first attempt to design a house which blossomed from the landscape of Southern California.

greater or lesser extent, beginning with a series of houses in California designed in the 1920s. These include the monumental Hollyhock House and four others built using a 'textile-block' construction system invented in 1906. The first and most delicate of the latter was built for Alice Millard, a former client from the Prairie Style period who was now widowed and wanted to run her rare book and antique business from home. The budget was tight and the client small – hence the name Wright gave the house, La Miniatura. He persuaded her to buy a cheap 'unbuildable' site in a small ravine, which had two beautiful eucalyptus trees and struck him as typically Californian. The plan consists of two interlocking squares; the one nearer the road contains the entrance loggia and a garage, while to the rear is a three-storey cubic volume. At ground level are the servant's room, kitchen and dining room, which opens onto a terrace overlooking a small pond. Above are a double-height living room and guest room, and on the top floor Mrs Millard's bedroom, also double height, with a balcony overlooking the living room and a door leading onto a terrace on the garage roof.

La Miniatura Pasadena, California, USA, 1922–3, Frank Lloyd Wright

With his textile-block system Wright aimed, as he put it, to 'take that despised outcast of the building industry – the concrete block' and 'make it live as a thing of beauty – textured like the trees'. For the Millard House he designed three units: a plain one, used mainly for solid internal partitions; a cross-shaped pattern, which could be embossed or perforated, and left permeable for screen walls or sealed by casting in glass; and a type with a square boss on its face and U-shaped channels in its sides, which used back-to-back to form piers. The 40-centimetre (16-inch) square grid of the blocks controlled all the vertical and horizontal dimensions – even those you cannot see, like the spacing of the floor joists. The square motifs in the blocks established additional controlling dimensions for details like mullions and transoms. They appeared to extend outwards in all four directions, permeating the surfaces and making clear the meaning of 'textile' block: the spaces are woven as a continuous three-dimensional fabric, supressing, so as not to disturb the system, the reinforced concrete columns and beams that were structurally necessary.

'Standardization was the soul of the machine,' Wright explained, 'and here I was the Weaver taking it as a principle, knitting a great future for it.' Several of Wright's key ideas have been persuasively linked to the nineteenth-century German architect Gottfried Semper, whose theory of the 'Four Elements' (earthwork, hearth, framework/roof and lightweight enclosure) were widely discussed in Chicago in the 1890s. They are clearly legible in the Prairie houses and it seems likely that in developing the weaving analogy Wright had in mind Semper's discussion of textiles as one of the earliest forms of enclosure, and of the transposition of ideas from one medium to another. If the Greeks could emulate timber construction in stone, why could he not 'weave' in concrete? Externally, Wright's exquisite perspective looking down on the house beside its pond stressed graphically the link to the eucalyptus trees. But to my eyes the blocks do not seem so much to be 'textured like the trees' as studded with flowers, like those other beguiling images of earthly paradise, Persian carpets. What is unmistakable is the pervasive organic quality, the feeling that the house has blossomed from its site, like plants luxuriating in the sun. The Millard House

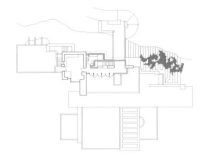

Fallingwater Bear Run, Pennsylvania, USA, 1935–9, Frank Lloyd Wright

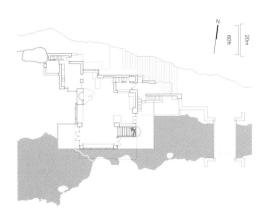

Above, left and opposite
Fallingwater, Bear Run, Pennsylvania,
USA, 1935–9, Frank Lloyd Wright.
Designed 'to the music of the stream',
Fallingwater was a structural and
compositional tour de force which
represented a lyrical peak in Wright's
search for the 'Natural House'.

was a convincing beginning to Wright's search for 'a distinctly genuine expression of California', and in later and larger designs in the series he went on to break up the block-like character and develop the plans along out-reaching diagonals.

Among twentieth-century buildings Fallingwater, built at Bear Run in north-west Pennsylvania in 1935–9, is probably second only to Sydney Opera House in public recognition. The clients were Edgar and Liliane Kaufmann, owners of the Kaufmann department store in nearby Pittsburgh. They were introduced to Wright through their son, Edgar Jr, who had started work the previous year as an apprentice at the Taliesin Fellowship, Wright's combined office and school. They decided to commission a 'forest retreat' on their 650-hectare (1600-acre) estate in the Allegheny Mountains, and the idea of building a house 'to the music of the stream' occurred to Wright on his first visit. It took nine months to mature and the first time he touched paper was during the two hours it took his client to drive from Milwaukee to Taliesin, after Kaufmann had 'phoned ahead to ask if it would be all right to come and see the drawings'. The design was living in his mind and the plans and sections Wright hastily set down defined all its essential features. He named it 'Fallingwater' just before Kaufmann arrived.

The house was structured as a series of reinforced concrete trays, cantilevered from a rock ledge next to the stream and supported by orthogonally arranged load-bearing walls and piers. They were of local stone, specially quarried nearby and laid, like those at Taliesin, in irregularly coursed horizontal beds, the thinner of which project to form narrow ledges: the result is indeed more like eroded sedimentary rock than a conventional wall. The plan is organized around a 'great room' which, as in the Prairie houses, moves from entrance and hearth to glazed screens and open terraces – towards which you gravitate, drawn by the sound of falling water. The hearth is the surface of an enormous boulder, which emerges through the shiny flagstone floor like a rock in a stream. It had added significance for the Kaufmanns, having been Edgar's favourite resting-spot before the house was built.

The terraces cantilever dramatically more than 5 metres (16 feet) out over the stream below – seen from the bridge as you approach the effect of suspension in space is staggering – and the main room not only opens out but up, through a glazed concrete trellis, and down, through a sliding glass hatch onto a concrete staircase, hung by steel bars and descending to the stream. Wright thought it might be possible to deepen the stream for swimming at this point, but the stair was as much an excuse to create the symbolically necessary connection. Above and to the rear of the living room, the bedrooms pinwheel around the large chimney, each a miniature of the space you have left, with its own fire and floating terrace.

Wright described the house as 'an extension of the cliff' and anchored it back with a concrete trellis that continues the plane of the first-floor tray through the rear stone wall. One of the beams forms a semi-circle to wrap around the trunk of a tree, emphasizing the integration with nature. Framed and contrasted, the ridges on the tree's bark are echoed in the striated surfaces of the stones behind. Like all the exposed concrete, the beams are painted a pale peach-cream. Wright originally wanted to coat them with gold leaf, and when even this

most enthusiastic of clients deemed that too expensive he explored aluminium as an alternative. Then he experimented with a paint containing mica flakes, which he thought would be more sympathetic to the stone. The choice of finish was critical, as the concrete trays are almost all one sees on approaching the house through the woods. Wright's intentions are clarified by an observation Lewis Mumford made shortly after the house was completed: 'The stones represent, as it were, the earth theme; the concrete slabs are the water theme'. Wright always thought of concrete as a fluid material – of which the spiralling Guggenheim Museum in New York became the ultimate expression – and detailed it, as here, with rounded edges and corners. He wanted the surfaces to come alive by both responding to, and evoking, the light flashing from the running water or flickering through the foliage. Gold leaf would also have given the illusion, he said, of the glisten of water on dying autumnal leaves.

Throughout his life Wright was fascinated by natural processes, especially the large-scale ones revealed by geology. He thought of stone as the 'basic material of our planet' which reveals the laws of 'cosmic change', and whereas Taliesin had been an essentially static expression of the relative permanence of geologic features – in terms of human time – Fallingwater was an image of flux. At one end of the timescale the structure and volumes of this extraordinarily dynamic composition evoke the processes of transformation and erosion that affect rocks. At the other, by heightening our awareness of the ever-changing forest light and sounds of moving water, they provide a vivid reminder that life is perpetual flux.

Unlike Wright's earlier work, Fallingwater was sufficiently Modern to satisfy MOMA's criteria and in 1938 they gave it a one-building exhibition, emphasizing the apparent links to the International Style. The similarities were, however, superficial. Developments in Europe surely contributed to the elimination of ornament and a greater freedom in planning, but Wright's work never followed a set of stylistic formulae and was grounded in unchanging principles whose expression could vary dramatically according to the demands of the site, climate and materials. This was made abundantly clear in the project on which he began work in 1937, his winter home and studio in the desert near Phoenix, which he named Taliesin West. The plan was based on the earlier design, but overlaid with a diagonal geometry that rendered it dynamic, and established – partly by luck, partly by judgement – alignments to major features in the surrounding landscape. The building was anchored to the desert not so much by careful siting as by calculated orientation.

Taliesin West Scottsdale, Arizona, USA, 1937–8, Frank Lloyd Wright

At one level, like its namesake in Wisconsin, Taliesin West can be interpreted as a response to the physical landscape. The battered walls, made of what Wright called 'desert rubble stone', echo the surrounding mountains, which he described as 'spotted like the leopard's skin', and to reinforce the link their surfaces are grooved horizontally to suggest the erosion patterns found in desert canyons. But just as clearly, the forms were intended to recall the site's cultural history. Characteristic Toltec-Mayan profiles are evoked and, in places, the forms bring to mind a wide-bellied basket or jar. Visitors were given pointers in this direction by the petroglyph stone that greeted their arrival and by large jars placed at key points around the complex. The latter recalled the idea, expressed by the Chinese philosopher Lao-

Above Taliesin West, Scottsdale, Arizona, USA, 1937–8, Frank Lloyd Wright. In his new winter home and studio, Wright combined the now familiar 'geological' response to the landscape with an interest in the traces of the desert site's archaeological history.
Opposite Fallingwater, Bear Run, Pennsylvania, USA, 1935–9, Frank Lloyd Wright. Light and and space seem to cascade through the trellis and staircase, which leads down from the living room to a plunge pool in the stream.

Below and opposite Kaufmann Desert House, Palm Springs, California, USA, 1946–7, Richard Neutra. The intense sun and clear forms of the desert proved an ideal foil to the crisp planes and flowing space of modern architecture, and in this house – one of many he built after the war – Neutra crystallized an influential image of a new expression of house and garden for Southern California.

Kaufman Desert House Palm Springs, California, USA, 1946–7, Richard Neutra

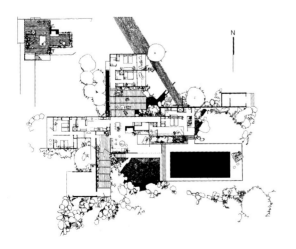

Tzu and frequently reiterated by Wright, that the reality of architecture is the 'space within'. In this context their significance was increased by the possibility, which intrigued Wright, that the earliest buildings in the desert might have been made in imitation of baskets or jars.

The long duration of archaeological and geological time was emphasized by the comparatively ephemeral nature of the roofs, canvas supported by rough-sawn redwood trusses, which Wright envisaged being replaced cyclically as the Fellowship made its annual migration from Taliesin East to West. Externally, the structural system resulted in a jagged profile, with thin, boldly projecting timber trusses alternating with stepped layers of canvas. The jagged, almost aggressive profile, was again a response to the landscape because, as Wright observed, 'in all this astounding desert there is not one hard undotted line to be seen'. Spatially, the contrasts are similarly extreme: the 30-metre (98-foot) long drafting room, originally open along one side, evoked the spirit of a tent, while other spaces were cave-like enclosures cut into the sloping ground.

When Taliesin West was built, Phoenix was little more than a large town of 65,000 inhabitants and the road that passed the site had not even been paved. Reaching it became a pilgrimage, and over the twenty years before his death Wright refined the spiral processional route around the site, framing a distant view here, adding another petroglyph there. Its logic had more to do with the positioning of ancient temples than functional site planning. He liked to quote his wife's observation that it 'looked like something we had been excavating, not building', and to his friend Elizabeth Gordon, editor of *House Beautiful*, the massive walls seemed 'as if they had been cast in place 100,000 years ago'. In his search for permanence and monumentality Wright anticipated the major shift in architecture precipitated by the Second World War, which was typified in Europe by the later work of Le Corbusier, and with suburban sprawl now lapping around its edges Taliesin West's challenge to what Wright saw as the all too time-bound 'degeneracy' of modern civilization seems both urgent and tragic.

Before considering Wright's smaller Usonian houses, it is worth comparing Taliesin West with another seminal desert house. It was built, like Fallingwater, for Edgar J. Kaufmann but known as the Desert House because Kaufmann never openly acknowledged ownership while Wright was alive, lest the latter be offended that it was by his former assistant, Richard Neutra. The plan, with its three wings pinwheeling out from a central fire, was clearly indebted to Wright, but whereas Wright chose to emulate the desert's textures and colours, Neutra opted for an abstract architecture of floating planes and reflective surfaces 'to make the rocks more rocky', as he put it. Around the house he created a 'natural' garden of indigenous rocks and cacti, anticipating ideas promoted in magazines in the 1950s as appropriate to the Californian climate and landscape. Here, as so often later, until worries about water shortages and the future of the planet began to change attitudes, it was contrasted with a verdant oasis of neatly mown lawn around the large, rectangular swimming pool. Neutra's vision, echoed in the work of a new generation of architects, helped to define the modern Californian lifestyle. In the post-war climate of growing optimism about the material pleasures being unleashed by the world's most powerful economy, Wright's heroic vision of life in

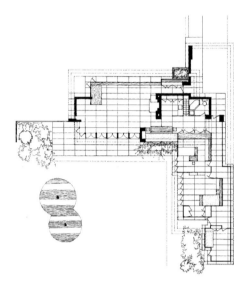

Jacobs House Madison, Wisconsin, USA, 1936, Frank Lloyd Wright

the desert might just as well have been on another planet.

During the late 1920s Wright developed a vision of the city based on 'Ruralism', in direct opposition to Le Corbusier's *Urbanisme*. Both were responses to the car, but where Le Corbusier envisaged vast apartment blocks in a continuous green park criss-crossed by elevated highways, Wright proposed an agrarian alternative, an endless but radically restructured suburbia. The basic unit was a 4-square-mile module, derived from the Jefferson grid of the Louisiana Purchase and intended to function as a semi-autonomous community. He devised new systems of finance to eliminate land speculation and envisaged each American citizen claiming their birthright of a house on an acre of land. He designed prototype houses for a variety of income levels and called the most basic 'Usonians'. In 1934, with work hard to come by in the Depression, he put his apprentices to work on a vast model of a square-mile section of his ideal city, exhibited the following year in New York, Pittsburgh and Washington D.C. to considerable press interest.

In 1936 Wright had his first chance to build a Usonian house. At 116 square metres (1250 square feet) the Jacobs House, built for a journalist/author and his wife in Madison, Wisconsin, is a small three-bedroom home by American standards. Wright despised the convention of placing a dwelling in the centre of its plot on a tiny lawn, like a plantation house in severely reduced circumstances, and instead developed an L-shaped plan to frame the garden. The house was positioned close to the boundary, with its back to the street and only the high-level windows to the bedroom corridor visible to public gaze. At the heart of the plan was the kitchen – Wright soon started calling it the workplace – from which Mrs Jacobs could command the house like a captain on the bridge of a ship. The dining and living areas formed part of a continuous living space, articulated by solid brick piers and surrounded by long runs of book-shelving and a screen of glazed opening doors. The bathroom was placed next to the kitchen to minimize service runs, and the three bedrooms ran off in a staggered tail of accommodation served by a one-sided corridor. Outside, the car was left by the door under the shelter of a carport – a Wright invention.

To keep down costs, Wright developed a highly efficient construction system for the Usonian house. Masonry was concentrated around the service core and kept to the minimum needed for load bearing and wind bracing. The other walls were either glazed or of a board-and-batten sandwich panel of extreme thinness – in long runs, bookshelves were actually needed for structural stiffening. The stripes of the battens provided a vertical module, while horizontally the houses were laid out on a 60 x 120-centimetre (2 x 4-foot) module, to suit the sizes of plywood and other sheet materials. This grid was marked in the painted concrete floor slab as a perpetual reminder of the underlying discipline. The overhanging roof prevented unwanted solar gain in summer, but allowed the low summer sun in to warm the interior. The brick walls and floor – into which heating pipes were embedded – acted as a 'thermal flywheel', releasing the heat absorbed during the day as free warmth in the evening. Wright's use of underfloor heating was novel, inspired, he said, by Japanese and Korean examples. The principle, of course, goes back to the Romans and had been revived in England in 1907 by Arthur

Above and opposite Jacobs House, Madison, Wisconsin, USA, 1936, Frank Lloyd Wright. The first of Wright's numerous 'Usonian' houses, it was built using a highly economical construction system. The L-shaped plan pivots around the hearth and kitchen, presenting almost blank walls to the outside and opening to the garden which its wings reach out to enclose.

Henry Barker, who used piped hot water in the walls of churches and houses: Wright may well have known of Barker's books.

Wright's drawings make it clear that he thought of the garden as the most important 'room' in the Jacobs House. In organic architecture, he said, 'we have no longer an outside and an inside as two separate things. Now the outside may come inside, and the inside may and does go outside'. He rejected air-conditioning because it cut us off from the natural climate and his vision of 'The Natural House' – the title of a 1954 book – envisaged direct contact with nature as vital to physical and mental health. 'Whether people are fully conscious of this or not, they actually derive countenance and sustenance from the "atmosphere" of the things they live in or with. They are rooted in them just as a plant is in the soil'. The Usonian House was ecological and energy-efficient before its time.

The January 1938 issue of *Architectural Forum* was devoted to Wright's solution to the 'small house problem' and he presented the Jacobs House in pragmatic terms. He made no claims about its beauty, but stressed the practical, cost-saving benefits of his methods – by using his paying apprentices as general contractors he managed to drag the costs down even further, building some houses for as little as $1500. He built numerous Usonians, developing a series of superbly resolved plan types and often startling his clients by giving their small homes his personal attention. Wright's reputation as one of the foremost architects of the twentieth or any other century rests on his major houses and a handful of public buildings, but in light of our current concerns few designs in this book seem more prescient, or pertinent to the new century, than his modestly-sized Usonians.

Wright was by no means alone in evincing a concern for energy efficiency in the 1930s because in part it was a response to government calls during the Depression to reduce costs and speed up residential construction. In 1932 the Royal Institute of British Architects had published what proved to be an influential manual, showing how to track the sun's movement across a building's elevations, and illustrated a device called a heliodon, developed to model this motion. The Chicago practice of Keck and Keck began designing houses to trap solar energy during the 1930s and a project like their Kellett House, built in Wenasha, Wisconsin in 1939, shows a mature understanding of the principles involved. To the north, its curving elevation – designed to maximize views of Lake Winnebago – has minimal glazing, while to the south a two-storey solarium allowed morning and low winter sun into the core to heat the house. The glazing was protected from high summer sun by a deep, visor-like roof, and the overhang was lightened visually by rectangular openings designed primarily to relieve wind pressure. The roof retained water in summer to reduce solar transmission, and in winter could be drained to avoid booming noises from the sound of cracking ice. While building a house in Madison, across town from the Jacobs House, William Keck visited Wright at Taliesin and was particularly intrigued by his ideas on underfloor heating, incorporating them in the Kellett and many later houses. When *House Beautiful* published an article on the Kellett House in 1942 it appeared under the title, 'What Houses will be Like after the War'.

In 1920, six years before completing the Lovell Beach House (see p.54), Rudolf Schindler was working in California on Wright's Hollyhock House. In

Opposite Kellett House, Wenasha, Wisconsin, USA, 1939, Keck and Keck. Opening to the sun and to views over Lake Winnebago, the Kellett House was amongst the first to be designed using modern 'passive solar' techniques. The overhanging, visor-like roof protects the glazing from high summer sun, and has holes to provide relief from wind pressure.

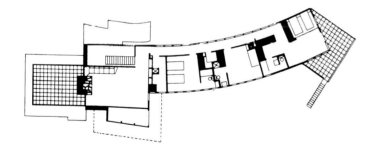

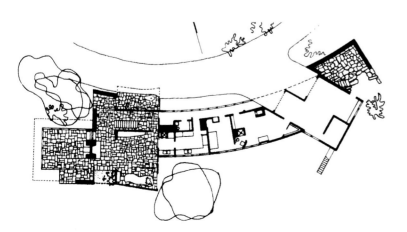

response to the benign climate, the basic idea for the house was, as Aline Barnsdall put it, that it should be as much 'outside as inside'. It was organized around a courtyard, and the main bedroom – which Schindler detailed – was conceived as a tent-like space hovering over the trees. The other important influence on Schindler's ideas was Irving Gill who, like Wright, originally hailed from Chicago. Inspired by the local Spanish mission buildings, Gill built several cubic, whitewashed, flat-roofed, asymmetrical houses – such as the Dodge House of 1915–16 – which were totally devoid of ornamentation. They were seen as proto-Modern by Pevsner and others, but are better understood as a local flowering of Arts and Crafts principles than as unwitting 'anticipations' of what came later.

Schindler-Chace House Los Angeles, California, USA, 1921–2, Rudolf Schindler

All these early influences, filtered through the floating world of Japan, can be discerned in Schindler's first and finest building, a double house built for himself, his wife and their friends Clyde and Marian Chace on North Kings Road, West Hollywood, from 1921 to 1922. The inspiration sprang from a camping and horse-riding trip the Schindlers took in Yosemite Valley: they wanted a house as open to nature as a tent. After teaming up with the Chaces, they decided that each couple should have an L-shaped wing with, as they explained in a letter to Pauline Schindler's parents, who were to lend most of the funds, 'large studio rooms – with concrete walls on three sides, the front open (glass) to the outdoors – a real California scheme. On the roof two "sleeping baskets" are provided – for open-air sleeping – with temporary covers for rainy nights'. The open garden fronts were fitted with large sliding doors, above which two cantilevered beams supported an overhanging roof, sliding light fittings and movable partitions. The varied roof levels, rooftop sleeping baskets, and close integration between the rooms and patios produced a complex, three-dimensional interlocking of house and garden which anticipated the relaxed Californian lifestyle that emerged after 1945. Schindler went on to develop a formal language based on wood framing and stucco, producing a steady stream of fine domestic projects into the early 1950s. But none, save the Lovell Beach House, rivalled the clarity and poetry of the Schindler-Chace houses.

Above Dodge House, Los Angeles, California, USA, 1915–16, Irving Gill. Although often linked to the abstraction of the International Style, the cubic forms and white rendered surfaces of Gill's houses grew out of the local Spanish Mission Style and became a model for others seeking a regional style for California.

Wright's Hollyhock House also played a decisive role in the life of Harwell Hamilton Harris. He visited the house in 1925, while still a sculpture student, and discovered, he later said, 'sculpture on a completely different scale'. It was a Road-to-Damascus experience. He decided to become an architect, and the sense of privacy, sculptural form and love of nature he encountered in Wright would inform all his work. He visited the Schindler-Chace house in 1928, where he met Schindler and a toga-clad Dione Neutra – who, with her husband Richard, had replaced the Chaces four years earlier. When Neutra himself arrived he promptly offered Harris a job – as assistant on the Lovell Health House (see pp.54–5), which would prove to be the finest American example of the International Style. By 1939 when Mr and Mrs Lee Blair, directors at the Walt Disney Studios, came to commission a house from Harris he was beginning to experiment with wood in a way that would in turn influence Neutra and Schindler and contribute to the formation of the so-called 'Redwood school' of California modernists. The Blairs' site was precipitously steep and their brief modest, just one bedroom, a small studio, and living space. Harris's response was as simple as

Above and right Schindler-Chace House, Los Angeles, California, USA, 1921–2, Rudolf Schindler. Melding influences from the emerging modern architecture of Europe, Irving Gill, Wright and Japan, this was the first house to capture a vision of the relaxed California lifestyle which would be the ideal for many after 1945.

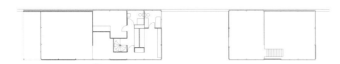

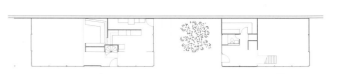

Opposite, top Blair House, Los Angeles, California, USA, 1939, Harwell Hamilton Harris. Designed for two directors at the Walt Disney Studios, this small house stepped dramatically down its steep site in the Hollywood Hills. Harris's bold use of timber proved a major influence on the California 'Redwood School' after the war.

Opposite and below Eames House, Los Angeles, California, USA, 1949, Charles and Ray Eames. The most widely influential of the Case Study Houses promoted by John Entenza through his magazine *Arts and Architecture*, the Eames House, with its enviably relaxed use of industrial building technology, came to epitomize the new Californian architecture and lifestyle.

Eames House Los Angeles, California, USA, 1949, Charles and Ray Eames

it was elegant. He disposed the three elements of accommodation on separate floors, the rear edge resting on the ground, and the front on the rear of the floor below, whose roof became a terrace. He used grass matting, plywood walls and Celotex ceilings throughout, and each room had a wall of glass opening into a garden or terrace. Low furniture, mostly by Aalto, was sparsely scattered to enhance the feeling of space.

Harris had published in 1935, as a list of nine dos and don'ts, the principles on which the Blair House and others were based. His article appeared in *California Arts and Architecture*, and three years later another of his clients, John Entenza, became editor of the magazine. Entenza, who had been working for MGM, set about transforming the magazine from an unadventurous regional publisher of homes, gardens and theatre reviews into a leading vehicle for progressive ideas. Articles on serious modern architecture started appearing. 'California' was dropped from the title in 1943 and in the same year he ran a competition for a worker's house entitled 'Design for Postwar Living'. Then, in January 1945, he launched the 'Case Study House Program' to promote new housing in which social and aesthetic ideals and innovation went hand in hand. In place of 'speculation in the form of talk and reams of paper', said Entenza, he would show real houses built for real clients, and mostly by young architects using innovative materials. It would make his magazine one of the most influential in the world.

Entenza's programme came to worldwide fame in 1949 with the completion in Los Angeles of Case Study House # 8 by, and for, Charles and Ray Eames. The couple were already renowned as the designers of what the architect Eliot Noyes described in *Arts and Architecture* as the 'most important group of furniture ever developed in this country'. The Eames House was designed in 1945, in partnership with Eero Saarinen, but when the materials arrived on site in the autumn of 1948 Charles Eames radically altered his ideas. The delicate, cubic house of glass and steel that resulted was made using standard lattice beams and window sections, and seemed to be as 'natural' to them as Wright's houses were to their very different, organic materials. Taut and neat, it was bathed in sunlight filtered by a stand of mature eucalyptus trees and filled with exquisite furniture, plants and items from the Eames's ever-growing collection.

The Eames House consists of two two-storey pavilions ranged against a 60-metre (200-foot) long retaining wall. The house itself is eight bays long, the last of which is open on two sides (each bay is 2.25 metres/7 feet wide by 6 metres/20 feet deep); a first-floor sleeping loft covers part of the volume. An open courtyard, four bays wide, separates the house from the five-bay studio. Both house and studio are enclosed by slender black steel-framed industrial window sections, horizontally proportioned like Japanese *shoji* screens. Much of the exterior is glazed, with a mixture of glass from clear to translucent, and the regularity is further broken by cross-braces, white or primary-coloured infill panels and occasional subdivisions within the large modules. Inside, the ribbed underside of the ceiling is exposed and painted white, as are all the steel beams, and a spiral stair with slender plywood treads leads up to the sleeping loft, where *shoji*-like panels can be slid across the glazed wall to modify the light. What makes the space magical is the light: sunshine, bathing or dappling the floor; even daylight,

Above Case Study House #16, Los Angeles, California, USA, 1952–3, Craig Ellwood. The first of Ellwood's three Case Study houses was conceived as a weightless floating world, seen at its most evanescent at night when the back-lit translucent screens to the bedroom courts transform it into a shimmering field of light.

Opposite Bass House, Los Angeles, California, USA, 1958, Buff, Straub and Hensman. The twentieth of the Case Study houses and atypical in its use of a timber frame, barrel-vaulted living space, and highly site-specific design – it was built around the mature Italian Stone Pine, which has since had to be cut down.

Case Study House # 22 Los Angeles, California, USA, 1959–60, Pierre Koenig

filtered by the translucent glass; and the ever-changing play of shadows from the eucalyptus on the translucent surfaces, flickering like the brushstrokes in Far Eastern calligraphy.

Dumped on a suburban plot, deprived of its filtered light, and emptied of its artfully arranged contents the Eames House would lose much of its magic. The eucalyptus outside, and the plants, furniture, objects and decorations inside, are as much part of the architecture as the fabric of the building. The house represented, as Entenza put it, 'an attempt to state an idea rather than a fixed architectural pattern'. In this it was in striking contrast, as we shall see, to the steel and glass houses being built at the same time on the East Coast. The consummately artful yet relaxed ordinariness of the Eames House struck a chord with a new generation of designers. Its appeal was augmented by fascination with the increasingly sophisticated American consumer products, from pop-up toasters to automatic dishwashers. Charles and Ray Eames were lauded in magazines around the world, and by the mid 1960s their house was established as one of the iconic achievements of post-war architecture. To his friend Peter Smithson, Charles Eames was 'a natural California Man, using his native resources and know-how – of the film-making, the aircraft and the advertising industries – as others drink water; that is almost without thinking'. With its elegant, all pervasive displays of objects and images from around the world the Eames House was like a showroom. It became a favourite setting for fashion shoots with magazines like *Life* and *Vogue* and was a perfect emblem for the burgeoning consumer society.

The Case Study House Program ran until 1964, by when twenty-seven houses, as well as a few apartments, had been completed. Among the most radical was # 18 (1956–8), the third of Craig Ellwood's contributions designed using a prefabricated steel frame and panel system. The result was about as minimal as architecture can get, wonderfully light and delicate, with paper-thin roof planes floating above the entrance and carport: a later owner transformed it into a Mediterranean-style villa.

Another in the series, Case Study House # 22 (1959–60), the Stahl House by Pierre Koenig, has come to epitomize the glamour of Los Angeles. This is thanks in part to a magnificent night-time photograph by Julius Shulman – whose images did much to promote the Californian vision of modernity – and even more to its use as a location for countless advertising, fashion and film shoots. The house is perched high in the Hollywood Hills and visitors are greeted by a view of more than a hundred square miles of the city laid out temptingly below them like a luxurious carpet. It feels much larger than its 214 square metres (2300 square feet), and it is difficult to grasp that on completion it was regarded as economical, rather than the epitome of luxury it has become. The only solid wall faces the street; behind, all the perimeter is of minimally-framed glass, in sheets up to 6 metres (20 feet) wide, giving the house a 270-degree panorama of the city. The plan is L-shaped, with a core of services in the corner, bedrooms in one wing and an open-plan kitchen-dining-living space in the other. In the embrace of the wings are a small terrace and the obligatory swimming pool. Like Mies van der Rohe, Koenig worked, as Reyner Banham aptly put it, by 'elegant omission' and the house seems to float

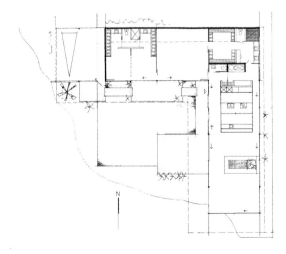

Above and opposite Case Study House #22 (Stahl House), Los Angeles, California, USA, 1959–60, Pierre Koenig. Dramatically cantilevered out from its site high in the Hollywood Hills and more luxurious than earlier Case Study designs, the Stahl House came to epitomize the freedom and glamour of Southern California.

effortlessly on air. In architecture the appearance of ease is usually hard-won and here the cantilevered wing sits on 75-centimetre (30-inch) deep concrete beams supported by up to 10.5-metre (35-foot) deep concrete caissons. The Stahl family have lived happily in their house for over thirty years, but contrary to predictions in magazines at the time its compelling expression of the Southern Californian version of the good life did not herald the arrival of steel as an important material in mainstream housing.

The Case Study Houses are the best known and most ambitious of many efforts to promote modern ways of living in the aftermath of the Second World War. In 1945 the editors of New York's *Architectural Forum* magazine published a book entitled, *Tomorrow's House: How to Plan your Post-war Home Now*. It explained, room by room, how superior a modern, functionally planned house was to the tired 'period' styles and was illustrated almost entirely by modern, if not always strictly Modern, examples. The following year MOMA brought out *If You Want to Build a House* by Elizabeth B. Mock which, not surprisingly, was more forthright in its promotion of Modern design for modern living. 'Light and space work together and they have much more to do with our feeling of well-being than is generally granted,' Mock explained, adding that, the 'advantages of freedom in space and generous uniform light are peculiar to modern architecture'. There was a small but steadily growing market for individually designed modern houses but, with a single and singular exception, volume house-builders failed to respond to the many calls. The exception was Joseph Eichler and he operated, not surprisingly, in California.

Eichler was born in 1900 in New York, and migrated with his parents to San Francisco in the 1920s. In 1942, he moved his own young family into a rented house designed by Frank Lloyd Wright and fell in love with modern architecture. After discovering simple post-and-beam construction in 1947 through the work of Earl 'Flat-top' (after his houses' flat-roofs) Smith, he decided to set up his own house-building company. Two years later the first recognizable 'Eichler House' was built to designs by Bob Anshen. Over the next eighteen years, before his main business went bankrupt in 1967 due to the rising cost of materials and the demand for air-conditioning (which his designs could not economically accommodate), Eichler built over 10,000 houses in the Bay Area and what we now know as Silicon Valley. The standard formula was simple: a blank elevation to the street; rear and, depending on the site, side walls of glass; fenced gardens; post-and-beam roofs, typically with a shallow pitch to a central ridge; boarded ceilings and, aş in Wright's Usonians, radiant-heated concrete floors. It is said that by the mid-1950s every self-respecting Bay Area resident could spot an Eichler, a level of recognition no other speculatively built house has ever enjoyed, and by 1972 when the influential *Sunset* magazine, gospel of the California lifestyle, surveyed its readers, over 60 percent were found to own an Eichler home.

I know of no mass-built modern houses to compare with the quality or popularity of Eichler's. They exemplified the new relaxed lifestyles that flourished in California's benign coastal climate, which was rarely too hot or too cold and sufficiently dry to prevent insects becoming a nuisance, still less a threat. In the 1950s the West retained something of the frontier spirit, and in California social freedom came to be identified with living in an open-plan house with glass walls

Opposite The houses built in the San Francisco Bay Area by Joseph Eichler, such as this typical example designed by architect A. Quincy Jones, made the new architecture available to large numbers of middle-class Californians – some 10,000 of these and similar houses were sold during the 1950s and 1960s.

Above Breuer House, New Canaan, Connecticut, USA, 1947, Marcel Breuer. The combination of a masonry base surmounted by a cantilevered timber-clad first floor proved widely influential, and was typical of the less doctrinaire modernism practised by Gropius, Breuer and other European *emigrés* after settling on the East Coast of the USA.

Above and below Demonstration house, Museum of Modern Art, New York, USA, 1949, Marcel Breuer. Built as part of MOMA's campaign to promote modern architecture, the butterfly-roof form (probably derived from a little known project by Le Corbusier) was widely imitated.

that fused inside and out. The dream of a Modern house affordable by the majority had finally become a reality, and an active Eichler network still flourishes in California, with its own magazine, website and advice on maintaining and improving the homes.

Seen from California, the East Coast of America was a foreign country, and modern architecture was different there. The Ivy League universities, home to several distinguished schools of architecture based on Beaux-Arts principles, encouraged an academic attitude that was the antithesis of the freewheeling 'can-do' approach which drove innovation in the West. When, in 1937, Walter Gropius accepted an offer to direct the department of architecture at Harvard, where he was joined by Marcel Breuer, it was seen as an important victory for the Modern cause. The following year the university invited Sigfried Giedion, secretary of CIAM, to give the Charles Eliot Norton lectures, which were published in 1941 as the massively influential book, *Space, Time and Architecture: The Growth of a New Tradition*. Harvard produced a stream of graduates trained in modern architecture, but in many essentials the academic tradition persisted and Gropius's belief in teamwork and anonymity increasingly resulted in banality rather than hard-won simplicity.

Breuer left Harvard for practice in New York in 1946 and the following year built his own house in New Canaan, Connecticut. Its timber-clad box cantilevered from a masonry lower floor with a very shallow pitched roof was elegant and polite, as was the showhouse he built in the garden of the Museum of Modern Art in 1949. As the officially sanctioned face of modern architecture in the East this proved very popular, and its distinctive butterfly roof was widely imitated. It might well have been inspired by Le Corbusier's Errazuriz House project in Chile of 1930, but whereas there the roof was locked into the structure of the house, following the slope of the ramp and responding to the views, in Breuer's it was reduced to a decorative motif with scant relationship to the spatial organization.

1949 also saw the completion of Philip Johnson's Glass House. The historian/critic had become an architect and disciple of Mies van der Rohe, and during the following half century would undergo several dramatic stylistic reincarnations. Johnson's was the first all-glass house to be completed, but it was based on a 1945 design by Mies — who was now head of architecture at the Illinois Institute of Architecture in Chicago — for Dr Edith Farnsworth, though her house was not built until 1951. The site of the Farnsworth House at Plano, Illinois, was prone to flooding so Mies raised the ground floor by 1.5 metres (5 feet), slinging rectangular floor and roof planes between eight H-section columns. Both beams and columns are oversized according to conventional structural requirements, the former to ensure that the planes remained perfectly level, with no trace of sag, and the columns to suit the size Mies deemed correct visually.

A broad flight of steps leads up to a third rectangular plane, hovering above the ground on stubby columns, from where identical steps rise onto a covered terrace at the end of the fully-glazed volume. Inside is a freestanding, primavera wood-veneered core containing two bathrooms, a galley kitchen and a fireplace. Privacy was afforded by shantung silk curtains, and as in the Tugendhat House, Mies's own furniture was intended to be laid out in perfect islands on cream-coloured rugs. Inside and out, the floors are of travertine and the detailing minimal and meticulous. The paving is perfectly flat with open joints for drainage, and the columns are welded to the face of the beams, with all traces of work removed by grinding the welds flat and painting the steel white. When tapped, the steelwork rings like a tuning fork.

Edith Farnsworth was single. A successful nephrologist, she met Mies at a party and mentioned that she was thinking of building a weekend house; he naturally offered his services. They became good friends, but probably nothing more (contrary to popular assumptions), and she was won over to Mies's vision of architecture. As the project progressed, however, she realized that he saw her as a patron rather than client, a means to execute his unyielding less-is-more vision of the Modern house. With tradesmen questioning the wisdom of some of Mies's plumbing and electrical arrangements and the costs reaching almost double the $40,000 estimate – already a lot of money for a house of this size – Dr Farnsworth became increasingly distressed and put the matter in the hands of her lawyer, prompting Mies to countersue for his fees.

After a long legal battle Mies eventually won an out-of-court settlement, but the legal case was as nothing compared to the fight in the press. In interviews Farnsworth made her house sound completely uninhabitable – though she chose to remain there for twenty years – and it became the focus of a campaign against the vices of the new Modern aesthetic and the 'self-chosen elite who are trying to tell us what we should like and how we should live', as an article in the April 1953 issue of *House Beautiful* put it. Dr Farnsworth found the lack of an enclosed bedroom unsettling, and disliked the fact that while her guests had a separate bathroom they were expected to sleep on a sofa or a mattress on the floor. She tried to tame Mies's rigorous geometry by furnishing the house with family heirlooms rather than Mies's designs, but eventually gave up the struggle and in 1971 sold it to Peter Palumbo, a developer and Mies enthusiast who lived in London. Palumbo installed the furniture Mies intended, and happily used the house as a vacation home for his young family, responding enthusiastically to its aesthetic qualities. The sight of lime tree leaves silhouetted on the silk curtains by the dawn sun, he says, 'is a scene no Japanese print could capture to greater effect'.

In the architectural world the reception of the Farnsworth House echoed Palumbo's enthusiasm, and it was widely regarded as the ultimate expression of the open plan and of Mies's ideal of *beinahe nichts*, 'almost nothing'. Palumbo recalls that Mies told him he would prefer him not to hang pictures on the house's primavera core, adding, 'I give you the space, it's open plan, you do what you like'. But of course the architect was being disingenuous. The difficulty with Mies's version of the open plan was that its 'freedom' could quickly become a new kind of tyranny, every bit as demanding – and to Farnsworth, intimidating – as the *Gesamtkunstwerken* of an architect like Josef Hoffmann. Where Le Corbusier designed light, easily moved furniture, and was happy to mix classic old styles with new designs in an interior, Mies's work was deliberately heavy and intended to be installed like sculptures by the architect-curator. Where Mies's designs of the 1920s had been dynamic, asymmetrical and quintessentially Modern, those of the post-war period were destined to be static, symmetrical and

Farnsworth House Plano, Illinois, USA, 1946–51, Ludwig Mies van der Rohe

Below and overleaf Farnsworth House, Plano, Illinois, USA, 1946–51, Ludwig Mies van der Rohe. The combination of exquisite materials, visually (if not always technically) flawless detailing, and an open plan divided only by the free-standing service core represented the apotheosis of Mies's less-is-more aesthetic.

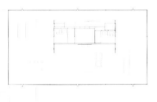

essentially neo-classical in spirit. The Farnsworth House, with its frozen perfection and hidden symmetries, marked the point at which the die was cast.

Glass House New Canaan, Connecticut, USA, 1949, Philip Johnson

Philip Johnson's Glass House, although inspired by Mies's design, looked to his commercial projects in Chicago for guidance in detailing the steelwork. It sits like a diminutive temple at the centre of a terraced lawn, with the columns at the corners to form a static, closed box. In place of the rectangular primavera core he used a cylinder of brick containing a hearth and bathroom: to spectators gazing in from outside it might almost be a parody of the all-American home. Introducing the project in 1950 Johnson said, 'Perhaps if there is ever to be "decoration" in our architecture it may come from the manipulation of stock structural elements such as these', and went on to suggest that the more playful use of structure might develop into a 'mannerist' phase like that which followed Renaissance Classicism. Trained as a historian, he thought in terms of style; living as a gay man, he never dreamt of proposing his house as a model for the American family; and being the heir to a substantial fortune, he had the resources to indulge his architectural fantasies. Johnson almost immediately complemented the Glass House with a guest house in which a glass living pavilion sat over a masonry bunker containing the sleeping accommodation and bathrooms. He remodelled the austere base in 1953, turning it into a camp stage set with a palatial bedroom, canopied like a fantasy from the Arabian Nights.

In retrospect, Johnson's Glass House looks less like the Modern masterpiece it was declared at the time, and more like a commentary upon the nature of modernity. For Johnson, the radical, innovative drive that inspired early Modern architecture and was still thriving on the West Coast seemed altogether too earnest. He opted for the knowing manipulation of a chosen vocabulary or set of stylistic tropes. Throughout his long, multi-faceted career Philip Johnson has had an uncanny knack for anticipating, and often catalyzing, a new trend. The East Coast soon polarized between an academic, anti-historicist Functionalism, promoted by Gropius and his colleagues at Harvard, and a concern for a 'New Monumentality', of which the Glass House can be seen as the first, perhaps unwitting, manifesto. Johnson's later public buildings were prime exemplars of this new trend, and Yale University, under the chairmanship of George Howe, the academic focus.

The most gifted and original architect to emerge on the East Coast after 1945 was Louis Kahn. He was a late starter and from 1950 to 1951, after twenty years in practice, much of them spent building public housing projects and some as an assistant to George Howe, he took a mid-career break as resident architect at the American School in Rome. He travelled the Mediterranean, experiencing Greek, Roman and Egyptian architecture for the first time. Overwhelmed by what he had seen, he returned to America determined to rethink his art from the ground up. He rediscovered the room as the basis of architecture; he divided accommodation between 'served' and 'servant' spaces – a kitchen serves a dining room, a pantry the kitchen, and so on; and he took absolutely nothing for granted. To Kahn, cutting holes in walls to make windows violated the wall's integrity. He sought ways of generating forms from a rigorous inner spatial and constructional logic, playing with repeating units or cells and trying to find a basis for every

Opposite Glass House, New Canaan, Connecticut, USA, 1949, Philip Johnson. Having christened the International Style before the Second World War, Johnson began to practise what he preached after it. His temple-like glass and steel house is the jewel in a luxurious estate developed for his own use.

decision in the 'way a thing wants to be', not in what the designer might want to impose on it from outside.

Esherick House Chestnut Hill, Pennsylvania, USA, 1961, Louis Kahn

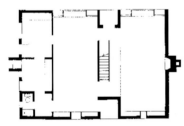

Private houses provided Kahn with an ideal vehicle for testing his ideas and we can seem them at play in the Esherick House, completed in Chestnut Hill, Philadelphia, in 1961. The plan is governed by a square module and divided into alternating bands of served and servant spaces. The layout emulates a seventeenth-century Colonial type, with a chimney at each end and two rooms separated by a staircase; the living room is double height. The principal spaces are lit through large glazed openings at high level, while views are provided by articulating the walls to form narrow slots rather than providing conventional 'windows'. This increases the apparent thickness of the walls and modulates the light through reflection off the deep embrasures. A 'thick wall' became a favourite device for organizing small servant spaces, and here seats and bookshelves are also built into the walls. The entrance is a dark square recess, cut out of the main volume, adding to the feeling both of abstraction and monumentality. The folding of the wall suggests mass, while at the same time revealing the thinness of timber-frame construction. Despite the chimneys and reference to a Colonial plan type, it is a very un-house-like object, with few conventional indicators of size.

In his search for monumentality Kahn's buildings became increasingly massive and rigid. But while he rejected the lightness, flexibility and flowing space of modern architecture he declared that, 'Le Corbusier was always my teacher, although no-one knew it at the time'. He rejected some of its central tenets such as transparency and spatial continuity, yet he saw his work as part of the evolving tradition of a radical modernism. The same, increasingly, could not be said of many of his colleagues for whom, as for Philip Johnson, architecture was once again becoming a question of style. For most the chosen style was still 'Modern', conspicuously so in a design like Paul Rudolph's Arthur W. Milam Residence at Jacksonville Beach, Florida (1960–62). The spatial organization is highly accomplished, flowing around a galleried double-height living room; every dimension is controlled by the stack-bonded concrete blocks; and the interiors are protected by a boldly articulated *brise-soleil* inspired by Le Corbusier and reminiscent of the Shodhan House. Seen from outside the *brise-soleil* is apparently completely freestanding, living its own sculptural life. It is a virtuoso piece of late-modern design, and also an example of the mannerism predicted by Johnson, playing games with the Corbusian rather than Miesian vocabulary. For all its accomplishment, this and similar work signalled the exhaustion of modern architecture, not its creative extension. Post-Modernism was beckoning: the Modern was about to be rejected, and then reinvented as one stylistic option among many.

Some of the most radically innovative houses of the post-war period in America were designed under the influence of Wright and outside the mainstream currents of ideas by John Lautner and Bruce Goff. Lautner was perhaps the only architect trained in Wright's Taliesin Fellowship to produce original independent work. Where most of Wright's buildings seem to grow out of their site and hug the ground, Lautner's mature designs frequently thrust and rotate out into space. In what is probably his best known project, the octagonal

Elrod House Palm Springs, California, USA, 1968, John Lautner

Bavinger House Oklahoma City, Oklahoma, USA, 1949, Bruce Goff

Malin Residence completed in 1960 in the Hollywood Hills and known as 'Chemosphere', this tendency reached its most extreme expression. In response to a site so steep local contractors considered it unbuildable, the entire house was cantilevered and propped from a single concrete column, a massive version of Buckminster Fuller's Dymaxion House.

Chemosphere is understandably popular, but by no means typical. Lautner is a master of *in situ* concrete, which he pushed to extremes of fluidity in his later works, and like Wright he always sought to draw inspiration from a site. That for the Elrod House, built in Palm Springs in 1968, had been bulldozed flat to turn it into a saleable 'lot'. But the ridge-top location was superb, with beautiful panoramic mountain views, and noticing the tops of outcrops poking through the soil Lautner had the land excavated by more than 2 metres (6.6 feet) to leave them standing proud. As in the living room of Fallingwater, the house incorporated the rocks, its black slate floor lapping around them like an oily sea. At night the specially designed circular carpet – its pattern of circles very Wrightian – seems to float like an island in space, hovering above the flickering lights of Palm Springs below. As if to outdo Pierre Koenig's classic Case Study House # 22, a similar feeling was created in the master bedroom of the Sheats Residence, built above Los Angeles in 1963. The effect was heightened in 1969 after a remodelling for the new owner, Jim Goldstein, in which the large and apparently frameless sheets of glass at the corner could slide at the touch of a button.

Lautner's detailing and choice of finishes sometimes hover uneasily on the edge of stylization – Jim Goldstein's bedroom might almost have escaped from the Starship Enterprise – but are nothing compared to those of Bruce Goff, whom the critic Charles Jencks dubbed the 'Michelangelo of Kitsch'. He worked in the mid-West and to his many detractors Goff's houses are little more than festivals of bad taste, with thick piled carpets climbing out of conversation pits to cover walls and ceilings, orange outdoor carpet in place of 'proper' roofing, vast beds cantilevered from anthracite pylons, all-gold bathrooms lit by crystals, and doors encrusted with glass beads and sequins. New Age before its time, Goff saw this exuberance as echoing that of nature and below the glitzy surfaces lurks an organizational talent of a high order, revealed by the sophisticated geometrical control of the spaces. To those without the stomach for the later work, the Bavinger House of 1949 in Oklahoma City remains his masterpiece.

Gene Bavinger was a young professor of art at Oklahoma University, where Goff headed the architecture department, and his wife Nancy was a ceramicist. After the arrival of their son they bought a site in a ravine and wrote to Goff explaining that they did not wish to live in the 'usual conglomeration of boxes with holes cut in them for doors and windows' but wanted 'a large open space in which all their needs could be satisfied' – including a lot of tropical plants and a pool for fish. The Bavingers loved the sandstone on the site and wanted to build the house themselves, with the help of students. It took several years, and was never really finished in the conventional sense.

Goff could not have wished for a more inspiring brief or site. His response was to use the natural stone to build a wall almost 30 metres (100 feet) long which

Above Sheats Residence, Los Angeles, California, USA, 1963, remodelled for Jim Goldstein, 1969, John Lautner. As if to outdo Pierre Koenig's similarly dramatic Stahl House also in Los Angeles, the glass walls of the master bedroom can be retracted at the touch of a button.
Opposite Malin Residence ('Chemosphere'), Los Angeles, USA, 1960, John Lautner. Perched precariously on an 'unbuildable' site in the Hollywood Hills, the Chemosphere became an instant emblem of the West Coast's can-do mentality.

took the form of a logarithmic spiral rising from the ground and coiling itself around a steel pole from which the roof, floors and stairs were suspended. 'Floors' is not quite the right word, however. Goff called them 'living area bowls': there are five, and they are dish-shaped, fabricated from welded steel bars and – yes! – clad in gold carpet. Curtains provided the only form of privacy and furniture was built-in: the beds, for example, were sunk into the bowls to lie flush with the floor. The kitchen and bathroom were tucked into the masonry core – which became like one of Kahn's servant spaces – and the entire house was a conservatory for plants and birds. As an expression of the clients' way of life the Bavinger House was as inventive and persuasive as anything we have considered. The freedom to live how you want, unconstrained by government regulation and the tyranny of accepted rules of taste, remains central to the mid-Western version of the American Dream. In Bruce Goff this rugged individualism found its poet.

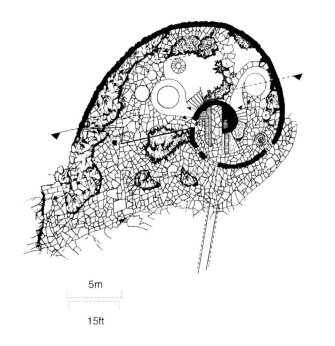

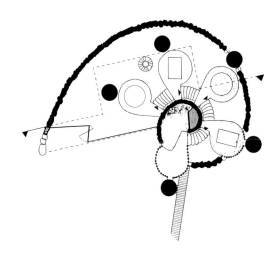

5m

15ft

Opposite and above Bavinger House, Oklahoma City, Oklahoma, USA, 1949, Bruce Goff. Built for a young art professor, his ceramicist wife and their new-born son, the Bavinger House was planned as a continuous, open-plan spiral of space in which tropical plants, birds, fish and the young family could co-exist in a unique symbiosis.

scandinavian modern

A young girl stands with her back to us, hands linked casually behind her neck, blonde hair and bare skin glowing in the low sun. She is at the edge of what appears to be a pond formed from run-off gathered around the base of a rock outcrop, and looks back to a single-storey house, a door invitingly ajar and windows flung open to the sun and air. The pond is actually a small swimming pool and this artfully composed idyll – in Europe, one of the most widely reproduced images of the immediate post-war period – illustrates the house and garden of the architect Sven Markelius, director of city planning in Stockholm. It was built in 1945 and the design was more innovative than it appears. The walls were made from a novel prefabricated timber system of Markelius's own design; the roof trusses bore only on the perimeter walls to allow complete freedom in positioning partitions; and it was heated using hot air distributed through floor grilles.

Markelius House Kevinge, Sweden, 1945, Sven Markelius

Visually, however, it wore its technical innovations lightly. Timber boarding painted with traditional dull yellow oil paint has replaced the smooth white surfaces of Functionalism, of which Markelius had been a distinguished exponent. But what was radically new was the fusion of the house with a seemingly natural garden in the heart of suburban Kevinge, not in the depths of the countryside. Markelius's daughter, the photograph tells us, is completely at home in this sylvan world, and what is presented is a compelling image of the free, modern life that awaits her and her generation.

The presentation plan is just as revealing as the photograph. Inside the house Markelius drew every piece of furniture, not in some ideal arrangement, as in a Mies design, but to convey a sense of habitation. The house, we can see, is organized around a large, informal room where the family eat, relax and listen to the piano. Outside, everything is described in even more exhaustive detail, from the car, two bicycles and child's tricycle under the generous entrance canopy, through the meticulously rendered paved surfaces, to individual shrubs and trees. As an image of the good life its message is as clear as the photograph: in the aftermath of the Second World War, life is going to be lived close to nature in a more informal way. Enter the house and we find a world of white walls, floors scattered with rugs, a fair-face (no applied finish) brick fireplace and a mixture of traditional-looking wicker chairs and unostentatious contemporary wooden furniture. The missionary zeal of the Heroic Period has gone. The machine must still be put to use – the structure is, after all, prefabricated – but it no longer demands an overtly machine-age style, nor precludes the use of natural materials – of wooden rather than steel furniture. Ideas anticipated in the work of Aalto and others in the 1930s are poised to dominate the mainstream.

Markelius's house was one of several built in the late 1940s and early 1950s in which a new way of living was given architectural expression, in a style now known as Scandinavian Modern. This was the European counterpart to the so-called Contemporary style of post-war California, with which it shared many similarities in terms of both lifestyle and design. Its influence would similarly be felt worldwide, most directly through the wooden furniture that became almost ubiquitous in the Western world during the late 1950s and '60s. Like most styles offered for popular consumption through magazines, Scandinavian Modern is a distillation of ideas drawn from disparate sources. It did not spring up overnight,

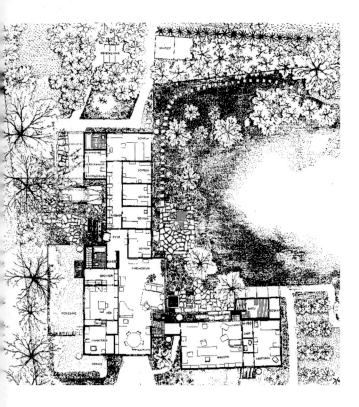

Above and opposite Markelius House, Kevinge, Sweden, 1945, Sven Markelius. System-built yet reassuringly traditional in feeling, Markelius's house and its natural-seeming garden exemplified the ideals of the 'softened' modernism of post-war Swedish architecture.

but can be readily traced to the vision of an unpretentious family life, with children at its centre and filled with sunlight and fresh air, projected so successfully half a century earlier by Carl and Karin Larsson. And these values in turn were very much in evidence at the event that marked the official launch of Functionalism in the Nordic countries: the hugely popular 1930 Stockholm Exhibition, co-ordinated and partly designed by Gunnar Asplund.

Like the Weissenhof in Stuttgart the Stockholm Exhibition presented fully furnished model houses and apartments to an amazed public, but unlike Stuttgart it was never intended to leave a permanent legacy of buildings. This enabled Asplund to design it as a festive market place for new ideas. Sigfried Giedion declared that there had been 'no exhibition to rival this one for overall effect' and in his newspaper reviews Alvar Aalto caught its mood perfectly. 'The exhibition speaks out for joyful and spontaneous everyday life,' he wrote, and 'consistently propagates a healthy and unpretentious lifestyle based on economic realities. . . the deliberate social message that the Stockholm Exhibition is intended to convey is expressed in the architectural language of pure, spontaneous joy. There is a festive elegance, but also a childlike lack of inhibition about it all. . . This is not a composition of glass, stone, and steel, as a visitor who despises functionalism might imagine; it is a composition of houses, flags, floodlights, flowers, fireworks, happy people, and clean tablecloths.'

In an influential article entitled 'The New Empiricism: Sweden's Latest Style', published in 1947, the British *Architectural Review* welcomed the new developments, but recognized that a house like Markelius's might easily be mistaken for 'local builder's bungalow style'. They stressed its technical innovations and quoted Sven Backström to explain for those readers who might be troubled by the apparent rejection of the 'objectivity' of 1930s Functionalism that the new style was an attempt to extend its rationality by bringing to bear the insights of the science of psychology. 'Today we have reached the point where all the elusive psychological factors have again begun to engage our attention,' explained Backström. 'To interpret such a programme as a reaction and a return to something that is past and to pastiches is definitely to misunderstand the development of architecture in this country.'

Ränangen House Djursholm, Sweden, 1951, Leonie and Charles-Edouard Geisendorf

In Sweden Markelius's house was followed by several others in which the now familiar Scandinavian style was crystallized. The Ränangen House, built in Djursholm near Stockholm in 1951 by Leonie and Charles-Edouard Geisendorf, offered a relaxed combination of brickwork and full-height glazing panels, several with vertical, grey-stained boarding to one side or below the window to fill out the panel. Internally, the fire sat to one side of a large fair-face brick wall, and slight changes of ceiling plane – variously finished in plaster or narrow timber boarding – marked places of rest and transition. Stig Ancker's summer house in Halland, completed two years later, also epitomized the new approach. Externally it is a simple cubic composition of white-painted blockwork walls, with a low-pitch interlocking tiled roof and dark-stained window frames and timber-boarded doors. Inside it has boarded walls, floors and ceilings, with simple, modern-looking kitchen furniture and colourfully striped woven rugs on the floor. Interiors like this would feature in countless interior design magazines.

Opposite Ränangen House, Djursholm, Sweden, 1951, Leonie and Charles-Edouard Geisendorf. With its relaxed combination of natural materials, clean planar surfaces and large windows, the design and furnishing of the Ränangen House epitomized the essence of what would later be known as the 'Scandinavian Modern' style.

Above Sugden House, Watford, England, 1955–6, Alison and Peter Smithson. Rejecting the influential architecture emanating from Sweden as sentimental, in the Sugden House the Smithsons transformed the post-war English developer's vernacular into something altogether tougher.

As with its Californian counterpart, the influence of Japan was crucial to the emergence of what we now think of as quintessentially Scandinavian. When Alvar Aalto's library in Viipuri opened in 1935 Gustaf Strengell wrote that, 'the interiors of the building display Japanese characteristics in many places. Observe the pale, light colouring which give the rooms not just their charming airy quality but actually a scent. Quite particularly the Japanese streak appears in the choice of pale wood only – birch, pine, beech – for the panelling and furnishings, and it is even more striking in the treatment of smooth surfaces: in true Japanese manner, they are not treated at all, but "left in their natural state", which is both attractive to the eye and pleasing to the touch.' As we have seen, Aalto also made extensive use of lime-washed brickwork and timber boarding in his own house and studio, also completed in 1935. In the same year, in his lecture entitled 'Rationalism and Man', he argued that a truly rational architecture must extend to psychological issues. In essence, the elements of Scandinavian Modern were formulated in the 1930s, but it took a decade and a world war for them to enter the mainstream.

The new manner was not, however, without its critics. In the Göth House of 1950 in Uppsala, designed by two young architects Bengt Edman and Lennart Holm, for example, we see an altogether tougher architecture of severely cubic form. It has unrelieved brick walls in which the internal partitions register as vertical zips in the joint pattern and a ribbon window sits below an exposed steel lintel. The architects shared an office with Gunnar Asplund's son Hans who commented, with a hint of sarcasm, that they were 'Neo-Brutalists'. He repeated the term to some English architect-friends who took it back home where it was adapted by Alison and Peter Smithson and others who styled themselves exponents of New Brutalism. The phrase caught on. It was intended as a riposte to what its proponents saw as the abandonment of rigorous architectural standards by an older generation eager to embrace the 'softened modernism' of the New Empiricism – which the editors of *The Architectural Review* allied to the English Picturesque tradition and suburbia. New Brutalism, the Smithsons declared, was 'an ethic not an aesthetic'.

Extolling traditional Japanese architecture as the manifestation of 'a general conception of Life, a sort of reverence for the natural world and, from that, for the materials of the built world', the Smithsons saw architecture 'as the direct result of a way of life'. They were therefore more interested in peasant dwelling forms than past architectural styles. Equally, by placing 'reverence for materials' at the centre of the New Brutalist ethic they were trying to return architecture to the intellectual heart of the Modern Movement. Despite its avowedly broad scope, New Brutalism became identified stylistically with an architecture of massive plasticity and coarse surfaces – exemplified by Le Corbusier's Unité at Marseilles and his Jaoul houses, which were appropriated as early and representative examples. But when the Smithsons came to design a house (1955–6) for an engineer at Ove Arup, Derek Sugden, and his wife Jean, they attempted to give contemporary expression to the English way of life rather than dogmatically use a specific formal language. Indeed, this would have been difficult given that the planning constraints on the site on the edge of Watford dictated secondhand London stock bricks, a tiled roof and standard steel windows.

Above, below and right Ancker
Summer House, Halland, Sweden,
1953, Stig Ancker. Austere, white-
painted blockwork walls frame
interiors epitomizing the new sense of
domesticity exemplified by light
timber-boarded floors, woven rugs and
simple, unpretentious fittings.

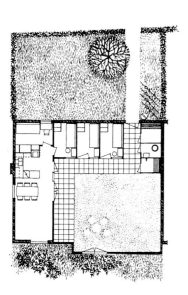

Below and opposite Utzon House,
Hellebaek, Denmark, 1952, Jørn
Utzon. Sited like a dam at the head of
a small valley, Utzon's house melded
influences from Mies van der Rohe,
Wright's Usonians and Japan with
native Danish brick-building traditions
to create an architecture of
unmistakable authority.

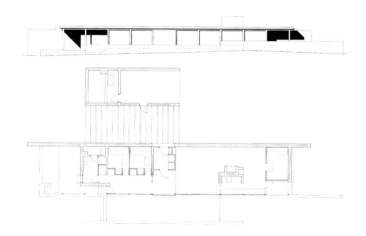

Utzon House Hellebaek, Denmark, 1952, Jørn Utzon

The English, the Smithsons argued, are so attached to the small-windowed
Tudor cottage and suspicious of the large glazed areas of modern architecture,
that their post-war houses are merely pre-war houses with enlarged windows.
These divide the elevation into vertical strips in which neither wall nor windows
dominate. By using unusual L-shaped openings and positioning the windows
irregularly they hoped to 'allow the brickwork to flow together and coalesce with
the roof to form a solid mass, with the appearance of all-round protection once
the characteristic of English popular architecture'. The planners took some
persuading – an earlier scheme was rejected – and many observers found the
deviation from the familiar disturbing. An Australian newspaper awarded the
Sugden House the 'Gruyère Prize', but in retrospect its artful manipulation of
conventions can be seen to have anticipated by almost a decade the more widely
trumpeted celebration of the 'ordinary' by Robert Venturi in America.

Not all Scandinavian architecture was as softened – or soft-centred, as its
critics saw it – as the Swedish version. In Denmark several of the best known
houses could, with little difficulty, have been aligned with the declared values of
New Brutalism, if not always with the forms through which they were expressed.
Again, Japan played a vital role. Tetsuro Yoshida's book *Das Japanische
Wohnhaus*, published in 1935, proved a revelation with its detailed cultural and
technical explanations of the Japanese house. Cast in terms that would appeal to
Functionalists, it explained the close relationship to the climate and way of life
and emphasized how the houses were built using a 'kit' of standard components.
1935 also saw the construction of the Zui-Ki-Tei teahouse in the grounds of the
Ethnographic Museum in Stockholm, which was documented in detail in the
leading Swedish journal *Byggmästaren*. As Sweden was neutral during the war, it
became a place of refuge for architects from other Scandinavian countries, who
naturally took the opportunity to see the Zui-Ki-Tei at first hand. Its influence was
felt throughout the Nordic states, but nowhere as keenly as in Denmark, and
nowhere more originally than in the work of the most talented member of the
post-war generation of architects, the Dane Jørn Utzon (whose house on
Majorca, Can Lis, we considered in Chapter 4, pages 124–7).

Utzon spent three years working in Stockholm during the war
and in 1949 won a scholarship to travel to Mexico and the
United States, where he spent a week with Frank Lloyd Wright
at Taliesin East and met Mies van der Rohe in Chicago. In 1952, when he came
to build his own house on a large wooded plot at Hellebaek in northern Zealand,
he managed to meld a series of influences – those of Wright's Usonian houses,
Mies's Farnsworth House and of Japanese architecture – into a distinctive,
original whole. The house was sited at the head of a shallow valley across which
he threw up a solid wall, like a dam, against the north winds and, in its shelter, a
low brick platform. The rigour is unyielding. The wall is broken only once, by the
main entrance, and as a consequence the study and children's bedrooms have
only roof lights – in protest, his young daughter tried to scrape her own tiny
opening in the wall.

Spatially, the house unfolds in layers between parallel wall-planes and around a
service core. Internally, the boarding on the partitions stops short of the ceiling
and floor, to allow the roof and floor planes to float visually, and the doors are full

height in the Miesian manner. Utzon used modular elements to allow for the possibility of change, a theme that became the basis of the 'Espansiva' house-building system commissioned fifteen years later by the Danish timber industry. At Hellebaek he worked with a limited palette of materials – stained timber and a mellow, yellow brick – and handled them with a control that was a hallmark of Danish tradition. Its inspirations may have been exotic, but for many architects Utzon's house at Hellebaek came to define what a modern Danish house should look and – just as important – feel like.

To encourage people to build their own houses, the Danish government promoted a low-interest state loan scheme. Utzon was counting on one when he embarked on his ambitious Hellebaek project at the age of thirty-four. To qualify, it was normally obligatory to use an architect to prepare the plans, and the system enabled many architects both to build for themselves and to try out ideas on small, easily managed commissions. There were limits to how experimental you could be, however, and Utzon's house turned out to be ineligible for a loan because it had too much glazing and underfloor heating – a novelty designed using a Californian manual. For clients wanting something more conventional than his own house, Utzon developed a line of Wright-inspired houses that can best be described as Utzonian. Most were built for young middle-class families under the state loan scheme at modest cost. They were often adapted from the Hellebaek plan but with concessions to everyday needs such as windows in the north wall and no central core – which rendered them spatially more conventional. The use of dark-stained exposed roof timbers and fair-face or white painted brickwork also brought them closer to the familiar image of Scandinavian Modern architecture.

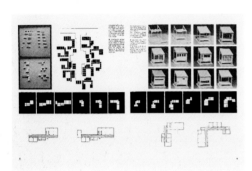

Middlebøe House Lake Furesö, Denmark, 1953, Jørn Utzon

Utzon worked by a set of guiding principles, not a 'style', as is clear from the Middlebøe House overlooking Lake Furesö near Copenhagen, completed in 1953. To take advantage of the views he decided to raise the main floor a full storey, and because access to the site was difficult he returned to the ideas on prefabrication which he had only been able to hint at in the modular co-ordination of his own house. He devised a simple, but highly unusual, system of framing based on precast concrete components, in which the beams merely rest under gravity on rectangular double columns. The inner section of the columns rises only to the first floor, the outer one through both floors to support the roof. Both columns are double squares in plan, and the beams overlap across their tops, so that the structure steps in and out along the façade. The end beams are standard lengths and project beyond the columns, suggesting the possibility of extension.

The black and red colour scheme of the Middlebøe House was inspired by Chinese timber construction, and the influence of Mies's Farnsworth House is again evident, although the scale is smaller and the accommodation for a family more complex. To preserve the openness of the plan the bathroom was shrunk to a minimal shower room, whose viability Utzon demonstrated in a sketch showing the clients taking their ablutions: it was later extended. A similarly compact galley kitchen backs up against the shower room, with a preparation counter opposite. The south-facing deck, framed by the structure and situated well above the mosquitoes' hunting height below, provides the ideal place to enjoy the lake,

Above Espansiva prototype house, Hellebaek, Denmark, 1969, Jørn Utzon. This ingenious timber-building system, commissioned to challenge the dominance of brick construction in Danish housing, reflected Utzon's love of traditional Japanese houses. Very few were built as financing fell foul of the major banks.
Opposite Middlebøe, Lake Furesö, Denmark, 1953, Jørn Utzon. Elevated to enjoy views of the lake, the design recalls Mies's Farnsworth House but was built using a concrete frame and timber secondary structure. The red and black colour scheme reflects Utzon's lifelong interest in Chinese architecture.

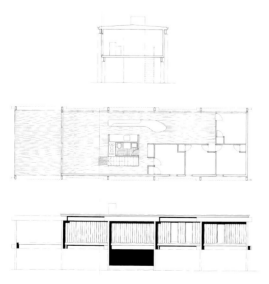

Above Sørensen House, Jaegersborg, Denmark, 1955, Erik Chr. Sørensen. Japanese influence is evident in the modular planning around a sequence of courtyards, exposed timber structure and elegantly detailed gardens.

which the living and dining areas address through full-height glazing. The lake becomes the focus of living, *in* the house, but *with* nature.

The Middlebøe house found no imitators, but Utzon's Hellebaek house, on the other hand, was widely emulated around Copenhagen. 1956 saw the completion of a one-family house in Søllerød by Børge Glahn and Ole Helweg and of his own house by Bertel Udsen. The former was directly derived from Utzon's design, but lost the spatial subtlety of the original by developing it into a more compartmentalized, L-shaped plan, while Udsen's was more successful in retaining the planar layering of the space by allowing the scheme to develop either side of the 'closed' wall. In Erik Chr. Sørensen's own house, completed in Jaegersborg in 1955, the debts to Japan are more obvious than those to Utzon, although the handling of out-reaching brick walls probably owed something to him. The plan was organized around a sequence of courtyards in which Danish versions of the natural garden were displayed to full effect.

A similar continuity between inside and out is evident in one of the most accomplished houses of the period, built in 1958 by Halldor Gunnløgsson for himself at Rungsted Strandvej looking out over Øre Sound north of Copenhagen. The open plan unfolds between two unbroken flank walls, with the spaces, column-and-beam structure and window divisions conforming strictly to a 2 x 2 metre (6.5 x 6.5 foot) module. Deep beams span between the flank walls, along each window wall and down the centre of the 8-metre- (26-foot-) wide plan, supported by columns at 4-metre (13-foot) centres. Above them, evenly spaced roof beams establish a counterpoint to the module, and cantilever at each end to protect the terraces. Between the beams the ceiling is boarded flush with its underside and the pine is left in its natural colour to contrast with the dark-stained structural elements. The flank walls and chimneys are plastered and painted white, and the floors finished with bright grey Swedish marble. Timber decks, flush with the internal floor, run along each edge, one looking out to sea, the other into a large terrace garden. The meticulously controlled interior, in which Miesian and Japanese ideals are fused, is perfectly complemented by Poul Kjærholm's furniture, epitomising the Danish sense of *quality*. This was a word used frequently to convey not only the understated elegance and refinement for which Danish design in the 1950s became renowned, but also an appropriate balance between form and material, production and cost, innovation and tradition. Danish design in its heyday exemplified the informality and freedom of the Scandinavian lifestyle, while retaining an underlying classical discipline which largely disappeared in Sweden after 1945.

No architect better epitomized these qualities than Arne Jacobsen who, having been a pioneer of Functionalism, re-established his position as a leading Danish architect with a group of houses in Søholm, designed in 1950 and completed over the next five years. Threaded between the mature trees of an old estate, the houses were cranked at 45 degrees to the road to optimize their exposure to the sun and to the views across Strandvej to Øre Sound. In plan, the more eye-catching of the two house-types is intricate yet surprisingly compact, with all the living spaces, bar one bedroom above the garage, ranged between cross-walls placed 4 metres (13 feet) apart. Jacobsen's houses were widely admired but, being so specific to their site, not easily emulated.

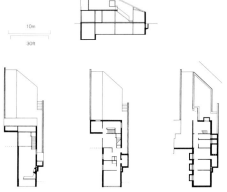

Above Gunnløgson House,
Rungsted, Strandvej, Denmark, 1958,
Halldor Gunnløgson. The structural
clarity, Miesian planning, natural
materials and understated detailing of
this fine house exemplify the classical
virtues of Danish architecture.
Left Link-houses, Søholm,
Copenhagen, Denmark, 1950–55,
Arne Jacobsen. Ingeniously organized
in plan and section, this influential
group of houses was designed to
make the most of a difficult site which
enjoyed views across the coast road
to Øre Sound.

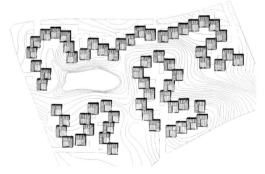

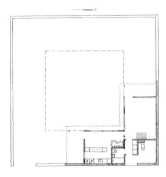

Above Skåne Houses, competition project, Sweden, 1954, Jørn Utzon. The courtyard house fascinated Utzon and his winning design in this competition proposed a house which could grow and change like the family occupying it. The idea's potential achieved its most poetic expression in the Fredensborg Housing (**top**).

Kingo Houses Helsingør, Denmark, 1965, Jørn Utzon

Opposite Kingo Houses, Helsingør, Denmark, 1957–9, Jørn Utzon. This development of more compact houses of the type proposed for Skåne was built at Utzon's initiative. The distinctive, sentinel-like chimneys were inspired by Iranian wind-catchers and were widely imitated.

In 1954 a competition was organized in Sweden specifically to develop models for low-cost suburban housing around the edges of towns in the southern region of Skåne. It was won by Jørn Utzon with a proposal for courtyard houses based on a 20-metre (65-foot) square bounded by a high wall, within which a wide strip of building could develop in response to a family's changing needs. Utzon's ideas exemplified the Scandinavian concern with the house as an expression of the values of everyday life. He invented a life-history for each house, and the plans show how the accommodation could expand from a small, three-room, L-shaped dwelling to cope with the arrival of children, divorce and subsequent setting-up of a small bakery, provision of guest accommodation, or pursuit of a hobby such as boat building. As in Markelius's house the plans and sections are drawn fully furnished and planted, to evoke the sense of organic life and change.

The courtyard form is one of the oldest and most universal of types, and Utzon's fascination with it had both domestic and exotic roots. The traditional Danish farm house, ranged around a central yard, provided a local prototype, while his studies of Chinese and Islamic architecture confirmed its potential as the unit of a development – or entire town. The type was also coming back into favour elsewhere. In 1957 the landscape architect Ian McHarg – the leading pioneer of ecological planning and design – published a major review article in the *Architects' Year Book* documenting examples built worldwide 'over the last twenty years'. These demonstrated that the court house could 'provide the essence of the best freestanding country houses' and create 'a residential environment as humane as it is urbane'.

Versions of Utzon's houses were built around Lund, but as so often in post-war Sweden the final designs were not under his control, so he decided to take things into his own hands in Denmark. Eventually, in 1957, he persuaded the mayor of Helsingør to make available some nine acres of undulating land and formed a collaboration with the Kingohusene company to undertake the development of the Kingo houses, as they became known. They were intended for low-paid workers and teachers, and Utzon reduced the square to 15 metres (49 feet) and developed two alternative house-types.

Despite the vernacular precedents, the Kingo houses were initially seen by many as alien, and acquired nicknames like 'Roman Houses' and 'Arab City' – entirely appropriately as Islamic towns were a prime inspiration. Roland Rainer, whose books Utzon greatly admired, described a traditional Iranian town as a 'total environment', a 'single, freely formed sculpture. . . "made in one casting"' in which 'room, house, street and square appear to be as perfectly adjusted to body measurements, patterns of movement, living conditions and social structure as to the climate'. It was just such a unity Utzon aimed at and he suppressed all extraneous details to achieve it. The chimneys, modelled on Iranian wind-catchers, grow solidly from the perimeter walls, and windows in the outside walls were kept to a minimum and screened by timber slats.

The Kingo houses came to the attention of Danes Worldwide, an organization to help nationals working abroad keep in touch with all things Danish. The result was a small retirement community for returning expatriates, built on a superb, gently sloping site near the royal castle of Fredensborg. In addition to the

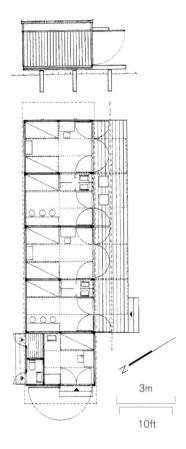

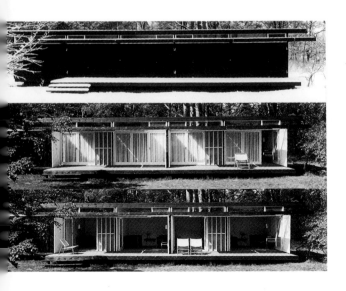

sequences of courtyard houses there was to be a communal building with dining room, lounge and a small hotel for guests. The scheme was completed in 1965, well after Utzon left to work full-time in Sydney on the Opera House, but before leaving he established the principles to be followed in designing the walls of the individual courtyards. The builder's tender included an allowance for a standard number of bricks, and each wall was to be individually designed by one of Utzon's assistants sitting in the courtyard and determining by eye – according to possible views, exposure, overlooking, orientation, etc – an appropriate configuration. Utzon's inspiration was a lecture he had heard in Stockholm, in which Alvar Aalto proposed a branch of flowering cherry as a model for a housing scheme – each flower the same, yet each unique, according to its relationship to its neighbours, the sun, wind, and so on.

Something similar had been attempted in the Kingo houses, but too many identical walls were repeated: at Fredensborg the result is masterly. The gently undulating greensward framed by a continuous built fabric feels as timeless as the Islamic and medieval European settlements that were its ultimate inspiration. The balance between privacy and community, repetition and variety, is finely struck, and just as important as the designed variation of the private courtyards is the individuality that comes from Utzon's boldness in fitting the houses to the sloping land. Some, at the ends of the long terraces, stand almost 3 metres (10 feet) out of the ground. They are given no special treatment, such as a window overlooking the farmland beyond, and confront the open landscape with unbroken walls of brickwork up to 7 metres (23 feet) high. The result suggests a small city-wall. It is breached only once, and the view down between the gable ends, across the grass to the terraces beyond, seems, for a moment, like a glimpse of Umbria.

Utzon's courtyard houses were widely admired and emulated in Denmark. The Ved Stampedammen courtyard houses in Usserød, completed in 1965 by Frederiksen, Hammer, Moldenhawer and Paulsen for example, were modelled directly on the Kingo project but executed in the white-painted brick style that originated in the private houses of the 1950s and was widely adopted in the 1960s. In a terrace of houses in Overrød, completed in 1963, Bertel Udsen framed the houses with bold, L-shaped walls and emulated the 'city-wall' appearance Utzon achieved, while the terraced houses in Carlsminderpark in Søllerød, by Henrik Iversen and Harald Plum, echo Utzon's formal language, including the distinctive chimneys.

The summer house continued to provide Scandinavian architects with outstanding opportunities for experimentation, and again Japanese influence was very much to the fore. Just how varied were the outcomes of the continuing fascination with the Japanese house can be seen by examining contrasting examples. The first, designed in 1957 by Vilhelm Wohlert (renowned for the Japanese-inspired Louisiana Museum, designed with Jørgen Bo) was a guest annex at the great physicist Niels Bohr's summer residence. Wohlert's design adapts the openness and seasonal flexibility of traditional Japanese architecture to the Nordic climate and in plan is simplicity itself. Two double and two single rooms are placed in line, entered directly from the outside via a south-facing deck, with a separate nanny's room entered from the short, west-facing end.

3m

10ft

Above Fredensborg Housing,
Fredensborg, Denmark, 1962–5, Jørn
Utzon. The continuous fabric of yellow
brick walls and tiled roofs, punctuated
by the cubic chimneys, has a unity
reminiscent of medieval settlements,
and successfully accommodated a rich
variety of private worlds within the
dwellings and courtyards.

Opposite Nils Bohr summer house
(guest annex), Tisvilde, Denmark, 1957,
Vilhelm Wohlert. Built for the inventor
of Quantum Theory, this annex to his
summer-house changed from a
secretive black box in winter to an
open belvedere in summer.

Above Kaapeli, Lingonsö, Finland,
1969, Kaija and Heikki Siren. This
private 'chapel' for nature-worship,
which forms part of the Sirens'
summer-house, evokes memories of
ancient Japanese Shinto shrines like
those periodically re-built at Ise.

Opposite, bottom Span houses,
Ham Common, Surrey, England, 1956,
Eric Lyons. The landscaped public
space and combinations of tile-
hanging, timber-boarding and render
reflected Scandinavian influence in
the most innovative speculatively built
modern housing on offer in England.

In the winter it is completely sealed, a mysterious black-stained wooden box with only a clerestory to hint at the possibility of habitation. Shutters at each end and a pair in the middle swing open to reveal glazed doors with broad, white-painted frames. They can be fixed open at 90 degrees to subdivide the terrace, providing privacy and shelter, or turned inwards to leave the sun terrace completely open. The large window shutters, painted black outside and white inside, can be lifted up into a horizontal position to form a sun roof, and the windows then fold away to open the interior completely.

During the 1960s many leading Finnish architects again became preoccupied with industrialization, and in 1967 Arno Ruusuvuori was commissioned by the well known fashion and fabric company Marimekko to design an experimental summer house using simple prefabricated components. The result was simple but strikingly elegant, a long, thin box with a covered porch linking house to sauna. It was emulated two years later by two young architects, Kristian Gullichsen (son of the family who built the Villa Mairea) and Juhani Pallasmaa, in the industrialized summer house system they named 'Moduli'. In total contrast, and also completed in 1969, is the sitting room Kaija and Heikki Siren added to their summer residence at Lingonsö. The site is an isolated island of rock and the fully glazed space is framed with four substantial hand-hewn columns, cut to receive similarly robust beams. With its elevated, cantilevered floor and projecting roof it almost recalls a rudimentary Greek temple, but the ultimate inspiration was Japanese – the Japan of the sixth century Ise Shrine, rebuilt almost every twenty years since, not of Edo period modularization which inspired Ruusuvuori and the younger generation.

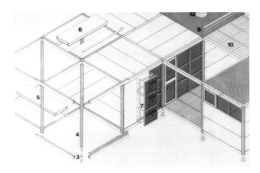

Above 'Moduli' summer-house system, Finland, 1969, Gullichsen and Pallasmaa. Miesian discipline combines with the Finnish love of natural materials in this elegant system-built house.

Kaapeli Lingonsö, Finland, 1969, Kaija and Heikki Siren

Designing it as a space from which to contemplate nature, the Sirens named their new room Kaapeli – 'Chapel'. At first sight the contrast with the Moduli system could hardly be more complete, but in much of the best Scandinavian architecture the two poles – organic/mechanical, craft-made/machine-made – can both be discerned. In the Villa Mairea, we may recall, Aalto used steel columns but wrapped them with rattan, both as a reference to nature and to humanize the industrial product, rendering it warm and tactile. Similarly, although the Siren's Kaapeli is conspicuously handmade, its geometry and tectonic expression are rigorous, utterly devoid of the sentimentality so often associated with the handcrafted. Similarly, too, the Moduli system uses wood, not steel or aluminium, and even as austerely systematic a design as this retains those links to nature that are widely seen as the essence of the Scandinavian contribution to modern architecture. Nowhere, arguably, did the Scandinavian influence receive a greater welcome from architects and a progressive section of the public than in England, and it is with two English examples that we will conclude our discussion.

The continuing reluctance of English popular taste to come to terms with modern architecture was much discussed in the architectural press. By the mid 1950s, however, in the wake of the 1951 Festival of Britain, education by the BBC and women's magazines, and the arrival of such exotic continental delights as espresso bars, there was a small but tangible demand for more modern houses. The need was most famously met by Span Builders and their architect Eric Lyons. Span advertised in *The Observer* and *The Sunday Times*, which were

read almost exclusively by literate professionals. They built initially in salubrious outer London suburbs such as Richmond, Twickenham and Blackheath, and Lyons often worked in the teeth of opposition from amenity societies and local planners to whom the houses still seemed dangerously modern. To describe the Span style as overtly Scandinavian would be misleading, but the relaxed combination of brick cross-walls, tile hanging, weather-boarding and large areas of glazing was an English version of the easy-going 'New Empiricism' that found such a receptive audience in Britain. Internally, the house plans daringly opened up the familiar semi-detached house-type, offering a continuous ground floor with living room to the front and dining/kitchen to the rear. Even more innovative, and clearly marked by Scandinavian examples, was the creation of a continuous, richly planted public landscape, beautifully scaled to the houses. The elimination of front gardens was unheard of in private housing in the UK at the time, but it became a main selling feature in Span's advertisements.

Turn End Haddenham, England, 1967, Peter Aldington

A smaller shared landscape also formed part of the remarkable group of three houses – known as Turn End – created by Peter Aldington in Haddenham. The site was acquired in 1963 and the houses completed in 1967. Aldington still lives in the largest of them, more land has been acquired, and under his care the garden has evolved into an exquisite, quintessentially English setting. He conceived the houses as a series of walled enclosures and when asked to cite the influences on his work named his student heroes – Mies, Wright and Le Corbusier. Their impress is apparent in the open-plan, loft-cum-gallery, built-in seating and Jaoul-like toughness of the masonry. But the ambience is far closer to some of the Scandinavian examples we have examined, and details such as the split roof section with high-level glazing, close-spaced mullions and tile-capped chimneys immediately recall Jacobsen's Søholm houses and the detailing of Aalto and Utzon.

Stylistically, these houses did not set out to be radically innovative. What makes them exemplary is the way in which English picturesque and vernacular traditions are combined with the tougher, evolving language of modern architecture and then fitted into a traditional village. By preserving existing buildings, using local materials and details – such as the distinctive lime-rendered and tile-topped walls – and planning the three houses as an intricate, interlocking composition, Aldington achieved an organic unity that is a riposte to the all too familiar pattern of treating each house in a development in splendid isolation from its neighbours. But finally what makes them unique is the magical, seamless unity of interior and exterior, house and garden. Few houses built in Britain in the twentieth century can rival them as richly habitable places to live.

Above, below and opposite Turn End, Haddenham, England, 1963–7, Peter Aldington. Melding forms and materials drawn from the local vernacular with Continental – not least Scandinavian – influences, Peter Aldington created a marvellously habitable group of three houses which fit seamlessly into a small English village.

from post-modern houses to postmodern dwelling

In 1966 the Museum of Modern Art in New York published the first of its 'Papers on Architecture'. Entitled *Complexity and Contradiction in Architecture*, and written by the Philadelphia architect Robert Venturi, it was later seen to mark the arrival of Post-Modernism though the style was only christened a decade or so later by Charles Jencks. By the now ubiquitous term 'Post-Modern' Jencks meant an architecture that rejected the central assumptions of modern architecture – abstraction, spatial continuity, truth to materials, etc – and addressed itself primarily to issues of communication and style. Architecture was seen as a language that, by drawing on historic styles, popular culture and its own more recent past, could communicate with a variety of audiences. The term postmodern – no capitals, and with the hyphen now increasingly commonly dropped – gradually came into use to describe a more far-reaching cultural phenomenon which one of its leading theorists, Jean-François Lyotard, argues began with the transition to the so-called post-industrial age towards the end of the 1950s. In this chapter we will begin by looking at Post-Modern houses in the narrower, stylistic sense, and then move on to consider broader issues centred around the ideas of 'dwelling' and 'place'.

Vanna Venturi House Chestnut Hill, Pennsylvania, USA, 1962–4, Robert Venturi

The house Robert Venturi built for his mother Vanna Venturi in Philadelphia's leafy suburb of Chestnut Hill (1962–4) is the first emblematic building of Post-Modernism. At a glance the front elevation resembles the classic child's drawing of 'house': gabled and symmetrical, with a big central chimney, a door in the middle and windows either side. Look again and you find it is anything but simple. The gable is split down the middle, the fissure coming to rest on an expressed lintel though which is drawn the line of an arch. The windows are all different but linked by a rudimentary stringcourse. To the left are large and small squares, to the right a miniature Corbusian ribbon window which slides into the corner and destabilizes the sense of solidity that the rest of the façade might seem designed to evoke.

Walk round to the back and symmetry is again asserted – by the overall form, emphasized by a lunette window at high level – and then denied by three different openings whose form clearly has more to with the internal requirements. This is what Venturi meant by 'complexity and contradiction'; it is also an example of what Jencks later called 'double-coding', the pernicious idea that buildings should communicate high-brow aesthetic meanings to the architecturally literate, and simpler, familiar messages for the man-in-the-street. The literate, for example, were meant to 'spot' that the split gable might be a knowing reference to Luigi Moretti's apartments on the Via Parioli in Rome, illustrated on page 29 of Venturi's book, or to various Mannerist villas – Mannerism being one of his favourite styles.

The complexities of Venturi's architecture are by no means skin deep. In plan, symmetry was asserted and then 'accommodated' (he used the word in a particular sense) to the functional requirements. The kitchen balances a bedroom, but not exactly, and the chimney and stair battle for supremacy at the centre of the composition. The stair is wider at its bottom than at the top, as befits the transition from 'public' downstairs to 'private' upstairs, and cleverly sliced by an angled wall which eases open the entrance porch to make room for the double entrance doors. At three of the four corners, recesses and a covered veranda

Above and opposite Vanna Venturi House, Chestnut Hill, Pennsylvania, USA, 1962–4, Robert Venturi. The house Venturi designed for his mother exemplified his ideas on 'complexity and contradiction in architecture' and was later hailed as one of the first manifestos of Post-Modern design. Although deliberately house-like, the gabled front elevation plays games with symmetry reminiscent of Le Corbusier's Villa Stein at Garches.

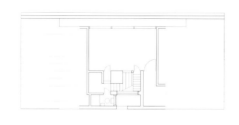

reveal the thinness of the walls, turning the front and rear elevations into screens – an effect reinforced by the parapets in which they terminate.

The Vanna Venturi house was undeniably clever, and Venturi proved to be one of the most artful planners of his generation, drawing ideas as freely from Le Corbusier and Aalto as from historical architecture. He became increasingly obsessed with architecture as imagery, however, and later took his students to Las Vegas to study the casinos and roadside signs as 'an architecture of communication'. The book *Learning from Las Vegas* appeared in 1972 and in it Venturi, his wife Denise Scott-Brown and colleague Steve Izenour indulged in a High Camp reverie of the city's relentless kitsch. Buildings, they declared, could be considered either Ducks or Decorated Sheds. The former, named after a Long Island restaurant in the shape of a duck, included all form-follows-function buildings which try to communicate though manipulating the form of the entire building, while the latter encompassed fancy, communicative façades or signs that screened some cheap building to the rear. It was a deeply cynical reduction, but epitomized a growing fascination with the idea of architecture as a language operating through culturally determined codes rather than the abstract properties of space, form and structure – an idea explored at length in Charles Jencks's influential 1977 book *The Language of Post-Modern Architecture.*

Jencks dated the 'death of modern architecture' with oft-quoted precision: it passed away, he declared, on 'July 15, 1972 at 3.32pm' when several slab-blocks of Minoru Yamasaki's Pruitt-Igoe development, a twenty-year-old, award-winning public housing project in St-Louis, Missouri, were dynamited. Like many other critics and theorists in the 1970s Jencks borrowed ideas from the linguistic theories of Saussure, Chomsky and others. Through their preoccupation with space and structure, he argued, Modernist architects had neglected vital semantic and symbolic aspects of architecture and thereby cut themselves off from the wider culture. Jencks's advocacy of style, language and meaning was to lead architects in startlingly disparate directions. Venturi, Charles Moore, Robert Stern and Michael Graves, all prolific house builders, moved inexorably towards increasingly self-conscious re-uses of historic styles, whereas others – most famously the New York Five – treated the architecture of the Heroic Period, the 1920s, as a stylistic resource.

Trubek and Wislocki Houses Nantucket, Massachusetts, USA, 1971–2, Robert Venturi

Venturi's Trubek and Wislocki houses of 1971–2 on Nantucket, Massachusetts, are clearly derived from the Shingle-style houses for which the island is renowned, but at the same time allude to other, more distant architectures. Their placement, turning towards each other as if in conversation, was, according to Venturi, influenced by the Greek temples at Selinus. The larger house boasts a Palladian gable to suggest a grander scale, but is then deflated by having its corner sliced diagonally in deference to the direction of approach. As in his mother's house, what seems at first familiar, even conventional, turns out to be complex. Thus, for example, on one house the veranda is 'conventional', added to the rear of the house, in the other it cuts into the volume in a thoroughly Modernist way. The windows, similarly, are commonplace sashes eccentrically distributed in response to internal requirements. The idea is given a different spin in the Tucker House of 1975, in Katonah, New York, which exaggerates almost to the point of caricature the familiar form of 'house'. The pyramidal roof is like a giant hat, and its profile is repeated inside to frame the fireplace. Venturi's explanation for the tapering, tower-like form was, however, refreshingly straightforward: it looked better among the aspens, and involved cutting down fewer trees.

The architect Robert Stern was one of the first to recognize Venturi's talents, giving him pride of place in the 1965 edition of the Yale architecture journal, *Perspecta*, which he edited while still a student. Stern has always regarded himself as an adapter rather than inventor, an informed eclectic content to work with the ideas of others, variously refining, exaggerating and distorting their forms. His Wiseman House (1965–7), a year-round vacation home in Montauk, New York, is patently indebted to the Vanna Venturi House, in both plan and elevation, but it plays games with the prototype. The front elevation has been expanded laterally to address the distant views by means of diagonal corners to create a bigger scale, and the lunette window has been vastly enlarged to make a huge arch — part window, part open frame — defining the edge of a roof-top terrace.

Venturi's Brant House of 1971, in Bermuda, likewise appears to have been an inspiration for Stern's much larger house of 1974–6 in Westchester County, New York, which turned the idea of the screen wall used by Venturi into a leitmotif of the whole composition. A curving screen sweeps across half the entrance front, framing the entrance and sheltering a private outdoor space for the servants, while to the rear a symmetrical, bowed screen wall reduces the apparent length of the elevation and provides solar protection. It is echoed inside, in the form of the symmetrical wall framing the kitchen, one of several examples of what Stern describes as 'formal interventions which are assembled by the observer as he moves through the spaces'; these are encountered on promenades that culminate in open vistas across the garden. If this sounds suspiciously like a description of a 1920s villa by Le Corbusier it is hardly surprising, because the Corbusian syntax is also much in evidence here. The shallow, S-shaped wall dividing the two servants' bedrooms is surely a knowing reference to the almost identical partition of the maid's room in the Cook House, thus a clue to the ultimate inspiration behind Stern's repeated layering of space. The walls, of cream-coloured stucco with two narrow terracotta stripes forming a rudimentary cornice, are intended, Stern says, to remind us of Tuscan villas, Fallingwater and 1930s Hollywood, but the prevailing influence is unmistakably Art Deco. Rambling and picturesque, the house is a large-scale exercise in the decorative use of space and surfaces; skilful in its way, but by comparison with the Corbusian models on which it drew, slack and devoid of a strong controlling idea.

During the late 1970s and 1980s Stern's work became more overtly derivative of past styles. A large house in Llewellyn Park, New Jersey emulated French Classicism externally while inside it mixed traditional rooms and flowing spaces; another at King's Point, New York played games with broken symmetry but was cast in a more consistently Classical manner. The Shingle style that had inspired Stern's first house in Montauk was followed more closely in the Bozzi House at East Hampton, New York, of 1983. This appears to be a faithful rendition of a house that might have been designed a century earlier, but on closer inspection it turns out to question many of the underlying assumptions of the style. The

Above and opposite Private
House, Westchester County, New
York, USA, 1974–6, Robert Stern. Art
Deco colours and styling combine with
Corbusian spatial layering in this
rambling, picturesque composition.

chimney is detached at one end of the composition, not integral to it as a spatial and social focus; the porch is Classical and added on, not cut out of the main volume as was usual in the classic Shingle style houses; the eyebrow dormer-windows are a familiar feature of East Hampton Shingle style houses, but Stern's are apparently unrelated to the rest of the composition and deeper than usual, more like applied features than delicate incisions into the roof covering propped open by slivers of glass; the gridded screen on the west elevation is borrowed from William Ralph Emerson's Hemenway House of 1883, but whereas there the corner is marked by a thicker post, Stern neither registers the different structural condition nor closes the corner visually.

Vincent Scully, we may recall, identified in the Shingle style a feeling of organic wholeness in the way the richly articulated masses were 'indicative of plastic volumes within'. In Stern's reworking of the style that wholeness is consistently denied; he does not aim at formal or spatial coherence but strings together forms and spaces calculated, as Gavin Macrae-Gibson has argued, to bring back memories of Atlantic resorts and traditional summers by the sea. Stern's method is scenographic rather than architectonic: no longer able to believe in the possibility of building a better world, the Bozzi House invites us to inhabit images of a past one.

Michael Graves began his career as a member of the self-styled New York Five, who achieved widespread recognition with a manifesto-like compilation of their work published in 1975 as *Five Architects*. The book was square and white. The cover featured only the architects' surnames in block letters and the work it contained was avowedly modern – pure 'White' as opposed to the eclectic 'Grey' of Venturi and his ilk. Graves was then the master of what were popularly dubbed 'Cubist kitchens', highly-worked – or over-worked, according to your taste – essays in post-Corbusian abstraction tacked onto unsuspecting houses around Princeton University where he taught. Graves made a rapid transition to an overtly Post-Modern style, however, and his Government Building in Portland, Oregon, of 1980–82 became the public flagship of the movement. In the Plocek House, designed in 1976 and completed in 1982 on a steep, wooded site in Waren, New Jersey, the future direction of his work was clear.

Like Palladio's Villa Madama, which provided a model, the plan is organized around two axes; they begin with tapering entrances at different levels, cross in a circular hall carved out of what Graves calls the 'stair column', and then move on. The long axis terminates in a mural entitled *Archaic Landscape*, painted by Graves above the large fireplace, while the cross axis disappears through the library window to end nowhere in particular, thanks to the client's failure to build the projected keystone-shaped pool house. The plan is composed of traditional rooms, some wholly contained by walls, others defined by perforated screens, and abounds in symmetries and sub-symmetries.

Externally, the modelling is intended to suggest the traditional Classical tripartite division into *piano rustica, piano nobile* and *corona aedificii* but Graves's Classicism is far from orthodox. The stair column which begins as a circular void at the ground floor emerges above as a freestanding cylindrical drum, and then blossoms into a conical, wood-framed 'capital' below a skylight

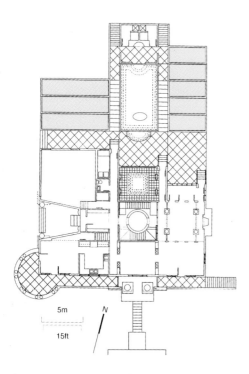

5m
15ft
N

Plocek House Warren, New Jersey, USA, 1976–82, Michael Graves

Above and opposite Plocek House, Warren, New Jersey, USA, 1976–82, Michael Graves. Cross-axial planning and broken symmetries confirm an underlying Classical discipline, which is overlaid by an eclectic range of details, from the cubic corner windows to entrances reminiscent of Egyptian pylons.

which allows light into the centre of the house. The windows are mostly square rather than upright and on either side of the main entrance two eminently Modernist projecting cubes of glass dissolve the corner, only to rest on rudimentary cylindrical columns. The side entrance, on the other hand, recalls Egyptian pylons and might almost be contrived to intimidate rather than welcome. You enter through a tall, narrow slot which expands into a keystone-shaped void; this was intended to be projected into the garden as the unbuilt pool house but it is now somewhat forlorn, an unconsummated example of Post-Modern wit.

Unlike later, more stylistically earnest Post-Modern Classicism, the Plocek House simulates thickness and mass but does not seriously attempt to convince you its walls are solid and heavy. You hardly need to tap them to know that they are hollow, that slender timber framing rather than masonry lies behind the rendered surface. Despite this, the gap between material substance and visual effect is disturbing. The house offers itself as a commentary on the world rather than as a piece of it, a feeling reinforced inside by the built-in cabinetry, furniture, lamps and rugs, all designed by Graves, which contrive to give it the air of a film set rather than somewhere palpably real. The effect is hardly coincidental, for Graves's work epitomizes the values of our media-dominated world. Permanence, for so long a hallmark of architecture, is here a product of the building's appearance, of the Classical language it deploys, not of its material substance. Post-Modernism was always meant to be ironic in its use of past styles, but the real irony is that less than twenty years after its completion Graves's return to the supposedly timeless language of Classicism should already seem so old fashioned, like last month's hit record or last season's fashions.

During the late 1970s and early 1980s Charles Jencks seemed able to discover or invent a new style every few months, disseminated as special issues of *Architectural Design* magazine with such titles as 'Post-Modern Classicism', 'Free-Style Classicism', 'Abstract Representation' and 'Late-Modern Architecture'. Jencks put his money where his mouth was by teaming up with the English architect Terry Farrell to convert and extend a London villa into his own 'Thematic House', published in 1985 in the glossy, overweening book *Symbolic Architecture*. By then, however, the tide was turning against the superficial pillaging of architectural history for forms and 'meanings', and whereas *The Language of Post-Modern Architecture* reportedly sold over 100,000 copies, *Symbolic Architecture* was destined to linger in the publisher's warehouse for years to come.

The term Post-Modern in architecture increasingly came to be identified with witty, ironic or in other ways unorthodox interpretations of Classical architecture, and its brief time in the limelight had more to do with media and marketing than with lasting architectural quality. But as Jencks rightly pointed out, the term could equally well apply to the New York Five. The two most important members of this group were Richard Meier, who based his work on a self-conscious reworking of Le Corbusier's 1920s villas – which, by the end of his life, Le Corbusier himself reportedly came to dislike; and Peter Eisenman, who treated architecture as a self-referential language. Eisenman was inspired to a lesser extent by Le Corbusier and more by the layered structures of Giuseppe Terragni and plastic energy of De Stijl.

Smith House Darien, Connecticut, USA, 1965, Richard Meier

The Smith House of 1965 exemplifies Meier's early work. It sits on a magnificent half hectare (one-and-a-half acre) site overlooking Long Island Sound, set back from the rocky shoreline among trees. Spatially the house is divided into two zones: a three-storey block of cellular rooms and, in front, a triple-height volume stratified but not compartmentalized by three platforms. Structurally, the rooms are enclosed by timber-framed walls with pierced openings, and the open zone is demarcated by columns and beams, permitting large areas of glass. The contrast is further heightened by placing an enclosed stair in one corner of the cellular zone and an open outdoor stair diagonally opposite to provide alternative links between floors.

Anyone receptive to the abstract language of modern architecture can hardly fail to find this white beacon of modernity set amid pristine nature aesthetically appealing. Meier's version of the Corbusian language is thoughtfully worked out and skilfully deployed, but it is also almost completely lacking in the tension and subtlety that made its model so potent. By the 1960s the dream of universality represented by the architecture of the Heroic Period was widely realized to be no longer tenable, and Meier's choice is, therefore, stylistic. Whereas the Modern Movement aspired to a twentieth-century vernacular, Meier offers a particular 'modern style' as his selling feature in the increasingly global marketplace. It proved a shrewd choice and he built a substantial career – museums, university buildings, corporate headquarters, a city hall – on the basis of a few years of Le Corbusier's endlessly inventive career: no matter that the language became mannered and stretched beyond its capacity, it *sold*.

The most original thinker presented in *Five Architects* was Peter Eisenman. He called his contributions 'Cardboard Architecture' and presented two projects, the laconically named House I and House II. Whereas most Post-Modernists concentrated on language as a semantic system he turned to syntax, to the grammatical and other structures that make linguistic communication possible. Emulating the 'generative grammars' of Noam Chomsky, Eisenman derived his houses from transformational rules that were purely formal in their operation. An initial set of what he called 'formal conditions' – an array of grids, planes and volumes – was variously shifted, translated and rotated to generate bewilderingly complex structures from which he could distil a sequence of habitable spaces. 'Such a logical structure of space,' said Eisenman, 'aims not to comment on the country house as a cultural symbol but to be neutral with respect to its existing social meanings.' Like the Minimalist sculptures of Sol Lewitt and Donald Judd produced around the same time, early Eisenman houses were hermetic, autonomous works: their form bore no relation to their site, nor did their organization spring from the pattern of activities they might house.

For Eisenman, however, House I and House II, and two further projects that followed them, still 'contained many preconceptions which upon reflection seemed to me to be culturally conditioned'. In particular, he felt they had been designed from the outside in rather than from the centre out, a process that would enable him to challenge the whole idea of 'façade'. In House VI, completed

House VI West Cornwall, Connecticut, USA, 1972–5, Peter Eisenman

in 1975 for the photographer Dick Frank and his wife Suzanne, an architectural historian, Eisenman set about inverting these preconceptions about the nature of architecture. He again used

Above, left and right House VI, West Cornwall, Connecticut, USA, 1972–5, Peter Eisenman. In his self-styled 'cardboard architecture' Eisenman subjected the planar language of Modernism to complex formal transformations using rules which he likened to the syntax of a natural language.

Opposite Smith House, Darien, Connecticut, USA, 1965, Richard Meier. Often magnificently sited, as here, Meier's houses are seductive essays in the manner of Le Corbusier's Twenties villas.

Above House at Ballyweelin, County Sligo, Ireland, 1983, O'Donnell and Tuomey. Although rooted in Irish Classicism and immediately at home in the landscape, the design reflects contemporary debates about the tectonic virtues of 'Doricism', notably in the exposed roof structure above the terrace which looks out to the sea.
Opposite Casa Rotonda, Stabio, Switzerland, 1981, Mario Botta. Split down a central axis and oriented to the four points of the compass, the cylindrical house ignores its suburban neighbours to address the wider landscape.

'diagrammed transformations' but saw the house not as an end product of the process, but as a record of it. The resulting solids and voids, columns and planes, were not a resolved composition, but an invitation to the mind to reorder them, and in the process question their 'meaning'. The house is permeated by vertical and horizontal slots, some glazed, some open, which seem to imply the existence of a 'virtual house' of absent columns and beams to be perceived in parallel with the real, physical one. And as if to reinforce this reading, each has its own staircase: a green one which connects the two floors, and a red one which goes nowhere and merely hangs in space as a 'sign' – like an anti-stair escaped from an Escher engraving.

Both clients and critics were responsive to House VI's visual and intellectual pleasures. Suzanne Frank described the 'series of slots, beams, and columns that unfold when viewed from the bedroom' as 'an effect as spellbinding as the movement of bits of glass on mirrors in a kaleidoscope'; the sociologist Robert Gutman recalled the first glimpse of the house as 'literally breathtaking – one of the superb visual experiences of modern design'; and Kenneth Frampton declared it 'canonical' on account of its 'dense orchestration of impacted form, comprised simultaneously and to the same degree of planes, transparencies, volumes and masses'. As a home, even a vacation home, however, it proved problematic. A column makes conversation around the dining table difficult: even after 'mental relocation' it remains insistently present. A window in the floor of what became the master bedroom required the clients to sleep in separate beds; guests had to cross the master bedroom to reach the bathroom; the kitchen worktops were too high to work at comfortably except when seated on a stool – a great inconvenience for Dick Frank who photographs food and is a keen cook; and views of the beautiful site from the living spaces were largely cut off by solid planes.

In 1988 the Franks decided to renovate their thirteen-year-old house. It was leaking – Eisenman, they said, was somewhat cavalier about details such as roof-flashings – and they had had enough of sleeping in separate beds and putting up with the other idiosyncrasies. The renovation took four years and, like the saga of the Farnsworth House, became something of a *cause célèbre*. Eisenman declared the house had lost its edge, but finally seemed to be reconciled to its new life. In the intervening years, as his work developed in new directions, he had also become clearer about the wider implications of his ideas. The novelist William Gass hinted at them when he wrote as follows about House VI: 'The world of this house was Copernican. Its spaces did not flow from me as though I were their source and centre. Its surfaces were not the limits of my sight and movement, places for paintings, shepherds of privacy, backgrounds for my furniture. Nor did the floor exist to support my rugs or serve to assure me, always, that I was safe on the hard and even earth.' Eisenman and a growing coterie of New York intellectuals based their work on the theory that in the wake of the Holocaust and Hiroshima it was no longer possible to sustain the classical, Western belief in the centrality of human values. The task of architecture, therefore, was to 'de-centre' the human subject: in House VI the owners finally chose to re-centre parts of the house around their needs.

In Europe, the most searching manifestation of Post-Modernism was the so-called neo-Rationalist movement associated with the Italians Aldo Rossi and Giorgio Grassi, the German Oswald Mathias Ungers, and the Luxemburg-born brothers Rob and Leon Krier. Their preoccupation was with restructuring the city, using traditional urban blocks and house types to create a fabric for monumental public buildings. The individual house did not loom large in their concerns, but their ideas were widely influential, not least in the Ticino, the Italian-speaking canton of Switzerland where Mario Botta produced a string of distinctive houses in the late 1970s and '80s. Botta's houses typically have strong, closed forms cut with bold openings and are planned symmetrically about a central axis. They are invariably built of concrete block which contrasts with delicate glass and steel windows, roof lights and stairs – the stairs sometimes designed to flex slightly under load to emphasize the solidity of the walls.

Casa Rotonda Stabio, Switzerland, 1981, Mario Botta

Casa Rotonda in Stabio, completed in 1981, is typical of Botta's early work. Aligned to the four points of the compass it stands in defiant isolation, a riposte to the amorphous suburban sprawl around it. The openings are scaled to the horizons and calculated to cut out views of the immediate surroundings and direct attention to untouched landscapes further afield. On the street side the walls step open on either side of the stair to make space for two cars. This allows the stair to stand free in a blockwork tower, whose curved top corbels out to meet the larger cylinder of the house – and in the process suggests a rudimentary column and capital. The reference is entirely conscious, but in no sense is it an applied motif, still less a Post-Modern joke. Botta saw his work as an attempt to propose a 'a new equilibrium between man and his surroundings' and to 'recapture the initial values from which the dwelling was made'.

Similar motives inspired a house at Ballyweelin in County Sligo, Ireland, built by O'Donnell and Tuomey in 1983. The language is gently Classical – almost the vernacular in Ireland – and the simple form, oriented towards the view, contains a subtle sequence of spaces in which changes of level and ceiling height describe rooms of varying importance. The organization is axial, but never simplistically symmetrical, and the fireplace breaks the enfilade to divert you onto the terrace to view the ocean.

Stylistic Post-Modernism in Europe was led by design rather than architecture, above all by the work of Ettore Sottsass Jr and the Alchymia studio he founded with Andrea Branzi, Alessandro Mendini and others in 1976. Their brilliantly coloured and often wilfully dysfunctional forms were later turned into marketable products under the name Memphis. In the mid-1980s Sottsass turned his attention increasingly to architecture and produced a string of houses composed from almost toy-like elements – triangular, gutter-less roofs, cubes and chunky columns. They did not, however, gain comparable international recognition.

In Norway Jan Digerud and Jon Lundberg came, ephemerally, to international notice with two houses in Kongsvinger (1971–3) and Jessheim (1979–81). The distinguished historian and theorist Christian Norberg-Schulz felt able to praise them as an 'important, enriching contribution to Norwegian wooden architecture' but in retrospect the houses appear to be little more than clumsy reworkings of American examples, the planning lacking Venturi's subtlety and the elevations ponderous and overloaded with motifs. In Denmark, an overtly Venturi-inspired

New House Sussex, England, 1986, John Outram

Opposite New House, Sussex, England, 1986, John Outram. Although unmistakably classical in inspiration, the monumental exterior is strikingly inventive formally and constructionally, and harbours a richly articulated sequence of spaces, many of which enjoy outstanding views over open countryside.

house was built as early as 1965 near Jeeling by Ole Ramsgaard Thomsen, and four years later the leading Swedish architect Peter Celsing built a self-conscious exercise in historically-referenced complexities and contradictions for himself in Drottningholm.

Despite the superficially Post-Modern features of his work, the English architect and self-professed Classicist, John Outram, rejects being classified as 'post' anything. His Classicism is of a singularly unorthodox and inventive kind and like most innovative, practising architects, he does not think of his work as belonging to, still less reviving, a particular style, but as a contribution to the ever-expanding language of Architecture. Outram delights in Classicism's other, and to many architects, uncomfortable side: the polychrome colours, primitivism and mixed-up iconography that were rediscovered in the eighteenth century, much to the embarrassment of many later, dryly correct Neo-Classicists. Relishing the physicality and substance of Classical buildings he could never be satisfied by the timber-frame and stucco versions built across the Atlantic, but he has no worries about mixing traditional and synthetic materials – which he likes to invent. Wherever possible, the colours are integral to the materials rather than applied to their surfaces, and his office is scattered with samples of specially coloured concretes with strange aggregates. Outram's designs are guided by what he calls 'generative fictions', personal narratives about the idea of Arcadia and the reconciliation of human culture and nature through Classical mimesis.

'New House', so named to preserve its owner's privacy, was completed in 1986 in the county of Sussex in southern England.

It occupies a large estate, replete with lake, 1200 deer and a neo-Gothic orangery, to which it is attached. The plan is a traditional H-shape, with an entry court on one side and a south-facing terrace on the other. The terrace, and the living and dining rooms which frame two sides of it, enjoy fine views down to the lake, and the entire plan sits on a square base like a vast, vestigial stylobate, gridded and elaborately paved, with 'absent' columns marked by circular insets. The structure is of steel set within hollow, 90-centimetre- (3-foot-) square columns which house services. They are clad in banded layers of precast concrete, which Outram thinks of as like geological strata: sedimentation and the action of water are a recurring theme in the choice and finishes of the materials. The base of each column has an exposed pebble aggregate; above it is a narrower band, acid-etched to reveal a crushed limestone aggregate with its marine fossils; most of the shaft is then clad in what he calls 'blitz-crete', concrete ground down to reveal large pieces of brick in the aggregate. The capitals are cubes out of which a sphere surfaces as if through water: made of black concrete, and with black marble aggregate, they are lacquered to look permanently wet and variously house rainwater overflows and floodlights. Between the capitals, not on them, are green lintel beams and arches, and below them the infill-walls are faced in travertine banded with brick.

Inside this massive-looking frame the interior is surprisingly light and airy. The richness of colours and materials, and attention to detail, are breathtaking and endlessly inventive: pink and yellow plywood ceilings, for example, sit happily with luxuriously inlaid wooden doors and stone floors. The shallow dome of the library brings to mind England's most inventive interpreter of Classicism, Sir John Soane,

Opposite Moore House, Orinda, California, USA, 1962, Charles Moore. The Modernist open plan is here transformed into a multiplicity of specific 'places' by changes of light, level and enclosure. The four-poster aedicules define sitting and bathing areas, whilst sliding windows and panels dissolve the corners in summer.
Below Casa Andreis, Scandriglia, Italy, 1964–7, Paolo Portoghesi. The plan illustrates how the Modernist field of space defined by orthogonal planes is transformed to generate a sequence of places in the surrounding landscape.

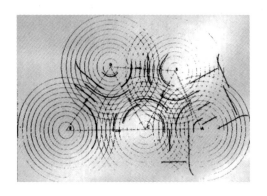

but in no sense does the design feel derivative. It is Classical, certainly, but a thoroughly modern Classicism designed, as Outram explained, in 'direct response to the saturated greens and dense colours that glow in southern England's cool, dim, stormy light with its shafts of brilliant sunlight'. For Outram, soaked in the traditions of his discipline, architecture has a 10,000-year history which 'like the heritage of the rainforests is the best place to find the "cure" to all our ills'. His work is not an attempt to pillage the past in search of forms with which to construct an artificial present, but rather to extend a living past into the future.

Stylistic Post-Modernism enjoyed greater success in commercial than residential architecture, and despite the vast amount of publicity and critical attention it attracted proved to be a surprisingly short-lived episode. The broader critique of modern architecture, recognized retrospectively as postmodern, had a more lasting impact. It focussed initially on the idea of 'place', which we used in discussing the regional adaptations of modernism in Chapter 4, and on the role of architecture in enabling us to 'dwell' in the world. Some of the key ideas were first articulated in short, poetic texts by Aldo van Eyck. In 1962, for example, he wrote that 'it is not merely what space sets out to effect in human terms, that gives it place, but what it is able to gather and transmit. . . what you should try to accomplish is built meaning. So get close to the meaning and build'. Christian Norberg-Schulz provided the most sustained body of theory for this approach, drawing on disparate intellectual sources. Initially he explored existential philosophy and Gestalt psychology, and later the German phenomenologist Martin Heidegger, whose ideas became almost ubiquitous in architectural literature during the 1980s, following the belated discovery of his essay *Bauen, Wohnen, Denken* (Building, dwelling, thinking), originally given at a 1951 conference on 'Man and Space' in Darmstadt.

As its title suggests, Norberg-Schulz's 1971 book *Existence, Space and Architecture* was framed as a challenge to the 'naïve realism', as he put it, of Giedion's *Space, Time and Architecture*. Far from being simply an abstract continuum in which we happen to exist, Norberg-Schulz argued, space as we experience and live it is concrete, compounded of things 'out there' in the environment and 'in here' in our heads. Contrary, for example, to the uniform three-dimensionality of the Schröder House or Eisenman's House VI, space – whether up and down, front and back, even left and right – is qualitatively different. Floors and ceilings may be designed abstractly as planes, but we experience them as above and below us, which brings to our perceptions a range of associations and expectations, not least with the earth and sky. To feel at home in the world, Norberg-Schulz argued, the environment needs to have an 'imageable structure' which offers rich possibilities of identification, enabling us to *dwell*, to belong to a place. Building has traditionally been one of the principal means by which we take possession of part of the world. Understood in these terms the 'meaning' of architecture is not, as Jencks framed it, a problem of communication or language, but of giving spatial form to a way of life in a particular location and culture.

Norberg-Schulz illustrated his ideas on 'existential space' – the precursor to 'place' in his writing – with Casa Andreis of 1964–7, by the Italian architect Paolo Portoghesi. The design can be seen as a commentary on the orthogonal planar

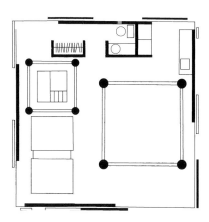

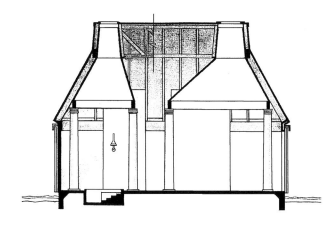

Moore House Orinda, California, USA, 1962, Charles Moore

structures of De Stijl. In place of abstract flat planes, the walls are generated from grids of circles drawn around a series of centres external to the house, establishing a more concrete interplay between building and site and creating a multiplicity of specific 'places' both within the house and in the landscape around it. The walls themselves are concrete, incised with vertical grooves to emphasize their rising movement, a feeling reinforced by the polished aluminium tubes applied to their ends to reflect ground and sky. The design was too idiosyncratic to have a wide impact, however, and it was in the USA, largely independent of European theorizing, that the place-making approach was most extensively realized in the design of houses. The protagonists were Charles Moore, Donlyn Lyndon and Gerald Allen, whose 1974 book *The Place of Houses* was aimed, like those produced just after the Second World War, at potential clients who might want a custom-built house.

The Place of Houses is profusely illustrated with a catholic collection of examples, ancient and modern, including many of the authors' own designs. Its key messages are all present in two small Californian houses by Moore: the Bonham House of 1961 and his own in Orinda completed the following year. Situated in a redwood forest in Santa Cruz County, the diminutive Bonham House makes up in importance what it lacks in stature by asserting its presence among this lofty company of trees with a huge, industrial-looking steel window, as high as the 4.2-metre- (13-feet-) square living space behind it is deep. The main space is supplemented by what Moore called 'saddlebags' (we met them in Bernard Maybeck's Guty Hyde Chick House, which could have been an inspiration) on opposite sides, one containing the kitchen and bathroom, the other a dining alcove. The floor sinks down into that necessity of Californian life, the conversation pit – here gathered around the stove – and rises via narrow, winding steps to the sleeping deck above it. A raised level around the perimeter doubles as display space and seating for the parties that were one of the main reasons why its owner wanted a weekend retreat.

The volume is open and continuous but transformed into a multiplicity of places by the numerous changes in level and light. The same multiplicity-in-unity is achieved, using different architectural means, in the highly personal version of the Californian good life Moore built for himself in Orinda in 1962. The site lies in one of the valleys behind San Francisco, filled with golden grass for most of the year and dotted with Live Oaks. The house is sited in the middle of a roughly circular lawn made by a previous owner in anticipation of building there and, as if in response, the plan is square and open. The roof is pyramidal, but asymmetrically pitched to allow for a roof light along the ridge, and the simplicity of the resulting form evokes an archetypal hut.

The interior is articulated by two square aedicules – miniature shelters consisting of four columns and a white-painted, lopsided pyramidal ceiling, which rises to the roof light. The roof has dark-stained rafters and boarding and is dimly lit by the remaining section of roof light, so that columns and bright light combine to define two distinct places – and imply others around them – within the continuum of the house. The first becomes the main sitting area; the second, and smaller, an oversized sunken bath, 'a celebration of the act of bathing here

liberated from the cramped conventional bathroom', as Moore described it. All four corners can be dissolved by sliding open glazed or solid barn doors. Like a Japanese house this one can be transformed according to season, but unlike a Modernist house there is not, Moore pointed out, 'an imperceptible merging of inside and out, rather the excitement of a boundary that can be leaned out over'.

The Orinda house manifested Moore's lifestyle and taste in detail as well as overall organization. The columns were selected, not designed: with classical entasis and rudimentary capitals, they were recycled from an old factory and then 'lovingly scraped, washed, and painted at their capitals'. The perimeter walls are layered to provide niches in which some of the fruits of his collecting are displayed, as if in a miniature museum: a little self-conscious for some tastes, perhaps, but clearly suited to his. And that is one of the central messages of *The Place of Houses*. Contrary to the exhortations of the 1920s to develop a shared modern lifestyle, Moore and his colleagues extolled the merits of the house as an expression of individual personality: 'You bind together the goods and trappings of your life together with your dreams to make a place that is your own'. Theirs was explicitly and unashamedly a theory of architecture for the consumer society, but sadly while Moore's early work offered the promise of something light and inventive, it quickly degenerated into a cardboard Classicism of no lasting interest.

Moore's early work exerted a considerable influence in America, however, and a house like that which Eugene Kupper completed in 1979 for the singer-songwriter Harry Nilsson and his wife Una would be almost unthinkable without it. Organized around a long, colonnaded spine it consists of a richly layered bunch of places, to borrow Aldo van Eyck's definition of a house, defined by different levels according to the sloping site and variously coloured to respond to different qualities of light. True to the principle of making the house as personal as possible, the nave-like spine is intended as an allusion to Una's Irish Catholic upbringing, but it ends ironically in a bath adjacent to a pulpit-like outdoor platform. The house can equally well be read as a theatre or hillside castle: through the playful manipulation of familiar symbols it invites many interpretations, and insists on none.

Cornford House Cambridge, England, 1967, Colin St. John Wilson

At first sight the Cornford House in Cambridge, designed by Colin St. John Wilson and completed in 1967, appears to belong to a completely different world to the Nilssons' theatrical showpiece. Look again, however, and you notice that it is also informed by a place-making sensibility. This can be seen both in plan – the square rooms defined by a combination of walls and freestanding columns have an obvious affinity with the aedicules at Moore's Orinda house – and in the subtle interplay of opposites: heavy brick against light timber; outside against inside, mediated by clearly articulated 'inbetween realms' (another Aldo van Eyck term); and shared/communal versus individual/private spaces. The similarities are not coincidental: Wilson came into direct contact with the new American thinking in 1960 through a teaching appointment at Yale, where Moore later became chairman, and through his colleague C. J. Long, who studied there as a postgraduate.

Illustrating a house like St. John Wilson's in a chapter on postmodernism may seem strange, because it so clearly belongs to the search for new possibilities

Above and opposite Cornford House, Cambridge, England, 1967, Colin St John Wilson. Although firmly rooted in the tectonic and compositional disciplines of modern architecture, this house reflects the interest in place-making central to the post-war European critique of the Modernist orthodoxy.

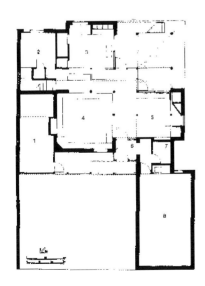

211

Above Private Residence, Lake Berryessa, California, USA, 1990, Christopher Alexander. Built using 'pattern languages' rather than conventionally designed, this rambling, site-inflected house attempts to recapture what Alexander believes are the timeless, humane values ignored by what he has called the 'giant scam' of modern architecture.

within modern architecture, free of International style clothing, but firmly committed to the broader values of the Modern Movement. But if a specifically 'Modern' architecture is to be identified as that which embodied the dream of a universal, machine-age style applicable in all climates and cultures, then almost everything of interest since 1945 has to be considered postmodern in the broad sense of the term. Such niceties of historiography are, however, of little concern to practising architects and life itself has a happy knack of turning apparent trends upside down. How many of those in the 1970s who confidently proclaimed the death of modern architecture would have predicted that the 1990s would witness a worldwide resurgence of interest in exploring and extending the twentieth century's most radical body of ideas, Modernism?

To Christopher Alexander, debating the relative merits of Modernism and Post-Modernism was supremely irrelevant because in his view the 'invented series of conceptions about space and volume and style' which underpin both are a 'giant scam. . . not connected to real human feelings, but only the artificially constructed aesthetic rules of a design intelligentsia.' Although trained as an architect, and a long-term professor of architecture at the University of California at Berkeley, Alexander has always marched to a different drummer. In the 1960s he was a leading advocate of systematic design methods, and then in 1978 he launched a comprehensive alternative theory of architecture with the book *The Timeless Way of Building*, a heady mixture of pseudo-scientific analysis, misty-eyed reverie at the delights of the ordinary, and ancient Oriental wisdom.

Alexander believes that beautiful, humane buildings of all periods and cultures are governed by intricate relationships among their parts and with the environment, which he attempts to describe using what he calls 'patterns'. He had published 253 examples the previous year in the book *A Pattern Language* and his ultimate aim was to empower people to become their own architects and builders. Central to Alexander's method is his conviction that many 'design' problems can only be solved working on site and in the process of building, not on a drawing board. While his solutions were too radical to be widely embraced, his critique raised issues that go back to the Arts and Crafts movement and will continue to resurface in our post-industrial economies.

Architects, hardly surprisingly, did not care to be told their ideas were not only unnecessary but often inimical to the task of making beautiful places, and when Alexander stopped theorizing and started building, the results, to most architects' eyes, only confirmed their doubts. The rambling, site-inflected plan of the residence on Lake Berryessa, California is typical of the loose, additive structures that generally emerge from working with pattern languages, and the formal resolution, with its vague memories of Classicism, is altogether less persuasive than the similarly site-responsive, but conventionally designed house on the Cinnamon Hill in Lunuganga, Sri Lanka, which Geoffrey Bawa completed in 1994. Bawa shares Alexander's belief that designs should be improvisations on site rather than premeditated exercises in abstract ideas: he produced only one drawing as the house emerged from inside out, configured in response to the site and in close harmony with nature. Both the bedrooms incorporate antique windows positioned to frame magnificent views of the lake and their en-suite bathrooms are roofless, ceiled by

House on Cinnamon Hill Lunuganga, Sri Lanka, 1994, Geoffrey Bawa

foliage and with living tree roots as towel rails. It hardly matters whether you describe such a house as post- or pre-modern: it is manifestly a wonderful place to dwell, achieving that timelessness to which Alexander aspires.

Above and left House on Cinnamon Hill, Lunuganga, Sri Lanka, 1994, Geoffrey Bawa. Improvising in response to the site rather than imposing preconceived abstract forms, Bawa here achieves the relaxed, timeless quality that Alexander admires in traditional architecture.

213

continuity and transformations

Although stylistic Post-Modernism proved to be a short-lived episode, the broader postmodern critique cut deep, rendering untenable the belief in a simple-minded modernity of unending progress and universal truths. Global information and entertainment technologies promoted a climate of pluralism and perpetual change. This led many architects, delighted with the multiplicity of the postmodern world, to explore the formal possibilities of fragmentation as a mirror of unruly vitality, and to use the house as a vehicle for an unprecedented freedom of sculptural expression. Others, believing the task of architecture was to create islands of calm and order amid the all-embracing clamour, pursued reductively abstract forms – often referred to, sometimes misleadingly, as 'minimalist' – or sought to ground their work in local cultures and places to counter the pervasive homogenization of environments and experience.

Modernism may no longer have been tenable as a system of values and beliefs, but predictions of its death as a formal repertoire proved greatly exaggerated, and by the 1990s a widespread neo-modern revival which built on the aesthetic and spatial possibilities first explored in the 1920s was evident worldwide. Core ideas such as spatial continuity and transparency were re-examined and transformed, frequently with a new emphasis on the materiality of the forms, and the issues of place, climate and culture discussed in Chapter 4 provided an ongoing and, in the case of climate, increasingly urgent agenda.

After more than twenty years spent designing competent but unremarkable buildings in and around Los Angeles, Frank Gehry burst onto the international scene in 1978 with one of the most influential house-conversions in architectural history. Struck by how much more exciting timber-framed houses looked during construction than when neatly finished in the owner's preferred 'style', when he

Gehry House Santa Monica, California, USA, 1978, Frank Gehry

came to remodel and extend his own home in Santa Monica, Gehry set about taking it apart to reveal the hidden layers of structure, sheathing and insulation – his methods recall the work of the architect-turned-sculptor Gordon Matta-Clark, famous for slicing timber buildings in two and, in 1972, exhibiting segments of walls in a New York loft-gallery. In Gehry's transformed house, white-painted casement windows suddenly found themselves on inside walls, figural incidents in ad hoc assemblages of timber boards and struts through which, layer upon layer, light filtered into the interior. The extensions, Gehry said, resembled boxes dropped on the old building and then casually frozen in space at odd angles, framed in wood and glass or chain-link fencing and variously clad in raw plywood or metal siding. In the kitchen and dining room, built over the old driveway, you discover an eminently serviceable tarmac floor beneath a forest of angled struts.

Inspired by Californian artist-friends who insisted on the primacy of perception, not concepts, in the shaping of form, Gehry worked intuitively using a kind of architectural *bricolage* – the collage-like technique Picasso invented to make sculptures over sixty years before. His transformed house was immediately interpreted as a challenge to conventional notions of domesticity and a commentary on the chaotic vitality of the sprawling megalopolis of Los Angeles; later, in an authentic postmodern critique, Kurt Forster saw it as an attempt to break out of his identity as a male, Canadian-Jewish immigrant. Gehry pursued this gritty, casual-seeming style in several later projects, but for the Winton Guest

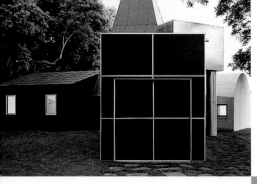

Top Winton Guest House, Wayzata, Minnesota, USA, 1983, Frank Gehry. Like a giant still-life set on the green baize of the lawn, the composition provided a dramatic contrast to the Philip Johnson-designed house for which it became an annex.

Above and left Lawson Westen House, Los Angeles, California, USA, 1988-91, Eric Owen Moss. Where Frank Gehry composes by eye, Moss prefers to use complex 'geometric mappings' to generate deconstructive forms, with results which strike many as apt metaphors for the chaos and vitality of Los Angeles.

House in suburban Wayzata, Minnesota, completed in 1983, he developed a different, equally radical approach. The clients lived in an elegant, Philip Johnson-designed brick box, but needed extra space for their children and visitors. The harsh climate demanded sound construction and, despite choosing Gehry, the Wintons were not interested in anything in his by then celebrated improvisational manner. What he delivered was an architectural still life, a series of objects placed on a lush green lawn, traversed almost imperceptibly, Japanese-style, by irregularly placed stones.

The rooms of the Winton Guest House are attached to the corners of a tall living room, a distorted square with a pyramidal roof, clad in sheet metal and evoking a giant chimney: a parody, almost, of Wright's archetypal dwelling. The hearth is a freestanding brick cube – the same brick as the Johnson house – from which, skewed in plan, rises a square chimney. Detailed with none of the normal concessions to weather, such as copings and cills, nor to gravity – expressed lintels or arches – it resembles a sculptural installation as much as a building. One bedroom is vaulted and covered – roof as well as walls – in limestone, the other in black sheeting, while the kitchen and garage are sheathed in Finnish plywood, and above them a stone-clad sleeping loft stands on a cylindrical metal column. The only reminder of Gehry's earlier manner comes inside, with a fragment of deliberately exposed rough carpentry and chicken wire below the stairs.

In the Winton Guest House Gehry offered a critique of the endlessly repetitive suburbia epitomized for many Americans by Levittown in New Jersey. By breaking the house down into individualized elements, not only did the whole become unique, but each part could assume different meanings for its inhabitants – 'ideas you have liked, places you have liked, bits and pieces of your life that you would like to recall,' as he put it. Treating the individual building as a miniature settlement was hardly new, but the result certainly was, and like Gehry's own house the Winton Guest House can now be seen as an early manifestation of a growing fascination for composing with visually or figuratively charged fragments. A similar sensibility is at work in another Los Angeles architect, Eric Owen Moss, but whereas Gehry works almost entirely by eye, like a traditional sculptor, Moss dissects and reassembles forms on the drawing board or computer screen.

Lawson Westen House Los Angeles, California, USA, 1988–91, Eric Owen Moss

The Lawson Westen House, designed by Moss between 1988 and 1991 and completed two years later, is generated by a series of complex 'geometric mappings' derived from the cylindrical kitchen which is the physical and symbolic heart of the dwelling. The centre of its conical roof is displaced laterally and the cone sliced vertically to make a deck with a view to the Pacific. The parabolic curve created by the cut is pulled down towards the street, creating the curved roof, whose gable end is marked by a strangely angled, cross-mullioned square window; the gable is then 'excavated' to reveal an identical window, conventionally aligned. These products of geometric deconstruction are overlaid by apparently ad hoc elements of structure, revealed or concealed according to taste rather than system, with results that are sculptural rather than tectonic. The garden front, for example, features a boldly projecting section of roof and laminated rafters tied or propped – it is not obvious which – by tubular steel members, one straight, the other

Below Open House Project, Malibu, California, 1983-90, Coop Himmelb(l)au. Although unbuilt, this project was one of the most influential of the 1980s, capturing more completely than any of their realized buildings the lightness and expressionism of Coop Himmelb(l)au's deconstructive style.

Open House Project Malibu, California, 1983–90 (unbuilt), Coop Himmelb(l)au

cranked as if fractured, and tied back to the façade with a steel cable.

The formal fragmentation and dissolution encountered in the houses of Gehry and Moss seem especially apt as responses to the chaos and dynamism of Los Angeles, but they were also to be found in the work of a diverse range of architects whose work was rooted in different attitudes, ideas and locales. The convergence was sufficiently striking for critics and magazines to scent a new style and like the International style it was duly christened at New York's MOMA, in the exhibition 'Deconstructivist Architecture' of 1990. The name – quickly reduced to Decon – had in fact been in use for a while and combined allusions to the fashionable school of textual criticism known as deconstruction with the exuberant forms of Russian Constructivism rediscovered in the era of glasnost. The connections between Gehry's intuitive manipulations of form, Peter Eisenman's ever-more esoteric theorizing, and the automatist techniques of the Austrians Wolf Prix and Helmut Swiczinsky – who practised as Coop Himmelb(l)au – were intellectually tenuous, as the MOMA catalogue readily acknowledged, but the fascination with fragmentation did reflect a widespread shift in sensibility.

The most influential Decon project – the Open House at Malibu, by Coop Himmelb(l)au – was never built, although they worked on it for six years, from 1983 to 1990. It began life as a much acclaimed project and following its publication in 1984 the architects were approached by an 81-year-old client who wished to build it. A site was found in 1987, but the client died three years later as construction was beginning; the site and design were marketed through Sotheby's International Realty, but it remains unrealized. Coop Himmelb(l)au was formed in 1968 and is rare among the utopian groups from the late 1960s in retaining its radicalism while also producing convincing mature work. They believe that a work of art should emerge in a moment of automatic self-expression and base their designs on sketches, produced with eyes shut, which they think capture the essence of an idea. The spiky, jagged lines and planes of the Open House are translations into steel and glass of such an original sketch, and generate an exceptionally dynamic form that looks as if it has just touched down from outer space to explore an alien planet.

In place of the orderly, planned world of Modernist dreams, Decon architects offered ecstatic responses to a bewilderingly multifarious world that which seemed to defy systematization. Although new to mainstream architecture, such perspectives had much in common with the techniques of fragmentation, collage and automatism developed in early Modernist art as responses to a world torn apart by war and competing ideologies. Decon buildings, by contrast, were predicated on a world order so apparently stable that it led the historian Francis Fukuyama famously to proclaim 'The End of History': it requires exceedingly sophisticated engineering and a highly developed construction industry to make buildings which can indulge in the luxury of looking as if they are falling apart. For all its radical pretensions Decon quickly became, especially in the USA, the new academy, a manner briefly almost as ubiquitous in schools of architecture as Beaux-Arts classicism had been a century before. Even the best Decon works teetered on the brink of a descent into meaningless, self-indulgent form-making, and the ever nimble Charles Jencks's attempt, in his 1991 book *The Architecture*

Villa dall'Ava Saint-Cloud, France, 1991, Rem Koolhaas/OMA

Above Villa dall'Ava, Saint-Cloud, France, 1991, Rem Koolhaas/OMA. Like much of Koolhaas's work, the house is an ironic commentary on Modernism – the roof-top swimming pool aligned on the Eiffel Tower is surely a knowing reference to the Surrealist roof-garden of the Bestegui apartment, for which Le Corbusier appropriated the Arc de Triomphe as part of the composition.

of the Jumping Universe, to interpret them as exemplars of the chaotic order revealed by the 'new sciences of complexity' proved less successful than some of his earlier stylistic classifications.

Decon can also be interpreted as an essentially decorative repertoire of devices designed to stimulate jaded senses, and as such inevitably locked into the cycle of excitement, exploitation and rejection typical of a media-culture in which appearance dominates substance. For one of the most influential architects at work in the late twentieth century, the Dutchman Rem Koolhaas, founder of the Office of Metropolitan Architecture (OMA), this was the inescapable condition of the time, to which he responded by exploring architecture as an ironic language of signs. Appropriately, his first major domestic project, the Villa dall'Ava completed in 1991 in the Paris suburb of Saint-Cloud, was commissioned by the publisher of several of France's leading architectural magazines.

At one level the Villa dall'Ava can be read as a commentary on classic Modern houses: the layered organization recalls Mies's Tugendhat House, while Le Corbusier seems to lurk around almost every corner. The open, almost fully glazed ground floor sits on a concrete base clad, like the Villa de Mandrot, in random stone, and the pavilions at each end are ribbon-windowed reminders of the nearby Villa Savoye. A long ramp connects the lower entry level to the top of the base and, as in the Corbusian model, is played off against a spiral stair which links the entrance hall directly to the daughter's bedroom two storeys above. But this is no orthodox *hommage* since Koolhaas takes every opportunity to parody his sources. The front pavilion is supported on a structurally irrational forest of slender columns which jut randomly in all directions, while to the rear the pavilion has a reassuringly familiar *piloti* in one corner, but no apparent means of support in the other.

In defiance of the stuccoed houses all around, Koolhaas clads the bedrooms not with white render but with corrugated metal – blue aluminium to the street, copper to the rear. Finally, on the roof, in place of the Corbusian celebration of the natural delights of *soleil, espace et verdure*, he offers us green Astroturf and a synthetic-blue lap pool, aligned on the Eiffel Tower, which looks as if it has been flown in straight from Hollywood – to the knowing, of course, it recalls Pierre Koenig's seminal Case Study House # 22 (see p. 148). For all its luxury, the roof seems deliberately inhospitable: Astroturf and water form an unbroken plane; there are no inviting ledges or reassuring balustrades; and in place of the Villa Savoye's sinuous, guitar-shaped screen is a potato-shaped fence of orange poly-something-or-other mesh more usually encountered protecting roadworks.

Koolhaas's other major house, completed in 1998 and one of the finest of the decade, is a large private villa on a hillside outside Bordeaux, part of the *jardin anglais* of an old mansion and close to a disused quarry. Shortly before design work began the father of the family who commissioned it was left paralysed following a car crash, unable to walk and barely able to talk. He told Koolhaas, 'This house is my world; please make it as complex as possible,' and in response it was designed on three floors, like a classical villa but with radically contrasting characters. A dramatically cantilevered concrete sleeping bunker is precariously poised over a glass house of Californian clarity and openness, which in turn sits on a travertine-clad

House at Bordeaux France, 1998, Rem Koolhaas/OMA

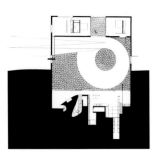

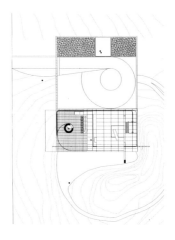

Opposite, below and right House at Bordeaux, France, 1998, Rem Koolhaas/OMA. In this tour de force of a house, a transparent world of glass is sandwiched between a stone-clad 'cave' and a dramatically cantilevered concrete box. Linking these different worlds is a room-sized elevator platform for the wheelchair-bound client.

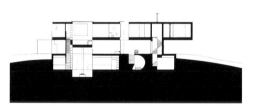

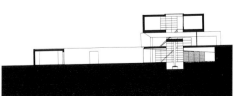

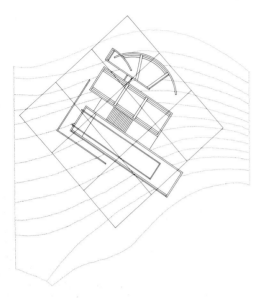

cave-like base. The interlocking of inside and out is more like a Chinese puzzle than an orthodox spatial continuum. Near the centre of the plan is a large, room-sized section of the floor which is a lift-cum-vertical office moving hydraulically between levels to connect kitchen and wine cellar to library and finally bedroom. The house is like a labyrinth, in which you encounter a bewildering array of experiences: the refinement of travertine and lightness and polish of aluminium; cave-like spaces which simulate natural erosion; earth-coloured concrete of determined rawness; and the transparent world sandwiched between. Most surprising, perhaps, is that it seems everywhere to court danger, with unexpected, vertiginous drops: not what regulations normally dictate for someone with severe disabilities, and all the more liberating as a result.

To the Japanese architect Tadao Ando, the chaotic environment of the modern metropolis – and few appear more chaotic than Tokyo or his native Osaka – constitute a threat to both the diversity of regional cultures and to the individual's capacity to develop a stable identity through an inner, personal life. Ando achieved national recognition in the late 1970s following the completion of the Row House Sumiyoshi in Osaka, a reinterpretation of a traditional wooden terraced house which provides a key to all his later work. The house confronts the street with a concrete façade, bare but for a single top-lit recess to one side of which is the entrance door. Beyond lie two, two-storey cubes of accommodation placed either side of an open, similarly proportioned court, across which runs a narrow bridge to connect the upper floors: walking from living to dining room, bedroom to bathroom, involves going outdoors, regardless of the weather. To most Westerners the arrangement appears bizarre, but in Japan it connects with a long tradition of living close to nature. Traditional houses were all but uninsulated, and had a toilet at the bottom of the garden – its chilly delights were the subject of a famous eulogy by the novelist Jun'ichiro Tanizaki.

The Koshino House, completed in 1982 in a national park in Ashiya, Hyogo, brought Ando to worldwide attention as one of the most potent talents of his generation. It consists of two wings linked by an underground passage: a two-storey block containing living room, kitchen-dining room and master bedroom; and a long single-storey block housing a row of six children's bedrooms and two *tatami* rooms for guests. The house is dug into the site and entered at the upper level, from where a narrow stair leads down into the double-height living room. You enter along a wall of unbroken concrete, lit by a continuous slit of glazing between roof and wall through which, at the chosen hour, a raking slice of sun moves across the end wall and then dissolves the blank rear wall in a blaze of light – the performance recalls the living room of Utzon's Can Lis (see p. 124). Two large openings, placed to exclude sight of nearby properties, allow views of the falling ground, trees and distant hills. As in a traditional Japanese house the views are sliced off, partial, inviting the imagination to complete the scene in the mind – very different from the spatial continuity realized by the full-height glazing of Modernist houses.

The handling of openings is but one of several subtle interplays between Western modernism and Japanese tradition typical of Ando's work. Compared with the rambling, echelon form of Classic houses like Katsura, the seventeenth-century imperial villa in Kyoto, the plan looks severely 'rational' – but like a

Koshino House Ashiya, Hyogo Prefecture, Japan, 1979–82, Tadao Ando

Above and opposite Koshino House, Ashiya, Hyogo Prefecture, Japan, 1979-82, Tadao Ando. Conceived as a 'bastion of resistance' against the consumerism which was sweeping away Japanese traditions, the interior opens to controlled views of nature, near and far, celebrating the passage of the sun and clouds overhead.

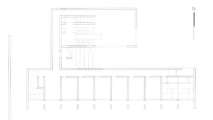

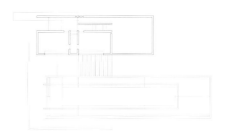

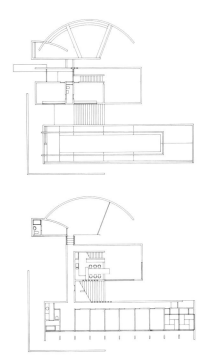

Opposite, above and right

Koshino House, Ashiya, Hyogo
Prefecture, Japan, 1979–82,
extension 1983–4, Tadao Ando.
Designed to complement the
orthogonal world of the original house,
the extension is framed by a quarter-
circular wall and manages the rare
trick of making the new composition
feel as resolved as the original.

Opposite Bom Jesus House, Porto, Portugal, 1994, Eduardo Souto de Moura. An essay in combining modernity and tradition, minimalist abstraction with robust stonework – the latter intended to anchor the house to the site and to the local building vernacular.

Below Antonio Carlos Siza House, Santo Tirso, Portugal, 1978, Alvaro Siza. When moving through it the house is reminiscent of the seemingly ad hoc juxtapositions of a Mediterranean village, but in plan the forms are seen to be controlled by subtle geometric alignments.

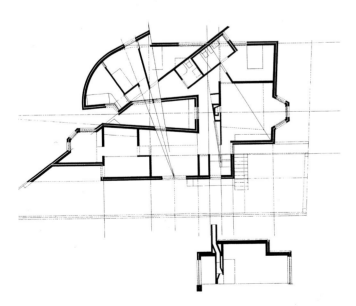

Japanese garden it is structured around a series of what Ando calls 'scenic locations' designed to heighten our awareness of nature. The concrete-paved terrace and steps – a reinterpretation of the traditional *kare sansui* or 'dry garden' of gravel – celebrate sun and rain, while in the bedroom corridor narrow glazed slits (reminiscent of a passage in Luis Barragán's Gilardi House, completed in 1977) follow the steps outside and create a dramatic interplay of light and shade. Internally, by projecting a long table from the sunken kitchen level across the living room floor, Ando both links the two spaces and offers the inhabitant the choice between sitting, Western-style, on chairs or Japanese-style, on the floor. The carpet echoes the colour of traditional *tatami* mats, but the modular control of the spaces is taken over by the 1.8- metre- (6-foot-) wide by 0.9-metre- (3-foot-) high grid of the concrete formwork. The concrete itself is of extraordinary quality, made with a blue-grey sand and rendered almost as insubstantial as paper screens by the play of light.

Four years after completing the house Ando was asked to add a studio. Placed completely underground to the north of the living room, the retaining wall is a quarter-circle in plan and also lit by a narrow horizontal slit: the complex, intersecting curves of light and shadow are a perfect counterpoint to the orthogonal world of the original house, and the addition achieves the rare trick of making the total composition feel more complete. The Koshino House was a weekend/holiday home for a well-known fashion designer, but many of Ando's clients were 'ordinary' – businessmen and teachers, for example – to whom the houses represented an opportunity to reconnect to Japanese traditions in a modern way.

In the West, Ando's work has frequently been linked to the Minimalist art that emerged in the USA in the 1960s, but although he was greatly influenced by Modernist abstraction the austerity of his forms is best understood in the context of Japanese religious and aesthetic traditions. In this respect, the simplicity of the archetypal forms of Shinto shrines, and its pantheistic nature-worship, are as important as the more familiar 'minimalist' aesthetics associated with Zen Buddhism. Ando's work was widely influential, but an architecture based on similarly austere means was already developing independently in parallel with it in Europe. The expressions varied, but were all grounded in what Vittorio Gregotti aptly described as the 'suppression of redundancy in artistic practice' and grew out of a re-evaluation of the Modern Movement in the light of local traditions – the cubic, whitewashed vernacular buildings of the South, or the Protestant love of precision and sparseness typical of much Swiss architecture.

In the Antonio Carlos Siza House, completed in Santo Tirso in Portugal in 1978, Alvaro Siza developed an intricate series of spaces around a small patio. Although controlled by complex internal geometric relationships, they nonetheless managed to evoke the relaxed, timeless world of traditional villages and materialized as crisp, rendered surfaces with precise openings. In a holiday house on the Quinta do Lago estate in the Algarve, built in 1984, Siza's fellow-countryman Eduardo Souto de Moura combined references to vernacular buildings of southern Portugal with a highly articulated roofscape inspired by Le Corbusier. The result evokes a miniature walled settlement but the precision of the surfaces and almost complete absence of detail yield a heightened abstraction which is wholly modern.

Bom Jesus House Porto, Portugal, 1994, Souto de Moura

In later work such as the Bom Jesus House in Porto of 1994 Souto de Mora combined minimalist, abstract forms – the rectangular planes of the pool and pure white wall, for example – with materials drawn from past and present construction techniques. These include the undressed granite that supports the terrace of the principal floor, and the exposed steel, I-section columns. The granite echoes an existing boundary wall and, like the planes in Mies's early projects, runs out into the landscape. But whereas in Mies's Brick Country House the walls could be interpreted as disappearing to infinity, here the granite is used to anchor the house firmly to the site and to local building traditions, while at the same time asserting its modernity. The openings, framed with variously sized stones and lintels, have no dividing mullions and become either reflecting planes or disappear like the black holes on a Classical drawing, while in the entrance hall the rough stone is set against a conspicuously machine-made stair of slender timber treads floating on a sculptural steel frame.

In Switzerland a similar determination to reduce architectural expression to essentials is strongly marked in the work of, among others, Luigi Snozzi and Herzog and de Meuron. Like Mario Botta, Snozzi practises in Ticino and sees himself as part of a regionalist school that seeks to reinterpret early Modernism, in particular the villas of Le Corbusier, in the light of the *genius loci* of a site. Unlike the ideal Corbusian villas, Snozzi's houses are inseparable from a specific topography and views. The Casa Bernasconi (1988–9) in Carona, for example, is entered via a steep stair sculpted to the land; its three-storey garden front gives no hint of the double-height volume within because single-storey glazing has been used to emphasize the link to the lap pool and better dramatize the distant panorama of mountain peaks.

In their Stone House, built in the Ligurian mountains near Tavole in Italy, Herzog and de Meuron use rubble-stone walls to connect both to the local architecture and to the rocky landscape. These walls are then framed in a concrete skeleton, which marks on the exterior the positions of the internal floors and walls, and is extended out to form a pergola over the terrace. Theoretically 'endless', the frame is intended to suggest the abstract world of modern serial production, while the walls and internal planning – simple rooms connecting one to another, with no differentiated corridors – relate to timeless peasant traditions.

In their different ways all these architects – Siza, Souto de Mora, Snozzi and Herzog and de Meuron – are concerned with reconciling the international with the regional, the global with the local, and in the process they deploy deliberately reduced architectural means. A similar impulse can be seen at work in Ireland in the development of O'Donnell and Tuomey from advocates of traditional typologies in the 1980s towards a locally grounded architecture of abstraction in the 1990s. The Hudson House, completed in Navan in 1998, still has a markedly urban character, a miniature city in which a three-storey 'tower' of bedrooms and cave-like living room are organized around three small courts, but all stylistic references to Classical architecture have disappeared in favour of a direct, Ando-like expression of the concrete construction – and, as if in direct emulation of the Japanese master, the circulation between the living and sleeping areas is external, across the central court.

Opposite Casa Bernasconi, Carona, Switzerland, 1988-9, Luigi Snozzi. Like all Snozzi's houses, Casa Bernasconi is carefully attuned to the site. The continuous glazing, for example, dramatizes the panorama of distant mountains rather than expressing the double-height living room within.

Right Stone House, Tavole, Italy, Herzog and de Meuron. The concrete frame, which marks the floors and extends as a pergola, signifies the 'global', placeless nature of modern production, and is infilled with local stone which, like the arrangement of non-specific rooms inside, emulates peasant traditions.

Below Hudson House, Navan, Ireland, 1998, O'Donnell and Tuomey. Conceived as an urban fragment, with external circulation between living and sleeping spaces, the house is rendered in concrete which recalls the widely influential work of Tadao Ando.

The work we have so far considered can only loosely be described as 'minimalist' certainly when compared with the far more reductive style of David Pawson and Claudio Silvestrin, who worked in partnership in London between 1987 and 1989, completing several shop interiors and apartments and a widely acclaimed holiday house on Majorca for the art dealer Hans Neuendorf and his family. Before deciding on a career in architecture Pawson had spent four years in Japan, where he seriously contemplated entering a Buddhist monastery and became enamoured of a traditional lifestyle in which almost all possessions are hidden away from view in cupboards.

For the Majorca house Pawson and Silvestrin looked to Luis Barragán, not Japan, for inspiration, designing it as a fortress-like enclosure of 9-metre- (30-foot-) high pale brown rendered walls. Approached up a long flight of widely spaced steps, which also define a series of shallow terraces against a wall of gradually diminishing height, it is entered through a square atrium. The enclosing walls are broken only sparsely, save for a cavernous opening from which a lap pool projects into the landscape like a raised pier – inspired by the peerless raised tank Barragán threaded between eucalyptus trees on the San Cristobal estate in Mexico City in 1967. Internally, the clutter of loose furniture was kept to a minimum by building-in as much as possible, and such necessities as washbasins were designed as intersecting planes and hemispheres of marble.

The Neuendorf House popularized an approach to design that Pawson happily embraced as Minimalist, and in 1996 he published a book of images which inspired his work. Entitled simply *Minimum* it proved a surprising commercial success: after the conspicuous consumption and stylistic excesses of the 1980s, something more timeless and restrained was widely promoted in style magazines during the 1990s, making other architects suspicious of the Minimalist label. During this period the impulse to aesthetic reduction embraced a surprisingly wide range of architecture, from the classically proportioned, geometrically purified white box the German architect O. M. Ungers built for himself in 1995 in Cologne, to the similarly immaculate Skywood House in Middlesex, England, that was inspired by the Barcelona Pavilion and completed in 1998 by Graham Phillips, the managing director at Foster and Partners. Most minimalist of all, perhaps, in the means he deploys is the Spaniard Campo Baeza, though he is as emphatic as Ando in his rejection of the label: his aim, he says, is 'to do more with less' in search of what he calls 'essential space'.

Like the Row House in Sumiyoshi, Campo Baeza's Gaspar House, completed in 1991 in Zahora near Cadiz, creates an introverted paradise open to the sky but shut off from the rest of the world. The published presentation includes a medieval image of the Garden of Eden, and like a medieval *hortus conclusus* the house is situated in a walled enclosure, 18 metres (59 feet) square with 3.6-metre (12-foot) high boundaries. The square is divided into three rectangles: the internal spaces occupy the central zone and are flanked by patios, like a transformation of the archetypal Roman atrium house. To emphasize the unity of inside and out, the limestone floor runs as a continuous plane across the compound, and both house and patios are sub-divided by 2-metre- (6.6-foot-) high 'thick walls' which, internally,

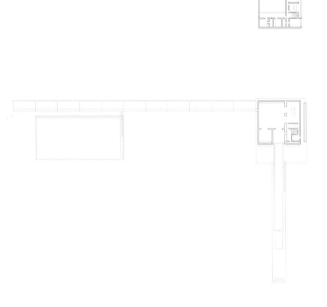

Neuendorf House Majorca, Spain, 1987–9, Pawson and Silvestrin

Gaspar House Zahora, Spain, 1991, Campo Baeza

Above and opposite Neuendorf House, Majorca, Spain, 1987-9, Pawson and Silvestrin. Whereas many architects during the 1980s favoured increasingly minimal means, in the Neuendorf House this becomes overtly Minimal. Furniture, details and clutter were eliminated in order to free the mind to enjoy the pleasures of pure form, space and light.

From aesthetic reduction to minimalism:
Top Ungers House, Cologne, 1995,
O. M. Ungers.
Above and left Skywood House,
Middlesex, England, 1998, Graham
Phillips.
Opposite Gaspar House, Zahora,
Spain, 1991, Campo Baeza.

Above Tallon House, Dublin, Ireland, 1970, Ronnie Tallon. Although clearly inspired by the Farnsworth House, the plan, with bedrooms either side of an open living space, was like that of countless traditional Irish houses.
Below Goulding Studio, Enniskerry, Ireland, 1973, Ronnie Tallon. Canyon-houses had been the subject of a travelling exhibition sponsored by the American company Bethlehem Steel in 1959 and here Tallon demonstrated that he could cantilever with the best of them.

Private House Rotterdam, The Netherlands, 1991, Mecanoo

contain storage cupboards and separate the bedrooms, bathroom and kitchen from the main living space. The latter rises to 4.5 metres (14.7 feet) while the service blocks are continuous with the enclosing walls. The only glazing is in four large square openings, placed at the intersection of the low walls and the main pavilion. They offer magical views through the walled spaces and generate what Baeza calls 'horizontal light', which by eliminating shadows has the effect of dematerializing rather than rendering form. In the Gaspar House, Baeza achieved an elemental simplicity and grandeur with modest means: it was built for a schoolteacher, and the accommodation occupies only 120 square metres (1291 square feet).

Architecture in the Minimalist vein was but one manifestation of the continuing interest in the high modern virtues of abstraction, transparency and spatial continuity. Miesian designs, indebted to the Farnsworth House and derivatives by Craig Ellwood in California, continued to be built into the 1980s. Some of the most elegant were the work of Ronnie Tallon in Ireland (a partner in Scott Tallon Walker): his own house, completed in 1970, was framed in white-painted steel and had an open living space with bedrooms at each end – just like a traditional old Irish house, he explained. Three years later, with the Goulding Studio, Tallon outdid the Americans at cantilevering a house off a steep, canyon-like hillside. At the same period, when Michael and Patty Hopkins built their house in Hampstead, London in 1977 they turned to the Eames House for inspiration.

While the Hopkins were happy to live with their young family in a fully glazed interior shielded and divided only by venetian blinds, other architects increasingly sought ways to retain the openness while adapting it to the needs of different sites and lifestyles. In 1991, in the Karlingse district of Rotterdam, Erik van Egeraat and Francine Houben (partners in Mecanoo before van Egeraat's departure), completed an urban house and studio for themselves which offered a lesson in combining privacy and openness. A two-storey living pavilion is placed above an enclosed garage and studio and kept as open as possible to enjoy views through to water on each side – service spaces are packed along the blank wall close to a neighbour to keep the volumes open. To the front, double-height glazing, set back behind shallow metal balconies, offers views north to a small lake, while to the rear an ad hoc arrangement of glazed and solid panels responds to the spaces within. The side elevation is closed at ground level by a plane of concrete, and above it a fully glazed wall is protected by bamboo canes which can be moved back and forth hydraulically in an aluminium frame: an inventive reinterpretation of the *shoji* screens seen on a recent trip to Japan. Although the architects denied any conscious attempt to link to Dutch traditions, the intricately layered and gridded composition also inevitably brings to mind Rietveld's Schroeder House.

The development of secondary, non-structural layers became a favourite device for controlling both solar penetration and transparency. In the Kern House (1997) in Lochau Austria, Baumschlager and Eberle wrapped a glass box completely with wooden louvres. Near the ground the louvres lie flat against the house and as they rise they gradually angle back, opening views out but still providing protection from prying eyes – and simultaneously recalling traditional log-built houses. The Rosebery House (1994–7) in Queensland, Australia by Brit

236

Above Private House, Rotterdam, The Netherlands, 1991, Mecanoo. Openness and transparency are adapted to an exposed urban site, with the glazed end wall screened by retractable bamboo canes inspired by Japanese shoji screens.

Right Kern House, Lochau, Austria, 1997, Baumschlager and Eberle. A glass house lurks behind the continuous screen of louvres, which angle back to open up views of the landscape from the first floor.

Top right Hopkins House, London, England, 1976, Michael Hopkins. The house was planned as a continuous gridded space, to be sub-divided as the needs of a growing family required, and built, like the Eames House, using standard steel components.

Andresen and Peter O'Gorman is similarly almost completely engulfed in vertical battens of Australian eucalyptus wood. Here the 'landscape screen', as the architects called it, mediates between the scale of the house and the landscape, filtering the passage of light in and views out and enabling the fully glazed pavilions to feel both open and protected.

On a densely wooded, lakeside site outside São Paolo in Brazil, Andrade Morettin achieved a similarly modified transparency using cellular polycarbonate panels. The D'Alessandro House, built for two young photographers in 1998, is a reworking of the Miesian glass box and consists of a transparent 'light box' and a 'thick wall' containing the bathroom and kitchen; at night, a retractable curtain defines a private cube for sleeping, and in one corner glass replaces polycarbonate to allow unmediated views of the lake. The main pavilion of the architect Barton Myers' own house, completed the same year in Toro Canyon, Montecito, California, builds on the tradition of seamless integration between interior and landscape established by Koenig's Case Study Houses. But here the delicate glass box has become an imposing, steel-framed loft space of distinctly industrial provenance, complete with large up-and-over glass doors and galvanized external roller-shutters to defend the interior against bush fires.

Spatially, none of the houses we have considered in this chapter moved beyond possibilities established half a century earlier, and even the most innovative designs of the last two decades are inventive developments and transformations of Modernist themes rather than radically new propositions. Two much admired houses in Belgium completed in the early 1990s, for example, reinterpreted classic Miesian and Corbusian types. The first, Villa Maesen by Stéphane Beel, built in 1992 in Zedelgem, is sited in the kitchen garden of a castle and approached along a beech-lined drive. In deference to this imposing context Beel stretched the classic flat-roofed pavilion, represented by the Farnsworth House, into a 7-metre- (23-foot-) wide wall of accommodation which he placed 7 metres (23 feet) from the rear wall of the garden, recreating the volume of the house as a void. A continuous suite of open plan spaces and private terraces – outdoor rooms reminiscent of Ando's walled courtyards – overlooks the garden, and the house is long enough to break through an old dividing wall, enabling occupants to walk between a formal garden and orchard.

The house in Brasschaat near Antwerp, completed in 1993 by Xaveer de Geyter, project architect for Rem Koolhaas's Villa dall'Ava, inverts the classic Corbusian villa. It is entered by vehicle at roof level, up a short ramp complete with official-looking entry barrier. On the roof sits the square steel-and-glass pavilion of the double garage, oddly angled like a Greek temple on its acropolis. Such angled alignments were the subject of a celebrated reverie in Le Corbusier's *Vers une Architecture* and here the element which the vulgar, *arriviste* houses of the wealthy neighbourhood seek to suppress is celebrated – and floodlit at night lest anyone miss the point. To enter the house you descend via a ramp into a plan which is more Koolhaasian than Corbusian, zoned in parallel bands divided by bookshelves and cupboards and articulated by varied materials – light blue-green tiles, wooden floors, profiled aluminium cladding.

Corbusian precedents are equally apparent in the Double House (1997) in

Villa Maesen Zedelgem, Belgium, 1992, Stéphane Beel

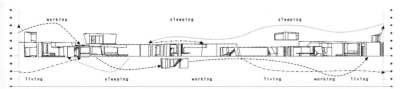

Utrecht by de architectengroep and MVRDV (the partners of the latter are noted followers of Koolhaas), where two four-storey houses are dramatically interlocked in a manner reminiscent of Le Corbusier's 1928 project for a Villa at Carthage. A similar influence, at further remove, can be seen in the Möbius House by Van Berkel and Bos, completed in 1999 at Het Gooi in the Netherlands. Designing it around a continuous linear cycle of living, working and sleeping, the architects made bold claims that it was based on process and movement and rejected autonomous object-making. The complex interlocking of form and space, glass and concrete, and the exceptional fluidity with which the concrete is handled are certainly impressive, but despite the theoretical baggage the house can be understood as a sophisticated composition which plays with, rather than rejects or transcends, Modernist norms.

The proliferation of increasingly personal 'theories' and 'narratives' around which buildings are purportedly designed became a conspicuous feature of much architecture in the closing years of the century. A distinguished example of the genre is the Stretto House built near Dallas, Texas in 1992, which was the subject of a short monograph by its architect, the New York based Steven Holl. After looking at the 'Texas vernacular materials of concrete block and metal roofs', Holl says, he explored the need for shade from the high sun, which led to studies of shadow and overlap, which in turn found an analogy in the overlapping ponds, linked by a stream, on the site. After discussion with a former student, who was also a professionally trained pianist, the musical idea of *stretto* – in which a subject is answered before it is completed – led him to adopt the four-movement, *stretto*-rich Music for Strings, Percussion and Celeste by Bartók as a model: light and space would echo the division between percussion and string sounds and the rich instrumental textures of the music. And so the vocabulary of the building emerged: lightweight metal roofs overlapping masonry spatial 'dams'; space made 'aqueous' and fluid by overlapping floor and roof planes, by an arched wall which pulled light down from a skylight, and by materials handled, according to Holl, to preserve memories of their liquid state – poured concrete, cast glass, terrazzo.

The musical model may have informed aspects of the house's organization, but it was hardly needed to achieve a by then relatively conventional spatial composition. The suavely sophisticated spaces and detailing, which can be readily understood as a skilful, if rather mannered, exercise in the 'destruction of the box' also had more to do with De Stijl and the Italian master of material juxtaposition Carlo Scarpa, than with Bartók. Similarly, the study of the 'Texas vernacular' cannot justifiably be said to have led to anything particular to Texas. What Holl claims to offer is an architecture derived almost autonomously from context and musical analogy; what we see is undeniably skilful but not notably original. Genuinely new ideas in architecture are rare, but in a culture that values novelty more than imaginative development, many architects feel obliged to press their claims with imposing and often esoteric theoretical ideas.

Like Holl in Texas, numerous architects during the 1980s and 1990s espoused a concern to 'get close to the context and build', but in the wake of the literal or heavy-handedly playful historicism of Post-Modernism the deployment of regional traditions required a light touch to avoid lapsing into nostalgia. Clark and

Stretto House Dallas, Texas, USA, 1992, Steven Holl

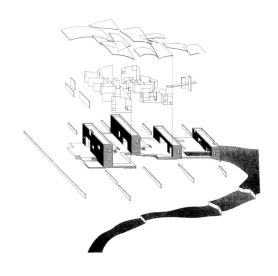

Above and right Stretto House,
Dallas, Texas, USA, 1992, Steven Holl.
Although inspired by the musical idea
of *stretto*, this skilful composition can
be readily understood in terms of
Modernist tropes from De Stijl to
Carlo Scarpa.
Opposite bottom Double House,
Utrecht, The Netherlands, 1997, de
architectengroep and MVRDV. Two
four-storey houses are dramatically
interlocked to deny any reading of
individual territory.

Opposite top and overleaf
Möbius House, Het Gooi,
The Netherlands, 1999, van Berkel
and Bos. The house was designed
around a continuous cycle of living,
expressed in forms and spaces of
conspicuous fluidity.

Left Morrison House, London, England, 1992, Graham Morrison (Allies and Morrison). The brick walls, slate roof and rendered porch of the surrounding Victorian villas are transformed into a modern composition of volumes and planes.

Top Reid House, Johns Island, South Carolina, USA, 1987, Clark and Menefee. The elements are familiar from the region – from boarding to shed-roofed porch – but the proportions and refined detailing are unmistakably contemporary.

Above Private House, Bad Tölz, Germany, 1996, Fink and Jocher. The shallow-pitch roof, timber boarding and louvres echo the traditional log-built houses, and sliding shutters enable the house to turn into an almost solid wooden box, like an agricultural store.

Above Concord House, Concord, Massachusetts, USA, 1994, Machado and Silvetti. The New England vernacular is given a twist by boldly coloured trapezoidal volumes projecting from the façade.

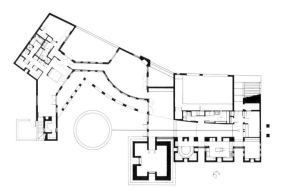

Above Fuller House, near Phoenix, Arizona, USA, 1984–6, Antoine Predock. The complex, processional sequence of volumes unfolds between sunrise- and sunset-viewing platforms.
Overleaf Zuber House, near Phoenix, Arizona, USA, 1989, Antoine Predock. The 'runway to anywhere', lit from below at night through cracks in the paving, projects out from one of two square towers which punctuate the bar of a T-shaped plan.

Menefee explain their Reid House, built on Johns Island, South Carolina in 1987, by reference to the shed-roofed porches, butane tanks and other accretions found on local rural buildings, but the house could never be mistaken for a traditional structure. The areas of glazing are too large, the detailing too delicate, and touches like the abstract acroteria too artful – but for all these refinements it still succeeds in feeling very much of its place. As, too, does Machado and Silvetti's Concord House of 1994 in Concord, Massachusetts, where the garden front juxtaposes the ubiquitous material of New England buildings – white-painted clapboarding – with two singular, trapezoidal volumes which grow unexpectedly from the main volume.

Faced with tough local planning requirements in Blackheath, London, Graham Morrison of Allies and Morrison had no option but to use traditional brickwork and a pitched roof for his own house, completed in 1992. In a further gesture to the context he included a white-rendered cubic version of the porches found on the surrounding Victorian villas, but by treating the walls and wafer-thin roof as planes he managed to achieve a convincingly modern expression. In a house completed in 1996 on the edge of an old village in Upper Bavaria, near the German Alps, Fink and Jocher responded to constructional forms evolved in response to the severe weather. But in place of horizontal logs or boarding they used narrow vertical strips; the roof is shallow pitched but with deeper than normal overhangs, painted white underneath to reflect light into the interior; and the glazed openings are far larger than in older houses, but can be protected by sliding timber shutters to restore the sense of solidity.

In America, the majority of the most innovative houses continued to be built as responses to rural rather than urban sites. Those of Antoine Predock, for example, seem inseparable from the deserts of New Mexico and Arizona. Like Wright before him, Predock is fascinated by the native adobe architecture, whose walls, he says, 'act as a bridge between earth and sky'. Given generous budgets and open, previously unsettled sites, many of Predock's houses are more like small settlements rather than individual buildings. The Treaster Gray Residence, completed in Tesuque in 1985, resembles a New Mexican village climbing the flank of a ridge, while the Fuller House of 1984–6, in the Sonoran desert north of Phoenix, Arizona is organized as a processional sequence of spaces in response to the passage of the sun. Between sunrise- and sunset-viewing platforms the house unfolds as an abstraction of the landscape, replete with an interior 'canyon' in which lie a channel of flowing water, a kitchen and dining 'boulder', and the miniature mountain of the pyramidal den – a rather inflated gesture for such a small room.

In the Zuber House, completed three years later on another desert site outside Phoenix, Predock abandoned adobe construction and references to pueblo architecture. The T-shaped plan is divided into a leg, deeply recessed into the mountain and constructed of rough concrete blocks whose aggregate echoes the mountain's colour, and a bar-shaped 'panoramic house' finished with grey-green stucco resembling the desert floor. The junction between the plan elements is marked by two square towers, rotated through 45 degrees. From one springs a metal bridge which ends poised high above the desert. It is aligned to local aircraft flight patterns and at night the open joints of the limestone paving are lit

McDonald House Stinson Beach, California, USA, 1992, Stanley Saitowitz

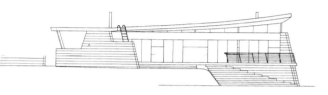

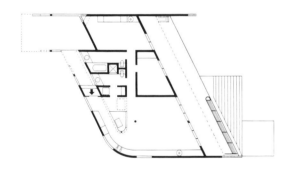

Above and opposite McDonald
House, Stinson Beach, California, USA,
1992, Stanley Saitowitz.
Below Casa Garau-Agusti, Barcelona,
Spain, 1988-93, Enric Miralles.

from below, transforming the bridge that leads nowhere into an imaginary runway to anywhere.

Stanley Saitowitz's Halfway House in the Transvaal, which we considered in Chapter 4, is an outstanding example of site-specific design and in 1992, some years after moving to California, he completed the McDonald House, a vacation home in Stinson Beach a few miles north of San Francisco's Golden Gate Bridge. Before visiting the site he had visions of pounding surf and acres of open sand, but what he found was a placid lagoon – so he set about making the house a metaphor for the absent sea. The parallelogram-shaped plan, a Saitowitz trademark, harbours a full width deck and anchors the house to the water's edge. Inland, it has one rounded corner, like a sea cave scoured by water, while the flank walls run out to present raking, prow-like forms to the lagoon and protect the deck from wind. The redwood-sheathed walls will weather to what the architect calls 'a driftwood crust' and protect, shell-like, an iridescent white interior. Above, the roof ebbs and flows gently across, barely touching the walls and rising, like the crest of a gentle wave, to reveal a shallow triangle of light, echoed in triangular cut-outs in the walls which further dissolve the sense of enclosure. Detailed with refreshing simplicity, and animated by odd slices of sun and the play of light reflected from the water onto the ceiling, the interior perfectly captures the spirit of relaxation by the sea.

A glance at the plans of the Casa Garau-Agusti (1988–93) by Enric Miralles might suggest that they were inspired by the spirit of fragmentation discussed earlier, but in fact the complex geometry developed in response to the site. Situated on a plot in suburban Barcelona with mundane houses to either side and a view across a shallow valley to a picturesque church, the walls and windows twist and angle in search of views, to settle into the topography and to avoid visual contact with the neighbours. The approach has its roots in the work of Miralles's distinguished predecessor in Barcelona, Antonio Coderch, whose site-responsive Casa Ugalde we encountered in Chapter 4 (p. 100), and is echoed in the work of John and Patricia Patkau, for whom every project begins with a search for what they call its 'found potential'. Rejecting the universal models of Classicism and Modernism, they seek to ground their designs in the particularities of place, programme and materials, and to make them part of a continuum with the natural world.

The Patkaus' first decade of practice culminated with the completion of the Barnes House in 1992. Sited on the edge of an open, rocky outcrop in five acres of forested land, it enjoys outstanding views of the Strait of Georgia and mainland British Columbia to the north and the rocky shoreline of Vancouver Island to the north-west. The irregular, compacted form is itself boulder-like and emerges from a plan developed by wedging the spaces into the tapering ravine. Or so it appears: in fact, while following the nature of the site closely, the plans and sections also artfully juxtapose two geometries, two kinds of space: orthogonal and non-orthogonal, figurative and abstract, strong and weak. The ultimate roots lie in Aalto and the approach serves to heighten both the experience of the landscape and the feeling of interiority. The orthogonal spaces, their walls thickened by built-in cabinets, are cave-like retreats, while the weaker, non-orthogonal zones direct the eye to the spectacular views and defer to the

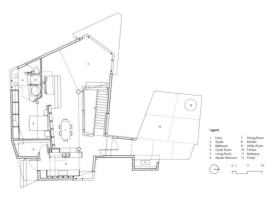

Legend

1	Entry	7	Dining Room
2	Studio	8	Kitchen
3	Bathroom	9	Utility Room
4	Guest Room	10	Terrace
5	Living Room	11	Barbeque
6	Master Bedroom	12	Firepit

252

Busk House Bamble, Norway, 1987–90, Sverre Fehn

Above Busk House, Bamble, Norway, 1987–90, Sverre Fehn. The house seems to grow out of the rocky ridge, its solidity emphasized by the tree-like angled struts of the overhanging roofs and canopies.
Opposite Barnes House, British Columbia, Canada, 1992, Patkau Architects. Below the boldly structured folded plane of the roof, orthogonal cave-like rooms retreat from freely planned spaces which open to the landscape.
Below Brick House, Baerum, Norway, 1987, Sverre Fehn. The projecting, nose-like chimney marks one end of a central axis along which are ranged the elements of earth (walled garden), air (white-tiled court), fire and water (bath).

landscape which forms the visual boundary of these weakly defined spaces. Similar contrasts are cultivated in the construction. Delicately detailed steel railings and connections are set against the heavy, monolithic surfaces of the concrete floors, stucco-clad, timber-framed walls and substantial roof timbers, while a one-centimetre-thick (0.4 inch) steel-plate canopy projects dramatically beyond the large opening to the north-west, a thin, perfectly horizontal surface in sharp contrast to the thick, folded planes of the roof.

The Busk House, completed in 1990 by the Norwegian architect Sverre Fehn, expresses a similar concern to lock the design into the land. The site is a large area of rocky, tree- and scrub-covered terrain in the Oslo fjord and the width of the main body of the house was determined by a massive boulder that closes one end of the chosen location. The house's alignment follows the rocky terrain to the south-west, a sheer concrete wall rising directly from the granite and folding round at each end of the house to contain the fire at one end and a plunge pool off the master bedroom at the other. In a showhouse for the brick industry completed in Baerum in 1987 Fehn made an even more elemental celebration central to the design, organizing the rooms around an axis along which earth (garden), air (white-tiled atrium), fire (hearth) and water (the bath) were aligned.

The perceived solidity of the concrete wall of the Busk House is enhanced by the layered timbers and angled struts of the overhanging roof canopies and, on the opposite elevation, by a long, glazed colonnade. The line of columns springs from an existing tree on the site and takes the occupants metaphorically out into nature to move between rooms – and literally so at each end, where it is unglazed. To contrast with the linear main block, Fehn designed the children's bedrooms as a freestanding timber tower – 'a little fortress for the daughters' as he put it – linked by a glazed bridge and connected vertically by a spiral stair housed in a wooden cylinder, which rises into a fully glazed study. 'In Norway,' Fehn says, 'you are still aware that you have to destroy nature in order to build.' His work is both an attempt to minimize the inevitable damage and to celebrate nature by deriving the architecture metaphorically from her: in the Busk House, the terrain-hugging main block, colonnade and timber roofs read clearly as abstractions of rocks, tree trunks and branches.

Through his work and teaching as professor of architecture in Oslo Fehn has exerted a strong influence over a gifted new generation of young Norwegian architects, including Carl-Viggo Hølmebakk whose summerhouse in Risor was completed in 1997. The client loved the many pine trees so the site was surveyed with a computerized level to provide exceptionally detailed plans of both trees and topography. The plan locks itself around several pines, which are captured in courtyards or rise through decks, and a special foundation system was adopted using concrete stub columns whose position could be adjusted as necessary to miss tree roots. The heights of the rooms also varied, to slip under branches, and the openings were carefully attuned to the views, final decisions often being taken on site. In the same year, Lacaton and Vassal were faced with a similar brief – to place a house on a beautiful, pine-covered site overlooking the Bassin d'Arcachon in Bordeaux without destroying any trees. They opted for a lightweight aluminium box, elevated on columns and built around six trees. The

253

continuity and transformations

Above Doctor's House, Paderborn, Germany, 1998, Thomas Herzog. An accomplished modernist composition which is also designed to maximize the use of passive energy and renewable resources.

Opposite, top and bottom Private house, Cap-Ferrat, France, 1997, Lacaton and Vassal. The machine in the garden – a lightweight aluminium box skewered by mature trees.

Opposite, middle Summer house, Risør, Noway, 1997, Carl-Viggo Hølmebakk. Here the rooms and decks flow with calculated precision around and under the tree trunks and branches.

Below House in Regensburg, Germany, 1979, Thomas Herzog. An early example of passive solar design, demonstrative in its maximal exposure of sloping, south-facing glazing.

openings for the tree trunks were fitted with transparent plastic sheets and flexible rubber gaskets around the trunks enable the house to be sealed and the trees to move and grow. Below, the reflective surface of the corrugated aluminium cladding makes for a magical undercroft.

These two pine-respecting houses say much about the differences between the Nordic and French attitudes to nature – in which Romantic fusion and Classical counterpoint are still very much to the fore – and even more about the shift in values that had been apparent since the 1960s. As the environmental consequences of economies and value-systems predicated on unlimited growth became increasingly apparent the concern with 'green' issues gathered force. Initially, little of architectural consequence was produced. Houses were earth-sheltered, or buried, had 'passive' and 'active' solar collectors – such as conservatories and heat-absorbing solar panels – or were built with unusual materials like the straw-block house erected by Klas Anhelm at the Ararat Exhibition in Stockholm in 1976. These houses frequently showed little concern for the visual consequences of their green philosophy. Indeed they were sometimes designed to offend conventional sensibilities by rejecting the aesthetic norms that were considered as bankrupt as the ecologically destructive societies that produced them. This radical spirit lived on in an ecological community built in Torup in Denmark as late as 1991, based on that icon of alternative culture, the geodesic dome. But by then green issues had firmly entered the mainstream and during the final decade of the century competitions for model energy-efficient homes proliferated worldwide.

Among the first architects to produce a sustained and architecturally convincing body of work addressing environmental issues was Thomas Herzog, a professor of design at Munich Technical University. His house in Regensburg was completed in 1979 and used one of the classic strategies of passive solar design – a linear plan with a south-facing, fully glazed buffer zone. Running across the main, inner house this was designed to capture solar energy by absorbing it in the heavy stone floor. In the Regensburg project the glazing ran down to the ground as part of a triangular wedge, and the whole house was raised slightly off the site to protect tree roots and escape the high water table. In a house in Waldmohr completed five years later Herzog opted for a compact 'thermal onion' plan, placing the rooms requiring the most heat – such as bathrooms – at the centre of a square-within-a-diamond scheme. A two-storey conservatory fills the south-facing elevation, and the east and west sides are protected by trellises covered by deciduous climbing plants whose leaves drop in winter to allow useful solar gain.

Herzog's later house for a doctor near Paderborn in Germany, completed in 1998, does not appear overtly 'environmental', but on analysis proves to be as rigorously thought through as his more programmatic earlier projects. Two double-height pavilions are linked to each other and to an earlier surgery by an intermediate, single-storey space that is glazed to the south-east and runs along a heavily insulated wall providing protection from the road. The pavilions are fully glazed to the south and protected from solar gain by the projecting roof and climbing plants; service spaces such as the bathrooms and sauna are housed in small concrete boxes in the connecting space, which also acts as a gallery for the doctor's modern art collection. In winter it becomes like an orangery, with only background heating from an underfloor system.

Sun Valley House Sun Valley, Idaho, USA, 1986, Arne Bystrom

In total contrast to Herzog's quiet, modestly scaled proposals is the Sun Valley House, completed in Idaho in 1986 by Arne Bystrom. A bold gesture addressing a vast landscape, it combines a heavy, bracketed timber roof – a familiar symbol of shelter from the Far East to northern Europe – with a Wright-inspired base variously cut into and projecting from the earth. Beneath the roof the plan is cranked 45 degrees to face due south; the mono-pitch roof slope exactly matches the low December sun to maximize solar gain, and it projects far enough to exclude the high summer sun from the interior. Heat gathered passively in the 'solar gallery' is stored in rock bins, and water circulates through an array of active metal-and-glass solar collectors which hang somewhat incongruously beneath the heavy timbers.

While conspicuously living up to its name, the Sun Valley House also embodies a problem evident in much 'green' design, torn between our urge to go back to nature and to the earth, and our desire to sustain an acceptable standard of living using sophisticated high-tech devices. No such equivocation is apparent in the solar house at Breisach-am-Rhein, completed in 1996 by Thomas Spiegelhalter. This extraordinary deconstructivist collage, bristling with solar collectors and photovoltaic panels and writhing restlessly in response to aspect and prospect, inevitably raises other questions: it might harness energy efficiently, but its overall use of resources would hardly stand up to an environmental audit.

Demonstration eco-houses are particularly susceptible to the proliferation of environmental gizmos, often resulting, as James Wines recently observed, in 'too little home and too much technology'. The Australian 'House of the Future' (or Monier House), built in 1992 in Swan Valley to competition-winning designs by Kimberly Ackert and Robert Dawson-Browne, was an exception. It integrated a range of active and passive solar collectors without overwhelming the spaces, and insulated the cool, south-facing elevation with a rammed-earth wall composed of an iron-rich soil mixed with 4 percent cement – a modification of a traditional way of building that is gradually coming back into use in diverse climates.

Frustrated by the house-building industry's continuing reluctance to embrace technology wholeheartedly, the Austrian architects Driendl and Steixner built Standard Solar House in Langenschönbichl in 1992. To admit more light and simplify construction, it uses all-glass walls with full-height, solid, opening panels for ventilation on all but the heavily insulated north elevation. On the southern, living side familiar passive solar strategies are employed, with external aluminium blinds to exclude excess sun. Along the north side, sunlight enters through a high, south-facing clerestory to be absorbed by the thick stone cladding of the insulated concrete wall; the stone then gives up its heat to water circulating in pipes in the wall, which take it away to a ground storage tank. The architects claim the house undercut standard building costs by 20 percent and, occupied by a family of five, is costing 40 percent less than normal to heat.

In a private house in Lyon-St Just, Jourda and Perraudin took a different tack. Accepting at face value the tendency of passive-solar designs to turn into

Above House of the Future, Swan Valley, Australia, 1992, Ackert and Dawson-Browne. Unlike many exhibition designs bristling with environmental technology, this house manages to integrate active and passive devices successfully into a visually calm form.

Right Solar House, Breisach-am-Rhein, Germany, 1996, Thomas Spiegelhalter. Deconstructivist collage meets solar energy.

Opposite Sun Valley House, Idaho, USA, 1986, Arne Bystrom. The all-sheltering roof and pervasive forty-five degree geometry struggle to hold together an array of solar collectors and sun-spaces.

Above Private house, Lyon-St Just, France, Jourda and Perraudin. A standard greenhouse construction system is used to make an eco-friendly house with the addition of canvas, insulation and planting.

Right Architects' Own House, Lyons, France, Jourda and Perraudin. This cheap steel-framed box has a dramatic fabric structure to keep most of the rain off the roof membrane, and plywood barrel-vaults to expand the living space.

Above, below and overleaf

Crescent House, Wiltshire, England,
1999, Ken Shuttleworth. By the end
of the century, efficient passive solar
design could be effortlessly combined
with Modernist abstraction in
sophisticated designs such as this.

Crescent House Wiltshire, England, 1999, Ken Shuttleworth

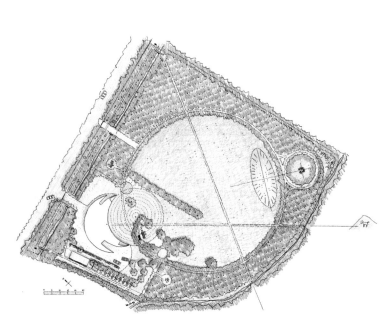

greenhouses, they built a simple, 21-metre- (69-foot-) long glass shed using a commercially produced system, and then modified it using a combination of fixed insulation panels, layers of canvas, and internal and external planting. In their own house in Lyons they opted for a simple steel frame and the cheapest of flat roofs, and then unfurled a dramatic fabric structure over the whole structure. Supported on a forest of light steel struts, the canopy provided protection from weather during construction, keeps most of the rain off the flat roof and offers solar shading. Plywood barrel vaults give added dignity and volume to the living/dining area, whereas in contrast the bedrooms are reduced to tiny pods. Jourda and Perraudin believe in providing only what is essential, and in minimizing a structure's impact on the earth: like Glenn Murcutt's elegant pavilions, whose work also demonstrates a serious concern with the use of resources, their house seems determined to 'touch this earth lightly'.

By the mid 1990s sophisticated software packages to predict the environmental performance of buildings were widely available and the basic principles of passive design were becoming a natural part of many architects' design processes, not the province of experts or the ideologically committed. At first sight Ken Shuttleworth's Crescent House (1999), with its artful crescent-moon plan, crisp white surfaces, unbroken glazed wall, open, light-filled interior and elegant formal landscape, might appear to be a sophisticated essay in late-Modern design rather than a serious attempt to address environmental issues: in fact it is both. To begin with, over a thousand deciduous trees were planted on the five-acre site, which lies in an area of outstanding natural beauty on the edge of the Marlborough Downs in Wiltshire in south-west England. The trees near the house reduce the chilling effect of the wind and provide welcome shade in summer, while allowing valuable sunshine through in winter.

Shuttleworth, a director of Foster and Partners, subjected the design to typically thorough technical studies which suggested that a south/south-east orientation was optimal for the large glazed wall, making the most of early morning gains but avoiding overheating in summer. The interior is generously day-lit and naturally cross ventilated, and even the chimney plays its part, acting as a ventilation stack in hot weather. Concrete was chosen as the main structural material because it was available from a plant across the road from the site, and secondhand timber from the run-down house which formerly occupied the land was used extensively in making the form-work. The heavy concrete walls, which store heat and even out thermal changes in the interior, are wrapped externally in 10 centimetres (4 inches) of CFC-free insulation; on the roof, the thickness of insulation is doubled. The building systems are designed to make use of photovoltaic panels, recycled rainwater and a nearby well when they become economically viable.

Crescent House, like the other houses we have considered in this final chapter, belongs to an evolving and increasingly mature, diverse and responsive tradition of modern architecture. Aesthetically, its roots lie in the abstraction explored in the 1920s, and to the majority of people such a thoroughgoing expression of modernity at the domestic scale remains alien, not least because it simply refuses to look like a 'proper house'. Herzog and de Meuron's Rudin House, built in 1993

Rudin House Leymen, France, .1993, Herzog and de Meuron

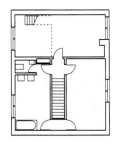

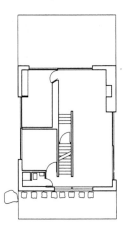

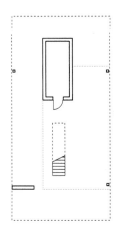

at Leymen in France, is in part a commentary on this dilemma. Seen across the fields it appears quintessentially house-like: symmetrical, gabled, rooted in the ground, and with holes for windows and doors, just like a child's drawing. Move closer, however, and it becomes utterly strange. It appears to be made of only one material, concrete (although in fact there is a membrane on the roof), and as a result looks unfinished; the openings are larger than normal and not neatly symmetrical; far from being rooted securely in the ground, it is raised precariously on a platform, like an architectural model on a cardboard base; and where, you suddenly wonder, is the front door?

The missing door turns out to be under the house, approached up a staircase which might be retractable but, like everything else, is made of concrete. Once inside you discover that the plan is ordinary, the section and finishes less so. The tall, narrow stairwell around which the rooms are organized reaches high up to a skylight, yet the daylight is mixed with the different colour spectrum emanating from a long horizontal strip of fluorescent tubes. The walls are lined with adobe, made with straw and loam from the surrounding land; on the lower floor, close to the fields, the finish is a natural sand colour, while the stairwell and upper floor are painted white. Despite your first impressions, there is little reassuringly conventional about the Rudin House, which has more to do with recent fine art practices than traditional house building. The mixture of natural and artificial light emulates the explorations of 'Light and Space' artists like Dan Flavin, while the adobe revetment of the ground floor echoes the emphasis on materiality in the work of American Minimalists such as Donald Judd, who built an adobe wall in the courtyard of the house he designed for himself in Marfa, Texas.

The Rudin House operates by different rules to the total works of art with which we began this exploration of the twentieth-century house, but it is still conceived as a work of art, a commentary on 'houseness' and also a house itself. As commonly understood, however, houses and works of art are very different creatures. A house should be accommodating and open to interpretation, allowing different occupants to change its decoration and adapt its rooms to their taste and requirements, not totally controlled from plan to teaspoon, or exquisitely tuned like a gallery installation. Culturally, it must be widely accessible, not the expression of abstruse ideas, and it should grow old with grace, not appear hopelessly outmoded by the next twist of fashion in a changing world. A work of art, on the other hand, can – and most contemporary artists and critics would doubtless say, should – be challenging and unconventional, and may legitimately make demands on its audience by way of attention and prior knowledge.

All architecture, to a greater or lesser extent, seeks to subject life to a system of spatial and aesthetic order, and the tension between the house as a work of art and a setting for everyday life runs acutely through the twentieth century. Even the supposedly liberating free plan could produce its own kind of tyranny: it is no coincidence that a disproportionate number of the houses we have explored are second homes, to be enjoyed in the more relaxed atmosphere of weekends or vacations, or are manifestos built by architects for their own occupation. The most eminently liveable of the great twentieth-century dwellings – one thinks of the Schröder and Sarabhai houses, many of Wright's, from Fallingwater to the

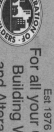
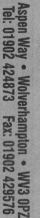

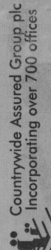
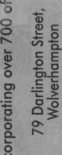

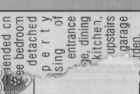

Opposite and below Rudin House, Leymen, France, 1993, Herzog and de Meuron. At first sight as house-like as any child's (or Post-Modernist's) dream, on closer inspection this all-concrete structure turns out to be a knowing exercise in late-modern design.

Usonians, the Villa Mairea, Niemeyer and Barragán houses, Utzon's Can Lis – succeed in reconciling these often conflicting poles, but the gulf between the ideals they represent and the general culture of housing hardly needs stating. The story of the twentieth-century house is an exhilarating journey through architectural ideas of great originality, and in the West, in the wealthiest society in history, the house's future as a vehicle for architectural expression and experimentation seems assured. Indeed, in an increasingly bureaucratized world it may prove to be the one building type over which the architect retains something close to traditional control.

further reading, index, credits, and acknowledgments

The literature on modern architecture is vast and a comprehensive bibliography of the houses discussed in this book could occupy many pages. These suggestions for further reading have been chosen for their accessibility and availability, to enable readers to broaden and deepen their interest in the work and ideas discussed in this book.

On modern architecture generally:
William Curtis: *Modern Architecture Since 1900* (London: Phaidon Press, 3rd edn, 1996)
Kenneth Frampton: *Modern Architecture: A critical history* (London: Thames and Hudson, 3rd edn, 1992)

On specific periods/styles:
Peter Davey: *Arts and Crafts Architecture* (London: Phaidon Press, 1995)
Lesley Jackson: *'Contemporary'* (London: Phaidon Press, 1994)
Richard Weston: *Modernism* (London: Phaidon Press, 1996)

Houses:
Esther McCoy: *Blueprints for Living: History and Legacy of the Case Study Houses* (Cambridge, MA: MIT Press, 1989)
John Welsh: *Modern House* (London: Phaidon Press, 1995)
Neil Jackson: *The Modern Steel House* (London: Spon, 1996)
Olivier Boissière: *Twentieth-Century Houses, Europe* (Paris: Terrail, 1998)
Anatxu Zabalbeascoa: *Houses of the Century* (Corte Madera: Gingko Press, 1998)
Clare Melhuish: *Modern House II* (London: Phaidon Press, 1999)
Susan Doubilet and Daralice Boles: *European House Now* (London: Thames and Hudson, 1999)
Robert McCarter, Richard Weston, James Steele: *Twentieth Century Houses* (London: Phaidon Press, 1999; Fallingwater, Villa Mairea, and the Eames House)
Nicolas Pople: *Experimental Houses* (London: Laurence King, 2000)

Theoretical/topical:
Christian Norberg-Schulz: *The Concept of Dwelling* (New York: Rizzoli, 1985)
Charles Moore, Donlyn Lyndon, Gerald Allen: *The Place of Houses* (New York: Henry Holt, 1979)
James Wines: *Green Architecture* (Cologne: Taschen, 2000)

Individual architects:
Richard Weston: *Alvar Aalto* (London: Phaidon Press, 1995)
Yukio Futagawa, ed.: *Tadao Ando, 1972–1987* (Tokyo: A.D.A. Edita, 1987)
Antonio Riggen Martínez: *Luis Barragán* (New York: Monacelli Press, 1996)
Pat Kirkham: *Charles and Ray Eames* (Cambridge, MA: MIT Press, 1995)
Eduard F. Sekler: *Josef Hoffmann* (Princeton: Princeton University Press, 1985)
William Curtis: *Le Corbusier: Forms and Ideas* (London: Phaidon Press, 199?)
Tim Benton: *The Villas of Le Corbusier, 1920–1930* (New Haven and London: Yale University Press, 1987)
Roberto Schezen: *Adolf Loos: Architecture 1903–1932* (New York: Monacelli Press, 1996)

All Frank Lloyd Wright pictures and drawings are
© ARS, NY and DACS, London 2002

All Le Corbusier pictures and drawings are
© FLC/ADAGP, Paris and DACS, London 2002

4 Julius Shulman
6 Hiroshi Kobayoshi/Tadao Ando Architect &
  Associates
8/9 Michael Freeman
12/13 Arcaid/Niall Clutton
14 Martin Charles
15 RIBA
16 Martin Charles)
17 Arcaid/Mark Fiennes
18 Martin Charles © DACS 2002
19t Author © DACS 2002
19b Archipress/Marc Loiseau
20 Archipress
21 Institut Mathildenhöhe, Darmstadt
22 & 23b Philippe Garner
23t Angelo Hornak
24t Author
24b Rauno Traskelin
25t&c Carl Larsson-Garden, Sundborn
25b Bridgeman Art Library/Nationalmuseum,
  Stockholm
26 ESTO/Roberto Schezen
27 Author
28t & 29 Julius Shulman
30 Maybeck Coll (1956–1) Environmental
  Design Archive, University of California,
  Berkeley
32 Pavel Stecha © DACS 2002
35 Arcaid/Richard Bryant
36 Frank den Oudsten & Assoc.
37 Index/Reus Perez
38 ESTO/Roberto Schezen
40 Pavel Stecha
41 Frank den Oudsten & Assoc. © DACS 2002
44 Fondation le Corbusier
45 Archipress/Lucien Hervé
46 Paul Harris
47t Martin Charles
47b Peter Kent
48t Pavel Stecha © DACS 2002
49 Pavel Stecha © DACS 2002
50/51 Pavel Stecha © DACS
52 Archipress/Lucien Hervé
53 Archipress/Franck Eustache
54 Michael Freeman
55 Michael Freeman
56/57 Michael Freeman
58 Architectural Association/F.R.Yerbury
59tl Author
59cl RIBA
59cr Arcaid/Amyas Connell
59 Gabriele Basilico
61t&c Hans Scharoun Archiv, Stiftung Archiv
  der Akademie der Künste, Berlin
61b Kari Haavisto
62t Eileen Gray Archive
62b/63 Philippe Garner
64/65 Martin Charles © ADAGP, Paris and
  DACS, London 2002
67 Fondation Le Corbusier
68 Author
69 Esto/Peter Aaron
71 Lucia Moholy, Bauhaus Archiv, Berlin
72&73 Frank den Oudsten & Assoc

76 Author
77t Netherlands Architecture Institute
77 Frank den Oudsten & Assoc.
79 Archipress/Peter Cook
80/81 Archipress/Peter Cook
82 & 84r Buckminster Fuller 'Your Private Sky'
  Lars Muller Publishers, Baden © Estate of
  Buckminster Fuller
85t photo by Albert Frey: Architecture & Design,
  Coll University Art Museum, UCSB
85c&b Richard Horden
86 Martin Charles ©ADAGP, Paris and DACS,
  London 2002
87 MNAM/CCI Centre Pompidou © ADAGP,
  Paris and DACS, London, 2002
88t&b Martin Charles © ADAGP, Paris and
  DACS, London 200
89t Architects Journal
89b Architectural Association
90/91 Architecture & Design Coll, University
  Art Museum, UCSB
92t&b Fondation Le Corbusier & DACS
93t Architecture & Design Coll, University Art
  Museum, UCSB
93b Julius Shulman
94 Author
95t Author
95b Esto/Roberto Schezen
96/97 Author
99 Martin Charles
100t Architecture Museum, Norway
100b Marte Catalan, Barcelona
101 Architects Journal
102 Esto/Roberto Schezen
103 Wolfgang Voigt
106/7 Lina Bo Bardi Archive, Brazil/Amaldo
  Pappalardo, 1998
109 Archipress/Michel Much
110/111 Barragán Foundation, Switzerland,
  photos by Armando Salas Portugal
112&113b Esto/Roberto Schezen
113t Architectural Association/©Barry Cameron
114 Bridgeman Art Library/Roger Last
115 Stanley Saitowitz
116,118&119 Max Dupain & Associates
120 Edward Cullinan & Assoc.
121 Martin Charles
122&123 Arcaid/Richard Einzig
124 Author
125 Ralph Erskine
126&127r Author
127l John Pardey
128/9 Julius Shulman
130&131 Paul Rocheleau
132 Julius Shulman
134&135 Paul Rocheleau
136 Author
137 Michael Freeman
138 Julius Shulman
140&141 Paul Rocheleau
143 Chicago Historical Society/Hedrich
  Blessing
144 Julius Shulman
145t Michael Freeman
145b Joachim Schumacher
146t University of Texas, Architectural Drawings
  Collection
146c Tim Street-Porter
146b&147 Julius Shulman
148 Michael Freeman

149, 150, 151&153 Julius Shulman
154t Esto/Wayne Andrews
154b Esto/Ezra Stoller ©DACS 2002
155 ©DACS 2002
156&157 Paul Rocheleau
159 Norman McGrath
160t Esto/Bill Maris
160b Esto/Ezra Stoller
161 Arcaid/Alan Weintraub
162 Julius Shulman
163 Arcaid/Alan Weintraub
164 Julius Shulman
166/7 Juhani Pallasmaa
169 Arkitekturmuseet, Sweden/Bo Tongren
170 Max Plunger
172 Author
173t Max Plunger
173b Arkitekturmuseet, Sweden/Sundahl, Sune
174,175b&176 Bent Ryberg
175t John Pardey
177t Keld Helm Petersen
177br Bent Ryberg
177bl John Pardey
178 FinnChristoffersen Fotograf
179t Keld Helmer Petersen
179b Kjeld Vindum
180t Author
180b Bent Ryberg
181t Author
182 Vilhelm Wohlert
183 Bent Ryberg
184 Kaari Haavisto
185t Juhani Pallasma
185b Architects Journal
186/&187 Arcaid/Richard Bryant
188/89 Paul Rocheleau
190 Arcaid
191 George Pohl/VSBA
194/5 Tom Bernard/VSBA
196 & 197 Edmund Stoecklean/Robert Stern
199 Norman McGrath/Michael Graves
202 Esto/Scott Francis
203 Paul Rocheleau
204 O'Donnell & Tuomey
205 Alo Zanetta/Mario Botta
206&207 John Outram
210 A.F.Kersting/Colin St. John Wilson assisted
  by MJLong
211 Martin Charles
212 Esto/Mark Darley
213 Channa Daswatte/Geoffrey Bawa
214/5 Hiroshi Kobayshi/Tadao Ando
216 Timothy Hursley
217 Tim Street Porter
218t Grant Mudford
218c&b Tom Bonner
220 Coop Himmelb(l)au
221, 222&223 Hans Weslemann/OMA
225 Hiroshi Kobayashi Tadao Ando
226 Tomio Ohashi/Tadao Ando
227 Hiroshi Kobayashi/Tadao Ando
229 Luis Seixas Ferreira Alves Souto de Moura
230 Luigi Snozzi
231t Margherita Spiluttini
231b Dennis Gilbert
233 Arcaid/Richard Bryant
234t Stefan Muller
234c&b Graham Phillips/Foster & Partners
235 Hisao Suzuki
236t Ronnie Tallon/Scott Tallon Walker

236b Author
237t ©2001 Matthew Weinreb/imagefind.com
237c Daria Scagliola & Stijn Brakkee/ Mecanoo
237b Eduard Hueber/Architectural Photo Inc.
238t Jon Linkins/Andresen O'Gorman
238b Lieve Blancqaert/Stéphane Beel
239 Hans Werlemann
240/41 Grant Mudford
242 MVRDV/Christian Richters
243 Paul Warchol Studio
245 Christian Richters
246t Clark & Menefee/Charles Menefee
246c Fink & Jocher
246b Peter Cook
247t Esto/Peter Aaaron
247b, 248 & 249 Timothy Hursley
250&251t Stanley Saitowitz
251b Hisao Suzuki
252 John & Patricia Patkau © James Dow
253 Sverre Fehn
253b Author
254t&b Lacaton & Vassal/Philippe Ruault
254c Carl-Viggo Hølmebakk
255t Dieter Liestner/Herzog
255b Richart Schenkirz/Herzog
256 Arne Bystrom
257t Esto/Scott Francis
257b Friedrich Busam/Architekturphoto
258 Archipress
259, 260/61 Ken Shuttleworth/Foster &
  Partners/Nigel Young
263 Margherita Spiluttini

author's acknowledgments

I would like to thank: my colleagues Malcolm Parry and John Pardey for observations and architectural stimulation; my father Don Weston for reading and commenting on drafts from the perspective of the 'interested layman'; Mary-Jane Gibson for her flexibility and persistence in pursuit of images; Keith Lovegrove for the fresh and elegant layout; and, at Laurence King, the commissioning editor Philip Cooper and project editor Liz Faber, who were unfailingly helpful and polite throughout the book's gestation.